MIND OF AN OUTLAW

———

MIND OF AN OUTLAW

SELECTED ESSAYS

Norman Mailer

Edited and with a Preface by Phillip Sipiora
Introduction by Jonathan Lethem

RANDOM HOUSE
NEW YORK

Copyright © 2013 by the Estate of Norman Mailer
Introduction copyright © 2013 by Jonathan Lethem
Editor's Preface copyright © 2013 by Phillip Sipiora

Published in the United States by Random House, an imprint of
The Random House Publishing Group, a division of Random House LLC,
a Penguin Random House Company, New York.

RANDOM HOUSE and the HOUSE colophon are registered trademarks of
Random House LLC.

All of the essays in this collection except "Freud" have been previously published.
Original Publication and Permission Credits are located on pages 595–596.

Library of Congress Cataloging-in-Publication Data
Mailer, Norman.
[Essays. Selections]
Mind of an outlaw: selected essays / Norman Mailer ; edited by Phillip Sipiora ;
introduction by Jonathan Lethem.
pages cm
Includes bibliographical references and index.
ISBN 978-0-8129-9347-9
eBook ISBN 978-0-679-64565-8
I. Sipiora, Phillip, editor of compilation.   II. Title.
PS3525.A4152A6 2013
814'.54—dc23
2013015716

Printed in the United States of America on acid-free paper

www.atrandom.com

2   4   6   8   9   7   5   3   1

First Edition

Book design by Christopher M. Zucker

Contents

———

2000s

Introduction

Jonathan Lethem

LET US SUPPOSE that a writer has sat down at his desk, aligned his fingers to familiar postures of readiness at the bare existential stage where wait QWERT and YUIOP—those unhelpful companions, mute as Beckett's clowns—let us go and suppose the writer has offered himself here to a situation that is, on its face, impossible, a battle almost certainly lost before it begins.

Well, the odds are awfully good that the writer who has put himself in this position is Norman Mailer—unless it happens to be, as at this moment, another writer attempting to introduce Mailer's *Selected Essays* and at the same time beguilingly ape Mailer's typical strategy in arriving at a topic. Whether awarding *Waiting for Godot* a negative review without having seen it (as Mailer once did in his column in *The Village Voice*); or pegging his long consideration of the death penalty—in *Parade* magazine, no less!—on the defense of a flip provocation he'd made on *The Phil Donohue Show*, where he'd claimed "we need a little capital punishment"; or prefacing his skirmish with feminism with a digression on how he'd spent a day mistakenly believing he'd won the Nobel Prize; or insistently reminding his readers that he wrote a lot of his books hurriedly, to satisfy contracts or make child-support payments—or, really, whenever frontloading nearly any stirring hypothesis with a prominent reminder of *who* it was that was doing the hypothesizing—Norman Mailer was a writer who never met a corner he didn't wish to paint himself into. It is one thing to go looking for fights. Certainly this is our default image of Mailer: provocateur, bare-knuckle brawler. It is another thing to go into so many fights having artfully tied one hand behind one's back. Sometimes both hands. If Mailer's favorite quote, from André Gide, was "Please do not understand me too quickly," it might often seem he baited his most significant forays into prose with a temptation to the reader to dismiss him almost *immediately*.

And here, tasked with giving a proper *envoi* to what I do believe is a great reader's voyage of a book, I've gone and "done a Mailer"—I'm burying the man before I even begin to try to figure out how to praise him. My excuse is that he seems to demand it, by the logic of his own self-demolitions: Watch Mailer climb out of the hole once again, folks! I'll commit another Mailer gesture, then, and quote myself. This, from the first and only other time I tried to write about the man:

> In hindsight, Mailer looked in the late fifties to have become a radar detector for the onset of . . . the postmodern cultural condition generally—in his declared topics, his appetite to engulf every dissident impulse and the whole atmosphere of paranoia and revelation that saturated the sixties, though he delivered barely any fiction to reflect it, in his predictions in essays like "Superman Comes to the Supermarket"; in his self-annihilating advocacy of Burroughs's *Naked Lunch;* in his desperate, dashed-off forays in *Why Are We in Vietnam?* and *An American Dream,* and so on. The reason Mailer couldn't arrive at a satisfactory postmodern style (even as he saw his one firm achievement in *The Naked and the Dead* mummified by ironic treatments of his war by Heller, Vonnegut, and Pynchon) was because postmodernism as an art practice extended from modern-

ism, to which Mailer had never authentically responded in the first place. This might have been Mailer's dirty secret: He was still back with James T. Farrell's *Studs Lonigan* in the soul of his aesthetics, even as the rest of his intelligence raced madly downfield, sometimes sprinting decades past his contemporaries. . . .

So defend indefensible Mailer. [His best books are:] *Advertisements for Myself, The Armies of the Night,* the two campaign books, and, er, parts of *The Fight,* parts of *Of a Fire on the Moon,* parts of *Cannibals and Christians* . . . parts of etc. Parts, always parts. The novelist Darin Strauss, confessing his Mailer-thing to me when I confessed mine, said, "Other writers are inconsistent book to book, but Mailer's inconsistent within books, sometimes even within paragraphs. . . ." I wonder: Does anyone credit Mailer this postmodern way, as a purveyor of fragments, a centrifuge of sentences? Mailer's false accents—Texas, Patrician, boxer-tough—are like Orson Welles's false noses.

Reading that now, it seems to me that despite how I'd assumed a (rather Maileresque) posture as the lone voice in the wilderness, I really fell in with the rough consensus: that Mailer, self-appointed great novelist with no definitively great novels to his credit, found his greatness instead in his nonfiction voice—in the volcanic river of his "New Journalism," from the *Village Voice* columns through to when, in the eighties, he (largely) recommitted himself to novels. A consensus that Mailer's great subject was himself, not in the usual personal-essayist's sense of "a private man revealed," but as a public entity, an existential shadowboxer and buffoonish slumming-patrician refusenik, moving through American history as a kind of disastrous recording angel, a lightning rod for exemplary controversies, a cautionary tale he alone couldn't learn from. In the words of Harold Bloom, "he is his own supreme fiction. . . . the author of 'Norman Mailer,' a lengthy, discontinuous, and perhaps canonical fiction."

So, do I agree with Bloom, and with myself? Yes and yes, there's no doubt; it's for this reason I'll go on thinking *Advertisements for Myself* is Mailer's greatest book, simply because it frames the drama of the construction of this voice, the thrilling resurrection of his personality as his greatest asset after the public pratfalls accompanying his second and third novels. That book sails aloft on Mailer's delighted discovery of the voice's elasticity and reach. (Then again, *Armies of the Night* is *Advertisements*'s equal, for it is in the march on the Pentagon that the voice discovers its greatest subject and fiercest power of implication.) Everywhere, Mailer negotiates with imagined persecutors and pursuers, those who'd keep him from feeling all he feels, suspecting all he suspects, attempting all he'd attempt (as well as what he wouldn't ever get around to attempting), yet never in despair. Never hounded. Always with an exhilaration more magnanimous than nose-thumbing, as though to say: There you go! You're pushing me and I'm pushing back, and don't you see how it brings out the best in us both! To turn on Mailer his own praise of Marlon Brando, he's "our greatest actor . . . and he is also our National Lout." For, though his chosen emblem was the boxer (a Hemingwayesque overcompensation for the apparent passivity of the writer's craft), Mailer's is really a method actor's style—and Brando's career is as near to the impossible space Mailer's gestures carved for himself in postwar American culture: always promising more than he could deliver, always inserting his own brooding self-consciousness between his audience and his ostensible creative task—and then providing captivating evidence of how, at its best, that obtrusive presence could be as much an artistic opportunity as it was a disaster area.

So, yes, Mailer as stylist, yes, Mailer as essayist, yes, but also *no,* because it could never be so simple: Mailer's essays are those of a novelist, and they would be even if he quit reminding us it was so. It's not merely how the essays gain energy from the theatricality of the novelist turning almost in irritation from his main task—will he *ever* be allowed to reel in that big fish?—but that where these essays explode most into greatness is in their capacities for portraiture, scene-making, fictional conjecture, passages of free indirect style worthy of any Flaubertian master.

"Norman Mailer" may demand the ironic title as this novelist's greatest character, but he has other great ones: "Dick Nixon," "Pat Nixon," "Barbara Bush," "Bob Dole" (I'm tempted just to say "the Republican Party"), "Ernest Hemingway," "Henry Miller," "Robert Lowell," "Jack Henry Abbott," and so on. These characters are, by definition, floated into a realm somewhere between fiction and non-, full of Mailer's projections and yearnings (in at least one case with disastrous results: In a brilliant intuition, Mailer compares his prison pen pal Abbott to Chauncey Gardiner, the lead character from Jerzy Kosinski's *Being There,* without grasping the deadly implications of his own insight). In any event, on the page, they become indelibly vivid, persuasive players on crucial stages of Mailer's devising, in dramas in which he never fails to persuade us of the stakes. The very best instances have all Mailer's seemingly guileless gestures coming together to form thought-experiments of stunning impact. Take, for example, that *Parade* essay on the death penalty. As we groan our way into Mailer's unsavory defense of his passing remark in favor of execution, the novelist sneaks up on us with a haunting evocation of the meaning of an execution *within* prison walls, in the minds of the guards and the prisoners. From there he widens the horizon, invoking a complicity that forces readers both to challenge easy—"liberal"—assumptions, and to dabble at least momentarily in Mailer's take on the American twentieth century, which he views (if you'll pardon a feeble paraphrase—he wouldn't) as reassuring itself with an uneasy delusory layer of science, law, and reason, one covering a cauldron full of uncanny forces, of outrageous stirrings of hatred and desire.

I'll stop there—to isolate Mailer's "ideas" from the context of a style at once aphoristic, discursive, and performative is to hang them out to dry as much as would be the case with those of Nietzsche and G. K. Chesterton, his companion talents in dialectics, provocation, and paradox. As in the case of Nietzsche and Chesterton, you'll be forced to argue with Mailer's thinking, and it is certain that in many cases you'll want to reject it—but to do so, you must enter the ground of his thinking as it is enacted here: with genius.

Editor's Preface

Phillip Sipiora

NORMAN MAILER WAS arguably the foremost public intellectual of the second half of the twentieth century. With the publication of his first novel in 1948, *The Naked and the Dead,* he emerged as one of America's most important creative writers and soon thereafter established himself as a potent and provocative essayist, film-maker, playwright, short-fiction writer, poet, biographer, journal-ist, cultural and political commentator, and media star. His ubiquitous presence over the decades in print and on the airwaves—William F. Buckley Jr.'s *Firing Line, The Dick Cavett Show, The Tonight Show Starring Johnny Carson,* and *Charlie Rose*—is proof that he possessed a mind and personality that immensely engaged the public. While the span between his first novel and his last, *The Castle in the Forest,* was a remarkable fifty-nine years, the complexity and heterogeneity of his vast, deep interests are best represented in his essays. For Mailer the essay, even more than his fiction, provided a forum in which he could unrelent-ingly confront the social, political, and cultural crises of the day. In his essays, Mailer's persistent curiosity—coupled with his dis-cursive prose—engages, opposes, clarifies, complicates, and rig-orously challenges whatever subjects he takes on.

As the founding editor of *The Mailer Review* and a member of the Norman Mailer Society board of directors, I have worked closely with Mailer's oeuvre for more than ten years. I knew Mailer personally; I teach his works and write about him frequently. Yet shaping this collection was a daunting process because I could include only a small fraction of his most powerful work. Mailer had written so much that the excluded essays ended up far exceeding in number those ultimately selected. I began the compilation of this volume by separating the essays into thematic categories: Prisms of the Self, Arts and Letters, the Political Arena, Race, Gender, Culture and Counterculture, American Sexuality, the Metaphor of Sport, War and Peace, Crime and Punishment, the Art of Writing, and Cosmology. These were useful for narrowing down the most interesting, relevant, and representative essays from six decades. However, the categories ultimately felt limiting, reductive, and exclusive. How does one confidently assign a "sexual" essay to either Gender or American Sexuality? Therefore, to avoid issues of overlap and confusion, the essays appear here chronologically. Although I consulted with a number of Mailer scholars, editors, other writers, librarians, archivists, and members of Mailer's family in choosing these essays, this table of contents is not meant to be hierarchical, exhaustive, or by any means definitive. It is a beginning in arranging the work of a most complex writer.

Early on, I employed a simple principle of inclusion: Select only the very best essays in the Mailer canon. Two critical criteria were influence and staying power. Classic essays like "The White Negro" and "Mind of an Outlaw" were mandatory inclusions because of their continued importance over the years and their roles in establishing and representing the Mailer persona. I unearthed more obscure gems by combing through old issues of *Esquire, The Village Voice, Saturday Review, The New York Review of Books, The Paris Review, The New Yorker,* and *Parade,* as well as *Playboy, Architectural Forum, The Harvard Advocate,* and *Dissent.* This sort of research highlighted not only the striking range and complexity of his essays (as illustrated by the original categories) but also the exceptionally diverse nature of the vehicles for his work, something that distinguishes him from many of his contemporaries. From the 1940s into the new millennium he published essays next to advertisements for typewriter repair, Fruit-Fresh anti-browning preservative, and special-edition Playmates' books. Looking through these decades of American journalism, I was reminded of how adaptable Mailer was to new times and new challenges and of how he was able to engage so effectively with diverse audiences. He demonstrated an unparalleled intellectual flexibility while never losing his edge and his sense of urgency.

Through the essay form, readers gain the closest access to Mailer because there are fewer veils separating the expositor from his listeners. In the very first sentence of 1948's "A Credo for the Living," twenty-five-year-old Mailer declares, "I must admit that I enjoy this opportunity to write a word or two about my own politics." The full-throated vitality of young Mailer's personality thus announces itself, carrying the same self-confidence and intellectual bravery that the mature Mailer would demonstrate time after time. With these early lines, readers enter a transaction that allows—and requires—them to meet Mailer personally. While reading Mailer's essays, we become intimate with his inimitable intellect and forms of expression. We are taken into the depths of critical issues that Mailer has plumbed more profoundly than we ever could. But we are also forced to reexamine our beliefs, whether casual or deeply held. When Mailer proffers a position, he demands that we engage with him, that we become active participants or stop reading. Both writer and reader are tested in this exchange.

Mailer has been taking on America in this way since the 1940s. His ongoing confrontation with the country he loved (and did not love) was always in the spirit of productive intellectual engagement that would, ideally, lead to a further freeing of the American spirit. Mailer wrote, "Our noble idea of democracy was forever being traduced, sullied, exploited, and downgraded." Every fiber in Mailer's being fought the onslaught of assaults against the country that he served throughout his life, as in his lifelong critique of government and governmental abuse of authority. From his criticism of the devastating failure of the Vietnam War to his late essays attacking America's war acts in Iraq, Mailer tried to live a life of affirmative rebellion.

Mailer's acute political consciousness is explicitly connected to his view of art and the artist. In his mid-1950s essay "What I Think of Artistic Freedom," Mailer describes the social responsibilities of the artist: "It is the artist, embodying the most noble faculty of man—his urge to rebel—who is forever enlarging the walls." A cornerstone of Mailer's approach to restructuring the political and social landscapes was the strategic use of productive conflict. A politically sensitive artist cannot be aloof and uninvolved. Mailer followed this prescription his entire adult life. Never was a public intellectual so intimately interconnected with his audience through constant appearances in print and electronic media, especially television. There were other celebrated novelists who commented publicly on events (James Baldwin and Gore Vidal, for example), and there were other public intellectuals, like William F. Buckley, Jr., who were consistently in the fray of controversy, but no single person rose to Mailer's stature, and certainly no one has filled the void left by his death. Mailer established a complex persona that, I would argue, performed public service at its very best.

In these pages, a previously unpublished essay on Sigmund Freud gives sharp insight into Mailer's conception of public responsibility. Freud is described less as a pioneering theoretical psychiatrist than as a public doctor, one who administers to the generic ills that plague twentieth-century society. According to Mailer, Freud, more than his findings, was the antidote to the vast range of threats to contemporary living. Society, with its wars and poverty and hypocrisies, was sick and barbaric and threatening to become even worse without Freud's ameliorating contributions, especially his emphasis on the importance of a civilizing culture. Mailer obviously felt a strong kinship with Freud, whom he describes as "a lower-middle-class middle-European Jew who rose in bourgeois society." His description of Freud's mental acuity could easily be a description of himself: "[H]e was capable of the finest intellectual distinctions." Freud and Mailer were interlocutors, mediating the tense, ongoing negotiation between cultural values and their representatives. Mailer often spoke for (and of) himself, of course, but he also felt a responsibility to speak for us all in his investigation into the collective remembrance of time and change.

This characterization is not to say that Mailer was a narrow ideologue. He was, first and foremost, an interrogative intellectual for whom the cast of a question was even more important than the reach of its answer. Foremost among his identities is that of a probing, hectoring teacher—the very best kind of educator. Mailer never fully lets go of either his reader-student or his topic. A common mode in his writing-teaching included an unrelenting questioning of his subject matter, infused with an unceasing challenge to the status quo, as we see in his probing analysis of the existential minority as part of his theory of violence in "The White Negro." In Mailer's view, the existential minority comprises individuals who are neither inherently good nor bad but who represent a series of divergent perspectives (such as feeling superior while also doubting this sense of superiority). In other words, individuals might *appear* to exhibit contradictory thinking or actions when in actuality they are reflecting different views that they hold at different times because they are deeply conflicted—a tension that reveals itself as existential angst. Mailer was keenly aware of the rich texture of contradictions that make up human beliefs but believed that these contradictions offer considerable flexibility in one's choices throughout life. In posing these possibilities, Mailer promotes a sensibility that recognizes the importance of divergent thought and behavior.

Mailer's intellectual opponents, who included James Baldwin; Norman Podhoretz; William F. Buckley, Jr.; Gore Vidal; and Irving Howe; did not always acknowledge the suppleness of the Mailer mind, but his debates with others (and with himself) for more than six decades reveal a man fully capable of being persuaded. Mailer's detractors routinely disagreed, oftentimes with exceptional fervor, with his interpretation of events and the inferences he drew from those interpretations. Above all else,

Mailer had a mind guided by reason. His well-known political self-designation (often taken as oxymoronic) was "left conservative," and Mailer's unwillingness to entrench himself in hard-and-fast alliances is demonstrated by this early identification in "A Credo for the Living": "I feel myself to the left of the Progressive Party and to the right of the Communist Party." This sentiment from the 1940s echoes a later Mailer quotation that provides a glimpse into his sense of the complexities of the fierce, unceasing political struggle of his time: "It may yet take an alchemy of Left and Right to confound the corporate center." Mailer's stances are necessarily fluid and constantly under pressure from within for critical reconsideration, reformulation, and rearticulation, which is where the inevitable inconsistency comes in.

This inconsistency—a valuable, fascinating by-product of the forces at work within Mailer's intellectual matrix—is reflected in his shifting attitude toward homosexuality. In "The Homosexual Villain," Mailer describes his early representations of homosexuality: "I have been as guilty as any contemporary novelist in attributing unpleasant, ridiculous, or sinister connotations to the homosexual (or more accurately, bisexual) characters in my novels." Mailer had earlier felt that "there was an intrinsic relation between homosexuality and 'evil,'" and does not spare himself from tough criticism as he accuses himself of bigotry: "I had been acting as a bigot in this matter, and 'bigot' was one word I did not enjoy applying to myself. With that came the realization I had been closing myself off from understanding a very large part of life." Mailer was willing to change his mind publicly when warranted, no matter the consequences to perceptions of his personal consistency.

This ability to adjust his beliefs continually reminds the reader of the ethical texture of Mailer's thinking. His ethos is strategically important because it requires the reader to be aware of his or her own ethical stance on issues. If a reader is in conflict with Mailer's positions, he or she shares an obligation with Mailer to base any resistance on ethics. Mailer's writing, throughout his career, is founded upon considerations of what is "right" under the present circumstances. Further, Mailer subscribed to Fitzgerald's belief that "the test of a first-rate intelligence is the ability to hold two opposed ideas in the mind at the same time, and still retain the ability to function." For Mailer, contrariety was a necessary condition of any intellectual activity, whether thinking, speaking, or writing; it is a catalyst for debate as well as lubrication for honest thinking and writing. Mailer well understood the importance of paying attention to the machinery of discourse. When he assumed contrary positions, as he did throughout his life, he knew that one of its effects would be to enrich the debate. This sensibility is most evident in Mailer's engagement with feminism, which resulted in occasional stormy confrontations with hecklers while on lecture tours or planned face-to-face conflicts on television. Mailer knew that theatricality and rhetorical performance were integral nourishments to his role as an intellectual outlaw, but it should also be pointed out that he maintained long-term, close friendships with feminists, including Gloria Steinem and Diana Trilling. Mailer was an intellectual performer of staggering proportions, and it was no surprise that he would rely on theatricality to generate emotions and interest in his audience.

What is the state of the expository Mailer in his later years? As always, he was engaged as fully as possible, carrying the responsibilities of a public person fighting for progressive humanist ideas. Indeed, his antiwar sentiment continued until his final breath. A book written weeks before the beginning of the Iraq war, *Why Are We at War?*, was published in his eightieth year. Yet despite the tens of thousands of pages he left us with, a mystery about Mailer remains, a sense that the public intellectual is ultimately irreducible and indefinable. F. Scott Fitzgerald once said that "[T]here never was a good biography of a good novelist. There couldn't be. He is too many people, if he's any good." For the same reason, no preface to the essays of Norman Mailer could ever hope to capture even a fragment of his complex and intertwined personalities. Mailer, surely by volition, repels reductive, singular definition. He is an outlaw public intellectual who can only be understood, however insufficiently, as a complex plural construction. Mailer demands a great deal from himself, and if you engage with this collection, he demands much from you, too. Yet readers who approach the essays with a Maileresque energy and intellectual flexibility—and readers who have a bit of the outlaw in themselves—will finish this book challenged and rewarded.

1940s

———

A Credo for the Living

(1948)

I MUST ADMIT that I enjoy this opportunity to write a word or two about my own politics. In the thirties it was common enough for authors to send out a barrage of credos and countercredos, but today—because, perhaps, this is a period of less hope and greater concentration—the tendency has been to pool our efforts in the Progressive Party, and to leave the refinements, the definitions-of-position, to those authors who have deserted the Left to create political parties of three or four members.

A long sentence, the above. My apologies.

Now my own politics, naturally, have a certain relation to *The Naked and the Dead*.

The Naked and the Dead was a parable. It was a parable about the movement of men through history, and how history operates; and specifically it was a novel about America's destiny and the historical paths America was to follow after the war. (I was a very ambitious young man at the time I wrote it.) It was not a bitter book. It tried to explore the outrageous proportions of cause and effect, of effort and recompense, in a sick society, and in that sense it is a book with a certain grim humor. Its function was not to seek for affirmations, but meanings, and for that reason perhaps it has been called a novel without hope.

I think actually it is a novel with a great deal of hope. It finds man corrupted, confused to the point of helplessness, but it also finds that there are limits beyond which man cannot be pushed, and it finds that even in man's corruption and sickness there are yearnings and inarticulate strivings for a better world, a life with more dignity.

I have written these words about "hope," because hope moves people politically. Although I do not think that "hope" has anything to do with the merits of a novel, I think it has a great deal to do with an author's political activity or lack of it.

Thus, with a delay or two, we come to the credo. I suppose that politically I am an ignorant Marxist. I mean by that a confession that I cannot in all honesty call myself a Marxist when I have read so few of the basic works of Marxist theory. But politically in terms of specific objectives, of specific legislation and specific projects, I am in agreement with a great many tenets of the Left. To focus it more finely I might say that I feel myself to the left of the Progressive Party and to the right of the Communist Party.

I have come to this station by way of certain basic assumptions. I feel, and this is most directly important, that the need today is to approach "issues and questions"—those ponderous words which are the bane of all leftist writing—with an attitude that problems are complex, and their solutions are complex. Out of the swill and the honey which has been strewn over the Soviet Union, it is rarely stated that the USSR is an immense country, and that evaluations of it must be as many-faceted and various as evaluations of the United States.

A book which saw America through a Negro chain gang in Georgia, or from a nightclub on Fifty-Second Street or from a peaceful farm in Iowa, would be hardly a definitive work on the United States. By the same token almost every approach to the USSR has been that limited and that special. It is my diffident opinion that Russia is neither Arcadia nor a black police state in which every man slaughters his brother. It is an immense nation with wonderful things and bad things, and it is a state which like all states is in the midst of a historical process, and is moving and changing.

But when the last war ended, it was not Russia which sought to take over Europe by force. It was the United States. A deep revolutionary movement that was spontaneous and natural, and came to being out of the miseries and lessons of the Second World War, was created in Western Europe. Communism was the answer for Western Europe, and it would have been a more satisfactory answer than the mangle of present-day political life there. We opposed it as a nation not because Communism in Europe would have been a threat to America's existence, but because it would have been a threat to the present economic organization of America.

It is perfectly ridiculous to assume that if Europe had gone Communist, Russia would have engaged in a war with us. Both Russia and the countries of Western Europe would have had their own crucial problems of reconstruction. It would have taken decades, as it may now take centuries, to have restored those countries to healthy productive societies. In the process America would have been influenced by what was occurring in Europe, might gradually and peacefully have oriented itself toward socialism.

That would have meant the end of the present ruling society in America. And in the instinctive appreciation of a dangerous problem that ruling societies always exhibit, the campaign to identify the Soviet Union with the worst ogres of a nightmare was begun. Its success was a reflection of the neurosis of America.

America is in a moral wilderness today, torn between a Christian ethic now enfeebled, a capitalist ethic, and a new sexual ethic whose essence is sadistic. When one contemplates the staggering frustrations and animosities of American life, I think there is hope to be found in the fact that there is resistance, and that there is a political party, the Progressive Party, which will

poll millions of votes, millions of protests, against the campaign
to make America fascist in preference to letting it move socialist.

My hope for the future depends upon more than those millions
of votes. It is heartening for us to remember that the economic
rulers of America have their problems too. They have satisfied
temporarily the spiritual frustration of America life by feeding
Americans upon anti-Russian hysteria. But hatred, except in rare
cases, is only a temporary food. The basic problems of Americans, the spiritual problems, remain unsolved, and there is no
way short of fascism or war for the present ruling groups to solve
those problems.

There is resistance to fascism, and there is resistance to war. I
think it is childish of us to assume that it is impossible for Americans to move toward the Progressive Party. History is filled with
waves and counterwaves. My hope and my belief in America is
that unlike Germany, there will be more and more resistance
created as we move closer to the solution of the fascism and war
that the reactionaries will present us.

In the meantime I will act politically for those things in which
I believe. If it will take courage so much the better. We shall all
find our courage. The beauty in man is that under the press of
circumstances he develops what he must possess.

1950s

Freud

(circa mid-1950s)

FOR FREUD IT WAS UNTHINKABLE not to have a civilization—no matter what price must be paid in individual suffering, in neurosis, in the alienation of man from his instincts,* the alternative—a return to barbarism, to the primitive, was simply beyond the cultural shaping of Freud's life. As a lower-middle-class middle-European Jew who rose in bourgeois society, he was not only the mirror but finally the essence of German culture. It could be argued that the nature of the Jews, the meaning of the Jews, is not to find themselves as a people, but to re-create within themselves, as works of art, the models of a culture which is forever alien to them. So it is possible that the finest understanding of manners, of snobbery, of power, or equally of bourgeois stability can be grasped only by an outsider who can never take such values for granted but must acquire them by imaginative exercises of will, talent, and social courage. Freud was not born to become a respected young neurologist in Viennese medical society at the age of forty; it took the application of his early ambition, the

------

* An excursion could be made into a parallelism between Marx and Freud, for Marx, the first of the social psychologists, created the psychic exposition of how the worker is alienated from his work.

subjugation of a good part of his more rebellious instincts, to acquire the training, the habits, and the *manners* of a Viennese doctor. No surprise, then, if at the moment of engaging his second career, with that long heroic passage through the underwater currents of the dream, at whose end he was to create no less than the most pervasive religion of the twentieth century, the rational gloomy ethic of psychoanalysis, it was enough to ask of him that he be ready to turn the foundations of Western society into a new view of marriage, family, and man. One could hardly ask for more: that the view be revolutionary, that the search be not for foundations but dynamic. Freud was ready to endanger his security in the bourgeois world [he had attained] in order to save that world—his unadmitted love was always for the middle class, but it was simply not within the bounds of one hero to wreak two upheavals upon thought. Society was sick, Freud could see it, but of necessity the answer for him was to redefine the nature of man in such a way as to keep society intact and Freud in his study and consulting room. If civilization was top-heavy in its structures and institutions, and instinct was therefore crippled in its expression, and able to achieve beauty (melancholy beauty, be it said) only through sublimation, then so it must be. Man, for whatever reason, and the ultimate reason was mysterious—Freud had no flair for the mystical—man for whatever reason must accept himself as a crippled being who could become less crippled but never whole—in return his civilization would presumably evolve and become less tragic. But it was a spartan view. In return for austerity, and *pure* psychoanalysis was austere, severe, unrelenting (as opposed to the more amiable and *friendly* varieties which proliferate in a pleasure-loving America today), man would at least be given the dignity of maintaining his civilization. How middle-class and Jewish this is can hardly be exaggerated. Part of the paradox in Freud's style of mind was that he was capable of the finest intellectual distinctions, and the subtlest engagements of the opposite point of view in debate, while possessing almost no original capacity as a philosopher. At a very high level, he is the Jewish businessman raised to apotheosis, [even to the cigar,] and the sum of his philosophy in a depressed state could come to not much more than the heavy sigh of: "I've never had a particularly good time in my life, and the world is dog eat dog, but I've raised a family and I've taken care of them, and who knows, the kids never listen to the parents anyway, but maybe they'll make a better world, although I doubt it. The big thing is to do your duty, 'cause otherwise it would all be chaos. I mean, where would we be if everybody went around doing what they wanted to do?"

This gloomy view could be maintained in Freud's time, at least until the First World War; afterward, Freud's sense of the possibilities darkened further, his speculative toe entered the new deep waters of mysticism as Thanatos was added to Eros, the death instinct engaged in a dialectic with libido. But mysticism is the executioner of the middle-class ethic. The stability of the bourgeois has always depended upon a schizophrenic separation of the power of religion-as-an-institution from religion as a personal revelation of Heaven, Hell, Eternity, the soul, God, and human destiny. Mysticism has the nasty faculty of joining one's public and private life, it presents as its ultimate threat the subordination of reason to instinct, even as society rules instinct by reason. Freud was the last genius of twentieth-century society, only the epigones have followed. And as he was dying in 1939, the wreckage of his world was about him, the last engineer of civilization was hearing the bulkheads blow as he went under into that dark night about which he had refused to speculate.

And a dark night it was, because the war upon instinct which was the progressive rationale of the nineteenth century, the—for so long it seemed victorious—achievement of the Victorian period, was blown beyond recognition in the concentration camps and the atomic bomb. The dam of civilization burst before pent-up floods of instinct, and even as gates were carried away in the wash, so the crippling irony remained, the debris of civilization dissolved into the instinct, and altered the language of instinct; men were not murdered by the million but liquidated, atomic residue was not a slow fatality but a fallout. Perhaps it is better to use Freud's image of the rider and the steed, reason controlling instinct, superego the reins, id the horse, and the rider as ego encouraging or punishing the separate heats of the animal. By that image, the wildness of the horse is controlled at the expense of the horseman's fatigue, but one goes where one wishes to go, if not always at the desired rate. This was the central image of Freud's psychology, civilization mounted upon the noble savage, but the results were unexpected. For the animal was controlled not a little too much but incommensurately too much, and as it came closer to death, so the horse went wild and headed for a cliff. But the rider was also insane, his fatigue was equally cruel, horse and rider had never been suited to one another, and in the gallop to the cliff, the rider was using his spurs, not his reins, they are at the moment of danger of leaping over together, each of them poisoned, berserk with frustration.

With Freud's love for the English, the idea must have been that somehow one would muddle through.

It would not be worth saying Freud had an umbilical respect for the meanings of anxiety and dread, if it were not that his disciples have reduced these concepts to alarm bells and rattles of malfunction in a psychic machine. Anxiety and dread are treated by them as facts, as the clashing of gears in a neurotic net. The primitive understanding of dread—that one was caught in a dialogue with gods, devils, and spirits, and so was naturally consumed with awe, shame, and terror, has been all but forgotten. We are taught that we feel anxiety because we are driven by unconscious impulses which are socially unacceptable; dread we are told is a repetition of infantile experiences of helplessness. It is induced in us by situations which remind our unconscious of weaning and other early deprivations. What is never discussed: the possibility that we feel anxiety because we are in danger of losing some part or quality of soul unless we act, and not dangerously; or the likelihood that we feel dread when intimations of our death inspire us with disproportionate terror, a horror not merely because we are going to die, but to the contrary because we are going to die badly and suffer some unendurable stricture of eternity. These explanations are altogether outside the close focus of the psychological sciences in the twentieth century. No, our century, at least our American century, is a convalescent home for the shell-shocked veterans of a two-thousand-year war—that huge struggle within Christianity to liberate or to destroy the vision of man.

The Homosexual Villain

———

(1955)

THOSE READERS OF *One* who are familiar with my work may be somewhat surprised to find me writing for this magazine. After all, I have been as guilty as any contemporary novelist in attributing unpleasant, ridiculous, or sinister connotations to the homosexual (or more accurately, bisexual) characters in my novels. Part of the effectiveness of General Cummings in *The Naked and the Dead*—at least for those people who thought him well conceived as a character—rested on the homosexuality I was obviously suggesting as the core of much of his motivation. Again, in *Barbary Shore,* the "villain" was a secret police agent named Leroy Hollingsworth whose sadism and slyness were essentially combined with his sexual deviation.

At the time I wrote those novels, I was consciously sincere. I did believe—as so many heterosexuals believe—that there was an intrinsic relation between homosexuality and "evil," and it seemed perfectly natural to me, as well as *symbolically* just, to treat the subject in such a way.

The irony is that I did not know a single homosexual during all those years. I had met homosexuals of course, I had recognized a few as homosexual, I had "suspected" others, I was to realize years later that one or two close friends were homosexual, but I had never known one in the human sense of knowing, which is to look at your friend's feelings through his eyes and not your own. I did not *know* any homosexual because obviously I did not want to. It was enough for me to recognize someone as homosexual, and I would cease to consider him seriously as a person. He might be intelligent or courageous or kind or witty or virtuous or tortured—no matter. I always saw him as at best ludicrous and at worst—the word again—sinister. (I think it is by the way significant that just as many homosexuals feel forced and are forced to throw up protective camouflage, even boasting if necessary of women they have had, not to mention the thousand smaller subtleties, so heterosexuals are often eager to be so deceived for it enables them to continue friendships which otherwise their prejudices and occasionally their fears might force them to terminate.)

Now, of course, I exaggerate to a certain degree. I was never a roaring bigot, I did not go in for homosexual baiting, at least not face-to-face, and I never could stomach the relish with which soldiers would describe how they had stomped some faggot in a bar. I had, in short, the equivalent of a "gentleman's anti-Semitism."

The only thing remarkable about all this is that I was hardly living in a small town. New York, whatever its pleasures and discontents, is not the most uncivilized milieu, and while one would go too far to say that its attitude toward homosexuals bears correspondence to the pain of the liberal or radical at hearing someone utter a word like "nigger" or "kike," there is nonetheless considerable tolerance and considerable propinquity. The hard-and-fast separations of homosexual and heterosexual society are often quite blurred. Over the past seven or eight years I had had more than enough opportunity to learn something about homosexuals if I had wanted to, and obviously I did not.

It is a pity I do not understand the psychological roots of my change of attitude, for something valuable might be learned from it. Unfortunately, I do not. The process has seemed a rational one to me, rational in that the impetus apparently came from reading and not from any important personal experiences. The only hint of my bias mellowing was that my wife and I had gradually become friendly with a homosexual painter who lived next door. He was pleasant, he was thoughtful, he was a good neighbor, and we came to depend on him in various small ways. It was tacitly understood that he was homosexual, but we never talked about it. However, since so much of his personal life was not discussable between us, the friendship was limited. I accepted him the way a small-town banker fifty years ago might have accepted a "good" Jew.

About this time I received a free copy of *One* which was sent out by the editors to a great many writers. I remember looking at the magazine with some interest and some amusement. Parts of it impressed me unfavorably. I thought the quality of writing generally poor (most people I've talked to agree that it has since improved), and I questioned the wisdom of accepting suggestive ads in a purportedly serious magazine. (Indeed, I still feel this way no matter what the problems of revenue might be.) But there was a certain militancy and honesty to the editorial tone, and while I was not sympathetic, I think I can say that for the first time in my life I was not unsympathetic. Most important of all, my curiosity was piqued. A few weeks later I asked my painter friend if I could borrow his copy of Donald Webster Cory's *The Homosexual in America.*

Reading it was an important experience. Mr. Cory strikes me as being a modest man, and I think he would be the first to admit that while his book is very good, closely reasoned, quietly argued, it is hardly a great book. Nonetheless, I can think of few books which cut so radically at my prejudices and altered my ideas so profoundly. I resisted it, I argued its points as I read, I was often annoyed, but what I could not overcome was my growing depression that I had been acting as a bigot in this matter, and "bigot" was one word I did not enjoy applying to myself. With that came the realization I had been closing myself off from understanding a very large part of life. This thought is always disturbing to a writer. A writer has his talent, and for all one knows, he is born with it, but whether his talent develops is to some degree responsive to his use of it. He can grow as a person or he can shrink, and by this I don't intend any facile parallels between moral and artistic growth. The writer can become a bigger hoodlum if need be, but his alertness, his curiosity, his reaction to life must not diminish. The fatal thing is to shrink, to be interested in less, sympathetic to less, desiccating to the point where life itself loses its flavor, and one's passion for human understanding changes to weariness and distaste.

So, as I read Mr. Cory's book, I found myself thinking in effect, *My God, homosexuals are people too.* Undoubtedly, this will seem incredibly naïve to the homosexual readers of *One* who have been all too painfully aware that they are indeed people, but prejudice is wed to naïveté, and even the sloughing of prejudice, particularly when it is abrupt, partakes of the naïve. I have not tried to conceal that note. As I reread this article I find its tone ingenuous, but there is no point in trying to alter it. One does not become sophisticated overnight about a subject one has closed from oneself.

At any rate I began to face up to my homosexual bias. I had been a libertarian socialist for some years, and implicit in all my beliefs had been the idea that society must allow every individual his own road to discovering himself. Libertarian socialism (the first word is as important as the second) implies inevitably that one have respect for the varieties of human experience. Very basic to everything I had thought was that sexual relations, above everything else, demand their liberty, even if such liberty should amount to no more than compulsion or necessity. For, in the reverse, history has certainly offered enough examples of the link between sexual repression and political repression. (A fascinating thesis on this subject is *The Sexual Revolution* by Wilhelm Reich.) I suppose I can say that for the first time I understood homosexual persecution to be a political act and a reactionary act, and I was properly ashamed of myself.

On the positive side, I found over the next few months that a great deal was opening to me—to put it briefly, even crudely, I felt that I understood more about people, more about life. My life-view had been shocked and the lights and shadows were being shifted, which is equal to saying that I was learning a great deal. At a perhaps embarrassingly personal level, I discovered another benefit. There is probably no sensitive heterosexual alive who is not preoccupied at one time or another with his latent homosexuality, and while I had no conscious homosexual desires, I had wondered more than once if really there were not something suspicious in my intense dislike of homosexuals. How pleasant to discover that once one can accept homosexuals as real friends, the tension is gone with the acceptance. I found that I was no longer concerned with latent homosexuality. It seemed vastly less important, and paradoxically enabled me to realize that I am actually quite heterosexual. Close friendships with homosexuals had become possible without sexual desire or even sexual nuance—at least no more sexual nuance than is present in all human relations.

However, I had a peculiar problem at this time. I was on the way to finishing *The Deer Park,* my third novel. There was a minor character in it named Teddy Pope who is a movie star and a homosexual. Through the first and second drafts he had existed as a stereotype, a figure of fun; he was ludicrously affected and therefore ridiculous. One of the reasons I resisted Mr. Cory's book so much is that I was beginning to feel uneasy with the characterization I had drawn. In life there are any number of ridiculous people, but at bottom I was saying that Teddy Pope was ridiculous because he was homosexual. I found myself dissatisfied with the characterization even before I read *The Homosexual in America,* it had already struck me as being compounded too entirely of malice, but I think I would probably have left it that way. After Mr. Cory's book, it had become impossible. I no longer believed in Teddy Pope as I had drawn him.

Yet a novel which is almost finished is very difficult to alter. If it is at all a good book, the proportions, the meanings, and the interrelations of the characters have become integrated, and one does not violate them without injuring one's work. Moreover, I have developed an antipathy to using one's novels as direct expressions of one's latest ideas. I therefore had no desire to

change Teddy Pope into a fine virtuous character. That would be
as false, and as close to propaganda, as to keep him the way he
was. Also, while a minor character, he had an important relation
to the story, and it was obvious that he could not be transformed
too radically without recasting much of the novel. My decision,
with which I am not altogether happy, was to keep Teddy Pope
more or less intact, but to try to add dimension to him. Perhaps
I have succeeded. He will never be a character many readers admire, but it is possible that they will have feeling for him. At least
he is no longer a simple object of ridicule, nor the butt of my
malice, and I believe *The Deer Park* is a better book for the change.
My hope is that some readers may possibly be stimulated to envisage the gamut of homosexual personality as parallel to the
gamut of heterosexual personality even if Teddy Pope is a character from the lower half of the spectrum. However, I think it is
more probable that the majority of homosexual readers who
may get around to reading *The Deer Park* when it is published will
be dissatisfied with him. I can only say that I am hardly satisfied
myself. But this time, at least, I have discovered the edges of the
rich theme of homosexuality rather than the easy symbolic equation of it to evil. And to that extent I feel richer and more confident as a writer. What I have come to realize is that much of my
homosexual prejudice was a servant to my aesthetic needs. In
the variety and contradiction of American life, the difficulty of
finding a character who can serve as one's protagonist is matched
only by the difficulty of finding one's villain, and so long as I was
able to preserve my prejudices, my literary villains were at hand.
Now, the problem will be more difficult, but I suspect it may be
rewarding too, for deep down I was never very happy nor proud
of myself at whipping homosexual straw boys.

A last remark. If the homosexual is ever to achieve real social
equality and acceptance, he too will have to work the hard row of
shedding his own prejudices. Driven into defiance, it is natural,
if regrettable, that many homosexuals go to the direction of assuming that there is something intrinsically superior in homo-

sexuality, and carried far enough it is a viewpoint which is as stultifying, as ridiculous, and as antihuman as the heterosexual's prejudice. Finally, heterosexuals are people too, and the hope of acceptance, tolerance, and sympathy must rest on this mutual appreciation.

What I Think of Artistic Freedom

(1955)

TO SAY ANYTHING ABOUT "artistic freedom" in a few pages is of course almost impossible. One has the doubtful choice of making a few private remarks or else listing a series of platitudes. If I choose the second procedure it is because the platitude for all its obvious disadvantages has nonetheless a particular advantage we are too likely to forget—in every cliché is buried a truth, and to contemplate a cliché, to explore it, to search for its paradoxes and attempt to resolve them is a most characteristic activity of thought, if indeed it is not thought itself, for in a very real sense every word in a language is a small cliché flattening the variety of experience it attempts to illumine. And some words are large clichés, meaningless to some, infinite to others; we need only think of "God," "Life," "Adventure," "Color"—whichever word one chooses.

There is one further preface I must make. For years I have been alternately attracted to Marxism and anarchism, and in the tension between the two I suppose I have found the themes for my novels. So I do not write this credo with any idea of being a champion of America or the West. As a practical matter, and one can hardly scorn such an important practical matter, there is

more liberty to express unpopular, radical, "useless," or dangerous ideas in the United States than there is in the Soviet Union
or the "Eastern Democracies." Nonetheless it is done at one's
disadvantage if not one's outright danger, and the advertisers of
America's artistic liberties often neglect to mention that our unpopular ideas are invariably buried in tangential newspapers and
magazines whose circulation is pitifully small. Still, this is better
than total zero. Stalinism, in its churchly wisdom, has recognized
for decades that nothing is more difficult to anticipate than the
movement and growth of ideas; therefore it permits no expression beyond the most clearly defined limits.

There was a period some years ago when I was half attracted
to Stalinism, and so I am not unfamiliar with the muscular appeal it offers many intellectuals. "Poor frustrated spindly thinker,"
Stalinism is constantly saying, "when will you realize that your
problems are not the problems of the world, and that all men
must eat before one man can be privileged to think indepen-
dently." Like all absolute assertions it presents a part of the
whole. For it is undeniable that there is shame as well as dignity
to thought so long as only a few have leisure enough to search
for it. The lie, however, and it is the organic contradiction of
Stalinism that it cannot recognize this lie which has haunted it,
confused it, and even created the insoluble tangles of its very
economic inefficiency, has been the lie, the arrogance, of assuming that human development can proceed on a half-truth. The
false humility of Stalinist self-criticism is always arrogance, for
there is no arrogance like declaring that one's past works and
actions led people in bad directions. It assumes the ridiculous
conceit that one's present works are therefore good.

Out of this arrogance Stalinism has defined what the artist is,
has allocated his specific work, has granted him a specific collective importance, and has denied him a private voice. Like most
Western artists I have been tormented more than once by the
nightmare of possessing a private voice. All too often one's work
seems meaningless, isolated, and one's accomplishments pitiful.
Yet it must never be forgotten that despair about the meaning of
one's work is more vital to the creative process than social ap-

proval. To create, one must first destroy; to be capable of love one must be able to hate, and nothing dulls love and hatred into their pallid social equivalent so much as social approval. Only when the artist is ready to accept despair, isolation, contraction, and spiritual exile can he be able to find the expansive energies and the unrestrained enthusiasm which continue the essential dialectic of human progress. The genius of Marx was that he was a mystic as well as a rationalist, and the intellectual deterioration of Socialism, not to mention the mental petrifaction of Stalinism, comes from denying the mystical element in Marxism and championing the rational. In human history there is finally one umbilical conflict: it is man versus society. For society always consists of the search for the single understanding, the "One," the rational judgment, the established value or the value to be established; the spectrum of society runs the unilinear gamut of those things admired absolutely to those things detested absolutely. Implicit in every social view is the concealed notion that society (which is One) is good, and man (who is multiple) is thereby bad, man who is mysterious and finally undefinable for he includes the expanding sum of all those things (people, thought, the Self, experience, the universe—one may extend the list indefinitely), all those things man must forever love-and-hate, hate-and-love. So, society, which is necessary to enable man to grow, is also the prison whose walls he must perpetually enlarge. The paradox of this relation—half wedding, half prison—is that without man there cannot be society, yet society must always seek to restrain man, and the total socialization of man is the social view that one man is good and another man is bad.

It is the artist, embodying the most noble faculty of man—his urge to rebel—who is forever enlarging the walls. An artist who is not ahead of his time is not an artist—he is merely a social producer—and one does not need to be a Marxist to remember that Marx's most compassionate agony was felt for the horror of separating man from his creative tools. The Stalinists by converting their artists to social producers have exercised the crippling vanity of total society for they have made the error, I believe, of assuming that society can foresee the future when only man can do that. They have gelded the artist of his real and exciting purpose which is never to fashion huge social products, book editions running to five million copies and dachas and medals and *social* esteem, but rather is the deeper purpose to awake—if it be in but one other person and that in ways the artist did not expect nor even desire—the knowledge that what we see today as simple will later be understood as complex and what we think is complex will appear simple, that in the bad man there is good and in the good man bad, that everything if we look at it carefully enough, even a stranger's comment on the weather, is a door of perception opening to other doors. That is the artist's purpose—to open doors—and it is arrogance for the bureaucrat, no matter how intelligent, devoted, and subjectively convinced of his moral purity he may be (I take the exceptional bureaucrat), to decide that the artist's function is to describe the glories of the room in which one remains. That is to make the artist a prisoner in a museum, a trustee in uniform, doomed forever to whine irritably at children that they must keep their fingers off the paintings.

Raison d'Être

———

(1956)

MANY YEARS AGO I remember reading a piece in the newspapers by Ernest Hemingway and thinking: "What windy writing." That is the penalty for having a reputation as a writer. Any signed paragraph which appears in print is examined by the usual sadistic literary standards, rather than with the easy tolerance of a newspaper reader pleased to get an added fillip for his nickel.

But this is a fact of life which any professional writer soon learns to put up with, and I know that I will have to put up with it since I doubt very much if this column is going to be particularly well written. That would take too much time, and it would be time spent in what is certainly a losing cause. Greenwich Village is one of the better provinces—it abounds in snobs and critics. That many of you are frustrated in your ambitions, and undernourished in your pleasures, only makes you more venomous. Quite rightly. If I found myself in your position, I would not be charitable either. Nevertheless, given your general animus to those more talented than yourselves, the only way I see myself becoming one of the cherished traditions of the Village is to be actively disliked each week.

At this point it can fairly be asked: "Is this your only reason for

writing a column?" And the next best answer I suppose is: "Egotism. My search to discover in public how much of me is sheer
egotism." I find a desire to inflict my casual opinions on a half-
captive audience. If I did not, there would always be the danger
of putting these casual opinions into a new novel, and we know
what a terrible thing that is to do.

I also feel tempted to say that novelists are the only group of
people who should write a column. Their interests are large, if
shallow, their habits are sufficiently unreliable for them to find
something to say quite often, and in most other respects they are
more columnistic than the columnists. Most of us novelists who
are any good are invariably half-educated; inaccurate, albeit brilliant upon occasion; insufferably vain of course; and—the indispensable requirement for a good newspaperman—as eager to
tell a lie as the truth. (Saying the truth makes us burn with the
desire to convince our audience, whereas telling a lie affords
ample leisure to study the result.)

We good novelists also have the most unnewspaperly virtue of
never praising fatherland and flag unless we are sick, tired, generally defeated, and want to turn a quick dishonest buck. Nobody but novelists would be asked to write columns if it were not
for the sad fact that newspaper editors are professionally and
obligatorily patriotic, and so never care to meet us. Indeed,
even *The Village Voice,* which is remarkably conservative for so
young a paper, and deeply patriotic about all community affairs,
etc., etc., would not want me either if they were not so financially
eager for free writing, and a successful name to go along with it,
that they are ready to put up with almost anything. And I, as a
minority stockholder in the *Voice* corporation, must agree that
this paper does need something added to its general languor
and whimsy.

At any rate, dear reader, we begin a collaboration which may
go on for three weeks, three months, or, the Lord forbid, for
three-and-thirty years. I have only one prayer—that I weary of
you before you tire of me. And therefore, so soon as I learn to
write columns in a quarter of an hour instead of the unprofitable
fifty-two minutes this has taken, we will all know better if our tri-

fling business is going to continue. If it does, there is one chance
in a hundred—make it a hundred thousand—that I will become
a habitual assassin-and-lover of a columnist who will have something superficial or vicious or inaccurate to say about many of
the things under the sun, and who knows but what some of the
night.

On Lies, Power, and Obscenity

(1956)

A WARNING: The column this week is difficult. True to my commitment to the *Voice*, I wrote it quickly. Because I do not want to lose all my readers at once, I suggest that all but the slowest readers pass me by this time. If you are not in a mood to think, or if you have no interest in thinking, then let us ignore each other until the next column. And if you do go on from here, please have the courtesy to concentrate. The art of careful writing is beginning to disappear before the mental impotence of such lazy audiences as the present one. Thought, after all, is one of the two prime pleasures available (at least theoretically) in a rational democracy, the other being sensual love, politely called the pursuit of happiness.

SINCE A NEWSPAPER column is supposed to be concerned with communication, it would not be the worst idea to attempt to trace what communication might be.

Thought begins somewhere deep in the unconscious—an unconscious which conceivably is divine—or if finite may still be vast enough in its complexity to bear comparison to an ocean.

Out of each human being's vast and mighty unconscious, perhaps from the depths of our life itself, up over all the forbiddingly powerful and subterranean mental mountain ranges which forbid expression, rises from the mysterious source of our knowledge the small self-fertilization of thought, conscious thought.

But for a thought to live (and so give us dignity) before it disappears, unexpressed and perhaps never to be thought again, it must be told to someone else: to one's mate, to a good friend, or occasionally to a stranger. It is in the act of telling a thought that the thought—no matter how unlikely—may be convincing to another, and inspiring him or her to some small action. Needless to say that small action is not likely to be the one we have suggested, but it is an action to which we have been the tangential father. We have at least, no matter how crudely or ineptly, succeeded in communicating something, and the actions of others, as well as our own, are the result. In the rigorous sense there is no communication unless action has resulted, be it immediately or in the unknown and indefinite future. Communication which does not lead to new action is not communication—it is merely the abortive presentation of new social ideas or the monotonous transportation of old ones.

Lies

But an old social idea is a lie. Where it is not sheer premeditated falsity (four-fifths of gossip columnists' spew, for example) it is at best a description of something which no longer exists. Society at any moment is the stubborn retarded expression of mankind's previous and partially collected experience. Yet our previous experience is the past, it is our knowledge of death, and theologians to the side (for I frankly am all but ignorant of theology) I would argue most seriously that growth is a greater mystery than death. All of us can understand failure, we all contain failure and death within us, but not even the successful man can begin to describe the impalpable elations and apprehensions of growth.

When we can all agree, including odd dialectical idealists like myself, that history is not foreseeable and the future is unknown, we must also agree that although society is a machine, it does not determine man's fate, but merely processes nine-tenths of his possibilities on the basis of what society has learned from the past. Since we are all in the process of changing, since we are already in the privacy of our minds far ahead of the life we see around us (for civilized man has always been outraged by what he sees, or else there would be no civilization)—since we are all advanced in our dreams beyond the practical social possibilities open to our immediate time, that present *living* time which is all but strangled by the slow mechanical determinations of society, we know and feel that whatever happens to us will happen as the reaction between our urgent desires to express ourselves, to discover the passionate attachment of our lives, and the resistant, mechanical network of past social ideas, platitudes, and lies.

Power

Only it is difficult to express oneself. The act of writing something (which one expects or hopes will be published) is a social act, it becomes—even at its best—all but a lie. To communicate socially (as opposed to communicating personally or humanly) means that one must accept the sluggish fictions of society for at least nine-tenths of one's expression in order to present deceptively the remaining tenth which may be new. Social communication is the doom of every truly felt thought. (Naturally, all men who wish to communicate seek social communication nonetheless, for it is the only way to influence great numbers of people in a relatively short time.)

To communicate socially is to communicate by way of the mass media—movies, radio, television, advertising, newspapers, best-selling novels, etc.—which is to communicate by way of the largest and most debased common denominator—which in turn is equivalent to communicating very little, for procedurally one becomes part of a machine which is antithetical to one's individual existence. Antithetical, I say, because this machine attempts to direct the fortunes of men by the obsolete and hence impractical results of the past. As one writes, one enters an external network of expectations, consequences, fears, cupidities, social fashions: in short, reward or punishment turns the language and alters the thought. This is true even of the most serious attempts to communicate, by artists let us say, or the occasional creative scholar. Once one enters the land of massive social communication, of network communication, once one becomes attached to the machine belt of the mass media—specifically, in our case, the assembly line of the columnist—there is no desire to retain even the father's ghost of a thought. There is only power for the sake of power, and it is cowardly power for it masquerades in coy and winsome forms. On the surface there is only the attempt to entertain in a conventional way. (Obviously, to entertain and yet say nothing new is quite a difficult game, which is why perhaps columnists, commercial writers, and so forth are paid so well.)

Therefore, I propose to try something I do not believe I can accomplish. I will try to write for you (this column to the contrary) as if I were talking in my living room, or in yours. So my opinions will be half-formed, if not totally inarticulate, but at least they can be awkwardly close to the questions I am really thinking about.

Obscenity

Even so, I promise very very little. For example I will be able to use no obscenities, and obscenities communicate a great deal in the living room and indeed in other places as well. For what are obscenities finally but our poor debased gutturals for the magical parts of the human body, and so they are basic communication, for they awake, no matter how uneasily, many of the questions, riddles, aches, and pleasures which surround the enigma of life.

No, I will not be able to use obscenities—what a pity!—

because a little social fact which is too often forgotten is that obscene language, which is used at least once in a while by 95 percent of the people living in this country, would forbid the passage of this newspaper through the mails. And there are other restrictions, stories I cannot tell about unpleasant people in the daily news, people who are pusillanimous, or archly vicious, or hypocritical, or worse, or simply no good, stories I cannot tell because this paper would be sued for libel. (Ah, well, perhaps we will find a way yet.)

So these restrictions and all others sadden me, because I would like to express myself properly, and the true communication of soul to soul is speeded on its way, as every soldier and ex-soldier knows, by the foul language God gave our tongues, along with everything else He gave us including malicious stories, women, society, pain, pleasure, lights and darks, and all the other mysterious dualities of our mysterious universe.

Therefore, brethren, let me close this sermon by asking the grace for us to be aware, if only once in a while, that beyond the mechanical communication of all of society's obvious and subtle networks, there remains the sense of life, the sense of creative spirit (we are all creative if it is for no less than to create new life itself), and therefore the sense no matter how dimly felt of some expanding and not necessarily ignoble human growth.

With this worthy homilectic come to a close, I promise next week to offer some diversion. Perhaps even some dialogue. If I say so myself, I am rather good at that.

Nomination of Ernest Hemingway
for President: Part I

———

(1956)

UNTIL NOW, I believe I have been fairly regular about covering some facet of what I promised to deliver the week before. This once, however, I would like to beg my readers' all-but-nonexistent indulgence and postpone the fateful nomination of Democratic candidate until next week.

There are various reasons for this, but the most direct is the news-box which appeared on page 1 of the *Voice* last week. It went:

> Who's Norman Mailer's candidate for president? Those readers who turn to page 5 and read "Quickly" slowly, might find some clue. In any case there's a $10 prize for the first correct solution received at this office. (His choice, by the way, is in a sealed envelope pasted on to the center of the Village Voice window. You can see it there from the street.)

Now this was a trifle misleading, since there were no portentous clues in last week's column. I had said to the gentleman who wrote the news-box that there might be a few hints in all my columns taken together, but this was unfortunately garbled a bit in transmission. So, as an apology for neglecting to look at the news box in galleys, I will double the ante to $20, and give a few more pointed suggestions.

The greatest clues of course are buried in those parts of my character which have been revealed week by week. What it comes down to is who, by God, would that megalomaniac Mailer nominate besides himself? And of course the wise man—if there is one among you—would answer: "Why, even a bigger megalomaniac."

Clue #2. Last week I had a line in answer to Dr. Y. which went: "Sleep is wisdom for gladiators like yourself." So your columnist demonstrated indirectly that in his cold bitter soul, he has respect for gladiators who are on their feet. Therefore, Candidate X must fulfill this condition as well.

Clue #3. Candidate X would approve of slow readers.

Clue #4. Candidate X must of course be Hip, and yet not display himself unduly as a hipster. Perhaps we can assume that he was one of the germinal influences in the birth of the hipster.

Clue #5. (And this should be enough.) My passion, as a few slow readers may have realized by now, is to destroy stereotypes, categories, and labels. So Candidate X, who has never been considered (to my knowledge) as a political candidate for anything, by either party—as indeed was once true of Eisenhower—is nonetheless an important figure in American life. To a degree he has affected the style of American manners. If he were drafted as a candidate, the emanations of his personality might loosen the lugubrious rhetorical daisy chains of liberal argument which so deaden the air about all these Demo-bureaucratic candidates.

The rest of this column I wish to give over to a little talk about politics, most of which will be, as usual, in the first person. I have not voted since 1948, and I doubt if I will vote in 1956 even if, by some fantastic mischance, Candidate X would be drafted. (My sole motive in all this is to look for a good time. I want the next presidential campaign to be an interesting circus, rather than the dreary set of opposed commercials it now promises to be.) In my time I have been consecutively a sort of fellow-traveler (as was fitting for my earnest youth), a radical-at-liberty, disenchanted by the USSR on closer study, yet never quite enthusiastic about our own glorious fatherland and flag; and at present I have ended temporarily as what I have always been by temperament, an anarchist, or perhaps more accurately, a rebel. So it is obvious to anyone who knows me well that for me to write about a Democratic candidate is pretty much a tongue-in-cheek performance.

Still, most of you will be taking your vote seriously, and to go on like this is only to offend you further. Most people, given their massage by propaganda, believe that a man who doesn't vote is a little lower than a man who beats his mother, or, to be more psychically exact, a son who strikes his father. And perhaps even the Mailer would come off his mountain long enough to vote, if he felt any confidence that the Republican or Democratic Party was relatively the least bit more effective—for a given year—at going in historical directions one might think to be encouraging. But the curious contradictions of power and party politics are such that if I were to vote on this principle, I would be forced ever so slightly toward the Republicans. Not because I like them, mind you—I rather dislike them, they are such unconscionable hypocrites. Yet the disagreeable fact of power in these politically depressed years—like it or leave it—is that the Republican Party is a little more free to act, precisely because it does not have to be afraid of the Republicans, whereas the Democrats do. If the Democrats had the presidency, any relatively happy political action would be attacked by the Republicans as Communist-inspired; in power themselves, the Republicans find the objective situation (that is, the passive logic of events) pushes the same action and legislation upon them. So, reluctantly, they introduce what is necessary, and the predominantly Republican press and mass media accept it. (As an example, think of the end of the war in Korea, or the antisegregation efforts: I believe quite seriously that we would still be at war in Korea if the Democrats had won in '52, for one can only begin to imagine the Republican fury at making peace—the hearty howling cries that for the first time in America's proud history we had lost a war, and so forth, and so forth. So, too, with antisegregation. If the Democrats had tried to carry it through, the Republicans would have been rather pleased to collect the various little Democratic parties in the South.)

I know this is unpleasant to all of you who believe that truth and untruth are separate, but then I have no particular desire to bring you pleasure. The antitheses of power are such today that I believe the party in power must adopt the opposite in office of what it announced as its desires when it was out of power. It is metaphorically similar to the change in personality which you may have noticed in some of your friends who came to marriage after living together for years.

NEXT WEEK: CANDIDATE X WILL BE NAMED, AND THE PRIZEWINNER, IF THERE SHOULD BE ONE, WILL BE GIVEN HIS OR HER $20.

Nomination of Ernest Hemingway
for President: Part II

————

(1956)

YES, IT MAY SEEM a trifle fantastic at the first approach, but the man I think the Democrats ought to draft for their presidential candidate in 1956 is Ernest Hemingway.

I have had this thought in mind for some months, and have tried to consider its merits and demerits more than once. You see, I am far from a worshipper of Hemingway, but after a good many years of forever putting him down in my mind, I came to decide that like him or not, he was one of the two counterposed aesthetic forces in the American novel today—the other being Faulkner of course—and so his mark on history is probably assured.

Now, what I think of Hemingway as a writer would be of interest to very few people, but I underline that I am not a religious devotee of his work in order to emphasize that I have thought about him as a presidential candidate without passion or self-involvement (or at least so I believe it to be). As for his merits and even more important his possibilities for victory, I will try to discuss them quickly in the limits of this column.

To begin with, the Democratic Party has the poorest of chances against Eisenhower, and whether it be Stevenson, Kefauver, or some other political half-worthy, the candidate's personality would suffer from his unfortunate resemblance to a prosperous undertaker. There is no getting around it—the American people tend to vote for the candidate who gives off the impression of having experienced some pleasure in his life, and Eisenhower, whatever his passive vicissitudes, looks like he has had a good time now and again. I would submit that this is one of the few healthy aspects of our unhealthy country—it is indeed folk wisdom. A man who has had good times has invariably also suffered (as opposed to the unfortunate number of people who have avoided pain at the expense of avoiding pleasure as well), and the mixture of pain and pleasure in a man's experiences is likely to give him the proportion, the common sense, and the charm a president needs.

Hemingway, I would guess, possesses exactly that kind of charm, possesses it in greater degree than Eisenhower, and so he would have some outside chance to win. His name is already better known in America than was Stevenson's in 1951, and his prestige in Europe would be no mean factor in the minds of the many overeducated middlebrows who think in such collectivized words as our-prestige-in-Europe. There are, after all, as passing examples, Hemingway's Nobel Prize and his fluency in French, Spanish, and Italian.

In the small towns of America, where Eisenhower has such strong roots, Hemingway, by the grace of his thorough knowledge of hunting and fishing, would exercise a most human and direct appeal to the instincts of small-town men. On the other hand, city women would also be drawn toward him. It has been my experience that a man who has been married a few times interests more women than not. It is of course defeating to say this out loud, but then there would be no need for the Democrats to advertise it, the Republicans might consider it wiser to refrain from dirty politics, and the word would get around from living room to living room.

Another of Hemingway's political virtues is that he has an interesting war record, and that he succeeded in becoming a man of more physical courage than most—and this is no easy nor unexhausting attainment for a major writer. Whether the Village will like it or not, most Americans like warriors, indeed so much that they have been ready to swallow the bitter pill of an Army general in office. Yet I think they are not so far submerged into the hopeless conformity which plagues us, as to ignore the independent initiative of a general-at-liberty like Hemingway, who came so close to taking Paris in the last war with only a few hundred men.

Again, Hemingway might be inclined to speak simply, and so far as politics goes, freshly, and the energy this would arouse in the minds of the electorate, benumbed at present by the turgid Latinisms of the Kefauvers, the Stevensons, and the Eisenhowers, is something one should not underestimate, for almost never has the electorate been given the opportunity to have their minds stimulated.

Finally, Hemingway's lack of a previous political life is an asset, I would argue, rather than a vice. Politics has become static in America, and Americans have always distrusted politicians. (Which distrust indeed accounts for a great deal of Eisenhower's original appeal.) The glimmer of hope on all our murky horizons is that civilization may be coming to the point where we will return to voting for individual men (or individual women) rather than for political ideas, those political ideas which eventually are cemented into the social network of life as a betrayal of the individual desires which gave birth to them—for society, I will argue, on the day I get the wit, is the assassin of us all.

The above is for people who like a point-by-point discussion. What it comes down to by rebel rule-of-Hip is that Hemingway is probably a good bit more human than Eisenhower or the others, and so there might be a touch more color in our Roman Empire. More than that is unfair to expect of any president.

Now, for those who believe that a nominating speech must have a little warmth, and even—I tighten my stomach for this— a little sentimentality, I suppose I ought to go on to say that Hemingway is one of the few people in our national life who has tried to live with a certain passion for capturing what he desired, and I believe he indeed succeeded in earning a degree of the self-respect for which he has always searched, and yet at the same time he was able, with what writing pains only another serious writer (good or not) can know, to write his novels as well; and so no matter what his faults of character, and they must be many, I have the feeling that he probably has achieved a considerable part of his dream—which was to be more than most—and this country could stand a man for president, since for all too many years our lives have been guided by men who were essentially women, which indeed is good for neither men nor women. So to me Ernest Hemingway looks like the best practical possibility in sight, because with all his sad and silly vanities, and some of his intellectual cowardices, I suspect that he's still more real than most, you know?

P.S. Since my endorsement can only cause Hemingway various small harms, I promise to any Democratic Party leader who hears of this, and is wise enough to see the political sex appeal of drafting Ernest Hemingway, that I will devote my political time to attacking old Hemingway for whatever small number of voters I will influence by reverse English to vote for him. You see, friends and constituents of this paper, one advantage of being a village villain is that one is always certain of influencing events by arguing the opposite of what one really wants.

The White Negro

(1957)

Our search for the rebels of the generation led us to the
hipster. The hipster is an enfant terrible turned inside
out. In character with his time, he is trying to get back
at the conformists by lying low. . . . You can't interview a
hipster because his main goal is to keep out of a society
which, he thinks, is trying to make everyone over in its
own image. He takes marijuana because it supplies him
with experiences that can't be shared with "squares."
He may affect a broad-brimmed hat or a zoot suit, but
usually he prefers to skulk unmarked. The hipster may
be a jazz musician; he is rarely an artist, almost never a
writer. He may earn his living as a petty criminal, a hobo,
a carnival roustabout, or a freelance moving man in
Greenwich Village, but some hipsters have found a safe
refuge in the upper income brackets as television com-
ics or movie actors. (The late James Dean, for one, was
a hipster hero.) . . . It is tempting to describe the hipster
in psychiatric terms as infantile, but the style of his in-
fantilism is a sign of the times; he does not try to en-
force his will on others, Napoleon-fashion, but contents

himself with a magical omnipotence never disproved
because never tested. . . . As the only extreme noncon-
formist of his generation, he exercises a powerful if underground appeal for conformists, through newspaper
accounts of his delinquencies, his structureless jazz, and
his emotive grunt words.

—"BORN 1930: THE UNLOST GENERATION"
BY CAROLINE BIRD, *Harper's Bazaar*, FEB. 1957

PROBABLY, WE WILL NEVER be able to determine the psychic havoc
of the concentration camps and the atom bomb upon the unconscious mind of almost everyone alive in these years. For the
first time in civilized history, perhaps for the first time in all of
history, we have been forced to live with the suppressed knowledge that the smallest facets of our personality or the most minor
projection of our ideas, or indeed the absence of ideas and the
absence of personality, could mean equally well that we might
still be doomed to die as a cipher in some vast statistical operation in which our teeth would be counted, and our hair would be
saved, but our death itself would be unknown, unhonored, and
unremarked, a death which could not follow with dignity as a
possible consequence to serious actions we had chosen, but
rather a death by deus ex machina in a gas chamber or a radioactive city; and so if in the midst of civilization—that civilization
founded upon the Faustian urge to dominate nature by mastering time, mastering the links of social cause and effect—in the
middle of an economic civilization founded upon the confidence that time could indeed be subjected to our will, our psyche
was subjected itself to the intolerable anxiety that death being
causeless, life was causeless as well, and time deprived of cause
and effect had come to a stop.

The Second World War presented a mirror to the human condition which blinded anyone who looked into it. For if tens of
millions were killed in concentration camps out of the inexora-
ble agonies and contradictions of superstates founded upon the
always insoluble contradictions of injustice, one was then obliged
also to see that no matter how crippled and perverted an image

of man was the society he had created, it was nonetheless his creation, his collective creation (at least his collective creation from the past), and if society was so murderous, then who could ignore the most hideous of questions about his own nature?

Worse. One could hardly maintain the courage to be individual, to speak with one's own voice, for the years in which one could complacently accept oneself as part of an elite by being a radical were forever gone. A man knew that when he dissented, he gave a note upon his life which could be called in any year of overt crisis. No wonder then that these have been the years of conformity and depression. A stench of fear has come out of every pore of American life, and we suffer from a collective failure of nerve. The only courage, with rare exceptions, that we have been witness to has been the isolated courage of isolated people.

II

It is on this bleak scene that a phenomenon has appeared: the American existentialist—the hipster, the man who knows that if our collective condition is to live with instant death by atomic war, relatively quick death by the State as *l'univers concentrationnaire,* or with a slow death by conformity with every creative and rebellious instinct stifled (at what damage to the mind and the heart and the liver and the nerves no research foundation for cancer will discover in a hurry), if the fate of twentieth-century man is to live with death from adolescence to premature senescence, why then the only life-giving answer is to accept the terms of death, to live with death as immediate danger, to divorce oneself from society, to exist without roots, to set out on that uncharted journey into the rebellious imperatives of the self. In short, whether the life is criminal or not, the decision is to encourage the psychopath in oneself, to explore that domain of experience where security is boredom and therefore sickness, and one exists in the present, in that enormous present which is without past or future, memory or planned intention, the life where a man must go until he is beat, where he must gamble with his energies through all those small or large crises of courage and unforeseen situations which beset his day, where he must be with it or doomed not to swing. The unstated essence of Hip, its psychopathic brilliance, quivers with the knowledge that new kinds of victories increase one's power for new kinds of perception; and defeats, the wrong kind of defeats, attack the body and imprison one's energy until one is jailed in the prison air of other people's habits, other people's defeats, boredom, quiet desperation, and muted icy self-destroying rage. One is Hip or one is Square (the alternative which each new generation coming into American life is beginning to feel), one is a rebel or one conforms, one is a frontiersman in the Wild West of American nightlife, or else a Square cell, trapped in the totalitarian tissues of American society, doomed willy-nilly to conform if one is to succeed.

A totalitarian society makes enormous demands on the courage of men, and a partially totalitarian society makes even greater demands, for the general anxiety is greater. Indeed if one is to be a man, almost any kind of unconventional action often takes disproportionate courage. So it is no accident that the source of Hip is the Negro for he has been living on the margin between totalitarianism and democracy for two centuries. But the presence of Hip as a working philosophy in the subworlds of American life is probably due to jazz, and its knifelike entrance into culture, its subtle but so penetrating influence on an avant-garde generation—that postwar generation of adventurers who (some consciously, some by osmosis) had absorbed the lessons of disillusionment and disgust of the Twenties, the Depression, and the War. Sharing a collective disbelief in the words of men who had too much money and controlled too many things, they knew almost as powerful a disbelief in the socially monolithic ideas of the single mate, the solid family, and the respectable love life. If the intellectual antecedents of this generation can be traced to such separate influences as D. H. Lawrence, Henry Miller, and Wilhelm Reich, the viable philosophy of Hemingway fits most of their facts: in a bad world, as he was to say over and over again (while taking time out from his parvenu snobbery and dedicated gourmandise), in a bad world there is no love nor mercy nor charity nor justice unless a man can keep his courage—and this indeed fitted some of the facts. What fitted the need of the adventurer even more precisely was Hemingway's categorical imperative that what made him feel good became therefore The Good.

So no wonder that in certain cities of America, in New York of course, and New Orleans, in Chicago and San Francisco and Los Angeles, in such American cities as Paris and Mexico, D.F., this particular part of a generation was attracted to what the Negro had to offer. In such places as Greenwich Village, a ménage à trois was completed—the bohemian and the juvenile delinquent came face-to-face with the Negro, and the hipster was a fact in American life. If marijuana was the wedding ring, the child was the language of Hip, for its argot gave expression to abstract states of feeling which all could share—at least all who were Hip. And in this wedding of the white and the black it was the Negro who brought the cultural dowry. Any Negro who wishes to live must live with danger from his first day, and no experience can ever be casual to him, no Negro can saunter down a street with any real certainty that violence will not visit him on his walk. The cameos of security for the average white: mother and the home, job and the family, are not even a mockery to millions of Negroes; they are impossible. The Negro has the simplest of alternatives: live a life of constant humility or ever-threatening danger. In such a pass where paranoia is as vital to survival as blood, the Negro had stayed alive and begun to grow by following the need of his body where he could. Knowing in the cells of his existence that life was war, nothing but war, the Negro (all exceptions admitted) could rarely afford the sophisticated inhibitions of civilization, and so he kept for his survival the art of the primitive, he lived in the enormous present, he subsisted for his Saturday night kicks, relinquishing the pleasures of the mind for the more obligatory pleasures of the body, and in his music he gave voice to the character and quality of his existence, to his rage and the infinite variations of joy, lust, languor, growl, cramp, pinch, scream, and despair of his orgasm. For jazz is orgasm, it is the music of orgasm, good orgasm and bad, and so it spoke across a nation, it had the communication of art even where it was watered, perverted, corrupted, and almost killed, it spoke in no matter what laundered popular way of instantaneous existential states to which some whites could respond, it was indeed a communication by art because it said, "I feel this, and now you do too."

So there was a new breed of adventurers, urban adventurers who drifted out at night looking for action with a black man's code to fit their facts. The hipster had absorbed the existentialist synapses of the Negro, and for practical purposes could be considered a white Negro.

To be an existentialist, one must be able to feel oneself—one must know one's desires, one's rages, one's anguish, one must be aware of the character of one's frustration and know what would satisfy it. The overcivilized man can be an existentialist only if it is chic, and deserts it quickly for the next chic. To be a real existentialist (Sartre admittedly to the contrary) one must be religious, one must have one's sense of the "purpose"—whatever the purpose may be—but a life which is directed by one's faith in the necessity of action is a life committed to the notion that the substratum of existence is the search, the end meaningful but mysterious; it is impossible to live such a life unless one's emotions provide their profound conviction. Only the French, alienated beyond alienation from their unconscious, could welcome an existential philosophy without ever feeling it at all; indeed only a Frenchman by declaring that the unconscious did not exist could then proceed to explore the delicate involutions of consciousness, the microscopically sensuous and all but ineffable frissons of mental becoming, in order finally to create the theology of atheism and so submit that in a world of absurdities the existential absurdity is most coherent.

In the dialogue between the atheist and the mystic, the atheist is on the side of life, rational life, undialectical life—since he conceives of death as emptiness, he can, no matter how weary or despairing, wish for nothing but more life; his pride is that he does not transpose his weakness and spiritual fatigue into a romantic longing for death, for such appreciation of death is then all too capable of being elaborated by his imagination into a universe of meaningful structure and moral orchestration.

Yet this masculine argument can mean very little for the mystic. The mystic can accept the atheist's description of his weakness, he can agree that his mysticism was a response to despair. And yet . . . and yet his argument is that he, the mystic, is the one finally who has chosen to live with death, and so death is his experience and not the atheist's, and the atheist by eschewing the limitless dimensions of profound despair has rendered himself incapable to judge the experience. The real argument which the mystic must always advance is the very intensity of his private vision—his argument depends from the vision precisely because what was felt in the vision is so extraordinary that no rational argument, no hypotheses of "oceanic feelings," and certainly no skeptical reductions can explain away what has become for him the reality more real than the reality of closely reasoned logic. His inner experience of the possibilities within death is his logic. So, too, for the existentialist. And the psychopath. And the saint and the bullfighter and the lover. The common denominator for all of them is their burning consciousness of the present, exactly that incandescent consciousness which the possibilities within death have opened for them. There is a depth of desperation to the condition which enables one to remain in life only by engaging death, but the reward is their knowledge that what is happening at each instant of the electric present is good or bad for them, good or bad for their cause, their love, their action, their need.

It is this knowledge which provides the curious community of feeling in the world of the hipster, a muted cool religious revival to be sure, but the element which is exciting, disturbing, nightmarish perhaps, is that incompatibles have come to bed, the inner life and the violent life, the orgy and the dream of love, the desire to murder and the desire to create, a dialectical conception of existence with a lust for power, a dark, romantic, and yet undeniably dynamic view of existence for it sees every man and woman as moving individually through each moment of life forward into growth or backward into death.

III

It may be fruitful to consider the hipster a philosophical psychopath, a man interested not only in the dangerous imperatives of his psychopathy but in codifying, at least for himself, the suppositions on which his inner universe is constructed. By this premise the hipster is a psychopath, and yet not a psychopath but the negation of the psychopath for he possesses the narcissistic detachment of the philosopher, that absorption in the recessive nuances of one's own motive which is so alien to the unreasoning drive of the psychopath. In this country where new millions of psychopaths are developed each year, stamped with the mint of our contradictory popular culture (where sex is sin and yet sex is paradise), it is as if there has been room already for the development of the antithetical psychopath who extrapolates from his own condition, from the inner certainty that his rebellion is just, a radical vision of the universe which thus separates him from the general ignorance, reactionary prejudice, and self-doubt of the more conventional psychopath. Having converted his unconscious experience into much conscious knowledge, the hipster has shifted the focus of his desire from immediate gratification toward that wider passion for future power which is the mark of civilized man. Yet with an irreducible difference. For Hip is the sophistication of the wise primitive in a giant jungle, and so its appeal is still beyond the civilized man. If there are ten million Americans who are more or less psychopathic (and the figure is most modest) there are probably not more than one hundred thousand men and women who consciously see themselves as hipsters, but their importance is that they are an elite with the potential ruthlessness of an elite, and a language most adolescents can understand instinctively for the hipster's intense view of existence matches their experience and their desire to rebel.

Before one can say more about the hipster, there is obviously much to be said about the psychic state of the psychopath—or, clinically, the psychopathic personality. Now, for reasons which may be more curious than the similarity of the words, even many people with a psychoanalytical orientation often confuse the psychopath with the psychotic. Yet the terms are polar. The psychotic is legally insane, the psychopath is not; the psychotic is almost always incapable of discharging in physical acts the rage of his frustration, while the psychopath at his extreme is virtually as incapable of restraining his violence. The psychotic lives in so misty a world that what is happening at each moment of his life is not very real to him, whereas the psychopath seldom knows any reality greater than the face, the voice, the being of the particular people among whom he may find himself at any moment. Sheldon and Eleanor Glueck describe him as follows:

> The psychopath . . . can be distinguished from the person sliding into or clambering out of a "true psychotic" state by the long tough persistence of his anti-social attitude and behaviour and the absence of hallucinations, delusions, manic flight of ideas, confusion, disorientation, and other dramatic signs of psychosis.

The late Robert Lindner, one of the few experts on the subject, in his book *Rebel Without a Cause: The Hypnoanalysis of a Criminal Psychopath,* presented part of his definition in this way:

> the psychopath is a rebel without a cause, an agitator without a slogan, a revolutionary without a program: in other words, his rebelliousness is aimed to achieve goals satisfactory to himself alone; he is incapable of exertions for the sake of others. All his efforts, hidden under no matter what disguise, represent investments designed to satisfy his immediate wishes and desires. . . . The psychopath, like the child, cannot delay the pleasures of gratification; and this trait is one of his underlying, universal characteristics. He cannot wait upon

erotic gratification which convention demands should
be preceded by the chase before the kill: he must rape.
He cannot wait upon the development of prestige in
society: his egoistic ambitions lead him to leap into
headlines by daring performances. Like a red thread
the predominance of this mechanism for immediate
satisfaction runs through the history of every psychopath. It explains not only his behavior but also the violent nature of his acts.

Yet even Lindner, who was the most imaginative and most sympathetic of the psychoanalysts who have studied the psychopathic
personality, was not ready to project himself into the essential
sympathy—which is that the psychopath may indeed be the perverted and dangerous front-runner of a new kind of personality
which could become the central expression of human nature
before the twentieth century is over. For the psychopath is better
adapted to dominate those mutually contradictory inhibitions
upon violence and love which civilization has exacted of us, and
if it be remembered that not every psychopath is an extreme
case, and that the condition of psychopathy is present in a host
of people including many politicians, professional soldiers,
newspaper columnists, entertainers, artists, jazz musicians, call
girls, promiscuous homosexuals, and half the executives of Hollywood, television, and advertising, it can be seen that there are
aspects of psychopathy which already exert considerable cultural
influence.

What characterizes almost every psychopath and part-
psychopath is that they are trying to create a new nervous system
for themselves. Generally we are obliged to act with a nervous
system which has been formed from infancy, and which carries
in the style of its circuits the very contradictions of our parents
and our early milieu. Therefore, we are obliged, most of us, to
meet the tempo of the present and the future with reflexes and
rhythms which come from the past. It is not only the "dead
weight of the institutions of the past" but indeed the inefficient
and often antiquated nervous circuits of the past which strangle

our potentiality for responding to new possibilities which might be exciting for our individual growth.

Through most of modern history, "sublimation" was possible: at the expense of expressing only a small portion of oneself, that small portion could be expressed intensely. But sublimation depends on a reasonable tempo to history. If the collective life of a generation has moved too quickly, the "past" by which particular men and women of that generation may function is not, let us say, thirty years old, but relatively a hundred or two hundred years old. And so the nervous system is overstressed beyond the possibility of such compromises as sublimation, especially since the stable middle-class values so prerequisite to sublimation have been virtually destroyed in our time, at least as nourishing values free of confusion or doubt. In such a crisis of accelerated historical tempo and deteriorated values, neurosis tends to be replaced by psychopathy, and the success of psychoanalysis (which even ten years ago gave promise of becoming a direct major force) diminishes because of its inbuilt and characteristic incapacity to handle patients more complex, more experienced, or more adventurous than the analyst himself. In practice, psychoanalysis has by now become all too often no more than a psychic bloodletting. The patient is not so much changed as aged, and the infantile fantasies which he is encouraged to express are condemned to exhaust themselves against the analyst's nonresponsive reactions. The result for all too many patients is a diminution, a "tranquilizing" of their most interesting qualities and vices. The patient is indeed not so much altered as worn out—less bad, less good, less bright, less willful, less destructive, less creative. He is thus able to conform to that contradictory and unbearable society which first created his neurosis. He can conform to what he loathes because he no longer has the passion to feel loathing so intensely.

The psychopath is notoriously difficult to analyze because the fundamental decision of his nature is to try to live the infantile fantasy, and in this decision (given the dreary alternative of psychoanalysis) there may be a certain instinctive wisdom. For there is a dialectic to changing one's nature, the dialectic which underlies all psychoanalytic method: it is the knowledge that if one is to change one's habits, one must go back to the source of their creation, and so the psychopath exploring backward along the road of the homosexual, the orgiast, the drug addict, the rapist, the robber, and the murderer seeks to find those violent parallels to the violent and often hopeless contradictions he knew as an infant and as a child. For if he has the courage to meet the parallel situation at the moment when he is ready, then he has a chance to act as he has never acted before, and in satisfying the frustration—if he can succeed—he may then pass by symbolic substitute through the locks of incest. In thus giving expression to the buried infant in himself, he can lessen the tension of those infantile desires and so free himself to remake a bit of his nervous system. Like the neurotic he is looking for the opportunity to grow up a second time, but the psychopath knows instinctively that to express a forbidden impulse actively is far more beneficial to him than merely to confess the desire in the safety of a doctor's room. The psychopath is ordinately ambitious, too ambitious ever to trade his warped brilliant conception of his possible victories in life for the grim if peaceful attrition of the analyst's couch. So his associational journey into the past is lived out in the theater of the present, and he exists for those charged situations where his senses are so alive that he can be aware actively (as the analysand is aware passively) of what his habits are, and how he can change them. The strength of the psychopath is that he knows (where most of us can only guess) what is good for him and what is bad for him at exactly those instants when an old crippling habit has become so attacked by experience that the potentiality exists to change it, to replace a negative and empty fear with an outward action, even if—and here I obey the logic of the extreme psychopath—even if the fear is of himself, and the action is to murder. The psychopath murders—if he has the courage—out of the necessity to purge his violence, for if he cannot empty his hatred then he cannot love, his being is frozen with implacable self-hatred for his cowardice. (It can of course be suggested that it takes little courage for two strong eighteen-year-old hoodlums, let us say, to beat in the brains of a candy

store keeper, and indeed the act—even by the logic of the psychopath—is not likely to prove very therapeutic, for the victim is
not an immediate equal. Still, courage of a sort is necessary, for
one murders not only a weak fifty-year-old man but an institution
as well, one violates private property, one enters into a new relation with the police and introduces a dangerous element into
one's life. The hoodlum is therefore daring the unknown, and
so no matter how brutal the act it is not altogether cowardly.)

At bottom, the drama of the psychopath is that he seeks love.
Not love as the search for a mate, but love as the search for an
orgasm more apocalyptic than the one which preceded it. Orgasm is his therapy—he knows at the seed of his being that good
orgasm opens his possibilities and bad orgasm imprisons him.
But in this search, the psychopath becomes an embodiment of
the extreme contradictions of the society which formed his character, and the apocalyptic orgasm often remains as remote as the
Holy Grail, for there are clusters and nests and ambushes of violence in his own necessities and in the imperatives and retalia-
tions of the men and women among whom he lives his life, so
that even as he drains his hatred in one act or another, so the
conditions of his life create it anew in him until the drama of his
movements bears a sardonic resemblance to the frog who
climbed a few feet in the well only to drop back again.

Yet there is this to be said for the search after the good orgasm: when one lives in a civilized world, and still can enjoy none
of the cultural nectar of such a world because the paradoxes on
which civilization is built demands that there remain a culture-
less and alienated bottom of exploitable human material, then
the logic of becoming a sexual outlaw (if one's psychological
roots are bedded in the bottom) is that one has at least a running competitive chance to be physically healthy so long as one
stays alive. It is therefore no accident that psychopathy is most
prevalent with the Negro. Hated from outside and therefore hating himself, the Negro was forced into the position of exploring
all those moral wildernesses of civilized life which the Square
automatically condemns as delinquent or evil or immature or
morbid or self-destructive or corrupt. (Actually the terms have

equal weight. Depending on the telescope of the cultural clique from which the Square surveys the universe, "evil" or "imma-ture" are equally strong terms of condemnation.) But the Negro, not being privileged to gratify his self-esteem with the heady sat-isfactions of categorical condemnation, chose to move instead in that other direction where all situations are equally valid, and in the worst of perversion, promiscuity, pimpery, drug addiction, rape, razor-slash, bottle-break, what-have-you, the Negro discov-ered and elaborated a morality of the bottom, an ethical differ-entiation between the good and the bad in every human activity from the go-getter pimp (as opposed to the lazy one) to the rela-tively dependable pusher or prostitute. Add to this the cunning of their language, the abstract ambiguous alternatives in which from the danger of their oppression they learned to speak ("Well, now, man, like I'm looking for a cat to turn me on. . . ."), add even more the profound sensitivity of the Negro jazzman who was the cultural mentor of a people, and it is not too diffi-cult to believe that the language of Hip which evolved was an artful language, tested and shaped by an intense experience and therefore different in kind from white slang, as different as the special obscenity of the soldier which in its emphasis upon "ass" as the soul and "shit" as circumstance, was able to express the existential states of the enlisted man. What makes Hip a special language is that it cannot really be taught—if one shares none of the experiences of elation and exhaustion which it is equipped to describe, then it seems merely arch or vulgar or irritating. It is a pictorial language, but pictorial like nonobjective art, imbued with the dialectic of small but intense change, a language for the microcosm, in this case, man, for it takes the immediate experi-ences of any passing man and magnifies the dynamic of his movements, not specifically but abstractly so that he is seen more as a vector in a network of forces than as a static character in a crystallized field. (Which, latter, is the practical view of the snob.) For example, there is real difficulty in trying to find a Hip substi-tute for "stubborn." The best possibility I can come up with is "That cat will never come off his groove, dad." But groove im-plies movement, narrow movement but motion nonetheless.

There is really no way to describe someone who does not move at all. Even a creep does move—if at a pace exasperatingly more slow than the pace of the cool cats.

IV
—

Like children, hipsters are fighting for the sweet, and their language is a set of subtle indications of their success or failure in the competition for pleasure. Unstated but obvious is the social sense that there is not nearly enough sweet for everyone. And so the sweet goes only to the victor, the best, the most, the man who knows the most about how to find his energy and how not to lose it. The emphasis is on energy because the psychopath and the hipster are nothing without it since they do not have the protection of a position or a class to rely on when they have overextended themselves. So the language of Hip is a language of energy, how it is found, how it is lost.

But let us see. I have jotted down perhaps a dozen words, the Hip perhaps most in use and most likely to last with the minimum of variation. The words are man, go, put down, make, beat, cool, swing, with it, crazy, dig, flip, creep, hip, square. They serve a variety of purposes, and the nuance of the voice uses the nuance of the situation to convey the subtle contextual difference. If the hipster moves through his night and through his life on a constant search with glimpses of Mecca in many a turn of his experience (Mecca being the apocalyptic orgasm) and if everyone in the civilized world is at least in some small degree a sexual cripple, the hipster lives with the knowledge of how he is sexually crippled and where he is sexually alive, and the faces of experience which life presents to him each day are engaged, dismissed, or avoided as his need directs and his lifemanship makes possible. For life is a contest between people in which the victor generally recuperates quickly and the loser takes long to mend, a perpetual competition of colliding explorers in which one must grow or else pay more for remaining the same (pay in sickness, or depression, or anguish for the lost opportunity), but pay or grow.

Therefore one finds words like go, and make it, and with it, and swing: "Go" with its sense that after hours or days or months or years of monotony, boredom, and depression one has finally had one's chance, one has amassed enough energy to meet an exciting opportunity with all one's present talents for the flip (up or down) and so one is ready to go, ready to gamble. Movement is always to be preferred to inaction. In motion a man has a chance, his body is warm, his instincts are quick, and when the crisis comes, whether of love or violence, he can make it, he can win, he can release a little more energy for himself since he hates himself a little less, he can make a little better nervous system, make it a little more possible to go again, to go faster next time and so make more and thus find more people with whom he can swing. For to swing is to communicate, is to convey the rhythms of one's own being to a lover, a friend, or an audience, and— equally necessary—be able to feel the rhythms of their response. To swing with the rhythms of another is to enrich oneself—the conception of the learning process as dug by Hip is that one cannot really learn until one contains within oneself the implicit rhythm of the subject or the person. As an example, I remember once hearing a Negro friend have an intellectual discussion at a party for half an hour with a white girl who was a few years out of college. The Negro literally could not read or write, but he had an extraordinary ear and a fine sense of mimicry. So as the girl spoke, he would detect the particular formal uncertainties in her argument, and in a pleasant (if slightly Southern) English accent, he would respond to one or another facet of her doubts. When she would finish what she felt was a particularly well-articulated idea, he would smile privately and say, "Other-direction . . . do you really believe in that?"

"Well . . . no," the girl would stammer, "now that you get down to it, there is something disgusting about it to me," and she would be off again for five more minutes.

Of course the Negro was not learning anything about the merits and demerits of the argument, but he was learning a great deal about a type of girl he had never met before, and that was what he wanted. Being unable to read or write, he could hardly be interested in ideas nearly as much as in lifemanship, and so he eschewed any attempt to obey the precision or lack of precision in the girl's language, and instead sensed her character (and the values of her social type) by swinging with the nuances of her voice.

So to swing is to be able to learn, and by learning take a step toward making it, toward creating. What is to be created is not nearly so important as the hipster's belief that when he really makes it, he will be able to turn his hand to anything, even to self-discipline. What he must do before that is find his courage at the moment of violence, or equally make it in the act of love, find a little more of himself, create a little more between his woman and himself, or indeed between his mate and himself (since many hipsters are bisexual), but paramount, imperative, is the necessity to make it because in making it, one is making the new habit, unearthing the new talent which the old frustration denied.

Whereas if you goof (the ugliest word in Hip), if you lapse back into being a frightened stupid child, or if you flip, if you lose your control, reveal the buried weaker more feminine part of your nature, then it is more difficult to swing the next time, your ear is less alive, your bad and energy-wasting habits are further confirmed, you are farther away from being with it. But to be with it is to have grace, is to be closer to the secrets of that inner unconscious life which will nourish you if you can hear it, for you are then nearer to that God which every hipster believes is located in the senses of his body, that trapped, mutilated, and nonetheless megalomaniacal God who is It, who is energy, life, sex, force, the yoga's *prana*, the Reichian's orgone, Lawrence's "blood," Hemingway's "good," the Shavian life-force; "It"; God; not the God of the churches but the unachievable whisper of mystery within the sex, the paradise of limitless energy and perception just beyond the next wave of the next orgasm.

To which a cool cat might reply, "Crazy, man!"

Because, after all, what I have offered above is a hypothesis, no more, and there is not the hipster alive who is not absorbed in his own tumultuous hypotheses. Mine is interesting, mine is way out (on the avenue of the mystery along the road to "It"), but still I am just one cat in a world of cool cats, and everything interesting is crazy, or at least so the Squares who do not know how to swing would say.

(And yet crazy is also the self-protective irony of the hipster. Living with questions and not with answers, he is so different in his isolation and in the far reach of his imagination from almost everyone with whom he deals in the outer world of the Square, and meets generally so much enmity, competition, and hatred in the world of Hip, that his isolation is always in danger of turning upon itself and leaving him indeed just that, crazy.)

If, however, you agree with my hypothesis, if you as a cat are way out too, and we are in the same groove (the universe now being glimpsed as a series of ever-extending radii from the center), why then you say simply "I dig," because neither knowledge nor imagination comes easily, it is buried in the pain of one's forgotten experience, and so one must work to find it, one must occasionally exhaust oneself by digging into the self in order to perceive the outside. And indeed it is essential to dig the most, for if you do not dig you lose your superiority over the Square, and so you are less likely to be cool (to be in control of a situation because you have swung where the Square has not, or because you have allowed to come to consciousness a pain, a guilt, a shame, or a desire which the other has not had the courage to face). To be cool is to be equipped, and if you are equipped it is more difficult for the next cat who comes along to put you down. And of course one can hardly afford to be put down too often, or one is beat, one has lost one's confidence, one has lost one's will, one is impotent in the world of action and so closer to the demeaning flip of becoming a queer, or indeed closer to dying, and therefore it is even more difficult to recover enough energy to try to make it again, because once a cat is beat he has nothing to give, and no one is interested any longer in making it with him. This is the terror of the hipster—to be beat—because once the sweet of sex has deserted him, he still cannot give up the

search. It is not granted to the hipster to grow old gracefully—
he has been captured too early by the oldest dream of power, the
gold fountain of Ponce de Leon, the fountain of youth where the
gold is in the orgasm.

To be beat is therefore a flip, it is a situation beyond one's experience, impossible to anticipate—which indeed in the circular
vocabulary of Hip is still another meaning for flip, but then I
have given just a few of the connotations of these words. Like
most primitive vocabularies each word is a prime symbol and
serves a dozen or a hundred functions of communication in the
instinctive dialectic through which the hipster perceives his experience, that dialectic of the instantaneous differentials of existence in which one is forever moving forward into more or
retreating into less.

V

It is impossible to conceive a new philosophy until one creates a
new language, but a new popular language (while it must implicitly contain a new philosophy) does not necessarily present its
philosophy overtly. It can be asked then what really is unique in
the life-view of Hip which raises its argot above the passing verbal
whimsies of the bohemian or the lumpen proletariat.

The answer would be in the psychopathic element of Hip
which has almost no interest in viewing human nature, or better,
in judging human nature from a set of standards conceived a
priori to the experience, standards inherited from the past.
Since Hip sees every answer as posing immediately a new alternative, a new question, its emphasis is on complexity rather than
simplicity (such complexity that its language without the illumination of the voice and the articulation of the face and body remains hopelessly incommunicative). Given its emphasis on
complexity, Hip abdicates from any conventional moral responsibility because it would argue that the result of our actions are
unforeseeable, and so we cannot know if we do good or bad, we
cannot even know (in the Joycean sense of the good and the

bad) whether unforeseeable, and so we cannot know if we do
good or bad, we cannot be certain that we have given them energy, and indeed if we could, there would still be no idea of what
ultimately they would do with it.

Therefore, men are not seen as good or bad (that they are
good-and-bad is taken for granted) but rather each man is
glimpsed as a collection of possibilities, some more possible than
others (the view of character implicit in Hip) and some humans
are considered more capable than others of reaching more possibilities within themselves in less time, provided, and this is the
dynamic, provided the particular character can swing at the right
time. And here arises the sense of context which differentiates
Hip from a Square view of character. Hip sees the context as
generally dominating the man, dominating him because his
character is less significant than the context in which he must
function. Since it is arbitrarily five times more demanding of
one's energy to accomplish even an inconsequential action in an
unfavorable context than a favorable one, man is then not only
his character but his context, since the success or failure of an
action in a given context reacts upon the character and therefore affects what the character will be in the next context. What
dominates both character and context is the energy available at
the moment of intense context.

Character being thus seen as perpetually ambivalent and dynamic enters then into an absolute relativity where there are no
truths other than the isolated truths of what each observer feels
at each instant of his existence. To take a perhaps unjustified
metaphysical extrapolation, it is as if the universe which has usually existed conceptually as a Fact (even if the Fact were Berke-
ley's God) but a Fact which it was the aim of all science and
philosophy to reveal, becomes instead a changing reality whose
laws are remade at each instant by everything living, but most
particularly man, man raised to a neomedieval summit where
the truth is not what one has felt yesterday or what one expects
to feel tomorrow but rather truth is no more nor less than what
one feels at each instant in the perpetual climax of the present.

What is consequent therefore is the divorce of man from his

values, the liberation of the self from the superego of society. The only Hip morality (but of course it is an ever-present morality) is to do what one feels whenever and wherever it is possible, and—this is how the war of the Hip and the Square begins—to be engaged in one primal battle: to open the limits of the possible for oneself, for oneself alone because that is one's need. Yet in widening the arena of the possible, one widens it reciprocally for others as well, so that the nihilistic fulfillment of each man's desire contains its antithesis of human cooperation.

If the ethic reduces to Know Thyself and Be Thyself, what makes it radically different from Socratic moderation with its stern conservative respect for the experience of the past is that the Hip ethic is immoderation, childlike in its adoration of the present (and indeed to respect the past means that one must also respect such ugly consequences of the past as the collective murders of the State). It is this adoration of the present which contains the affirmation of Hip, because its ultimate logic surpasses even the unforgettable solution of the Marquis de Sade to sex, private property, and the family, that all men and women have absolute but temporary rights over the bodies of all other men and women—the nihilism of Hip proposes as its final tendency that every social restraint and category be removed, and the affirmation implicit in the proposal is that man would then prove to be more creative than murderous and so would not destroy himself. Which is exactly what separates Hip from the authoritarian philosophies which now appeal to the conservative and liberal temper—what haunts the middle of the twentieth century is that faith in man has been lost, and the appeal of authority has been that it would restrain us from ourselves. Hip, which would return us to ourselves, at no matter what price in individual violence, is the affirmation of the barbarian, for it requires a primitive passion about human nature to believe that individual acts of violence are always to be preferred to the collective violence of the State; it takes literal faith in the creative possibilities of the human being to envisage acts of violence as the catharsis which prepares growth.

Whether the hipster's desire for absolute sexual freedom contains any genuinely radical conception of a different world is of course another matter, and it is possible, since the hipster lives with his hatred, that many of them are the material for an elite of storm troopers ready to follow the first truly magnetic leader whose view of mass murder is phrased in a language which reaches their emotions. But given the desperation of his condition as a psychic outlaw, the hipster is equally a candidate for the most reactionary and most radical of movements, and so it is just as possible that many hipsters will come—if the crisis deepens—to a radical comprehension of the horror of society, for even as the radical has had his incommunicable dissent confirmed in his experience by precisely the frustration, the denied opportunities, and the bitter years which his ideas have cost him, so the sexual adventurer deflected from his goal by the implacable animosity of a society constructed to deny the sexual radical as well may yet come to an equally bitter comprehension of the slow relentless inhumanity of the conservative power which controls him from without and from within. And in being so controlled, denied, and starved into the attrition of conformity, indeed the hipster may come to see that his condition is no more than an exaggeration of the human condition, and if he would be free, then everyone must be free. Yes, this is possible too, for the heart of Hip is its emphasis upon courage at the moment of crisis, and it is pleasant to think that courage contains within itself (as the explanation of its existence) some glimpse of the necessity of life to become more than it has been.

It is obviously not very possible to speculate with sharp focus on the future of the hipster. Certain possibilities must be evident, however, and the most central is that the organic growth of Hip depends on whether the Negro emerges as a dominating force in American life. Since the Negro knows more about the ugliness and danger of life than the White, it is probable that if the Negro can win his equality, he will possess a potential superiority, a superiority so feared that the fear itself has become the underground drama of domestic politics. Like all conservative political fear it is the fear of unforeseeable consequences, for the

Negro's equality would tear a profound shift into the psychology, the sexuality, and the moral imagination of every White alive.

With this possible emergence of the Negro, Hip may erupt as a psychically armed rebellion whose sexual impetus may rebound against the antisexual foundation of every organized power in America, and bring into the air such animosities, antipathies, and new conflicts of interest that the mean empty hypocrisies of mass conformity will no longer work. A time of violence, new hysteria, confusion, and rebellion will then be likely to replace the time of conformity. At that time, if the liberal should prove realistic in his belief that there is peaceful room for every tendency in American life, then Hip would end by being absorbed as a colorful figure in the tapestry. But if this is not the reality, and the economic, the social, the psychological, and finally the moral crises accompanying the rise of the Negro should prove insupportable, then a time is coming when every political guidepost will be gone, and millions of liberals will be faced with political dilemmas they have so far succeeded in evading, and with a view of human nature they do not wish to accept. To take the desegregation of the schools in the South as an example, it is quite likely that the reactionary sees the reality more closely than the liberal when he argues that the deeper issue is not desegregation but miscegenation. (As a radical I am of course facing in the opposite direction from the White Citizens' Councils—obviously I believe it is the absolute human right of the Negro to mate with the White, and matings there will undoubtedly be, for there will be Negro high school boys brave enough to chance their lives.) But for the average liberal whose mind has been dulled by the committeeish cant of the professional liberal, miscegenation is not an issue because he has been told that the Negro does not desire it. So, when it comes, miscegenation will be a terror, comparable perhaps to the derangement of the American Communists when the icons to Stalin came tumbling down. The average American Communist held to the myth of Stalin for reasons which had little to do with the political evidence and everything to do with their psychic necessities. In this sense it is equally a psychic necessity for the liberal to believe that the Negro and even the reactionary Southern White eventually are fundamentally people like himself, capable of becoming good liberals too if only they can be reached by good liberal reason. What the liberal cannot bear to admit is the hatred beneath the skin of a society so unjust that the amount of collective violence buried in the people is perhaps incapable of being contained, and therefore if one wants a better world one does well to hold one's breath, for a worse world is bound to come first, and the dilemma may well be this: given such hatred, it must either vent itself nihilistically or become turned into the cold murderous liquidations of the totalitarian state.

VI

No matter what its horrors the twentieth century is a vastly exciting century for its tendency is to reduce all of life to its ultimate alternatives. One can well wonder if the last war of them all will be between the blacks and the whites, or between the women and the men, or between the beautiful and ugly, the pillagers and managers, or the rebels and the regulators. Which of course is carrying speculation beyond the point where speculation is still serious, and yet despair at the monotony and bleakness of the future have become so ingrained in the radical temper that the radical is in danger of abdicating from all imagination. What a man feels is the impulse for his creative effort, and if an alien but nonetheless passionate instinct about the meaning of life has come so unexpectedly from a virtually illiterate people, come out of the most intense conditions of exploitation, cruelty, violence, frustration, and lust, and yet has succeeded as an instinct in keeping this tortured people alive, then it is perhaps possible that the Negro holds more of the tail of the expanding elephant of truth than the radical, and if this is so, the radical humanist could do worse than to brood upon the phenomenon. For if a revolutionary time should come again, there would be a crucial difference if someone had already delineated a neo-Marxian calculus aimed at comprehending every circuit and process of society from ukase to kiss as the communications of human energy—a calculus capable of translating the economic relations of man into his psychological relations and then back again, his productive relations thereby embracing his sexual relations as well, until the crises of capitalism in the twentieth century would yet be understood as the unconscious adaptations of a society to solve its economic imbalance at the expense of a new mass psychological imbalance. It is almost beyond the imagination to conceive of a work in which the drama of human energy is engaged, and a theory of its social currents and dissipations, its imprisonments, expressions, and tragic wastes are fitted into some gigantic synthesis of human action where the body of Marxist thought, and particularly the epic grandeur of *Das Kapital* (that first of the major *psychologies* to approach the mystery of social cruelty so simply and practically as to say that we are a collective body of humans whose life-energy is wasted, displaced, and procedurally stolen as it passes from one of us to another)—where particularly the epic grandeur of *Das Kapital* would find its place in an even more godlike view of human justice and injustice, in some more excruciating vision of those intimate and institutional processes which lead to our creations and disasters, our growth, our attrition, and our rebellion.

From Surplus Value to the Mass Media

(1959)

NO ONE CAN WORK his way through *Das Kapital* without etching on his mind forever the knowledge that profit must come from loss—the lost energy of one human being paying for the comfort of another; if the process has become ten times more subtle, complex, and untraceable in the modern economy, and conceivably a hundred times more resistant to the careful analysis of the isolated radical, it is perhaps now necessary that some of us be so brash as to cut a trail of speculation across subjects as vast as the title of this piece.

Let me start with a trivial discrepancy. Today one can buy a can of frozen orange juice sufficient to make a quart for 30 cents. A carton of prepared orange juice, equal in quality, costs 45 cents. The difference in price is certainly not to be found by the value of the container, nor in the additional cost of labor and machinery which is required to squeeze the oranges, since the process which produces frozen orange juice is if anything more complex—the oranges must first be squeezed and then frozen. Of course orange juice which comes in quart cartons is more expensive to ship, but it is doubtful if this added cost could account for more than 2 or 3 cents in the price. (The factors are complex, but may reduce themselves as follows: The distributor for cartons of prepared orange juice is generally the milk companies, who are saved most of the costs of local distribution by delivering the orange juice on their milk route. While the cost of shipping whole oranges is greater, because of their bulk, than cans of frozen juice, it must be remembered that the largest expense in freight charges is loading and unloading, and the majority of freshly picked oranges have in any case to be shipped by freight to a freezer plant, converted, and shipped again.) What is most likely is that the price is arrived at by some kind of developed if more or less unconscious estimation by the entrepreneur of what it is worth to the consumer not to be bothered with opening a can, mixing the frozen muddle with three cans of water, and shaking. It is probable that the additional 12 or 13 cents of unnecessary price rise has been calculated in some such ratio as this: The consumer's private productive time is worth much more to him than his social working time, because his private productive time, that is, the time necessary to perform his household functions, is time taken away from his leisure. If he earns $3 an hour by his labor, it is probable that he values his leisure time as worth ideally two or three times as much, let us say arbitrarily $6 an hour, or 10 cents a minute. Since it would take three or four minutes to turn frozen orange juice into drinkable orange juice, it may well be that a covert set of values in the consumer equates the saving of 3 or 4 minutes to a saving of 30 or 40 *ideal* cents of his pleasure time. To pay an extra 12 actual cents in order to save this 40 ideal cents seems fitting to his concept of value. Of course, he has been deprived of 10 actual cents—the extra comfort should have deprived him of no more than 2 of his actual cents. So the profit was extracted here from a disproportionate exploitation of the consumer's need to protect his pleasure time rather than from an inadequate repayment to the worker for his labor. (Such contradictions to this thesis as the spate of Do-It-Yourself hobbies, or magazine articles about the problem of what to do with leisure, are of too serious a nature to dismiss with a remark—it can however be suggested that the general hypothesis may not be contradicted: the man who is bored with his leisure time, or so industrious as to work at handicrafts, can still resent inroads upon his leisure which he has not chosen. Indeed it might be argued that the tendency to be attracted to private labor-saving devices is greatest in the man who doesn't know what to do with himself when he is at home.)

At any rate, if the hypothesis sketched here should prove to have any economic validity, the consequences are worth remarking. When the source of profit is extracted more and more (at one remove or another) from the consumer's at-home working time, the consumer is paying a disproportionate amount for the desire to work a little less in his leisure time. Over the economy as a whole, this particular germ of profit may still be minuscule, but it is not at all trivial once one includes the expenses of the war economy whose costs are paid by taxation, an indirect extraction of leisure time from the general consumer, who then has noticeably less money in his leisure to pursue the sports, occupations, and amusements which will restore to his body the energy he has spent in labor. (To take the matter into its real complexity, the conflicting anxieties of living in a war-and-pleasure-oriented environment opens most men and women to a daily spate of psychic havoc whose damages can be repaired only by the adequate exercise of a *personal* leisure appropriate to each, exactly that leisure which the war economy must impoverish.) By this logic, the root of capitalist exploitation has shifted from the proletariat-at-work to the mass-at-leisure who now may lose so much as four or five *ideal* hours of extra leisure a day. The old exploitation was vertical—the poor supported the rich. To this vertical exploitation must now be added the horizontal exploitation of the mass by the State and by Monopoly, a secondary exploitation which is becoming more essential to a modern capitalist economy than the direct exploitation of the proletariat. If the origin of this secondary exploitation has come out of the proliferation of the machine with its consequent and relative reduction of the size of the proletariat and the amount of surplus value to be accumulated, the exploitation of mass leisure has been accelerated by the relative contraction of the world market. Through the postwar years, prosperity has been maintained in

America by invading the wage earner in his home. Nineteenth-century capitalism could still find its profit in the factory; when the worker was done, his body might be fatigued but his mind could look for a diversion which was relatively free of the industry for which he worked. So soon, however, as the surplus labor of the proletariat comes to be replaced by the leisure value given up by the consumer, the real expropriator of the wage earner has to become the mass media, for if the domination of leisure time is more significant to the health of the economy than the exploitation of the working time, the stability of the economy derives more from manipulating the psychic character of leisure than forcibly subjecting the working class to its productive role. It is likely that the survival of capitalism is no longer possible without the creation in the consumer of a series of psychically disruptive needs which circle about such wants and emotions as the desire for excessive security, the alleviation of guilt, the lust for comfort and new commodity, and a consequent allegiance to the vast lie about the essential health of the State and the economy, an elaborated fiction whose bewildering interplay of real and false detail must devil the mass into a progressively more imperfect apperception of reality and thus drive them closer to apathy, psychosis, and violence. Nineteenth-century capitalism exhausted the life of millions of workers; twentieth-century capitalism can well end by destroying the mind of civilized man.

If there is a future for the radical spirit, which often enough one can doubt, it can come only from a new revolutionary vision of society, its sicknesses, its strengths, its conflicts, contradictions and radiations, its self-created incapacity to solve its evasions of human justice. There is the root of social problem. An injustice half corrected results in no more than a new sense of injustice and suppressed violence in both parties, which is why revolutionary situations are meaningful and liberal situations are not, for liberal solutions end by compromising a society in the nausea of its past and so bog the mass mind further into the institutionalization of social habits and methods for which no one has faith, and from which one cannot extract the psychic marrow of culture upon which everyone in a civilization must depend. If this revolutionary vision is to be captured by any of us in a work or works, one can guess that this time it will explore not nearly so far into that jungle of political economy which Marx charted and so opened to rapid development, but rather will engage the empty words, dead themes, and sentimental voids of that mass media whose internal contradictions twist and quarter us between the lust of the economy (which radiates a greed to consume into us, with sex as the invisible salesman) and the guilt of the economy which must chill us with authority, charities for cancer, and all reminder that the mass consumer is only on drunken furlough from the ordering disciplines of church, FBI, and war.

Quick Evaluations on the Talent in the Room

———

(1959)

THE ONLY ONE of my contemporaries who I felt had more talent than myself was James Jones. And he has also been the one writer of my time for whom I felt any love. We saw each other only six or eight times over the years, but it always gave me a boost to know that Jim was in town. He carried his charge with him, he had the talent to turn a night of heavy drinking into a great time. I felt then and can still say now that *From Here to Eternity* has been the best American novel since the war, and if it is ridden with faults, ignorances, and a smudge of the sentimental, it has also the force of few novels one could name. What was unique about Jones was that he had come out of nowhere, self-taught, a clunk in his lacks, but the only one of us who had the beer-guts of a broken-glass brawl. What must next be said is sad, for Jones has sold out badly over the years. There is not a man alive he cannot charm if he chooses to, and the connection of that gift to his huge success made him a slave of our time, for it handcuffed the rebel in him. Like Styron, like myself, like Kerouac, he has been running for president as well as sticking at his work, and it was near tragic to watch the process as he imprisoned his anger, and dwindled without it.

I do not know that one can judge him. His first virtues are an appetite for life and an animal sense of who has the power, and maybe it would have been worse for Jones to deny himself. So he spent years hobnobbing with gentlemanly shits and half-assed operators and some of it had to rub off on him, especially since he had no art for living with his weaknesses, and a blind vanity which locked him out of his faults and took him on a long trip away from anyone whose mind could see into his holes.

The debacle of *Some Came Running* is, however, more of Scribner's fault than his own. They handled him like poltroons. There was no one in the house who had guts enough to say that *Some Came Running* was a washerwoman at twelve hundred pages, and could be fair at four hundred. So a little of Jones's very best writing was lost in the dreary wastes and tiresome egotisms of his most accurate if caterpillarish portrait of the Midwest.

Next came *The Pistol,* a dud. More vanity. The God of Sir Jones looking for his nose and wondering about applause.

Yet Jones could do ten bad novels and I would never write him off, not even if it seemed medically evident he had pickled his brain in the gin. For Jones, like a bull, is most dangerous when almost dead, and with a rebel whiff of self-respect all hell might break loose. If Jones stops trying to be the first novelist to end as a multimillionaire; if he gives up the lust to measure his talent by the money he makes; if he dares not to castrate his hatred of society with a literary politician's assy cultivation of it, then I would have to root for him because he may have been born to write a great novel.

So may William Styron have been born, only I wonder if anyone who gets to know him well could wish him on his way. I will try to be fair about his talent, but I do not know if I can, because I must speak against the bias of finding him not nearly as big as he ought to be.

Styron wrote the prettiest novel of our generation. *Lie Down in Darkness* has beauty at its best, is almost never sentimental, even has whispers of near-genius as the work of a twenty-three-year-old. It would have been the best novel of our generation if it had not lacked three qualities: Styron was not near to creating a man who could move on his feet, his mind was uncorrupted by a new idea, and his book was without evil. There was only Styron's sense of the tragic: misunderstanding—and that is too small a window to look upon the world we have known.

Since then only a remarkably good short novel, *The Long March,* has appeared by Styron. But he has been working hard over the years on a second novel, *Set This House on Fire,* and I hear it is done. If it is at all good, and I expect it is, the reception will be a study in the art of literary advancement. For Styron has spent years oiling every literary lever and power which could help him on his way, and there are medals waiting for him in the mass media. If he has written a book which expresses some real part of his complex and far from pleasant view of the American character, if this new novel should prove to have the bite of a strong and critical consciousness, then one can hardly deny him his avidity as a politician for it is not easy to work many years on a novel which has something hard and new to say without trying to shape the reception of it. But if Styron has compromised his talent, and written what turns out to be the most suitable big book of the last ten years, a *literary* work which will deal with sec- ondhand experience and all-but-deep proliferation on the smoke of passion and the kiss of death, if he has done no more than fill a cornucopia of fangless perceptions which will please the conservative power and delight the liberal power, offend no one, and prove to be ambitious, traditional, innocuous, artful, and in the middle, breathy and self-indulgent in the beauty of its prose, evocative to the tenderhearted and the reviewers of books, then Styron will receive a ravingly good reception, for the mass media is aching for such a novel like a tout for his horse. He will be made the most important writer of my generation. But how much more potent he will seem to us, his contemporaries and his competitors, if he has had the moral courage to write a book equal to his hatred and therefore able to turn the consciousness of our time, an achievement which is the primary measure of a writer's size.

Truman Capote I do not know well, but I like him. He is tart as a grandaunt, but in his way he is a ballsy little guy, and he is the most perfect writer of my generation, he writes the best sentences word for word, rhythm upon rhythm. I would not have changed two words in *Breakfast at Tiffany's,* which will become a small classic. Capote has still given no evidence that he is serious about the deep resources of the novel, and his short stories are too often saccharine. At his worst he has less to say than any good writer I know. I would suspect he hesitates between the attractions of Society, which enjoys and so repays him for his unique gifts, and the novel he could write of the gossip column's real life, a major work, but it would banish him forever from his favorite world. Since I have nothing to lose, I hope Truman fries a few of the fancier fish.

Kerouac lacks discipline, intelligence, honesty, and a sense of the novel. His rhythms are erratic, his sense of character is nil, and he is as pretentious as a rich whore, as sentimental as a lollipop. Yet I think he has a large talent. His literary energy is enormous, and he had enough of a wild eye to go along with his instincts and so become the first figure for a new generation. At his best, his love of language has an ecstatic flux. To judge his worth it is better to forget about him as a novelist and see him instead as an action painter or a bard. He has a medieval talent, he is a teller of frantic court tales for a dead king's ears, and so in the years of James Madison's Avenue, he has been a pioneer. For a while I worried about him as a force from the political right which could lead Hip into a hole, but I liked him when I met him, more than I would have thought, and felt he was tired, as indeed why should he not be, for he has traveled in a world where the adrenaline devours the blood.

Saul Bellow knows words but writes in a style I find self-willed and unnatural. His rhythms have a twitch. There were some originalities and one or two rich sections to *Augie March* (which is all I know of his work) but at its worst it was a travelogue for timid intellectuals and so to tell the truth I cannot take him seriously as a major novelist. I do not think he knows anything about people, nor about himself. He has a whacky, almost psychotic lack of responsibility to the situations he creates, and his narrative disproportions are elephantiastical in their anomaly. This judgment is not personal, for we met only once, under easy circumstances, and had a mild conversation which left me neither remembering nor dismembering him as a man.

Since writing the above, I have read his short novel *Seize the Day*. It is, I think, the first of the cancer novels. Its miserable hero, Tommy Wilhelm, leads a life of such hopeless obstacles to the dreams of gentle love trapped in his flesh, that one would diagnose him as already in a precancerous stage. That Wilhelm bursts into tears and weeps before the bier of a stranger in a funeral parlor, in that surprisingly beautiful ending to *Seize the Day*, is the first indication for me that Bellow is not altogether hopeless on the highest level. But before he can begin to command the respect he has been given too quickly by the flaccid taste of these years, he must first give evidence, as must Styron, that he can write about men who have the lust to struggle with the history about them, for it is not demanding to write about characters considerably more defeated than oneself since the writer's ego is rarely in danger of being punished by too much self-perception, and compassion can be poured over one's work like cream from a pitcher.

If one does not request an apocalyptic possibility for literature, then I have been needlessly severe on Bellow, for his work does no obvious harm, but I think one must not be easy on art which tries for less than it can manage, or in the example of Augie March, does something worse, muddles the real and the false in such ambitious copulation that the mind of the reader is debauched. Augie is an impossible character, and his adventures could never have happened, for he is too timid a man ever to have moused into more than one or two cruel corners of the world. But there it is: to simulate a major mood, Bellow must create a world which has none of the psychic iron of society, none of the facts and nuance of that social machine which is geared to catch all but the most adept of adventurers by weakness and need.

When and if I come to read *Henderson the Rain King*, let me hope I do not feel the critic's vested interest to keep a banished writer in limbo, for I sense uneasily that without reading it, I have already the beginnings of a negative evaluation for it since I doubt that I would believe in Henderson as a hero.

Algren has something which is all his own. I respect him for staying a radical, yet I do not feel close to his work. Probably it is too different from my own. If I say that I do not think he will ever do a major work until he overcomes his specialty—that ghoulish and weirdly sentimental sense of humor which is pure Algren and so skitters him away from the eye of his meanings—well, I offer this without the confidence that I see into him. Of all the writers I know, he is the Grand Odd-Ball. Once he took me to a lineup in Chicago, and I could have sworn the police and the talent on the line had read *The Man with the Golden Arm* for they caught the book perfectly, those cops and those crooks, they were imitating Algren. Yet all the while Nelson laughed like a mad tourist from Squaresville who was hearing these things for the first time.

Salinger is everyone's favorite. I seem to be alone in finding him no more than the greatest mind ever to stay in prep school. What he can do, he does well, and it is his, but it is finally not very lively to live on a campus where bully-muscle always beats those who feel but feel weak. I cannot see Salinger soon emerging onto the battleground of a major novel.

Of course, this opinion may come from nothing more graceful than envy. Salinger has had the wisdom to choose subjects which are comfortable, and I most certainly have not, but since the world is now in a state of acute discomfort, I do not know that his wisdom is honorable.

Paul Bowles opened the world of Hip. He let in the murder, the drugs, the incest, the death of the Square (Port Moresby), the call of the orgy, the end of civilization; he invited all of us to these themes a few years ago, and he wrote one short story, "Pages from Cold Point," a seduction of a father by a son, which is one of the best short stories ever written by anyone. Yet I am not ready to think of Bowles as a major novelist—his characters are without life, and one does not feel that the author ever lived with them. He does not love them and certainly he does not hate them—he is as bored with his characters as they are bored with each other, and this boredom, the breath of Bowles's work, is not the boredom of the world raised to the cool relations of art, but rather is a miasma from the author. One can never disregard Paul Bowles, however, for whatever his lacks, his themes have been adventurous and pure.

Vance Bourjaily is an old acquaintance and upon occasion we are friends. I thought his first two novels were insignificant, and it seemed to me he stayed in existence because of really nice gifts as a politician. (Since very few people in the literary world have any taste—they are much too tense with fashion—the virtue of being a good literary politician is that one can promote one's own fashion, be put in vogue, and so relax the bite of the snob to the point where he or she can open the mouth and sup upon the message.) But I never understood Bourjaily because I kept expecting him to go Madison Avenue, I was certain he would sell out sooner or later. Instead he did the opposite, wrote a novel called *The Violated,* which is a good long honest novel filled with an easy sense of life and detail about pieces and parts of my generation, a difficult book to do, and Bourjaily did it with grace, and had a few things to say. He is the first of my crowd to have taken a major step forward, and if his next novel is as superior to *The Violated* as was *The Violated* to his early work, he could end up being champion for a while. But I doubt if he could hold the title in a strong field, for his taint is to be cute.

Chandler Brossard is a mean pricky guy who's been around, and he'd have been happier as a surgeon than a novelist, but he is original, and parts I read of *The Bold Saboteurs* were sufficiently interesting for me to put the book away—it was a little too close to some of my own notions. Brossard has that deep distaste for weakness which gives work a cold poetry. I like him as a man but I think there are too many things he does not understand; in common with many of us he is too vain about his strengths, too blind to his lacks, and since he has not had the kind of recognition he wanted and maybe deserved, I get the feeling he has temporarily lost enthusiasm for the race. Yet it would not surprise me if he appeared with a major work in ten or fifteen years, or however long it takes for the rest of the world to become as real to him as Chandler Brossard.

Something of the same may be said of Gore Vidal. He is one of the few novelists I know who has a good formal mind. We spent an hour once talking about my play of *The Deer Park*, and it was the best criticism I ever received from one of my competitors— incisive, detached, with a fine nose for what was slack in the play or insufficiently developed. The best of it was that he took my play on its own terms and criticized it in context rather than wasting our mutual hour in a set of artillery and counterbattery barrages about the high aesthetic of the theatre. Since his remarks were helpful to my play, and he knew they would improve the work, I thought it generous of him and more than decent. Since then I have seen sides of him I thought not so nice, and I do not know that one could call him a friend. I mention this not to comment on Vidal's character but to correct the balance— I do not feel that I owe him a favor, and so my comments on his work may be considered more or less objective.

Not that I have the definitive word to say. While the considerable body of his work (the largest of my generation) still presents no single novel which is more successful than not (at least in

those of his novels which I've read), he has developed a variety
of styles, and he has continued to experiment. In his essays,
where he is at his best, he often brings a brave and cultivated wit
to the pomades of the national suet. But in his fiction it seems
difficult for him to create a landscape which is inhabited by people. At his worst he becomes his own jailer and is imprisoned in
the recessive nuances of narcissistic explorations which do not
go deep enough into himself, and so end as gestures and postures. But if Vidal does not lose his will, he could still be most
important, for he has the first requirement of an interesting
writer—one cannot predict his direction. Still I cannot resist suggesting that he is in need of a wound which would turn the prides
of his detachment into new perception.

I've read two stories by Anatole Broyard. They are each first-rate,
and I would buy a novel by him the day it appeared.

One writer who was not properly applauded was Myron
Kaufmann, whose *Remember Me to God* was one of the most honest novels written since the war. Kaufmann is not a fine writer,
and his work is perhaps too solid, too sober, and too lacking in
innovation to attract quick attention, but he had more to say
about the deadening of individuality in the American Jew than
anyone I can remember, and of the novels about Jews which I
have read, his is easily the best since Meyer Levin's *The Old Bunch*.
Kaufmann's talents as a realist are so complete, and his eye for
detail is so sharp, that he is bound to become important if he can
amass a body of work against the obstacle of writing in a time
whose first love is self-deception.

Calder Willingham is a clown with the bite of a ferret, and he
suffers from the misapprehension that he is a mastermind. He
has written what may be the funniest dialogue of our time, and if
Geraldine Bradshaw, his second novel, had been half as long, it

would have been the best short novel any of us did. But it is hard
to bet on Calder, for if he ever grows up, where will he go? He
lacks ideas, and is as indulgent to his shortcomings as a fat old
lady to her Pekingese. This said, it must also be admitted that he
is one of the few writers who can make an evening, and once he
put me down with the economy of a Zen master. I had just finished *Natural Child,* and happened to run into him at the White
Horse Tavern. "Calder," I said, coming on like Max Lerner, "I'd
like to talk to you about your book. I liked parts of it and didn't
like other parts."

"Nawmin," said Calder. "Could you lend me two bucks? I
haven't had breakfast yet."

That Ralph Ellison is very good is dull to say. He is essentially a
hateful writer: when the line of his satire is pure, he writes so
perfectly that one can never forget the experience of reading
him—it is like holding a live electric wire in one's hand. But Ellison's mind, fine and icy, tuned to the pitch of a major novelist's
madness, is not always adequate to mastering the forms of rage,
horror, and disgust which his eyes have presented to his experience, and so he is forever tumbling from the heights of pure
satire into the nets of a murderously depressed clown, and *Invisible Man* insists on a thesis which could not be more absurd, for
the Negro is the least invisible of all people in America. (That
the white does not see each Negro as an individual is not so significant as Ellison makes it—most whites can no longer see each
other at all. Their experience is not as real as the experience of
the Negro, and their faces have been deadened in the torture
chamber of the overburdened American conscience. They have
lost all quick sense of the difficulty of life and its danger, and so
they do not have faces the way Negroes have faces—it is rare for
a Negro who lives it out to reach the age of twenty without having a face which is a work of art.)

Where Ellison can go, I have no idea. His talent is too exceptional to allow for casual predictions, and if one says that the way
for Ellison may be to adventure out into the white world he

knows so well by now, and create the more difficult and conceivably more awful invisibility of the white man—well, it is a mistake to write prescriptions for a novelist as gifted as Ellison.

James Baldwin is too charming a writer to be major. If in *Notes of a Native Son* he has a sense of moral nuance which is one of the few modern guides to the sophistications of the ethos, even the best of his paragraphs are sprayed with perfume. Baldwin seems incapable of saying "Fuck you" to the reader; instead he must delineate the cracking and the breaking and the melting and the hardening of a heart which could never have felt such sensuous growths and little deaths without being emptied as a voice. It is a pity, because Baldwin is not without courage. His second novel, *Giovanni's Room,* was a bad book but mostly a brave one, and since his life has been as fantastic and varied as the life of any of my fellow racketeers, and he has kept his sensitivity, one itches at times to take a hammer to his detachment, smash the perfumed dome of his ego, and reduce him to what must be one of the most tortured and magical nerves of our time. If he ever climbs the mountain, and really tells it, we will have a testament, and not a noble toilet water. Until then he is doomed to be minor.

I have a terrible confession to make—I have nothing to say about any of the talented women who write today. Out of what is no doubt a fault in me, I do not seem able to read them. Indeed I doubt if there will be a really exciting woman writer until the first whore becomes a call girl and tells her tale. At the risk of making a dozen devoted enemies for life, I can only say that the sniffs I get from the ink of the women are always fey, old hat, Quaintsy Goysy, tiny, too dykily psychotic, crippled, creepish, fashionable, frigid, outer-Baroque, *maquillée* in mannequin's whimsy, or else bright and stillborn.[*] Since I've never been able to read Virginia

* With a sorry reluctance to spoil the authority of this verdict, I have to admit that the early work of Mary McCarthy, Jean Stafford, and Carson McCullers gave me pleasure.

Woolf, and am sometimes willing to believe it can conceivably be my fault, this verdict may be taken fairly as the twisted tongue of a soured taste, at least by those readers who do not share with me the ground of departure—that a good novelist can do without everything but the remnant of his balls. If to this, I add that the little I have read of Herbert Gold reminds me of nothing so much as a woman writer, well I do not know that I have to be aware now of still another such acquaintance.

There are fifty fine writers who could be mentioned, and the odds are not that the first of us to become major will come from their host. More likely we are to hear from writers altogether unknown, working in silence, here, nowhere, and there.[*] But since I can speak only of people with whose work and/or person I am knowledgeable, I can do no more than tip my hat to such men and boys of good repute as William Gaddis, Harvey Swados, Harold Humes, William Humphrey, Wright Morris, Bernard Malamud, John Philips, and all the other respected old and new styles of our piggish time.

I will cease with the comment that the novelists will grow when the publishers improve. Five brave publishing houses (a miracle) would wear away a drop of nausea in the cancerous American conscience, and give to the thousand of us or more with real talent the lone-wolf hope that we can begin to explore a little more of that murderous and cowardly world which will burst into madness if it does not dare a new art of the brave.

---

[*] The ten episodes from *Naked Lunch* that were printed in *Big Table* were more arresting, I thought, than anything I've read by an American in years. If the rest of William Burroughs's book is equal to what was shown, and if the novel proves to be a novel and not a collage of extraordinary fragments, then Burroughs will deserve rank as one of the most important novelists in America, and may prove comparable in his impact to Jean Genet.

The Mind of an Outlaw

(1959)

IN HIS REVIEW OF *The Deer Park,* Malcolm Cowley said it must have been a more difficult book to write than *The Naked and the Dead.* He was right. Most of the time, I worked on *The Deer Park* in a low mood; my liver, which had gone bad in the Philippines, exacted a hard price for forcing the effort against the tide of a long depression, and matters were not improved when nobody at Rinehart & Co. liked the first draft of the novel. The second draft, which to me was the finished book, also gave little enthusiasm to the editors, and open woe to Stanley Rinehart, the publisher. I was impatient to leave for Mexico, now that I was done, but before I could go, Rinehart asked for a week in which to decide whether he wanted to do the book. Since he had already given me a contract which allowed him no option not to accept the novel (a common arrangement for writers whose sales are more or less large), any decision to reject the manuscript would cost him a sizable advance. (I learned later he had been hoping his lawyers would find the book obscene, but they did not, at least not then in May 1954.) So he had really no choice but to agree to put the book out in February, and gloomily he consented. To cheer him a bit, I agreed to his request that he delay paying me my advance until publication, although the first half was due on delivery of the manuscript. I thought the favor might improve our relations.

Now, if a few of you are wondering why I did not take my book back and go to another publishing house, the answer is that I was tired. I was badly tired. Only a few weeks before, a doctor had given me tests for the liver, and it had shown itself to be sick and depleted. I was hoping that a few months in Mexico would give me a chance to fill up again.

But the next months were not cheerful. *The Deer Park* had been done as well as I could do it, yet I thought it was probably a minor work, and I did not know if I had any real interest in starting another book. I made efforts of course: I collected notes, began to piece together a few ideas for a novel given to bullfighting, and another about a concentration camp. I wrote *David Riesman Reconsidered* during this time, and *The Homosexual Villain;* read most of the work of the other writers of my generation (I think I was looking for a level against which to measure my third novel), went over the galleys when they came, changed a line or two, sent them back. Keeping half busy I mended a bit, but it was a time of dull drifting. When we came back to New York in October, *The Deer Park* was already in page proof. By November, the first advertisement was given to *Publishers' Weekly.* Then, with less than ninety days to publication, Stanley Rinehart told me I would have to take out a small piece of the book— six not-very-explicit lines about the sex of an old producer and a call girl. The moment one was ready to consider losing those six lines they moved into the moral center of the novel. It would be no tonic for my liver to cut them out. But I also knew Rinehart was serious, and since I was still tired, it seemed a little unreal to try to keep the passage. Like a miser I had been storing energy to start a new book: I wanted nothing to distract me now. I gave in on a word or two, agreed to rewrite a line, and went home from that particular conference not very impressed with myself. The next morning I called up the editor in chief, Ted Amussen, to tell him I had decided the original words had to be put back.

"Well, fine," he said, "fine. I don't know why you agreed to anything in the first place."

A day later, Stanley Rinehart halted publication, stopped all ads (he was too late to catch the first run of *Publishers' Weekly*, which was already on its way to England with a full page for *The Deer Park*) and broke his contract to do the book. I was started on a trip to find a new publisher, and before I was done the book had gone to Random House, Knopf, Simon & Schuster, Harper's, Scribners, and unofficially to Harcourt Brace. Someday it would be fine to give the details, but for now little more than a few lines of dialogue and an editorial report:

Bennett Cerf: This novel will set publishing back twenty years.

Alfred Knopf to an editor: Is this your idea of the kind of book which should bear a Borzoi imprint?

The lawyer for one publishing house complimented me on the six lines, word for word, which had excited Rinehart to break his contract. This lawyer said, "It's admirable the way you get around the problem here." Then he brought out more than a hundred objections to other parts of the book. One was the line, "She was lovely. Her back was adorable in its contours." I was told that this ought to go because "the principals are not married, and so your description puts a favorable interpretation upon a meretricious relationship."

Hiram Haydn had lunch with me some time after Random House saw the book. He told me he was responsible for their decision not to do it, and if I did not agree with his taste, I had to admire his honesty—it is rare for an editor to tell a writer the truth. Haydn went on to say that the book never came alive for him, even though he had been ready to welcome it. "I can tell you that I picked the book up with anticipation. Of course I had heard from Bill, and Bill had told me that he didn't like it, but I never pay attention to what one writer says about the work of another. . . ." Bill was William Styron, and Haydn was his editor. I had asked Styron to call Haydn the night I found out Rinehart had broken his contract. One reason for asking the favor of Styron was that he sent me a long letter about the novel after I had shown it to him in manuscript. He had written, "I don't like *The*

Deer Park, but I admire sheer hell out of it." So I thought to impose on him.

Other parts of the account are not less dreary. The only generosity I found was from the late Jack Goodman. He sent me a photostat of his editorial report to Simon & Schuster, and because it was sympathetic, his report became the objective estimate of the situation for me. I assumed that the book when it came out would meet the kind of trouble Goodman expected, and so when I went back later to work on the page proofs I was not free of a fear or two. But that can be talked about in its place. Here is the core of his report:

> Mailer refuses to make any changes . . . . (He) will consider suggestions, but reserves the right to make final decisions, so we must make our decision on what the book now is.
>
> That's not easy. It is full of vitality and power, as readable a novel as I've ever encountered. Mailer emerges as a sort of post-Kinsey F. Scott Fitzgerald. His dialogue is uninhibited and the sexuality of the book is completely interwoven with its purpose, which is to describe a segment of society whose morality is nonexistent. Locale is evidently Palm Springs. Chief characters are Charles Eitel, movie director who first defies the House Un-American Committee, then becomes a friendly witness, his mistress, a great movie star who is his ex-wife, her lover who is the narrator, the head of a great movie company, his son-in-law, a strange, tortured panderer who is Eitel's conscience, and assorted demimondaines, homosexuals, actors.
>
> My layman's opinion is that the novel will be banned in certain quarters and that it may very well be up for an obscenity charge, but this should of course be checked by our lawyers. If it were possible to recognize this at the start, to have a united front here and treat the whole issue positively and head-on, I would be for our publishing. But I am afraid such unanimity may be impossible

of attainment and, if so, we should reject, in spite of the fact that I am certain it will be one of the best-selling novels of the next couple of years. It is the work of a serious artist.

The eighth house was G. P. Putnam. I didn't want to give it to them, I was planning to go next to Viking, but Walter Minton kept saying, "Give us three days. We'll give you a decision in three days." So we sent it over to Putnam, and in three days they took it without conditions, and without a request for a single change. I had a victory, I had made my point, but in fact I was not very happy. I had grown so wild on my diet of polite letters from publishing houses who didn't want me that I had been looking forward to collecting rejections from twenty houses, publish *The Deer Park* at my own expense, and try to make a kind of publishing history. Instead I was thrown in with Walter Minton, who has since attracted some fame as the publisher of *Lolita*. He is the only publisher I ever met who would make a good general. Months after I came to Putnam, Minton told me, "I was ready to take *The Deer Park* without reading it. I knew your name would sell enough copies to pay your advance, and I figured one of these days you're going to write another book like *The Naked and the Dead*," which is the sort of sure hold of strategy you can have when you're not afraid of censorship.

Now I've tried to water this account with a minimum of tears, but taking *The Deer Park* into the nervous system of eight publishing houses was not so very good for my own nervous system, nor was it good for getting to work on my new novel. In the ten weeks it took the book to travel the circuit from Rinehart to Putnam, I squandered the careful energy I had been hoarding for months; there was a hard comedy at how much of myself I would burn up in a few hours of hot telephone calls; I had never had any sense for practical affairs, but in those days, carrying *The Deer Park* from house to house, I stayed as close to it as a stagestruck mother pushing her child forward at every producer's office. I was amateur agent for it, messenger boy, editorial consultant, Machiavelli of the luncheon table, fool of the five-o'clock drinks; I was learning the publishing business in a hurry, and I made a hundred mistakes and paid for each one by wasting a new bout of energy.

In a way there was sense to it. For the first time in years I was having the kind of experience which was likely to return some day as good work, and so I forced many little events past any practical return, even insulting a few publishers en route as if to discover the limits of each situation. I was trying to find a few new proportions to things, and I did learn a bit. But I'll never know what that novel about the concentration camp would have been like if I had gotten quietly to work when I came back to New York and *The Deer Park* had been published on time. It is possible I was not serious about the book, it is also possible I lost something good, but one way or the other, that novel disappeared in the excitement, as lost as "the little object" in *Barbary Shore,* and it has not stirred since.

The real confession is that I was making a few of my mental connections those days on marijuana. Like more than one or two of my generation, I had smoked it from time to time over the years, but it never had meant anything. In Mexico, however, down in my depression with a bad liver, pot gave me a sense of something new about the time I was convinced I had seen it all, and I liked it enough to take it now and again in New York.

Then *The Deer Park* began to go like a beggar from house to house and en route Stanley Rinehart made it clear he was going to try not to pay the advance. Until then I had had sympathy for him. I thought it had taken a kind of displaced courage to be able to drop the book the way he did. An expensive moral stand, and wasteful for me; but a moral stand. When it turned out that he did not like to bear the expense of being that moral, the experience turned ugly for me. It took many months and the service of my lawyer to get the money, but long before that the situation had become real enough to drive a spike into my cast-iron mind. I realized in some bottom of myself that for years I had been the sort of comic figure I would have cooked to a turn in one of my books, a radical who had the nineteenth-century naïveté to believe that the people with whom he did business were (1) gentlemen, (2) fond of him, and (3) respectful of his ideas, even if in disagreement with them. Now, I was in the act of learning that I was not adored so very much; that my ideas were seen as nasty; and that my fine America which I had been at pains to criticize for so many years was in fact a real country which did real things and ugly things to the characters of more people than just the characters of my books. If the years since the war had not been brave nor noble in the history of the country, which I certainly thought and do think, why then did it come as surprise that people in publishing were not as good as they used to be, and that the day of Maxwell Perkins was a day which was gone, really gone, gone as Greta Garbo and Scott Fitzgerald? Not easy, one could argue, for an advertising man to admit that advertising is a dishonest occupation, and no easier was it for the working novelist to see that now were left only the cliques, fashions, vogues, snobs, snots, and fools, not to mention a dozen bureaucracies of criticism; that there was no room for the old literary idea of oneself as a major writer, a figure in the landscape. One had become a set of relations and equations, most flourishing when most incorporated, for then one's literary stock was ready for merger. The day was gone when people held on to your novels no matter what others might say. Instead one's good young readers waited now for the verdict of professional young men, academics who wolfed down a modern literature with an anxiety to find your classification, your identity, your corporate literary earnings, each reference to yourself as individual as a carloading of homogenized words. The articles which would be written about you and a dozen others would be done by minds which were expert on the aggregate and so had senses too lumpy for the particular. There was a limit to how much appraisal could be made of a work before the critic exposed his lack of the critical faculty, and so it was naturally wiser for the mind of the expert to masticate the themes of ten writers rather than dissect the difficulties of any one.

I had begun to read my good American novels at the end of an era—I could remember people who would talk wistfully about the excitement with which they had gone to bookstores because it was publication day for the second novel of Thomas Wolfe. My adolescent crush on the profession of the writer had been more lasting than I could have guessed. I had even been so simple as to think that the kind of people who went into publishing were still most concerned with the few writers who made the profession not empty of honor, and I had been taking myself seriously. I had been thinking I was one of those writers.

Instead I caught it in the face and deserved it for not looking at the evidence. I was out of fashion and that was the score; that was all the score; the publishing habits of the past were going to be of no help for my *Deer Park*. And so, as the language of sentiment would have it, something broke in me, but I do not know if it was so much a loving heart as a cyst of the weak, the unreal, and the needy, and I was finally open to my anger. I turned within my psyche I can almost believe, for I felt something shift to murder in me. I finally had the simple sense to understand that if I wanted my work to travel further than others, the life of my talent depended on fighting a little more, and looking for help a little less. But I deny the sequence in putting it this way, for it took me years to come to this fine point. All I felt then was that I was an outlaw, a psychic outlaw, and I liked it, I liked it a good sight better than trying to be a gentleman, and with such a set of emotions accelerating one on the other, I mined down deep into the murderous message of marijuana, the smoke of the assassins, and for the first time in my life I knew what it was to make your kicks.

I could write about that here, but it would be a mistake. Let the experience stay where it is, and on a given year it may be found again in a novel. For now it is enough to say that marijuana gives a great deal to the senses and burns out much of the mind. In the end, you pay for what you get. If you get something big, the cost will equal it. There is a moral economy to one's vice, but you learn that last of all. I still had the thought it was possible to find something which cost nothing. Thus, *The Deer Park* resting at Putnam, and new friends found in Harlem, I was off on that happy ride where you discover another duchy of jazz every night and the drought of the past is given a rain of new sound.

What has been dull and dead in your ears is now tart to the taste, and there is sweet in the illusion of how fast you can change. To keep up with it all, I began to log a journal, a wild set of thoughts and outlines for huge projects—I wrote one hundred thousand words in eight weeks, more than once twenty pages a day in a style which came willy-nilly from the cramp of the past, a lock-step jargon of sociology and psychology that sours my teeth when I look at those pages today. Yet this journal has the start of more ideas than I will have again; ideas which came so fast and so rich that sometimes I think my brain was dulled by the heat of their passage. (With all proportions kept, one can say that cocaine may have worked a similar good and ill upon Freud.)

The journal wore down by February, about the time *The Deer Park* had once been scheduled to appear. By then I had decided to change a few things in the novel, nothing in the way of law-yers' deletions, just a few touches for style. They were not happy about this at Putnam. Minton argued that some interest in the book would be lost if the text were not identical to Rinehart's page proofs, and Ted Purdy, my editor, told me more than once that they liked the book "just the way it is." Besides, there was thought of bringing it out in June as a summer book.

Well, I wanted to take a look. After all, I had been learning new lessons. I began to go over the page proofs, and the book read as if it had been written by someone else. I was changed from the writer who had labored on that novel, enough to be able to see it without anger or vanity or the itch to justify myself. Now, after three years of living with the book, I could at last admit the style was wrong, that it had been wrong from the time I started, that I had been strangling the life of my novel in a po-etic prose which was too self-consciously attractive, false to the life of my characters, especially false to the life of my narrator who was the voice of my novel and so gave the story its air. He had been a lieutenant in the Air Force, he had been cool enough and hard enough to work his way up from an orphan asylum, and to allow him to write in a style which at its best sounded like Nick Carraway in *The Great Gatsby* must of course blur his charac-ter and leave the book unreal. Nick was legitimate, out of fair family, the Midwest and Princeton—he would write as he did, his style was himself. But the style of Sergius O'Shaughnessy, no matter how good it became (and the Rinehart *Deer Park* had its moments), was a style which came out of nothing so much as my determination to prove I could muster a fine style.

If I wanted to improve my novel, yet keep the style, I would have to make my narrator fit the prose, change his past, make him an onlooker, a rich pretty boy brought up let us say by two old-maid aunts, able to have an affair with a movie star only by luck and/or the needs of the plot which would give me a book less distracting, well written, but minor. If, however, I wanted to keep that first narrator, my orphan, flier, adventurer, *germ*—for three years he had been the frozen germ of some new theme— well, to keep him I would need to change the style from the inside of each sentence. I could keep the structure of my book, I thought, it had been put together for such a narrator, but the style could not escape. Probably I did not see it all so clearly as I now suggest. I believe I started with the conscious thought that I would tinker just a little, try to patch a compromise, but the navigator of my unconscious must already have made the choice, because it came as no real surprise that after a few days of changing a few words, I moved more and more quickly toward the eye of the problem, and in two or three weeks, I was tied to the work of doing a new *Deer Park*. The book was edited in a way no editor could ever have time or love to find; it was searched sentence by sentence, word for word, the style of the work lost its polish, became rough, and I can say real, because there was an abrupt and muscular body back of the voice now. It had been there all the time, trapped in the porcelain of a false style, but now as I chipped away, the work for a time became exhilarating in its clarity—I never enjoyed work so much—I felt as if finally I was learning how to write, learning the joints of language and the touch of a word, I felt as if I came close to the meanings of sound and could say which of two close words was more female or more forward. I even had a glimpse of what Flaubert must have felt, for as I went on tuning the book, often five or six words would pile above one another in the margin at some small crisis of choice.

(Since the Rinehart page proof was the usable copy, I had little space to write between the lines.) As I worked in this fine mood, I kept sending pages to the typist, yet so soon as I had exhausted the old galley pages, I could not keep away from the new type-written copy—it would be close to say the book had come alive, and was invading my brain.

Soon the early pleasure of the work turned restless; the consequences of what I was doing were beginning to seep into my stamina. It was as if I were the captive of an illness whose first symptoms had been excitement, prodigies of quick work, and a confidence that one could go on forever, but that I was by now close to a second stage where what had been quick would be more like fever, a first wind of fatigue upon me, as if at the end of the drunken night a clammy cold was waiting. I was going to move at a pace deadly to myself, loading and overloading whatever little centers of the mind are forced to make the hard decisions. In ripping up the silk of the original syntax, I was tearing into any number of careful habits as well as whatever subtle fleshing of the nerves and the chemicals had gone to support them.

For six years I had been writing novels in the first person; it was the only way I could begin a book, even though the third person was more to my taste. Worse, I seemed unable to create a narrator in the first person who was not overdelicate, oversensitive, and painfully tender, which was an odd portrait to give, because I was not delicate, not physically; when it was a matter of strength I had as much as the next man. In those days I would spend time reminding myself that I had been a bit of an athlete (house football at Harvard, years of skiing), that I had not quit in combat, and that my ideas had never been weak, nor my personality too small. Yet the first person seemed to paralyze me, as if I had a horror of creating a voice which could be in any way larger than me. I had dug a psychological trench for myself, had become mired in a false style for every narrator I tried. If now I had been in a fight, had found out that no matter how weak I could be in certain ways, I was also steady enough to hang on to six important lines, that may have given me new respect for myself. I don't know, but for the first time I was able to use the first person in a way where I could suggest some of the stubbornness and belligerence I also might have, I was able to color the empty reality of that first person with some real feeling of how I had always felt, which was to be outside, for Brooklyn where I grew up is not the center of anything. So I was able to create an adventurer whom I believed in, and as he came alive for me, the other parts of the book which had been stagnant for a year and more also came to life, and new things began to happen to Eitel my director and to Elena his mistress, and their character changed. It was a phenomenon. I learned how real a novel is. Before, the story of Eitel had been told by O'Shaughnessy of the weak voice, now by a confident young man: when the new narrator would remark that Eitel was his best friend and so he tried not to find Elena too attractive, the man and woman he was talking about were larger than they had once been. I was no longer telling of two nice people who fail at love because the world is too large and too cruel for them; the new O'Shaughnessy had moved me by degrees to the more painful story of two people who are strong as well as weak, corrupt as much as pure, and fail to grow despite their bravery in a poor world, because they are finally not brave enough, and so do more damage to one another than to the unjust world outside them. Which for me was exciting, for here and there *The Deer Park* now had the rare tenderness of tragedy. The most powerful leverage in fiction comes from point of view, and giving O'Shaughnessy courage gave passion to the others.

But the punishment was commencing for me. I was now creating a man who was braver and stronger than me, and the more my new style succeeded, the more was I writing an implicit portrait of myself as well. There is a shame about advertising yourself that way, a shame which became so strong that it was a psychological violation to go on. Yet I could not afford the time to digest the self-criticism backing up in me, I was forced to drive myself, and so more and more I worked by tricks, taking marijuana the night before and then drugging myself into sleep with an overload of Seconal. In the morning I would be lithe with new perception, could read new words into the words I had already, and so could go on in the pace of my work, the most scrupulous part of my brain too sluggish to interfere. My powers of logic became weaker each day, but the book had its own logic, and so I did not need close reason. What I wanted, and what the drugs gave me, was the quick flesh of associations, and there I was often oversensitive, could discover new experience in the lines of my text like a hermit savoring the revelation of Scripture; I saw so much in some sentences that more than once I dropped into the pit of the amateur: since I was receiving such emotion from my words, I assumed everyone else would be stimulated as well, and on many a line I twisted the phrase in such a way that it could read well only when read slowly, about as slowly as it would take for an actor to read it aloud. Once you write that way, the quick reader (who is nearly all your audience) will stumble and fall against the vocal shifts of your prose. Then you had best have the cartel of a Hemingway, because in such a case it is critical whether the reader thinks it is your fault or is so in awe of your reputation that he returns on the words, throttles his pace, and tries to discover why he is so stupid as not to swing on the off-bop of your style.

An example: In the Rinehart *Deer Park* I had this—

"They make Sugar sound so good in the newspapers," she declared one night to some people in a bar, "that I'll really try him. I really will, Sugar." And she gave me a sisterly kiss.

I happened to change that very little, I put in "said" instead of "declared" and later added, "older sister," so that it now read:

"And she gave me a sisterly kiss. Older sister."

Just two words, but I felt as if I had revealed some divine law of nature, had laid down an invaluable clue—the kiss of an older sister was a worldly universe away from the kiss of a younger sister—and I thought to give myself the Nobel Prize for having brought such illumination and *division* to the cliché of the sisterly kiss.

Well, as an addition it wasn't bad fun, and for two words it did a bit to give a sense of what was working back and forth between Sergius and Lulu, it was another small example of Sergius's hard eye for the world, and his cool sense of his place in it, and all this was to the good, or would have been for a reader who went slowly, and stopped, and thought. But if anyone was in a hurry, the little sentence, "Older sister," was like a finger in the eye: it jabbed the unconscious, and gave an uncomfortable nip of rhythm to the mind.

I had five hundred changes of this kind. I started with the first paragraph of the book, on the third sentence which pokes the reader with its backed-up rhythm. "Some time ago," and I did that with intent, to slow my readers from the start, like a fighter who throws his right two seconds after the bell and so gives the other man no chance to decide on the pace.

There was a real question, however, whether I would slow the reader down or merely irritate him to distraction, and so as I worked on further, at some point beginning to write paragraphs and pages to add to the new Putnam galleys, the attrition of the drugs and the possibility of failure began to depress me, and Benzedrine entered the balance, and I was on the way to wearing badly. Because, determined or no that they would read me slowly, praying my readers would read me slowly, they would do nothing of the sort if the reviews were poor. As I started to worry this, it grew worse, because I knew in advance that three or four of my major reviews had to be bad, *Time* magazine for one, because Max Gissen was the book review editor, and I had insulted him in public once by suggesting that the kind of man who worked for a mind so exquisitely and subtly totalitarian as Henry Luce was not likely to have any ideas of his own. The daily *New York Times* would be bad because Orville Prescott was well known for his distaste of books too forthrightly sexual; and *Saturday Review* would be bad. That is, they would probably be bad; the mentality of their reviewers would not be above the level of their dean of reviewers, Mr. Maxwell Geismar, and Geismar didn't seem to know that my second novel was titled *Barbary Shore* rather than *Barbary Coast*. I could make a list, but what is more to the point is that I was thinking of the reviews before I was done with the book, and this doubtful occupation came out of the kind of inner knowledge I had of myself in those days. I knew what was good for my energy and what was poor, and so I knew that for the vitality of my work in the future, and yes even the quantity of my work, I needed a success and I needed it badly if I were to shed the fatigue I had been carrying since *Barbary Shore.* Some writers receive not enough attention for years, and so learn early to accommodate the habits of their work to little recognition. I think I could have done that when I was twenty-five, but now it was a little late; I had gone through the psychic labor of changing a good many modest habits so I could live as a man with a name which could arouse quick reactions in strangers. If that started as an overlarge work, because I started as a decent but scared boy, well, I had learned to like success—in fact I had come to depend on it, or at least my new habits did.

When *Barbary Shore* was ambushed in the alley, the damage to my nervous system was slow but thorough. My status dropped immediately—America is a quick country—but my ego did not permit me to understand that, and I went through tiring years of subtle social defeats because I did not know that I was no longer as large to others as I had been. I was always overmatching myself. To put it crudely, I would think I was dropping people when they were dropping me. And of course my unconscious knew better. There was all the waste of ferocious if unheard discussion between the armies of ego and id; I would get up in the morning with less snap in me than I had taken to sleep. Six or seven years of breathing that literary air taught me a writer stayed alive in the circuits of such hatred only if he were unappreciated enough to be adored by a clique, or was so overbought by the public that he excited some defenseless nerve in the snob. I knew if *The Deer Park* were a powerful bestseller (the magical figure had become one hundred thousand copies for me) that I would then have won. I would be the first serious writer of my generation to have a bestseller twice, and so it would not matter what was said about the book. Half of publishing might call it cheap, dirty, sensational, second-rate, and so forth and so forth, but it would be weak rage and could not hurt, for the literary world suffers a spot of the national taint—a serious writer is certain to be considered major if he is also a bestseller; in fact, no one is convinced of his value until his books do well. Steinbeck is given more size than Dos Passos, John O'Hara is taken seriously by people who dismiss Farrell, and indeed it took three decades and a Nobel Prize before Faulkner was placed on a level with Hemingway. For that reason, it would have done no good if someone had told me at the time that the financial success of a writer with major talent was probably due more to what was meretricious in his work than what was central. The argument would have meant nothing to me—all I knew was that seven publishing houses had been willing to dismiss my future, and so if the book did poorly, a good many people were going to congratulate themselves on their foresight and be concerned with me even less. I could see that if I intended to keep on writing the kind of book I wanted to write, I needed the energy of new success like I needed blood. Through every bit of me, I knew *The Deer Park* had damn well better make it, or I was close to some serious illness, a real apathy of the will. Every now and again I would have the nightmare of wondering what would happen if all the reviews were bad, as bad as *Barbary Shore*. I would try to tell myself that could not happen, but I was not certain, and I knew that if the book received a unanimously bad press and still showed signs of selling well, it was likely to be brought up for prosecution as obscene. As a delayed convulsion from the McCarthy years, the fear of censorship was strong in publishing, in England it was critically bad, and so I also knew that the book could lose such a suit—there might be no one of reputation to say it was serious. If it were banned, it could sink from sight. With the reserves I was throwing into the work, I no longer knew if I were ready to take another beating—for the first time in my life I had worn down to the edge, I could see through to the other side of my fear, I knew a time could come when I would be no longer my own man, that I might lose what I had liked to think was the incorruptible center of my strength (which of course I had had money and freedom to cultivate). Already the signs were there—I was beginning to avoid new lines in the Putnam *Deer Park* which were legally doubtful, and once in a while, like a gambler hedging a bet, I toned down individual sentences from the Rinehart *Deer Park,* nothing much, always a matter of the new O'Shaughnessy character, a change from "at last I was able to penetrate into the mysterious and magical belly of a movie star," to what was more in character for him: "I was led to discover the mysterious brain of a movie star." Which "brain" in context was fun for it was accurate, and "discover" was a word of more life than the legality of "penetrate," but I could not be sure if I were chasing my new aesthetic or afraid of the cops. The problem was that *The Deer Park* had become more sexual in the new version, the characters had more force, the air had more heat, and I had gone through the kind of galloping self-analysis which makes one very sensitive to the sexual nuance of every gesture, word, and object—the book now seemed overcharged to me, even a terror of a novel, a cold chisel into all the dull mortar of our guilty society. In my mind it became a more dangerous book than it really was, and my drug-hipped paranoia saw long consequences in every easy line of dialogue. I kept the panic in its place, but by an effort of course, and once in a while I would weaken enough to take out a line because I could not see myself able to defend it happily in a court of law. But it was a mistake to nibble at the edges of censoring myself, for it gave no life to my old pride that I was the boldest writer to come out of my flabby time, and I think it helped to kill the small chance of finding my way into what could have been a novel as important as *The Sun Also Rises.*

But let me spell it out a bit: originally *The Deer Park* had been about a movie director and a girl with whom he had a bad affair, and it was told by a sensitive but faceless young man. In changing the young man, I saved the book from being minor, but put a disproportion upon it. Because my narrator became too interesting, and not enough happened to him in the second half of the book, and so it was to be expected that readers would be disappointed by this part of the novel.

Before I was finished, I saw a way to write another book altogether. In what I had so far done, Sergius O'Shaughnessy was given an opportunity by a movie studio to sell the rights to his life and get a contract as an actor. After more than one complication, he finally refused the offer, lost the love of his movie star Lulu, and went off wandering by himself, off to become a writer. This episode had never been an important part of the book, but

I could see that the new Sergius was capable of accepting the offer, and if he went to Hollywood and became a movie star himself, the possibilities were good, for in O'Shaughnessy I had a character who was ambitious, yet in his own way moral, and with such a character, one could travel deep into the paradoxes of the time.

Well, I was not in shape to consider that book. With each week of work, bombed and sapped and charged and stoned with lush, with pot, with Benny, saggy, Miltown, coffee, and two packs a day, I was working live, and overalert, and tiring into what felt like death, afraid all the way because I had achieved the worst of vicious circles in myself, I had gotten too tired. I was more tired than I had ever been in combat, and so as the weeks went on, and publication was delayed from June to August and then to October, there was only a worn-out part of me to keep protesting into the pillows of one drug and the pinch of the other that I ought to have the guts to stop the machine, to call back the galleys, to cease—to rest, to give myself another two years, and write a book which would go a little farther to the end of my particular night.

But I had passed the point where I could stop. My anxiety had become too great. I did not know anything anymore, I did not have that clear sense of the way things work which is what you need for the natural proportions of a long novel, and it is likely I would not have been writing a new book so much as arguing with the law. Of course another man might have had the stamina to write the new book and manage to be indifferent to everything else, but it was too much to ask of me. By then I was like a lover in a bad, but uncontrollable affair; my woman was publication, and it would have cost too much to give her up before we were done. My imagination had been committed; to stop would leave half the psyche in limbo.

Knowing, however, what I had failed to do, shame added momentum to the punishment of the drugs. By the last week or two, I had worn down so badly that, with a dozen pieces still to be fixed, I was reduced to working hardly more than an hour a day. Like an old man, I would come up out of a Seconal stupor with

four or five times the normal dose in my veins, and drop into a
chair to sit for hours. It was July, the heat was grim in New York,
the last of the book had to be in by August 1. Putnam's had been
more than accommodating, but the vehicle of publication was
on its way, and the book could not be postponed beyond the
middle of October or it would miss all chance for a large fall sale.
I would sit in a chair and watch a baseball game on television, or
get up and go out in the heat to a drugstore for sandwich and
malted—it was my outing for the day: the walk would feel like a
patrol in a tropical sun, and it was two blocks, no more. When I
came back, I would lie down, my head would lose the outer wrap-
pings of sedation, and with a crumb of Benzedrine, the first
snake or two of thought would wind through my brain. I would
go for some coffee; it was a trip to the kitchen, but when I came
back I would have a scratchboard and pencil in hand. Watching
some afternoon horror on television, the boredom of the performers coming through their tense hilarities with a bleakness to
match my own, I would pick up the board, wait for the first
sentence—like all working addicts I had come to an old man's
fine sense of inner timing—and then slowly, but picking up
speed, the actions of the drugs hovering into collaboration like
two ships passing in view of one another, I would work for an
hour, not well but not badly either. (Pages 195 to 200 were written this way.) Then my mind would wear out, and new work was
done for the day. I would sit around, watch more television, and
try to rest my dulled mind, but by evening, a riot of bad nerves
was on me again, and at two in the morning I'd be having the
manly debate of whether to try sleep with two double capsules or
settle again for my need of three.

Somehow I got the book done for the last deadline. Not
perfectly—doing just the kind of editing and small rewriting I
was doing. I could have used another two or three days, but I got
it almost the way I wanted, and then I took my car up to the Cape
and lay around in Provincetown with my wife, trying to mend,
and indeed doing a fair job because I came off sleeping pills and

the marijuana and came part of the way back into that world which has the proportions of the ego. I picked up on *The Magic Mountain,* took it slowly, and lowered *The Deer Park* down to modest size in my brain. Which events proved was just as well.

A few weeks later we came back to the city, and I took some mescaline. Maybe one dies a little with the poison of mescaline in the blood. At the end of a long and private trip which no quick remark should try to describe, the book of *The Deer Park* floated into mind, and I sat up, reached through a pleasure garden of velveted light to find the tree of a pencil and the bed of a notebook, and brought them to union together. Then, out of some flesh in myself I had not yet known, with the words coming one by one, in separate steeps and falls, hip in their turnings, all cool with their flights, like the touch of being coming into other being, so the last six lines of my bloody book came to me, and I was done. And it was the only good writing I ever did directly from a drug, even if I paid for it with a hangover beyond measure.

That way the novel received its last sentence, and if I had waited one more day it would have been too late, for in the next twenty-four hours, the printers began their cutting and binding. The book was out of my hands.

Six weeks later, when *The Deer Park* came out, I was no longer feeling eighty years old, but a vigorous hysterical sixty-three, and I laughed like an old pirate at the indignation I had breezed into being with the equation of sex and time. The important reviews broke about seven good and eleven bad, and the out-of-town reports were almost three-to-one bad to good, but I was not unhappy because the good reviews were lively and the bad reviews were full of factual error, indeed so much so that it would be monotonous to give more than a good couple.

Hollis Alpert in the *Saturday Review* called the book "garish and gauche." In reference to Sergius O'Shaughnessy, Alpert wrote: "He has been offered $50,000 by Teppis to sell the rights to his rather dull life story. . . ." As a matter of detail, the sum was

$20,000, and it must have been mentioned a half dozen times in the pages of the book. Paul Pickrel in *Harper's* was blistering about how terrible was my style and then quoted the following sentence as an example of how I was often incomprehensible:

"(He) could talk opening about his personal life while remaining a dream of espionage in his business operations."

I happened to see Pickrel's review in *Harper's* galleys, and so was able to point out to them that Pickrel had misquoted the sentence. The fourth word was not "opening" but "openly." *Harper's* corrected his incorrect version, but of course left his remark about my style.

More interesting is the way reviews divided in the New York magazines and newspapers. *Time,* for example, was bad, *Newsweek* was good; *Harper's* was terrible but *The Atlantic* was adequate; the New York daily *Times* was very bad, the Sunday *Times* was good; the daily *Herald Tribune* gave a mark of zero, the Sunday *Herald Tribune* was better than good; *Commentary* was careful but complimentary, the *Reporter* was hysterical; the *Saturday Review* was a scold, and Brendan Gill writing for *The New Yorker* put together a series of slaps and superlatives which went partially like this: " . . . a big, vigorous, rowdy, ill-shaped, and repellent book, so strong and so weak, so adroit and so fumbling, that only a writer of the greatest and most reckless talent could have flung it between covers."

It's one of the three or four lines I've thought perceptive in all the reviews of my books. That Malcolm Cowley used one of the same words in saying *The Deer Park* was "serious and reckless" is also, I think, interesting, for reckless the book was—and two critics, anyway, had the instinct to feel it.

One note appeared in many reviews. The strongest statement of it was by John Hutchens in the New York daily *Herald Tribune:* " . . . the original version reputedly was more or less rewritten and certain materials eliminated that were deemed too erotic for public consumption. And, with that, a book that might at least have made a certain reputation as a large shocker wound up as a cipher."

I was bothered to the point of writing a letter to the twenty-odd newspapers which reflected this idea. What bothered me was that I could never really prove I had not "eliminated" the book. Over the years all too many readers would have some hazy impression that I had disemboweled large pieces of the best meat, perspiring in a coward's sweat, a publisher's directive in my ear. (For that matter, I still get an occasional letter which asks if it is possible to see the unbowdlerized *Deer Park.*) Part of the cost of touching the Rinehart galleys was to start those rumors, and in fact I was not altogether free of the accusation, as I have tried to show. Even the six lines which so displeased Rinehart had been altered a bit; I had shown them once to a friend whose opinion I respected, and he remarked that while it was impossible to accept the sort of order Rinehart had laid down, still a phrase like the "fount of power" had a Victorian heaviness about it. Well, that was true, it was out of character for O'Shaughnessy's new style, and so I altered it to the "thumb of power" and then other changes became desirable, but the mistake I made was to take a small aesthetic gain on those six lines and lose a larger clarity about a principle.

What more is there to say? The book moved fairly well, it climbed to seven and then to six on the *New York Times* bestseller list, stayed there for a week or two, and then slipped down. By Christmas, the tone of the *Park* and the Christmas spirit being not all that congenial, it was just about off the lists forever. It did well, however; it would have reached so high as three or two or even to number one if it had come out in June and then been measured against the low sales of summer, for it sold over fifty thousand copies after returns, which surprised a good many in publishing, as well as disappointing a few, including myself. I discovered that I had been poised for an enormous sale or a failure—a middling success was cruel to take. Week after week I kept waiting for the book to erupt into some dramatic change of pace which would send it up in sales instead of down, but that never happened. I was left with a draw, not busted, not made, and since I was empty at the time, worn out with work, waiting for the quick transfusions of a generous success, the steady sales of the book left me deeply depressed. Having reshaped my words with an intensity of feeling I had not known before, I could not understand why others were not overcome with my sense of life, of sex, and of sadness. Like a starved revolutionary in a garret, I had compounded out of need and fever and vision and fear nothing less than a madman's confidence in the identity of my being and the wants of all others, and it was a new dull load to lift and to bear, this knowledge that I had no magic so great as to hasten the time of the apocalypse, but that instead I would be open like all others to the attritions of half success and small failure. Something godlike in my confidence began to leave, and I was reduced in dimension if now less a boy. I knew I had failed on the biggest hand I had ever held.

Now a few years have gone by, more years than I thought, and I have begun to work up another hand, a new book which will be the proper book of an outlaw, and so not publishable in any easy or legal way. I'll say here only that O'Shaughnessy will be one of the three heroes, and that if I'm to go all the way this time, the odds are that my beat senses will have to do the work without the fires and the wastes of the minor drugs.

But that is for later, and the proper end to this account is the advertisement I took in *The Village Voice*. It was bought in November 1955, a month after publication, it was put together by me and paid for by me, and it was my way, I now suppose, of saying goodbye to the pleasure of a quick triumph, of making my apologies for the bad flaws in the bravest effort I had yet pulled out of myself, and certainly for declaring to the world (in a small way, mean pity) that I no longer gave a sick dog's drop for the wisdom, the reliability, and the authority of the public's literary mind, those creeps and old ladies of vested reviewing.

Besides, I had the tender notion—believe it if you will—that the ad might after all do its work and excite some people to buy the book.

But here it is:

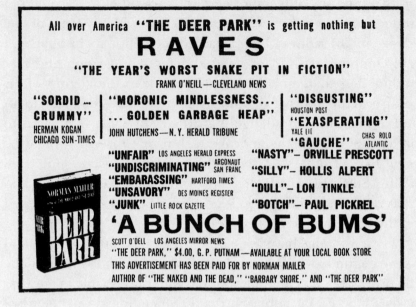

1960s

Superman Comes to the Supermarket

(1960)

FOR ONCE LET US TRY to think about a political convention without losing ourselves in housing projects of fact and issue. Politics has its virtues, all too many of them—it would not rank with baseball as a topic of conversation if it did not satisfy a great many things— but one can suspect that its secret appeal is close to nicotine. Smoking cigarettes insulates one from one's life, one does not feel as much, often happily so, and politics quarantines one from history; most of the people who nourish themselves in the political life are in the game not to make history but to be diverted from the history which is being made.

If that Democratic Convention which has now receded behind the brow of the summer of 1960 is only half remembered in the excitements of moving toward the election, it may be exactly the time to consider it again, because the mountain of facts which concealed its features last July has been blown away in the winds of High Television, and the man in the street (that peculiar political term which refers to the quixotic voter who will pull the lever for some reason so salient as "I had a brown-nose lieutenant once with Nixon's looks," or "that Kennedy must have false teeth"), the not so easily estimated man in the street has forgotten most of what happened and could no more tell you who Kennedy was fighting against than you or I could place a bet on who was leading the American League in batting during the month of June.

So to try to talk about what happened is easier now than in the days of the convention, one does not have to put everything in—an act of writing which calls for a bulldozer rather than a pen—one can try to make one's little point and dress it with a ribbon or two of metaphor. All to the good. Because mysteries are irritated by facts, and the 1960 Democratic Convention began as one mystery and ended as another.

Since mystery is an emotion which is repugnant to a political animal (why else lead a life of bad banquet dinners, cigar smoke, camp chairs, foul breath, and excruciatingly dull jargon if not to avoid the echoes of what is not known), the psychic separation between what was happening on the floor, in the caucus rooms, in the headquarters, and what was happening in parallel to the history of the nation was mystery enough to drown the proceedings in gloom. It was on the one hand a dull convention, one of the less interesting by general agreement, relieved by local bits of color, given two half hours of excitement by two demonstrations for Stevenson, buoyed up by the class of the Kennedy machine, turned by the surprise of Johnson's nomination as vice president, but, all the same, dull, depressed in its overall tone, the big fiestas subdued, the gossip flat, no real air of excitement, just moments—or as they say in bullfighting—details. Yet it was also, one could argue—and one may argue this yet—it was also one of the most important conventions in America's history, it could prove conceivably to be the most important. The man it nominated was unlike any politician who had ever run for president in the history of the land, and if elected he would come to power in a year when America was in danger of drifting into a profound decline.

Depression obviously has its several roots: it is the doubtful protection which comes from not recognizing failure, it is the psychic burden of exhaustion, and it is also, and very often, the discipline of the will or the ego which enables one to continue working when one's unadmitted emotion is panic. And panic it was I think which sat as the largest single sentiment in the breast of the collective delegates as they came to convene in Los Angeles. Delegates are not the noblest sons and daughters of the Republic; a man of taste, arrived from Mars, would take one look at a convention floor and leave forever, convinced he had seen one of the drearier squats of Hell. If one still smells the faint living echo of carnival wine, the pepper of a bullfight, the rag, drag, and panoply of a jousting tourney, it is all swallowed and regurgitated by the senses into the fouler cud of a death gas one must rid oneself of—a cigar-smoking, stale-aired, slack-jawed, butt-littered, foul, bleak, hardworking, bureaucratic death gas of language and faces ("Yes, those *faces*," says the man from Mars: lawyers, judges, ward heelers, mafiosi, Southern goons and grandees, grand old ladies, trade unionists and finks), of pompous words and long pauses which lie like a leaden pain over fever, the fever that one is in, over, or is it that one is just behind history? A legitimate panic for a delegate. America is a nation of experts without roots; we are always creating tacticians who are blind to strategy and strategists who cannot take a step, and when the culture has finished its work the institutions handcuff the infirmity. A delegate is a man who picks a candidate for the largest office in the land, a president who must live with problems whose borders are in ethics, metaphysics, and now ontology; the delegate is prepared for this office of selection by emptying wastebaskets, toting garbage, and saying yes at the right time for twenty years in the small political machine of some small or large town; his reward, one of them anyway, is that he arrives at an invitation to the convention. An expert on local catch-as-catch-can, a small-time, often mediocre practitioner of small-town political judo, he comes to the big city with nine-tenths of his mind made up, he will follow the orders of the boss who brought him. Yet of course it is not altogether so mean as that: his opinion is listened to—the boss will consider what he has to say as one interesting factor among five hundred, and what is most important to the delegate, he has the illusion of partial freedom. He can, unless he is severely honest with himself—and if he is, why sweat out the low levels of a political

machine?—he can have the illusion that he has helped to choose
the candidate, he can even worry most sincerely about his choice,
flirt with defection from the boss, work out his own small political gains by the road of loyalty or the way of hard bargain. But
even if he is there for more than the ride, his vote a certainty in
the mind of the political boss, able to be thrown here or switched
there as the boss decides, still in some peculiar sense he is reality
to the boss, the delegate is the great American public, the bar he
owns or the law practice, the piece of the union he represents,
or the real estate office, is a part of the political landscape which
the boss uses as his own image of how the votes will go, and if the
people will like the candidate. And if the boss is depressed by
what he sees, if the candidate does not feel right to him, if he has
a dull intimation that the candidate is not his sort (as, let us say,
Harry Truman was his sort, or Symington might be his sort, or
Lyndon Johnson), then vote for him the boss will if he must; he
cannot be caught on the wrong side, but he does not feel the
pleasure of a personal choice. Which is the center of the panic.
Because if the boss is depressed, the delegate is doubly depressed, and the emotional fact is that Kennedy is not in focus,
not in the old political focus, he is not comfortable; in fact it is a
mystery to the boss how Kennedy got to where he is, not a mystery in its structures; Kennedy is rolling in money, Kennedy got
the votes in primaries, and, most of all, Kennedy has a jewel of a
political machine. It is as good as a crack Notre Dame team, all
discipline and savvy and go-go-go, sound, drilled, never dull,
quick as a knife, full of the salt hipper-dipper, a beautiful machine; the boss could adore it if only a sensible candidate were
driving it, a Truman, even a Stevenson, please God a Northern
Lyndon Johnson, but it is run by a man who looks young enough
to be coach of the freshman team, and that is not comfortable at
all. The boss knows political machines, he knows issues, farm
parity, Forand health bill, Landrum-Griffin, but this is not all so
adequate after all to revolutionaries in Cuba who look like beatniks, competitions in missiles, Negroes looting whites in the
Congo, intricacies of nuclear fallout, and NAACP men one does
well to call Sir. It is all out of hand, everything important is off
the center, foreign affairs is now the lick of the heat, and sena-

tors are candidates instead of governors, a disaster to the old family style of political measure where a political boss knows his governor and knows who his governor knows. So the boss is depressed, profoundly depressed. He comes to this convention resigned to nominating a man he does not understand, or let us say that, so far as he understands the candidate who is to be nominated, he is not happy about the secrets of his appeal, not so far as he divines these secrets; they seem to have too little to do with politics and all too much to do with the private madnesses of the nation which had thousands—or was it hundreds of thousands—of people demonstrating in the long night before Chessman was killed, and a movie star, the greatest, Marlon the Brando, out in the night with them. Yes, this candidate for all his record; his good, sound, conventional liberal record has a patina of that other life, the second American life, the long electric night with the fires of neon leading down the highway to the murmur of jazz.

> I was seeing Pershing Square, Los Angeles, now for the first time . . . the nervous fugitives from Times Square, Market Street SF, the French Quarter—masculine hustlers looking for lonely fruits to score from, anything from the legendary $20 to a pad at night and breakfast in the morning and whatever you can clinch or clip; and the heat in their holy cop uniforms, holy because of the Almighty Stick and the Almightier Vagrancy Law; the scattered junkies, the small-time pushers, the queens, the sad panhandlers, the lonely, exiled nymphs haunting the entrance to the men's head, the fruits with the hungry eyes and jingling coins; the tough teen-age chicks—"dittybops"—making it with the lost hustlers . . . all amid the incongruous piped music and the flowers—twin fountains gushing rainbow colored: the world of Lonely America squeezed into Pershing Square, of the Cities of Terrible Night, downtown now trapped in the City of lost Angels . . . and the trees hang over it all like some type of apathetic fate.
>
> —JOHN RECHY, *Big Table 3*

Seeing Los Angeles after ten years away, one realizes all over again that America is an unhappy contract between the East (that Faustian thrust of a most determined human will which reaches up and out above the eye into the skyscrapers of New York) and those flat lands of compromise and mediocre self-expression, those endless half-pretty repetitive small towns of the Middle and the West whose spirit is forever horizontal and whose marrow comes to rendezvous in the pastel monotonies of Los Angeles architecture.

So far as America has a history, one can see it in the severe heights of New York City, in the glare from the Pittsburgh mills, by the color in the brick of Louisburg Square, along the knotted greedy facades of the small mansions on Chicago's North Side, in Natchez's antebellum homes, the wrought-iron balconies off Bourbon Street, a captain's house in Nantucket, by the curve of Commercial Street in Provincetown. One can make a list; it is probably finite. What culture we have made and what history has collected to it can be found in those few hard examples of an architecture which came to its artistic term, was born, lived, and so collected some history about it. Not all the roots of American life are uprooted, but almost all, and the spirit of the supermarket, that homogeneous extension of stainless surfaces and psychoanalyzed people, packaged commodities and ranch homes, interchangeable, geographically unrecognizable, that essence of a new postwar SuperAmerica is found nowhere so perfectly as in Los Angeles's ubiquitous acres. One gets the impression that people come to Los Angeles in order to divorce themselves from the past, here to live or try to live in the rootless pleasure world of an adult child. One knows that if the cities of the world were destroyed by a new war, the architecture of the rebuilding would create a landscape which looked, subject to specifications of climate, exactly and entirely like the San Fernando Valley.

It is not that Los Angeles is altogether hideous, it is even by degrees pleasant, but for an Easterner there is never any salt in the wind; it is like Mexican cooking without chile, or Chinese egg rolls missing their mustard; as one travels through the endless repetitions of that city which is the capital of suburbia with its milky pinks, its washed-out oranges, its tainted lime-yellows of pastel on one pretty little architectural monstrosity after another, the colors not intense enough, the styles never pure, and never sufficiently impure to collide on the eye, one conceives the people who live here—they have come out to express themselves, Los Angeles is the home of self-expression, but the artists are middle-class and middling-minded; no passions will calcify here for years in the gloom to be revealed a decade later as the tessellations of hard and fertile work, no, it is all open, promiscuous, borrowed, half bought, a city without iron, eschewing wood, a kingdom of stucco, the playground for mass men—one has the feeling it was built by television sets giving orders to men. And in this land of the pretty-pretty, the virility is in the barbarisms, the vulgarities, it is in the huge billboards, the screamers of the neon lighting, the shouting farm-utensil colors of the gas stations and monster drugstores, it is in the swing of the sports cars, hot rods, convertibles, Los Angeles is a city to drive in, the boulevards are wide, the traffic is nervous and fast, the radio stations play bouncing, blooping, rippling tunes, one digs the pop in a pop tune, no one of character would make love by it but the sound is good for swinging a car, electronic guitars and Hawaiian harps.

So this is the town the Democrats came to, and with their unerring instinct (after being with them a week, one thinks of this party as a crazy, half-rich family loaded with poor cousins, traveling always in caravans with Cadillacs and Okie Fords, Lincolns and quarter-horse mules, putting up every night in tents to hear the chamber quartet of Great Cousin Eleanor invaded by the Texas-twanging steel-stringing geetarists of Bubber Lyndon, carrying its own mean high school principal, Doc Symington, chided for its manners by good Uncle Adlai, told the route of march by Navigator Jack, cut off every six months from the rich will of Uncle Jim Farley, never listening to the mechanic of the caravan, Bald Sam Rayburn, who assures them they'll all break down unless Cousin Bubber gets the concession on the garage; it's the Snopes family married to Henry James, with the labor unions thrown in like a Yankee dollar, and yet it's true, in tranquillity one recollects them with affection, their instinct is good, crazy-family good) and this instinct now led the caravan to pick the Biltmore Hotel in downtown Los Angeles for their family get-together and reunion.

The Biltmore is one of the ugliest hotels in the world. Patterned after the flat roofs of an Italian Renaissance palace, it is eighty-eight times as large, and one-millionth as valuable to the continuation of man, and it would be intolerable if it were not for the presence of Pershing Square, that square block of park with cactus and palm trees, the three-hundred-and-sixty-five-day-a-year convention of every junkie, pothead, pusher, queen (but you have read that good writing already). For years Pershing Square has been one of the three or four places in America famous to homosexuals, famous not for its posh, the chic is round-heeled here, but because it is one of the avatars of good old masturbatory sex, dirty with the crusted sugars of smut, dirty rooming houses around the corner where the score is made, dirty-book-and-photograph stores down the street, old-fashioned out-of-the-Thirties burlesque houses, cruising bars, jukeboxes, movie houses; Pershing Square is the town plaza for all those lonely, respectable, small-town homosexuals who lead a family life, make children, and have the Philbrick psychology (How I Joined the Communist Party and Led Three Lives). Yes, it is the open-air convention hall for the small-town inverts who live like spies, and it sits in the center of Los Angeles, facing the Biltmore, that hotel which is a mausoleum, that Pentagon of traveling salesmen the party chose to house the headquarters of the Convention.

So here came that family, cursed before it began by the thundering absence of Great-uncle Truman, the delegates dispersed over a run of thirty miles and twenty-seven hotels: the Olympian Motor Hotel, the Ambassador, the Beverly Wilshire, the Santa Ynez Inn (where rumor has it the delegates from Louisiana had some midnight swim), the Mayan, the Commodore, the Mayfair, the Sheraton-West, the Huntington-Sheraton, the Green, the Hayward, the Gates, the Figueroa, the Statler Hilton, the Hollywood Knickerbocker—does one have to be a collector to list such names?—beauties all, with that up-from-the-farm Los Angeles décor, plate glass windows, patio and terrace, foam rubber mattress, pastel paints, all of them pretty as an ad in full-page color, all but the Biltmore where everybody gathered every day— the newsmen, the TV, radio, magazine, and foreign newspaper-men, the delegates, the politicos, the tourists, the campaign managers, the runners, the flunkies, the cousins and aunts, the wives, the grandfathers, the eight-year-old girls, and the twenty-eight-year-old girls in the Kennedy costumes, red and white and blue, the Symingteeners, the Johnson Ladies, the Stevenson La-dies, everybody—and for three days before the convention and four days into it, everybody collected at the Biltmore, in the lobby, in the grill, in the Biltmore Bowl, in the elevators, along the corridors, three hundred deep always outside the Kennedy suite, milling everywhere, every dark-carpeted gray-brown hall of the hotel, but it was in the gallery of the Biltmore where one first felt the mood which pervaded all proceedings until the conven-tion was almost over, that heavy, thick, witless depression which was to dominate every move as the delegates wandered and gawked and paraded and set for a spell, there in the gallery of the Biltmore, that huge depressing alley with its inimitable hotel color, that faded depth of chiaroscuro which unhappily has no depth, that brown which is not a brown, that gray which has no pearl in it, that color which can be described only as hotel-color because the beiges, the tans, the walnuts, the mahoganies, the dull blood rugs, the moaning yellows, the sick greens, the grays, and all those dumb browns merge into that lack of color which is an overlarge hotel at convention time, with all the small-towners wearing their set, starched faces, that look they get at carnival, all fever and suspicion, and proud to be there, eddying slowly back and forth in that high block-long tunnel of a room with its arched ceiling and square recesses filling every rib of the arch with artwork, escutcheons and blazons and other art, pic-tures I think, I cannot even remember, there was such a hill of cigar smoke the eye had to travel on its way to the ceiling, and at one end there was galvanized pipe scaffolding and workmen re-pairing some part of the ceiling, one of them touching up one of the endless squares of painted plaster in the arch, and another worker, passing by, yelled up to the one who was working on the ceiling: "Hey, Michelangelo!"

Later, of course, it began to emerge and there were portraits one could keep, Symington, dogged at a press conference, declaring with no conviction that he knew he had a good chance to win, the disappointment eating at his good looks so that he came off hard-faced, mean, and yet slack—a desperate dullness came off the best of his intentions. There was Johnson, who had compromised too many contradictions and now the contradictions were in his face: when he smiled the corners of his mouth squeezed gloom; when he was pious, his eyes twinkled irony; when he spoke in a righteous tone, he looked corrupt; when he jested, the ham in his jowls looked to quiver. He was not convincing. He was a Southern politician, a Texas Democrat, a liberal Eisenhower; he would do no harm, he would do no good, he would react to the machine, good fellow, nice friend—the Russians would understand him better than his own.

Stevenson had the patina. He came into the room and the room was different, not stronger perhaps (which is why ultimately he did not win), but warmer. One knew why some adored him; he did not look like other people, not with press lights on his flesh; he looked like a lover, the simple truth, he had the sweet happiness of an adolescent who has just been given his first major kiss. And so he glowed, and one was reminded of Chaplin, not because they were the least alike in features, but because Charlie Chaplin was luminous when one met him and Stevenson had something of that light.

There was Eleanor Roosevelt, fine, precise, hand-worked like ivory. Her voice was almost attractive as she explained in the firm, sad tones of the first lady in this small town why she could not admit Mr. Kennedy, who was no doubt a gentleman, into her political house. One had the impression of a lady who was finally becoming a woman, which is to say that she was just a little bitchy about it all; nice bitchy, charming, it had a touch of art to it, but it made one wonder if she were not now satisfying the last passion of them all, which was to become physically attractive, for she was better-looking than she had ever been as she spurned the possibilities of a young suitor.

Jim Farley. Huge. Cold as a bishop. The hell he would consign you to was cold as ice.

Bobby Kennedy, the archetype Bobby Kennedy, looked like a West Point cadet, or, better, one of those reconstructed Irishmen from Kirkland House one always used to have to face in the line in Harvard house football games. "Hello," you would say to the ones who looked like him as you lined up for the scrimmage after the kickoff, and his type would nod and look away, one rock glint of recognition your due for living across the hall from one another all through freshman year, and then bang, as the ball was passed back, you'd get a bony king-hell knee in the crotch. He was the kind of man never to put on the gloves with if you wanted to do some social boxing, because after two minutes it would be a war, and ego-bastards last long in a war.

Carmine DeSapio and Kenneth Galbraith on the same part of the convention floor. DeSapio is bigger than one expects, keen and florid, great big smoked glasses, a suntan like Man-Tan—he is the kind of heavyweight Italian who could get by with a name like Romeo—and Galbraith is tall-tall, as actors say, six foot six it could be, terribly thin, enormously attentive, exquisitely polite, birdlike, he is sensitive to the stirring of reeds in a wind over the next hill. "Our gray eminence," whispered the intelligent observer next to me.

Bob Wagner, the mayor of New York, a little man, plump, groomed, blank. He had the blank, pomaded, slightly worried look of the first barber in a good barbershop, the kind who would go to the track on his day off and wear a green transparent stone in a gold ring.

And then there was Kennedy, the edge of the mystery. But a sketch will no longer suffice.

> it can be said with a fair amount of certainty that the essence of his political attractiveness is his extraordinary political intelligence. He has a mind quite unlike that of any other Democrat of this century. It is not literary, metaphysical and moral, as Adlai Stevenson's is. Kennedy is articulate and often witty, but he does not seek verbal polish. No one can doubt the seriousness of his

concern with the most serious political matters, but one
feels that whereas Mr. Stevenson's political views derive
from a view of life that holds politics to be a mere fraction of existence, Senator Kennedy's primary interest is
in politics. The easy way in which he disposes of the
question of Church and State—as if he felt that any reasonable man could quite easily resolve any possible conflict of loyalties—suggests that the organization of
society is the one thing that really engages his interest.
          —RICHARD ROVERE: *The New Yorker,* JULY 23, 1960

The afternoon he arrived at the convention from the airport,
there was of course a large crowd on the street outside the Biltmore, and the best way to get a view was to get up on an outdoor
balcony of the Biltmore, two flights above the street, and look
down on the event. One waited thirty minutes, and then a honk-
ing of horns as wild as the getaway after an Italian wedding
sounded around the corner, and the Kennedy cortege came
into sight, circled Pershing Square, the men in the open and
leading convertibles sitting backward to look at their leader,
and finally came to a halt in a space cleared for them by the
police in the crowd. The television cameras were out, and a
Kennedy band was playing some circus music. One saw him immediately. He had the deep orange-brown suntan of a ski instructor, and when he smiled at the crowd his teeth were
amazingly white and clearly visible at a distance of fifty yards.
For one moment he saluted Pershing Square, and Pershing
Square saluted him back, the prince and the beggars of glamour staring at one another across a city street, one of those very
special moments in the underground history of the world, and
then with a quick move he was out of his car and by choice
headed into the crowd instead of the lane cleared for him into
the hotel by the police, so that he made his way inside surrounded by a mob, and one expected at any moment to see him
lifted to its shoulders like a matador being carried back to the
city after a triumph in the plaza. All the while the band kept
playing the campaign tunes, sashaying circus music, and one

had a moment of clarity, intense as déjà vu, for the scene which had taken place had been glimpsed before in a dozen musical comedies; it was the scene where the hero, the matinee idol, the movie star comes to the palace to claim the princess, or what is the same, and more to our soil, the football hero, the campus king, arrives at the dean's home surrounded by a court of open-singing students to plead with the dean for his daughter's kiss and permission to put on the big musical that night. And suddenly I saw the convention, it came into focus for me, and I understood the mood of depression which had lain over the convention, because finally it was simple: the Democrats were going to nominate a man who, no matter how serious his political dedication might be, was indisputably and willy-nilly going to be seen as a great box-office actor, and the consequences of that were staggering and not at all easy to calculate.

Since the First World War, Americans have been leading a double life, and our history has moved on two rivers, one visible, the other underground; there has been the history of politics, which is concrete, factual, practical, and unbelievably dull if not for the consequences of the actions of some of these men; and there is a subterranean river of untapped, ferocious, lonely and romantic desires, that concentration of ecstasy and violence which is the dream life of the nation.

The twentieth century may yet be seen as that era when civilized man and underprivileged man were melted together into mass man, the iron and steel of the nineteenth century giving way to electronic circuits which communicated their messages into men, the unmistakable tendency of the new century seeming to be the creation of men as interchangeable as commodities, their extremes of personality singed out of existence by the psychic fields of force the communicators would impose. This loss of personality was a catastrophe to the future of the imagination, but billions of people might first benefit from it by having enough to eat—one did not know—and there remained citadels of resistance in Europe where the culture was deep and roots were visible in the architecture of the past.

Nowhere, as in America, however, was this fall from individual man to mass man felt so acutely, for America was at once the first and most prolific creator of mass communications and the most rootless of countries, since almost no American could lay claim to the line of a family which had not once at least severed its roots by migrating here. But, if rootless, it was then the most vulnerable of countries to its own homogenization. Yet America was also the country in which the dynamic myth of the Renaissance—that every man was potentially extraordinary— knew its most passionate persistence. Simply, America was the land where people still believed in heroes: George Washington; Billy the Kid; Lincoln, Jefferson; Mark Twain, Jack London, Hemingway; Joe Louis, Dempsey, Gentleman Jim; America believed in athletes, rumrunners, aviators; even lovers, by the time Valentino died. It was a country which had grown by the leap of one hero past another—is there a county in all of our ground which does not have its legendary figure? And when the West was filled, the expansion turned inward, became part of an agitated, overexcited, superheated dream life. The film studios threw up their searchlights as the frontier was finally sealed, and the romantic possibilities of the old conquest of land turned into a vertical myth, trapped within the skull, of a new kind of heroic life, each choosing his own archetype of a neo–Renaissance man, be it Barrymore, Cagney, Flynn, Bogart, Brando, or Sinatra, but it was almost as if there were no peace unless one could fight well, kill well (if always with honor), love well and love many, be cool, be daring, be dashing, be wild, be wily, be resourceful, be a brave gun. And this myth, that each of us was born to be free, to wander, to have adventure and to grow on the waves of the violent, the perfumed, and the unexpected, had a force which could not be tamed no matter how the nation's regulators— politicians, medicos, policemen, professors, priests, rabbis, ministers, *idéologues,* psychoanalysts, builders, executives and endless communicators—would brick in the modern life with hygiene upon sanity, and middlebrow homily over platitude; the myth would not die. Indeed a quarter of the nation's business must have depended upon its existence. But it stayed alive for more than that—it was as if the message in the labyrinth of the genes would insist that violence was locked with creativity, and adventure was the secret of love.

Once, in the Second World War and in the year or two which followed, the underground river returned to earth, and the life of the nation was intense, of the present, electric; as a lady said, "That was the time when we gave parties which changed people's lives." The Forties was a decade when the speed with which one's own events occurred seemed as rapid as the history of the battlefields, and for the mass of people in America a forced march into a new jungle of emotion was the result. The surprises, the failures, and the dangers of that life must have terrified some nerve of awareness in the power and the mass, for, as if stricken by the orgiastic vistas the myth had carried up from underground, the retreat to a more conservative existence was disorderly, the fear of Communism spread like an irrational hail of boils. To anyone who could see, the excessive hysteria of the Red wave was no preparation to face an enemy, but rather a terror of the national self: free-loving, lust-looting, atheistic, implacable—absurdity beyond absurdity to label Communism so, for the moral products of Stalinism had been Victorian sex and a ponderous machine of material theology.

Forced underground again, deep beneath all *Reader's Digest* hospital dressings of Mental Health in Your Community, the myth continued to flow, fed by television and the film. The fissure in the national psyche widened to the danger point. The last large appearance of the myth was the vote which tricked the polls and gave Harry Truman his victory in '48. That was the last. Came the Korean War, the shadow of the H-bomb, and we were ready for the General. Uncle Harry gave way to Father, and security, regularity, order, and the life of no imagination were the command of the day. If one had any doubt of this, there was Joe McCarthy with his built-in treason detector, furnished by God, and the damage was done. In the totalitarian wind of those days, anyone who worked in government formed the habit of being not too original, and many a mind atrophied from disuse and private shame. At the summit there was benevolence without leadership, regularity without vision, security without safety, rhetoric without life. The ship drifted on, that enormous warship of the United States, led by a secretary of state whose cells were seceding to cancer, and as the world became more fantastic—Africa turning itself upside down, while some new kind of machine man was being made in China—two events occurred which stunned the confidence of America into a new night: the Russians put up their Sputnik, and Civil Rights—that reluctant gift to the American Negro, granted for its effect on foreign affairs—spewed into real life at Little Rock. The national Ego was in shock: the Russians were now in some ways our technological superiors, and we had an internal problem of subject populations equal conceivably in its difficulty to the Soviet and its satellites. The fatherly calm of the General began to seem like the uxorious mellifluences of the undertaker.

Underneath it all was a larger problem. The life of politics and the life of myth had diverged too far, and the energies of the people one knew everywhere had slowed down. Twenty years ago a post-Depression generation had gone to war and formed a lively, grousing, by times inefficient, carousing, pleasure-seeking, not altogether inadequate army. It did part of what it was supposed to do, and many, out of combat, picked up a kind of private life on the fly, and had their good time despite the yaws of the military system. But today in America the generation which respected the code of the myth was Beat, a horde of half-begotten Christs with scraggly beards, heroes none, saints all, weak before the strong, empty conformisms of the authority. The sanction for finding one's growth was no longer one's flag, one's career, one's sex, one's adventure, not even one's booze. Among the best in the newest of the generations, the myth had found its voice in marijuana, and the joke of the underground was that when the Russians came over they could never dare to occupy us for long because America was too Hip. Gallows humor. The poorer truth might be that America was too Beat, the instinct of the nation so separated from its public mind that apathy, schizophrenia, and private beatitudes might be the pride of the welcoming committee any underground could offer.

Yes, the life of politics and the life of the myth had diverged too far. There was nothing to return them to one another, no common danger, no cause, no desire, and, most essentially, no hero. It was a hero America needed, a hero central to his time, a man whose personality might suggest contradiction and mysteries which could reach into the alienated circuits of the underground, because only a hero can capture the secret imagination of a people, and so be good for the vitality of his nation; a hero embodies the fantasy and so allows each private mind the liberty to consider its fantasy and find a way to grow. Each mind can become more conscious of its desire and waste less strength in hiding from itself. Roosevelt was such a hero, and Churchill, Lenin and de Gaulle; even Hitler, to take the most odious example of this thesis, was a hero, the hero-as-monster, embodying what had become the monstrous fantasy of a people, but the horror upon which the radical mind and liberal temperament foundered was that he gave outlet to the energies of the Germans and so presented the twentieth century with an index of how horrible had become the secret heart of its desire. Roosevelt is of course a happier example of the hero; from his paralytic leg to the royal elegance of his geniality he seemed to contain the country within himself; everyone from the meanest starving cripple to an ambitious young man could expand to the optimism of an improving future because the man offered an unspoken promise of a future which would be rich. The sexual and the sex-starved, the poor, the hardworking and the imaginative well-to-do could see themselves in the president, could believe him to be like themselves. So a large part of the country was able to discover its energies because not as much was wasted in feeling that the country was a poisonous nutrient which stifled the day.

Too simple? No doubt. One tries to construct a simple model. The thesis is after all not so mysterious; it would merely nudge the notion that a hero embodies his time and is not so very much better than his time, but he is larger than life and so is capable of giving direction to the time, able to encourage a nation to discover the deepest colors of its character. At bottom the concept of hero is antagonistic to impersonal social progress, to the belief that social ills can be solved by social legislating, for it sees a country as all but trapped in its character until it has a hero who reveals the character of the country to itself. The implication is that without such a hero the nation turns sluggish. Truman for example was not such a hero, he was not sufficiently larger than life, he inspired familiarity without excitement, he was a character but his proportions came from soap opera: Uncle Harry, full of salty common sense and small-minded certainty, a storekeeping uncle.

Whereas Eisenhower has been the antihero, the regulator. Nations do not necessarily and inevitably seek for heroes. In periods of dull anxiety, one is more likely to look for security than a dramatic confrontation, and Eisenhower could stand as a hero only for that large number of Americans who were most proud of their lack of imagination. In American life, the unspoken war of the century has taken place between the city and the small town; the city which is dynamic, orgiastic, unsettling, explosive, and accelerating to the psyche; the small town which is rooted, narrow, cautious, and planted in the life-logic of the family. The need of the city is to accelerate growth; the pride of the small town is to retard it. But since America has been passing through a period of enormous expansion since the war, the double-four years of Dwight Eisenhower could not retard the expansion, it could only denude it of color, character, and the development of novelty. The small-town mind is rooted—it is rooted in the small town—and when it attempts to direct history the results are disastrously colorless because the instrument of world power which is used by the small-town mind is the committee. Committees do not create, they merely proliferate, and the incredible dullness wreaked upon the American landscape in Eisenhower's eight years has been the triumph of the corporation. A tasteless, sexless, odorless sanctity in architecture, manners, modes, styles has been the result. Eisenhower embodied half the needs of the nation, the needs of the timid, the petrified, the sanctimonious, and the sluggish. What was even worse, he did not divide the nation as a hero might (with a dramatic dialogue as the result); he merely excluded one part of the nation from the other. The result was an alienation of the best minds and bravest impulses from the faltering history which was made. America's need in those years was to take an existential turn, to walk into the night-mare, to face into that terrible logic of history which demanded that the country and its people must become more extraordi-nary and more adventurous, or else perish, since the only alter-native was to offer a false security in the power and the panacea of organized religion, family, and the FBI, a totalitarianization of the psyche by the stultifying techniques of the mass media which would seep into everyone's most private associations and so leave the country powerless against the Russians even if the denoue-ment were to take fifty years, for in a competition between totali-tarianisms the first maxim of the prizefight manager would doubtless apply: "Hungry fighters win fights."

Some part of these thoughts must have been in one's mind at the moment there was the first glimpse of Kennedy entering the Biltmore Hotel; and in the days which followed, the first mystery—the profound air of depression which hung over the convention—gave way to a second mystery which can be an-swered only by history. The depression of the delegates was un-derstandable: no one had too much doubt that Kennedy would be nominated, but if elected he would be not only the youngest president ever to be chosen by voters, he would be the most con-ventionally attractive young man ever to sit in the White House, and his wife—some would claim it—might be the most beautiful First Lady in our history. Of necessity the myth would emerge once more, because America's politics would now be also Amer-ica's favorite movie, America's first soap opera, America's best-seller. One thinks of the talents of writers like Taylor Caldwell or Frank Yerby, or is it rather *The Fountainhead* which would contain such a fleshing of the romantic prescription? Or is it indeed one's own work which is called into question? "Well, there's your first hipster," says a writer one knows at the convention, "Sergius O'Shaughnessy born rich," and the temptation is to nod, for it could be true, a war hero, and the heroism is bona fide, even exceptional, a man who has lived with death, who, crippled in the back, took on an operation which would kill him or restore him to power, who chose to marry a lady whose face might be too

imaginative for the taste of a democracy which likes its first ladies
to be executives of home management, a man who courts political suicide by choosing to go all out for a nomination four, eight,
or twelve years before his political elders think he is ready, a man
who announces a week prior to the convention that the young
are better fitted to direct history than the old. Yes, it captures the
attention. This is no routine candidate calling every shot by safety's routine book ("Yes," Nixon said, naturally but terribly tired
an hour after his nomination, the TV cameras and lights and
microphones bringing out a sweat of fatigue on his face, the
words coming very slowly from the tired brain, somber, modest,
sober, slow, slow enough so that one could touch emphatically
the cautions behind each word, "Yes, I want to say," said Nixon,
"that whatever abilities I have, I got from my mother." A tired
pause . . . dull moment of warning, " . . . and my father." The
connection now made, the rest comes easy, " . . . and my school
and my church." Such men are capable of anything).

One had the opportunity to study Kennedy a bit in the days
that followed. His style in the press conferences was interesting.
Not terribly popular with the reporters (too much a contemporary, and yet too difficult to understand, he received nothing like
the rounds of applause given to Eleanor Roosevelt, Stevenson,
Humphrey, or even Johnson), he carried himself nonetheless
with a cool grace which seemed indifferent to applause, his manner somehow similar to the poise of a fine boxer, quick with his
hands, neat in his timing, and two feet away from his corner
when the bell ended the round. There was a good lithe wit to his
responses, a dry Harvard wit, a keen sense of proportion in disposing of difficult questions—invariably he gave enough of an
answer to be formally satisfactory without ever opening himself
to a new question which might go further than the first. Asked by
a reporter, "Are you for Adlai as vice president?" the grin came
forth and the voice turned very dry, "No, I cannot say we have
considered *Adlai* as a vice president." Yet there was an elusive
detachment to everything he did. One did not have the feeling
of a man present in the room with all his weight and all his mind.
Johnson gave you all of himself, he was a political animal, he

breathed like an animal, sweated like one, you knew his mind was entirely absorbed with the compendium of political fact and maneuver; Kennedy seemed at times like a young professor whose manner was adequate for the classroom, but whose mind was off in some intricacy of the Ph.D. thesis he was writing. Perhaps one can give a sense of the discrepancy by saying that he was like an actor who had been cast as the candidate, a good actor, but not a great one—you were aware all the time that the role was one thing and the man another—they did not coincide, the actor seemed a touch too aloof (as, let us say, Gregory Peck is usually too aloof) to become the part. Yet one had little sense of whether to value this elusiveness, or to beware of it. One could be witnessing the fortitude of a superior sensitivity or the detachment of a man who was not quite real to himself. And his voice gave no clue. When Johnson spoke, one could separate what was fraudulent from what was felt, he would have been satisfying as an actor the way Broderick Crawford or Paul Douglas is satisfying; one saw into his emotions, or at least had the illusion that one did. Kennedy's voice, however, was only a fair voice, too reedy, near to strident, it had the metallic snap of a cricket in it somewhere, it was more impersonal than the man, and so became the least impressive quality in a face, a body, a selection of language, and a style of movement which made up a better-than-decent presentation, better than one had expected.

With all of that, it would not do to pass over the quality in Kennedy which is most difficult to describe. And in fact some touches should be added to this hint of a portrait, for later (after the convention), one had a short session alone with him, and the next day, another. As one had suspected in advance the interviews were not altogether satisfactory, they hardly could have been. A man running for president is altogether different from a man elected president: the hazards of the campaign make it impossible for a candidate to be as interesting as he might like to be (assuming he has such a desire). One kept advancing the argument that this campaign would be a contest of personalities, and Kennedy kept returning the discussion to politics. After a while one recognized this was an inevitable caution for him. So

there would be not too much point to reconstructing the dialogue since Kennedy is hardly inarticulate about his political attitudes and there will be a library vault of text devoted to it in the
newspapers. What struck me most about the interview was a passing remark whose importance was invisible on the scale of politics, but was altogether meaningful to my particular competence.
As we sat down for the first time, Kennedy smiled nicely and said
that he had read my books. One muttered one's pleasure. "Yes,"
he said, "I've read . . ." and then there was a short pause which
did not last long enough to be embarrassing in which it was yet
obvious no title came instantly to his mind, an omission one was
not ready to mind altogether since a man in such a position must
be obliged to carry a hundred thousand facts and names in his
head, but the hesitation lasted no longer than three seconds or
four, and then he said, "I've read *The Deer Park* and . . . the others," which startled me for it was the first time in a hundred similar situations, talking to someone whose knowledge of my work
was casual, that the sentence did not come out, "I've read *The
Naked and the Dead* . . . and the others." If one is to take the worst
and assume that Kennedy was briefed for this interview (which is
most doubtful), it still speaks well for the striking instincts of his
advisers.

What was retained later is an impression of Kennedy's manners, which were excellent, even artful, better than the formal
good manners of Choate and Harvard, almost as if what was creative in the man had been given to the manners. In a room with
one or two people, his voice improved, became low-pitched,
even pleasant—it seemed obvious that in all these years he had
never become a natural public speaker and so his voice was con-
stricted in public, the symptom of all orators who are ambitious,
throttled, and determined.

His personal quality had a subtle, not quite describable intensity, a suggestion of dry pent heat perhaps, his eyes large, the
pupils gray, the whites prominent, almost shocking, his most
forceful feature: he had the eyes of a mountaineer. His appearance changed with his mood, strikingly so, and this made him
always more interesting than what he was saying. He would seem

at one moment older than his age, forty-eight or fifty, a tall, slim, sunburned professor with a pleasant weathered face, not even particularly handsome; five minutes later, talking to a press conference on his lawn, three microphones before him, a television camera turning, his appearance would have gone through a metamorphosis, he would look again like a movie star, his coloring vivid, his manner rich, his gestures strong and quick, alive with that concentration of vitality a successful actor always seems to radiate. Kennedy had a dozen faces. Although they were not at all similar as people, the quality was reminiscent of someone like Brando whose expression rarely changes, but whose appearance seems to shift from one person into another as the minutes go by, and one bothers with this comparison because, like Brando, Kennedy's most characteristic quality is the remote and private air of a man who has traversed some lonely terrain of experience, of loss and gain, of nearness to death, which leaves him isolated from the mass of others.

> The next day while they waited in vain for rescuers, the wrecked half of the boat turned over in the water and they saw that it would soon sink. The group decided to swim to a small island three miles away. There were other islands bigger and nearer, but the Navy officers knew that they were occupied by the Japanese. On one island, only one mile to the south, they could see a Japanese camp. McMahon, the engineer whose legs were disabled by burns, was unable to swim. Despite his own painfully crippled back, Kennedy swam the three miles with a breast stroke, towing behind him by a life-belt strap that he held between his teeth the helpless McMahon . . . it took Kennedy and the suffering engineer five hours to reach the island.

The quotation is from a book which has for its dedicated unilateral title *The Remarkable Kennedys,* but the prose is by one of the best of the war reporters, the former *Yank* editor, Joe McCarthy, and so presumably may be trusted in such details as this.

Physical bravery does not of course guarantee a man's abilities in the White House—all too often men with physical courage are disappointing in their moral imagination—but the heroism here is remarkable for its tenacity. The above is merely one episode in a continuing saga which went on for five days in and out of the water, and left Kennedy at one point "miraculously saved from drowning (in a storm) by a group of Solomon Island natives who suddenly came up beside him in a large dugout canoe." Afterward, his back still injured (that precise back injury which was to put him on crutches eleven years later, and have him search for "spinal-fusion surgery" despite a warning that his chances of living through the operation were "extremely limited"), he asked to go back on duty and became so bold in the attacks he made with his PT boat "that the crew didn't like to go out with him because he took so many chances."

It is the wisdom of a man who senses death within him and gambles that he can cure it by risking his life. It is the therapy of the instinct, and who is so wise as to call it irrational? Before he went into the Navy, Kennedy had been ailing. Washed out of freshman year at Princeton by a prolonged trough of yellow jaundice, sick for a year at Harvard, weak already in the back from an injury at football, his trials suggest the self-hatred of a man whose resentment and ambition are too large for his body. Not everyone can discharge their furies on an analyst's couch, for some angers can be relaxed only by winning power, some rages are sufficiently monumental to demand that one try to become a hero or else fall back into that death which is already within the cells. But if one succeeds, the energy aroused can be exceptional. Talking to a man who had been with Kennedy in Hyannis Port the week before the convention, I heard that he was in a state of deep fatigue.

"Well, he didn't look tired at the convention," one commented.

"Oh, he had three days of rest. Three days of rest for him is like six months to us."

One thinks of that three-mile swim with the belt in his mouth and McMahon holding it behind him. There are pestilences which sit in the mouth and rot the teeth—in those five hours how much of the psyche must have been remade, for to give vent to the bite in one's jaws and yet use that rage to save a life: it is not so very many men who have the apocalyptic sense that heroism is the First Doctor.

If one had a profound criticism of Kennedy it was that his public mind was too conventional, but that seemed to matter less than the fact of such a man in office because the law of political life had become so dreary that only a conventional mind could win an election. Indeed there could be no politics which gave warmth to one's body until the country had recovered its imagination, its pioneer lust for the unexpected and incalculable. It was the changes that might come afterward on which one could put one's hope. With such a man in office the myth of the nation would again be engaged, and the fact that he was Catholic would shiver a first existential vibration of consciousness into the mind of the white Protestant. For the first time in our history, the Protestant would have the pain and creative luxury of feeling himself in some tiny degree part of a minority, and that was an experience which might be incommensurable in its value to the best of them.

As yet we have said hardly a word about Stevenson. And his actions must remain a puzzle unless one dares a speculation about his motive, or was it his need?

So far as the people at the convention had affection for anyone, it was Stevenson, so far as they were able to generate any spontaneous enthusiasm, their cheers were again for Stevenson. Yet it was obvious he never had much chance because so soon as a chance would present itself he seemed quick to dissipate the opportunity. The day before the nominations, he entered the Sports Arena to take his seat as a delegate—the demonstration was spontaneous, noisy, and prolonged; it was quieted only by Governor Collins's invitation for Stevenson to speak to the delegates. In obedience perhaps to the scruple that a candidate must not appear before the convention until nominations are done,

Stevenson said no more than: "I am grateful for this tumultuous and moving welcome. After getting in and out of the Biltmore Hotel and this hall, I have decided I know whom you are going to nominate. It will be the last survivor." This dry reminder of the ruthlessness of politics broke the roar of excitement for his presence. The applause as he left the platform was like the dying fall-and-moan of a baseball crowd when a home run curves foul. The next day, a New York columnist talking about it said bitterly, "If he'd only gone through the motions, if he had just said that now he wanted to run, that he would work hard, and he hoped the delegates would vote for him. Instead he made that lame joke." One wonders. It seems almost as if he did not wish to win unless victory came despite himself, and then was overwhelming. There are men who are not heroes because they are too good for their time, and it is natural that defeats leave them bitter, tired, and doubtful of their right to make new history. If Stevenson had campaigned for a year before the convention, it is possible that he could have stopped Kennedy. At the least, the convention would have been enormously more exciting, and the nominations might have gone through half a dozen ballots before a winner was hammered into shape. But then Stevenson might also have shortened his life. One had the impression of a tired man who (for a politician) was sickened unduly by compromise. A year of maneuvering, broken promises, and detestable partners might have gutted him for the election campaign. If elected, it might have ruined him as a president. There is the possibility that he sensed his situation exactly this way, and knew that if he were to run for president, win and make a good one, he would first have to be restored, as one can indeed be restored, by an exceptional demonstration of love—love, in this case, meaning that the party had a profound desire to keep him as their leader. The emotional truth of a last-minute victory for Stevenson over the Kennedy machine might have given him new energy; it would certainly have given him new faith in a country and a party whose good motives he was possibly beginning to doubt. Perhaps the fault he saw with his candidacy was that he attracted only the nicest people to himself and there were not enough of them.

(One of the private amusements of the convention was to divine some of the qualities of the candidates by the style of the young women who put on hats and clothing and politicked in the colors of one presidential gent or another. Of course, half of them must have been hired models, but someone did the hiring and so it was fair to look for a common denominator. The Johnson girls tended to be plump, pie-faced, dumb sexy Southern; the Symingteeners seemed a touch mulish, stubborn, good-looking pluggers; the Kennedy ladies were the handsomest; healthy, attractive, tough, a little spoiled—they looked like the kind of girls who had gotten all the dances in high school and/or worked for a year as an airline hostess before marrying well. But the Stevenson girls looked to be doing it for no money; they were good sorts, slightly horsy-faced, one had the impression they had played field hockey in college.) It was indeed the pure, the saintly, the clean-living, the pacifistic, the vegetarian who seemed most for Stevenson, and the less humorous in the Kennedy camp were heard to remark bitterly that Stevenson had nothing going for him but a bunch of Goddamn Beatniks. This might even have had its sour truth. The demonstrations outside the Sports Arena for Stevenson seemed to have more than a fair proportion of tall, emaciated young men with thin, wry beards and three-string guitars accompanied (again in undue proportion) by a contingent of ascetic, face-washed young Beat ladies in sweaters and dungarees. Not to mention all the Holden Caulfields one could see from here to the horizon. But of course it is unfair to limit it so, for the Democratic gentry were also committed half en masse for Stevenson, as well as a considerable number of movie stars, Shelley Winters for one: after the convention she remarked sweetly, "Tell me something nice about Kennedy so I can get excited about him."

What was properly astonishing was the way this horde of political half-breeds and amateurs came within distance of turning the convention from its preconceived purpose, and managed at least to bring the only hour of thoroughgoing excitement the convention could offer.

But then nominating day was the best day of the week and

enough happened to suggest that a convention out of control would be a spectacle as extraordinary in the American scale of spectator values as a close seventh game in the World Series or a tied fourth quarter in a professional football championship. A political convention is after all not a meeting of a corporation's board of directors; it is a fiesta, a carnival, a pig-rooting, horse-snorting, band-playing, voice-screaming medieval get-together of greed, practical lust, compromised idealism, career advancement, meeting, feud, vendetta, conciliation, of rabble-rousers, fistfights (as it used to be), embraces, drunks (again as it used to be), and collective rivers of animal sweat. It is a reminder that no matter how the country might pretend it has grown up and become tidy in its manners, bodiless in its legislative language, hygienic in its separation of high politics from private life, that the roots still come grubby from the soil, and that politics in America is still different from politics anywhere else because the politics has arisen out of the immediate needs, ambitions, and cupidities of the people, that our politics still smell of the bedroom and the kitchen rather than having descended to us from the chill punctilio of aristocratic negotiation.

So. The Sports Arena was new, too pretty of course, tasteless in its design—it was somehow pleasing that the acoustics were so bad for one did not wish the architects well; there had been so little imagination in their design, and this arena would have none of the harsh grandeur of Madison Square Garden when it was aged by spectators' phlegm and feet over the next twenty years. Still it had some atmosphere; seen from the streets, with the spectators moving to the ticket gates, the bands playing, the green hot-shot special editions of the Los Angeles newspapers being hawked by the newsboys, there was a touch of the air of promise that precedes a bullfight, not something so good as the approach to the Plaza Mexico, but good, let us say, like the entrance into El Toreo of Mexico City, another architectural monstrosity, also with seats painted, as I remember, in rose pink, and dark, milky sky blue.

Inside, it was also different this nominating day. On Monday and Tuesday the air had been desultory, no one listened to the

speakers, and everybody milled from one easy chatting conversation to another—it had been like a tepid kaffeeklatsch for fifteen
thousand people. But today there was a whip of anticipation in
the air, the seats on the floor were filled, the press section was
working, and in the gallery people were sitting in the aisles.

Sam Rayburn had just finished nominating Johnson as one
came in, and the rebel yells went up, delegates started filing out
of their seats and climbing over seats, and a pullulating dance of
bodies and bands began to snake through the aisles, the posters
jogging and whirling in time to the music. The dun color of the
floor (faces, suits, seats, and floorboards), so monotonous the
first two days, now lit up with life as if an iridescent caterpillar
had emerged from a fold of wet leaves. It was more vivid than
one had expected, it was right, it felt finally like a convention,
and from up close when one got down to the floor (where your
presence was illegal and so consummated by sneaking in one
time as demonstrators were going out, and again by slipping a
five-dollar bill to a guard) the nearness to the demonstrators
took on high color, that electric vividness one feels on the sidelines of a football game when it is necessary to duck back as the
ball carrier goes by, his face tortured in the concentration of the
moment, the thwomp of his tackle as acute as if one had been hit
oneself.

That was the way the demonstrators looked on the floor.
Nearly all had the rapt, private look of a passion or a tension
which would finally be worked off by one's limbs, three hundred
football players, everything from seedy delegates with jowl-
sweating shivers to livid models, paid for their work that day, but
stomping out their beat on the floor with the hypnotic adulatory
grimaces of ladies who had lived for Lyndon these last ten years.

Then from the funereal rostrum, whose color was not so rich
as mahogany nor so dead as a cigar, came the last of the requests
for the delegates to take their seats. The seconding speeches
began, one minute each; they ran for three and four, the minor-
league speakers running on the longest as if the electric antennae of television was the lure of the Sirens, leading them out.
Bored cheers applauded their concluding Götterdämmerungen

and the nominations were open again. A favorite son, a modest demonstration, five seconding speeches, tedium.

Next was Kennedy's occasion. Governor Freeman of Minnesota made the speech. On the second or third sentence his television prompter jammed, an accident. Few could be aware of it at the moment; the speech seemed merely flat and surprisingly void of bravura. He was obviously no giant of extempore. Then the demonstration. Well-run, bigger than Johnson's, jazzier, the caliber of the costumes and decoration better chosen: the placards were broad enough, "Let's Back Jack," the floats were garish, particularly a papier-mâché or plastic balloon of Kennedy's head, six feet in diameter, which had nonetheless the slightly shrunken, over-red, rubbery look of a toy for practical jokers in one of those sleazy off–Times Square magic-and-gimmick stores; the band was suitably corny; and yet one had the impression this demonstration had been designed by some hands-to-hip interior decorator who said, "Oh, joy, let's have fun, let's make this *true* beer hall."

Besides, the personnel had something of the Kennedy élan, those paper hats designed to look like straw boaters with Kennedy's face on the crown, and small photographs of him on the ribbon, those hats which had come to symbolize the crack speed of the Kennedy team, that Madison Avenue cachet which one finds in the bars like P. J. Clarke's, the elegance always giving its subtle echo of the Twenties so that the raccoon coats seem more numerous than their real count, and the colored waistcoats are measured by the charm they would have drawn from Scott Fitzgerald's eye. But there, it occurred to one for the first time that Kennedy's middle name was just that, Fitzgerald, and the tone of his crack lieutenants, the unstated style, was true to Scott. The legend of Fitzgerald had an army at last, formed around the self-image in the mind of every superior Madison Avenue opportunist that he was hard, he was young, he was In, his conversation was lean as wit, and if the work was not always scrupulous, well, the style could aspire. If there came a good day . . . he could meet the occasion.

———————

The Kennedy snake dance ran its thirty lively minutes, cheered its seconding speeches, and sat back. They were so sure of winning, there had been so many victories before this one, and this one had been scouted and managed so well, that hysteria could hardly be the mood. Besides, everyone was waiting for the Stevenson barrage which should be at least diverting. But now came a long tedium. Favorite sons were nominated, fat mayors shook their hips, seconders told the word to constituents back in Ponderwaygot County, treacly demonstrations tried to hold the floor, and the afternoon went by; Symington's hour came and went, a good demonstration, good as Johnson's (for good cause—they had pooled their demonstrators). More favorite sons, Governor Docking of Kansas declared "a genius" by one of his lady speakers in a tense go-back-to-religion voice. The hours went by, two, three, four hours, it seemed forever before they would get to Stevenson. It was evening when Senator Eugene McCarthy of Minnesota got up to nominate him.

The gallery was ready, the floor was responsive, the demonstrators were milling like bulls in their pen waiting for the *toril* to fly open—it would have been hard not to wake the crowd up, not to make a good speech. McCarthy made a great one. Great it was by the measure of convention oratory, and he held the crowd like a matador, timing their *oles*!, building them up, easing them back, correcting any sag in attention, gathering their emotion, discharging it, creating new emotion on the wave of the last, driving his passes tighter and tighter as he readied for the kill. "Do not reject this man who made us all proud to be called Democrats, do not leave the prophet without honor in his own party." One had not heard a speech like this since 1948 when Vito Marcantonio's voice, his harsh, shrill, bitter, street urchin's voice screeched through the loudspeakers at Yankee Stadium and lashed seventy thousand people into an uproar.

"There was only one man who said let's talk sense to the American people," McCarthy went on, his muleta furled for the *naturales*. "There was only one man who said let's talk sense to the American people," he repeated. "He said the promise of America is the promise of greatness. This was his call to greatness. . . .

Do not forget this man. . . . Ladies and gentlemen, I present to you not the favorite son of one state, but the favorite son of the fifty states, the favorite son of every country which has not seen him but is secretly thrilled by his name." Bedlam. The kill. "Ladies and gentlemen, I present to you Adlai Stevenson of Illinois." Ears and tail. Hooves and bull. A roar went up like the roar one heard the day Bobby Thompson hit his home run at the Polo Grounds and the Giants won the pennant from the Dodgers in the third playoff game of the 1951 season. The demonstration cascaded onto the floor, the gallery came to its feet, the Sports Arena sounded like the inside of a marching drum. A tidal pulse of hysteria, exaltation, defiance, exhilaration, anger, and roaring desire flooded over the floor. The cry which had gone up on McCarthy's last sentence had not paused for breath in five minutes, and troop after troop of demonstrators jammed the floor (the Stevenson people to be scolded the next day for having collected floor passes and sent them out to bring in new demonstrators) and still the sound mounted. One felt the convention coming apart. There was a Kennedy girl in the seat in front of me, the Kennedy hat on her head, a dimpled healthy brunette; she had sat silently through McCarthy's speech, but now, like a woman paying her respects to the power of natural thrust, she took off her hat and began to clap herself. I saw a writer I knew in the next aisle; he had spent a year studying the Kennedy machine in order to write a book on how nomination is won. If Stevenson stampeded the convention, his work was lost. Like a reporter at a mine cave-in I inquired the present view of the widow. "Who can think," was the answer, half frantic, half elated, "just watch it, that's all." I found a cool one, a New York reporter, who smiled in rueful respect. "It's the biggest demonstration I've seen since Wendell Willkie's in 1940," he said, and added, "God, if Stevenson takes it, I can wire my wife and move the family on to Hawaii."

"I don't get it."

"Well, every story I wrote said it was locked up for Kennedy."

Still it went on, twenty minutes, thirty minutes, the chairman could hardly be heard, the demonstrators refused to leave. The lights were turned out, giving a sudden theatrical shift to the sense of a crowded church at midnight, and a new roar went up, louder, more passionate than anything heard before. It was the voice, it was the passion, if one insisted to call it that, of everything in America which was defeated, idealistic, innocent, alienated, outside and Beat, it was the potential voice of a new third of the nation whose psyche was ill from cultural malnutrition, it was powerful, it was extraordinary, it was larger than the decent, humorous, finicky, half-noble man who had called it forth, it was a cry from the Thirties when Time was simple, it was a resentment of the slick technique, the oiled gears, and the superior generals of Fitzgerald's Army; but it was also—and for this reason one could not admire it altogether, except with one's excitement—it was also the plea of the bewildered who hunger for simplicity again, it was the adolescent counterpart of the boss's depression before the unpredictable dynamic of Kennedy as president, it was the return to the sentimental dream of Roosevelt rather than the approaching nightmare of history's oncoming night, and it was inspired by a terror of the future as much as a revulsion of the present.

Fitz's Army held; after the demonstration was finally down, the convention languished for ninety minutes while Meyner and others were nominated, a fatal lapse of time because Stevenson had perhaps a chance to stop Kennedy if the voting had begun on the echo of the last cry for him, but in an hour and a half depression crept in again and, emotions spent, the delegates who had wavered were rounded into line. When the vote was taken, Stevenson had made no gains. The brunette who had taken off her hat was wearing it again, and she clapped and squealed when Wyoming delivered the duke and Kennedy was in. The air was sheepish, like the mood of a suburban couple who forgive each other for cutting in and out of somebody else's automobile while the country club dance is on. Again, tonight, no miracle would occur. In the morning the papers would be moderate in their description of Stevenson's last charge.

One did not go to the other convention. It was seen on television, and so too much cannot be said of that. It did however confirm one's earlier bias that the Republican Party was still a party of church ushers, undertakers, choirboys, prison wardens, bank presidents, small-town police chiefs, state troopers, psychiatrists, beauty parlor operators, corporation executives, Boy Scout leaders, fraternity presidents, tax board assessors, community leaders, surgeons, Pullman porters, head nurses, and the fat sons of rich fathers. Its candidate would be given the manufactured image of an ordinary man, and his campaign, so far as it was a psychological campaign (and this would be far indeed), would present him as a simple, honest, dependable, hard-working, ready-to-learn, modest, humble, decent, sober young man whose greatest qualification for president was his profound abasement before the glories of the Republic, the stability of the mediocre, and his own unworthiness. The apocalyptic hour of Uriah Heep.

It would then be a campaign unlike the ones which had preceded it. Counting by the full spectrum of complete Right to absolute Left, the political differences would be minor, but what would be not at all minor was the power of each man to radiate his appeal into some fundamental depths of the American character. One would have an inkling at last if the desire of America was for drama or stability, for adventure or monotony. And this, this appeal to the psychic direction America would now choose for itself was the element most promising about this election, for it gave the possibility that the country might be able finally to rise above the deadening verbiage of its issues, its politics, its jargon, and live again by an image of itself. For in some part of themselves the people might know (since these candidates were not old enough to be revered) that they had chosen one young man for his mystery, for his promise that the country would grow or disintegrate by the unwilling charge he gave to the intensity of the myth, or had chosen another young man for his unstated oath that he would do all in his power to keep the myth buried and so convert the remains of Renaissance man as rapidly as possible into mass man. One might expect them to choose the enigma in preference to the deadening certainty. Yet one must doubt America's bravery. This lurching, unhappy, pompous, and

most corrupt nation—could it have the courage finally to take
on a new image for itself, was it brave enough to put into office
not only one of its ablest men, its most efficient, its most conquis-
tadorial (for Kennedy's capture of the Democratic Party deserves
the word), but also one of its more mysterious men (the national
psyche must shiver in its sleep at the image of Mickey Mantle–
cum–Lindbergh in office, and a First Lady with an eighteenth-
century face). Yes, America was at last engaging the fate of its
myth, its consciousness about to be accelerated or cruelly depressed in its choice between two young men in their forties
who, no matter how close, dull, or indifferent their stated politics might be, were radical poles apart, for one was sober, the
apotheosis of opportunistic lead, all radium spent, the other
handsome as a prince in the unstated aristocracy of the American dream. So, finally, would come a choice which history had
never presented to a nation before—one could vote for glamour
or for ugliness, a staggering and most stunning choice—would
the nation be brave enough to enlist the romantic dream of itself, would it vote for the image in the mirror of its unconscious,
were the people indeed brave enough to hope for an accelera-
tion of Time, for that new life of drama which would come from
choosing a son to lead them who was heir apparent to the psychic loins? One could pause: it might be more difficult to be a
president than it ever had before. Nothing less than greatness
would do.

Yet if the nation voted to improve its face, what an impetus
might come to the arts, to the practices, to the lives and to the
imagination of the American. If the nation so voted. But one
knew the unadmitted specter in the minds of the Democratic
delegates: that America would go to sleep on election eve with
the polls promising Kennedy a victory on the day to come, yet in
its sleep some millions of Democrats and Independents would
suffer a nightmare before the mystery of uncharted possibilities
their man would suggest, and in a terror of all the creativities
(and some violences) that mass man might now have to dare
again, the undetermined would go out in the morning to vote
for the psychic security of Nixon the way a middle-aged man past

adventure holds to the stale bread of his marriage. Yes, this election might be fearful enough to betray the polls, and no one in America could plan the new direction until the last vote as counted by the last heeler in the last ambivalent ward, no one indeed could know until then what had happened the night before, what had happened at three o'clock in the morning on that long dark night of America's search for a security cheaper than her soul.

An Evening with Jackie Kennedy

Being an Essay in Three Acts

(1962)

A FEW OF YOU MAY REMEMBER that on February 14, last winter, our
First Lady gave us a tour of the White House on television. For
reasons to be explained in a while, I was in no charitable mood
that night and gave Mrs. Kennedy a close scrutiny. Like anybody
else, I have a bit of tolerance for my vices, at least those which do
not get into the newspapers, but I take no pride in giving a hard
look at a lady when she is on television. Ladies are created for an
encounter face-to-face. No man can decide a lady is trivial until
he has spent some minutes alone with her. Now while I have
been in the same room with Jackie Kennedy twice, for a few minutes each time, it was never very much alone, and for that matter
I do not think anyone's heart was particularly calm. The weather
was too hectic. It was the summer of 1960, after the Democratic
Convention, before the presidential campaign had formally
begun, at Hyannis Port, site of the Summer White House—those
of you who know Hyannis ("High-anus," as the natives say) will
know how funny is the title—all those motels and a Summer
White House too: the Kennedy compound, an enclosure of three
summer homes belonging to Joe Kennedy, Sr., RFK, and JFK,
with a modest amount of lawn and beach to share among them.

In those historic days the lawn was overrun with journalists, cameramen, magazine writers, politicians, delegations, friends and neighboring gentry, government intellectuals, family, a prince, some Massachusetts state troopers, and red-necked hard-nosed tourists patrolling outside the fence for a glimpse of the boy. He was much in evidence, a bit of everywhere that morning, including the lawn, and particularly handsome at times as one has described elsewhere (*Esquire,* November, 1960), looking like a good version of Charles Lindbergh at noon on a hot August day. Well, Jackie Kennedy was inside in her living room sitting around talking with a few of us, Arthur Schlesinger, Jr., and his wife, Marian, Prince Radziwill, Peter Maas the writer, Jacques Lowe the photographer, and Pierre Salinger. We were a curious assortment indeed, as oddly assembled in our way as some of the do-gooders and real baddies on the lawn outside. It would have taken a hostess of broad and perhaps dubious gifts, Perle Mesta, no doubt, or Ethel Merman, or Elsa Maxwell, to have woven some mood into this occasion, because pop! were going the flashbulbs out in the crazy August sun on the sun-drenched terrace just beyond the bay window at our back, a politician—a stocky machine type sweating in a dark suit with a white shirt and white silk tie—was having his son, seventeen perhaps, short, chunky, dressed the same way, take a picture of him and his wife, a Mediterranean dish around sixty with a bright, happy, flowered dress. The boy took a picture of father and mother, father took a picture of mother and son—another heeler came along to take a picture of all three—it was a little like a rite surrounding droit du seigneur, as if afterward the family could press a locket in your hand and say, "Here, here are contained three hairs from the youth of the Count, discovered by me on my wife next morning." There was something low and greedy about this picture-taking, perhaps the popping of the flashbulbs in the sunlight, as if everything monstrous and overreaching in our insane public land were tamped together in the foolproof act of taking a sun-drenched picture at noon with no shadows and a flashbulb—do we sell insurance to protect our cadavers against the corrosion of the grave?

And I had the impression that Jackie Kennedy was almost suffering in the flesh from their invasion of her house, her terrace, her share of the lands, that if the popping of the flashbulbs went on until midnight on the terrace outside she would have a tic forever in the corner of her eye. Because that was the second impression of her, of a lady with delicate and exacerbated nerves. She was no broad hostess, not at all; broad hostesses are monumental animals turned mellow: hippopotami, rhinoceri, plump lion, sweet gorilla, warm bear. Jackie Kennedy was a cat, narrow and wild, and her fur was being rubbed every which way. This was the second impression. The first had been simpler. It had been merely of a college girl who was nice. Nice and clean and very merry. I had entered her house perspiring—talk of the politician, I was wearing a black suit myself, a washable, the only one in my closet not completely unpressed that morning, and I had been forced to pick a white shirt with button-down collar: all the white summer shirts were in the laundry. What a set-to I had had with Adele Mailer at breakfast. Food half-digested in anger, sweating like a goat, tense at the pit of my stomach for I would be interviewing Kennedy in a half hour, I was feeling not a little jangled when we were introduced, and we stumbled mutually over a few polite remarks, which was my fault I'm sure more than hers for I must have had a look in my eyes—I remember I felt like a drunk marine, who knows in all clarity that if he doesn't have a fight soon it'll be good for his character but terrible for his constitution.

She offered me a cool drink—iced verbena tea with a sprig of mint no doubt—but the expression in my face must have been rich because she added, still standing by the screen in the doorway, "We do have something harder of course," and something droll and hard came into her eyes as if she were a very naughty eight-year-old indeed. More than one photograph of Jackie Kennedy had put forward just this saucy regard—it was obviously the life of her charm. But I had not been prepared for another quality, of shyness conceivably. There was something quite remote in her. Not willed, not chilly, not directed at anyone in particular, but distant, detached as the psychologists say, moody and ab-

stracted the novelists used to say. As we sat around the coffee
table on summer couches, summer chairs, a pleasant living room
in light colors, lemon, white, and gold seeming to predominate,
the sort of living room one might expect to find in Cleveland,
may it be, at the home of a fairly important young executive
whose wife had taste, sitting there, watching people go by, the
group I mentioned earlier kept a kind of conversation going. Its
center, if it had one, was obviously Jackie Kennedy. There was a
natural tendency to look at her and see if she was amused. She
did not sit there like a movie star with a ripe olive in each eye for
the brain, but in fact gave conversation back, made some of it,
laughed often. We had one short conversation about Provincetown, which was pleasant. She remarked that she had been staying no more than fifty miles away for all these summers but had
never seen it. She must, I assured her. It was one of the few fishing villages in America which still had beauty. Besides it was the
Wild West of the East. The local police were the Indians and the
beatniks were the poor hardworking settlers. Her eyes turned
merry. "Oh, I'd love to see it," she said. But how did one go? In
three black limousines and fifty police for escort, or in a sports
car at four A.M. with dark glasses? "I suppose now I'll never get to
see it," she said wistfully.

She had a keen sense of laughter, but it revolved around the
absurdities of the world. She was probably not altogether unlike
a soldier who has been up at the front for two weeks. There was
a hint of gone laughter. Soldiers who have had it bad enough
can laugh at the fact some trooper got killed crossing an open
area because he wanted to change his socks from khaki to green.
The front lawn of this house must have been, I suppose, a kind
of no-man's-land for a lady. The story I remember her telling was
about Stash, Prince Radziwill, her brother-in-law, who had gone
into the second-story bathroom that morning to take a shave and
discovered, to his lack of complete pleasure, that a crush of tourists was watching him from across the road. Yes, the house had
been besieged, and one knew she thought of the sightseers as a
mob, a motley of gargoyles, like the horde who riot through the
last pages in *The Day of the Locust*.

Since there was an air of self-indulgence about her, subtle but precise, one was certain she liked time to compose herself. While we sat there she must have gotten up a half dozen times to go away for two minutes, come back for three. She had the exasperated impatience of a college girl. One expected her to swear mildly. "Oh, Christ!" or "Sugar!" or "Fudge!" And each time she got up, there was a glimpse of her calves, surprisingly thin, not unfeverish. I was reminded of the legs on those adolescent Southern girls who used to go out together and walk up and down the streets of Fayetteville, North Carolina, in the summer of 1944 at Fort Bragg. In the petulant Southern air of their boredom many of us had found something humorous that summer, a mixture of laughing, heat, innocence, and stupidity which was our cocktail vis-à-vis the knowledge we were going soon to Europe or the other war. One mentions this to underline the determinedly romantic aura in which one had chosen to behold Jackie Kennedy. There was a charm this other short summer of 1960 in the thought a young man with a young attractive wife might soon become president. It offered possibilities and vistas; it brought a touch of life to the monotonies of politics, those monotonies so profoundly entrenched into the hinges and mortar of the Eisenhower administration. It was thus more interesting to look at Jackie Kennedy as a woman than as a probable First Lady. Perhaps it was out of some such motive, such a desire for the clean air and tang of unexpected montage, that I spoke about her in just the way I did later that afternoon.

"Do you think she's happy?" asked a lady, an old friend, on the beach at Wellfleet.

"I guess she would rather spend her life on the Riviera."

"What would she do there?"

"End up as the mystery woman, maybe, in a good murder case."

"Wow," said the lady, giving me my reward.

It had been my way of saying I liked Jackie Kennedy, that she was not at all stuffy, that she had perhaps a touch of that artful madness which suggests future drama.

My interview the first day had been a little short, and I was invited back for another one the following day. Rather nicely, Senator Kennedy invited me to bring anyone I wanted. About a week later I realized this was part of his acumen. You can tell a lot about a man by whom he invites in such a circumstance. Will it be a political expert or the wife? I invited my wife. The presence of this second lady is not unimportant, because this time she had the conversation with Jackie Kennedy. While I was busy somewhere or other, they were introduced. Down by the Kennedy family wharf. The Senator was about to take Jackie for a sail. The two women had a certain small general resemblance. They were something like the same height, they both had dark hair, and they had each been wearing it in a similar style for many years. Perhaps this was enough to create a quick political intimacy. "I wish," said Jackie Kennedy, "that I didn't have to go on this corny sail, because I would like very much to talk to you, Mrs. Mailer." A stroke. Mrs. M. did not like many people quickly, but Jackie now had a champion. It must have been a pleasant sight. Two attractive witches by the water's edge.

II

Jimmy Baldwin once entertained the readers of *Esquire* with a sweet and generously written piece called *The Black Boy Looks at the White Boy* in which he talked a great deal about himself and a little bit about me, a proportion I thought well taken since he is on the best of terms with Baldwin and digs next to nothing about this white boy. As a method, I think it has its merits.

After I saw the Kennedys I added a few paragraphs to my piece about the convention, secretly relieved to have liked them, for my piece was most favorable to the Senator, and how would I have rewritten it if I had not liked him? With several mishaps it was printed three weeks before the election. Several days later, I received a letter from Jackie Kennedy. It was a nice letter, generous in its praise, accurate in its details. She remembered, for example, the color of the sweater my wife had been wearing, and mentioned she had one like it in the same purple.

I answered with a letter which was out of measure. I was in a Napoleonic mood, I had decided to run for mayor of New York; in a few weeks, I was to zoom and crash—my sense of reality was extravagant. So in response to a modestly voiced notion by Mrs. Kennedy that she wondered if the "impressionistic" way in which I had treated the convention could be applied to the history of the past, I replied in the cadence of a Goethe that while I was now engaged in certain difficulties of writing about the present, I hoped one day when work was done to do a biography of the Marquis de Sade and the "odd strange honor of the man."

I suppose this is as close to the edge as I have ever come. At the time, it seemed reasonable that Mrs. Kennedy, with her publicized interest in France and the eighteenth century, might be fascinated by de Sade. The style of his thought was, after all, a fair climax to the Age of Reason.

Now sociology has few virtues, but one of them is sanity. In writing such a letter to Mrs. Kennedy I was losing my sociology. The Catholic wife of a Catholic candidate for president was not likely to find de Sade as familiar as a tea cozy. I received no reply. I had smashed the limits of such letter writing. In politics a break in sociology is as clean as a break in etiquette.

At the time I saw it somewhat differently. The odds were against a reply, I decided, three-to-one against, or eight-to-one against. I did not glean they were eight-hundred-to-one against. It is the small inability to handicap odds which is family to the romantic, the desperate, and the insane. "That man is going to kill me," someone thinks with fear, sensing a stranger. At this moment, they put the odds at even money, they may even be ready to die for their bet, when, if the fact could be measured, there is one chance in a thousand the danger is true. Exceptional leverage upon the unconscious life in other people is the strength of the artist and the torment of the madman.

Now if I have bothered to show my absence of proportion, it is because I want to put forward a notion which will seem criminal to some of you, but was believed in by me, is still believed in by me, and so affects what I write about the Kennedys.

Jack Kennedy won the election by one hundred thousand
votes. A lot of people could claim therefore to be the mind behind his victory. Jake Arvey could say the photo finish would have
gone the other way if not for the track near his Chicago machine. J. Edgar Hoover might say he saved the victory because he
did not investigate the track. Lyndon Johnson could point to LBJ
Ranch, and the vote in Texas. *Time* magazine could tell you that
the abstract intrepidity of their support for Nixon gave the duke
to Kennedy. Sinatra would not be surprised if the late ones who
glommed onto Kennedy were not more numerous than the early
risers he scattered. And one does not even need to speak of the
corporations, the Mob, the money they delivered by messenger,
the credit they would use later. So if I came to the cool conclusion I had won the election for Kennedy with my piece in *Esquire,*
the thought might be high presumption, but it was not unique. I
had done something curious but indispensable for the
campaign—succeeded in making it dramatic. I had not shifted
one hundred thousand votes directly, I had not. But a million
people might have read my piece and some of them talked to
other people. The cadres of Stevenson Democrats whose morale
was low might now revive with an argument that Kennedy was
different in substance from Nixon. Dramatically different. The
piece titled *Superman Comes to the Supermarket* affected volunteer
work for Kennedy, enough to make a clean critical difference
through the country. But such counting is a quibble. At bottom
I had the feeling that if there were a power which made presidents, a power which might be termed Wall Street or Capitalism
or the Establishment, a Mind or Collective Mind of some Spirit,
some Master, or indeed *the* Master, no less, that then perhaps my
article had turned that intelligence a fine hair in its circuits. This
was what I thought. Right or wrong, I thought it, still do, and tell
it now not to convince others (the act of stating such a claim is
not happy), but to underline the proprietary tone I took when
Kennedy invaded Cuba.

"You've cut . . ." I wrote in *The Village Voice,* April 27,
1961: ". . . the shape of your plan for history, and it

smells . . . rich and smug and scared of the power of the worst, dullest and most oppressive men of our land."

There was more. A good deal more. I want to quote more. Nothing could ever convince me the invasion of Cuba was not one of the meanest blunders in our history:

"You are a virtuoso in political management but you will never understand the revolutionary passion which comes to those who were one way or another too poor to learn how good they might have been; the greediness of the rich had already crippled their youth.

"Without this understanding you will never know what to do about Castro and Cuba. You will never understand that the man is the country, revolutionary, tyrannical . . . hysterical . . . brave as the best of animals, doomed perhaps to end in tragedy, but one of the great figures of the twentieth century, at the present moment a far greater figure than yourself."

Later, through the grapevine which runs from Washington to New York, it could be heard that Jackie Kennedy was indignant at this piece, and one had the opportunity to speculate if her annoyance came from the postscript:

I was in a demonstration the other day . . . five literary magazines (so help me) which marched in a small circle of protest against our intervention in Cuba. One of the pickets was a very tall poetess with black hair which reached near to her waist. She was dressed like a medieval varlet, and she carried a sign addressed to your wife:
Jacqueline, *vous avez*
perdu vos artistes
"Tin soldier, you are depriving us of the Muse."

Months later, when the anger cooled, one could ask oneself what one did make of Washington now, for it was not an easy

place to understand. It was intelligent, yes, but it was not original; there was wit in the detail and ponderousness in the program; vivacity, and dullness to equal it; tactical brilliance,
political timidity; facts were still superior to the depths, criticism was less to be admired than the ability to be amusing—or
so said the losers; equality and justice meandered; bureaucratic
canals and locks; slums were replaced with buildings which
looked like prisons; success was to be admired again, self-
awareness dubious; television was attacked, but for its violence,
not its mendacity, for its lack of educational programs, not its
dearth of grace. There seemed no art, no real art in the new
administration, and all the while the new administration pro-
claimed its eagerness to mother the arts. Or as Mr. Collingwood said to Mrs. Kennedy, "This administration has shown a
particular affinity for artists, musicians, writers, poets. Is this
because you and your husband just feel that way or do you
think that there's a relationship between the government and
the arts?"

"That's so complicated," answered Mrs. Kennedy with good
sense. "I don't know. I just think that everything in the White
House should be the best."

Stravinsky had been invited of course and Robert Frost. Pablo
Casals, Leonard Bernstein, Arthur Miller, Tennessee.

"But what about us?" growled the apes. Why did one know
that Richard Wilbur would walk through the door before Allen
Ginsberg; or Saul Bellow and J. D. Salinger long before William
Burroughs or Norman Mailer? What special good would it do to
found an Establishment if the few who gave intimations of high
talent were instinctively excluded? I wanted a chance to preach
to the president and to the First Lady. "Speak to the people a
little more," I would have liked to say, "talk on television about
the things you do not understand. Use your popularity to be
difficult and intellectually dangerous. There is more to greatness than liberal legislation." And to her I would have liked to
go on about what the real meaning of an artist might be, of how
the marrow of a nation was contained in his art, and one deadened artists at one's peril, because artists were not so much

gifted as endowed; they had been given what was secret and best in their parents and in all the other people about them who had been generous or influenced them or made them, and so artists embodied the essence of what was best in the nation, embodied it in their talent rather than in their character, which could be small, but their talent—this fruit of all that was rich and nourishing in their lives—was related directly to the dreams and the ambitions of the most imaginative part of the nation. So the destiny of a nation was not separate at all from the fate of its artists. I would have liked to tell her that every time an artist failed to complete the full mansion, jungle, garden, armory, or city of his work the nation was subtly but permanently poorer, which is why we return so obsessively to the death of Tom Wolfe, the broken air of Scott Fitzgerald, and the gloomy smell of the vault which collects already about the horror of Hemingway's departure. I would have liked to say to her that a war for the right to express oneself had been going on in this country for fifty years, and that there were counterattacks massing because there were many who hated the artist now, that as the world dipped into the totalitarian trough of the twentieth century there was a mania of abhorrence for whatever was unpredictable. For all too many, security was the only bulwark against emptiness, eternity and death. The void was what America feared. Communism was one name they gave this void. The unknown was Communist. The girls who wore dungarees were Communist, and the boys who grew beards, the people who walked their dog off the leash. It was comic, but it was virulent, and there was a fanatic rage in much too much of the population. Detestation of the beatnik seethed like rabies on the mouths of small-town police officers.

Oh, there was much I wanted to tell her, even—exit sociology, enter insanity—that the obscene had a right to exist in the novel. For every fifteen-year-old who would be hurt by premature exposure, somewhere another, or two or three, would emerge from sexual experience which had been too full of moral funk onto the harder terrain of sex made alive by culture, that it was the purpose of culture finally to enrich all of the psyche, not just part of us, and damage to particular people in passing was a price we must pay. Thirty thousand Americans were killed each year by automobile crashes. No one talked of giving up the automobile: it was necessary to civilization. As necessary, I wanted to say, was art. Art in all its manifestations. Including the rude, the obscene, and the unsayable. Art was as essential to the nation as technology. I would tell her these things out of romantic abundance, because I liked her and thought she would understand what one was talking about, because as First Lady she was queen of the arts, she was our Muse if she chose to be. Perhaps it would not be altogether a disaster if America had a Muse.

Now it is not of much interest to most of you who read this that a small but distinct feud between the editors of *Esquire* and the writer was made up around the New Year. What is not as much off the matter was the suggestion, made at the time by one of these editors, that a story be done about Jackie Kennedy.

One liked the idea. What has been written already is curious prose if it is not obvious how much one liked the idea. Pierre Salinger was approached by the magazine, and agreed to present the same idea to Mrs. Kennedy. I saw Salinger in his office for a few minutes. He told me: not yet a chance to talk to the Lady, but might that evening. I was leaving Washington. A few days later, one of the editors spoke to him. Mrs. Kennedy's answer: negative.

One didn't know. One didn't know how the idea had been presented, one didn't know just when it had been presented. It did not matter all that much. Whatever the details, the answer had come from the core. One's presence was not required. Which irritated the vanity. The vanity was no doubt outsized, but one thought of oneself as one of the few writers in the country. There was a right to interview Mrs. Kennedy. She was not only a woman looking for privacy, but an institution being put together before our eyes. If the people of America were to have a symbol, one had the right to read more about the creation. The country would stay alive by becoming more extraordinary, not more predictable.

III

Nor with a kind eye then did I watch Mrs. Kennedy give the nation a tour. One would be fair. Fair to her and fair to the truth of one's reactions. There was now an advantage in not having had the interview.

I turned on the program a minute after the hour. The image on the screen was not of Mrs. Kennedy, but the White House. For some minutes she talked, reading from a prepared script while the camera was turned upon old prints, old plans, and present views of the building. Since Jackie Kennedy was not visible during this time, there was an opportunity to listen to her voice. It produced a small continuing shock. At first, before the picture emerged from the set, I thought I was turned to the wrong station, because the voice was a quiet parody of the sort of voice one hears on the radio late at night, dropped softly into the ear by girls who sell soft mattresses, depilatories, or creams to brighten the skin.

Now I had heard the First Lady occasionally on newsreels and in brief interviews on television, and thought she showed an odd public voice, but never paid attention, because the first time to hear her was in the living room at Hyannis Port and there she had been clear, merry, and near excellent. So I discounted the public voice, concluded it was muffled by shyness perhaps or was too urgent in its desire to sound like other voices, to sound, let us say, like an attractive small-town salesgirl, or like Jackie Kennedy's version of one; the gentry in America have a dim ear for the nuances of accent in the rough, the poor, and the ready. I had decided it was probably some mockery of her husband's political ambitions, a sport upon whatever advisers had been trying for years to guide her to erase whatever was too patrician or cultivated in her speech. But the voice I was hearing now, the public voice, the voice after a year in the White House had grown undeniably worse, had nourished itself on its faults. Do some of you remember the girl with the magnificent sweater who used to give the weather reports on television in a swarmy singsong tone? It

was a self-conscious parody, very funny for a little while.
"Temperature—forty-eight. Humidity—twenty-eight. Prevailing
winds." It had the style of the pinup magazine, it caught their
prose. "Sandra Sharilee is 37-25-37, and likes to stay in at night."
The girl who gave the weather report captured the voice of those
pinup magazines, dreamy, narcissistic, visions of sex on the
moon. And Jackie Kennedy's voice, her public voice, might as
well have been influenced by the weather girl. What madness is
loose in our public communication. And what self-ridicule that
consciously or unconsciously, wittingly, willy-nilly, by the aid of
speech teachers or all on her stubborn own, this was the manufactured voice Jackie Kennedy chose to arrive at. One had heard
better ones at Christmastime in Macy's selling gadgets to the
grim.

The introduction having ended, the camera moved onto
Jackie Kennedy. We were shown the broad planes of the First
Lady's most agreeable face. Out of the deep woods now. One
could return to them by closing one's eyes and listening to the
voice again, but the image was reasonable, reassuringly stiff. As
the eye followed Mrs. Kennedy and her interlocutor, Charles
Collingwood, through the halls, galleries and rooms of the White
House, through the Blue Room, the Green Room, the East
Room, the State Dining Room, the Red Room; as the listeners
were offered a reference to Dolly Madison's favorite sofa, or
President Monroe's Minerva clock, Nellie Custis's sofa, Mrs. Lincoln's later poverty, Daniel Webster's sofa, Julia Grant's desk, An-
drew Jackson's broken mirror, the chest President Van Buren
gave to his grandson, as the paintings were shown to us, paintings entitled *Niagara Falls, Grapes and Apples, Naval Battle of 1812,
Indian Guides, A Mountain Glimpse, Mouth of the Delaware;* as one
contemplated the life of this offering, the presentation began to
take on the undernourished, overdone air of a charity show, a
telethon for a new disease. It was not Mrs. Kennedy's fault—she
strove honorably. What an agony it must have been to establish
the sequence of all these names, all these objects. Probably she
knew them well, perhaps she was interested in her subject—
although the detached quality of her presence on this program

made it not easy to believe—but whether or not she had taken a
day-to-day interest in the booty now within the White House, still
she had had a script partially written for her, by a television writer
with black horn-rimmed glasses no doubt, she had been obliged
to memorize portions of this script, she had trained for the part.
Somehow it was sympathetic that she walked through it like a
starlet who is utterly without talent. Mrs. Kennedy moved like a
wooden horse. A marvelous horse, perhaps even a live horse, its
feet hobbled, its head unready to turn for fear of a flick from the
crop. She had that intense wooden lack of rest, that lack of comprehension for each word offered up which one finds only in a
few of those curious movie stars who are huge box office. Jane
Russell comes to mind, and Rita Hayworth when she was sadly
cast, Jayne Mansfield in deep water, Brigitte Bardot before she
learned to act. Marilyn Monroe. But one may be too kind. Jackie
Kennedy was more like a starlet who will never learn to act because the extraordinary livid unreality of her life away from the
camera has so beclouded her brain and seduced her attention
that she is incapable of the simplest and most essential demand,
which is to live and breathe easily with the meaning of the words
one speaks.

This program was the sort of thing Eleanor Roosevelt could
have done, and done well. She had grown up among objects like
this—these stuffed armchairs, these candelabra—no doubt they
lived for her with some charm of the past. But Jackie Kennedy
was unconvincing. One did not feel she particularly loved the
past of America—not all of us do for that matter, it may not even
be a crime—but one never had the impression for a moment
that the White House fitted her style. As one watched this tame,
lackluster, and halting show, one wanted to take the actress by
the near shoulder. Because names, dates, and objects were boring down into the very secrets of her being—or so one would lay
the bet—and this encouraged a fraud which could only sicken
her. By extension it would deaden us. What we needed and what
she could offer us was much more complex than this public
image of a pompadour, a tea-dance dress, and a Colonial window
welded together in committee. Would the Kennedys be no more

intelligent than the near past, had they not learned America was not to be saved by Madison Avenue, that no method could work which induced nausea faster than the pills we push to carry it away?

Afterward one could ask what it was one wanted of her, and the answer was that she show herself to us as she is. Because what we suffer from in America, in that rootless moral wilderness of our expanding life, is the unadmitted terror in each of us that bit by bit, year by year, we are going mad. Very few of us know really where we have come from and to where we are going, why we do it, and if it is ever worthwhile. For better or for worse we have lost our past, we live in that airless no-man's-land of the perpetual present, and so suffer doubly as we strike into the future because we have no roots by which to project ourselves forward, or judge our trip.

And this tour of the White House gave us precisely no sense of the past. To the contrary, it inflicted the past upon us, pummeled us with it, depressed us with facts. I counted the names, the proper names, and the dates in the transcript. More than two hundred items were dumped upon us during that hour. If one counts repetitions, the number is closer to four hundred. One was not being offered education, but anxiety.

We are in the Green Room—I quote from the transcript:

> Mr. Collingwood: What other objects of special interest are there in the room now?
>
> Mrs. Kennedy: Well, there's this sofa which belonged to Daniel Webster and is really one of the finest pieces here in this room. And then there's this mirror. It was George Washington's and he had it in the Executive Mansion in Philadelphia, then he gave it to a friend and it was bought for Mount Vernon in 1891. And it was there until Mount Vernon lent it to us this fall. And I must say I appreciate that more than I can say, because when Mount Vernon, which is probably the most revered house in this country, lends something to the White House, you know they have confidence it will be taken care of.

A neurotic may suffer agonies returning to his past, so may a nation which is not well. The neurotic recites endless lists of his activities and offers no reaction to any of it. So do we teach with empty content and by rigid manner where there is anxiety in the lore. American history disgorges this anxiety. Where, in the pleasant versions of it we are furnished, can we find an explanation for the disease which encourages us to scourge our countryside, stifle our cities, kill the physical sense of our past, and throw up excruciatingly totalitarian new office buildings everywhere to burden the vista of our end? This disease, is it hidden in the evasions, the injustices, and the prevarications of the past, or does it come to us from a terror of what is yet to come? Whatever, however, we do not create a better nation by teaching schoolchildren the catalogs of the White House. Nor do we use the First Lady decently if she is flattered in this, for catalogs are imprisonment to the delicate, muted sensitivity one feels passing across Jackie Kennedy from time to time like a small summer wind on a good garden.

Yes, before the tour was over, one had to feel compassion. Because silly, ill-advised, pointless, empty, dull, and obsequious to the most slavish tastes in American life as was this show, still she was trying so hard, she wanted to please, she had given herself to this work, and it was hopeless there was no one about to tell her how very hopeless it was, how utterly without offering to the tormented adventurous spirit of American life. At times, in her eyes, there was a blank, full look which one could recognize. One had seen this look on a nineteen-year-old who was sweet and on the town and pushed too far. She slashed her wrists one night and tried to scar her cheeks and her breast. I had visited the girl in the hospital. She had blank eyes, a wide warm smile, a deadness in her voice. It did not matter about what she spoke— only her mouth followed the words, never her eyes. So I did not care to see that look in Jackie Kennedy's face, and I hoped by half—for more would be untrue—that the sense one got of her in newspaper photographs, of a ladygirl healthy and on the bounce, might come into her presence before our deadening sets. America needed a lady's humor to leaven the solemnities of our toneless power: finally we will send a man to Mars and the Martians will say, "God, he is dull."

Yes, it is to be hoped that Jackie Kennedy will come alive. Because I think finally she is one of us. By which I mean that she has not one face but many, not a true voice but accents, not a past so much as memories which cannot speak to one another. She attracts compassion. Somewhere in her mute vitality is a wash of our fatigue, of existential fatigue, of the great fatigue which comes from being adventurous in a world where most of the bets are covered cold and statisticians prosper. I liked her, I liked her still, but she was a phony—it was the cruelest thing one could say, she was a royal phony. There was something very difficult and very dangerous she was trying from deep within herself to do, dangerous not to her safety but to her soul. She was trying, I suppose, to be a proper First Lady and it was her mistake. Because there was no need to copy the Ladies who had come before her. Suppose America had not yet had a First Lady who was even remotely warm enough for our needs? Or sufficiently imaginative? But who could there be to advise her in all that company of organized men, weaned on the handbook of past precedent? If she would be any use to the nation she must first regain the freedom to look us in the eye. And offer the hard drink. For then three times three hurrah, and hats, our hats, in the air. If she were really interested in her White House, we would grant it to her, we would not begrudge her the tour, not if we could believe she was beginning to learn the difference between the arts and the safe old crafts. And indeed there was a way she could show us she was beginning to learn, it was the way of the hostess; one would offer her one's sword when Henry Miller was asked to the White House as often as Robert Frost and Beat poetry's own Andy Hardy—good Gregory Corso—could do an Indian dance in the East Room with Archibald MacLeish. America would be as great as the royal rajah of her arts when the Academy ceased to be happy as a cherrystone clam, and the weakest of the Beat returned to form. Because our tragedy is that we diverge as countrymen further and further away from one another, like a spaceship broken apart in flight which now drifts mournfully in isolated orbits, satellites to each other, planets none, communication faint.

Suicides of Hemingway and Monroe

————

(1962)

YOUR COLUMNIST would warn you. These pieces will be written two months before publication. The art is to anticipate what may be interesting in sixty days. I was talking about this with a columnist. "Write your column so it can still be read with pleasure ten years from now," he said. Good advice. I will try to entertain some of you. I will try to drive others a little closer to their deaths.

This week the news is of Marilyn Monroe and the drug thalidomide. In sixty days most of you will have forgotten thalidomide so I remind you now that it was the drug which gave tranquillity to pregnant women suffering from morning sickness. As a side effect it seemed to affect embryos. They grew little flippers for arms. In West Germany, five thousand of them grew that way. It encouraged a joke:

"Darling," said the German bride, new and pregnant, "these pills seem to have an odd effect on me."

"Don't worry, dear," says husband, "doctor knows what he's doing."

The joke is sexually displaced. It is men who distrust doctors. Women adore them. If a hero cares enough about a lady he must be ready to enter the lists against Richard Burton, Fidel Castro,

Jack Kennedy, Cary Grant, Paul Getty, Yuri Gagarin, Sinatra, Glenn, early Brando or middle Pinza, it does not matter. If one wants a woman enough, there is some kind of chance. Do not give up, advises your columnist. Do not, unless your lady is an actress or a beauty and your opponent is a doctor or a psychoanalyst. Then it is hopeless.

"Darling," says the German bride, "these pills seem to have an odd effect on me."

"Throw them out," says her groom.

"Are you being stupid again?" cries she. "Doctor knows what he's doing."

I know a doctor who's intelligent, cynical, and an expert on cancer research. He heads a program in a New York hospital. He was fascinated by thalidomide. Thought it might represent a breakthrough. "It means we are able to affect the direction of evolution."

"To what end?" I asked.

He shrugged. Not interested in that. It is not the end but the immediate power which calls to scientists. In modern man there is a profound rage against nature. One hears it everywhere: in the sound of an air conditioner, the electronic hiss of a public address system, in automobiles passing on a superhighway. One feels this invasion upon nature when one touches a plastic toy. I hate the thought of children using plastic toys. I would as soon give them blown-up prophylactics for dolls.

And then there's the cry of nature answering back.

I am torn in two, says the air. Take away your jet planes.

Stop screaming, pal. We need the jets to get there.

Get where?

Move on, says fuzz.

The worst story I ever heard about Jack Kennedy was that he sat on his boat one day eating chicken and threw the half-chewed bones into the sea.

So few people understand what I mean, it forces me to explain that you don't give the carcass of an animal to the water. It was meant to seep back into the earth.

Of course we pump our sewage out to sea, a sewage which was meant to return to the land, but then in a thousand years we may discover that the worst plagues of man, the cancer and the concentration camps, the housing projects and the fallout, the mass media and the mass nausea come from a few social vices, from the manufacture of the mirror, from the introduction of tobacco to Europe, from the advance of sanitation. Science may have been born the day a man came to hate nature so profoundly that he swore he would devote himself to comprehending her, and secretly to stifling her.

There is nothing wrong with hating nature. It is less bad than being the sort of columnist who admonishes his readers to love nature. What is bad is to fear death so completely that one loses the nerve to contemplate it. Throwing a chicken bone into the sea is bad because it shows no feeling for the root of death, which is burial. Of course Kennedy might have muttered "Sorry, old man" as he tossed the bone. That is the difficulty with anecdotes. One cannot determine the nuance. I have the conceit that if I had been there I might have sensed whether Kennedy was genuinely rueful, oblivious to the fact, or acting like a dick, a house dick.

Some will now mutter: Can't the man be left alone? Is he entitled to no private life? The answer is: none. He is a young man who has chosen to be president. He is now paying part of the price. I suspect he is ready to pay it.

Rare was the czar or king who did not have a witness in his chamber to sniff the passing of the state. Arthur Schlesinger?

The root of death is burial. I was never particularly fond of Joe DiMaggio. His legend left me cold. But I have respect for the way he chose to give Marilyn Monroe a small funeral. If she had never been a movie star, if she had been one of those small, attractive blondes who floats like spray over the Hollywood rocks, a little drink here, bit of a call girl there, bing, bam, bad marriage, nice pot, easy head, girlfriend, headshrinker, fuzz, dope, miscarriage and lowering night, if she had been no more than that, just a misty little blonde who hurt no one too much and went down inch by inch, inevitably, like a cocker spaniel in a quickbog, well then she would have ended in some small Hollywood parlor with fifteen friends invited.

Probably she was like that by the end. Sleeping pills are the great leveler. If everyone in America took four capsules of Nembutal a night for two thousand nights we would all be the same when we were done. We would all be idiots.

Any writer who takes the pills year after year ought to be able to write the tale of a club fighter whose brain turns slowly drunk with punishment. But that is the book which is never written. We learn the truth by giving away pieces of our tongue. When we know it all, there is no tongue left. Is it then one rises at dawn for the black flirtation, slips downstairs, slips the muzzle into the mouth, cool gunmetal to balm the void of a lost tongue, and goes blasting off like a rocket. Here come I, eternity, cries Ernest, I trust you no longer. You must try to find me now, eternity. I am in little pieces.

Hemingway and Monroe. Pass lightly over their names. They were two of the people in America most beautiful to us.

I think Ernest hated us by the end. He deprived us of his head. It does not matter so much whether it was suicide or an accident— one does not put a gun barrel in one's mouth, tickle the edge of an accident, and fail to see that people will say it's suicide. Ernest, so proud of his reputation. So fierce about it. His death was awful. Say it. It was the most difficult death in America since Roosevelt. One has still not recovered from Hemingway's death. One may never.

But Monroe was different. She slipped away from us. She had been slipping away from us for years. Now it is easy to say that her actions became more vague every year. I thought she was bad in *The Misfits,* she was finally too vague, and when emotion showed, it was unattractive and small. But she was gone from us a long time ago.

If she had done Grushenka in *The Brothers Karamazov* the way she announced she would all those years ago, and if she had done it well, then she might have gone on. She might have come all the way back into the vault of herself where the salts of a clean death and the rot of a foul death were locked together. We take the sleeping pills when the sense of a foul and rotten death has become too certain, we look for the salt in the Seconal. Probably to stay alive Monroe had to become the greatest actress who ever lived. To stay alive Hemingway would have had to write a better book than *War and Peace*.

From *The Deer Park:* "There was that law of life, so cruel and so just, which demanded that one must grow or else pay more for remaining the same." I think that line is true. I think it is biologically true. And I think its application is more ferocious in America than anywhere I know. Because we set ourselves out around the knoll and get ready to play King of the Hill. Soon one of us is brave enough to take the center and insist it belongs to us. Then there is no rest until the new king is killed. Our good America. We are the nation of amateur kings and queens.

Each month our column will end with a small sentence. Make ready for our last cattle king, Robert Ruark. Robert Ruark has the kind of personality Ernest Hemingway would have had if Ernest Hemingway had been a bad writer.

Punching Papa

(1963)

TALKING TO CALLAGHAN one day, Fitzgerald referred to Hemingway's ability as a boxer, and remarked that while Hemingway was probably not good enough to be heavyweight champion of the world, he was undoubtedly as good as Young Stribling, the light heavyweight champion. "Look, Scott," said Callaghan, "Ernest is an amateur. I'm an amateur. All this talk is ridiculous." Unconvinced, Fitzgerald asked to come along to the gym at the American Club and watch Hemingway and Callaghan box. But Callaghan has let the reader in earlier on one small point. Hemingway, four inches taller and forty pounds heavier than Callaghan, "may have thought about boxing, dreamed about it, consorted with old fighters and hung around gyms," but Callaghan "had done more actual boxing with men who could box a little and weren't just taking exercise or fooling around."

So on a historic afternoon in June in Paris in 1929, Hemingway and Callaghan boxed a few rounds, with Fitzgerald serving as timekeeper. The second round went on for a long time. Both men began to get tired, Hemingway got careless. Callaghan caught him a good punch and dropped Hemingway on his back. At the next instant Fitzgerald cried out, "Oh, my God! I let the round go four minutes."

"All right, Scott," Ernest said. "If you want to see me getting the shit knocked out of me, just say so. Only don't say you made a mistake."

According to Callaghan's estimate, Scott never recovered from that moment. One believes it. For months later, a cruel and wildly inaccurate story about this episode appeared in the *Herald Tribune* book section. It was followed by a cable sent collect to Callaghan by Fitzgerald at Hemingway's insistence. HAVE SEEN STORY IN HERALD TRIBUNE. ERNEST AND I AWAIT YOUR CORREC-TION. SCOTT FITZGERALD.

Since Callaghan had already written such a letter to the paper, none of the three men could ever forgive each other.

The story offers a fine clue to the logic of Hemingway's mind, and tempts the prediction that there will be no definitive biography of Hemingway until the nature of his personal torture is better comprehended. It is possible Hemingway lived every day of his life in the style of the suicide. What a great dread is that. It is the dread that sits in the silences of his short declarative sentences. At any instant, by any failure in magic, by a mean defeat, or by a moment of cowardice, Hemingway could be thrust back again into the agonizing demands of his courage. For the life of his talent must have depended on living in a psychic terrain where one must either be brave beyond one's limit, or sicken closer into a bad illness, or, indeed, by the ultimate logic of the suicide, must advance the hour in which one would make another reconnaissance into one's death.

That may be why Hemingway turned in such fury on Fitzgerald. To be knocked down by a smaller man could only imprison him further into the dread he was forever trying to avoid. Each time his physical vanity suffered a defeat, he would be forced to embark on a new existential gamble with his life. So he would naturally think of Fitzgerald's little error as an act of treachery, for the result of that extra minute in the second round could only be a new bout of anxiety that would drive his instinct into ever more dangerous situations. Most men find their profoundest passion in looking for a way to escape their private and secret torture. It is not likely that Hemingway was a brave man who sought danger for the sake of the sensations it provided him.

What is more likely the truth of his long odyssey is that he struggled with his cowardice and against a secret lust to suicide all of
his life, that his inner landscape was a nightmare, and he spent
his nights wrestling with the gods. It may even be that the final
judgment on his work may come to the notion that what he
failed to do was tragic, but what he accomplished was heroic, for
it is possible he carried a weight of anxiety within him from day
to day that would have suffocated any man smaller than himself.
There are two kinds of brave men: those who are brave by the
grace of nature, and those who are brave by an act of will. It is the
merit of Callaghan's long anecdote that the second condition is
suggested to be Hemingway's own.

Some Children of the Goddess

(1963)

THE LAST TIME I remember talking about the novel was a year ago, last June or July, and it was in a conversation with Gore Vidal. We were reminiscing in mutually sour fashion over the various pirates, cutthroats, racketeers, assassins, pimps, rape artists, and general finks we had encountered on our separate travels through the literary world, and we went on at length, commenting—Gore with a certain bitter joy, I with some uneasiness—upon the decline of the novel in recent years. We were speaking as trade unionists. It was not that the American novel was necessarily less good than it had been immediately after the war, so much as that the people we knew seemed to care much less about novels. The working conditions were not as good. One rarely heard one's friends talking about a good new novel anymore; it was always an essay in some magazine or a new play which seemed to occupy the five minutes in a dinner party when writers are discussed rather than politicians, friends, society or, elevate us, foreign affairs. One could not make one's living writing good novels anymore. With an exception here and there, it had always been impossible, but not altogether—there had used to be the long chance of having a bestseller. Now with paperback books, even a serious novel with extraordinarily good reviews was lucky to sell thirty thousand copies—most people preferred to wait a year and read the book later in its cheap edition.

So we went on about that, and the professional mediocrity of book reviewers and the indifference of publishers, the lack of community among novelists themselves, the backbiting, the glee with which most of us listened to unhappy news about other novelists, the general distaste of the occupation—its lonely hours, its jealous practitioners, its demands on one's character, its assaults on one's ego, its faithlessness as inspiration, its ambushes as fashion. Since we had both begun again to work on a novel after many years of working at every other kind of writing, there was a pleasant irony to all we said. We were not really as bitter as we sounded.

Finally, I laughed. "Gore, admit it. The novel is like the Great Bitch in one's life. We think we're rid of her, we go on to other women, we take our pulse and decide that finally we're enjoying ourselves, we're free of her power, we'll never suffer her depredations again, and then we turn a corner on a street, and there's the Bitch smiling at us, and we're trapped. We're still trapped. We know the Bitch has still got us."

Vidal gave that twisted grin of admiration which is extracted from him when someone else has coined an image which could fit his style. "Indeed," he said, sighing, "the novel *is* the Great Bitch."

We've all had a piece of her, Nelson Algren, Jack Kerouac, myself, Ross Lockridge, Thomas Heggen, Truman Capote, John Horne Burns, Calder Willingham, Gore Vidal, Chandler Brossard, Walter Van Tilburg Clark, Vance Bourjaily, William Humphrey, Willard Motley, Wright Morris, William Gaddis, Alex Trocchi—as well as the writers I'm going to talk about here, specifically James Jones, William Styron, Joseph Heller, John Updike, Philip Roth, Jimmy Baldwin, William Burroughs, Saul Bellow, J. D. Salinger—and all the writers there's not been time to read or write about this trip: James Purdy, Walker Percy, J. F. Powers, Ken Kesey, John Hawkes, Mark Harris, Louis Auchin-

closs, John Hersey, Clancy Sigal, J. P. Donleavy, Bernard Malamud, and how many others I've missed, and all the women, all
the lady writers, bless them. But one cannot speak of a woman
having a piece of the Bitch.

Let me list the novels I wish to discuss. They are *The Thin Red
Line; Set This House on Fire; Naked Lunch; Catch-22; Rabbit, Run;
Letting Go; Another Country; Henderson the Rain King; Franny and
Zooey;* and *Raise High the Roof Beam, Carpenters.* They are not necessarily the best novels to have been written in America in the
last few years, although if one could pick the best ten books of
fiction which have been done in this country for the period, four
or five of the titles on my list might have to be included. I chose
these particular volumes by a particular test which might as well
be explained.

It is impossible to read each good novel as it comes out. If
you're trying to do your own work, it's distracting. Generally you
stay away from the work of contemporaries for a year or two at a
time: it saves a good deal of reading. It is amazing how many
much-touted novels disappear in eighteen months. The underlying force in book reviewing is journalism. The editor of a book
review has a section which he hopes to make as interesting to the
owner of the newspaper as any other department. If, for two or
three days, a newspaper is filled with news about a murder, one
can be certain it is treated implicitly as the most exciting murder
in the last twenty years. So with war novels, first novels, novels
about homosexuality, politics, novels by authors of the Establishment, and historical novels. If I had a chapter of a novel for each
review I've read of a new war novel which was said to be as good
as *The Naked and the Dead* or *From Here to Eternity,* I would have
fifty chapters. One never knows, of course. Maybe a few of these
books are as good as they're said to be, and even if they've since
disappeared, they will emerge again in ten or twenty years or in
a century, but it is easier and much more logical to ignore what
is said about a book when it first appears. There is too much direct and personal interest in the initial opinions, and much too
much logrolling. The editor of a large book review is of course
not owned by the Book-of-the-Month Club, but on the other

hand the editor would just as soon not give more than two or three bad reviews in a year to book club choices. Nor is his attitude dissimilar when it comes to choosing a reviewer for the novel which a big publishing house has chosen for its big book of the season. Robert Ruark, James Michener, Allen Drury will pick up their occasional roasts and slams, but considering how bad their books can be, it's impressive what attention they get. The slack (since a book review, depending on local tradition, can have just a certain proportion of good reviews) is taken up by misassigning small, determined literary types onto most of the really good novels, which then receive snide treatment and/or dismissal. *Catch-22*, for example, was reviewed on page fifty of *The New York Times Book Review*. Since this causes a vague uneasiness afterward in the book review editor, there are always good young writers like Updike and Roth who get on the approved list and get many too many good reviews from bad reviewers. The point is that any serious novelist knows enough to stay out of the flurry which hits a new book. Every year whether the books deserve it or not, four or five first novelists will be provided a brilliant debut and four or five respectable young novelists will receive the kind of review which "enhances their reputation as one of the most serious and dedicated voices in the vineyard of literature."

So you stay away. If your friends keep talking about certain books, and young writers, and girls at cocktail parties, if the talk is intriguing because as the months go by, you begin to have less and less of a clear impression of the books, then they come to install themselves on your reading list. And every year, or two years, or three, you go off on a binge for a month and gorge on the novels of your contemporaries and see how they made out on their night with the Bitch. But of course there are many books which you know are good and yet never get around to reading. For example, I had a lot of respect for *The Violated* by Vance Bourjaily. It gave me the feeling Bourjaily was capable of writing a major novel before he was through. His next book was *Confessions of a Spent Youth*. I dipped into it, and it seemed good to me, but it was good in the way of *The Violated;* it did not seem to go further. What I heard about it did not contradict my impression. So although Bourjaily was a friend, I never got around to reading *Confessions of a Spent Youth*. I still think that in ten years Bourjaily can be one of our four or five major novelists. He has great stamina and very decent insights which ride on a fine oil of humor, but the implicit logic of my method directed me away from Vance's last novel. It was not that I didn't think it would be good, but rather that I didn't think it would be different from what I expected. And when you're a professional and a gentleman gangster, your taste is for new weapons, not improvements on the old ones.

Now this emphasis upon the personal method of the critic may have justification. Trotsky once wrote that you can tell the truth by a comparison of the lies. Every novelist who has slept with the Bitch (only poets and writers of short stories have a *Muse*) comes away bragging afterward like a GI tumbling out of a whorehouse spree—"Man, I made her moan," goes the cry of the young writer. But the Bitch laughs afterward in her empty bed. "He was so sweet in the beginning," she declares, "but by the end he just went, 'Peep, peep, peep.' " A man lays his character on the line when he writes a novel. Anything in him which is lazy, or meretricious, or unthought-out, or complacent, or fearful, or overambitious, or terrified by the ultimate logic of his exploration, will be revealed in his book. Some writers are skillful at concealing their weaknesses, some have a genius for converting a weakness into an acceptable mannerism of style. (One can even go so far as to say that Hemingway could never write a really good long sentence, and so cultivated the art of the short, whereas Faulkner could never express the simple very simply, and so flowered a great garden in the thicket of nonstop prose.)

The notion is that a writer, no matter how great, is never altogether great; a small part of him remains a liar. Tolstoy evaded the depths which Dostoyevsky opened; in turn Dostoyevsky, lacking Tolstoy's majestic sense of the proportions of things, fled proportion and explored hysteria. A writer is recognized as great when his work is done, but while he is writing, he rarely feels so great. He is more likely to live with the anxiety of "Can I do it?

Should I let up here? Should I reconnoiter there? Will dread overwhelm me if I explore too far? or depression deaden me if I do not push on? Can I even do it?" As he writes, the writer is re-shaping his character. He is a better man and he is worse, once he has finished a book. Potentialities in him have been devel-oped, other talents have been sacrificed. He has made choices on his route and the choices have shaped him. By this under-standing, a genius is a man of large talent who has made many good choices and a few astounding ones. He has had the wit to discipline his cowardice and he has had the courage to be bold where others might cry insanity. Yet no matter how large his ge-nius, we can be certain of one thing—he could have been even greater. Dostoyevsky was a very great writer, but if he had tried to be even greater he would either have cracked up or found impe-tus to write the *Confessions of a Great Sinner.* And if he had, the history of the world might have been different for it. It is even possible that Dostoyevsky died in anguish, complimenting him-self not at all for *The Brothers Karamazov* but hating himself for having so wasted a part of his talent that the greatest novel of them all was not written and he went with terror into death be-lieving he had failed his Christ.

The example is extreme. Just so. There is a kind of critic who writes only about the dead. He sees the great writers of the past as simple men. They are born with a great talent, they exercise it, and they die. Such critics see the mastery in the work; they ne-glect the subtle failures of the most courageous intent, and the dramatic hours when the man took the leap to become a great writer. They do not understand that for every great writer, there are a hundred who could have been equally great but lacked the courage. For that reason it may be better to think of writers as pole vaulters than as artists. Pole vaulting is an act. The man who wins is the man who jumps the highest without knocking off the bar. And a man who clears the stick with precise form but eigh-teen inches below the record commands less of our attention. The writer, particularly the American writer, is not usually—if he is interesting—the quiet master of his craft; he is rather a being who ventured into the jungle of his unconscious to bring back a sense of order or a sense of chaos, he passes through ambushes in his sleep and, if he is ambitious, he must be ready to engage the congealed hostility of the world. If a writer is really good enough and bold enough he will, by the logic of society, write himself out onto the end of a limb which the world will saw off. He does not go necessarily to his death, but he must dare it. And some of us do go into death: Ross Lockridge, Thomas Heggen, Thomas Wolfe most especially, firing the passions which rotted his brain on those long paranoid nights in Brooklyn when he wrote in exaltation and terror on the top of a refrigerator. And Hemingway who dared death ten times over and would have had to dare it a hundred more in order to find more art, because each time he passed through death the sweet of new creativity was offered.

Well, few of us dare death. With the trinity of booze, coffee, and cigarettes, most of us voyage out a part of the way into our jungle and come back filled with pride at what we dared, and shame at what we avoided, and because we are men of the middle and shame is an emotion no man of the middle can bear for too long without dying, we act like novelists, which is to say that we are full of spleen, small gossip, hatred for the success of our enemies, envy at the fortunes of our friends, ideologues of a style of fiction which is uniquely the best (and is invariably our own style), and so there is a tendency for us to approach the books of our contemporaries like a defense attorney walking up to a key witness for the prosecution. The average good novelist reads the work of his fellow racketeers with one underlying tension—find the flaw, find where the other guy cheated.

One cannot expect an objective performance therefore when one novelist criticizes the work of other novelists. It is better to realize that a group of men who are to a degree honest and to another extent deceitful (to the reader, or to themselves, or to both) are being judged by one of their peers who shares in the rough their proportions of integrity and pretense and is likely to have the most intense vested interest in advancing the reputation of certain writers while doing his best to diminish others. But the reader is at least given the opportunity to compare the lies, a gratuity he cannot always get from a good critic writing about a novelist, for critics implant into their style the fiction of disinterested passion when indeed *their* vested interest, while less obvious, is often more rabid, since they have usually fixed their aim into the direction they would like the novel to travel, whereas the novelist by the nature of his endeavor is more ready to change. One need not defend the procedure used here any further than to say it is preferable to warn a reader of one's prejudices than to believe the verdict of a review which is godly in its authority and psychologically unsigned.

I doubt if there is any book I read in the last few years which I approached with more unnatural passion than *Set This House on Fire*. Styron's first novel, *Lie Down in Darkness,* was published when he was twenty-six, and it was so good (one need today only compare it to *Rabbit, Run* to see how very good it was) that one felt a kind of awe about Styron. He gave promise of becoming a great writer, great not like Hemingway nor even like Faulkner, whom he resembled a bit, but great perhaps like Hawthorne. And there were minor echoes of Fitzgerald and Malcolm Lowry. Since his first novel had failed to make him a household word in America, he had a justifiable bitterness about the obscurity in which good young writers were kept. But it poisoned his reaction to everything. One of the traps for a writer of exceptional talent, recognized insufficiently, is the sort of excessive rage which washes out distinction. Styron was intensely competitive—all good young novelists are—but over the years envy began to eat into his character. Months before James Jones's *Some Came Running* was published (and it had the greatest advance publicity of any novel I remember—for publicity seemed to begin two years before publication), Styron obtained a copy of the galleys. There were long nights in Connecticut on "Styron's Acres" when he would entertain a group of us by reading absurd passages from Jones's worst prose. I would laugh along with the rest, but I was a touch sick with myself. I had love for Jones, as well as an oversized fear for the breadth of his talent, and I had enough envy in me to enjoy how very bad were the worst parts of *Some Came Running*. But there were long powerful chapters as well; some of the best writing Jones has ever done is found in that book. So I would laugh in paroxysms along with the others, but I was also realizing that a part of me had wanted *Some Came Running* to be a major book. I was in the doldrums, I needed a charge of dynamite. If *Some Came Running* had turned out to be the best novel any of us had written since the war, I would have had to get to work. It would have meant the Bitch was in love with someone else, and I would have had to try to win her back. But the failure of *Some Came Running* left me holding on to a buttock of the lady—if she had many lovers, I was still one of them. And so everything in me which was slack and conservative could enjoy Styron's burlesque readings. Yet I also knew I had lost an opportunity.

A few months later, I ceased seeing Styron—it would take a chapter in a novel to tell you why. I liked the boy in Styron, disliked the man, and had vast admiration for his talent. I was hardly the one to read *Set This House on Fire* with a cool mind. Nine years had gone by since *Lie Down in Darkness* was published, and the anticipation of the second novel had taken on grandiloquent proportions among his friends and his closest enemies. One knew it would be close to unbearable if his book were extraordinary; yet a part of me felt again what I had known with *Some Came Running*—that it would be good for me and for my work if Styron's novel were better than anything any of us had done. So I read it with a hot sense of woe, delighted elation, and a fever of moral speculations. Because it was finally a bad novel. A bad maggoty novel. Four or five half-great short stories were buried like pullulating organs in a corpse of fecal matter, overblown unconceived philosophy, Technicolor melodramatics, and a staggering ignorance about the passions of murder, suicide, and rape. It was the magnum opus of a fat spoiled rich boy who could write like an angel about landscape and like an adolescent about people. The minor characters were gargoyles, and badly drawn. Here and there quick portraits emerged, there was one excellent still life of an Italian police official who was Fascist, the set pieces were laid out nicely, but the vice of the talent insisted on dominating. Whenever Styron didn't know what to do with his men and women (which was often, for they repeated themselves as endlessly as a Southern belle), Styron went back to his landscape; more of the portentous Italian scenery blew up its midnight storm. But Styron was trying to write a book about good and evil, and his good was as vacuous as the spirit of an empty water bag:

> I can only tell you this, that as for being and nothing-
> ness, the one thing I did know was that to choose be-
> tween them was simply to choose being, not for the sake
> of being, or even the love of being, much less the desire
> to be forever—but in the hope of being what I could be
> for a time.

Which is a great help to all of us.

His evil character took on the fatal sin of an evil character: he was not dangerous but pathetic. A fink. Styron was crawling with all ten thumbs toward that ogre of mystery who guards the secrets of why we choose to kill others and quiver in dread at the urge to kill ourselves. But like a bad general who surrounds himself with a staff which daren't say no, Styron spent his time digging trenches for miles to the left and miles to the right, and never launched an attack on the hill before him. It was the book of a man whose soul had gotten fat.

And yet, much as I could be superior to myself for having taken him thus seriously, for having written predictions in *Advertisements for Myself* that he would write a very good book which the mass media would call great, much as I would grin each day after reading a hundred pages of hothouse beauty and butter bilge, much as I would think, "You don't catch the Bitch that way, buster, you got to bring more than a trombone to her boudoir," much so much as I was pleased at the moral justice which forbids a novelist who envied too much the life of others to capture much life in his own pages, I was still not altogether happy, because I knew his failure was making me complacent again, and so delaying once more the day when I would have to pay my respects to the lady.

And indeed I lost something by the failure of *Some Came Running* and *Set This House on Fire.* I never did get going far on my novel. I wrote a four-hour play and essays and articles, two hundred thousand words accumulated over the years since *Advertisements for Myself,* and I showed a talent for getting into stunts, and worse, much worse. Years went by. Now once again, in this season, ready to start my novel about the mysteries of murder and suicide,* I found by taking stock of psychic credit and debit that I had lost some of my competitive iron. I knew a bit of sadness about work. I did not feel sure I could do what I had now settled for doing, and to my surprise I was curious what others were up to. If I couldn't bring off the work by myself, it might be just as well if someone else could give a sign of being ready to make the attempt. In this sad dull mellow mood, feeling a little like a middle-aged mountaineer, I read at one stretch over three weeks the novels I want to write about here.

There was a time, I suspect, when James Jones wanted to be the greatest writer who ever lived. Now, if *The Thin Red Line* is evidence of his future, he has apparently decided to settle for being a very good writer among other good writers. The faults and barbarities of his style are gone. He is no longer the worst writer of prose ever to give intimations of greatness. The language has been filed down and the phrases no longer collide like trailer trucks at a hot intersection. Yet I found myself nostalgic for the old bad prose. I never used to think it was as bad as others did, it was eloquent and communicated Jones's force to the reader. It is not that *The Thin Red Line* is dishonest or narrow; on the contrary it is so broad and true a portrait of combat that it could be used as a textbook at the Infantry School if the Army is any less chicken than it used to be. But, sign of the times, there is now something almost too workmanlike about Jones. He gets almost everything in, horror, fear, fatigue, the sport of combat, the

* This novel was a continuation thematically of the long novel announced in *Advertisements for Myself.* It was put aside six months later to go to work on *An American Dream.*

hang-ups, details, tactics; he takes an infantry company through its early days in combat on Guadalcanal and quits it a few weeks later as a veteran outfit, blooded, tough, up on morale despite the loss of half the original men, gone, dead, wounded, sick, or transferred. So he performs the virtuoso feat of letting us know a little about a hundred men. One can even (while reading) remember their names. Jones's aim, after all, is not to create character but the feel of combat, the psychology of men. He is close to a master at this. Jones has a strong sense of a man's psychology and it carries quietly through his pages.

The Thin Red Line was of course compared to The Naked and the Dead, but apart from the fact that I am the next-to-last man to judge the respective merits of the two books, I didn't see them as similar. The Naked and the Dead is concerned more with characters than military action. By comparison it's a leisurely performance. The Thin Red Line is as crammed as a movie treatment. No, I think the real comparison is to The Red Badge of Courage, and I suspect The Red Badge of Courage will outlive The Thin Red Line. Yet I don't quite know why. The Thin Red Line is a more detailed book; it tells much more of combat, studies the variations in courage and fear of not one man but twenty men and gets something good about each one of them. Its knowledge of life is superior to The Red Badge of Courage. The Thin Red Line is less sentimental, its humor is dry to the finest taste, and yet . . . it is too technical. One needs ten topographical maps to trace the action. With all its variety, scrupulosity, respect for craft, one doesn't remember The Thin Red Line with that same nostalgia, that same sense of a fire on the horizon which comes back always from The Red Badge of Courage.

No, Jones's book is better remembered as satisfying, as if one had studied geology for a semester and now knew more. I suppose what was felt lacking is the curious sensuousness of combat, the soft lift of awe and pleasure that one was moving out onto the rim of the dead. If one was not too tired, there were times when a blade of grass coming out of the ground before one's nose was as significant as the finger of Jehovah in the Sistine Chapel. And this was not because a blade of grass was necessarily in itself so beautiful, or because hitting the dirt was so sweet, but because the blade seemed to be a living part of the crack of small-arms fire and the palpable flotation of all the other souls in the platoon full of turd and glory. Now, it's not that Jones is altogether ignorant of this state. The description he uses is "sexy," and one of the nicest things about Jim as a writer is his ease in moving from mystical to practical reactions with his characters. Few novelists can do this, it's the hint of greatness, but I think he steered *The Thin Red Line* away from its chance of becoming an American classic of the first rank when he kept the mystical side of his talents on bread and water, and gave his usual thoroughgoing company man's exhibition of how much he knows technically about his product. I think that is the mistake. War is as full of handbooks as engineering, but it is more of a mystery, and the mystery is what separates the great war novels from the good ones. It is an American activity to cover the ground quickly, but I guess this is one time Jones should have written two thousand pages, not four hundred ninety-five. But then the underlying passion in this book is not to go for broke, but to promise the vested idiots of the book reviews that he can write as good as anyone who writes a book review.

When you discuss eight or ten books, there is a dilemma. The choice is to write eight separate book reviews, or work to find a thesis which ties the books together. There is something lickspittle about the second method: "Ten Authors in Search of a Viable Theme," or "The Sense of Alienation in Eight American Novelists." A bed of Procrustes is brought in from the wings to stretch and shorten the separate qualities of the books. I would rather pick up each book by itself and make my connections on the fly. The thesis of the Bitch is thesis enough for me. Its application to Jones would say that *The Thin Red Line* is a holding action, a long distance call to the Goddess to declare that one still has one's hand in, expect red roses for sure, but for the time, you know, like there're contacts to make on the road, and a few johns to impress.

Another Country, by James Baldwin, is as different from *The Thin Red Line* as two books by talented novelists published in the same year can turn out to be. It does not deal with a hundred characters, but eight, and they are very much related. In fact there is a chain of fornication which is all but complete. A Negro musician named Rufus Scott has an affair with a white Southern girl which ends in beatings, breakdown, and near-insanity. She goes to a mental hospital, he commits suicide. The connection is taken up by his sister who has an affair with a white writer, a friend of Rufus's named Vivaldo Moore, who in turn gets into bed with a friend named Eric who is homosexual but having an affair with a married woman named Cass Silenski, which affair wrecks her marriage with her husband, Richard, another writer, and leaves Eric waiting at the boat for his French lover Yves. A summary of this sort can do a book no good, but I make it to trace the links. With the exception of Rufus Scott, who does not go to bed with his sister, everybody else in the book is connected by their skin to another character who is connected to still another. So the principal in the book, the protagonist, is not an individual character, not society, not a milieu, not a social organism like an infantry company, but indeed is sex, sex very much in the act. And almost the only good writing in the book is about the act. And some of that is very good indeed. But *Another Country* is a shocker. For the most part it is an abominably written book. It is sluggish in its prose, lifeless for its first hundred pages, stilted to despair in its dialogue. There are roles in plays called actorproof. They are so conceived that even the worst actor will do fairly well. So *Another Country* is writerproof. Its peculiar virtue is that Baldwin commits every gaffe in the art of novel writing and yet has a powerful book. It gets better of course; after the first hundred pages it gets a lot better. Once Eric, the homosexual, enters, the work picks up considerably. But what saves the scene is that Baldwin has gotten his hands into the meat and won't let go. All the sex in the book is displaced, whites with blacks, men with men, women with homosexuals; the sex is funky to suffocation, rich but claustrophobic, sensual but airless. Baldwin understands the existential abyss of love. In a world of Negroes and whites, nuclear fallout, marijuana, bennies, inversion, insomnia, and tapering off with beer at four in the morning, one no longer just falls in love—one has to take a brave leap over the wall of one's impacted rage and cowardice. And nobody makes it, not quite. Each of the characters rides his sexual chariot, whip out, on a gallop over a solitary track, and each is smashed, more or less by his own hand. They cannot find the juice to break out of their hatred into the other country of love. Except for the homosexuals who can't break into heterosexual love. Of all the novels talked about here, *Another Country* is the one which is closest to the mood of New York in our time, a way of saying it is close to the air of the Western world, it is at least a novel about matters which are important, but one can't let up on Baldwin for the way he wrote it. Years ago I termed him "minor" as a writer; I thought he was too smooth and too small. Now on his essays alone, on the long continuing line of poetic fire in his essays, one knows he has become one of the few writers of our time. But as a Negro novelist he could take lessons from a good journeyman like John Killens. Because *Another Country* is almost a major novel and yet it is far and away the weakest and worst near-major novel one has finished. It goes like the first draft of a first novelist who has such obvious stuff that one is ready, if an editor, to spend years guiding him into how to write, even as one winces at the sloppy company which must be kept. Nobody has more elegance than Baldwin as an essayist, not one of us hasn't learned something about the art of the essay from him, and yet he can't even find a good prose for his novel. Maybe the form is not for him. He knows what he wants to say, and that is not the best condition for writing a novel. Novels go happiest when you discover something you did not know you knew. Baldwin's experience has shaped his tongue toward directness, for urgency—the honorable defense may be that he has not time nor patience to create characters, milieu, and mood for the revelation of important complexities he has already classified in his mind.

Baldwin's characters maim themselves trying to smash through the wall of their imprisonment. William Burroughs gives what may be the finest record in our century of the complete psychic

convict. *Naked Lunch* is a book of pieces and fragments, notes
and nightmarish anecdotes, which he wrote—according to his
preface—in various states of delirium, going in and out of a heroin addiction. It is not a novel in any conventional sense, but
then there's a question whether it's a novel by any set of standards other than the dictum that prose about imaginary people
put between book covers is a novel. At any rate, the distinction is
not important except for the fact that *Naked Lunch* is next to impossible to read in consecutive fashion. I saw excerpts of it years
ago, and thought enough of them to go on record that Burroughs "may conceivably be possessed by genius." I still believe
that, but it is one thing to be possessed by genius, it is another to
be a genius, and *Naked Lunch* read from cover to cover is not as
exciting as in its separate pieces. Quantity changes quality, as
Karl Marx once put it, and fifty or sixty three-page bits about
homosexual orgies, castration, surgeon-assassins, and junkie fuzz
dissolving into a creeping green ooze leaves one feeling pretty
tough. "Let's put some blue-purple blood in the next rape," says
your jaded taste.

This is, however, quibbling. Some of the best prose in America
is graffiti found on men's-room walls. It is prose written in bone,
etched by acid, it is the prose of harsh truth, the virulence of the
criminal who never found his stone walls and so settles down on
the walls of the john, it is the language of hatred unencumbered
by guilt, hesitation, scruple, or complexity. Burroughs must be
the greatest writer of graffiti who ever lived. His style has the
snap of a whip, and it never relents. Every paragraph is quotable.
Here's a jewel among a thousand jewels:

> Dr. Benway . . . looks around and picks up one of those
> rubber vacuum cups at the end of a stick they use to
> unstop toilets . . . "Make an incision, Doctor Limpf. . . .
> I'm going to massage the heart." . . . Dr. Benway washes
> the suction cup by swishing it around in the toilet-
> bowl. . . .
>   Dr. Limpf: "The incision is ready, doctor."
>   Dr. Benway forces the cup into the incision and works

it up and down. Blood spurts all over the doctors, the nurse and the wall. . . .

Nurse: "I think she's gone, doctor."

Dr. Benway: "Well, it's all in the day's work."

Punch and Judy. Mr. Interlocutor and Mr. Bones. One, two, three, bam! Two, four, eight, bam! The drug addict lives with a charged wire so murderous he must hang his nervous system on a void. Burroughs's achievement, his great achievement, is that he has brought back snowflakes from this murderous void.

Once, years ago in Chicago, I was coming down with a bad cold. By accident, a friend took me to hear a jazz musician named Sun Ra who played "space music." The music was a little like the sound of Ornette Coleman, but further out, outer space music, close to the *eeee* of an electric drill at the center of a harsh trumpet. My cold cleared up in five minutes. I swear it. The anger of the sound penetrated into some sprung–up rage which was burning fuel for the cold. Burroughs's pages have the same medicine. If a hundred patients on terminal cancer read *Naked Lunch,* one or two might find remission. Bet money on that. For Burroughs is the surgeon of the novel.

Yet he is something more. It is his last ability which entitles him to a purchase on genius. Through the fantasies runs a vision of a future world, a half-demented welfare state, an abattoir of science fiction with surgeons, bureaucrats, perverts, diplomats, a world not describable short of getting into the book. The ideas have pushed into the frontier of an all-electronic universe. One holds on to a computer in some man-eating machine of the future which has learned to use language. The words come out in squeaks, spiced with static, sex coiled up with technology like a scream on the radar. Bombarded by his language, the sensation is like being in a room where three radios, two television sets, stereo hi-fi, a pornographic movie, and two automatic dishwashers are working at once while a mad scientist conducts the dials to squeeze out the maximum disturbance. If this is a true picture of the world to come, and it may be, then Burroughs is a great writer. Yet there is sadness in reading him, for one gets intimations of a mind which might have come within distance of Joyce, except that a catastrophe has been visited on it, a blow by a sledgehammer, a junkie's needle which left the crystalline brilliance crashed into bits.

Now beyond a doubt, of all the books discussed here, the one which most cheats evaluation is Joseph Heller's *Catch*-22. It was the book which took me longest to finish, and I almost gave it up. Yet I think that a year from now I may remember it more vividly than *The Thin Red Line*. Because it is an original. There's no book like it anyone has read. Yet it's maddening. It reminds one of a Jackson Pollock painting eight feet high, twenty feet long. Like yard goods, one could cut it anywhere. One could take out a hundred pages anywhere from the middle of *Catch*-22 and not even the author could be certain they were gone. Yet the length and similarity of one page to another gives a curious meat-and-potatoes to the madness; building upon itself the book becomes substantial until the last fifty pages grow suddenly and surprisingly powerful, only to be marred by an ending over the last five pages which is hysterical, sentimental, and wall-eyed for Hollywood.

This is the skin of the reaction. If I were a major critic, it would be a virtuoso performance to write a definitive piece on *Catch*-22. It would take ten thousand words or more. Because Heller is carrying his reader on a more consistent voyage through Hell than any American writer before him (except Burroughs who has already made the trip and now sells choice seats in the auditorium), and so the analysis of Joseph H.'s Hell would require a discussion of other varieties of inferno and whether they do more than this author's tour.

Catch-22 is a nightmare about an American bomber squadron on a made-up island off Italy. Its hero is a bombardier named Yossarian who has flown fifty missions and wants out. On this premise is tattooed the events of the novel, fifty characters, two thousand frustrations (an average of four or five to the page), and one simple motif: more frustration. Yossarian's colonel wants to impress his general and so raises the number of missions to fifty-five. When the pilots have fifty-four, the figure is lifted to sixty. They are going for eighty by the time the book has been done. On the way every character goes through a routine *on every page* which is as formal as a little peasant figure in a folk dance. Back in school, we had a joke we used to repeat. It went:

"Whom are you talking about?"

"Herbert Hoover."

"Never heard of him."

"Never heard of whom?"

"Herbert Hoover."

"Who's he?"

"He's the man you mentioned."

"Never heard of Herbert Hoover."

So it went. So goes *Catch-22*. It's the rock and roll of novels. One finds its ancestor in basic training. We were ordered to have clean sheets for Saturday inspection. But one week we were given no clean sheets from the post laundry so we slept on our mattress covers, which got dirty. After inspection, the platoon was restricted to quarters. "You didn't have clean sheets," our sergeant said.

"How could we have clean sheets if the clean sheets didn't come?"

"How do I know?" said the sergeant. "The regulations say you gotta have clean sheets."

"But we can't have clean sheets if there are no clean sheets."

"That," said the sergeant, "is tough shit."

Which is what *Catch-22* should have been called. The Army is a village of colliding bureaucracies whose colliding orders cook up impossibilities. Heller takes this one good joke and exploits it into two thousand variations of the same good joke, but in the act he somehow creates a rational vision of the modern world. Yet the crisis of reason is that it can no longer comprehend the modern world. Heller demonstrates that a rational man devoted to reason must arrive at the conclusion that either the world is mad and he is the only sane man in it, or (and this is the weakness of *Catch-22*—it never explores this possibility) the sane man is not really sane because his rational propositions are without existential reason.

On page 178, there is a discussion about God.

> "how much reverence can you have for a Supreme Being who finds it necessary to include such phenomena as phlegm and tooth decay in His divine system of creation. . . . Why in the world did He ever create pain?"
>
> "Pain?" Lieutenant Scheisskopf's wife pounced upon the word victoriously. "Pain is a useful symptom. Pain is a warning to us of bodily dangers."
>
> . . . "Why couldn't he have used a doorbell instead to notify us, or one of His celestial choirs?"

Right there is planted the farthest advance of the flag of reason in his cosmology. Heller does not look for any answer, but there is an answer which might go that God gave us pain for the same reason the discovery of tranquilizers was undertaken by the Devil: if we have an immortal soul some of us come close to it only through pain. A season of sickness can be preferable to a flight from disease, for it discourages the onrush of a death which begins in the center of oneself.

Give talent its due. *Catch-22* is the debut of a writer with merry gifts. Heller may yet become Gogol. But what makes one hesitate to call his first novel great or even major is that he has only grasped the inferior aspect of Hell. What is most unendurable is not the military world of total frustration so much as the midnight frustration of the half world, Baldwin's other country, where a man may have time to hear his soul, and time to go deaf, even be forced to contemplate himself as he becomes deadened before his death. (Much as Hemingway may have been.) That is when one becomes aware of the anguish, the existential angst, which wars enable one to forget. It is that other death—without war—where one dies by a failure of nerve, which opens the bloodiest vents of Hell. And that is a novel none of us has yet come back alive to write.

With the exception of *Another Country,* the novels talked about up to now have been books written for men. *Catch-22* was liked, I believe, by almost every man who read it. Women were puzzled. The world of a man is a world of surface slick and rock knowledge. A man must live by daily acts where he goes to work and works on the world some incremental bit, using the tools, instruments, and the techniques of the world. Thus a man cannot afford to go too deeply into the underlying meaning of a single subject. He prefers to become interested in quick proportions and contradictions, in the practical surface of things. A book like *Catch-22* is written on the face of solemn events and their cockeyed contradictions. So it has a vast appeal: it relieves the frustration men feel at the idiocy of their work. *Naked Lunch* fries the surface in a witch's skillet; the joy in reading is equal to the kick of watching a television announcer go insane before your eyes and start to croon obscenely about the president, First Lady, Barry Goldwater, Cardinal Spellman, J. Edgar. Somewhere in America somebody would take out his pistol and shoot the set. Burroughs shatters the surface and blasts its shards into the madness beneath. He rips the reader free of suffocation. Jones wrote a book which a dedicated corporation executive or an ambitious foreman would read with professional avidity because they would learn a bit about the men who work for them. *The Thin Red Line* brings detail to the surprises on the toughest part of the skin. So these three books are, as I say, books for men. Whereas *Another Country,* obsessed with that transcendental divide keeping sex from love, is a book more for women, or for men and women. So too is *Set This House on Fire.* And much the same can be said of *Rabbit, Run* and *Letting Go.*

On record are the opinions of a partisan. So it is necessary to admit that John Updike's novel was approached with animus. His reputation has traveled in convoy up the Avenue of the Establishment, *The New York Times Book Review* blowing sirens like a motorcycle caravan, the professional muse of *The New Yorker* sitting in the Cadillac, membership cards to the right, fellowships in his pocket. The sort of critics who are rarely right about a book—Arthur Mizener and Granville Hicks, for example—ride on his flanks, literary bodyguards. *Life* magazine blew its kiss of death into the confetti. To my surprise, *Rabbit, Run* was therefore a better book than I thought it would be. The Literary Establishment was improving its taste. Updike was not simply a junior edition of James Gould Cozzens. But of course the Establishment cannot nominate a candidate coherently. Updike's merits and vices were turned inside out. The good-girlish gentlemen of letters were shocked by the explicitness of the sex in *Rabbit, Run,* and slapped him gently for that with their fan, but his style they applauded. It is Updike's misfortune that he is invariably honored for his style (which is atrocious—and smells like stale garlic) and is insufficiently recognized for his gifts. He could become the best of our literary novelists if he could forget about style and go deeper into the literature of sex. *Rabbit, Run* moves in well-modulated spurts at precisely those places where the style subsides to a ladylike murmur and the characters take over. The trouble is that young John, like many a good young writer before him, does not know exactly what to do when action lapses, and so he cultivates his private vice, he *writes.* And there are long overfingered descriptions in exacerbated syntax, airless crypts of four or five pages, huge inner exertions reminiscent of weight lifters; a stale sweet sweat clings to his phrases.

Example: *Redbook, Cosmopolitan, McCall's.*

Boys are playing basketball around a telephone pole with a backboard bolted to it. Legs, shouts. The scrape and snap of Keds on loose alley pebbles seems to catapult their voices high into the moist March air blue above the wires. Rabbit Angstrom, coming up the alley in a business suit, stops and watches, though he's twenty-six and six-three. So tall, he seems an unlikely rabbit, but the breadth of white face, the pallor of his blue irises, and a nervous flutter under his brief nose as he stabs a cigarette into his mouth partially explain the nickname.

Example: *True Confessions.*

Outside in the air his fears condense. Globes of ether, pure nervousness, slide down his legs. The sense of outside space scoops at his chest.

Example: *Elements of Grammar.*

His hands lift of their own and he feels the wind on his ears even before, his heels hitting heavily on the pavement at first but with an effortless gathering out of a kind of sweet panic growing lighter and quicker and quieter, he runs. Ah: runs. Runs.

It's the rare writer who cannot have sentences lifted from his work, but the first quotation is taken from the first five sentences of the book, the second is on the next-to-last page, and the third is nothing less than the last three sentences of the novel. The beginning and end of a novel are usually worked over. They are the index to taste in the writer. Besides, trust your local gangster. In the run of Updike's pages are one thousand other imprecise, flatulent, wry-necked, precious, overpreened, self-indulgent, tortured sentences. It is the sort of prose which would be admired in a writing course overseen by a fussy old nance. And in Updike's new book, *The Centaur,* which was only sampled, the style has gotten worse. Pietisms are congregating, affirmations à la Archibald MacLeish.

The pity is that Updike has instincts for finding the heart of the conventional novel, that still-open no-man's-land between the surface and the deep, the soft machinery of the world and the subterranean rigors of the dream. His hero, Rabbit Angstrom, is sawed in two by the clear anguish of watching his private vision go at a gallop away from the dread real weight of his responsibility. A routine story of a man divided between a dull wife he cannot bear to live with and a blowsy tough tender whore he cannot make it with, the merit of the book is not in the simplicity of its problem, but in the dread Updike manages to convey, despite the literary commercials in the style, of a young man who is beginning to lose nothing less than his good American soul, and yet it is not quite his fault. The power of the novel comes from a sense, not absolutely unworthy of Thomas Hardy, that the universe hangs over our fates like a great sullen hopeless sky. There is real pain in the book, and a touch of awe. It is a novel which could have been important, it could have had a chance to stay alive despite its mud pies in prose, but at the very end the book drowns in slime. Updike does not know how to finish. Faced with the critical choice of picking one woman or another (and by the end, both women are in fearful need), his character bolts over a literal hill and runs away. Maybe he'll be back tomorrow, maybe he'll never be back, but a decision was necessary. The book ends as minor, a pop-out. One is left with the expectation that Updike will never be great; there is something too fatally calculated about his inspiration. But very good he can be, a good writer of the first rank with occasional echoes from the profound. First he must make an enemy or two of the commissioners on the Literary Mafia. Of course a man spends his life trying to get up his guts for such a caper.

Letting Go, by Philip Roth, has precisely the opposite merits and faults. As a novel, its strategy is silly, tiresome, and weak. But its style, while not noteworthy, is decent and sometimes, in dialogue, halfway nice. It is good time spent to read any ten pages in the book. The details are observed, the mood is calm, the point is always made. It is like having an affair with a pleasant attentive woman—the hours go by neatly. It is only at the end of a year that one may realize the preoccupations of the mistress are hollow, and the seasons have been wasted.

Letting Go is a scrupulous account in upper Jewish New Yorker genre of a few years in the lives of two English department college instructors, one married to that most coveted of creatures, a fragile dreary hang-up of a heroine, the other a bachelor and

lover of worried proportions. Very little happens. The wife goes
on being herself, the husband remains naturally frozen and
stingy, and the instructor-lover has a small literary breakdown.
One can say, well isn't this life? Didn't Chekhov and de Maupassant write about such things? And the answer is yes they did, in
five pages they did, and caught that mood which reminds us that
there is sadness in attrition and grinding sorrows for decency.
But Roth is not writing a book with a vision of life; on the contrary, one could bet a grand he is working out an obsession. His
concentration is appropriated by something in his life which has
been using him up in the past. Virtually every writer, come soon
or late, has a cramped-up love affair which is all but hopeless. *Of
Human Bondage* could be the case study of half the writers who
ever lived. But the obsession is opposed to art in the same way a
compulsive talker is opposed to good conversation. The choice
is either to break the obsession or enter it. The compulsive talker
must go through the herculean transformation of learning to
quit or must become a great monologuist. Roth tried to get into
the obsession—he gave six hundred pages to wandering around
in a ten-page story—but he did it without courage. He was too
careful not to get hurt on his trip and so he does not reveal himself: he does not *dig*. The novel skitters like a water fly from pollen spread to pollen spread; a series of good short stories
accumulate en route, but no novel. The iron law of the conventional novel, the garden novel, is that the meaning of the action
must grow on every page or else the book will wither. It is Updike's respectable achievement in *Rabbit, Run* that he writes just
such a book, or tries to until the last three pages when he van-
ishes like a sneak thief. Roth never gets into the game. One
senses a determined fight to maintain *Letting Go* as a collection
of intricately intercollected short stories.

But the short story has a tendency to look for climates of per-
manence—an event occurs, a man is hurt by it in some small way
forever. The novel moves as naturally toward flux. An event occurs, a man is injured, and a month later is working on something else. The short story likes to be classic. It is most acceptable
when one fatal point is made. Whereas the novel is dialectical. It

is most alive when one can trace the disasters which follow victory or the subtle turns that sometimes come from a defeat. A novel can be created out of short stories only if the point in each story is consecutively more interesting and incisive than the point before it, when the author in effect is drilling for oil. But Roth's short stories in *Letting Go* just dig little holes in many suburban lawns until finally the work of reading it becomes almost as depressing as must have been the work of writing it. Roth has to make a forced march in his next book, or at least, like Updike, get around to putting his foot in the whorehouse door. If he doesn't, a special Hell awaits his ambition—he will be called the rich man's Paddy Chayefsky, and Paddy without his grasp of poverty is nothing much at all.

It is necessary to say that the four stories about the Glass family by J. D. Salinger, published in two books called *Franny and Zooey* and *Raise High the Roof Beam, Carpenters,* seem to have been written for high school girls. The second piece in the second book, called *Seymour—An Introduction,* must be the most slovenly portion of prose ever put out by an important American writer. It is not even professional Salinger. Salinger at his customary worst, as here in the other three stories of the two books, is never bad—he is just disappointing. He stays too long on the light ice of his gift, writes exquisite dialogue and creates minor moods with sweetness and humor, and never gives the fish its hook. He disappoints because he is always practicing. But when he dips into Seymour, the Glass brother who committed suicide, when the cult comes to silence before the appearance of the star—the principal, to everyone's horror, has nausea on the stage. Salinger for the first time is engaged in run-off writing, free suffragette prose; his inhibitions (which once helped by their restraint to create his style) are now stripped. He is giving you himself as he is. No concealment. It feels like taking a bath in a grease trap.

Now, all of us have written as badly. There are nights when one comes home after a cancerously dull party, full of liquor but not drunk, leaden with boredom, somewhere out in Fitzgerald's long dark night. Writing at such a time is like making love at such a time. It is hopeless, it desecrates one's future, but one does it anyway because at least it is an act. Such writing is almost always unsprung. It is reminiscent of the wallflower who says, "To hell with inhibitions, I'm going to dance." The premise is that what comes out is valid because it is the record of a mood. So one records the mood. What a mood. Full of vomit, self-pity, panic, paranoia, megalomania, merde, whimpers, excuses, turns of the neck, flips of the wrist, transports. It is the bends of Hell. If you purge it, if you get sleep and tear it up in the morning, it can do no more harm than any other bad debauch. But Salinger went ahead and reread his stew, then sent it to *The New Yorker,* and they accepted it. Now, several years later, he reprints it in book covers.

There is social process at work here. Salinger was the most gifted minor writer in America. *The New Yorker*'s ability is to produce such writers. The paradox comes from the social fact that *The New Yorker* is a major influence on American life. Hundreds of thousands, perhaps millions of people in the most established parts of the middle class kill their quickest impulses before they dare to act in such a way as to look ridiculous to the private eye of their taste whose style has been keyed by the eye of *The New Yorker.* Salinger was the finest writer *The New Yorker* ever produced, but profoundly minor. The major writer like James Jones, indeed James Jones, leads the kind of inner life which enables him to study victories as well as defeats; Salinger was catapulted by a study of excruciating small defeats into a position of major importance. The phenomenon in the nation was the same those years. Men of minor abilities engaged America in major brinkmanships.

But it is always dangerous when the Literary Mafia (*The New Yorker,* the *Saturday Review, The New York Times Book Review, Time* magazine's book reviews, and the genteel elements in publishing) promote a minor writer into a major writer. A vested interest attaches itself to keeping the corpse of the violated standards buried. Readers who might be average keen in their sense of literary value find their taste mucked up. The greatest damage in this case, however, seems to have been to Salinger himself. Because a writer, with aristocratic delicacy of intent and nerves so subtle that only isolation makes life bearable for him, has been allowed to let his talent fester in that corrupt isolation. Salinger has been the most important writer in America for a generation of adolescents and college students. He was their leader in exile. The least he owed them for his silence was a major performance.

But it's a rare man who can live like a hermit and produce a major performance unless he has critics who are near to him and hard on him. No friend who worried about Salinger's future should have let him publish *Seymour—An Introduction* in *The New Yorker* without daring to lose his friendship first by telling him how awful it was. Yet there was too much depending on Salinger's interregnum—he was so *inoffensive,* finally. So a suspension of the critical faculty must have gone on in the institutional wheels of *The New Yorker* which was close to psychotic in its evasions.

As for the other three stories in the two books, they are not as good as the stories in *Nine Stories.* Affectations which were part once of Salinger's charm are now faults. An excessive desire to please runs through his pages. There is too much sweetness. He is too pleased with himself, too nice, he lingers too much over the happy facility of his details in a way Fitzgerald never would. He is no longer a writer so much as he is an entertainer, a slim much-beloved version of Al Jolson or Sophie Tucker; the music hall is in the root of his impulse as much as the dungeons and mansions of literature. Does one desire the real irony? There is nothing in *Franny and Zooey* which would hinder it from becoming first-rate television. It is genre with all the limitations of genre: catalogs of items in the medicine chest, long intimate family conversations with life, snap with mother, crackle and pop. If I were a television producer I'd put on *Franny and Zooey* tomorrow. And indeed in ten years they will. America will have moved from *One Man's Family* to the *Glass Family.* Which is progress. I'd rather have the Glass family on the air. But don't confuse the issue. The Glass stories are not literature, but television. And Salinger's work since *The Catcher in the Rye* is part of his long retreat from what is substantial, agonizing, uproarious, or close to awe and terror. *The Catcher in the Rye* was able to change people's lives. The new books are not even likely to improve the conversation in college dormitories. It is time Salinger came back to the city and got his hands dirty with a rough corruption or two, because the very items which composed the honor of his reputation, his resolute avoidance of the mass media and society, have now begun to back up on him. There is a taste of something self-absorptive, narcissistic, even putrefactive in his long contemplation of a lintless navel.

The value of past predictions by this critic may be judged by the following about Saul Bellow. It is taken from page 467 in *Advertisements for Myself*:

> When and if I come to read *Henderson the Rain King,* let me hope I do not feel the critic's vested interest to keep a banished writer in limbo, for I sense uneasily that without reading it, I have already the beginnings of a negative evaluation for it since I doubt that I would believe in Henderson as a hero.

Well, one might as well eat the crow right here. Henderson is an exceptional character, almost worthy of Gulliver or Huckleberry Finn, and it is possible that of all the books mentioned in this piece, *Henderson the Rain King* comes the closest to being a great novel. Taken even by its smallest dimension, and its final failure, it will still become a classic, a fine curiosity of a book quite out of the mainstream of American letters but a classic in the way *The Innocents Abroad,* or *The Ox-Bow Incident, The Informer,* or *A High Wind in Jamaica* is classic.

Bellow's main character, Henderson, is a legendary giant American, an eccentric millionaire, six-four in height, with a huge battered face, an enormous chest, a prodigious potbelly, a wild crank's gusto for life, and a childlike impulse to say what he thinks. He is a magical hybrid of Jim Thorpe and Dwight Mac-donald. And he is tormented by an inner voice which gives him no rest and poisons his marriages and pushes him to go forth. So he chooses to go to Africa (after first contemplating a visit to the Eskimos) and finds a native guide to take him deep into the interior.

The style gallops like Henderson, full of excess, full of light, loaded with irritating effusions, but it is a style which moves along. *The Adventures of Augie March* was written in a way which could only be called *all writing*. That was one of the troubles with the book. Everything was mothered by the style. But Henderson talks in a free-swinging easy bang-away monologue which puts your eye in the center of the action. I don't know if Bellow ever visited Africa, I would guess he didn't, but his imaginative faculty—which has always been his loot—pulls off a few prodigies. I don't know if any other American writer has done Africa so well. As for instance:

> I was in tremendous shape those first long days, hot as they were. At night, after Romilayu had prayed, and we lay on the ground, the face of the air breathed back on us, breath for breath. And then there were the calm stars, turning around and singing, and the birds of the night with heavy bodies, fanning by. I couldn't have asked for anything better. When I laid my ear to the ground, I thought I could hear hoofs. It was like lying on the skin of a drum.

After a series of tragicomic adventures, Henderson reaches a royal almost Oriental tribe with a culture built upon magic and death. He is brought to the king, Dahfu, who lives in a wooden palace attended by a harem of beautiful Amazons. (One could be visiting the royalest pad in Harlem.) Dahfu is a philosopher-king, large in size, noble, possessed of grace, complex, dignified, elegant, educated, living suspended between life and death. The king, delighted with his new friend, takes him into the secrets of his mind and his palace, and one begins to read the book with a vast absorption because Bellow is now inching more close to the

Beast of mystery than any American novelist before him. Dahfu is an exceptional creation, a profoundly sophisticated man with a deep acceptance of magic, an intellectual who believes that civilization can be saved only by a voyage back into the primitive, an expedition which he is of course uniquely suited to lead.

As the action explores its way down into an underworld of plot and magical omens, one ceases to know any longer whether Dahfu is potentially an emperor who can save the world, or a noble man lost in a Faustian endeavor. The book is on the threshold of a stupendous climax—for the first time in years I had the feeling I was going to learn something large from a novel—and then like a slow leak the air goes out of the book in the last fifty pages. Dahfu is killed in a meaningless action, Henderson goes home to his wife, and the mystery that Bellow has begun to penetrate closes over his book, still intact.

He is a curious writer. He has the warmest imagination, I think, of any writer in my generation, and this gift leads him to marvelous places—it is possible that Bellow succeeds in telling us more about the depths of the black man's psyche than either Baldwin or Ellison. He has a widely cultivated mind which nourishes his gift. He has a facility for happy surprises, and in Henderson, unlike Augie March, he has developed a nose for where the treasure is buried. Yet I still wonder if he is not too timid to become a great writer. A novelist like Jones could never have conceived *Henderson the Rain King* (no more could I), but I know that Jones or myself would have been ready to urinate blood before we would have been ready to cash our profit and give up as Bellow did on the possibilities of a demonically vast ending. The clue to this capitulation may be detected in Bellow's one major weakness, which is that he creates individuals and not relations between them, at least not yet. Augie March travels alone, the hero of *Seize the Day* is alone, Henderson forms passionate friendships but they tend to get fixed and the most annoying aspect of the novel is the constant repetition of the same sentiments, as if Bellow is knocking on a door of meaning which will not open for him. It is possible that the faculty of imagination is opposed to the gift of grasping relationships—in the act of coming to know somebody else well, the point of the imagination may be dulled by the roughness of the other's concrete desires and the attrition of living not only in one's own boredom but someone else's. Bellow has a lonely gift, but it is a gift. I would guess he is more likely to write classics than major novels, which is a way of saying that he will give intense pleasure to particular readers over the years, but is not too likely to seize the temper of our time and turn it.

For those who like the results of a horse race, it should be clear that the novels I liked the most in this round of reading were *Henderson, Naked Lunch,* and *Catch-22. The Thin Red Line* if not inspired was still impressive. *Another Country* suffered from too little style but compensated by its force. *Rabbit, Run* was better than expected but cloyed by too much writing. *Set This House on Fire* was rich in separate parts, and obese for the whole. *Letting Go* gave a demonstration of brilliant tactics and no novelistic strategy at all. *Franny and Zooey* and *Raise High the Roof Beam, Carpenters* was a literary scandal which came in last.

It has been said more than once that Tolstoy and Dostoyevsky divided the central terrain of the modern novel between them. Tolstoy's concern—even in the final pessimism of *The Kreutzer Sonata*—was with men-in-the-world, and indeed the panorama of his books carries to us an image of a huge landscape peopled with figures who changed that landscape, whereas the bulk of Dostoyevsky's work could take place in ten closed rooms: it is not society but a series of individuals we remember, each illuminated by the terror of exploring the mystery of themselves. This distinction is not a final scheme for classifying the novel. If one can point to *Moby-Dick* as a perfect example of a novel in the second category—a book whose action depends upon the voyage of Ahab into his obsession—and to *An American Tragedy* as a virile example of the first kind of novel, one must still come up short before the work of someone like Henry James, who straddles the categories, for he explores into society as if the world were a creature in a closed room and he could discover its heart. Yet the distinction is probably the most useful single guide we have to the novel and can even be given a modern application to Proust as a novelist of the developed, introspective, but still objective world, and Joyce as a royal, demented, most honorable traveler through the psyche. The serious novel begins from a fixed philosophical point—the desire to discover reality—and it goes to search for that reality in society, or else must embark on a trip up the upper Amazon of the inner eye.

It is this necessity to travel into one direction or the other up to the end which makes the writing of novels fatal for one's talent and finally for one's health, as the horns of a bull are final doom for the suit of lights. If one explores the world, one's talent must be blunted by punishment, one's artistic integrity by corruption: nobody can live in the world without shaking the hand of people he despises; so, an ultimate purity must be surrendered. Yet it is as dangerous to travel unguided into the mysteries of the Self, for insanity prepares an ambush. No man explores into his own nature without submitting to a curse from the root of biology since existence would cease if it were natural to turn upon oneself.

This difficulty has always existed for the novelist, but today it may demand more antithesis and more agony than before. The writer who would explore the world must encounter a society which is now conscious of itself, and so resistant (most secretly) to an objective eye. Detours exist everywhere. There was a time when a writer had to see just a little bit of a few different faces in the world and could know that the world was still essentially so simple and so phrased that he might use his imagination to fill in unknown colors in the landscape. Balzac could do that, and so could Zola. But the arts of the world suffered a curious inversion as man was turned by the twentieth century into mass man rather than democratic man. The heartland which was potential in everyone turned upon itself; people used their personal arts to conceal from themselves the nature of their work. They chose to become experts rather than artists. The working world was no longer a panorama of factories and banks so much as it was reminiscent of hospitals and plastic recreation centers. Society tended to collect in small stagnant pools. Now, any young man trying to explore that world is held up by pleasures which are not sufficiently intense to teach him and is dulled by injustices too elusive to fire his rage. The Tolstoyan novel begins to be impossible. Who can create a vast canvas when the imagination must submit itself to a plethora of detail in each joint of society? Who can travel to many places when the complexity of each pool sucks up one's attention like a carnivorous cess-fed flower? Of all the writers mentioned here, only Jones, Heller, and Burroughs even try to give a picture of the world, and the last two have departed from conventional reality before financing the attempt. It may be that James Jones is indeed the single major American writer capable of returning with a realistic vision of the complex American reality. But by his method, because of the progressively increasing confusion and contradiction of each separate corner in American society, he will have to write twenty or thirty books before he will have sketched even a small design.

Yet a turn in the other direction, into the world of the Self, is not less difficult. An intellectual structure which is cancerous and debilitating to the instinct of the novelist inhabits the crossroads of the inner mind. Psychoanalysis. An artist must not explore into himself with language given by another. A vocabulary of experts is a vocabulary greased out and sweated in committee and so is inimical to a private eye. One loses what is new by confusing it with what may be common to others. The essential ideas of psychoanalysis are reductive and put a dead weight on the confidence of the venture. If guilt, for example, is neurotic, a clumsy part of the functioning in a graceful machine, then one does not feel like a hero studying his manacles, nor a tragic victim regarding his just sentence, but instead is a skilled mechanic trying to fix his tool. Brutally, simply, mass man cannot initiate an inner voyage unless it is conducted by an expert graduated by an institution.

Set This House on Fire, Another Country, Rabbit, Run, Letting Go, Henderson, and the Glass stories were all amateur expeditions into the privacy of the Self, but they are also a measure of the difficulty, because one could sense the exhaustion of talent in

the fires on the way, as if a company of young untried men were
charging a hill which was mined and laid across with fire lanes
for automatic weapons.

Yet the difficulty goes beyond the country of psychoanalysis.
There are hills beyond that hill. The highest faces an abyss. Man
in the Middle Ages or the Renaissance, man even in the nineteenth century, explored deep into himself that he might come
closer to a vision of a God or some dictate from eternity, but that
exploration is suspect in itself today, and in the crucial climactic
transcendental moments of one's life, there is revealed still another dilemma. God, is it God one finds, or madness?

The religious temper of these books is significant. Of them all,
only *The Thin Red Line, Naked Lunch, Another Country,* and *Letting
Go* have no overt religious preoccupation. Yet altogether one
could make a kind of case that *Naked Lunch* and *Another Country*
are not divorced from religious obsessions. The suggestion of
still another frontier for the American novel is here. A war has
been fought by some of us over the last fifteen years to open the
sexual badlands to our writing, and that war is in the act of being
won. Can one now begin to think of an attack on the stockade—
those dead forts where the spirit of twentieth-century man, frozen in flop and panic before the montage of his annihilation,
has collected, like castrated cattle behind the fence? Can the feet
of those infantrymen of the arts, the novelists, take us through
the mansions and the churches into the palace of the Bitch
where the real secrets are stored? We are the last of the entrepreneurs, and one of us homeless guns had better make it, or the
future will smell like the dead air of the men who captured our
time during that huge collective cowardice which was the aftermath of the Second War.

The Executioner's Song

*I think if I had three good years to give
in study at some occupation
which was fierce and new*

and full of stimulation
I think I would become
                an executioner
        with time spent out in the field
        digging graves for bodies I had made
                the night before.
You see: I am bad at endings
My bowels move without honor
        and flatulence is an affliction
        my pride must welcome with gloom
It comes I know from preoccupation
        much too much with sex
Those who end well do not spend their time
        so badly on the throne

For this reason I expect the task
        of gravedigger welcomes me
I would like to kill well and bury well
Perhaps then my seed would not shoot
        so frantic a flare
If I could execute neatly
        (with respect for whatever romantic
                        imagination
gave passion to my subject's crime)
and if I buried well
(with tenderness, dispatch, gravity
and joy that the job was not jangled—
giving a last just touch of the spade
to the coffin
                in order to leave it
quivering
        like a leaf—for forget not
coffins quiver as the breath goes out
and the earth comes down)

Yes if I could kill cleanly
        and learn not to turn my back

on the face of each victim
as he chooses
                    what is last to be seen
in his eye,
            well, then perhaps,
then might I rise so high upon occasion
as to smite a fist of the Lord's creation
into the womb of that muse
which gives us poems
Yes, then I might
For one ends best when death is clean
            to the mind
                        and calm in its proportions
            fire in the orchard and flame at the root

Introducing Our Argument

———

(1966)

IN PROVINCETOWN, a friend brought a gift. She brought a big round metal GULF sign seven feet in diameter which another friend had discovered in the town dump and rescued. The hair of fashion came alert: we might make a coffee table. While we drank, we could look at the shading in the orange and blue letters. Poets in the room could contemplate the value of—GULF—even as a novitiate in yoga will fix on the resonance of *om*. Musicians could explore the tick of the cocktail glass against the metal. Intellectuals could . . .

What a deal intellectuals could do. There would be those to claim Pop art is the line where culture meets mass civilization, and so Pop art is the vehicle for bringing taste to the masses; others to argue the debauch of capitalism has come to the point where it crosses the doorstep and inhabits the place where you set your drink. And those to say fun; fun is the salvation of society.

It would go on: some might decide that putting a huge gasoline company's totem into one's private space helped to mock civilization and its hired man, the corporation; others would be certain the final victory of the corporation was near when we felt affection for the device by which a corporation advertised itself.

At last, nothing was done with the sign. I did not want to go through dialogue and the same dialogue about why it was there and whether it was good it was there, or bad it was there, and in truth I did not want the work of disposing of it when the fashion had passed. So I left the sign to rust on the beach, a mile from its burial ground on the dump.

List the symptoms. We live in a time which has created the art of the absurd. It is our art. It contains happenings, Pop art, camp, a theater of the absurd, a homosexual genius who spent thirty years as a thief; black humor is its wit; the dances are livid and solitary—they are also orgiastic: Orgy or masturbation?—the first question posed by the art of the absurd. So the second: Is the art rational or absurd? Do we have the art because the absurd is the patina of waste, and we are waiting in the pot for the big roar of waters when the world goes down the pipe? Or are we face-to-face with a desperate but most rational effort from the deepest resources of the unconscious of us all to rescue civilization from the pit and plague of its bedding, that gutted swinish foul old bedding on which two centuries of imperialism, high finance, moral hypocrisy, and horror have lain? The skulls of black men and the bowels of the yellow race are in that bed, the death of the Bride of the Sabbath is in that bed with the ashes of the concentration camp and the ashes of the Kabbala, moonshots fly like flares across black dreams, and the Beatles—demons or saints?—give shape to a haircut which looks from the rear like nothing so much as an atomic cloud. Apocalypse or debauch is upon us. And we are close to dead. There are faces and bodies like gorged maggots on the dance floor, on the highway, in the city, in the stadium; they are a host of chemical machines who swallow the product of chemical factories, aspirin, preservatives, stimulant, relaxant, and breathe out their chemical wastes into a polluted air. The sense of a long last night over civilization is back again; it has perhaps not been here so intensely in thirty years, not since the Nazis were prospering, but it is coming back.

Well, it has been the continuing obsession of this writer that the world is entering a time of plague. And the continuing metaphor for the obsession—a most disagreeable metaphor—has been cancer. The argument is old by now: its first assumption is that cancer is a disease different from other diseases, an ultimate disease against which all other diseases are in design to protect us.

The difficulty—for one can always convince the literary world to accept a metaphor if one remains loyal to it—is that my obsession is not merely an obsession, I fear, but insight into the nature of things, perhaps the deepest insight I have, and this said with no innocence of the knowledge that the plague can have its home within, and these condemnations come to no more than the grapplings of a man with a curse on his flesh, or even the probability that society partakes of the plague and its critic partakes, and each wars against the other, the man and the society each grappling with his own piece of the plague, as if, indeed, we are each of us born not only with our life but with our death, with our variety of death, good death and bad, and it is the act of each separate man to look to free himself from that part of his existence which was born with the plague. Some succeed, some fail, and some of us succeed nobly for we clear our own plague and help to clear the plague upon the world, and others succeed, others—are we those?—you don't know—who clear their plague by visiting it upon friends, passing their disease into the flesh and mind of near bodies, and into the circuits of the world. And they poison the wells and get away free, some of them—they get away free if there is a Devil and he has power, and that is something else we do not know. But the plague remains, that mysterious force which erects huge, ugly, and aesthetically emaciated buildings as the world ostensibly grows richer, and proliferates new diseases as medicine presumably grows wiser, nonspecific diseases, families of viruses, with new names and no particular location. And products deteriorate in workmanship as corporations improve their advertising, wars shift from carnage and patriotism to carnage and surrealism, sex shifts from whiskey to drugs. And all the food is poisoned. And the waters of the sea we are told. And there is always the sound of some electric motor in the ear.

In a modern world which produces mediocrities at an accelerating rate, and keeps them alive by surgical gymnastics which go beyond anyone's patience but the victim, the doctor, and the people who expect soon to be on the operating tables themselves; in a civilization where compassion is of political use and is stratified in welfare programs which do not build a better society but shore up a worse; in a world whose ultimate logic is war, because in a world of war all overproduction and overpopulation is possible since peoples and commodities may be destroyed wholesale—in a breath, a world of such hypercivilization is a world not of adventurers, entrepreneurs, settlers, social arbiters, proletarians, agriculturists, and other egocentric types of a dynamic society, but is instead a world of whirlpools and formlessness where two huge types begin to reemerge, types there at the beginning of it all: cannibals and Christians.

We are martyrs all these days. All that Right Wing which believes there is too much on earth and too much of it is second-rate, all of that Right Wing which runs from staunch Republicanism to the extreme Right Wing and then half around the world through the ghosts of the Nazis, all of that persecuted Right Wing which sees itself as martyr, knows that it knows how to save the world: one can save the world by killing off what is second-rate. So they are the cannibals—they believe that survival and health of the species comes from consuming one's own, not one's near-own, but one's own species. So the pure cannibal has only one taboo on food—he will not eat the meat of his own family. Other men he will of course consume. Their virtues he will conserve in his own flesh, their vices he will excrete, but to kill and to eliminate is his sense of human continuation.

Then come our Christians. They are the commercial. The commercial is the invention of a profoundly Christian nation—it proceeds to sell something in which it does not altogether believe, and it interrupts the mood. We are all of us Christians: Jews, liberals, Bolsheviks, anarchists, Socialists, Communists, Keynesians, Democrats, Civil Righters, beatniks, ministers, moderate Republicans, pacifists, Teach-inners, doctors, scientists, professors, Latin Americans, new African nations, Common Marketers, even Mao Tse-tung. Doubtless. From Lyndon Johnson to Mao Tse-tung, we are all Christians. We believe man is good if given a chance, we believe man is open to discussion, we believe science is the salvation of all, we believe death is the end of discussion; ergo we believe nothing is so worthwhile as human life. We think no one should go hungry. So forth. What characterizes Christians is that most of them are not Christian and have no interest left in Christ. What characterizes the cannibals is that most of them are born Christian, think of Jesus as Love, and get an erection from the thought of whippings, blood, burning crosses, burning bodies, and screams in mass graves. Whereas their counterpart, the Christians—the ones who are not Christian but whom we choose to call Christian—are utterly opposed to the destruction of human life and succeed within themselves in starting all the wars of our own time, since every war since the Second World War has been initiated by liberals or Communists; these Christians also succeed by their faith in science to poison the nourishment we eat and the waters of the sea, to alter the genetics of our beasts, and to break the food chains of nature.

Yet every year the girls are more beautiful, the athletes are better. So the dilemma remains. Is the curse on the world or on oneself? Does the world get better, no matter how, getting better and worse as part of the same process, or does the world get better in spite of the fact it is getting worse, and we are approaching the time when an apocalypse will pass through the night? We live after all in a time which interrupts the mood of everything alive.

Well, this is a book of writings on these themes. I will not pretend it is a book written with the clear cold intent to be always on one precise aim or another. I will not even pretend that all the targets are even necessarily on the same range or amenable to literary pieces. No, I would submit that everything here has been written in the years of the plague, and so I must see myself sometimes as physician more than rifleman, a physician half blind, not so far from drunk, his nerve to be recommended not at every occasion, nor his hand to hold at each last bed, but a noble physician nonetheless, noble at least in his ideal, for he is certain that there is a strange disease before him, an unknown illness, a phenomenon which partakes of mystery, nausea, and horror; if the nausea gives him pause and the horror fear, still the mystery summons, he is a physician, he must try to explore the mystery. So, he does, and by different methods too many a time. We will not go on to speak of the medicines and the treatment, of surgeon, bonesetter, lab analyst—no, the metaphor has come to the end of its way. These writings are then attempts in a dozen different forms to deal with mysteries which offer the presumption that there is an answer to be found, or a clue. So I proceed, even as a writer when everything goes well, and perhaps a few matters are uncovered and more I know are left to chase.

There are times when I think it is a meaningless endeavor— that the only way to hunt these intimations is in the pages of a novel, that that is the only way this sort of mystery can ever be detected. Such a time is on me again, so it is possible this collection will be the last for a period. The wish to go back to that long novel, announced six years ago, and changed in the mind by all of seven years, may be here again, and if that is so, I will have yet to submit to the prescription laid down by the great physician Dr. James Joyce—"silence, exile, and cunning," he said. Well, one hopes not; the patient is too gregarious for the prescription. What follows, at any rate, are some explorations of the theme stated here, some talk of Cannibals and Christians, some writings on politics, on literary matters, on philosophy—save us all—on philosophy.

Our Argument as Last Presented

———

(1966)

NOW I WILL GIVE YOU a set of equations. They are not mathematical, but metaphorical; and therefore full of science. I repeat: they are equations in the form of metaphor; so they are full of science. It is just that they are not scientific. For they are equations composed only of words. I am thus trying to say my equations are a close description of phenomena which cannot be measured by a scientist. Yet these observations are clear enough to say that interruption is shock, and shock deadens mood, but mood then stirs itself to rouse a wave. Why? Well, the sum of one's experience might suggest that it is probably in the nature of mood to restore itself by raising a wave. Of course, if the wave is too vigorous a response to the shock, new waste may be left behind. But if the wave is adequate to the impulse which begot it, the wave can clear the waste away. So we come to the measure of the absurd, and its enigma: some art movements serve to wash out the sludge of civilization, some leave us deeper in the pit. The art of the absurd is here to purify us or to swamp us—we do not know—suddenly, we are back at the GULF sign. Only now we must recognize that we are confronted by no less than the invisible church of modern science. No small matter. Science has built a wall across the route of metaphor: poets whine before experts.

The difficulty is that none of us, scientists first, are equipped to measure the achievements of science. That vast scientific work of the last fifty years has come most undeniably out of the collective efforts of the twentieth-century scientist, but the achievement came also out of the nineteenth century, the Enlightenment, and the Renaissance. Who may now measure where the creativity was finest? The scientists of the last five centuries were the builders of that foundation from which modern scientists have created a modern science. Only these ancestors may have been more extraordinary men. They were adventurers, rebels, courtiers, painters, diplomats, churchmen. Our scientists are only experts; those of the last decade are dull in person as experts, dull as Jonas Salk, they write jargon, their minds are narrow before they are deep. Their knowledge of life is incarcerated.

The huge industrial developments and scientific advances of the twentieth century—the automobile, antibiotics, radium, flight, the structure of the atom, relativity, the quantum theory, psychoanalysis, the atom bomb, the exploration of space—may speak not so much for the genius of the twentieth century as for the genius of the centuries which preceded it. Modern science may prove to be the final poisoned fruit of the rich European tree, and plague may disclose itself as the most characteristic invention of our time. For science was founded originally on metaphor, would go our Argument, and the twentieth century has shipped metaphor to the ghetto of poets. Consider: science began with the poetic impulse to treat metaphor as equal to equation; the search began at that point where a poet looked for a means (which only later became experiment) to measure the accuracy of his metaphor. The natural assumption was that his discovery had been contained in the metaphor, since good metaphor could only originate in the deepest experience of a man; so science still remained attached to poetic vision, and scientific insight derived from culture—it was not the original desire of science to convert nature, rather to reveal it. Faust was still unborn when Aristotle undertook his pioneer observations.

There is a danger in metaphor, however; the danger which is present in poetry: contradictory meanings collect too easily about the core of meaning; unconnected meanings connect themselves. So, science sought a methodology through experiment which would be severe, precise, and able to measure the verity of the insight in the metaphor. Experiment was conceived to protect the scientific artist from ambiguity.

Experiment, however, proliferated; as the scientist ceased to be a great amateur and became expert, experiment ran amok, and laboratory men of partial, determined, fanatic brilliance became the scientist's director rather than his assistant. The laboratory evicted the mind; the laboratory declared itself the womb of scientific knowledge; laboratory methodology grew as cumbersome as the labor codes of a theatrical union. Metaphor disappeared.

It was replaced by a rabidity of experiment, a fetishism of experiment. Mediocrity invaded science. Experiment became a faith, experiment replaced the metaphor as a means of inquiry, and technological development pushed far ahead of even the most creative intuition. Penicillin was discovered by accident, as a by-product of experiment—it did not come at the end of a poetic journey of the mind. No, it was an orphan and a bastard. And by similar mass methods were all the other antibiotics uncovered, by observing the bactericidal action of a million molds: those which gave the best laboratory evidence of success were marketed by drug companies. But the root of the success was not comprehended. There was no general theory to point to a particular mold for a specific disease. No metaphor. Metaphor had been replaced by gross assay.

Metaphor. The word has been used generously. Would an example be welcome? The Argument can try to provide it. A modern disease, for example, as it is comprehended in a laboratory, is explained to the laboratory technician, the student, and the layman, as a phenomenon made up of its own pimples, rash, swelling, and development, but the disease is not ever presented as a creature—real or metaphorical—a creature which might have an existence separate from its description, even as you and

I have an existence which is separate from the fact that we weigh so many pounds and stand so many inches tall. No, the symptom is stripped of its presence. Of course, psychoanalysis made an attempt to say that the root of one disease could be similar to the root of another whose symptoms were different; it was a way of hinting that the metaphor ought to return. Such an approach might have wished ultimately to demonstrate that a malfunction of the liver and an inflammation of the eyes were both connected to despair at one's position in society. But psychoanalysis was hungry, and dependent upon the sciences: like most welfare cases it was therefore not in a rush for poetry—rather it rushed to advertise the discovery of each new tranquilizer for each disorder in emotion. It was anxious to show itself respectable. So psychiatry became pharmacology.

Let us, however, try to travel in the other direction, let us look for an extreme metaphor of disease. Let us suppose that each specific ill of the body is not so much a dull evil to be disposed of by any chemical means whatever, but is, rather, a theatrical production presented by some company in oneself to some audience in oneself. To the degree then that our illness is painful, detailed, clear, and with as much edge as a sharply enunciated voice, the particular disease is a *success;* the communion of the body (the statement sent from stage to audience) is deep, is resonant. The audience experiences catharsis—at the end of the drama, the body is tired but enriched. By the logic of our metaphor, that is a good disease. The illness has waged conflict, drama, and distress through the body, and has obliged the body to sit in attention upon it, but now the body knows more. Its experience has become more profound, its intimate knowledge of its own disharmony is more acute.

By this reckoning, a disease is the last attempt (*at a particular level of urgency*) to communicate from one part of the body to the other, a last attempt to tell us that if we do not realize the function before us is now grievously out of harmony, then we will certainly sicken further. On the other hand, if the disease which presents itself is not accepted, if one's suffering is not suffered, if there are no statements of our suffering enunciated through the

caverns of the body, but if instead our disease is averted by antibiotic, or our pain is silenced by a sedative, then the attempted
communication of the illness has failed. The disease, having no
other expression, sinks, of necessity, into a lower and less elegant
condition, it retreats from a particular pain or conflict into a bog
of disharmony. Where one organ or two might have borne the
original stress, now ten organs share ubiquitous tension. A clear
sense of symptom tends to disappear. Infection begins to be replaced by virus, a way of saying the new diseases are not
classifiable—their symptoms reveal no characteristic form. One
is close to the plague.

If my metaphor is valid, then drugs to relieve pain, and antibiotics to kill infection, are invalid. They are in fact liquidators of
possibility, for they deaden the possibility of any quick dramatic
growth. A disease checked by an antibiotic has taught the body
nothing—nothing to terminate ambiguity—for the body does
not know how well it could have cured itself, or even precisely
what it had to cure. Yet ambiguity is the seat of disease. Ambiguity demands double communication to achieve a single purpose.
It demands we be ready for a particular course of action and yet
be ready for its exact opposite. So it demands double readiness
or double function for single use. Ambiguity is therefore waste.
A man brought back from death by chemicals his own body did
not manage to provide cannot know afterward if he should be
alive. Small matter, you may argue; he is much alive, is he not?
But he has lost biological dignity, he is crucially less alive in a part
of his mind and his body. That is one reason metaphors are not
encouraged near to science now, for one would then have to say
that the patient is alive, but his soul has died a degree.

So the Argument would demand that there be metaphors to
fit the vaults of modern experience. That is, in fact, the unendurable demand of the middle of this century, to restore the metaphor, and thereby displace the scientist from his center. Would
you call for another example? Think of the elaborate architecture in the structure of a protein molecule. The scientist will
describe the structure and list the properties of the molecule
(and indeed it took technological achievements close to genius

to reach that point) but the scientist will not look at the metaphorical meaning of the physical structure, its meaning as an architectural form. He will not ponder what biological or spiritual experience is suggested by the formal structure of the molecule, for metaphor is not to the present interest of science. It is instead the desire of science to be able to find the cause of cancer in some virus: a virus—you may count on it—which will be without metaphor. You see, that will then be equal to saying that the heart of the disease of all diseases is empty of meaning, that cancer is caused by a specific virus which has no character or quality and is in fact void of philosophy and bereft of metaphysics. All those who are there to claim that disease and death are void of meaning are there to benefit from such a virus, for next they can move on to say that life is absurd. We are back once again at the enigma surrounding the art of the absurd. Except now we have hints of the meaning. For if the Argument would propose that a future to life depends on creating forms of an intensity which will capture the complexity of modern experience and dignify it, illumine—if you will—its danger, then the art of the absurd reveals the wound in its own heart and the schizophrenia of its impulse, for the art of the absurd wars with one hand against the monotonies of all totalitarian form in politics, medicine, architecture, and media communication, and with the other, trembles and is numb to any human passion and is savage toward discourse, for the danger is palpable and the discovery of new meaning may live in ambush at the center of a primitive fire.

Well, enough of such metaphor. Let us go off to explore the tributaries of form.

The Crazy One

(1967)

TURNING THROUGH THE PAGES of this book one is captured finally
by a modest addiction. One keeps going back. As the pages are
toured for the tenth time, a small magic emerges. The flights,
the vulgarities, the comedy, and the religious dedication of the
bullfight return. Late afternoons of color—hues of lavender, sil-
ver, pink, orange silk and gold in the *traje de luces*—(feminine
indulgences only a bullfighter could entertain) now begin to
play in one's mind against the small sharp impact on the eyes of
horseballs falling like eggs between the frightened legs of the
horse, and the flanks of the bull glistening with the sheen of a
dark wet wood. And the blood. The bullfight always gets back to
the blood. It pours in gouts down the forequarters of the bull, it
wells from the hump of his *morillo* and moves in waves of bright
red along the muscles of his chest and the heaving of his sides. If
he has been killed poorly and the sword goes through his lung,
then the animal dies in vomitings of blood. If the matador is
working close to the animal, the suit of lights becomes stained—
the dark bloodstain is honorable, it is also steeped in horror.
Should the taste of your favorite herb come from the death of
some rare love, so the life of the bright red blood of an animal

river pouring forth becomes some other life as it darkens down to the melancholy hues of an old dried blood which speaks in some lost primitive tongue about the mysteries of death, color, and corruption. The dried blood reminds you of the sordid glory of the bullfight, its hint of the Renaissance when noble figures stated their presence as they paraded through the marketplace and passed by cripples with stumps for legs, a stump for a tongue, and the lewdest grin of the day. Yes, the spectrum of the bullfight goes from courage to gangrene.

In Mexico, the hour before the fight is always the best hour of the week. It would be memorable not to sound like Hemingway, but in fact you would get happy the night before just thinking of that hour next day. Outside the Plaza de Mexico, cheap cafés open only on Sunday, and huge as beer gardens, filled with the public (us tourists, hoodlums, pimps, pickpurses and molls, Mexican variety—which is to say the whores had headdresses and hindquarters not to be seen elsewhere on earth, for their hair rose vertically twelve inches from the head, and their posteriors projected horizontally twelve inches back into that space the rest of the whore had just marched through). The mariachis were out with their romantic haunting caterwauling of guitar, violin, songs of carnival and trumpet, their song told of hearts which were true and hearts which were broken, and the wail of the broken heart went right into the trumpet until there were times when drunk the right way on tequila or Mexican rum, it was perhaps the best sound heard this side of Miles Davis. You hear a hint of all that in the Tijuana Brass.

You see, my friends, the wild hour was approaching. The horrors of the week in Mexico were coming to term. Indeed, no week in Mexico is without its horrors for every last Mexican alive—it is a city and a country where the bones of the dead seem to give the smell of their char to every desert wind and auto exhaust and frying tortilla. The mournfulness of unrequited injustice hangs a shroud across the centuries. Every Mexican is gloomy until the instant he becomes happy, and then he is a maniac. He howls, he whistles, smoke of murder passes off his pores, he bullies, he beseeches friendship, he is a clown, a

brigand, a tragic figure suddenly merry. The intellectuals and
the technicians of Mexico abominate their national character
because it is always in the way. It puts the cracks in the plaster of
new buildings, it forgets to cement the tiles, it leaves rags in the
new pipes of new office buildings and forgets to put the gas cap
back on the tank. So the intellectuals and the technicians hate
the bullfight as well. You cannot meet a socialist in Mexico who
approves of the running of the bulls. They are trying to turn
Mexico into a modern country, and thus the same war goes on
there that goes on in three-quarters of the world—the battle-
front is the new highways to the suburbs, and the corporation's
office buildings, the walls of hospital white, and the myopic
sheets of glass. In Mexico, like everywhere else, it is getting
harder and harder to breathe in a mood through the pores of
the city because more and more of the city is being covered with
corporation architecture, with surgical dressing. To the vam-
pires and banshees and dried blood on the curses of the cactus
in the desert is added the horror of the new technology in an
old murder-ridden land. And four o'clock on Sunday is the beginning of release for some of the horrors of the week. If many
come close to feeling the truth only by telling a lie, so Mexicans
come close to love by watching the flow of blood on an animal's
flanks and the certain death of the bull before the bravery and/
or humiliation of the bullfighter.

I could never have understood it if someone tried to explain
ahead of time, and in fact, I came to love the bullfight long before I comprehended the first thing about why I did. That was
very much to the good. There are not too many experiences a
radical American intellectual could encounter in those days
(when the youngest generation was called the silent generation)
which invaded his sure sense of his own intellectual categories. I
did not like the first bullfights I saw, the formality of the ritual
bored me, the fights appeared poor (indeed they were), and the
human content of the spectacle came out atrocious. Narcissistic
matadors, vain when they made a move, pouting like a girl stood
up on Saturday night when the crowd turned on them, clumsy at
killing, and the crowd, brutal to a man. In the Plaza de Mexico,

the Indians in the cheap seats buy a paper cup of beer and when they are done drinking, the walk to the WC is miles away, and besides they are usually feeling sullen, so they urinate in their paper cup and hurl it down in a cascade of harvest gold, Indian piss. If you are an American escorting an American girl who has blond hair, and you have tickets in *Sol,* you buy your girl a cheap sombrero at the gate, for otherwise she will be a prime target of attention. Indeed, you do well not to sit near an American escorting a blonde whose head is uncovered, for the aim of a drunken Indian is no better than you when your aim is drunk. So no surprise if one's early detestation of the bullfight was fortified in kidney brew, Azteca.

Members of a minority group are always ready to take punishment, however, and I was damned if I was going to be excluded from still another cult. So I persisted in going to bullfights, and they were a series of lousy bullfights, and then the third or fourth time I got religion. It was a windy afternoon, with threats of rain, and now and then again ten minutes of rain, poisonous black clouds overhead, the chill gloom of a black sky on Sundays in Mexico, and the particular torero (whose name I could not recall for anything) was a clod. He had a nasty build. Little spindly legs, too big a chest, a butt which was broad and stolid, real peasant ass, and a vulgar worried face with a gold tooth. He was engaged with an ugly bull who kept chopping at the muleta with his horns, and occasionally the bull would catch the muleta and fling it in the air and trample it and wonder why the object was either dead or not dead, the bull smelling a hint of his own blood (or the blood of some cousin) on the blood of the muleta, and the crowd would hoot, and the torero would go over to his sword handler at the barrera, and shake his head and come out with a new muleta, and the bull would chop, and the wind would zig the muleta out of control, and then the matador would drop it and scamper back to the *barrera,* and the crowd would jeer and the piss would fly in yellow arcs of rainbow through the rain all the way down from the cheap seats, and the whores would make farting sounds with their spoiled knowledgeable mouths, while the aficionados would roll their eyes, and the sound of Mexican laughter, that operative definition of the echo of total disgust, would shake along like jelly-gasoline through the crowd.

I got a look at the bullfighter who was the center of all this. He was not a man I could feel something for. He had a cheap pimp's face and a dull, thoroughgoing vanity. His face, however, was now in despair. There was something going on for him more humiliating than humiliation—as if his life were going to take a turn into something more dreadful than anything it had encountered until now. He was in trouble. The dead dull fight he was giving was going to be death for certain hopes in his psyche. Somehow it was going to be more final than the average dead dull fight to which he was obviously all too accustomed. I was watching the despair of a profoundly mediocre man.

Well, he finally gave up any attempt to pass the bull, and he worked the animal forward with jerks of his muleta to left and right, a competent rather than a beautiful technique at best, and even to my untutored eye he was a mechanic at this, and more whistles, and then desperation all over that vain incompetent pimp's face, he profiled with his sword, and got it halfway in, and the animal took a few steps to one side and the other and fell over quickly.

The art of killing is the last skill you learn to judge in bullfighting, and the kill on this rainy afternoon left me less impressed than the crowd. Their jeers were replaced by applause (later I learned the crowd would always applaud a kill in the lung—all audiences are Broadway audiences) and the approbation continued sufficiently for the torero to take a tour of the ring. He got no ears, he certainly didn't deserve them, but he had his tour and he was happy, and in his happiness there was something suddenly likable about him, and I sensed that I was passing through some interesting emotions since I had felt contempt for a stranger and then a secret and most unsocialistic desire to see this type I did not like humiliated a little further, and then in turn I was quietly but most certainly overcome by his last-minute success sufficiently to find myself liking a kind of man I had never considered near to human before. So this bad bullfight in the rain had given a drop of humanity to a very dry area of my heart, and now I knew a little more and had something to think about which was no longer altogether in category.

We have presented the beginning of a history then—no, say it better—the origin of an addiction. For a drug's first appeal is always existential—our sense of life (once it is made alert by the sensation of its absence) is thereupon so full of need as the desire for a breath of air. The sense of life comes alive in the happy days when the addict first encounters his drug. But all histories of addiction are the same—particularly in the beginning. They fall into the larger category of the history of a passion. So I will spare each and every one of us the titles of the books I read on the running of the bulls, save to mention the climactic purchase of a three-volume set in leather for fifty 1954 dollars (now doubtless in value one hundred) of *Los Toros* by Cossio. Since it was entirely in Spanish, a language I read with about as much ease and pleasure as Very Old English, *Los Toros* remains in my library as a cornerstone of my largest mental department—*The Bureau of Abandoned Projects:* I was going to write *the* novel about bullfight, dig, digary.

Nor will I reminisce about the great bullfighters I saw, of the majesties of Arruza and the machismo of Procuna, the liquidities of Silverio and the solemnity of Cesar Giron, no, we will not micturate the last of such memory to tell a later generation about El Ranchero and Ortiz of the Orticina, and Angel Peralta the Rejoneador, nor of Manolete, for he was dead long before I could with confidence distinguish a bull from a heifer or a steer, and no more can I talk of Luis Miguel and Antonio, for neither of them have I seen in a fight, so that all I know of Ordoñez is his reputation, and of Dominguín his style, for I caught his work in a movie once and it was not work the way he made it look. No, enough of these qualifications for *afición.* The fact is that I do not dwell on Arruza and Procuna and Silverio and Giron and Peralta and Ranchero because I did not see them that often and in fact most of them I saw but once. I was always in Mexico in the summer, you see, and the summer is the *temporada de novillos,* which is to say it is the time when the *novilladas* are held, which is to say it is the time of the novices.

Now the fellow who is pushing up this preface for you is a great lover of the bullfight—make on it no mistake. For a great bullfight he would give up just about any other athletic or religious spectacle—the World Series in a minute, a pro football championship, a mass at the Vatican, perhaps even a great heavyweight championship—which, kids, is really saying it. No love like the love for four in the afternoon at the Plaza Mexico. Yet all the great matadors he saw were seen only at special festivals when they fought very small bulls for charity. The *novillada* is, after all, the time of the *novilleros,* and a *novillero* is a bullfighter approximately equal in rank to a Golden Gloves fighter. A very good *novillero* is like a very good Golden Gloves finalist. The Sugar Ray Robinsons and the Rocky Marcianos of the bullfighting world were glimpsed by me only when they came out of retirement long enough to give the equivalent of a snappy two-round exhibition. My love of bullfighting, and my experience of it as a spectator, was founded then by watching *novilleros* week after week over two separate summers in Mexico City. So I know as much about bullfighting as a man would know about boxing if he read a lot and heard a lot about great fighters and saw a few movies of them and one or two exhibitions, and also had the intense, if partial, fortune to follow two Golden Gloves tournaments all the way and to follow them with some lively if not always dependable instinct for discerning what was good and what was not so good in the talent before him.

After a while I got good at seeing the flaws and virtues in *novilleros,* and in fact I began to see so much of their character in their style, and began to learn so much about style by comprehending their character (for nearly everything good or bad about a novice bullfighter is revealed at a great rate) that I began to take the same furious interest and partisanship in the triumph of one style over another that is usually reserved for literary matters (is Philip Roth better than John Updike?—you know) or what indeed average Americans and some not so average might take over political figures. To watch a bullfighter have an undeserved triumph on Sunday afternoon when you detest his style is not the worst preparation for listening to Everett Dirksen nominate Barry Goldwater or hearing Lyndon Johnson give a lecture on TV about Amurrican commitments to the free universe. Everything bad and god-awful about the style of life got into the style of bullfighters, as well as everything light, delightful, honorable, and good.

At any rate, about the time I knew a lot about bullfighting, or as much as you could know watching nothing but *novilleros* week after week, I fell in love with a bullfighter. I never even met this bullfighter, I rush to tell you. I would not have wanted to meet him. Meeting him could only have spoiled the perfection of my love, so pure was my affection. And his name—not one in a thousand of you out there, dear general readers, can have heard of him—his name was El Loco. El Loco, the Crazy One. It is not a term of endearment in Mexico, where half the populace is crazy. To amplify the power of nomenclature, El Loco came from the provinces, he was God's own hick, and his real name was Amado Ramirez, which is like being a boy from Hicksville, Georgia, with a name like Beloved Remington. Yet there was a time when I thought Beloved Remington, which is to say Amado Ramirez, would become the greatest bullfighter in the whole world, and there were critics in Mexico City hoary with *afición* who held the same opinion (if not always in print). He came up one summer a dozen years ago like a rocket, but a rocket with one tube hot and one tube wet and he spun in circles all over the bullfighting world of Mexico City all through the summer and fall.

But we must tell more of what it is like to watch *novilleros.* You see, novice bullfighters fight bulls who are called *novillos,* and these bulls are a year younger and two to four hundred pounds lighter than the big fighting bulls up around a thousand pounds which matadors must face. So they are less dangerous. They can still kill a man, but not often does that happen—they are more likely to pound and stomp and wound and bruise a *novillero* than to catch him and play him in the air and stab him up high on the horns the way a terrible full-grown fighting bull can do. In consequence, the analogy to the Golden Gloves is imperfect, for a talented *novillero* can at his best look as exciting as, or more exciting than, a talented matador—the novice's beast is smaller and less dangerous, so his lack of experience is compensated for by his relative comfort—he is in less danger of getting killed. (Indeed, to watch a consummate matador like Carlos Arruza work with a new young bull is like watching Norman Mailer box with his three-year-old son—absolute mastery is in the air.)

Novilleros possess another virtue. Nobody can contest their *afición*. For every *novillero* who has a manager, and a rich man to house and feed him, and influential critics to bring him along on the sweet of a bribe or two, there are a hundred devoted all but unknown *novilleros* who hitch from *poblado* to *poblado* on back dirt roads for the hint of a chance to fight at some fiesta so small the results are not even phoned to Mexico City. Some of these kids spend years in the provinces living on nothing, half starved in the desire to spend a life fighting bulls, and they will fight anything—bulls who are overweight, calves who are under the legal limit, beasts who have fought before and so are sophisticated and dangerous. These provincial *novilleros* get hurt badly by wounds which show no blood, deep bruises in the liver and kidney from the flat of a horn, deep internal bleedings in the gut, something lively taken off the groin—a number of them die years later from malnutrition and chronic malfunctions of some number of those organs—their deaths get into no statistics on the fatalities of the bullfight.

A few of these provincial *novilleros* get enough fights and enough experience and develop enough talent, however, to pick up a reputation of sorts. If they are very lucky and likable, or have connections, or hump themselves—as some will—to rich homosexuals in the capital, then they get their shot. Listen to this. At the beginning of the *novillada,* six new bullfighters are brought in every Sunday to fight one bull each in the Plaza Mexico. For six or eight weeks this goes on. Perhaps fifty fighters never seen before in Mexico City have their chance. Maybe ten will be seen again. The tension is enormous for each *novillero.* If he fails to have a triumph or attract outstanding attention, then his years in the provinces went for nothing. Back again he will go to the provinces as a punishment for failing to be superb. Perhaps he will never fight again in the Plaza Mexico. His entire life depends on this one fight. And even this fight depends on luck. For any *novillero* can catch a poor bull, a dull mediocre cowardly bull. When the animal does not charge, the bullfighter, unless possessed of genius, cannot look good.

Once a *novillero* came into the Plaza on such an occasion, was hit by the bull while making his first pass, a veronica, and the boy and cape sailed into the air and came down together in such a way that when the boy rolled over, the cape wrapped around him like a tortilla, and one wit in *Sol,* full of the harsh wine of Mexico's harsh grapes, yelled out, "*Suerte de Enchiladas.*" The young bullfighter was named The Pass of the Enchiladas. His career could never be the same. He went on to fight that bull, did a decent honorable job—the crowd never stopped laughing. Suerte de Enchiladas. He was branded. He walked off in disgrace. The one thing you cannot be in any land where Spanish is spoken is a clown. I laughed with the rest. The bullfight is nine-tenths cruelty. The bullfight brews one's cruelty out of one's pores—it makes an elixir of cruelty. But it does something else. It reflects the proportions of life in Latin lands. For in Mexico it does not seem unreasonable that a man should spend years learning a dangerous trade, be rapped once by a bull, and end up ruined, a Suerte de Enchiladas. It is unfair, but then life is monstrously unfair, one knows that, one of the few gleams in the muck of all this dubious Mexican majesty called existence is that one can on occasion laugh bitterly with the gods. In the Spanish-Indian blood, the substance of one's dignity is found in sharing the cruel vision of the gods. In fact, dignity can be found nowhere else. For courage is seen as the servant of the gods' cruel vision.

On to Beloved Remington. He arrived in Mexico City at the end of the beginning of the *novillada* in the summer of 1954. He was there, I think, on the next to last of the early Sundays when six bulls were there for six *novilleros*. (In the full season of the *novillada,* when the best new young men have been chosen, there are six bulls for only three toreros—each kid then has two bulls, two chances.) I was not yet in Mexico for Amado Ramirez's first Sunday, but I heard nothing else from my bullfighting friends from the day I got in. He had appeared as the last of six *novilleros*. It had been a terrible day. All of the *novilleros* had been bad. He apparently had been the last and the worst, and had looked so clumsy that the crowd in derision had begun to applaud him. There is no sign of displeasure greater among the Mexican bull-fighting public than to turn their ovations upside down. But Ramirez had taken bows. Serious solemn bows. He had bowed so much he had hardly fought the bull. The Plaza Mexico had rung with merriment. It took him forever to kill the beast—he received a tumultuous ovation. He took a turn of the ring. A wit shouted *"Olé, El Loco."* He was named. When they cheer incompetence they are ready to set fire to the stadium.

El Loco was the sensation of the week. A clown had fought a bull in the Plaza Mexico and gotten out alive. The promoters put him on the following week as a seventh bullfighter, an extra added attraction. He was not considered worth the dignity of appearing on the regular card. For the first time that season, the Plaza was sold out. It was also the first fight I was to see of my second season.

Six young *novilleros* fought six mediocre bulls that day, and gave six mediocre fights. The crowd grew more and more sullen. When there is no good bullfight, there is no catharsis. One's money has been spent, the drinks are wearing down, and there has been no illumination, no moment to burn away all that spiritual sewer gas from the horrors of the week. Dull violence breeds, and with it, contempt for all bullfighters. An ugly Mexican bullfighting crowd has the temper of an old-fashioned street corner in Harlem after the police wagon has rounded up the nearest five studs and hauled them away.

Out came the clown, El Loco. The special seventh bullfighter. He was an apparition. He had a skinny body and a funny ugly face with little eyes set close together, a big nose, and a little mouth. He had very black Indian hair, and a tuft in the rear of his head stood up like the spike of an antenna. He had very skinny legs and they were bent at the knee so that he gave the impression of trudging along with a lunchbox in his hand. He had a comic ass. It went straight back like a duck's tail feathers.

His suit fit poorly. He was some sort of grafting between Ray Bolger and Charlie Chaplin. And he had the sense of self-importance to come out before the bull, he was indeed given a turn of the ring before he even saw the bull. An honor granted him for his appearance the week before. He was altogether solemn. It did not seem comic to him. He had the kind of somber extravagant ceremoniousness of a village mayor in a mountain town come out to greet the highest officials of the government. His knees stuck out in front and his buttocks in back. The Plaza rocked and rocked. Much applause followed by circulating zephyrs of laughter. And under it all, like a croaking of frogs, the beginnings of the biggest thickest Bronx raspberry anybody living ever heard.

Amado Ramirez went out to receive the bull. His first pass was a yard away from the animal, his second was six feet. He looked like a fifty-five-year-old peon ready to retire. The third pass caught his cape, and as it flew away on the horns, El Loco loped over to the *barrera* with a gait like a kangaroo. A thunderstorm of boos was on its way. He held out his arm horizontally, an injunction to the crowd, fingers spread, palm down, a mild deprecatory peasant gesture, as if to say, "Wait, you haven't seen nothing yet." The lip-farters began to smack. Amado went back out. He botched one pass, looked poor on a basic veronica. Boos, laughter, even the cops in the aisle were laughing. *Que payaso!*

His next pass had a name, but few even of the aficionados knew it, for it was an old-fashioned pass of great intricacy which spoke of the era of Belmonte and El Gallo and Joselito. It was a pass of considerable danger, plus much formal content (for a flash it looked like he was inclining to kiss a lady's hand, his cape draped over his back, while the bull went roaring by his unprotected ass). If I remember, it was called a *gallicina*, and no one had seen it in five years. It consisted of whirling in a reverse serpentina counterclockwise into the bull, so that the cape was wrapped around your body just like the Suerte de Enchiladas, except you were vertical, but the timing was such that the bull went by at the moment your back was to him and you could not see his horns. Then the whirling continued, and the cape flared out again. Amado was clumsy in his approach and stepped on his cape when he was done, but there was one moment of lightning in the middle when you saw clear sky after days of fog and smelled the ozone, there was an instant of heaven—finest thing I had yet seen in the bullfight—and in a sob of torture and release, "*Olé*" came in a panic of disbelief from one parched Mexican throat near to me. El Loco did the same pass one more time and then again. On the second pass, a thousand cried "*Olé*," and on the third, the Plaza exploded and fifty thousand men and women gave up the word at the same time. Something merry and corny as a gypsy violin flowed out of his cape.

After that, nothing but comedy again. He tried a dozen fancy passes, none worked well. They were all wild, solemn, courtly, and he was there with his peasant bump of an ass and his knobby knees. The crowd laughed with tears in their eyes. With the muleta he looked absurd, a man about to miss a train and so running with his suitcase. It took him forever to kill and he stood out like an old lady talking to a barking dog, but he could do no wrong now for this crowd—they laughed, they applauded, they gave him a tour of the ring. For something had happened in those three passes which no one could comprehend. It was as if someone like me had gotten in the ring with Cassius Clay and for twenty seconds had clearly outboxed him. The only explanation was divine intervention. So El Loco was back to fight two bulls next week.

If I remember, he did little with either bull, and killed the second one just before the third *aviso*. In a good season, his career would have been over. But it was a dreadful season. A couple of weeks of uneventful bullfights and El Loco was invited back. He looked awful in his first fight, green of face, timid, unbelievably awkward with the cape, morose and abominably prudent with the muleta. He killed badly. So badly in fact that he was still killing the bull when the third *aviso* sounded. The bull was let out alive. A dull sullen silence riddled with Mexican whistles. The crowd had had a bellyful of laughs with him. They were now getting very bored with the joke.

But the second bull he liked. Those crazy formal courtly passes, the *gallicinas*, whirled out again, and the horns went by his back six inches away. *Olé*. He went to put the banderillas in himself and botched the job, had to run very fast on the last pair to escape the bull and looked like a chicken as he ran. The cat-calls tuned up again. The crowd was like a bored lion uncertain whether to eat entrails or lick a face. Then he came out with the muleta and did a fine series of *derechazos,* the best seen in several weeks, and to everyone's amazement, he killed on the first *esto-cada.* They gave him an ear. He was the *triunfador* of the day.

This was the afternoon which confirmed the beginning of a career. After that, most of the fights are mixed in memory be-cause he had so many, and they were never without incident, and they took place years ago. All through the summer of 1954, he fought just about every week, and every week something hap-pened which shattered the comprehension of the most veteran bullfighting critic. They decided after this first triumph that he was a mediocre *novillero* with nothing particular to recommend him except a mysterious flair for the *gallicina* and a competence with the *derechazo.* Otherwise, he was uninspired with the cape and weak with the muleta. So the following week he gave an ex-hibition with the muleta. He did four *pases de pecho* so close and luminous (a pass is luminous when your body seems to lift with breath as it goes by) that the horns flirted with his heart. He did *derechazos* better than the week before, and finished with *mano-letinas.* Again he killed well. They gave him two ears. Then his second bull went out alive. A *fracaso.*

Now the critics said he was promising with the muleta but weak with the cape. He could not do a veronica of any value. So in one of the following weeks he gave five of the slowest, most luminous, most soaring veronicas anyone had ever seen.

Yet, for three weeks in a row, if he cut ears on one bull, he let the other go out alive. A bullfighter is not supposed to let his animal outlive three *avisos.* Indeed if the animal is not killed be-fore the first *aviso,* the torero is in disgrace already. Two *avisos* is like the sound of the knell of the bell in the poorhouse, and a bullfighter who hears the third *aviso* and has to let his bull go out alive is properly ready for hara-kiri. No sight, you see, is worse. It takes something like three to five minutes from the first *aviso* to the last, and in that time the kill becomes a pigsticking. Because the torero has tried two, three, four, five times, even more, to go in over the horns, and he has hit bone, and he has left the sword half in but in some abominable place like the middle of the back or the flank, or he has had a perfect thrust and the bull does not die and minutes go by waiting for it to die and the peons run up with their capes and try to flick the sword out by swirling cloth around the pommel guard and giving a crude Latin yank— nothing is cruder than a peon in a sweat for his boss. Sometimes they kick the bull in the nuts in the hope it will go down, and the crowd hoots. Sometimes the bull sinks to its knees and the *puntillero* comes in to sever its neck with a thrust of his dagger, but the stab is off-center, the spinal cord is not severed. Instead it is stimulated by the shock and the dying bull gets up and wanders all over the ring looking for its *querencia* while blood drains and drips from its wounds and the bullfighter, looking ready to cry, trots along like a farmer accompanying his mule down the road. And the next *aviso* blows. Such scenes are a nightmare for the torero. He will awaken from dreams where he is stabbing and stabbing over the horns with the *descabillar* and the bull does not drop but keeps jerking his head. Well, you receive this communication, I'm sure. A bull going out alive because the torero was not able to kill him in the allotted time is a sight about as bloody and attractive as a victim getting out of a smashed car and stumbling down the road, and the matador is about as popular as the man who caused the accident. The average torero can afford less than one occasion a year when three *avisos* are heard. El Loco was allowing an average of one bull a week to go out unkilled. One may get an idea of how good he was when he was good, if you appreciate a prizefighter who is so good that he is forgiven even if every other fight he decides to climb out of the ring and quit.

For a period, criticism of El Loco solidified. He had brilliant details, he was able on occasion to kill with inspiration, he had huge talent, but he lacked the indispensable ingredient of the bullfighter, he did not know how to get a good performance out of a bad bull. He lacked tenacity. So Ramirez created the more bizarre *faena* in anyone's memory, a fight which came near to shattering the rules of bullfighting. For on a given Sunday, he caught a very bad bull, and worked with him in all the dull, technical, unaesthetic ways a bullfighter has to work an unpromising beast, and chopped him to left and to right, and kept going into the bull's *querencia* and coaxing him out and this went on for minutes, while the public demonstrated its displeasure. And El Loco paid no attention and kept working with the bull, and then finally got the bull to charge and he made a few fine passes. But then the first *aviso* sounded and everyone groaned. Because finally the bull was going good, and yet Amado would have to kill him now. But Amado had his bull in shape and he was not going to give him up yet, and so with everyone on the scent of the loss of each second, he made *derechazos* and the pass with the muleta which looks like the *gaonera* with the cape, and he did a deliberate *adorno* or two and the second *aviso* sounded and he made an effort to kill and failed, but stayed very cool and built up the crowd again by taking the bull through a series of *naturales,* and with twenty seconds left before the third *aviso* and the Plaza in pandemonium he went in to kill and had a perfect *estocada* and the bull moved around softly and with dignity and died about ten seconds after the third *aviso,* but no one could hear the trumpet for the crowd was in a delirium of thunder, and every white handkerchief in the place was out. And Amado was smiling, which is why you could love him, because his pinched ugly little peasant face was full of a kid's decent happiness when he smiled. And a minute later there was almost a riot against the judges for they were not going to give him tail or two ears or even an ear—how could they if the bull had died after the third *aviso?*—and yet the tension of fighting the bull on the very edge of his time had given a quality to this fight which had more than a hint of the historic, for new emotions had been felt. The bullfighting public has a taste for new emotions equaled only by the lust for loot of a lady after new pleasures.

This account of triumphs is in danger of becoming as predictable as any account of triumphs since Caesar. Let us keep it alive with an account of the fiascos. Amado was simply unlike any bull-

fighter who had ever come along. When he had a great fight, or
even a great pass, it was unlike the passes of other fine *novilleros*—
the passes of El Loco were better than anything you had ever
seen. It was as if you were looking at the sky and suddenly a bird
materialized in the air. And a moment later disappeared again.
His work was frightening. It was simple, lyrical, light, illuminated,
but it came from nowhere and then was gone. When El Loco was
bad, he was not mediocre or dull, he was simply the worst, most
inept, and most comical bullfighter anyone had ever seen. He
seemed to have no technique to fall back on. He would hold his
cape like a shroud, his legs would bend at the knees, his sad ass
seemed to have an eye for the exit, his expression was morose as
Fernandel, and his feet kept tripping. He looked like a praying
mantis on its hind legs. And when he was afraid he had a nerve-
less incapacity to kill which was so hopeless that the moment he
stepped out to face his animal you knew he could not go near
this particular bull. Yet when he was good, the comic body suddenly straightened, the back took on the camber of the best back
any Spanish aristocrat chose to display, the buttocks retired into
themselves like a masterpiece of poise, and the cape and the
muleta moved slowly as full sails, or whirled like the wing of that
mysterious bird. It was as if El Loco came to be every comic Mexican who ever breathed the finest Spanish grace into his pores.
For five odd minutes he was as completely transformed as Charlie Chaplin's tramp doing a consummate impersonation of the
one and only Valentino, long-lost Rudolph.

He concluded the summer in a burst of honors. He had great
fights. One was the greatest fight I have ever seen. Afterward
they gave him a day where he fought six bulls all by himself, and
he went on to take his *alternativa* and became a full-fledged matador. But he was a Mexican down to the bones. The honors all
turned damp for him. I was not there the day he fought six bulls,
I had had to go back to America and never saw him fight again.
I heard about him only in letters and in bullfighting newspapers.
But the day he took on the six bulls I was told he did not have a
single good fight, and the day he took his *alternativa* to become
a matador, both his bulls went out alive, a disgrace too great even

for Amado. He fought a seventh bull. Gypsy magic might save him again. But the bull was big and dull and El Loco had no luck and no magic and just succeeded in killing him in a bad difficult dull fight. It was obvious he was afraid of the big bulls. So he relinquished his *alternativa* and went back to the provinces to try to regain his reputation and his nerve. And no one ever heard much of him again. Or at least I never did, but then I have not been back to Mexico. Now I suspect I'm one of the very few who remembers the happiness of seeing him fight. He was so bad when he was bad that he gave the impression you could fight a bull yourself and do no worse. So when he was good, you felt as if you were good too, and that was something no other torero ever gave me, for when they were good they looked impenetrable, they were like gods, but when Beloved Remington was good, the whole human race was good—he spoke of the great distance a man can go from the worst in himself to the best, and that finally is what the bullfight might be all about, for in dark bloody tropical lands possessed of poverty and desert and swamp, filth and treachery, slovenliness, and the fat lizards of all the worst lust, the excretory lust to shove one's own poison into others, the one thing which can keep the sweet nerve of life alive is the knowledge that a man cannot be judged by what he is every day, but only in his greatest moment, for that is the moment when he shows what he was intended to be. It is a romantic self-pitying impractical approach to the twentieth century's demand for predictable ethics, high production, dependability of function, and categorization of impulse, but it is the Latin approach. Their allegiance is to the genius of the blood. So they judge a man by what he is at his best.

Let me tell then of Amado's best fight. It came past the middle of that fine summer when he had an adventure every week in the plaza and we had adventures watching him, for he had fights so mysterious that the gods of the bulls and the ghosts of dead matadors must have come with the mothers and the witches of the centuries, homage to Lorca!, to see the miracles he performed. Listen! One day he had a sweet little bull with nice horns, regular, pleasantly curved, and the bull ran with gaiety, even aban-

don. Now we have to stop off here for an imperative explanation.
I beg your attention, but it is essential to discuss the attitudes of
afición to the *natural*. To them the *natural* is the equivalent of the
full parallel turn in skiing or a scrambling T-formation quarterback or a hook off a jab—it cannot be done well by all athletes
no matter how good they are in other ways, and the *natural* is a
dangerous pass, perhaps the most dangerous there is. The cloth
of the muleta has no sword to extend its width. Now the cloth is
held in the left hand, the sword in the right, and so the target of
the muleta which is presented for the bull's attraction is half as
large as it was before and the bullfighter's body is thus so much
bigger and so much more worthy of curiosity to the beast—
besides the bull is wiser now, he may be ready to suspect it is the
man who torments him and not the swirling sinister chaos of the
cloth in which he would bury his head. Moreover—and here is
the mystique of the *natural*—the bullfighter has a psychic communion with the bull. Obviously. People who are not psychic do
not conceive of fighting bulls. So the torero fights the bull from
his psyche first. And with the muleta he fights him usually with
his right hand from a position of authority. Switching the cloth
to the left hand exposes his psyche as well as his body. He feels
less authority—in compensation his instinct plays closer to the
bull. But he is so vulnerable! So a *natural* inspires a bullfighting
public to hold their breath, for danger and beauty come closest
to meeting right here.

It was *naturales* Amado chose to perform with this bull. He had
not done many this season. The last refuge of his detractors was
that he could not do *naturales* well. So here on this day he gave
his demonstration. Watch if you can.

He began his *faena* by making no exploratory pass, no *pase de
muerte,* no *derechazos,* he never chopped, no, he went up to this
sweet bull and started his *faena* with a series of *naturales,* with a
series of five *naturales* which were all linked and all beautiful and
had the Plaza in pandemonium because where could he go from
there? And Amado came up sweetly to the bull, and did five
more *naturales* as good as the first five, and then did five more
without moving from his spot—they were superb—and then

furled his muleta until it was the size of the page in an art book like this, and he passed the bull five more times in the same way, the horns going around his left wrist. The man and the bull looked in love with each other. And then after these twenty *naturales,* Amado did five more with almost no muleta at all, five series of five *naturales* had he performed, twenty-five *naturales*—it is not much easier than making love twenty-five times in a row— and then he knelt and kissed the bull on the forehead he was so happy, and got up delicately, and went to the *barrera* for his sword, came back, profiled to get ready for the kill. Everyone was sitting on a collective fuse. If he managed to kill on the first *estocada* this could well be the best *faena* anyone had ever seen a *novillero* perform, who knew, it was all near to unbelievable, and then just as he profiled, the bull charged prematurely, and Amado, determined to get the kill, did not skip away but held ground, received the charge, stood there with the sword, turned the bull's head with the muleta, and the bull impaled himself on the point of the torero's blade which went right into the proper space between the shoulders, and the bull ran right up on it into his death, took several steps to the side, gave a toss of his head at heaven, and fell. Amado had killed *recibiendo.* He had killed standing still, receiving the bull while the bull charged. No one had seen that in years. So they gave him everything that day, ears, tail, *vueltas* without limit—they were ready to give him the bull— a month later they even forgave him the six bad bulls he fought all by himself. But they could not forgive the two big bulls who went out alive on the day he took his *alternativa.* That was the end of Amado Ramirez in Mexico City.

But I will always have love for El Loco because he taught me how to love the bullfight, and how to penetrate some of its secrets. And finally he taught me something about the mystery of form. He gave me the clue that form is the record of a war. When Amado was happy and brave he delineated the form of bullfighting as bullfighting should be, and when he was awkward and afraid he engraved archetypes of clumsiness on the brain and offered models to avoid forever. Because he never had the ability most bullfighters, like most artists, possess to be false with their art, tasty yet phony, he taught something about life with every move he made, including the paradox that courage can be found in men whose conflict is caught between their ambition and their cowardice. He even taught me how to look for form in other places. Do you see the curve of a beautiful breast? It is not necessarily a gift of God—it may be the record life left on a lady of the balance of forces between her desire, her modesty, her ambition, her timidity, her maternity, and her sense of an impulse which cannot be denied. So go through the pictures which follow. If we were wise enough, bold enough, and scholars from head to motorcyclist's boot, we could extract the real history of Europe from the forms elucidated between man and beast in the sequences soon to be glimpsed beneath your hand, *torero de salon!*

Black Power

———

(1968)

ALLOW A SYMPOSIAST to quote from himself. The following is out of a new book called *The Armies of the Night*.

> Not for little humor had Negroes developed that odd humorless crack in their personality which cracked each other into laughter, playing on one side an odd mad practical black man who could be anything, wise chauffeur, drunken butler, young money-mad Pullman porter, Negro college graduate selling insurance—the other half was sheer psychopath, rocks in the ice cube, pocket oiled for the switchblade, I'll kill you Whitey, burn baby, all tuned to a cool. These Blacks moved through the New Left with a physical indifference to the bodies about them, as if ten Blacks could handle any hundred of these flaccid Whites, and they signaled to each other across the aisles, and talked in quick idioms and out, an English not comprehensible to any ear which knew nothing of the separate meanings of the same word at separate pitch (Maoists not for nothing these Blacks!) their hair carefully brushed out in every

direction like African guerrillas or huge radar stations on some lonely isle, they seemed to communicate with one another in ten dozen modes, with fingers like deaf and dumb, with feet, with their stance, by the flick of their long wrist, with the radar of their hair, the smoke of their will, the glide of their passage, by a laugh, a nod, a disembodied gesture, through mediums, seeming to speak through silent mediums among them who never gave hint to a sign. In the apathy which had begun to lie over the crowd as the speeches went on and on (and the huge army gathered by music, now was ground down by words, and the hollow absurd imprecatory thunder of the loudspeakers with their reductive echo—you must FIGHT . . . *fight* . . . fight . . . fite . . . ite . . . , in the soul-killing repetition of political jargon which reminded people that the day was well past one o'clock and they still had not started), the Blacks in the roped-in area about the speaker's stand were the only sign of active conspiracy, they were up to some collective expression of disdain, something to symbolize their detestation of the White Left—yes, the observer was to brood on it much of the next day when he learned without great surprise that almost all of the Negroes had left to make their own demonstration in another part of Washington, their announcement to the press underlining their reluctance to use their bodies in a White War. That was comprehensible enough. If the Negroes were at the Pentagon and did not preempt the front rank, they would lose face as fighters; if they were too numerous on the line, they would be beaten half to death. That was the ostensible reason they did not go, but the observer wondered if he saw a better.

There is an old tendency among writers of the Left when apologists for one indigestible new convulsion or another—they go in for a species of calculated reduction which attempts to introduce comfortable proportions into historic phenomena which are barbaric, heroic, monstrous, epic, and/or apocalyptic. (*New Republic* and *Nation* writers please stand!) So we may remember there was never much of a famine in the Ukraine, just various local dislocations of distribution; never real Moscow trials, rather the sort of predictable changing of the guard which accompanies virile epochs of history. The American labor unions were never really in danger of leaving the Left, just being led down the garden path by unscrupulous but limited leadership. Et cetera. So forth.

Now, Black Power. We are bound to hear before we are done that Black Power is merely a long-due corrective for premature and administratively betrayed efforts at integration—an indispensable period of self-development which will result in future integrations at a real level.

Like all such Left perspectives, it is wishful, pretty, programmatic, manipulable by jargon, and utterly stripped of that existential content which is indispensable to comprehending the first thing about Black Power.

The first thing to say, pretty or no, is that the Negro (that is the active volatile cadres of every militant Negro movement, SNCC, Black Muslims, etc., plus those millions of latently rebellious black masses behind them—which is what we will refer to when we speak of the Negro), yes, this Negro does not want equality any longer, he wants superiority, and wants it because he feels he is in fact superior. And there is some justice on his side for believing it. Sufficiently fortunate to be alienated from the benefits of American civilization, the Negro seems to have been better able to keep his health. It would take a liberal with a psychotic sense of moderation to claim that whites and Negroes have equally healthy bodies; the Negroes know they have become on the average physically superior, and this *against all the logic of America's medical civilization*—the Negroes get less good food ostensibly, no vitamins, a paucity of antibiotics, less medical care, less fresh air, less light and sanitation in living quarters. Let us quit the list—it is parallel to another list one could make of educational opportunities vs. actual culture (which is to say—real awareness of one's milieu). The Negro's relatively low rate of literacy seems to be in inverse relation to his philosophical capacity to have a comprehensive vision of his life, a large remark whose only support is existential—let us brood, brothers, on the superior cool of the Negro in public places. For the cool comes from a comprehensive vision, a relaxation before the dangers of life, a readiness to meet death, philosophy or amusement at any turn.

Commend us, while we are on lists, to the ability of the Negro to police himself, as opposed to the ability of the White to police others. At the Civil Rights March on Washington in 1963 with over a hundred thousand Negroes in town, no episodes of violence were reported—in the riots in the years which followed, fascinating patterns of cooperation among the rioters emerge. One may look, as government commissions do, for patterns of a plot; or one may do better to entertain the real possibility that the Negroes have psychic powers of mass impromptu collaboration which are mysterious, and by that measure, superior to the White.

What the Negro may have decided at this point, as Black Power emerges, is that he has gotten the worst and the least of civilization, and yet has been able to engage life more intensely. It is as if the cells of his body now know more than the white man—so his future potentiality is greater. Whether this is true, half true, or a species of madness is beyond anyone's capacity to know in this year, but the psychological reality is that breaking through his feelings of vast inferiority, a feeling of vast superiority is beginning to arise in the black man, and the antennae of this superiority lead not to developing the Negro to a point where he can live effectively as an equal in white society, but rather toward developing a viable modern culture of his own, a new kind of civilization. This is the real and natural intent of Black Power; not to get better schools, but to find a way to educate their own out of textbooks not yet written; not to get fair treatment from the police, but grapple instead with the incommensurable problem of policing one's own society—what will black justice be? Ergo, not to get a fair share of hospitals, but an opportunity to explore black medicine, herbs in place of antibiotics, witchcraft for cancer cures, surgical grace with the knife in preference to heart transfers. In parallel: not to get into unions, but to discover—it is far off in the distance—black notions of labor, cooperation, and the viability of Hip in production methods; not housing projects, but a new way to build houses; not shuttle planes, but gliders; not computers—rather psychic inductions.

Black Power moves then, obviously, against the technological society. Since the Negro has never been able to absorb a technological culture with success, even reacting against it with instinctive pain and distrust, he is now in this oncoming epoch of automation, going to be removed from the technological society anyway. His only salvation, short of becoming a city brigand or a government beggar, is to build his own society out of his own culture, own means, own horror, own genius. Or own heroic, tragic, or evil possibilities. For there is no need to assume that the black man will prove morally superior to the white man. Schooled in treachery, steeped in centuries of white bile, there are avalanches and cataracts of violence, destruction, inchoate rage and promiscuous waste to be encountered—there is well a question whether he can build his own society at all, so perverse are the conduits of his crossed emotions by now. But the irony is that the White would do well to hope the Black can build a world, for those well-ordered epochs of capitalism which flushed the white wastes down into the black heart are gone—the pipes of civilization are backing up. The irony is that we may even yet need a black vision of existence if civilization is to survive the death chamber it has built for itself. So let us at least recognize the real ground of Black Power—it is ambitious, beautiful, awesome, terrifying, and has to do with nothing so much as the most important questions of us all—What is man? Why are we here? Will we survive?

Looking for the Meat and Potatoes—Thoughts on Black Power

—————

(1969)

"You don't even know who you are," Reginald had said. "You don't even know, the white devil has hidden it from you, that you are of a race of people of ancient civilizations, and riches in gold and kings. You don't even know your true family name, you wouldn't recognize your true language if you heard it. You have been cut off by the devil white man from all true knowledge of your own kind. You have been a victim of the evil of the devil white man ever since he murdered and raped and stole you from your native land in the seeds of your forefathers."

—*The Autobiography of Malcolm X*

IN NOT TOO MANY YEARS, we will travel to the moon, and on the trip, the language will be familiar. We have not had our education for nothing—all those sanitized hours of orientation via high school, commercials, corporations, and mass media have given us one expectation: no matter how beautiful, insane, dangerous, sacrilegious, explosive, holy, or damned a new venture may be, count on it, fellow Americans, the language will be familiar. Are you going in for a serious operation, voting on the political future of the country, buying insurance, discussing nuclear disarmament, or taking a trip to the moon? You can depend on the one great American certainty—the public vocabulary of the discussion will suggest the same relation to the resources of the English language that a loaf of big-bakery bread in plastic bag and wax bears to the secret heart of wheat and butter and eggs and yeast.

Your trip to the moon will not deal needlessly with the vibrations of the heavens (now that man dares to enter eschatology) nor the metaphysical rifts in the philosophical firmament; no poets will pluck a stringed instrument to conjure with the pale shades of the white lady as you move along toward the lunar space. Rather, a voice will emerge from the loudspeaker, "This is your pilot. On our starboard bow at four o'clock directly below, you can pick out a little doojigger of land down there like a vermiform appendix, and that, as we say goodbye to the Pacific Coast, is Baja California. The spot of light at the nub, that little bitty illumination like the probe bulb in a cystoscope or comparable medical instrument, is Ensenada, which the guidebooks call a jeweled resort."

Goodbye to earth, hello the moon! We will skip the technological dividend in the navigator's voice as he delivers us to that space station which will probably look like a breeding between a modern convention hall and the computer room at CBS. Plus the packaged air in the space suits when the tourists, after two days of acclimation in air-sealed moon motels, take their first reconnoiter outside in the white moon dust while their good American bowels accommodate to relative weightlessness.

All right, bright fellow, the reader now may say—what does all this have to do with Black Power? And the author, while adept at dancing in the interstices of a metaphor, is going to come back nonetheless straight and fast with this remark—our American mass-media language is not any more equipped to get into a discussion of Black Power than it is ready to serve as interpreter en route to the moon. The American language has become a conveyer belt to carry each new American generation into its ordained position in the American scene, which is to say the corporate technological world. It can deal with external descriptions of everything which enters or leaves a man, it can measure the movements of that man, it can predict until such moment as it is wrong what the man will do next, but it cannot give a spiritual preparation for our trip to the moon any more than it can talk to us about death, or the inner experiences of real sex, real danger, real dread. Or Black Power.

If the preface has not been amusing, cease at once to read, for what follows will be worse: the technological American is programmed to live with answers, which is why his trip to the moon will be needlessly god-awful; the subject of Black Power opens nothing but questions, precisely those unendurable questions which speak of premature awakenings and the hour of the wolf. But let us start with something comfortable, something we all know, and may encounter with relaxation, for the matter is familiar:

> think of that black slave man filled with fear and dread, hearing the screams of his wife, his mother, his daughter being taken—in the barn, the kitchen, in the bushes! . . . *Think* of hearing wives, mothers, daughters, being *raped*! And you were too filled with fear of the rapist to do anything about it! . . . Turn around and look at each other, brothers and sisters, and *think* of this! You and me, polluted all these colors—and this devil has the arrogance and the gall to think we, his victims should *love* him!
>
> —*The Autobiography of Malcolm X*

"Okay," you say, "I know that, I know that already. I didn't do it. My great-grandfather didn't even do it. He was a crazy Swede. He never even saw a black skin. And now for Chrissake, the girls in Sweden are crazy about Floyd Patterson. I don't care. I say more power to him. All right," goes the dialogue of this splendid American now holding up a hand, "all right, I know about collective responsibility. If some Scotch-Irish planter wanted to tomcat in the magnolias, then I'll agree it's easier for me than for the victim to discern subtle differences between one kind of WASP and another, I'll buy my part of the ancestral curse for that Scotch-Irish stud's particular night of pleasure, maybe I'm guilty of something myself, but there are limits, man. All right, we never gave the Negro a fair chance, and now we want to, we're willing to put up with a reasonable amount of disadvantage, in fact, discomfort, outright inequality and inefficiency. I'll hire Negroes who are not as equipped in the productive scheme of things as whites; that doesn't mean we have to pay iota for iota on every endless misdemeanor of the past and suffer a vomit bag of bad manners to boot. Look, every student of revolution can tell you that the danger comes from giving the oppressed their first liberties. A poor man who wins a crazy bet always squanders it. The point, buddy, is that the present must forgive the past, there must be forgiveness for old sins, or else progress is impossible." And there is the key to the first door: progress depends upon anesthetizing the past. What if, says Black Power, we are not interested in progress, not your progress with packaged food for soul food, smog for air, hypodermics for roots, air-conditioning for breeze—what if we think we have gotten strong by living without progress and your social engineering, what if we think an insult to the blood is never to be forgotten because it keeps your life alive and reminds you to meditate before you urinate. Who are you to say that spooks don't live behind the left ear and ha'nts behind the right? Whitey, you smoke so much you can't smell, taste, or kiss—your breath is too bad. If you don't have a gun, I can poke you and run—you'll never catch me. I'm alive 'cause I keep alive the curse you put in my blood. Primitive people don't forget. If they do, they turn out no better than the civilized and the sick. Who are you, Whitey, to tell me to drop my curse, and join your line of traffic going to work? I'd rather keep myself in shape and work out the curse, natural style. There's always white women, ahem! Unless we decide they're too full of your devil's disease, hypocritical pus-filled old white blood, and so we stay black with black, and repay the curse by drawing blood. That's the life-giving way to repay a curse."

"Why must you talk this way?" says the splendid American. "Can't you see that there are white and whites, whites I do not begin to control? They wish to destroy you. They agree with your values. They are primitive whites. They think in blood for blood. In a war, they will kill you, and they will kill me."

"Well, daddy, I'm just putting you on. Didn't you ever hear of the hereafter? That's where it will all work out, there where us Blacks are the angels and honkies is the flunky. Now, let me take you by the tail, white cat, long enough to see that I want some more of these handouts, see, these homey horse balls and government aid."

The splendid American has just been left in the mire of a put-on and throwaway. How is he to know if this is spring mud or the muck of the worst Negro Hades?

> The native's relaxation takes precisely the form of a muscular orgy in which the most acute aggressivity and the most impelling violence are canalised, transformed, and conjured away. . . . At certain times on certain days, men and women come together at a given place, and there, under the solemn eye of the tribe, fling themselves into a seemingly unorganized pantomime, which is in reality extremely systematic, in which by various means—shakes of the head, bending of the spinal column, throwing of the whole body backwards—may be deciphered as in an open book the huge effort of a community to exorcise itself, to liberate itself . . . in reality your purpose in coming together is to allow the accumulated libido, the hampered aggressivity to dissolve as in a volcanic eruption. Symbolical killings, fantastic rite, imaginary mass murders—all must be brought out. The evil humours are undammed, and flow away with a din as of molten lava.
>
> —FRANTZ FANON, *The Wretched of the Earth*

Here is the lesson learned by the struggles of present-day colonial countries to obtain their independence: a war of liberation converts the energies of criminality, assassination, religious orgy, voodoo, and the dance into the determined artful phalanxes of

bold guerrilla armies. A sense of brotherhood comes to replace
the hitherto murderous clan relations of the natives. Once, that
propensity to murder each other had proved effective in keeping the peace—for the settler. Now, these violent sentiments
turn against the whites who constrain them. Just as the natives
upon a time made good servants and workers for the whites,
while reserving the worst of their characters for each other, now
they looked to serve each other, to cleanse the furies of their
exploited lives in open rude defiance against the authority.

This is the conventional explanation offered by any revolutionary spokesman for the Third World—that new world which
may or may not emerge triumphant in Latin America, Asia, and
Africa. It is a powerful argument, an uplifting argument, it stirs
the blood of anyone who has ever had a revolutionary passion,
for the faith of the revolutionary (if he is revolutionary enough
to have faith) is that the repressed blood of mankind is ultimately
good and noble blood. Its goodness may be glimpsed in the
emotions of its release. If a sense of brotherhood animates the
inner life of guerrilla armies, then it does not matter how violent
they are to their foe. That violence safeguards the sanctity of
their new family relations.

If this is the holy paradigm of the colonial revolutionary, its
beauty has been confirmed in places, denied in others. While
the struggles of the NLF and the North Vietnamese finally proved
impressive even to the most gung ho Marine officers in Southeast Asia, the horrors of the war in Biafra go far toward proving
the opposite. The suspicion remains that beneath the rhetoric of
revolution, another war, quite separate from a revolutionary war,
is also being waged, and the forces of revolution in the world are
as divided by this concealed war as the civilized powers who
would restrain them. It is as if one war goes on between the privileged and the oppressed to determine how the productive
wealth of civilization will be divided; the other war, the seed contained within this first war, derives from a notion that the wealth
of civilization is not wealth but a corporate productive poisoning
of the wellsprings, avatars, and conduits of nature; the power of
civilization is therefore equal to the destruction of life itself. It is,

of course, a perspective open to the wealthy as well as to the poor—not every mill owner who kills the fish in his local rivers with the wastes from his factory is opposed to protecting our wilderness preserve, not at all, some even serve on the State Conservation Committee. And our First Lady would try to keep billboards from defacing those new highways which amputate the ecology through which they pass. Of course, her husband helped to build those highways. But then the rich, unless altogether elegant, are inevitably comic. It is in the worldwide militancy of the underprivileged, undernourished, and exploited that the potential horror of this future war (concealed beneath the present war) will make itself most evident. For the armies of the impoverished, unknown to themselves, are already divided. Once victorious over the wealthy West—if ever!—they could only have a new war. It would take place between those forces on their side who are programmatic, scientific, more or less socialist, and near maniac in their desire to bring technological culture at the fastest possible rate into every backward land, and those more traditional and/or primitive forces in the revolution of the Third World who reject not only the exploitation of the Western world but reject the West as well, in toto, as a philosophy, a culture, a technique, as a way indeed of even attempting to solve the problems of man himself.

Of these colonial forces, black, brown and yellow, which look to overthrow the economic and social tyrannies of the white man, there is no force in Africa, Asia, or Latin America which we need think of as being any more essentially colonial in stance than the American Negro. Consider these remarks in *The Wretched of the Earth* about the situation of colonials:

> "The colonial world is a world cut in two. The dividing line, the frontiers are shown by barracks and police stations." (Of this, it may be said that Harlem is as separate from New York as East Berlin from West Berlin.)
> " . . . if, in fact, my life is worth as much as the settler's, his glance no longer shrivels me up nor freezes me, and his voice no longer turns me into stone. I am no longer

on tenterhooks in his presence; in fact, I don't give a damn for him. Not only does his presence no longer trouble me, but I am already preparing such efficient ambushes for him that soon there will be no way out but that of flight." (Now, whites flee the subways in New York.)

" . . . there is no colonial power today which is capable of adopting the only form of contest which has a chance of succeeding, namely, the prolonged establishment of large forces of occupation." (How many divisions of paratroops would it take to occupy Chicago's South Side?)

The American Negro is of course not synonymous with Black Power. For every Black militant, there are ten Negroes who live quietly beside him in the slums, resigned for the most part to the lessons, the action, and the treadmill of the slums. As many again have chosen to integrate. They live now like Negroid Whites in mixed neighborhoods, suburbs, factories, obtaining their partial peace within the white dream. But no American Negro is contemptuous of Black Power. Like the accusing finger in the dream, it is the rarest nerve in their head, the frightening pulse in their heart, equal in emotional weight to that passion which many a noble nun sought to conquer on a cold stone floor. Black Power obviously derives from a heritage of anger which makes the American Negro one man finally with the African, the Algerian, and even the Vietcong—he would become schizophrenic if he tried to suppress his fury over the mutilations of the past.

The confrontation of Black Power with American life gives us then not only an opportunity to comprehend some of the forces and some of the style of that war now smoldering between the global rich and the global poor, between the culture of the past and the intuitions of the future, but—since Black Power has more intimate, everyday knowledge of what it is like to live in an advanced technological society than any other guerrilla force on earth—the division of attitudes within Black Power has more to tell us about the shape of future wars and evolutions than any other militant force in the world. Technological man in his terminal diseases, dying of air he can no longer breathe, of packaged food he can just about digest, of plastic clothing his skin can hardly bear, and of static before which his spirit has near expired, stands at one end of revolutionary ambition—at the other is an inchoate glimpse of a world now visited only by the primitive and the drug-ridden, a world where technology shatters before magic and electronic communication is surpassed by the psychic telegraphy of animal mood.

Most of the literature of Black Power is interested entirely, or so it would seem, in immediate political objectives of the most concrete sort. Back in 1923, Marcus Garvey, father of the Back-to-Africa movement, might have written, "When Europe was inhabited by a race of cannibals, a race of savages, naked men, heathens and pagans, Africa was peopled with a race of cultured black men, who were masters in art, science and literature, men who were cultured and refined, men who, it was said, were like the gods," but the present leaders of Black Power are concerned with political mandate and economic clout right here. Floyd McKissick of CORE: "The Black Power Movement seeks to win power in a half dozen ways. These are:

"1. The growth of Black *political* power.
"2. The building of Black *economic* power.
"3. The improvement of the *self-image* of Black people.
"4. The development of Black *leadership*.
"5. The attainment of Federal *law enforcement*.
"6. The mobilization of Black *consumer power*."

These demands present nothing exceptional. On their face, they are not so different from manifestos by the NAACP or planks by the Democratic Party. A debater with the skill of William F. Buckley or Richard Nixon could stay afloat for hours on the lifesaving claim that there is nothing in these six points antithetical to conservatives. Indeed, there is not. Not on the face. For example, here is Adam Clayton Powell, a politician most respected by Black Power militants, on some of these points. Political power: "Where we are 20 percent of the jobs, judgeships, commissionerships, and all political appointments." Economic power: "Rather than a race primarily of consumers and stock boys, we must become a race of producers and stockbrokers." Leadership: "Black communities . . . must neither tolerate nor accept outside leadership—black or white." Federal law enforcement: "The battle against segregation in America's public school systems must become a national effort, instead of the present regional skirmish that now exists." Even consumer protest groups to stand watch on the quality of goods sold in a slum neighborhood are hardly revolutionary, more an implementation of good conservative buying practices. *Consumers Digest* is not yet at the barricades.

Indeed, which American institution of power is ready to argue with these six points? They are so rational! The power of the technological society is shared by the corporations, the military, the mass media, the trade unions, and the government. It is to the interest of each to have a society which is rational, even as a machine is rational. When a machine breaks down, the cause can be discovered; in fact, the cause must be capable of being discovered or we are not dealing with a machine. So the pleasure of working with machines is that malfunctions are correctable; satisfaction is guaranteed by the application of work, knowledge and reason. Hence, any race problem is anathema to power groups in the technological society, because the subject of race is irrational. At the very least, race problems seem to have the property of repelling reason. Still, the tendency of modern society to shape men for function in society like parts of a machine grows more powerful all the time. So we have the paradox of a conservative capitalistic democracy, profoundly entrenched in racial prejudice (and hitherto profoundly attracted to racial exploitation), now transformed into the most developed technological society in the world. The old prejudices of the men who wield power have become therefore inefficient before the needs of the social machine—so inefficient, in fact, that prejudiced as many of them are, they consider it a measure of their responsibility to shed prejudice. (We must by now move outside the center of power before we can even find Gen. Curtis LeMay.)

So the question may well be posed: If the demands formally presented by Black Power advocates like McKissick and Powell are thus rational, and indeed finally fit the requirements of the technological society, why then does Black Power inspire so much fear, distrust, terror, horror, and even outright revulsion among the best liberal descendants of the beautiful old Eleanor Roosevelt bag and portmanteau? And the answer is that an intellectual shell game has been played up to here. We have not covered McKissick's six points, only five. The sixth (point number three) was "The improvement of the *self-image* of Black people." It is here that sheer Black hell busts loose. A technological society can deal comfortably with people who are mature, integrated, goal-oriented, flexible, responsive, group-responsive, etc., etc.— the word we cannot leave out is "white" or white-oriented. The technological society is not able to deal with the self-image of separate peoples and races if the development of their self-image produces personalities of an explosive individuality. We do not substitute sticks of dynamite for the teeth of a gear and assume we still have an automotive transmission.

McKissick covers his third point, of course: "Negro history, art, music and other aspects of Black culture . . . make Black people aware of their contributions to the American heritage and to world civilization." Powell bastes the goose with orotundities of rhetorical gravy: "We must give our children a sense of pride in being black. The glory of our past and the dignity of our present must lead the way to the power of our future." Amen. We have been conducted around the point.

Perhaps the clue is that political Right and political Left are meaningless terms when applied conventionally to Black Power. If we are to use them at all (and it is a matter of real convenience), then we might call the more or less rational, programmatic, and recognizably political arm of Black Power, presented by McKissick and Powell, as the Right Wing, since their program can conceivably be attached to the programs of the technological society, whether Democrat or Republican. The straight-out political demands of this kind of Black Power not only can be integrated (at least on paper) into the needs of technological society, but must be, because—we would repeat—an exploited class creates disruption and therefore irrationality in a social machine; efforts to solve exploitation and disruption become mandatory for the power groups. If this last sentence sounds vaguely Marxist in cadence, the accident is near. What characterizes technological societies is that they tend to become more and more like one another. So America and the Soviet will yet have interchangeable parts, or at least be no more different than a four-door Ford from a two-door Chevrolet. It may thus be noticed that what we are calling the Right Wing of Black Power— the technological wing—is in the conventional sense interested in moving to the left. Indeed, after the Blacks attain equality—so goes the unspoken assumption—America will be able to progress toward a rational society of racial participation, etc., etc. What then is the Left Wing of Black Power? Say, let us go back to Africa, back to Garvey.

> We must understand that we are *replacing* a dying culture, and we must be prepared to do this, and be absolutely conscious of what we are replacing it with. We are sons and daughters of the most ancient societies on this planet. . . . No movement shaped or contained by Western culture will ever benefit Black People. Black power must be the actual force and beauty and wisdom of Blackness . . . reordering the world.
>
> —LEROI JONES

Are you ready to enter the vision of the Black Left? It is profoundly antitechnological. Jump into it all at once. Here are a few remarks by Ron Karenga:

> "The fact that we are Black is our ultimate reality. We were Black before we were born.

"The white boy is engaged in the worship of technology; we must not sell our souls for money and machines.
We must free ourselves culturally before we proceed politically.

"Revolution to us is the creation of an alternative . . .
we are not here to be taught by the world, but to teach
the world."

We have left the splendid American far behind. He is a straight-
punching all-out truth-sayer; he believes in speaking his mind;
but if LeRoi Jones—insults, absolute rejection, and consummate
bad-mouthing—is not too much for him, then Karenga will be
his finish. Karenga obviously believes that in the root is the answer to where the last growth went wrong—so he believes in the
wisdom of the blood, and blood-wisdom went out for the splendid American after reading *Lady Chatterley's Lover* in sophomore
year. Life is hard enough to see straight without founding your
philosophy on a metaphor.

Nonetheless the mystique of Black Power remains. Any mystique which has men ready to die for it is never without political
force. The Left Wing of Black Power speaks across the void to the
most powerful conservative passions—for any real conservatism
is founded on regard for the animal, the oak, and the field; it has
instinctive detestation of science, of the creation by machine.
Conservatism is a body of traditions which once served as the
philosophical home of society. If the traditions are now withered
in the hum of electronics; if the traditions have become almost
hopelessly inadequate to meet the computed moves of the technological society; if conservatism has become the grumbling of
the epicure at bad food, bad air, bad manners; if conservatism
lost the future because it enjoyed the greed of its privileged position to that point where the exploited depths stirred in righteous rage; if the conservative and their traditions failed because
they violated the balance of society, exploited the poor too sav-
agely, and searched for justice not nearly enough; if finally the
balance between property rights and the rights of men gave at
last too much to the land and too little to the living blood, still

conservatism and tradition had one last Herculean strength: they were of the marrow, they partook of primitive wisdom. The tradition had been founded on some half-remembered sense of primitive perception, and so was close to life and the sense of life. Tradition had appropriated the graceful movements with which primitive strangers and friends might meet in the depth of a mood, all animal in their awareness: lo! the stranger bows before the intense presence of the monarch or the chief, and the movement is later engraved upon a code of ceremony. So tradition was once a key to the primitive life still breathing within us, a key too large, idiosyncratic, and unmanageable for the quick shuttles of the electronic. Standing before technology, tradition began to die, and air turned to smog. But the black man, living a life on the fringe of technological society, exploited by it, poisoned by it, half-rejected by it, gulping prison air in the fluorescent nightmare of shabby garish electric ghettos, uprooted centuries ago from his native Africa, his instincts living ergo like nerves in the limbo of an amputated limb, had thereby an experience unique to modern man—he was forced to live at one and the same time in the old primitive jungle of the slums and the hygienic surrealistic landscape of the technological society. And as he began to arise from his exploitation, he discovered that the culture which had saved him owed more to the wit and telepathy of the jungle than the value of programs of the West. His dance had taught him more than writs and torts, his music was sweeter than Shakespeare or Bach (since music had never been a luxury to him but a need), prison had given him a culture deeper than libraries in the grove, and violence had produced an economy of personal relations as negotiable as money. The American Black had survived—of all the peoples of the Western world, he was the only one in the near seven decades of the twentieth century to have undergone the cruel weeding of real survival. So it was possible his manhood had improved while the manhood of others was being leached. He had at any rate a vision. It was that he was black, beautiful, and secretly superior—he had therefore the potentiality to conceive and create a new culture (perchance a new civilization), richer, wiser, deeper, more beautiful and profound than any he had seen. (And conceivably more demanding, more torrential, more tyrannical.) But he would not know until he had power for himself. He would not know if he could provide a wiser science, subtler schooling, deeper medicine, richer victual, and deeper view of creation until he had the power. So while some (the ones the Blacks called Negroes) looked to integrate into the supersuburbs of technologyland (and find, was their hope, a little peace for the kids), so others dreamed of a future world which their primitive lore and sophisticated attainments might now bring. And because they were proud and loved their vision, they were warriors as well, and had a mystique which saw the cooking of food as good or bad for the soul. And taste gave the hint. That was the Left of Black Power, a movement as mysterious, dedicated, instinctive, and conceivably bewitched as a gathering of Templars for the next Crusade. Soon their public fury might fall upon the fact that civilization was a trap, and therefore their wrath might be double, for they had been employed to build civilization, had received none of its gains, and yet, being allowed to enter now, now, this late, could be doomed with the rest. What a thought!

> When the *canaille roturière* took the liberating of beheading the high *noblesse,* it was done less, perhaps, to inherit their goods than to inherit their ancestors.
>
> —HEINRICH HEINE

But I am a white American, more or less, and writing for an audience of Americans, white and Negro in the main. So the splendid American would remind me that my thoughts are romantic projections, hypotheses unverifiable by any discipline, no more legitimate for discussion than melody. What, he might ask, would you do with the concrete problem before us. . . .

You mean: not jobs, not schools, not votes, not production, not consumption. . . .

No, he said hoarsely, law and order.

Well, the man who sings the melody is not normally consulted for the by-laws of the Arranger's Union.

Crap and craparoola, said the splendid American, what it all comes down to is: How do you keep the peace?

I do not know. If they try to keep it by force—we will not have to wait so very long before there are Vietnams in our own cities. A race which arrives at a vision must test that vision by deeds.

Then what would you do?

If I were king?

We are a republic and will never support a king.

Ah, if I were a man who had a simple audience with Richard Milhous Nixon, I would try to say, "Remember when all else has failed, that honest hatred searches for responsibility. I would look to encourage not merely new funding for businessmen who are Black, but Black schools with their own teachers and their own texts, Black solutions to Black housing where the opportunity might be given to rebuild one's own slum room by room, personal idiosyncrasy next to mad neighbor's style floor by floor, not block by block; I would try to recognize that an area of a city where whites fear to go at night belongs by all existential—which is to say natural—law to the Blacks, and would respect the fact, and so would encourage Black local self-government as in a separate city with a Black sanitation department run by themselves, a Black fire department, a funding for a Black concert hall, and most of all a Black police force responsible only to this city within our city and Black courts of justice for their own. There will be no peace short of the point where the Black man can measure his new superiorities and inferiorities against our own."

You are absolutely right but for one detail, said the splendid American. What will you do when they complain about the smog *our* factories push into *their* air?

Oh, I said, the Blacks are so evil their factories will push worse air back. And thus we went on arguing into the night. Yes, the times are that atrocious you can hardly catch your breath. "Confronted by outstanding merit in another, there is no way of saving one's ego except by love."

Goethe is not the worst way to say goodnight.

1970s

Millett and D. H. Lawrence

———

(1971)

OF COURSE, KATE MILLETT was not without her own kind of political genius in perceiving that any technologizing of the sexes into twin-unit living teams complete with detachable subunits (kids) might yet have to contend with the work of D. H. Lawrence. Not, of course, for any love of children; it would not be until his last book that one of Lawrence's romances would end with the heroine pregnant, tranquil, and fulfilled. No, Lawrence's love affairs were more likely to come in like winds off Wuthering Heights— but never had a male novelist written more intimately about women—heart, contradiction, and soul; never had a novelist loved them more, been so comfortable in the tides of their sentiment, and so ready to see them murdered. His work held, on the consequence, huge fascination for women. Since by the end he was also the sacramental poet of a sacramental act, for he believed nothing human had such significance as the tender majesties of a man and woman fucking with love, he was also the most appalling subversive to the single permissive sexual standard: the orgy, homosexuality, and the inevitable promiscuity attached to a sexual search repelled him, and might yet repel many of the young as they become bored with the similarity of the sexes.

Indeed, which case-hardened guerrilla of Women's Liberation might not shed a private tear at the following passage:

> And if you're in Scotland and I'm in the Midlands, and I can't put my arms round you, and wrap my legs round you, yet I've got something of you. My soul softly flaps in the little pentecost flame with you, like the peace of fucking. We fucked a flame into being. Even the flowers are fucked into being between the sun and the earth. But it's a delicate thing, and takes patience and the long pause.
>
> So I love chastity now, because it is the peace that comes of fucking. I love being chaste now. I love it as snowdrops love the snow. I love this chastity, which is the pause of peace of our fucking, between us now like a snowdrop of forked white fire. And when the real spring comes, when the drawing together comes, then we can fuck the little flame brilliant and yellow.

Yes, which stout partisan of Female Liberation would read such words and not go soft for the memory of some bitter bridge of love she had burned behind. Lawrence was dangerous. So delicate and indestructible an enemy to the cause of Liberation that to expunge him one would have to look for Millett herself. If she is more careful with Lawrence than with Miller, acting less like some literary Molotov, if her disrespect for quotation is in this place more guarded, if she even functions as a critic and so gives us a clue to the meaning of Lawrence's life and work, she has become twice adroit at hiding the real evidence. It is crucial to her case that Lawrence be the "counterrevolutionary sexual politician" she terms him, but since women love his work, and remember it, she is obliged to bring in the evidence more or less fairly, and only distort it by small moves, brief elisions in the quotation, the suppression of passing contradictions, in short bring in all the evidence on one side of the case and harangue the jury but a little further. Since she has a great deal of evidence, only a careful defense can overthrow her case. For Lawrence can be hung as a counterrevolutionary sexual politician out of his own words and speeches. There is a plethora of evidence—in his worst books. And in all his books there are unmistakable tendencies toward the absolute domination of women by men, mystical worship of the male will, detestation of democracy. There is a stretch in the middle of his work, out in such unread tracts as *Aaron's Rod* and *Kangaroo,* when the uneasy feeling arrives that perhaps it was just as well Lawrence died when he did, for he could have been the literary adviser to Oswald Mosley about the time Hitler came in, one can even ingest a comprehension of the appeal of fascism to Pound and Wyndham Lewis, for the death of nature lived already in the air of the contract between corporate democracy and technology, and who was then to know that the marriage of fascism and technology would be even worse, would accelerate that death. Still, such fear for the end of Lawrence is superficial. He was perhaps a great writer, certainly flawed, and abominably pedestrian in his language when the ducts of experience burned dry, he was unendurably didactic then, he was a pill and, at his worst, a humorless nag; he is pathetic in all those places he suggests that men should follow the will of a stronger man, a purer man, a man conceivably not unlike himself, for one senses in his petulance and in the spoiled airs of his impatient disdain at what he could not intellectually dominate that he was a mama's boy, spoiled rotten, and could not have commanded two infantrymen to follow him, yet he was still a great writer, for he contained a cauldron of boiling opposites—he was on the one hand a Hitler in a teapot, on the other he was the blessed breast of tender love, he knew what it was to love a woman from her hair to her toes, he lived with all the sensibility of a female burning with tender love—and these incompatibles, enough to break a less extraordinary man, were squared in their difficulty by the fact that he had intellectual ambition sufficient to desire the overthrow of European civilization; his themes were nothing if not immense—in *The Plumed Serpent* he would even look to the founding of a new religion based on the virtues of the phallus and the submission of women to the wisdom of that principle. But he was also the son of a miner, he came from hard practical small-minded people, stock descended conceivably from the Druids, but how many centuries had hammered the reductive wisdom of pounds and pennies into the

genes? So a part of Lawrence was like a little tobacconist from
the English Midlands who would sniff the smoke of his wildest
ideas—notions, we may be certain, that ran completely off the
end of anybody's word system—and hack out an irritable cough
at the intimate intricate knobby knotty contradictions of his
ideas when they were embodied in people. For if we can feel how
consumed he was by the dictatorial pressure to ram his sentiments into each idiot throat, he never forgets that he is writing
novels, and so his ideas cannot simply triumph, they have to be
tried and heated and forged, and finally be beaten into shape-
lessness against the anvil of his profound British skepticism,
which would not buy his ideas, not outright, for even his own
characters seem to wear out in them. Kate Leslie, the heroine of
The Plumed Serpent, a proud sophisticated Irish lady, falls in love
with one of the Mexican leaders of a new party, a new faith, a new
ritual, gives herself to the new religion, believes in her
submission—but not entirely! At the end she is still attached to
the ambivalence of the European mind. Lilly, the hero of *Aaron's
Rod,* finally preaches "deep fathomless submission to the heroic
soul in a greater man," and the greater man is Lilly, but he is a
slim small somewhat ridiculous figure, a bigger man for example
strikes him in front of his wife and he is reduced to regaining his
breath without showing he is hurt, he is a small hard-shelled nut
of contradictions, much like Lawrence himself, but the grandeur
of the ideas sounds ridiculous in the little cracked shell. Of
course, Lawrence was not only trying to sell dictatorial theorems,
he was also trying to rid himself of them. We can see by the literary line of his life that he moves from the adoration of his mother
in *Sons and Lovers* and from close to literal adoration of the womb
in *The Rainbow* to worship of the phallus and the male will in his
later books. In fact, Millett can be quoted to good effect, for her
criticism is here close to objective, which is to say not totally at
odds with the defense:

> *Aaron's Rod, Kangaroo,* and *The Plumed Serpent* are rather
> neglected novels, and perhaps justly so. They are un-
> questionably strident, and unpleasant for a number of

reasons, principally a rasping protofascist tone, an increasing fondness of force, a personal arrogance, and innumerable racial, class, and religious bigotries. In these novels one sees how terribly Lawrence strained after triumph in the "man's world" of formal politics, war, priest-craft, art and finance. Thinking of *Lady Chatterley* or the early novels, readers often equate Lawrence with the personal life which generally concerns the novelist, the relations of men and women—for whether he played a woman's man or a man's man, Lawrence was generally doing so before an audience of women, who found it difficult to associate him with the public life of male authority. After *Women in Love,* having solved, or failed to solve, the problem of mastering the female, Lawrence became more ambitious. Yet he never failed to take his sexual politics with him, and with an astonishing consistency of motive, made it the foundation of all his other social and political beliefs.

It is fair analysis as far as it goes, but it fails to underline the heroism of his achievement, which is that he was able finally to leave off his quest for power in the male world and go back to what he started with, go back after every bitterness and frustration to his first knowledge that the physical love of men and women, insofar as it was untainted by civilization, was the salvation of us all, there was no other. And in fact he had never ceased believing that, he had merely lost hope it could be achieved.

Millett's critical misdemeanor is to conceal the pilgrimage, hide the life, cover over that emotional odyssey that took him from adoration of the woman to outright lust for her murder, then took him back to worship her beauty, even her procreative beauty. Millett avoids the sympathy this might arouse in her female readers (which dead lover is more to be cherished after all than the one who returned at the end?), yes, avoids such huge potential sympathy by two simple critical stratagems: she writes about his last book first, which enables her to end her very long chapter on Lawrence with an analysis of his story "The Woman Who Rode Away." Since it may be the most savage of his stories, and concludes with the ritual sacrifice of a white woman by natives, Millett can close on Lawrence with the comment, "Probably it is the perversion of sexuality into slaughter, indeed, the story's very travesty and denial of sexuality, which accounts for its monstrous, even demented air." Not every female reader will remind herself that Lawrence, having purged his blood of murder, would now go on to write *Lady Chatterley*. But then Millett is not interested in the dialectic by which writers deliver their themes to themselves; she is more interested in hiding the process, and so her second way of concealing how much Lawrence has still to tell us about men and women is simply to distort the complexity of his brain into snarling maxims, take him at his worst and make him even worse, take him at his best and bring pinking shears to his context. Like a true species of literary mafia, Millett works always for points and the shading of points. If she can't steal a full point, she'll cop a half.

Examples abound, but it is necessary to quote Lawrence in some fullness; a defense of his works rests naturally on presenting him in uninterrupted lines, which indeed will be no hardship to read. Besides, the clearest exposure of the malignant literary habits of the prosecutor is to quote her first and thereby give everyone an opportunity to see how little she shows, how much she ignores, in her desire to steal the verdict.

> "You lie there," he orders. She accedes with a "queer obedience"—Lawrence never uses the word "female" in the novel without prefacing it with the adjectives "weird" or "queer": this is presumably done to persuade the reader that woman is a dim prehistoric creature operating out of primeval impulse. Mellors concedes one kiss on the navel and then gets to business:
>
> > "And he had to come into her at once, to enter the peace on earth of that soft quiescent body. It was the moment of pure peace for him, the entry into the body of a woman. She lay still, in a kind of sleep, always in a

kind of sleep. The activity, the orgasm was all his, all his; she could strive for herself no more."

This is the passage from which she has drawn her quotation:

"You lie there," he said softly, and he shut the door, so that it was dark, quite dark.

With a queer obedience, she lay down on the blanket. Then she felt the soft, groping, helplessly desirous hand touching her body, feeling for her face. The hand stroked her face softly, softly, with infinite soothing and assurance, and at last there was the soft touch of a kiss on her cheek.

She lay quite still, in a sort of sleep, in a sort of dream. Then she quivered as she felt his hand groping softly, yet with queer thwarted clumsiness among her clothing. Yet the hand knew, too, how to unclothe her where it wanted. He drew down the thin silk sheath, slowly, carefully, right down and over her feet. Then with a quiver of exquisite pleasure he touched the warm soft body, and touched her navel for a moment in a kiss. And he had to come into her at once, to enter the peace on earth of her soft, quiescent body. It was the moment of pure peace for him, the entry into the body of a woman.

She lay still, in a kind of sleep, always in a kind of sleep. The activity, the orgasm was his, all his; she could strive for herself no more. Even the tightness of his arms round her, even the intense movement of his body, and the springing seed in her, was a kind of sleep, from which she did not begin to rouse till he had finished and lay softly panting against her breast.

It is a modest example, but then it is a modest act and Constance Chatterley is exhausted with the deaths of the world she is carrying within—since they will make other kinds of love later, the prosecutor will have cause enough to be further enraged, but the example can show how the tone of Lawrence's prose is poisoned by the acids of inappropriate comment. "Mellors concedes one kiss on the navel and then gets to business." Indeed! Take off your business suit, Comrade Millett.

But it is hardly the time for a recess. We will want to look at another exhibit. The quoted lines up for indictment are from *Women in Love:*

> Having begun by informing Ursula he will not love her, as he is interested in going beyond love to "something much more impersonal and harder," he goes on to state his terms: "I've seen plenty of women, I'm sick of seeing them. I want a woman I don't see . . . I don't want your good looks, and I don't want your womanly feelings, and I don't want your thoughts nor opinions nor your ideas." The "new" relationship, while posing as an affirmation of the primal unconscious sexual being, to adopt Lawrence's jargon, is in effect a denial of personality in the woman.

Or is it Millett's denial of personality in Lawrence? Witness how our literary commissar will void the strength of Lawrence's style by cutting off our acquaintance with the marrow of his sensibility, the air of his senses. For Lawrence is always alert to the quiet ringing of the ether, the quick retreat of a mood, the awe of the thought about to be said, then left unsaid, then said after all. But his remarks cannot be chopped out of their setting. A bruised apple at the foot of a tree is another reality from a bruised apple in the Frigidaire.

> There was silence for some moments.
> "No," he said. "It isn't that. Only—if we are going to make a relationship, even of friendship, there must be something final and irrevocable about it."
> There was a clang of mistrust and almost anger in his voice. She did not answer. Her heart was too much contracted. She could not have spoken.

Seeing she was not going to reply, he continued, almost bitterly, giving himself away:

"I can't say it is love I have to offer—and it isn't love I want. It is something much more impersonal and harder—and rarer."

There was a silence, out of which she said:

"You mean you don't love me?"

She suffered furiously, saying that.

"Yes, if you like to put it like that. Though perhaps that isn't true. I don't know. At any rate, I don't feel the emotion of love for you—no, and I don't want to. Because it gives out in the last issues."

How different is all this from "going beyond love to 'something much more impersonal and harder,' " how much in fact we have the feeling they are in love.

"If there is no love, what is there?" she cried, almost jeering.

"Something," he said, looking at her, battling with his soul, with all his might.

"What?"

He was silent for a long time, unable to be in communication with her while she was in this state of opposition.

"There is," he said, in a voice of pure abstraction, "a final me which is stark and impersonal and beyond responsibility. So there is a final you, and it is there I would want to meet you—not in the emotional, loving plane—but there beyond, where there is no speech and no terms of agreement. There we are two stark, unknown beings, two utterly strange creatures, I would want to approach you, and you me. And there could be no obligation, because there is no standard for action there, because no understanding has been reaped from that plane. It is quite inhuman—so there can be no calling to book, in any form whatsoever—because one is outside the pale of all that is accepted, and nothing known applies. One can only follow the impulse, taking that which lies in front, and responsible for nothing, asking for nothing, giving nothing, only each taking according to the primal desire."

Ursula listened to this speech, her mind dumb and almost senseless, what he said was so unexpected and so untoward.

"It is just purely selfish," she said.

"If it is pure, yes. But it isn't selfish at all. Because I don't know what I want of you. I deliver *myself* over to the unknown, in coming to you, I am without reserves or defenses, stripped entirely, into the unknown. Only there needs the pledge between us, that we will both cast off everything, cast off ourselves even, and cease to be, so that that which is perfectly ourselves can take place in us."

As we shall soon see, Lawrence will go further than this, he will come to believe that a woman must submit—a most blood-enriching submission, bet on it—yet in that book where such submission takes place, in *The Plumed Serpent*, where Kate Leslie has her most profound sex with a man who insists on remaining a stranger and an Indian, the moral emerges that he wants her by the end, wants Kate Leslie just so deeply as she desires him. Lawrence's point, which he refines over and over, is that the deepest messages of sex cannot be heard by taking a stance on the side of the bank, announcing one is in love, and then proceeding to fish in the waters of love with a breadbasket full of ego. No, he is saying again and again, people can win at love only when they are ready to lose everything they bring to it of ego, position, or identity—love is more stern than war—and men and women can survive only if they reach the depths of their own sex down within themselves. They have to deliver themselves "over to the unknown." No more existential statement of love exists, for it is a way of saying we do not know how the love will turn out. What message more odious to the technologist? So Millett will accuse him endlessly of patriarchal male-dominated sex. But the domination of men over women was only a way station on the line of Lawrence's ideas—what he started to say early and ended saying late was that sex could heal, sex was the only nostrum which could heal, all other medicines were part of the lung-scarring smoke of factories and healed nothing, were poison, but sex could heal only when one was without "reserves or defenses." And so men and women received what they deserved of one another. Since Women's Lib has presented itself with the clear difficulty of giving modern woman a full hard efficient ego, Lawrence's ideas could not be more directly in the way. Still, it is painful to think that, quickly as men are losing any sense of fair play, women—if Millett can model for her sex—are utterly without it. Maybe Millett is not so much Molotov as Vishinsky. What a foul exhibit must now be displayed!

> Passive as she is, Connie fares better than the heroine of *The Plumed Serpent,* from whom Lawrentian man, Don Cipriano, deliberately withdraws as she nears orgasm, in a calculated and sadistic denial of her pleasure:
> "By a swift dark instinct, Cipriano drew away from this in her. When, in their love, it came back on her, the seething electric female ecstasy, which knows such spasms of delirium, he recoiled from her. . . . By a dark and powerful instinct he drew away from her as soon as this desire rose again in her, for the white ecstasy of frictional satisfaction, the throes of Aphrodite of the foam. She could see that to him, it was repulsive. He just removed himself, dark and unchangeable, away from her."

The passage restored will be of interest to any jury looking for further evidence on the virtues or deterrents of the clitoral come:

> She realised, almost with wonder, the death in her of the Aphrodite of the foam: the seething, frictional, ecstatic Aphrodite. By a swift dark instinct, Cipriano drew

away from this in her. When, in their love, it came back on her, the seething electric female ecstasy, which knows such spasms of delirium, he recoiled from her. It was what she used to call her "satisfaction." She had loved Joachim for this, that again, and again, and again he could give her this orgiastic "satisfaction," in spasms that made her cry aloud.

But Cipriano would not. By a dark and powerful instinct he drew away from her as soon as this desire rose again in her, for the white ecstasy of frictional satisfaction, the throes of Aphrodite of the foam. She could see that to him, it was repulsive. He just removed himself, dark and unchangeable, away from her.

And she, as she lay, would realise the worthlessness of this foam-effervescence, its strange externality to her. It seemed to come upon her from without, not from within. And succeeding the first moment of disappointment, when this sort of "satisfaction" was denied her, came the knowledge that she did not really want it, that it was really nauseous to her.

And he, in his dark, hot silence, would bring her back to the new, soft, heavy, hot flow, when she was like a fountain gushing noiseless and with urgent softness from the volcanic deeps. Then she was open to him soft and hot, yet gushing with a noiseless soft power. And there was no such thing as conscious "satisfaction." What happened was dark and untellable. So different from the friction which flares out in circles of phosphorescent ecstasy, to the last wild spasm which utters the involuntary cry, like a death-cry, the final love-cry. This she had known, and known to the end, with Joachim. And now this too was removed from her. What she had with Cipriano was curiously beyond her knowing: so deep and hot and flowing, as it were subterranean. She had to yield before it. She could not grip it into one final spasm of white ecstasy which was like sheer knowing.

And as it was in the love-act, so it was with him. She
could not know him. When she tried to know him,
something went slack in her, and she had to leave off.
She had to let be. She had to leave him, dark and hot
and potent, along with the things that are, but are not
known. The presence. And the stranger. This he was always to her.

Yes, sex was the presence of grace and the introduction of the
stranger into oneself. That was the only medicine for the lividities of the will. So Lawrence would preach, but he was a man in
torture. If Millett had wished to get around Lawrence in the easiest way for the advance of the Liberation, she would have done
better to have built a monument to him, and a bridge over his
work, rather than making the mean calculation she could bury
him by meretricious quotation. For Lawrence is an inspiration,
but few can do more than respect him on the fly (the way a Soviet official might duck into an Orthodox church to smell the
incense). The world has been technologized and technologized
twice again in the forty years since his death, the citizens are
technologized as well. Who will go looking for the "new, soft,
heavy, hot flow" or the "urgent softness from the volcanic deeps"
when the air of cities smells of lava and the mood of the streets is
like the bowels turned inside out? What he was asking for had
been too hard for him, it is more than hard for us; his life was,
yes, a torture, and we draw back in fear, for we would not know
how to try to burn by such a light.

Yet, he was a man more beautiful perhaps than we can guess,
and it is worth the attempt to try to perceive the logic of his
life, for he illumines the passion to be masculine as no other
writer, he reminds us of the beauty of desiring to be a man, for
he was not much of a man himself, a son despised by his father,
beloved of his mother, a boy and young man and prematurely
aging writer with the soul of a beautiful woman. It is not only that
no other man writes so well about women, but indeed is there a
woman who can? Useless for Millett to answer that here is a case
of one man commending another man for his ability to under-

stand women—what a vain and pompous assumption, she will hasten to jeer, but such words will be the ground meat of a dull cow. The confidence is that some of Lawrence's passages have a ring—perhaps it is an echo of that great bell which may toll whenever the literary miracle occurs and a writer sets down words to resonate with that sense of peace and proportion it is tempting to call truth. Yet whoever believes that such a leap is not possible across the gap, that a man cannot write of a woman's soul, or a white man of a black man, does not believe in literature itself. So, yes, Lawrence understood women as they had never been understood before, understood them with all the tortured fever of a man who had the soul of a beautiful, imperious, and passionate woman, yet he was locked into the body of a middling male physique, not physically strong, of reasonable good looks, a pleasant to somewhat seedy-looking man, no stud. What a nightmare to balance that soul! to take the man in himself, locked from youth into every need for profound female companionship, a man almost wholly oriented toward the company of women, and attempt to go out into the world of men, indeed even dominate the world of men so that he might find balance. For his mind was possessed of that intolerable masculine pressure to command which develops in sons outrageously beloved by their mothers—to be the equal of a woman at twelve or six or any early age that reaches equilibrium between the will of the son and the will of the mother, strong love to strong love, is all but to guarantee the making of a future tyrant, for the sense of where to find one's inner health has been generated by the early years of that equilibrium—its substitute will not be easy to create in maturity. What can then be large enough to serve as proper balance to a man who was equal to a strong woman in emotional confidence at the age of eight? Hitlers develop out of such balance derived from imbalance, and great generals and great novelists (for what is a novelist but a general who sends his troops across fields of paper?).

So we must conceive then of Lawrence arrogant with mother love and therefore possessed of a mind that did not believe any man on earth had a mind more important than his own. What a responsibility then to bring his message to the world, unique message that might yet save the world! We must conceive of that ego equal already to the will of a strong woman while he was still a child—what long steps had it taken since within the skull! He needed an extraordinary woman for a mate, and he had the luck to find his Frieda. She was an aristocrat and he was a miner's son, she was large and beautiful, she was passionate, and he stole her away from her husband and children—they could set out together to win the world and educate it into ways to live, do that, do all of that out of the exuberance of finding one another.

But she was a strong woman, she was individual, she loved him but she did not worship him. She was independent. If he had been a stronger man, he could perhaps have enjoyed such personal force, but he had become a man by an act of will, he was bone and blood of the classic family stuff out of which homosexuals are made, he had lifted himself out of his natural destiny, which was probably to have the sexual life of a woman, had diverted the virility of his brain down into some indispensable minimum of phallic force—no wonder he worshipped the phallus, he above all men knew what an achievement was its rise from the root, its assertion to stand proud on a delicate base. His mother had adored him. Since his first sense of himself as a male had been in the tender air of her total concern—now, and always, his strength would depend upon just such outsized admiration. Dominance over women was not tyranny to him but equality, for dominance was the indispensable elevator which would raise his phallus to that height from which it might seek transcendence. And sexual transcendence, some ecstasy where he could lose his ego for a moment, and his sense of self and his will, was life to him—he could not live without sexual transcendence. If he had had an outrageously unequal development—all fury to be a man and all the senses of a woman—there was a direct price to pay: He was not healthy. His lungs were poor, and he lived with the knowledge that he would likely have an early death. Each time he failed to reach a woman, each time he failed particularly to reach his own woman, he was dying a little. It is hopeless to read his books and try to understand the quirky changeable fury-

ridden relationships of his men and women without comprehending that Lawrence saw every serious love affair as
fundamental do-or-die: he knew he literally died a little more
each time he missed transcendence in the act. It was why he saw
lust as hopeless. Lust was meaningless fucking and that was the
privilege of the healthy. He was ill, and his wife was literally killing him each time she failed to worship his most proud and delicate cock. Which may be why he invariably wrote on the edge of
cliché—we speak in simples as experience approaches the enormous, and Lawrence lived with the monumental gloom that his
death was already in him, and sex—some transcendental variety
of sex—was his only hope, and his wife was too robust to recognize such tragic facts.

By the time of writing *Women in Love,* his view of women would
not be far from the sinister. One of the two heroines would succeed in driving her man to his death. His rage against the will of
women turns immense, and his bile explodes on the human
race, or is it the majority of the races?—these are the years when
he will have a character in *Aaron's Rod,* Lilly, his mouthpiece, say:

> I can't do with folk who teem by the billion, like the
> Chinese and Japs and Orientals altogether. Only vermin
> teem by the billion. Higher types breed slower. I would
> have loved the Aztecs and the Red Indians. I *know* they
> hold the element in life which I am looking for—they
> had living pride. Not like the flea-bitten Asiatics. Even
> niggers are better than Asiatics, though they are wallow-
> ers. The American races—and the South Sea Islanders—
> the Marquesans, the Maori blood. That was true blood.
> It wasn't frightened. All the rest are craven.

It is the spleen of a man whose organs are rotting in parts and so,
owner of a world-ego, he will see the world rotting in parts.

These are the years when he flirts with homosexuality but is
secretly, we may assume, obsessed with it. For he is still in need of
that restorative sex he can no longer find, and since his psyche
was originally shaped to be homosexual, homosexuality could

yet be his peace. Except it could not, not likely, for his mind
could hardly give up the lust to dominate. Homosexuality becomes a double irony—he must now seek to dominate men
physically more powerful than himself. The paradoxes of this
position result in the book *Aaron's Rod,* which is about a male
love affair (which never quite takes place) between a big man
and a little man. The little man does the housework, plays nurse-
maid to the big man when he is ill, and ends by dominating him,
enough to offer the last speech in the book:

> All men say, they want a leader. Then let them in their
> souls *submit* to some greater soul than theirs. . . . You,
> Aaron, you too have the need to submit. You, too, have
> the need livingly to yield to a more heroic soul, to give
> yourself. You know you have [but] perhaps you'd rather
> die than yield. And so, die you must. It is your affair.

He has separated the theme from himself and reversed the
roles, but he will die rather than yield, even though earlier in the
book he was ready to demonstrate that platonic homosexuality
saves. It is the clear suggestion that Aaron recovers only because
Lilly anoints his naked body, lays on hands after doctors and
medicines had failed:

> Quickly he uncovered the blond lower body of his pa-
> tient, and began to rub the abdomen with oil, using a
> slow, rhythmic, circulating motion, a sort of massage.
> For a long time he rubbed finely and steadily, then went
> over the whole of the lower body, mindless, as if in a sort
> of incantation. He rubbed every speck of the man's
> lower body—the abdomen, the buttocks, the thighs and
> knees, down to his feet, rubbed it all warm and glowing
> with camphorated oil, every bit of it, chafing the toes
> swiftly, till he was almost exhausted. Then Aaron was
> covered up again, and Lilly sat down in fatigue to look
> at his patient.

He saw a change. The spark had come back into the

sick eyes, and the faint trace of a smile, faintly luminous, into the face. Aaron was regaining himself. But Lilly said nothing. He watched his patient fall into a proper sleep.

Another of his heroes, Birkin, weeps in strangled tones before the coffin of Gerald. It is an earlier period in Lawrence's years of homosexual temptation; the pain is sharper, the passion is stronger. "He should have loved me," he said. "I offered him." And his wife is repelled, "recoiled aghast from him as he sat . . . making a strange, horrible sound of tears." They are the sickly sounds of a man who feels ready to die in some part of himself because the other man would never yield.

But homosexuality would have been the abdication of Lawrence as a philosopher-king. Conceive how he must have struggled against it! In all those middle years he moves slowly from the man who is sickened because the other did not yield to the man who will die because he himself will not yield. But he is bitter, and with a rage that could burn half the world. It is burning his lungs.

Then it is too late. He is into his last years. He is into the five last years of his dying. He has been a victim of love, and will die for lack of the full depth of a woman's love for him—what a near to infinite love he had needed. So he has never gotten to that place where he could deliver himself to the unknown, be "without reserves or defenses . . . cast off everything . . . and cease to be, so that that which is perfectly ourselves can take place in us," no, he was never able to go that far. By the time he began *Lady Chatterley,* he must have known the fight was done; he had never been able to break out of the trap of his lungs, nor out of the cage of his fashioning. He had burned too many holes in too many organs trying to reach into more manhood than the course of his nerves could carry, he was done; but he was a lover, he wrote *Lady Chatterley,* he forgave, he wrote his way a little further toward death, and sang of the wonders of creation and the glory of men and women in the rut and lovely of a loving fuck.

"When a woman gets absolutely possessed by her own will, her own will set against everything, then it's fearful, and she should be shot at last."

"And shouldn't men be shot at last, if they get possessed by their own will?"

"Ay!—the same!"

The remark is muttered, the gamekeeper rushes on immediately to talk of other matters, but it has been made, Lawrence has closed the circle, the man and the woman are joined, separate and joined.

Tango, Last Tango

———

(1973)

TO PAY ONE'S FIVE DOLLARS and join the full house at the Translux for the evening show of *Last Tango in Paris* is to be reminded once again that the planet is in a state of pullulation. The seasons accelerate. The snow which was falling in November had left by the first of March. Would our summer arrive at Easter and end with July? It is all that nuclear radiation, says every aficionado of the occult. And we pullulate. Like an anthill beginning to feel the heat.

We know that Spengler's thousand-year metamorphosis from culture to civilization is gone, way gone, and the century required for a minor art to move from commencement to decadence is off the board. Whole fashions in film are born, thrive, and die in twenty-four months. Still! It is only a half year since Pauline Kael declared to the readers of *The New Yorker* that the presentation of *Last Tango in Paris* at the New York Film Festival on October 14, 1972, was a date that "should become a landmark in movie history—comparable to May 29, 1913—the night *Le Sacre du Printemps* was first performed—in music history," and then went on to explain that the newer work had "the same kind of hypnotic excitement as the *Sacre*, the same primitive force, and the same jabbing, thrusting eroticism. . . . Bertolucci and Brando have altered the face of an art form." Whatever could have been shown onscreen to make Kael pop open for a film? "This must be the most powerfully erotic movie ever made, and it may turn out to be the most liberating movie ever made. . . ." Could this be our own Lady Vinegar, our quintessential cruet? The first frigid of the film critics was treating us to her first public reception. Prophets of Baal, praise Kael! We had obviously no ordinary hour of cinema to contemplate.

Now, a half year later, the movie is history, has all the palpability of the historic. Something just discernible has already happened to humankind as a result of it, or at least to that audience who are coming in to the Translux to see it. They are a crew. They have unexpected homogeneity for a movie audience, compose, indeed, so thin a sociological slice of the New York and suburban sausage that you cannot be sure your own ticket isn't what was left for the toothpick, while the rest of the house has been bought at a bite. At the least, there is the same sense of aesthetic oppression one feels at a play when the house is filled with a theater party. So, too, is the audience at *Tango* an infarct of middle-class anal majesties—if Freud hadn't given us the clue, a reader of faces could decide all on his own that there had to be some social connection between sex, shit, power, violence, and money. But these middle-class faces have advanced their historical inch from the last time one has seen them. They are this much closer now to late Romans.

Whether matrons or young matrons, men or boys, they are *swingers*. The males have wife-swapper mustaches, the women are department-store boutique. It is as if everything recently and incongruously idealistic in the middle class has been used up in the years of resistance to the Vietnamese War—now, bring on the Caribbean. Amazing! In America, even the Jews have come to look like the French middle class, which is to say that the egocentricity of the fascist mouth is on the national face. Perhaps it is the five-dollar admission, but this audience has an obvious obsession with sex as the confirmed core of a wealthy life. It is enough to make one ashamed of one's own obsession (although where would one delineate the difference?). Maybe it is that this audience, still in March, is suntanned, or at the least made up to look suntanned. The red and orange of their skins will match the famous "all uterine" colors—so termed by the set designer—of the interiors in *Last Tango*.

In the minute before the theater lights are down, what a tension is in the house. One might as well be in the crowd just before an important fight commences. It is years since one has watched a movie begin with such anticipation. And the tension holds as the projection starts. We see Brando and Schneider pass each other in the street. Since we have all been informed—by *Time* no less—we know they are going to take carnal occupation of each other, and very soon. The audience watches with anxiety as if it is also going to be in the act with someone new, and the heart (and for some, the bowels) shows a tremor between earthquake and expectation. Maria Schneider is so sexual a presence. None of the photographs has prepared anybody for this. Rare actresses, just a few, have flesh appeal. You feel as if you can touch them on the screen. Schneider has nose appeal—you can smell her. She is every eighteen-year-old in a miniskirt and a maxicoat who ever promenaded down Fifth Avenue in the inner arrogance that proclaims, "My cunt is my chariot."

We have no more than a few minutes to wait. She goes to look at an apartment for rent, Brando is already there. They have passed in the street, and by a telephone booth; now they are in an empty room. Abruptly Brando cashes the check Stanley Kowalski wrote for us twenty-five years ago—he fucks the heroine standing up. It solves the old snicker of how do you do it in a telephone booth?—he rips her panties open. In our new line of *New Yorker*-approved superlatives, it can be said that the cry of the fabric is the most thrilling sound to be heard in World Culture since the four opening notes of Beethoven's Fifth.* It is, in

---

* John Simon, as predictable in his critical reactions as a headwaiter, naturally thought *Last Tango* was part of the riffraff. Since it is Simon's temper to ignore details, he not only does not hear the panties tearing (some ears reside in the

fact, a hell of a sound, small, but as precise as the flash of a match above a pile of combustibles, a way for the director to say, "As you may already have guessed from the way I established my opening, I am very good at movie making, and I have a superb pair, Brando and Schneider—they are sexual heavyweights. Now I place my director's promise upon the material: you are going to be in for a grave and wondrous experience. We are going to get to the bottom of a man and a woman."

So intimates Bertolucci across the silence of that room, as Brando and Schneider, fully dressed, lurch, grab, connect, hump, scream, and are done in less than a minute, their orgasms coming on top of one another like trash cans tumbling down a hill. They fall to the floor, and fall apart. It is as if a hand grenade has gone off in their entrails. A marvelous scene, good as a passionate kiss in real life, then not so good because there has been no shot of Brando going up Schneider, and since the audience has been watching in all the somber awe one would bring to the first row of a medical theater, it is like seeing an operation without the entrance of the surgeon's knife.

One can go to any hard-core film and see fifty phalluses going in and out of as many vaginas in four hours (if anyone can be found who stayed four hours). There is a monumental abstractedness about hard core. It is as if the more a player can function sexually before a camera, the less he is capable of offering any other expression. Finally, the sexual organs show more character than the actors' faces. One can read something of the working conditions of a life in some young girl's old and irritated cunt, one can even see triumphs of the human spirit—old and badly burned labia which still come to glisten with new life, capital! There are phalluses in porno whose distended veins speak of the integrity of the hardworking heart, but there is so little specific content in the faces! Hard core lulls after it excites, and finally it puts the brain to sleep.

But Brando's real cock up Schneider's real vagina would have brought the history of film one huge march closer to the ulti-

---

music of the spheres) but announces that Schneider, beastly abomination, is wearing none.

mate experience it has promised since its inception (which is to reembody life). One can even see how on opening night at the Film Festival, it did not matter so much. Not fully prepared for what was to come, the simulated sex must have quivered like real sex the first time out. Since then we have been told the movie is great, so we are prepared to resist greatness, and have read in *Time* that Schneider said, " 'We were never screwing on stage. I never felt any sexual attraction for him . . . he's almost fifty you know, and'—she runs her hand from her torso to her midriff, 'he's only beautiful to here!' "

So one watches differently. Yes, they *are* simulating. Yes, there is something slightly unnatural in the way they come and fall apart. It is too stylized, as if paying a few subtle respects to Kabuki. The real need for the real cock of Brando into the depths of the real actress might have been for those less exceptional times which would follow the film long after it opened and the reaction had set in.

Since *Tango* is, however, the first major film with a respectable budget, a superbly skilled young director, an altogether accomplished cameraman, and a great actor who is ready to do more than dabble in improvisation, indeed will enter heavily into such near to untried movie science, so the laws of improvisation are before us, and the first law to recognize is that it is next to impossible to build on too false a base. The real problem in movie improvisation is to find some ending that is true to what has gone before and yet is sufficiently untrue to enable the actors to get out alive.

We will come back to that. It is, however, hardly time to let go of our synopsis. Real or simulated, opening night or months later, we know after five minutes that, at the least, we are in for a thoroughgoing study of a man and a woman, and the examination will be close. Brando rents the empty apartment; they will visit each other there every day. His name is Paul, hers is Jeanne, but they are not to learn each other's names yet. They are not to tell one another such things, he informs her. "We don't need names

here ... we're going to forget everything we knew. ... Everything outside this place is bullshit."

They are going to search for pleasure. We are back in the existential confrontation of the century. Two people are going to fuck
in a room until they arrive at a transcendent recognition or some
death of themselves. We are dealing not with a plot but with a
theme that is open range for a hundred films. Indeed we are face-
to-face with the fundamental structure of porno—the difference
is that we have a director who by the measure of porno is Eisen-
stein, and actors who are as gods. So the film takes up the simplest
and richest of structures. To make love in an empty apartment,
then return to a separate life. It is like every clandestine affair the
audience has ever had, only more so—no names! Every personal
demon will be scourged in the sex—one will obliterate the past!
That is the huge sanction of anonymity. It is equal to a new life.

What powerful biographical details we learn, however, on the
instant they part. Paul's wife is a suicide. Just the night before,
she has killed herself with a razor in a bathtub; the bathroom is
before us, red as an abattoir. A sobbing chambermaid cleans it
while she speaks in fear to Paul. It is not even certain whether
the wife is a suicide or he has killed her—that is almost not the
point. It is the bloody death suspended above his life like a bleed-
ing amputated existence—it is with that crimson torso before his
eyes that he will make love on the following days.

Jeanne, in her turn, is about to be married to a young TV director. She is the star in a videofilm he is making about French
youth. She pouts, torments her fiancé, delights in herself, delights in the special idiocy of men. She can cuckold her young
director to the roots of his eyes. She also delights in the violation
she will make of her own bourgeois roots. In this TV film she
makes within the movie she presents her biography to her fiancé's camera: she is the daughter of a dead Army officer who was
sufficiently racist to teach his dog to detect Arabs by smell. So she
is well brought up—there are glimpses of a suburban villa on a
small walled estate—it is nothing less than the concentrated family honor of the French Army she will surrender when Brando
proceeds a little later to bugger her.

These separate backgrounds divide the film as neatly between biography and fornication as those trick highball glasses which present a drawing of a man or a woman wearing clothes on the outside of the tumbler and nude on the inside. Each time Brando and Schneider leave the room we learn more of their lives beyond the room; each time they come together, we are ready to go further. In addition, as if to enrich his theme for students of film, Bertolucci offers touches from the history of French cinema. The life preserver in *Atalante* appears by way of homage to Vigo, and Jean-Pierre Léaud of *The 400 Blows* is the TV director, the boy now fully grown. Something of the brooding echo of *Le Jour se Lève* and Arletty is also with us, that somber memory of Jean Gabin wandering along the wet docks in the dawn, waiting for the police to pick him up after he has murdered his beloved. It is as if we are to think not only of this film but of other sexual tragedies French cinema has brought us, until the sight of each gray and silent Paris street is ready to evoke the lost sound of the *bal musette* and the sad near-silent wash of the Seine. Nowhere as in Paris can doomed lovers succeed in passing sorrow, drop by drop, through the blood of the audience's heart.

Yet as the film progresses with every skill in evidence, while Brando gives a performance that is unforgettable (and Schneider shows every promise of becoming a major star), as the historic buggeries and reamings are delivered, and the language breaks through barriers not even yet erected—no general of censorship could know the armies of obscenity were so near!—as these shocks multiply, and lust goes up the steps to love, something bizarre happens to the film. It fails to explode. It is a warehouse of dynamite and yet something goes wrong with the blow-up.

One leaves the theater bewildered. A fuse was never ignited. But where was it set? One looks to retrace the line of the story.

So we return to Paul trying to rise out of the bloody horizon of his wife's death. We even have some instinctive comprehension of how he must degrade his beautiful closet-fuck, indeed we are

even given the precise detail that he will grease her ass with butter before he buggers her family pride. A scene or two later, he
tricks forth her fear of him by dangling a dead rat which he offers to eat. "I'll save the asshole for you," he tells her. "Rat's asshole with mayonnaise."* (The audience roars—Brando knows
audiences.) She is standing before him in a white wedding
gown—she has run away from a TV camera crew that was getting
ready to film her pop wedding. She has rushed to the apartment
in the rain. Now shivering, but recovered from her fear, she tells
him she has fallen in love with somebody. He tells her to take a
hot bath, or she'll catch pneumonia, die, and all he'll get is "to
fuck the dead rat."

No, she protests, she's in love.

"In ten years," says Brando looking at her big breasts, "you're
going to be playing soccer with your tits." But the thought of the
other lover is grinding away at him. "Is he a good fucker?"

"Magnificent."

"You know, you're a jerk. 'Cause the best fucking you're going
to get is right here in this apartment."

No, no, she tells him, the lover is wonderful, a mystery . . . different.

"A local pimp?"

"He could be. He looks it."

She will never, he tells her, be able to find love until she goes
"right up into the ass of death." He is one lover who is not afraid
of metaphor. "Right up his ass—till you find a womb of fear. And
then maybe you'll be able to find him."

"But I've found this man," says Jeanne. Metaphor has continued long enough for her. "He's you. You're that man."

In the old scripted films, such a phrase was plucked with a
movie composer's chord. But this is improvisation. Brando's instant response is to tell her to get a scissors and cut the fingernails on her right hand. Two fingers will do. Put those fingers up
his ass.

---

* Dialogue from *Last Tango in Paris* was not entirely written in advance, but was
in part an improvisation. In other words, a small but important part of the
screenplay has in effect been written by Brando.

"*Quoi?*"

"Put your fingers up my ass, are you deaf? Go on."

No, he is not too sentimental. Love is never flowers, but farts and flowers. Plus every superlative test. So we see Brando's face before us—it is that tragic angelic mask of incommunicable anguish which has spoken to us across the years of his uncharted heroic depths. Now he is entering that gladiator's fundament again, and before us and before millions of faces yet to come she will be his surrogate bugger, real or simulated. What an entrance into the final images of history! He speaks to us with her body behind him, and her fingers just conceivably up him. "I'm going to get a pig," are the words which come out of his tragic face, "and I'm going to have a pig fuck you"—yes, the touch on his hole has broken open one gorgon of a fantasy—"and I want the pig to vomit in your face. And I want you to swallow the vomit. You going to do that for me?"

"Yeah."

"Huh?"

"Yeah!"

"And I want the pig to die while"—a profound pause—"while you're fucking him. And then you have to go behind, and I want you to smell the dying farts of the pig. Are you going to do that for me?"

"Yes, and more than that. And worse than before."

He has plighted a troth. In our year of the twentieth century how could we ever contract for love with less than five hundred pounds of pig shit? With his courage to give himself away, we finally can recognize the tragedy of his expression across these twenty-five years. That expression has been locked into the impossibility of ever communicating such a set of private thoughts through his beggar's art as an actor. Yet he has just done it. He is probably the only actor in the world who could have done it. He is taking the shit that is in him and leaving it on us. How the audience loves it. They have come to be covered. The world is not polluted for nothing. There is some profound twentieth-century malfunction in the elimination of waste. And Brando is onto it. A stroke of genius to have made a speech like that. Over and over, he is saying in this film that one only arrives at love by springing out of the shit in oneself.

So he seeks to void his eternal waste over the wife's suicide. He sits by her laid-out corpse in a grim hotel room, curses her, weeps, proceeds to wipe off the undertaker's lipstick, broods on her lover (who lives upstairs in the hotel), and goes through some bend of the obscure, for now, offstage, he proceeds to remove his furniture from the new apartment. We realize this as we see Jeanne in the empty rooms. Paul has disappeared. He has ordered her to march into the farts of the pig for nothing. So she calls her TV director to look at the empty apartment—should they rent it? The profound practicality of the French bourgeoisie is squatting upon us. She appreciates the value of a few memories to offer sauce for her lean marriage. But the TV director must smell this old cooking for he takes off abruptly after telling her he will look for a better apartment.

Suddenly Brando is before her again on the street. Has he been waiting for her to appear? He looks rejuvenated. "It's over," she tells him. "It's over," he replies. "Then it begins again." He is in love with her. He reveals his biography, his dead wife, his unromantic details. "I've got a prostate like an Idaho potato but I'm still a good stick man. . . . I suppose if I hadn't met you I'd probably settle for a hard chair and a hemorrhoid." They move on to a hall, some near mythical species of tango palace where a dance contest is taking place. They get drunk and go on the floor. Brando goes in for a squalid parody of the tango. When they're removed by the judges, he flashes his bare ass.

Now they sit down again and abruptly the love affair is terminated. Like that! She is bored with him. Something has happened. We do not know what. Is she a bourgeoise repelled by his flophouse? Or did his defacement of the tango injure some final nerve of upper French deportment? Too small a motive. Must we decide that sex without a mask is no longer love, or conclude upon reflection that no mask is more congenial to passion than to be without a name in the bed of a strange lover?

There are ten reasons why her love could end, but we know none of them. She merely wants to be rid of him. Deliver me from a fifty-year-old, may even be her only cry.

She tries to flee. He follows. He follows her on the Metro and all the way to her home. He climbs the spiraling stairs as she mounts in the slow elevator, he rams into her mother's apartment with her, breathless, chewing gum, leering. Now he is all cock. He is the memory of every good fuck he has given her. "This is the title shot, baby. We're going all the way."

She takes out her father's army pistol and shoots him. He murmurs, "Our children, our children, our children will remember . . ." and staggers out to the balcony, looks at the Paris morning, takes out his chewing gum, fixes it carefully to the underside of the iron railing in a move that is pure broth of Brando—culture is a goat turd on the bust of Goethe—and dies. The angel with the tragic face slips off the screen. And proud Maria Schneider is suddenly and most unbelievably reduced to a twat copping a plea. "I don't know who he is," she mutters in her mind to the oncoming *flics,* "he followed me in the street, he tried to rape me, he is insane. I do not know his name. I do not know who he is. He wanted to rape me."

The film ends. The questions begin. We have been treated to more cinematic breakthrough than any film—at the least—since *I Am Curious (Yellow).* In fact we have gone much further. It is hard to think of any film that has taken a larger step. Yet if this is "the most powerful erotic film ever made" then sex is as Ex-Lax to the lady. For we have been given a bath in shit with no reward. The film, for all its power, has turned inside out by the end. We have been asked to follow two serious and more or less desperate lovers as they go through the locks of lust and defecation, through some modern species of homegrown cancer cure, if you will, and have put up with their modern depths—shit on the face of the beloved and find love!—only to discover a peculiar extortion in the aesthetic. We have been taken on this tour down to the prostate big as an Idaho potato only to recognize that we never did get into an exploration of the catacombs of love, passion, infancy, sodomy, tenderness, and the breaking of emotional ice, instead only wandered from one onanist's oasis to another.

It is, however, a movie that has declared itself, by the power of its opening, as equal in experience to a great fuck, and so the measure of its success or failure is by the same sexual aesthetic. Rarely has a film's value depended so much on the power or lack of power of its ending, even as a fuck that is full of promise is ready to be pinched by a poor end. So, in *Tango*, there is no gathering of forces for the conclusion, no whirling of sexual destinies (in this case, the audience and the actors) into the same funnel of becoming, no flying out of the senses in pursuit of a new vision, no, just the full charge into a blank wall, a masturbator's spasm—came for the wrong reason and on the wrong thought— and one is thrown back, shattered, too ubiquitously electrified, and full of criticism for the immediate past. Now the recollected flaws of the film eat at the pleasure, even as the failed orgasm of a passionate act will call the character of the passion into question.

So the walk out of the theater is with anger. The film has been in reach of the greatness Kael has been talking about, but the achievement has only been partial. Like all executions less divine than their conception, *Tango* will give rise to mutations that are obliged to explore into dead ends. More aesthetic pollution to come! The performance by Brando has been unique, historic, without compare—it is just possible, however, that it has gone entirely in the wrong direction. He has been like a lover who keeps telling consummate dirty jokes until the ravaged dawn when the girl will say, "Did you come to sing or to screw?" He has come with great honor and dignity and exceptional courage to bare his soul. But in a solo. We are being given a fuck film without the fuck. It is like a Western without the horses.

Now the subtle sense of displacement that has hung over the movie is clear. There has been no particular high passion loose.

Brando is so magnetic an actor, Schneider is so attractive, and the scenes are so intimate that we assume there is sexual glue between their parts, but it is our libido which has been boiling that glue and not the holy vibration of the actors on the screen. If Kael has had a sexual liberation with *Tango,* her libido is not alone—the audience is also getting their kicks—by digging the snots of the celebrated. (Liberation for the Silent Majority may be not to attend a fuck but hear dirty jokes.) So the real thrill of *Tango* for five-dollar audiences becomes the peephole Brando offers us on Brando. They are there to hear a world-famous actor say in reply to "What strong arms you have,"

"The better to squeeze a fart out of you."

"What long nails you have."

"The better to scratch your ass with."

"Oh, what a lot of fur you have."

"The better to let your crabs hide in."

"Oh, what a long tongue you have."

"The better to stick in your rear, my dear."

"What's this for?"

"That's your happiness and my ha-penis."

Pandemonium of pleasure in the house. Who wants to watch an act of love when the ghost of Lenny Bruce is back? The crowd's joy is that a national celebrity is being obscene on screen. To measure the media magnetism of such an act, ask yourself how many hundreds of miles you might drive to hear Richard Nixon speak a line like: "We're just taking a flying fuck at a rolling doughnut," or "I went to the University of the Congo; studied whale fucking." Only liberal unregenerates would be so progressive as to say they would not drive a mile. No, one could start mass migrations if Nixon were to give Brando's pig-and-vomit address to the test of love.

Let us recognize the phenomenon. It would be so surrealistic an act, we could not pass Nixon by. Surrealism has become our objective correlative. A private glimpse of the great becomes the alchemy of the media, the fool's gold of the century of communication. In the age of television we know everything about the great but how they fart—the ass wind is, ergo, our trade wind. It is part of Brando's genius to recognize that the real interest of audiences is not in having him portray the tender passages and murderous storms of an unruly passion between a man and a woman, it is rather to be given a glimpse of his kinks. His kinks offer sympathetic vibration to their kinks. The affirmation of passion is that we rise from the swamps of our diapers—by whatever torturous route—to the cock and the cunt; it is the acme of the decadent to go from the first explosive bout of love in *Tango* down to the trimmed fingernails up his rectum.

Then follows the murder. Except it does not follow. It has been placed there from the beginning as the required ending in Bertolucci's mind, it has already been written into the screenplay first prepared with Trintignant and Dominique Sanda in mind. But complications and cast changes occurred. Sanda was pregnant, et cetera. Brando appeared, and Schneider was found. Yet the old ending is still there. Since it did not grow convincingly out of the material in the original script, it appears, after Brando's improvisation, to be fortuitous altogether.

In the original screenplay, the dialogue is so general and the characters so vague that one has to assume Trintignant, Sanda, and Bertolucci planned to give us something extraordinary precisely by overcoming their pedestrian script. It is as if Bertolucci purposely left out whole trunk lines of plot in order to discover them in the film. Only it was Brando who came along rather than Trintignant to make a particular character out of a general role, to "superimpose"—in accordance with Bertolucci's desire—his own character as Marlon Brando, as well as something of his life, and a good bit of his private obsessions. As he did that, however, the film moved away from whatever logic the script had originally possessed. For example, in the pre-Brando treatment, we would have been obliged to listen to the following:

LEON (alias Paul): I make you die, you make me die, we're two murderers, each other's. But who succeeds in realizing this is twice the murderer. And that's the biggest pleasure: watching you die, watching you come out of yourself, white-eyed, writhing, gasping, screaming so loud that it seems like the last time.

Oo la la! We are listening to a French intellectual. It is for good cause that Bertolucci wants to superimpose Brando's personality. Anything is preferable to Leon. And Brando most certainly obliterates this mouthy analysis, creates instead a character who is half noble and half a lout, an overlay drawn on transparent paper over his own image. Paul is an American, ex-boxer, ex-actor, ex–foreign correspondent, ex-adventurer, and now with the death of his wife, ex-gigolo. He is that character and yet he is Brando even more. He is indeed so much like Brando that he does not quite fit the part of Paul—he talks just a little too much, and is a hint too distinguished to be the proprietor of a cheap flophouse at the age of fifty—let us say that at the least Paul is close enough to the magnetic field of Marlon for an audience to be unable to comprehend why Jeanne would be repelled if he has a flophouse. Who cares, if it is Marlon who invites you to live in a flophouse? On the other hand, he is also being Marlon the Difficult, Marlon the Indian from the Underworld, Marlon the shade of the alienated, Marlon the young star who when asked on his first trip to Hollywood what he would like in the way of personal attention and private creature comfort, points to the nerve-jangled pet he has brought with him and says, "Get my monkey fucked."

Yes, he is studying whale-pronging in the Congo. He is the raucous out-of-phase voice of the prairie. Afterward, contemplating the failure, we realize he has been shutting Schneider off. Like a master boxer with a hundred tricks, he has been outacting her (with all his miser's hoard of actor's lore), has been stealing scenes from her while she is nude and he is fully dressed, what virtuosity! But it is unfair. She is brimming to let go. She wants to give the young performance of her life and he is tapping her out of position here, tricking her there—long after it is over we realize he does not want the fight of the century, but a hometown decision. He did not come to fuck but to shit. To defecate into the open-mouthed wonders of his audience and take his cancer cure in public. It is the fastest way! Grease up the kinks and bring in the pigs. We'd take a stockyard of pigs if he would get into what the movie is about, but he is off on the greatest solo of his life and artists as young as Schneider and Bertolucci are hardly going to be able to stop him.

So he is our greatest actor, our noblest actor, and he is also our National Lout. Could it be otherwise in America? Yet a huge rage stirs. He is so great. Can he not be even greater and go to the bottom of every fine actor's terror—which is to let go of the tricks that ring the person and enter the true arena of improvisation? It is there that the future of the film may exist, but we won't find out until a great actor makes the all-out effort.

But now we are back to the core of the failure in *Last Tango*. It is down in the difficulty of improvisation, in the recognition that improvisation which is anything less than the whole of a film is next to no improvisation. It has diminished from the dish to a spice that has been added to the dish (usually incorrectly). Bertolucci is a superb young director, adventurous, steeped in film culture, blessed with cinematic grace. He gives us a movie with high ambition, considerable risk, and a sense of the past. Yet he plows into the worst trap of improvisation—it is the simple refusal of filmmakers to come to grips with the implacable logic of the problem. One does not add improvisation to a script that is already written and with an ending that is locked up. No matter how agreeable the particular results may be, it is still the entrance of tokenism into aesthetics: "You blacks may work in this corporation, and are free to express yourselves provided you don't do anything a responsible white employee won't do." Stay true to the script. It reduces improvisation to a free play period in the middle of a strict curriculum.

The fundamental demand upon improvisation is that it begin with the film itself, which is to say that the idea for the film and the style of improvisation ought to come out of the same thought. From the beginning, improvisation must live in the premise rather than be added to it. The notion is not easy to grasp, and in fact is elusive. It may even be helpful to step away from *Tango* long enough to look at another example of possible improvisation. An indulgence is asked of the reader—to think about another kind of film altogether, a distracting hitch to the argument, but it may not be possible to bring focus to improvisation until we have other models before us.

So the following and imaginary film is offered: Orson Welles to play Churchill while Burton or Olivier does Beaverbrook in the week of Dunkirk. Let us assume we have the great good fortune to find these actors at the height of their powers, and have for auteur a filmmaker who is also a brilliant historian. To these beginnings, he adds a company of intelligent English actors and gives them the same historical material to study in order to provide a common denominator to everyone's knowledge. At this point the auteur and the company agree upon a few premises of plot. The auteur will offer specific situations. It will help if the episodes are sufficiently charged for the actors to lose their fear first of improvisation—which is that they must make up their lines.

Then a narrative action can begin to emerge out of the interplay of the characters, in much the way a good party turns out differently from the expectations of the hostess and yet will develop out of her original conception. With a script, actors try to convince the writer, if he is present, to improve their lines—with improvisation they must work upon their wits. Why assume that the wits of this company of intelligent English actors will have less knowledge of manner and history than an overextended scriptwriter trying to work up his remote conception of what Churchill and Beaverbrook might have been like? Why not assume Welles and Burton have a better idea? Are they not more likely to contain instinctive knowledge in their ambulating meat? Isn't the company, in its steeping as good British actors into their own history, able to reveal to us more of what such a week might have been like than any but the most inspired effort by a screenwriter?

We all contain the culture of our country in our unused acting skills. While Clark Gable could probably not have done an improvisation to save himself, since he had no working habits for that whatsoever, the suspicion still exists that Gable, if he had been able to permit himself, could have offered a few revelations on the life of Dwight D. Eisenhower, especially since Ike seems to have spent a good part of his life imitating Gable's voice. If violence can release love, improvisation can loose the unused culture of a film artist.

The argument is conceivably splendid, but we are talking about *historical* improvisation where the end is still known, and it is the details that are paramount. How simple (and intense) by comparison become the problems of doing a full improvisation for *Tango.* There we are given a fundamental situation, a spoiled girl about to be married, a distraught man whose wife is a suicide. The man and the girl are in the room to make love. We are back at the same beginning. But we can no longer project ahead! If the actors feel nothing for one another sexually, as Schneider has indicated in several interviews was the case for Brando and herself—she may even have been telling the truth—then no exciting improvisation is possible on sexual lines. (The improvisation would have to work on the consequences of a lack of attraction.) Actors do not have to feel great passion for one another in order to give a frisson to the audience, but enough attraction must exist to provide a live coal for improvisation to blow upon. Without some kernel of reality to an improvisation only a monster can continue to offer interesting lines. Once some little attraction is present, there is nothing exceptional about the continuation of the process. Most of us, given the umbilical relation of sex and drama, pump our psychic bellows on many a sensual spark, but then most affairs are, to one degree or another, improvisations, which is to say genuine in some part of their feeling and nicely acted for the rest. What separates professional actors from all of us amateur masses with our animal instinct for dissembling, our everyday acting, is the ability of the professional to take a small emotion in improvisation and go a long distance with it. In a scripted piece of work, some professionals need no relation to the other actor at all, they can, as Monroe once said, "wipe them out" and substitute another face. But improvisation depends on a continuing life since it exists in the no-man's-land between acting and uncalculated response, it is a *special* psychic state, at its best more real than the life to which one afterward returns, and so a special form of insanity. All acting is a corollary of insanity, but working from a script offers a highly controlled means of departing from one's own personality in order to enter another. (As well as the formal power to return.)

What makes improvisation fertile, luminous, frightening, and finally *wiggy* enough for a professional like Gable to shun its practice is that the actor is doing two things at once—playing at a fictitious role while using real feelings, which then begin to serve (rather than the safety of the script) to stimulate him into successive new feelings and responses, until he is in danger of pushing into emotional terrain that is too far out of his control.

If we now examine *Tango* against this perspective, the risks (once there is real sexual attraction between the man and the woman) have to multiply. They are after all not simply playing themselves, but have rather inserted themselves into highly charged creatures, a violent man with a blood-filled horizon and a spoiled middle-class girl with buried tyrannies. How, as they continue this improvisation, can they avoid falling in love, or coming to hate one another? With good film actors, there is even a very real danger that the presence of the camera crew will inflame them further since in every thespian is an orgiast screaming to get out.

So murder is the first dramatic reality between two such lovers in a continuing film of improvisation. They progress toward an end that is frighteningly open. The man may kill the woman, or the woman the man. For, as actors, they have also to face the shame of walking quietly away from one another, a small disaster when one is trying to build intensity, for such a quiet ending is equal to a lack of inspiration, a cowardice before the potential violence of the other. Improvisation is profoundly wicked when it works, it ups the ante, charges all dramatic potential, looks for collision. Yet what a dimension of dramatic exploration is also offered. For the actors can even fall in love, can truly fall in love, can go through a rite of passage together and so reach some locked crypt of the heart precisely because they have been photographed fucking together from every angle, and still—perhaps it is thereby—have found some private reserve of intimacy no one else can touch. Let the world watch. It is not near.

So the true improvisation that *Tango* called for should have moved forward each day on the actors' experience of the day before; it would thereby have offered more aesthetic excitement. Because of its danger! There is a very small line in the last recognitions of the psyche between real bullets in a gun and blanks. The madness of improvisation is such, the intensities of the will become such, that one hardly dares to fire a blank at the other actor. What if he or she is so carried away by excitement that they will refuse to fall? Bring on the real bullet, then. Bite on it.

Of course, literal murder is hardly the inevitable denouement in improvisation. But it is in the private design of each actor's paranoia. Pushed further together in improvisation than actors have gone before, who knows what literal risks might finally have been taken. That is probably why Brando chose to play a buffoon at a very high level and thereby also chose to put Schneider down. Finally we laugh at those full and lovely tits which will be good only for playing soccer (and she will choose to lose thirty pounds after the film is done—a whole loss of thirty pounds of pulchritude). Brando with his immense paranoia (it is hardly unjustified) may have concluded like many an adventurous artist before him that he was adventuring far enough. No need for more.

Still he lost an opportunity for his immense talent. If he has been our first actor for decades, it is because he has given us, from the season he arrived in *Streetcar,* a greater sense of improvisation out of the lines of a script than any other professional actor. Sometimes he seemed the only player alive who knew how to

suggest that he was about to say something more valuable than
what he did say. It gave him force. The lines other people had
written for him came out of his mouth like the final compromise
life had offered for five better thoughts. He seemed to have a
charged subtext. It was as if, whenever requested in other films
to say script lines so bad as "I make you die, you make me die,
we're two murderers, each other's," the subtext—the emotion of
the words he was using behind the words—became, "I want the
pig to vomit in your face." That was what gave an unruly, all but
uncontrolled, and smoldering air of menace to all he did.

Now, in *Tango,* he had nothing beneath the script, for his previous subtext was the script. So he appeared to us as a man orat-
ing, not improvising. But then a long speech can hardly be an
improvisation if its line of action is able to go nowhere but back
into the prearranged structures of the plot. It is like the aside of
a politician before he returns to that prepared text the press already has in their hands. So our interest moved away from the
possibilities of the film and was spent on the man himself, his
nobility and his loutishness. But his nature was finally a less interesting question than it should have been, and weeks would go by
before one could forgive Bertolucci for the aesthetic cacophony
of the end.

Still, one could forgive. For, finally, Bertolucci has given us a
failure worth a hundred films like *The Godfather.* Regardless of all
its solos, failed majesties, and off-the-mark horrors, even as a
highly imperfect adventure, it is still the best adventure in film to
be seen in this pullulating year. And it will open an abyss for Bertolucci. The rest of his life must now be an improvisation. Doubtless he is bold enough to live with that. For he begins *Last Tango*
with Brando muttering two words one can hardly hear. They are:
Fuck God.

The unmanageable in oneself must now offer advice. If Bertolucci is going to fuck God, let him really give the fuck. Then we
may all know a little more of what God is willing or unwilling to
forgive. That is, unless God is old and has indeed forgot, and we
are merely out on a sea of human anality, a collective Faust deprived of Mephisto and turning to shit. The choice, of course, is

small. Willy-nilly, we push on in every art and every technology toward the reembodiment of the creation. It is doubtless a venture more demented than coupling with the pig, but it is our venture, our white whale, and by it or with it shall we be seduced. On to the Congo with sex, technology, and the inflamed lividities of human will.

Genius

(1976)

PART OF THE CRISIS of the twentieth century is that nothing like a coherent view of personality seems able to exist. We live in every concept of human motivation, and they are all at odds. Our minds are obliged to entertain everything from the structured hydraulics of the Freudians, who tend to look at psychic disturbance as varieties of stopped-up plumbing, faulty pressure systems, and inoperative valves, to a hundred California-like conceptions of living it out—everything from Esalen to EST to Ram Dass—schools which see us as transmission belts for the universe: if my karma is taking a trip through you, yours may be off in premature exploration of the Bardol, be here now, man! The atomization is so complete that in compensation the world of legend descends to lower levels all the time. We have all the history to know better, but we still like our public personalities to be likable. There is a passion finally to find the president of the United States as comprehensible as the high school principal next door or the professional golfer up the road. We do not wish to encounter the possibility that any man who has walked, leaped, and been transported over the long road to the presidency can hardly still be simple. He has done too much damage to pure thought on his route. Therefore we allow legend to lap at the edges of our sentimentality. We content ourselves with the thought that Jerry Ford is basically a good guy. All the while we ignore the knowledge that any world leader who is so good and decent would crack up in three weeks out of his whole and total lack of relation to the questions he is having to decide every day. Nonetheless, we want our legend. In chaos, sugar us up.

So the authors who live best in legend offer personalities we can comprehend like movie stars. Hemingway and Fitzgerald impinge on our psyche with the clarity of Bogart or Cagney. We comprehend them at once. Faulkner bears the same privileged relation to a literary Southerner as Olivier to the London theatergoer. A grand and cultivated presence is enriching the marrow of your life. Nobody wishes to hear a bad story about Olivier or Faulkner.

Henry Miller, however, exists in the same relation to legend that antimatter shows to matter. His life is antipathetic to the idea of legend itself. Where he is complex, he is too complex—we do not feel the resonance of slowly dissolving mystery but the madness of too many knots; where he is simple, he is not attractive—his air is harsh. If he had remained the protagonist by which he first presented himself in *Tropic of Cancer*—the man with iron in his phallus, acid in his mind, and some kind of incomparable relentless freedom in his heart, that paradox of tough misery and keen happiness, that connoisseur of the spectrum of odors between good sewers and bad sewers, that noble rat gnawing on existence and impossible to kill—then he could indeed have been a legend, a species of Parisian Bogart or American Belmondo. Everybody would have wanted to meet this poet-gangster, barbarian-genius. He would have been the American and heterosexual equivalent of Jean Genet.

In fact, he could never have been too near to the character he made of himself in *Tropic of Cancer*. One part never fits. It is obvious he must be more charming than he pretends—how else account for all the free dinners he is invited to, the people he lives on, the whores who love him? There has to be something splendid about him. He may even seem angelic to his friends, or, perish the word, vulnerable. Anaïs Nin, when describing the apartment in Clichy that Miller kept with Alfred Perlès, made, we remember, the point that Miller was tidying the joint. "Henry keeps house like a Dutch housekeeper. He is very neat and clean. No dirty dishes about. It is all monastic, really, with no trimmings, no decoration."*

These few details are enough to suggest *Tropic of Cancer* is a fiction more than a fact. Which, of course, is not to take away a particle of its worth. Perhaps it becomes even more valuable. After all, we do not write to recapture an experience, we write to come as close to it as we can. Sometimes we are not very close, and yet, paradoxically, are nearer than if we had. Not nearer necessarily to the reality of what happened, but to the mysterious reality of what can happen on a page. Oil paints do not create clouds but the image of clouds; a page of manuscript can only evoke that special kind of reality which lives on the skin of the writing paper, a rainbow on a soap bubble. Miller is forever accused of caricature by people who knew his characters, and any good reader knows enough about personality to sense how much he must be leaving out of his people. Yet what a cumulative reality they give us. His characters make up a Paris more real than its paving stones until a reluctant wonder bursts upon us—no French writer no matter how great, not Rabelais, nor Proust, not Maupassant, Hugo, Huysmans, Zola, or even Balzac, not even Céline, has made Paris more vivid to us. Whenever before has a foreigner described a country better than its native writers? For in *Tropic of Cancer* Miller succeeded in performing one high literary act: he created a tone in prose which caught the tone of a period and a place. If that main character in *Tropic of Cancer* named Henry Miller never existed in life, it hardly matters—he is the voice of a spirit which existed at that time. The spirits of literature may be the nearest we come to historical truth.

For that matter, the great confessions of literature are apart from their authors. Augustine recollecting his sins is not the sin-

---

* *The Diary of Anaïs Nin*, vol. 1 (New York: Swallow Press and Harcourt, Brace & World, 1966), p. 62.

ner but the pieties. Julien Sorel is not Stendhal, nor the Seducer a copy of Kierkegaard. *On the Road* is close to Jack Kerouac, yet he gives a happier Kerouac than the one who died too soon. Proust was not his own narrator, even as homosexuality is not heterosexuality but another land, and if we take *The Sun Also Rises* as the purest example of a book whose innovation in style became the precise air of a time and a place, then even there we come slowly to the realization that Hemingway at the time he wrote it was not the equal of Jake Barnes—he had created a consciousness wiser, drier, purer, more classic, more sophisticated, and more judicial than his own. He was still naïve in relation to his creation.

The difference between Hemingway and Miller is that Hemingway set out thereafter to grow into Jake Barnes and locked himself for better and worse, for enormous fame and eventual destruction, into that character who embodied the spirit of an age. Whereas Miller, eight years older than Hemingway but arriving at publication eight years later, and so sixteen years older in 1934 than Hemingway was in 1926, chose to go in the opposite direction. He proceeded to move away from the first Henry Miller he had created. He was not a character but a soul—he would be various.

He was. Not just a *débrouillard*, but a poet; not just a splenetic vision but a prophet; no mere caricaturist, rather a Daumier of the written line; and finally not just master of one style but the prodigy of a dozen. Miller had only to keep writing *Tropic of Cancer* over and over and refining his own personality to become less and less separate from his book, and he could have entered the American life of legend. There were obstacles in his way, of course, and the first was that he was not publishable in America— the growth of his legend would have taken longer. But he had something to offer which went beyond Hemingway.

The cruelest criticism ever delivered of Henry James is that he had a style so hermetic his pen would have been paralyzed if one of his characters had ever entered a town house, removed his hat, and found crap on his head (a matter, parenthetically, of small moment to Tolstoy let us say, or Dostoyevsky, or Stendhal).

Hemingway would have been bothered more than he liked. Miller would have loved it. How did his host react to the shit? How did our host's wife? My God, the way she smacked her nostrils over the impact, you can be sure her thighs were in a lather.

In fact, Hemingway would have hated such a scene. He was trying to create a world where mood—which Hemingway saw as the staff of life—could be cultivated by the scrupulosity of the attention you paid to keeping mood aloft through the excellence of your gravity, courage, and diction.

The eye of every dream Hemingway ever had must have looked down the long vista of his future suicide—so he had a legitimate fear of chaos. He never wrote about the river—he contented himself, better, he created a quintessentially American aesthetic by writing about the camp he set up each night by the side of the river—that was the night we made camp at the foot of the cliffs just after the place where the rapids were bad.

Miller is the other half of literature. He is without fear of his end, a literary athlete at ease in earth, air, or water. I am the river, he is always ready to say, I am the rapids and the placids, I'm the froth and the scum and twigs—what a roar as I go over the falls. Who gives a fart. Let others camp where they may. I am the river and there is nothing I can't join.

Hemingway's world was doomed to collapse so soon as the forces of the century pushed life into a technological tunnel; mood to Hemingway, being a royal grace, could not survive grinding gears, surrealist manners—here's shit in your hat!— and electric machines which offered static, but Miller took off at the place where Hemingway ended. In *Tropic of Cancer* he was saying—and it is the force of the book—I am obliged to live in that place where mood is in the meat grinder, so I know more about it. I know all of the spectrum which runs from good mood to bad mood, and can tell you that a stinking mood is better than no mood. Life has also been designed to run in the stink.

Miller bounces in the stink. We read *Tropic of Cancer,* that book of horrors, and feel happy. It is because there is honor in the horror, and metaphor in the hideous. How, we cannot even begin to say. Maybe it is that mood is vastly more various, self-regenerative, hearty, and sly than Hemingway ever guessed. Maybe mood is not a lavender lady, but a barmaid with full visions of heaven in the full corruption of her beer breath, and an old drunk's vomit is a clarion call to some mutants of the cosmos just now squeezing around the bend. It is as if without courage, or militancy, or the serious cultivation of strength, without stoicism or good taste, or even a nose for the nicety of good guts under terrible pressure, Miller is still living closer to death than Hemingway, certainly he is closer if the sewer is nearer to our end than the wound.

History proved to be on Miller's side. Twentieth-century life was leaving the world of individual effort, liquor, and tragic wounds for the big-city garbage can of bruises, migraines, static, mood chemicals, amnesia, absurd relations, and cancer. Down in the sewers of existence where the cancer was being cooked, Miller was cavorting. Look, he was forever saying, you do not have to die of this crud. You can breathe it, eat it, suck it, fuck it, and still bounce up for the next day. There is something inestimable in us if we can stand the smell.

Considering where the world was going—right into the World-Wide Sewer of the Concentration Camps—Miller had a message which gave more life than Hemingway. "One reason why I have stressed so much the immoral, the wicked, the ugly, the cruel in my work is because I wanted others to know how valuable these are, how equally if not more important than the good things. . . . I was getting the poison out of my system. Curiously enough, this poison had a tonic effect for others. It was as if I had given them some kind of immunity."*

The legend, however, was never to develop. With his fingers and his nose and his toenails, he had gotten into the excrements of cancerland—he had to do no more than stay there, a dry sardonic demon, tough as nails, bright as radium. But he had had a life after all before this, tragic, twisted, near to atrophied in some of its vital parts, he was closer to the crud himself than he ever

* Jonathan Cott, "Reflections of a Cosmic Tourist," *Rolling Stone* (February 27, 1975), pp. 38–46, 57.

allowed. So he had to write himself out of his own dungeons and did in all the work which would follow *Tropic of Cancer* and some of the secrets of his unique, mysterious, and absolutely special personality are in his later work and we will yet live with him there, and try to comprehend him—a vital search. We would all know more if we could find him.

But for now let us take on the pleasure of *Tropic of Cancer.* Much of the first half is reprinted here.

Christ, Satan, and the Presidential Candidate: A Visit to Jimmy Carter in Plains

(1976)

PLAINS WAS DIFFERENT from what one expected. Maybe it was the name, but anticipation had been of a dry and dusty town with barren vistas, ramshackle warehouses, and timeless, fly-buzzing, sun-baked afternoons. Instead, Plains was green. As one approached, the fields were green and the trees were tall. The heat of southern Georgia was as hot in summertime as it promised to be, but there was shade under the elms, the pecan trees, and the oaks, and if the streets were wide, the foliage was rich enough to come together overhead. A surprising number of houses were big and white and wooden and looked to be fifty years old or more. Some were a hundred years old. They had porches and trees in the front yard, and lawns ran a good distance from the front door to the sidewalk while the grass to the rear of the house meandered leisurely into the backyard of the house on the street behind. Some homes might be newly painted, and some were shabby, but the town was pleasant and spread out for a population of 683 inhabitants. By comparison with meaner-looking places with a gas station, barbecue shack, general store, junkyard, empty lots, and spilled gasoline, a redneck redolence of dried ketchup and hamburger napkins splayed around thin-shanked, dusty trees, Plains felt peaceful and prosperous. It had the sweet deep green of an old-fashioned town that America has all but lost to the interstates and the ranch houses, the mobile homes and the condominiums, the neon strips of hotted-up truck stops and the static pall of shopping centers. Plains had an antiques store on the main street that must have been a hundred feet deep, and it was owned by Alton Carter, Jimmy Carter's uncle; Plains had a railroad running through the middle of the main street and a depot that was not more than twice as long as a tinker's wagon: Plains had an arcade one block long (the length of the main street), and all the stores were in the shade under the arcade, including a brand-new restaurant called the Back Porch with white tin ceilings fifteen feet high, four-blade propeller fan turning overhead, and chicken salad sandwiches with a touch of pineapple and a touch of pepper—tasty. Plains was that part of America which hitherto had been separate from the media, the part that offered a fundamental clue to the nature of establishment itself. One could pass through a hundred small towns in a state, and twenty or thirty might be part of a taproot for the establishment of its capital to draw upon. A place like Plains could be modest by the measure of its income and yet offer an unmistakable well-ordered patina, a promise that the mysterious gentility of American life was present, that there were still people interested in running things without showing the traces, that the small-town establishment remained a factor to be taken account of among all the other factors like exhaust roar and sewage slick and those plastic toylands stretching to the American horizon.

Maybe it was the architecture of the leading church in each town that gave the clue. Plains Baptist Church, now famous for the Sunday Bible classes for men conducted once a month (in his turn) by Jimmy Carter, had a fine architecture within. Painted white, with a ceiling of gracious wooden eaves and two splendid old chairs with red velvet seats on either side of the pulpit, it was an elegant church for a very small town, and its architect, whoever he had been—one could hope it was the town carpenter—must have lived a life that dwelt with ease in the proportions and needs of ecclesiastical space. The choir sang the hymns and the congregation sang with them, the words full of Christian exaltation, their sword of love quivering in the air, that secret in the strength of Christianity where the steel is smelted from the tears. "I will sing the wondrous story of the Christ who died for me," went the words, "how He left His home in glory for the cross of Calvary." When they came to sing "Bringing in the sheaves," or may it have been "When the roll is called up yonder, I'll be there," a member of the choir took out his harmonica and played it with feeling pure enough to take one back to the last campfires of a Confederate Army 111 years gone, the harmonica stirring old river reeds out of the tendrils of the past. It was a fine church service, and it gave the visitor from the North a little too much to think about, especially since he had spent a bemused hour in the basement of Plains Baptist Church somewhat earlier the same Sunday morning taking in Men's Bible Class 10 to 11 A.M. The basement, a schoolroom with institutional pale green walls, gray floor, gray metal seats, a blackboard, and a metal table up front for the deacons where Jimmy Carter sat, even an open window on the other side of which a ladder was leaning, had been relatively filled this Sunday with curious visitors, some press and two women from the media who had been allowed, as a political point (in the ongoing epic of women's liberation), to be admitted. They must have wondered what they were seeing. There was a devotion in the dry little voice, drier than gunpowder, of the deacon who interpreted the Scripture, a farmer or a shopkeeper, thin as jerky dried in the sun, a dry, late-middle-aged man with eyeglasses, hollow cheeks, and an ingrown devotion that resided in the dungeon clamor of his lungs. He spoke in a wispy Georgia snuffle, very hard to hear, and his piety being as close to him as the body of one young beloved clasping the body of another through the night, it was not the place to pull out a pad and start taking notes.

In the second row of seats, the first row being all but empty, sat the real stalwarts of the Bible class, seven or eight big Georgia farmers, pleased by the crowd of visitors in the class, bemused in their own right that the church, the town, the county was a cen-

ter suddenly of all the buzzing, insectlike instruments of the
media and the peculiar pale faces of the media people. The second row owned the basement. They nudged each other in the
ribs as they sat down next to one another. "Didn't see you sneak
in here," they said to each other. They were the meat and mind
of the South. They looked as if they had been coming here fifty
Sundays a year for twenty years, here to think whatever thoughts
they had on such occasions—one might be better situated to
read the minds of Martians—and they were impressive in their
mixture of hardworking bodies and hardworking hands, red
necks with work-wrinkle lines three-sixteenths of an inch deep,
and the classic ears of Southern farmers, big ears with large
flappy chewed-out lobes as if they had been pulled on like old
dugs over the ten thousand problems of their years. Men's Bible
class was teaching that Christian love was unselfish devotion to
the highest good of others, and up front Jimmy Carter sat silently at the metal table with a couple of other deacons, his face
calm, his mind attentive to one knew not necessarily what,
dressed in a gray-blue suit and harmonious tie, and the hour
passed and it was time to go upstairs to eleven o'clock service.

Somewhere the yeast must have been working in the religious
call, for in the early afternoon, a couple of hours after church,
when his private interview with Jimmy Carter took place, it
proved to be the oddest professional hour Norman Mailer ever
spent with a politician—it must have seemed twice as odd to
Carter. In retrospect, it quickly proved mortifying (no lesser
word will do), since to his embarrassment, Mailer did too much
of the talking. Perhaps he had hoped to prime Carter to the
point where they could have a conversation, but the subject he
chose to bring up was religion, and that was ill-chosen. A man
running for president could comment about Christ, he could
comment a little, but he could hardly afford to be too enthusiastic. Religion had become as indecent a topic to many a contemporary American as sex must have been in the nineteenth
century. If half the middle-class people in the Victorian period
held almost no conscious thoughts about sex, the same could
now be said of religion, except it might be even more costly to

talk about than sex, because religious conversations invariably sound insane when recounted to men or women who never feel such sentiments. Since it was a safe assumption that half of America lived at present in the nineteenth century and half in the twentieth, a journalist who had any respect for the candidate he was talking to would not ask an opinion on sex or religion. Still, Mailer persisted. He was excited about Carter's theological convictions. He wanted to hear more of them. He had read the transcript of Bill Moyers's one-hour TV interview with Carter ("People and Politics," May 6, 10:00 P.M., Public Broadcasting Service) and had been impressed with a few of Carter's remarks, particularly his reply to Moyers's question "What drives you?"

After a long silence Carter had said, "I don't know . . . exactly how to express it . . . I feel I have one life to live. I feel that God wants me to do the best I can with it. And that's quite often my major prayer. Let me live my life so that it will be meaningful." A little later he would add, "When I have a sense of peace and self-assurance . . . that what I'm doing is the right thing, I assume, maybe in an unwarranted way, that that's doing God's will."

These were hardly historic remarks, and yet on reflection they were certainly remarkable. There was a maw of practicality that engulfed presidents and presidential candidates alike. They lived in all those supermarkets of the mind where facts are stacked like cans; whether good men or bad, they were hardly likely to be part of that quintessential elevation of mind that can allow a man to say, "Let me live my life so that it will be meaningful." It was in the nature of politicians to look for *programs* to be meaningful, not the psychic substance of their lives. Reading the Moyers interview shortly before leaving for Plains must therefore have excited a last-minute excess of curiosity about Carter, and that was last-minute to be certain. Through all of the political spring when candidates came and went, Mailer had not gone near the primary campaigns. Working on a novel, he had made the whole decision not to get close to any of it. One didn't try to write seriously about two things at once. Besides, it was hard to tell much about Carter. Mailer thought the media had an inbuilt deflection that kept them from perceiving what was truly interesting in any new phenomenon. Since he rarely watched television any longer, he did not even know what Carter's voice was like, and photographs proved subtly anonymous. Still, he kept reading about Carter. In answer to the people who would ask, "What do you think of *him?*" Mailer would be quick to reply, "I suspect he's a political genius." It was all he knew about Carter, but he knew that much.

He also had to admit he enjoyed Carter's reaction to meeting Nixon and Agnew, McGovern and Henry Jackson, Hubert Humphrey, George Wallace, Ronald Reagan, Nelson Rockefeller, Ed Muskie. Carter confessed he had not been impressed sufficiently to think these men were better qualified to run the country than himself. Mailer understood such arrogance. He had, after all, felt enough of the same on meeting famous politicians to also think himself equipped for office, and had been brash enough to run for mayor of New York in a Democratic primary. Mailer had always assumed he would be sensational as a political candidate; he learned, however, that campaign work ran eighteen hours a day, seven days a week, and after a while it was not yourself who was the candidate but 50 percent of yourself. Before it was over, his belly was drooping—one's gut is the first to revolt against giving the same speech eight times a day. He came in fourth in a field of five, and was left with a respect for successful politicians. They were at least entitled to the same regard one would offer a professional athlete for his stamina. Later, brooding on the size of a conceit that had let him hope he could steal an election from veteran Democrats, Mailer would summarize his experience with the wise remark, "A freshman doesn't get elected president of the fraternity."

But Carter had. Carter must be a political genius. Nonetheless, Mailer felt a surprising lack of curiosity. Genius in politics did not interest him that much. He thought politics was a dance where you need not do more than move from right to left and left to right while evading the full focus of the media. The skill was in the timing. You tried to move to the left at that moment when you would lose the least on the right; to the right, when the damage would be smallest on the left. You had to know how to steer in and out of other news stories. It was a difficult skill, but hardly possessed of that upper aesthetic which would insist skill be illumined by a higher principle—whether elegance, courage, compassion, taste, or the eminence of wit. Politics called for some of the same skills you needed in inventing a new plastic. Politics called to that promiscuous material in the personality which could flow into many a form. Sometimes Mailer suspected that the flesh of the true politician would yet prove nonbiodegradable and fail to molder in the grave!

Still, there was no question in his mind that he would vote for Carter. In 1976 he was ready to vote for many a Democrat. It was not that Mailer could not ever necessarily vote for a Republican, but after eight years of Nixon and Ford, he thought the country could use a Democratic administration again. It was not that Ford was unendurable. Like a moderately dull marriage, Ford was endlessly endurable—one could even get fond of him in a sour way. Jerry Ford, after all, provided the clue to how America had moved in fifty years from George Babbitt to Jerry Ford. He even offered the peculiar security of having been shaped by forces larger than himself. Maybe that was why Ford's face suggested he would do the best he could with each problem as he perceived it: "Don't worry about me," said his face, "I'm not the least bit dialectical."

Of course, the president was only a handmaiden to the corporate spirit. The real question was whether the White House could afford another four years of the corporate spirit, that immeasurably self-satisfied public spirit whose natural impulse was to cheat on the environment and enrich the rich.

It was certainly time for the Democrats. He would probably vote for any Democrat who got the nomination. Nonetheless, it was irritating to have so incomplete an idea of Carter, to be so empty of any thesis as to whether he might be deemed ruthless, a computer, or saintly.

A day earlier, on the press plane to Albany, Georgia, he had felt—what with a few drinks inside him—that he was coming closer to what he wanted to discuss with Carter in the interview that would be granted next day. The sexual revolution had come out of a profound rejection of the American family—it had been a way of saying to the parents, "If you say sex is dirty, then it has to be good, because your lives are false!" But Carter would restore the family. Faithful, by public admission, to his wife for thirty years, he was in every way a sexual conservative. Since his economic proposals would appeal to progressives, he might be undertaking the Napoleonic proposition of outflanking two armies, Republicans and Democrats, from the right and the left. Yes, there was much to talk about with Carter. Even on the airplane, Mailer could feel his head getting overcompressed with themes of conversation arriving too early.

Jimmy Carter's home was on a side street, and you approached it through a barricade the Secret Service had erected. It was possible this was as unobtrusive a small-town street as the Secret Service had ever converted into an electronic compound with walkie-talkies, sentries, and lines of sight. The house was in a grove of trees, and the ground was hard-put to keep its grass, what with pine needles, pecan leaves, and the clay of the soil itself, which gave off a sandy-rose hue in the shade.

The rambling suburban ranch house in those trees spoke of California ancestry for its architecture, and a cost of construction between $50,000 and $100,000, depending on how recently it was built. The inside of the house was neither lavish nor underfurnished, not sumptuous or mean—a house that spoke of comfort more than taste. The colors laid next to one another were in no way brilliant, yet neither did their palette of soft shades depress the eye, for they were cool in the Georgia summer. Carter's study was large and dark with books, and there were busts of Kennedy and Lincoln, and his eight-year-old daughter Amy's comic book (starring Blondie) was on the floor. It was the only spot of red in all the room. Over his desk was a fluorescent light.

Maybe Carter was one of the few people in the world who could look good under fluorescent light. Wearing a pale blue button-down shirt open at the neck—pale blue was certainly his color—Carter had a quintessential American cleanliness, that silvery light of a finely tuned and supple rectitude that produces our best ministers and best generals alike, responsible for both the bogs of Vietnam and the vision of a nobler justice.

Now, sitting across the desk from Carter, he was struck by a quiet difference in Carter this Sunday afternoon. Maybe it was the result of church, or maybe the peril implicit for a politician in any interview—since one maladroit phrase can ruin a hundred good ones—but Carter seemed less generous than he had expected. Of course, Mailer soon knew to his horror that he was close to making a fool of himself, if indeed he had not done it already, because with his first question taking five minutes to pose, and then ten, he had already given a speech rather than a question. What anguish this caused, that he—known as criminally egomaniacal by common reputation, and therefore for years as careful as a reformed criminal to counteract the public expectation of him—was haranguing a future president of the United States. He had a quick recollection of the days when he ran for mayor and some fool or other, often an overly educated European newspaperman, would ask questions that consisted of nothing but long-suppressed monologues. To make matters worse, Carter was hardly being responsive in his answer—how could he be? Mailer's exposition dwelt in the bowels of that limitless schism in Protestantism—between the fundamental simplicities of good moral life as exemplified a few hours ago in Bible class and the insuperable complexities of moral examination opened by Kierkegaard, whose work, Mailer now told Carter with enthusiasm, looked to demonstrate that we cannot know the moral role we enact. We can feel saintly and yet be evil in the eyes of God, feel we are evil (on the other hand) and yet be more saintly than we expect; equally, we may do good even as we are feeling good, or be bad exactly when we expect we are bad. Man is alienated from his capacity to decide his moral worth. Maybe, Mailer suggested, he had sailed on such a quick theological course because Carter had quoted Kierkegaard on the second page of his autobiography. "Every man is an exception," Kierkegaard had written.

But it was obvious by the smile on Carter's face—a well of encouragement to elicit the point of this extended question—that Carter was not necessarily one of America's leading authorities on Kierkegaard. How foolish of Mailer to expect it of him—as if Norman in his turn had never quoted an author he had not lived with thoroughly.

Having failed with the solemnity of this exposition, but his voice nonetheless going on, beginning to wonder what his question might be—did he really have one, did he really enter this dialogue with the clean journalistic belief that ultimate questions were to be answered by presidential candidates?—he now began to shift about for some political phrasing he could offer Carter as a way out of these extensive hypotheses. The sexual revolution, Mailer said hopefully, the sexual revolution might be a case in point. And he now gave the lecture he had prepared the night before—that the family, the very nuclear family whose security Carter would look to restore, was seen as the enemy by a large fraction of Americans. "For instance," said Mailer, clutching at inspiration, "there are a lot of people in New York who don't trust you. The joke making the rounds among some of my friends is 'How can you put confidence in a man who's been faithful to the same woman for thirty years?' "

Carter's smile showed real amusement, as if he knew something others might not necessarily know. Of course, whether he was smiling to the left or right of this issue was another matter. Curiously encouraged by the ambiguous fiber of the smile, Mailer went on toward asking his first question. He had presented the joke, he suggested, to show the gulf of moral differences that awaited a Carter presidency—for instance, to talk of the drug problem just a moment, statistics reexamined showed that addicts deprived of heroin, or methadone, did not commit more crimes to get scarce heroin but instead took speed or barbiturates or pot, or even went to bourbon. The implication of this, Mailer said, is that there's a chasm in the soul that might have to be filled, a need precisely not to be oneself but rather to give oneself over to the Other, to give oneself to some presence outside oneself; the real answer to drug addiction might not be

in social programs but in coming to grips with the possibility that
Satanism was loose in the twentieth century. One question he
would like to ask in line with this was whether Carter thought
much about the hegemony of Satan, or did he—yes, this unasked
question was now being silently answered by Carter's eyes, yes,
Carter's concern was not with Satan but with Christ. On and on
went Mailer with considerable fever, looking, for instance, to
propose that one difference between Carter's religious point of
view as he, Mailer, presumed to comprehend it, and his own
might be that he had a notion of God as not clearly omnipotent
but rather as a powerful God at war with other opposed visions
in the universe—a ridiculous picture of God to present to Carter,
Mailer told the candidate, except that going back to the Moyers
interview, where Carter had certainly said that he felt he might
be doing God's will when he felt a sense of peace and self-
assurance—did it ever bother Carter, keeping Kierkegaard's
Principle of Uncertainty in mind, if he, Mailer, could, heh heh,
steal a title from Heisenberg—did it ever bother him that God
might be in anguish or rage at what He had not accomplished
across the heavens? For instance, there was the Hasidic tale of
Rabbi Zusya, who begged God to reveal himself in reward for
Zusya's devotions to him, and God finally replied by revealing
Himself, and Zusya crawled under the bed and howled in fear
like a dog, and said, "O God, please do not reveal yourself to
me." Did that story, that image of God, strike any chord in Carter,
was there any recognition that God, close to losing, could live in
wrath and horror? Christ, when all was said, had died on the
Cross, on a mission He believed would succeed and had failed.

Mailer ground down into silence, furious with himself for scat-
tering prodigious questions like buckshot. He looked across at
Carter. He was realizing all over again that the only insanity still
left in his head was this insane expectation he had of men in
public places.

Carter nodded sadly. He looked a little concerned. He had
every right to be. However would such an interview appear in
The New York Times?

Well, answered Carter soberly, thoughtfully, he was not certain that he could reply to everything that had been raised since their points of view were not the same in many respects. He was not, for instance, as devout and as prayerful as the press had perhaps made him out to be. Religion was something he certainly did and would live with, but he didn't spend as much time as people might expect exploring into the depths of these questions; perhaps—he suggested politely—he ought to be more concerned, but in truth, he did not think his personal beliefs were to be carried out by the government; there were limits to what government could do, yet in those limits, he thought much more could be done than was now being done. For example, he would recognize that there is little that government could do directly to restore the family. Welfare payments might, for example, be revised in such a way that fathers would not be directly encouraged to desert their families, as they were most ironically now encouraged to do, but he would admit that this, of course, was to the side of the question. He supposed, Carter said, that the answer, as he saw it, was in turning government around so that it would be more of a model. There was a yearning in this country for the restoration of something precious. "There's been a loss of pride in this country that I find catastrophic." The deterioration of family values was linked, Carter thought, to that loss of pride. It would be his hope that if he could get the actual workings of the government turned around, so that government was at once more efficient and more *sensitive,* then perhaps it could begin to serve as more of a model to counteract the fundamental distrust of people in relation to government, that is, their feeling they won't find justice. "The real answer is to get those of us who are running the government going right." You see, Carter went on to say, he was not looking to restore the family by telling people how to live; he did not wish to be president in order to judge them. "I don't care," he said in his quiet decent voice, as if the next words, while not wholly comfortable, had nonetheless to be said, "I don't care if people say ——," and he actually said the famous four-letter word that the *Times* has not printed in the 125 years of its publishing life.

He got it out without a backing-up of phlegm or a hitch in his rhythm (it was, after all, not the easiest word to say to a stranger), but it was said from duty, from the quiet decent demands of duty, as if he, too, had to present his credentials to that part of the twentieth century personified by his interviewer.

No, Carter went on, his function was not to be a religious leader but to bring the human factor back into economics. The same economic formula, he suggested, would work or not work depending on the morale of the people who were doing the work.

Mailer nodded. He believed as much himself. But he was still dissatisfied with his lack of contact on questions more fundamental to himself. Like a child who returns to the profitless point (out of obscure but certain sense of need), Mailer looked to return their conversation to Kierkegaardian ambiguities and so spoke of marijuana, for it was on marijuana, he told Carter, that he had had the first religious experience he had ever known—indeed, marijuana might even pose the paradox of arriving at mystical states for too little. One began to feel the vulnerability of God about the time one recognized a little more clearly in the unwinding of the centers of one's consciousness that one was consuming one's karma, possibly stripping—for no more than the pleasure of the experience—some of the resources of one's future lives. He asked Carter then if he had any belief in reincarnation, in the reincarnation of karma as our purgatory here on earth? And Carter said no, Carter said he believed we had our one life and our judgment. And then with that gentle seductiveness all good politicians have, Carter mentioned that his understanding was not wholly alien to drugs, his sons had experimented with marijuana a few years ago and had later done some work in the rehabilitation of addicts. He felt as if their experiences had helped them in such work.

Mailer was thinking morosely of the meeting of Sam Goldwyn and George Bernard Shaw to discuss making a film. Goldwyn had spoken of his admiration for Shaw's work, of his love of fine dramatic subjects, of the pleasures of aesthetics, and Shaw had finally replied, "Mr. Goldwyn, the difficulty is that you care only about art, and I am interested only in money." He had certainly been playing Goldwyn to Jimmy Carter's George Bernard Shaw—no, worse!

Mailer was finally beginning to feel the essential frustration of trying to talk about religion with Carter on equal terms. Carter had more troops, which is to say he had more habits. If you go to church every Sunday for most of your life, then you end with certain habits. You live in a dependable school of perception. In the case of Baptists, it might be living with the idea that if you were good enough and plucky and lucky and not hating your neighbor for too little, Christ was quietly with you. Certainly, if you had the feeling He was with you at all, He was with you in church on Sunday. So you could form the habit over the years of thinking about Him in a comfortable way.

Maybe Carter saw God in the little continuing revelations churchgoing offered on the personalities of one's friends. It was like enjoying a film or a bestselling novel. Cause and effect lived in a framework you could perceive. A good man had his character written on his face.

Whereas Mailer's love of God (we must assume he has some) owed too much to Kierkegaard, who could have said that a good man would have his character written on his face unless he wasn't a good man but an exceptional bad man with a good face— Mailer saw no reason why the Devil could not be the most beautiful creature God ever made. Yet, equally, a man could develop an evil face and a loving heart. There was the difference. Carter might be able to see hints of God in his neighbor; Mailer was forever studying old photographs of Gurdjieff and Rasputin.

They had come to the end of their hour. The author was feeling a dull relief that he would have, at least, another hour tomorrow. How fortunate that that had been scheduled in advance. He started to apologize in some roundabout form for how the first hour had gone, and Carter replied with his gracious smile: it was all right, he said, they had needed the first hour to loosen up, to become acquainted. Mailer left with the twice dull sense that he liked Carter more than Carter had any reason to like him.

Our Man at Harvard

(1977)

LET ME TELL YOU ABOUT the Somerset Maugham party that we gave
at *The Advocate* in the spring of 1942. The magazine was housed
then in a dark gray flat-roofed three-story building across the
street from the stern of *The Lampoon* (and indeed we were much
aware of being in their wake—*Lampoon* editors usually went to
Time; ours to oblivion). In those days *The Advocate* building was
as ugly from the exterior as it is now. A few small and dingy stores
occupied the ground floor; some mysterious never-seen tenants
were on the second; and *The Advocate* offices took up the third.
They were beautiful to me. One climbed a dull, carpeted stair-
case as dusty as a back road in Guerrero, used one's *Advocate* key
to go through the door at the top, and opened the suite, an entire floor-through of five rooms, five mystical chambers full of
broken-down furniture and the incomparable odor that rises
from old beer stains in the carpet and syrup-crusted empty Coke
bottles in the corners. It is a better odor than you would think,
sweet and alcoholic and faintly debauched—it spoke of little
magazines and future lands of literature, and the offices were
almost always empty in late afternoon, when the sunlight turned
the dust into a cosmos of angels dancing on a pin. Magicians

would have felt a rush of aphrodisia amid all this pendant funk and mote. Maybe I loved the *Advocate* offices more than anyone who was taken in my competition—I spent the spring of sophomore year at Harvard drinking Cokes by a table at the window that faced on *The Lampoon,* and I read old issues of the magazine. Once I was an authority on the early published work in *The Advocate* of T. S. Eliot, Edwin Arlington Robinson, Van Wyck Brooks, John Reed, Conrad Aiken, E. E. Cummings, and Malcolm Cowley—it must have been the nearest I ever came to extracting genealogical marrow from old print. Occasionally Marvin Barrett, the president, or Bowden Broadwater, Pegasus, would come through the office, give a start at seeing me at the same chair and table where he had glimpsed me on the last visit, and go off to do his work.

The following academic year, '41–'42, Bruce Barton, Jr., was elected president and John Crockett became Pegasus. We had troubles instantly. Barton, called Pete, was the son of Bruce Barton, Sr., an advertising magnate as well known in his period as was Nicholas Murray Butler, and for that matter one could find similarities. (Barton must have been the last of the advertising tycoons who believed passionately in a strenuous Jesus with muscles.)

His son, in compensation, was a gentleman. Pete Barton was the nicest guy a lot of us met at Harvard, and with his blond hair, good if somewhat pinched features and fundamental decency, he could have passed for Billy Budd if (1) he had not gone to Deerfield, which left him a little more patrician than yeoman in manner, and if (2) he had had more beef. But he was gentle, he was quietly literary, and his father had millions. Since *The Advocate* was in its usual cauldron of debt, no other man would have been so appropriate to serve as president. Barton might even have had a benign, well-financed, and agreeable administration if not for the new Pegasus, John Crockett, a man as talented as Claggart and equally riven in his soul by detestation of our Billy Budd.

Being innocent of Crockett's propensities for literary evil, we were a happy group coming into the office. The magazine would be ours. We would print what we wished. Our first issue, therefore, consisted of each of us putting in his own story. Crockett then took our gems to a printer in Vermont. This was, I think, in November. By February we still did not have a magazine. Crockett kept assuring us the printer would soon deliver. None of us ever called him. Crockett had promised us that the inexpensive rate he had managed to extract from the Linotype mills of the Vermont woods would be ruined forever if we broke any of our voices on the printer's ear. Therefore, we waited. Nervously, impatiently, suspiciously, we waited for the issue with our stories.

Instead, Crockett came back with the seventy-fifth anniversary edition of *The Advocate*, a little work of love Crockett had gotten together by himself over the last year—in truth, a prodigious push of Pegasusmanship—collecting poems, pieces, and comment from the fine ranks of Wallace Stevens, Horace Gregory, Djuna Barnes, Marianne Moore, Robert Hillyer, Frederic Prokosch, Mark Schorer, John Malcolm Brinnin, Richard Eberhart, Bowden Broadwater, and William Carlos Williams, plus a poem by John Crockett, "The Sulky Races at Cherry Park." It was a mammoth virtuoso literary crypto-CIA affair back in March of '42, and none of us on *The Advocate* had had the first clue as to what Crockett was cooking. As for the issue with our stories— Crockett promised to get to that next. The expression on his young but sour face told us what he thought of our stories. Crockett, incidentally, while not as well-featured as John Dean, had a great resemblance to him—I remember his tortoiseshell glasses, high forehead, and thin pale hair.

Pete Barton had been agitated for weeks at the long wait on our first issue. Painfully aware of his father's weight in the world, he was invariably overscrupulous never to push his own. He had suspended himself into a state of forbearance worthy of a Zen warrior considering the immense agitation the late appearance of the magazine had caused. When the anniversary issue appeared (to rich critical reception in the Boston papers, worse luck!), Barton finally demonstrated his father's blood. He called an emergency meeting where he calumniated himself for his derelictions of attention, took the full blame for the financial disaster of the issue (it had cost something like three times as much as more modest issues; our debt on the consequence had doubled overnight), and—Billy Budd to the last, absent even to intimations of a further notion to evil—stated that he would not ask for Crockett's resignation if he could expect his cooperation on future projects.

Crockett replied with a nod of his head and a profound turning of our collective head. Having heard, he said, that Somerset Maugham would be in the Boston area during April, he had sent an invitation to Maugham to come to a party that *The Advocate* would be happy to throw in his honor, and Maugham had accepted. Maugham had accepted.

This piece of news ran around the ring of Cambridge like a particle in a cyclotron. Nothing in four years at Harvard, not Dunkirk, Pearl Harbor, or the blitz, not even beating Yale and Princeton in the same season for the first time in years, could have lit Harvard up more. Not to be invited to that party was equal to signifying that one had mismanaged one's life.

The literary grandees of the faculty sent their early acceptance: F. O. Matthiessen, Theodore Spencer, and Robert Hillyer in the van; the officers of *The Lampoon* sucked around; housemasters' wives asked how things were *going* at *The Advocate*. On the night of the party, four hundred souls in four hundred bodies as large as Patrick Moynihan's and as delicate as Joan Didion's came to the small rooms on the third floor and packed themselves in so completely that you ended by bringing your drink to your lips around the wrist of the strange forearm in front of your face. The noise of cocktail gabble anticipated the oncoming shapings of time—one would not hear the sound again until the first jet planes fired up their engines at an airport. Drinks were passed overhead. If you did not reach at the right time, another hand plucked the drink. It did not matter. More was on its way. Glasses bounced like corks over white choppy Harvard hands. From time to time, word would pass like wind through grass that Maugham had just entered the building, Maugham was having trouble getting up the stairs, Maugham was through the door. Maugham was in the other room. We formed phalanxes to move into the other room; we did not budge. A phalanx cannot budge a volume that is impacted. The lovely smile of resignation was on the lips of faculty wives: it is the establishment smile that says, "Life is like that—the nearest pleasures are not to be tasted." After a half hour of such smiling into the face of a stranger as one brought one's arm around her neck to get at one's drink, the wind came through the grass again. Maugham, we heard, was at the door. Maugham was slowly going down the stair. Somerset Maugham was gone.

Hands passed drinks above the impacted mass. Eyes flashed in that hard gemlike smile of pride retained when opportunity is lost. In another half hour, there was a lessening of pressure on one's chest, and bodies began to separate. After a while, one could walk from room to room. What was the point? Maugham was gone.

It was only on the next day, after the claims of liars had been checked against the quiet evidence of reliable witnesses who had found themselves analogously empretzeled in every room and on the stairs, that the news came back. By every sound measure of verification, Somerset Maugham had never been in the *Advocate* building that night. Crockett, now confronted, confessed. Out of his unflappable funds of phlegm, he allowed that he had known for weeks Somerset Maugham was not coming—the great author had been kind enough to send a telegram in answer to the invitation. "Certainly not," it said.

It was too late to ask Crockett to resign. Due to the war and an accelerated graduation, our term as *Advocate* officers was up; the new president and Pegasus were in. Because of the party, we left with a debt that had just doubled again. *The Advocate* has never been solvent since.

A postscript: Pete Barton became a Navy officer and commanded a ship, came home, worked as quietly for *Time* as if he had been a *Lampoon* man, and died before he was forty. The only time I saw John Crockett again was about ten years ago in New York on a reunion at the Harvard Club. He was now in the State Department and had been stationed for years in Yugoslavia. He told delicious stories about idiotic conversations with Madame Tito at banquets in Zagreb. He looked to be as wicked as ever. Our cause was being well served in Yugoslavia. It occurs to me that the mag across the street never knew what a talent it missed when *The Advocate* got Crockett. Rest in peace, Pete Barton.

1980s

Before the Literary Bar

_____

(1980)

PROSECUTOR: Your Honor, our first and only witness will be the defendant, Norman Mailer.

THE COURT: He has waived his rights?

PROSECUTOR: Yes, Your Honor.

THE COURT: All right, let's put him on.

[The defendant is sworn]

Mr. Mailer, I will remind you of the charge. It is criminal literary negligence. On this charge, the court may find against you for censure in the first or second degree, or for reprimand. You may also be exonerated.

MAILER: I am aware of the charge, Your Honor.

PROSECUTOR: Mr. Mailer, I am holding in my hand a work entitled _Of Women and Their Elegance,_ which has your name on the cover as author. Would you describe it?

MAILER: It is a book of photographs by Milton Greene, with a text of fifty thousand words by myself.

PROSECUTOR: Fifty thousand words is the length of the average novel?

MAILER: Maybe half to two-thirds the length.

PROSECUTOR: Would you say this work presents itself as an autobiography by Marilyn Monroe?

MAILER: Originally, I wished to title it *Of Women and Their Elegance, by Marilyn Monroe as told to Norman Mailer,* but it was decided the title could prove misleading to the public, who might think the interview had actually taken place. I suppose it would be better to describe the text as a false autobiography. Or an imaginary memoir, since the story, but for a few recollections, only covers a period of three or four years in her life.

PROSECUTOR: It is made up.

MAILER: More or less made up.

PROSECUTOR: Could you be more specific?

MAILER: Much of the book is based on fact. I would say some of it is made up.

PROSECUTOR: Are you prepared to offer examples of fact and fiction as they occur in your pages?

MAILER: I can try.

PROSECUTOR: Let me read a passage to the court, written in the first person, which purports to be Marilyn Monroe's voice. The Amy she refers to is one Amy Greene, Milton Greene's wife. I will enter it as Exhibit A. It is taken from page 24 of Mr. Mailer's book.

THE COURT: All right, go ahead.

[The prosecution reads Exhibit A, page 24]

I went out shopping with Amy. She took me to Saks and Bonwit Teller's, and people lined up to look at me as soon as I got spotted. Women were ripping open the curtain in the dressing room, which was enough to do Amy in, if she hadn't been made of the toughest stuff. First, she discovered I wear no panties, and to make it worse, a bit of my natural odor came off with the removal of the skirt. Nothing drives people crazier than a woman with an aroma that doesn't come out of a bottle.

Maybe I should use deodorant, but I do like a little sniff of myself. It's a way of staying in touch.

Anyway, Amy turned her head at the sight of my pubic hair, which is, alas, disconcertingly dark, and then the curtains flew open, and shoppers gawked, three big mouths and big noses, and a tall, skinny salesman came over to shut the curtains and croaked, "Miss Monroe!" and disappeared forever. I had to laugh. I knew I'd changed his life. I think, sometimes, that's why I do it.

PROSECUTOR: Now, Mr. Mailer.
MAILER: Yessir.
PROSECUTOR: Did this scene occur?
MAILER: Yes. Mrs. Greene told me that hordes of shoppers did indeed gawk at Marilyn.
PROSECUTOR: And ripped open the curtain to the dressing room?
MAILER: It is my recollection that Mrs. Greene told me something of the sort.
PROSECUTOR: In a tape-recorded interview?
MAILER: [*Pauses*] Perhaps, in casual conversation. I am old friends with Mr. and Mrs. Greene, and we have had many unrecorded conversations about Marilyn Monroe as well.
PROSECUTOR: And you drew your impressions of Miss Monroe from these conversations, recorded and unrecorded?
MAILER: Some of my impressions.
PROSECUTOR: So Mrs. Greene told you that Miss Monroe was wearing no panties on this occasion?
MAILER: I don't recollect that Mrs. Greene told me that.
PROSECUTOR: Then how did you arrive at such a conclusion?
MAILER: On the basis of many conversations with many people who knew Marilyn Monroe, it seems to be established that Miss Monroe did not like to wear panties.
PROSECUTOR: So you took the liberty of deciding she was wearing none that day?
MAILER: It seemed a fair assumption. You try to be fair.
PROSECUTOR: You weren't just trying to sell copies?
DEFENSE: Objection. The witness is being manhandled.

THE COURT: Overruled. I want to hear the answer.

MAILER: I wasn't trying *just* to sell copies, although I didn't think the description would hurt sales—I'll give you that much. What I was trying to do, however . . .

PROSECUTOR: We're not interested in what you're trying to do, Mr. Mailer, but in what you did.

THE COURT: Let him give it.

MAILER: I was trying to get across Miss Monroe's sense of fun. She may not literally have been wearing no panties on that day, but it was in her nature to have been wearing none. I think she could certainly have been engaged in such a scene and have enjoyed it. So I chose to write it that way. It seemed right to me. That is what I must go by.

PROSECUTOR: I will continue with Exhibit A, page 24 to page 26.

[Reads]

After two days of such shopping, Amy said, "That's it, kiddo. From now on, we stay in the St. Regis and have everything brought up." I began to see how it worked. Some designers came by, friends of Amy's; I could tell by the way she said the name of one that it was another case of Laurence Olivier, Milton Greene, Joe DiMaggio, Arthur Miller, or Elia Kazan. First in category. So I said, "Oh, yes, Norman Norell, greatest dress designer in the world." And he had a couple of the second-greatests with him—George Nardiello, John Moore. They were the nicest men. It was not only that they were well groomed and slim and fit into their clothes like a beautiful hand has gone inside a beautiful glove, but they were so happy inside their suits. It was like the person within themselves also had a good suit which was their own skin. Moreover, they liked me. I could tell. Oh. I felt open as a sponge. I knew they were going to help me. Norell said, "Marilyn, everyone has a problem. I have a friend who's very ugly and she's the princess of fashion in New York. She takes that ugliness and makes it dramatic." Yet, he said, after she was done with her dress and coiffeur, she looked like a samurai warrior. You couldn't take your eyes off her. Besides, she was smart enough to wear jewelry that clanked and gonged with every move she made. You could have been in a Chinese temple. "Her little beauty tricks, if tried on anyone else, would have been a disaster," Norman Norell said and gave me my first lesson in style. "It's not enough to find the problem," he said, "and avoid it. Elegance is magic. The problem, *presto,* has to become the solution."

Sure enough, Norman Norell got around to informing me very kindly that my neck was too short, only he didn't put it that way. My neck, I was told, wasn't that long. I wouldn't be happy in a *Vogue* collar. Ruffles were death. "Let me," he said, "show you a shawl collar." I got it instantly. A nice, thin dinner-jacket set of lapels and a long V-neck. Society cleavage. I felt as if I had spent my life until that point being sort of very fluffy à la Hollywood. Now I could see the way Amy saw me with my head sitting on my shoulders like an armchair in the middle of a saggy floor.

PROSECUTOR: Mr. Mailer, would you say your account of conversations between Miss Monroe and Mr. Norell is factual?

MAILER: Miss Monroe met Norman Norell, he designed dresses for her, he had many conversations with her. I attempted to capture the flavor of those conversations as they might have occurred. They are imaginary conversations, but, hopefully, not too far away in mood from what was said.

PROSECUTOR: Not too far away in mood. But not in fact. In fact, they have no relation to what was said.

MAILER: Most conversations are lost. We reconstruct the past by our recollection of the mood fully as much as by our grasp of fact. When facts are skimpy, one hopes to do well at sensing the mood.

PROSECUTOR: I will continue Exhibit A, pages 26 and 27.

[Reads]

Of course, this new interest in clothes had all started on the trip to Palm Springs, when I told Milton I wanted to be immensely respected and he told me, "First step: Don't act like a slob." He held up a finger. "Be a woman."

"You say, 'Don't look like a slob.'"

"That dress you're wearing," said Milton. "It's a *shmatte.*"

"A what . . . ? No, don't tell me." I once saw a guy in a delicatessen spearing kosher pickles out of a barrel. That was what Yiddish sounded like to me. One more pickle on the prong.

"You want to be the greatest actress in the world," said Milton, "but you're exhibiting neither class nor taste. They call you a dumb blonde, and they are getting away with it. You have to carry yourself different. Don't walk around like you're nothing. Never forget you have something fantastic on the screen."

That was now prominent in my thoughts after meeting Norman Norell. I felt as if I was getting out from the carpet I had been living under all my life. I was beginning to see that class was not beyond me, nor was I beneath it.

PROSECUTOR: Would you say Miss Monroe's conversation with Milton Greene is also based on skimpy facts?

MAILER: Less skimpy. I take it from Mr. Greene's recollection. Of course, his conversations with Miss Monroe were held more than twenty-five years ago. In my case, I am not trying to delineate a boundary line between fact and fiction here. In this book, I want to explore the elusive nature of a most talented woman and artist.

PROSECUTOR: Let me now conclude Exhibit A with the rest of page 27.

It was the scene in *The Seven Year Itch* where I stand over a subway grating and my skirts blow up. Now I guess the studio had given me a white *shmatte* that night and tight white panties, and my hair had a hundred marcelled waves, and I certainly had no neck and lots of back and shoulders, where I was pleasantly plump, to say the least, but I paid no attention. I threw caution to the winds, which is one cliché I could die saying and hold it in my arms, I can't help it, give me a ton of caution to throw to the winds. There were two thousand people on the street, watching, and they had a million whistles. All the while Joe D. was on the outskirts of the crowd dying because he knew the secret of acting. Maybe it was because he was a ballplayer, but he knew it didn't have to be false when you acted that you were in love; sometimes it was real, and when that happened, it could be more real than anything else. So I guess he knew—no secrets between husband and wife; that's what the ceremony is for—guess he knew I was feeling a little moist every time my skirt blew up. Immortality would be immortalized if I ever took those white panties off. It's true, I wanted to throw myself to the crowd.

PROSECUTOR: Mr. Mailer, did your researches bring you to ask various friends of Miss Monroe's if, on this occasion when her skirts were flying, she wanted, and I quote from your text, "to throw myself to the crowd"?

MAILER: No, I asked no one.

PROSECUTOR: To your knowledge, she told no friends of such a feeling?

MAILER: No.

PROSECUTOR: Never mentioned it to you?

MAILER: I never met her.

DEFENSE: Would the court instruct my client that he need only answer the prosecutor's questions. He does not have to add supplementary information.

THE COURT: Mr. Mailer is now twice instructed.

PROSECUTOR: Norman Mailer, you never met Marilyn Monroe?

MAILER: No, but I sat behind her once at Actors' Studio.

[Laughter]

PROSECUTOR: On the basis of the firm insight you gathered from having once sat behind her, you presume to write of Marilyn Monroe's inner physical condition. You declare that she wanted to throw herself to the crowd.

MAILER: Yes.

PROSECUTOR: Would you call this a fair conclusion?

DEFENSE: Objection. The prosecutor is trying to make my client characterize his replies.

THE COURT: Sustained.

MAILER: I wish to answer anyway.

DEFENSE: Please obey the court.

MAILER: Your Honor, with all due respect to my own attorney, I wish to say that such perceptions and such liberties as I took on trying to enter Miss Monroe's mind are considered fair in literary practice.

PROSECUTOR: Objection. I think this ought to be cut off.

THE COURT: You started it. Let him go on.

MAILER: I have been thinking about Miss Monroe's life for many years. I have already written one other book about her, called *Marilyn,* and in that work did not enter her mind once. It was out of respect for the intricacies of her mind. I only dare in this case because I believe I know more about her by now. The experience of looking at Milton Greene's photographs of Marilyn Monroe over several years is part of that greater knowledge. Sides of her nature are revealed by Mr. Greene's photographs that I do not find anywhere else. I would also submit that I have been fair to Miss Monroe in my heart. In fact, I find her charming in those passages you read, and not at all maligned. She is a humorous woman.

PROSECUTOR: Mr. Mailer, concerning Exhibit A, which has just been read, you say you do not malign Miss Monroe but find her charming.

MAILER: Yessir.

PROSECUTOR: I will not argue with your conception of female charm. I will ask you instead to read aloud from Exhibit B, pages 83 and 84. May it please the court, Exhibit B is selected from a later part of the work but is concerned with earlier episodes in Miss Monroe's life when she was still in Hollywood. I believe this comes under the technical heading of "flashback."

MAILER: You could call it that.

[The defendant reads Exhibit B, pages 83 and 84]

Now, of course, even in those days I had a sheltered life. I wasn't respected, but I was sheltered. I might be considered the property of the studio and so be sent at a moment's notice with ten other girls to Denver or Modesto to help out with publicity, knowing full well that in such situations, the studio liked to hold the broadest view of publicity, that is—breed a little good-will. I wasn't being sent out in my sweater to strew ill will. All the same, it was a sheltered life. I might have to go through certain experiences with a big laugh when I was actually feeling a little queasy inside, but, still, who ever had to be afraid of a local movie reviewer or a small-town theater manager? Most of them didn't have poison in their system. In fact, they were really grateful, and some of them were nice people. Anyway, back on the studio lot, I also had to keep appointments. One day I saw three executives on the half hour—2:30 P.M., 3:30 P.M., and 4:30 P.M.—before going off to acting class in the evening, although, of course, those kind of assignments only took five minutes. "How are you, Mr. Farnsworth, how nice to see you again," and he had you behind the desk. Sometimes he never got out of his chair. Sometimes you never got off your knees. I knew the pleats on some executives' trousers better than their face. All the same, most of such people were not that rude, and I had an orphan's philosophy: Cheer up, it could be worse. They could take off their socks and ask you to kiss their feet.

   The key thing, however, was that I was on contract at the studio. A girl might have to do one little despicable deed or another, but you were not out there where you really had to know how to protect yourself. You were sort of more in the very bottom reaches of the middle class. You had to be obedient, that's all.

PROSECUTOR: Mr. Mailer, thank you for reading from your work. Would you summarize for the court your sources for this material.

MAILER: I would say it is based on general knowledge. I have read many books about Hollywood, I have known many people who lived and worked in Hollywood, I spent a year there myself in just the period of which the exhibit speaks, and have also drawn on many stories I heard about Miss Monroe's life during that period, or, for that matter, the life of many other starlets on studio contracts. I believe I can say that the scene described is not exceptional but common to life in Hollywood in the early fifties. It was well known that Miss Monroe had such a life during that period, and the scars of it were probably responsible in part for her future personality. I am trying to explain a woman of angelic appearance who, by the end of her career, was notoriously difficult to work with. Such scenes help me to understand her.

PROSECUTOR: Still, you are taking liberties with the facts.

MAILER: I would say this excerpt is factual. I can't certify it as a fact, but I believe it is a fact. She had the life of a stock girl on contract in Hollywood studios in the fifties. Her drama coach, Lee Strasberg, who is one of the beneficiaries of her will and had the highest regard for her talent, did say, "She was a call girl . . . she was on call for things the studio wanted." Arthur Miller once wrote, "She was chewed and spat out by a long line of grinning men! Her name floating in the stench of locker rooms and parlor-car cigar smoke!"

What is poignant about Marilyn is that all her life she wanted to become a lady. Elegance was as elusive and fearful and attractive and as awesome to her in these somewhat sordid early years as the hidden desire to be macho can feel to a young and wimpy intellectual.

THE COURT: Would Mr. Mailer define "wimpy"?

MAILER: Muscles like cold spaghetti might do it, Your Honor.

THE COURT: You are saying that women feel about elegance the way men feel about machismo?

MAILER: Well, sir, I would say many men decide to reject machismo. They see it as a trap that can dominate them. I expect many women feel that any undue longings toward elegance might direct them from more individual solutions to their lives. Nonetheless, I expect no man puts down machismo without a little uneasiness, and I think it is the same for women and elegance. The rejection of elegance can be haunting. Miss Monroe, having her voluptuous figure and no neck, was not free of the desire to be elegant. In fact, I think it was a major force in her life, a true source of motivation.

THE COURT: Hmmm.

PROSECUTOR: Mr. Mailer is doing his best to be his eloquent best. Still, you are saying, if I may dare to summarize, that your imaginary autobiography wishes to study her desire to rise above sordid beginnings, to become elegant.

MAILER: Something of the sort.

PROSECUTOR: Please forgive these inelegant expressions of your elegant intentions.

THE COURT: Will the prosecution forgo this? The prosecution is elegant enough for all of us.

PROSECUTOR: Thank you, Your Honor. Mr. Mailer, if I understand you correctly, you are saying that every excerpt read in court until now can be justified by you, whether factual or not, as material that can reasonably have occurred in Miss Monroe's life.

MAILER: Yes.

PROSECUTOR: Not literally true, but aesthetically true.

MAILER: Yessir. Well put.

PROSECUTOR: So you believe that up to here, through the exhibits cited, you have not maligned Miss Monroe's nature nor denigrated her character.

MAILER: I believe that.

PROSECUTOR: Even though you mix the real and the fictional, you have succeeded in giving a portrait of her that, hopefully, is more true than fact itself.

MAILER: Yessir.

PROSECUTOR: Would you also agree that when a portrait cheapens a character, the portrait can hurt the reader's mind, that is, injure his future powers of perception?

MAILER: Yessir. There are some who would say that is what the moral nature of literature is all about.

PROSECUTOR: How then would you characterize our next excerpt? Please read Exhibit B, page 88 to 91.

DEFENSE: Before Mr. Mailer begins, would the court again instruct the witness that he need only reply to the prosecutor's questions. He does not have to expatiate on them.

THE COURT: Maybe Mr. Mailer thinks he is being paid by the word.

[The defendant reads]

We passed through several rooms, and one had knives and guns on the wall, and another with zebra stripes for wallpaper, and then a room with nothing but filthy pictures all nicely framed, and the last room was big and had a photograph and a table with drinks, and a lot of couches on which guys and girls, and guys and guys, were lying around in a very dim purple light, just enough to see that there was a lot of purple nakedness in this neck of the woods, worse—I couldn't believe it. This was the first Hollywood party of the sort I'd grown up hearing about. I was used to walking in on a roommate who was under the covers with a fellow, but never anything like this. There were twenty people.

Then I saw our host. Bobby was naked except for cowboy boots and a Stetson hat, and he was walking a Doberman pinscher on a leash around the room, a huge female I suppose, because she had a diamond collar around her neck. But as the dog came up to one couple, it tried to mount, and I saw my mistake. She had a lot of male in the rear. Bobby was giggling like a two-year-old, because the dog kept jumping forcibly into all these lovers' midsts, if you can say such a thing. There were screams and shouts galore—"Bobby, get Romulus away! Bobby, you're a madman."

I would have thought our host was horrible, but when he came up to me, he gave the sweetest smile I'd seen in a year, as if he'd spent his childhood eating nothing but berries and grapes, and when he kissed me, his mouth was tender. I couldn't get over that, his mouth was as good as Edward's, who had the best mouth I'd ever kissed, but Bobby was also strong. I'd never been introduced to a man who was naked before, you learn so much that way, and his skin felt smooth as a seal and terrific to the touch. I couldn't keep my hands off. It was as if he was one boy who everybody had been rubbing love into since he was a baby. Oh, did his lower lip pout.

"Come on," he said, "you and me are going to leave these people."

He handed Romulus's leash to Rod and took me down the tunnel to a room at the other end that turned out to be another apartment. I didn't have time to look around; it didn't matter. We were on the floor. I was embarrassed for a little while, for I reeked of Rod, but Bobby de P. loved smells, I think he had a nose instead of a brain, and besides, he had his own aroma, as I have said. Maybe something in him had the answer to my secret, or maybe I had just been prepared for Bobby by that crazy ride with Rod, and so had kept nothing, absolutely nothing, with which to protect myself, but it was as if the very inside of me was pushing to get over to him as desperate as the feeling you know in a dream.

We went on all night. Somewhere in the middle I

said, "Oh, you're the best, I never knew anything like
this before," and I hadn't, I felt things start in me and go
flying off into the universe or somewhere, they were
sensations going out to far space, so I meant what I said,
except even as I opened my mouth, I knew I had always
had the same thing to say to any fellow who was any
good at all, in fact I had said it to Rod as soon as he
could hear me after the motorcycle stopped. I had even
been tempted to compliment Mr. Farnsworth (after all,
Farnsworth would say to himself, "Nobody sits in a chair
like me!"), it was exactly the remark to make if you
wanted to keep a fellow happy and on your string. I
once had eight great lovers on eight strings. Three more
and I would have run out of fingers. Saying it to Bobby
was true, however, I meant it, maybe I meant it for the
first time since I'd begun to say it, and Bobby just roared
with a crazy kind of laughter. Then we just started reaching into one another as if we were really going to catch
something never caught before.

After a while, we moved over to the bed, and later he
even turned on the lights, and there were a lot of mir-
rors. The room was full of antiques who sat there like
rich and famous people, and I could see the Persian rug
we had been doing it on, red and gold and purple and
green. The bed was the largest I'd been in till then. We
must have used every inch of it; he was one rich boy who
wouldn't stop. All through the night, there were knocks
on the door and people yelling, "Bobby, where are
you?" or "Join in the fun, for God's sake," but in the
morning, when we wandered out (and by then I was so
comfortable I wore nothing but high-heeled shoes, and
Mr. de P. was back in his Stetson hat), we came to the
dead smoky smell of old reefers and cartons of cigarette
butts in ashtrays and nobody around but the dog. Romulus was lying in the middle of the floor with his diamond collar gone and his throat cut. His eyes were
open, and he had the peculiar expression of a young

pup learning to sit on his hind legs. A simple dog look. Plus all that blood on the carpet which you couldn't see at first it was such a dark carpet.

Bobby started to blubber like a five-year-old kid. He cried and his belly shook a little and his big jaw looked really prominent the way a five-year-old kid with a big jaw can impress you with how mad they are going to be when they grow up. Then he came to a stop and knelt by the dog and got a little blood on his fingers and touched it to himself and to me, but so softly that I wasn't offended, as if that was a nice way to say goodbye to Romulus, and then we went back to the bedroom and made love, which turned out to be sweeter than anything because it was full of sorrow, and I cried for the baby in my stomach who would soon be gone and the dead dog and for myself, and felt very sweet toward Bobby.

Later that day I asked him, "Do you know who killed Romulus?" and he nodded.

I asked, "Are you going to do anything about it?"

"You bet," he said.

PROSECUTOR: We would like Mr. Mailer to continue directly to Exhibit B, page 92 to page 95. May it please the court, the new excerpt concludes the description after skipping over a brief account of the household of this Bobby de P., and his business connections, and his family.

[The defendant reads Exhibit B, page 92 to page 95]

Then I began to have this ferocious headache. When we weren't making love, I felt nauseated and wondered if it was morning sickness, and slowly, day by day, Bobby de P. and me began to fight. Except they weren't quarrels so much as savage displays, you might say, of bad nerves, after which we'd be off once more. All the while we'd

talk about getting married. Only it was like we were flip-
ping a switch. Maybe it was the benzedrine. He kept
feeding us pills until I couldn't sleep, and every time I
came near to something fabulous, my chest also came
near to exploding.

On the fifth day Bobby said to me, "You want to get
married?"

"Yes."

"Well, I'll get married."

"Let's," I said.

"We can't," he said. "I'm married already," and he bit
me on the lip. I flung him off. "You said you were divorced."

"She won't give it."

His wife was living with Rod. Rod, he told me, had
killed the dog and then stole the collar. Of course, that
diamond collar had used to belong to Bobby's wife, except that Bobby had taken it back from her the day they
broke up and put it on the dog.

"Rod is away now," he said, "on location in Utah.
Let's go over and visit my old lady."

"And tell her you want a divorce?"

He squeezed my arm so hard I could feel the bruise
instantly. "No," he said, "we'll finish her off like the dog."

What I couldn't believe was the excitement it gave
me. I was nearer to myself than I ever wanted to be. I
saw inside myself to the other soul, the one that never
spoke. It was ready to think of murder. In truth, my
headache went away.

"Let's drive up to her house," he said. "I'll do it and
you watch. Then we'll come back here. If we stick together, nobody can prove a thing. We can say we were in
bed."

I could see us looking at each other forever, one year
into the next. I could see my pictures in the newspapers.
STARLET QUESTIONED IN MURDER CASE. The pictures
would be printed in all the newspapers over the world.

A candle could burn in a dark church at such a thought. The idea that everyone would talk of me was beautiful. Killing Bobby's wife felt almost comfortable. Maybe if I hadn't seen Romulus with that funny expression on his face where he was dead but still seemed to be learning to sit on his paws, maybe if I hadn't seen something in that animal lying there so calmly after his throat was cut, I might have worried about Bobby's wife, but now I just felt as if it was all fair somehow. Maybe Bobby would even let me keep my baby. I remember thinking of how I felt when I first saw my face on film in *Scudda-Hoo! Scudda-Hay!* and decided I was very interesting, except I had what you might call a space in my expression. There was something in me that didn't show itself to others. Like: I'm ready to commit murder.

We got into Bobby's car and drove across Bel Air into Beverly Hills, and in one of the houses off Rodeo Drive was where she lived. It was dark, and there were no cars outside, and the garage was locked, so Bobby and I went to the back of the house. He found the wire to the burglar alarm and cut it and cracked the latch on the window. There we were standing in her kitchen. He looked in the rack for the carving knife and found one. Then we went up the stairs to her bedroom. I remember it was on the side that would have a view of the hills above Beverly Hills, and all the while he was doing this, despite the benzedrine, I never felt more calm as if, ha ha, I was on *This Is Your Life,* and they were talking about me looking for the woman's door. I even held Bobby's hand, the one that did not have the knife.

There was no lock to the master bedroom. By the light of the street lamps coming through the window, we could see that there was also no woman in the bed. The house was empty. We went through every room, but it was empty. Bobby's wife must have gone on location with Rod.

We went home. Before the night was over, Bobby beat me up, or at least he started to, but he was too drunk to catch me. I was awful sick of sex. I grabbed up my clothes and ran out the door and had the luck to find a taxi on those lonely streets and went home to Hollywood. I didn't even cry in the backseat. It just occurred to me that Bobby didn't even know my phone number or address, or even my last name, just my first, and maybe he would never try to find me, and he never did.

Two days later, I had the abortion. Whenever I looked into my mirror now in my apartment in the Waldorf Towers, on the thirty-seventh floor, I could still see how something ended in me that day, I don't know what, but it is still in my expression.

PROSECUTOR: Mr. Mailer, concerning these last two excerpts, what percentage of fact and fiction would you estimate are there?
MAILER: I would say those passages are fiction.
PROSECUTOR: This Bobby, as he is called, he is based on no one?
MAILER: No one.
PROSECUTOR: His wife?
MAILER: She is imaginary.
PROSECUTOR: The man named Rod?
MAILER: Equally fictional.
PROSECUTOR: Do you have knowledge that Miss Monroe at any time in her life made a compact to help a husband murder his wife?
MAILER: To my knowledge, she never did.
PROSECUTOR: There is nothing on record anywhere that she ever contemplated such an act?
MAILER: Not so far as I know.
PROSECUTOR: Did anyone suggest this possibility in an interview?
MAILER: No one.
PROSECUTOR: Yet, in a fictional situation, you make Marilyn Monroe accomplice to a conspiracy to commit murder.
MAILER: I suppose that's the legal description.
PROSECUTOR: How can you ever justify yourself? If Miss Monroe were alive, she could sue you for libel. And win.
DEFENSE: Objection.

THE COURT: Prosecution knows better than to draw conclusions.

PROSECUTOR: Forgive me, Your Honor. I consider the action of the defendant outrageous.

DEFENSE: Objection, Your Honor.

THE COURT: I'm putting the prosecution on notice.

PROSECUTOR: You wrote Exhibit B, pages 88 to 95, knowing there was no basis for them?

MAILER: No factual basis.

PROSECUTOR: What makes you think there is a fictional basis?

MAILER: I'm not sure a fictional basis is possible. I'm not even certain Marilyn Monroe could have gotten into such a situation, fictionally speaking, and still be Marilyn Monroe. I've pondered the question. All the while I was writing this book, I kept asking myself, Is this true to Marilyn?

PROSECUTOR: Are you telling us that you doubt your ethics?

MAILER: I call them in question.

PROSECUTOR: You think yourself guilty of literary malpractice?

MAILER: I hope not, but it's possible.

PROSECUTOR: We rest our case.

THE COURT: Let's take ten minutes.

[Recess]

DEFENSE: Your Honor, while court was out, I discussed his testimony with Mr. Mailer, and he has made clear to me again that he is not interested in an adversary proceeding so much as to ask the court for a discovery of his motives. That is the legal position out of which my questions will be asked.

THE COURT: You want to let us know where your questions are coming from.

DEFENSE: Yes, Your Honor.

THE COURT: I hope they are not coming from left field.

DEFENSE: It is my fervent hope, Your Honor.

THE COURT: Please proceed.

DEFENSE: Mr. Mailer, when you conceived this work, did you plan to have such scenes with the character named Bobby as are described in Exhibit B?

MAILER: I can say that I planned to have such passages, yes. There is a period in Marilyn Monroe's life about which very little is known. I would locate it during 1948, 1949, and 1950, sometime after she became a model but before she made *The Asphalt Jungle*. In those years, she was one of many girls around Hollywood, and there is no telling what kind of adventures she got into, or with what sort of men she went out, other than a few movie people we know she knew. So I thought I would try to invent some episode that might, in a few pages, capture the impact and probable horror of those years upon her.

THE COURT: Mr. Mailer, how did you form the conclusion that those years from 1948 to 1950 were horrible for Miss Monroe?

MAILER: On the basis of her later life, Your Honor. The tragedy that surrounds Marilyn Monroe is that as her career succeeded, so did she begin to come apart. It is tragic to be destroyed in the years of one's success. Right when she was most happily married is when she became most unhappily married. There is no simple explanation for such matters. We have to assume there are buried matters in the psyche.

THE COURT: Does that justify endowing her with murderous instincts?

MAILER: It is my understanding of Marilyn Monroe that she was murderous. I would say she was a killer in the way most of us are. On the set, she killed time and slaughtered expectations. She wore people out, she chilled their talent. Finally, with her husbands, she exhausted their hopes. She left not one death but a thousand little deaths in many of the people around her, nice people and awful people both, at least by her measure of nice and awful. When we slay indiscriminately, I think it is a sign we are trying to hold off our own doom. Any portrait of Marilyn Monroe that restricted itself to showing how attractive she could be in the panoply of all her tender wit had to be an untrue portrait which would mislead the reader.

DEFENSE: We wish to point out that the prosecution has offered excerpts that show Miss Monroe only in an unattractive or controversial light. Such passages are but a small part of this book, *Of Women and Their Elegance,* and give a distorted portrait.

MAILER: Yes, most of the time, in fact, since Marilyn Monroe is telling the story in her own voice, I did my best to show her as quintessentially charming.

THE COURT: Mr. Mailer, would you care to define your use of "charming"?

MAILER: Unpredictable but positive, Your Honor. We don't know how we'll get there, but we're looking to find our way to some-place nice. Miss Monroe is presented in most of my pages as nice.

DEFENSE: Exhibit C, page 96, may be an example of this, Your Honor.

[Defense reads]

I didn't like television because it made me want to burp. On the other hand, it was a little like having another person in the room. Nobody impressive, of course. Somebody who was pale and had a lot of stomach noises. Color TV was like they were putting makeup on that pale person. A very unhealthy person with a wheeze in his lungs and a twitch—if you got to know them well they would tell you about their operations. So I used to think TV was ridiculous. The entertainment industry, instead of understanding that they had this unhealthy individual who could only do a little bit, had it out in-stead working hard. Maybe one year it would come down with some awful disease, but in the meantime they were giving it dancing lessons.

DEFENSE: We will also offer Exhibit C, page 33, as typical of char-acteristic aspects of this work.

THE COURT: Do you object? I see you are standing.

PROSECUTOR: We will not object. Our case does not rest on the presence or absence of agreeable passages concerning Miss Monroe. It is based instead on one outrageously unfounded pre-sentation of her character.

DEFENSE: I proceed to read Exhibit C, page 33.

[Reads]

Once in a while, to put myself to sleep, I would think of
Amy's underwear, which was not only immaculate but
color-coordinated. If she was wearing a purple dress,
why, she would also put on a purple bra and a purple
girdle and a purple half-slip. "Why?" I asked her. "People can't see what you have on underneath."

"I like the feeling of being altogether in the color I
wear." I got it. She did everything for the inner feeling.
I was so impressed.

"Besides," said Amy, "if my husband comes wandering through while I'm getting dressed, I want him to see
something pretty. Why should I show Milton cotton underwear? With his eyes!"

Her lingerie cabinet was like a rainbow. All those colors arranged in a fan. When I thought about it, going to
sleep, the lingerie gave off sounds like organ pipes. I felt
so much love for Amy because we could be friends, she
who had every color of the rainbow for her underwear,
and I who never wore any.

DEFENSE: Would you say, Mr. Mailer, that it was to balance such
favorable impressions of Miss Monroe that you invented the
scenes concerning the imaginary man named Bobby?
MAILER: No, not to balance the portrait so much as to disturb it.
THE COURT: To disturb it?
MAILER: Yes, Your Honor. I did not wish to add to Miss Monroe's
legend but to shock its roots. So I decided to take a chance.
THE COURT: Can you expatiate on this chance you were taking?
MAILER: One reader, close to me, so hated the section in question
that it spoiled the manuscript for her. She is a practical woman,
just the sort of levelheaded reader one looks for, and I knew her
reaction would be common to many. Yet I felt no desire to re-

move that part—indeed, I knew I would keep it. For to contemplate my book without such a passage is intolerable. The work would then present Miss Monroe as sweet, charming, madcap, a natural soul. That could only deepen the confusion surrounding her life and her legend. We would be farther away from understanding how it is that someone so attractive could end so badly.

DEFENSE: Yet the prosecution has asked in effect why you chose the explanation you did.

MAILER: That still bothers me. The tone of the episode itself. There may have been a failure of invention. It is not easy to conceive of one powerful dramatic episode that will substitute satisfactorily for the sum of a thousand smaller episodes.

DEFENSE: Yet, what is this sum—to use your word—that you are trying to show the reader?

MAILER: It is Marilyn Monroe's unrecorded years in Hollywood. They must make up a large-size bag of foul encounters and small ruthless impulses that wakened in her one by one. In later years, I believe they were like a psychic cyst within her. Memories so bad cannot be called upon. It is exactly the memories we cannot face that destroy us. We are always carrying them uphill.

DEFENSE: So you felt it was fair to invent this extraordinary episode at the home of Bobby de P.?

MAILER: Yes. Fair to the reader, that is I wanted the reader to be jarred into comprehension of the size and spectrum of a movie star's soul. There is more to a movie star than we think, not less. I wanted to deepen the legend of Marilyn Monroe, not sweeten it. I thought it would be better for our comprehension of many things if we understood that art comes out of more contracts than are written, and the artist's inner negotiations with evil are often as comprehensive as the generosity of the artistic offering. So I do not think I was unfair to her at large. I expect the total of the little horrors she committed in those years would equal the one large horror I gave her. But whether I caught the taste and tone of her personality by that episode, or lost the flavor of her voice for a little while, is another matter.

DEFENSE: We rest.

THE COURT: A question. How would you feel, Mr. Mailer, if some other author were to characterize you in such extreme fashion after your death? Let me say I do not wish to rush that occasion. Still, how do you think you would feel?

MAILER: Your Honor, I have already been characterized in many books as if I were dead. Jacqueline Susann, from what I am told, depicted me as the improbable and repulsive villain of one of her novels. Mario Puzo once portrayed me as a fat man who smoked cigars and strangled a poodle with his bare hands on an airplane. That sounds more like a description of Puzo than myself. I also resent what Puzo's fiction had me doing. I owned a standard poodle once, and he was a great dog and lived to be eighteen years old. I do not go around killing poodles. Another writer gave one of his characters my name, literally! and then had him drop his pants obediently at gunpoint, for which compliance, he—I should say I—was shot in the anus and killed. There have been other such portraits. I do not say that because I have been, on occasion, poorly treated in print I have a right, therefore, to distort Marilyn Monroe's life. I say, rather, that I think uneasily of her opinion, and I hope she accepts, wherever she is, the equation I drew between her many lost episodes and the single one I gave her. For if I have been unfair to her, as I believe those authors have been unfair to me, then I must shift uncomfortably before any bar of judgment, since I know how deep is the contempt I hold for authors who would write about me and yet do not have the imagination to come up with some equivalent of my life that may be extreme but is fair. I would not like to think Miss Monroe feels an equal contempt for me. I guess that is all.

DEFENSE: Can we ask for an immediate verdict of exoneration?

THE COURT: Some might think your client lucky to escape hanging. I am going to take this under advisement. There is a lot to mull over here, and I am hardly going to let you off on the spot. I will say that I have read the book and consider it a serious enough work to give Mr. Mailer a fair opportunity of avoiding outright censure. But there is no escaping the conclusion that what he has done is downright dangerous. He almost certainly will be reprimanded for making up false and sordid episodes concerning public figures. What if a lot of bad authors were to act as Mr. Mailer has?

DEFENSE: They have, Your Honor. Ever since Gutenberg.

THE COURT: Well, I'm going to have to live with this for a while. Let me tell you that once again Mr. Mailer has done his best to take over my weekend. I'm going to close this court for now.

[Adjournment]

Until Dead: Thoughts on Capital Punishment

(1981)

I HATE THE QUESTION. It confuses me. Every time I am obliged to give an opinion whether capital punishment should or should not be abolished, I say something different. Once I was on *The Phil Donahue Show* trying to sell copies of my book *The Executioner's Song*. It's a poor way for a grown man to live, perched on a stage full of pale orange and pale blue plastic furniture, hot lights up, your stomach rumbling. There you are, trying to vend your creation. It behooves you to know on such occasions what you are talking about.

When my host asked about the death penalty, I *phumphered*. "I'm not for it," I allowed, "but I'm not against it, altogether, either. I think we need a little capital punishment."

Donahue said, "I don't understand how a little bit of shooting people and dropping cyanide tablets is good for us."

"Well," I replied, "I get mystical on this . . . I don't have a clear answer."

"You know, what you're saying," said Donahue, "is, 'Let's knock off three or four a year so we can feel strong.' "

"That's not what I'm saying," I told him, but maybe I was. I'm not sure I know now. Every time I contemplate the problem, I find finer reasons for confusion. The subject becomes bottom-

less. Of course, there are times when you have to live with questions you cannot answer in ten seconds. We may be face-to-face
with that difficulty now.

Certainly, it is easy to be against capital punishment. Should
you think of yourself as civilized and liberal, it is almost impossible not to wish it abolished. Capital punishment simply does not
appear to serve as a deterrent. In 1957, among the thirty-three
nations that chose not to exercise the death penalty, the number
of murders never increased. That gives pause.

Look at it. Some killings are committed in heat, and some in
the coldest regions of the heart, but a man who murders in passion is, by definition, blind to restraints. Passion, or for that matter, rage and panic, causes us to act in a way we never would if
our cautions were heard. On the other hand, anyone who murders by calculation can have a real fear of future execution, but
it is only one factor in his calculations. Even if it all goes wrong,
and he is caught and sentenced, there are still, by way of appeals,
many years between him and his execution, so much as a decade, conceivably two decades. In fact, such a death is so far away
that he is in more danger of being killed by a bust on the street.
(For how often can a cop make a street arrest in an atmosphere
free of the craziest tension?)

All right, replies the argument for deterrence: Change the calculations of the man who commits cold murder. Up the consequences. It sounds simple until you examine it. Up the
consequences.

As, for example, from an Associated Press release: "Turkey's
new military government hanged a leftist terrorist and a rightist
terrorist in front of their families before dawn today, informed
sources said. The execution ended an eight-year suspension of
capital punishment in Turkey and was aimed at deterring further terrorism."

Hanging a terrorist in front of his family will certainly deter
some of his friends—the timid ones. It will inspire the brave to
more martyrdom. SAVAK tortured political prisoners in Iran by
the thousands, and executed hundreds: the answer was provided
by the Ayatollah Khomeini. To up the consequences is to face
the consequences. It is a gamble. There may be more rather

than less violence. Besides, we would have to throw out the appeal system of the courts to speed up execution. You can't accelerate the law and bypass legal procedures without removing the safeguards that protect us against too little justice.

Well, then, continues the argument, keep the safeguards. Let the law take its time. But execute those killers even if it requires ten years.

It still won't work. If there is agreement about one common denominator to the psychopath—hot psychopaths and cold, calculating psychopaths—it is their need for quick gratification. Patience is not part of their powers. The present looms large, and the future seems hazy. To conceive of one's own execution in years to come does not offer much check against the immediate impulse to murder.

Deterrence is overwhelmed by the excitement which capital punishment offers the killer. Convicts are the first to comprehend that any man who can slay another has crossed a barrier not all others are ready to follow. Men who end up on death row have true charisma, therefore. They may live in cages and grow wild and demented in the isolation of their lives, but they are the most important figures in any prison. Everyone knows their names. Celebrity, we may as well recognize, is even more electrifying to a convict than to an entertainer. A man leading a dull life, full of oppression, who finds himself a little more choked with rage each year, will secretly be drawn to the idea of capital punishment as a release from the monotony of his existence. So it works as a stimulant long before it is felt as a deterrent. The fear of retribution, if there is any, is more likely to occur after the act, not before. In England in 1900, 250 men were hanged; 170 of them had previously witnessed an execution. 1900 is not 1980, but the burden of proof is hardly reduced since capital punishment was a daily event in those years.

Of course, you can find more sophisticated arguments than deterrence for bringing us back to capital punishment. Ed Koch, the mayor of New York, put himself on record against fellow liberals by declaring: "Society has the right to demonstrate its sense of moral outrage against particularly heinous crimes." The death sentence may not be a deterrent, but society can still feel fortified. In fact, if it is not ready to execute its extreme malefactors, then society may seem absurd to itself. A mass of good citizens does not like to sit around in impotent fury after a cheap hoodlum has savaged a young girl and dismembered her body.

There is trouble, however, with this idea as well. "Particularly heinous crimes," on closer examination, are almost never done by the kind of people society might be able to kill in good conscience. Atrocities are usually committed by poor, raddled wretches so schizophrenic in their inmost wheels that psychiatry itself is disturbed by a look into their minds. The gate of a mental hospital receives the killer rather than the sights of the executioner's gun, the straps of the electric chair, or the touch of the rope.

So the more one contemplates capital punishment, the less one can argue comfortably that it works. On the other side of the argument, it soon becomes clear that it may do much harm to society. Certainly it disturbs the law. Anyone familiar with courts and legal processes knows that justice likes to be concrete. Attorneys try to build a case by putting together ladders of evidence with no weak rungs. Thereby the judge or juror can mount to his conclusion and never have to step across a gap. When a court is asked to decide whether a penalty should be $5,000 or $10,000, legal precedent can be as well laid out as a good network of roads. But so soon as His Honor or the Peers of the Defendant are asked to consider the sentence of death, law has come to the end of its reason. It is awesome to give the verdict at that point. All concerned must take a leap. Contemplate the vertigo that spins in the half-remembered dreams of judges, lawyers, and juries when they must condemn the man (or, very occasionally, the woman) in the defendant's chair to a sentence of execution. It is one thing to read about a wanton slaying and tell your family they ought to kill the scummy son of a bitch who committed the act; it is another to sit on a jury and stare at your potential victim. He does not look that different now from anyone else. Yet you are going to order this stranger—and how strange he is—to death.

That can only inspire the deepest panic. In our dreams, we are always up before judgment. The penalties, the retribution, the outright torture we suffer in a nightmare suggests some more precipitous universe beyond the familiar world of law, society, and daily life, some existence where one is given prodigious sentences for every mistake. Think then of the boiling pits in any judge or juror who has to condemn another to death. What if he has missed some extenuating circumstance? How much will he have to pay in eternity for such an error? Capital punishment inspires pure dread in judges and juries. Your dream life can be changed forever by bringing in such a verdict.

Even the attorney who prosecuted Gary Gilmore did not want to go to the execution. Gilmore had killed two young married men on successive nights and spoke of it with icy detachment. Gilmore also had a bad record in jail. So the county attorney worked with all his skills to get the death penalty and succeeded. Yet he never believed Gilmore would be shot. Tacitly, he assumed that the sentence of death would not only be appealed, but eventually commuted to life imprisonment. Personally, he had no desire to see Gilmore dead.

He was not unique among prosecutors. Capital punishment is to the rest of all law as surrealism is to realism. It destroys the logic of the profession. Until one gets to capital punishment, law is a game. A most interesting, valuable, and serious game. To the degree that a case is brilliantly argued by both sides, justice, if not done, is at least approached. Law is a way of saying: Human nature being what it is, you cannot get justice itself, but you can, if the lawyers are good enough, get the next best thing to it. You may even find an approximation of justice.

Capital punishment, however, says: The penalty no longer fits the crime. You are being moved from the court to the tomb. The prosecuting attorney is transmuted into an avenging angel, and the judge, a god. What has that to do with legal camaraderie?

Opposing lawyers, trying to tear one another apart in court, also like to laugh afterward at the moves each pulled. Contending lawyers, out of court, are usually more friendly than athletes on rival teams—in fact, they are like athletes who are trying out for the same position. The law is built on the assumption that life is mad, and law offers the same stability society brings to restless humankind. Look, you fools, says society, the way we do it makes no one happy, but somehow, most of the time, you get through life in one piece.

Capital punishment is there, however, to say: How do you get through a death? The man is not dying of disease, or by one of those livid cracks in the bowl of time that speaks of sudden accidents, or spontaneous acts of mayhem. No, he is being murdered administratively. The state will do the job. Which is to say that a large group of people hired by the state—corrections officers— are suddenly in charge of an unprecedented event.

Now, prison guards, unlike other state employees, do not have lives that are high in security and low in risk—to that extent they are not the same as other bureaucrats. They are sitting on real dynamite, whereas a desk bureaucrat is only sitting on the explosiveness of his own anxieties. Yet prison guards are not so different either. What characterizes all state employees is that they want each day to be like the next day. Prison guards most of all. Each day, for eight hours, they must report to a city of convicts and try to administer it. These guards are like occupation soldiers in a foreign land. It is to their interest that everything remain the same. That is their safety. If breakfast is served to convicts at seven each morning, why, then, an execution at sunrise will require the authorities to keep the prisoners in their cells. That will disrupt the serving of breakfast. Convicts who have empty bellies in the morning can stage a riot by noon. Any disruption of routine could, conceivably, prove fatal to a guard.

So, the impact on a prison of even a solitary execution is vast. To the inmates, one of their own is going to be assassinated. As the citizens of a city-state whose boundaries are the penitentiary walls, they see it as one more outrage perpetrated by the occupying powers. Prisons may be administered by wardens and corrections officers, but they are kept in peace or are agitated by the prisoners, and it is the philosophy of the most determined convicts that gives the city-state its prevailing mood. Convicts do not necessarily see themselves as criminals, or maladjusted members of society. They can feel like occupied but unconquered partisans. A convict sees his own life from the inside, from *his* insides. His insides feel just as outraged by an injustice done to him as any law-abiding citizen.

Possibly, the convict is more outraged, since "law-abiding citizen" is just a couple of banal words, not an actual taxpayer. Which of us in the confessional of our heart would pretend to be law-abiding? No, we are usually full of guilt at all the little laws we break and do not pay for. Whereas the convict is suffering overt punishment. Often he does not feel wrong so much as trapped. The real criminals, goes prison lore, are on the outside slurping up fortunes at the money trough. A convict's rage at any injustice done to him is large, therefore, and his solidarity—it is the word—with other convicts can bear comparison to the feeling of Arab terrorists for border Arabs, or of Israeli commandos for Jews who have been victims of terrorists.

The authorities in a prison are hardly ignorant of this view. They live with it, after all. So they know what the impact of an execution will be on the peace of the daily routine. Yet that is only part of their problem. They also have to carry off the job without looking sadistic or ridiculous, and there is so little precedent for an execution. Indeed, before Gilmore, there had not been an execution in America for ten years. So almost all the steps will be untried. To a bureaucrat, lack of precedent is equal to lack of bread. In a state which does not have a professional executioner or hangman, but a statute which calls for a firing squad, the warden can go through many an anxious hour trying to decide who he will use.

It is, of course, not hard to find volunteers. For that matter, police officers will appear from everywhere on the day of the execution, and happy to be invited. To be there is a mark of status. It is also no surprise that a good many people have applied for the firing squad, all perfectly willing to pull a trigger as part of their duty to society. Of course, they have been refused. How could the state devise a psychological test that would protect society from the volunteer rifleman who might be a psycho himself? Only one conclusion is possible: State employees must pull the triggers. They cannot, however, be correction officers from the prison, or the convicts, listening to the gossip of the guards, might ferret out their identities. They must be state police instead.

Of course, the authorities also have to protect the firing squad from any feelings of future guilt. Ergo, they decide that one of the five riflemen will not draw a bullet but a blank. Then, goes the theory, nobody on the execution squad will know if his gun has fired a real round. Considerately, nobody wonders where you would find a skilled rifleman who does not know by the kick of his shoulder stock whether he has fired a real round. In the event, Gilmore's heart was certainly pierced by four bullets placed close enough together to be covered by a fifty-cent piece.

Any state of our union about to have an execution will have to confront some unaccustomed and large operations. Hundreds of press and media people are going to fly into the state capital. Demonstrators opposed to the execution will mass by the dozens, the hundreds, or will it be the thousands? One does not know in advance for what to get ready. It is the kind of panic that tempts state authorities to call in federal authorities for crowd control. Meanwhile, television cameras are going to be everywhere. A central obscenity soon dominates. It is that none of the locals, not even the children, escapes the knowledge that one man in their midst is going to be dead, and the state itself will be the killer. That proves more compelling than murder in the next neighborhood. Criminal slayings are horrible, but comprehensible. We all have a touch of murder inside us. There is, however, something repulsive, but withal riveting, about the state executing a man. That is like hearing of a human who walks around with a steel heart. You could not take your eyes off him. Today, we have a man behind bars who is absolutely alive but will be a corpse tomorrow. He is breathing eternity itself. Unless the law gives a reprieve.

That is the next possibility that attends all executions. Reprieve. It always sparks a circus of lawsuits. One legal intervention starts to jump on the back of another. To the courts, it is horrendous. Lawyers begin to look like charlatans and judges like clowns. Every safeguard written into law serves as fodder for a new headline. "YOU'RE ALL COWARDS!" GILMORE TELLS COURT. In the name of carrying out the law, the law seems ready to fall apart.

Then the hour of execution arrives. None of the press will see it, but no matter. They wait outside in hundreds of cars and vans that jam the prison parking lot. Through the night they start their motors to keep warm, and nip at the firewater in their flasks. If you cannot get drunk after freezing through a January night waiting for a man to be shot, when can you booze it up? The man was unknown six months ago, one more con with half his life in jail, now out on parole and getting into anonymous scrapes. By this night in January, he has become one of the best-known faces in the world. *Time* magazine, in the roundup at the end of the year, put his picture on the same two pages with Jimmy Carter and Rosalynn and Miz Lillian, put it there with Betty Ford and Mao Tse-tung and Henry Kissinger. What a deterrent!

To be fair, this was no ordinary execution. Gilmore was asking to be shot. Over and over, week after week, he had been saying that he preferred execution to life imprisonment. The question of capital punishment was being underlined in royal purple ink. So long as a man did not want to be killed, society could feel compassion and commute the sentence. But Gilmore was saying I do not want your compassion. Life imprisonment is not life. It is the misery of my body and the death of my soul. In public, he was virtually saying, and in private, in his letters, he was actually saying: I want to die so my soul can live.

Gilmore was thereby making a political statement. Society, he was declaring, has no rights over me. It only has power. It can kill me, but I will not allow it to tell me how I must live the rest of my life. He was striking a blow in favor of capital punishment. To liberals who believe society has some claim to determine the nature of your life, but no rights over your death, Gilmore was reversing all the signals.

Now the courts were in the shadow of another paradox. Suits were being brought to keep this man from his own execution even though he had asked for it. That made capital punishment the undeclared defendant. Society may have no right to carry out a death sentence, became the argument. In part, that was reaction in advance to the obscenity of the oncoming act. "We didn't tell you how we touched everything," a columnist, Bob Greene, would write after the press was allowed in the execution chamber. "We didn't tell you what we did to the death chair itself—the chair with the bullet holes in its leather back . . . didn't tell you how we inserted our fingers into the holes, and rubbed our fingers around, feeling for ourselves how deep and wide the death holes were." Obscenity, however, was not only in the aftermath but in the concept itself. For who, finally, went the liberal argument, had the right to be an executioner? Prosecutors and judges were not free of guilt nor pure of motive. Politicians were certainly not elevated above corruption. Yet they were also public officials. None of these people had the right to decide whether a prisoner should or should not live. Indeed, government officials often pushed for a death penalty because polls indicated it would hurt them politically if they didn't.

All the same, Gilmore had put the liberals in a quandary. He wished to die, and that was his private right. Yet, if it were suicide he desired, then, decided the liberals, pure suicide was what he should choose. He must not call on the state and all the machinery of the state to be his accomplice. There were more than five hundred men on death row in the fifty American states. Gilmore's death might encourage other states to go back to capital punishment after a hiatus of ten years in which no one had been executed. That moratorium, obtained by a few landmark cases in the Supreme Court, had to be kept. The prevention of capital punishment was a line of defense against the taking of life by the state for other reasons. If government officials grew accustomed to committing judicial murder, it would eventually—went the reasoning—seem less unnatural to execute people for political crimes. Kill yourself if you must, said the liberals to Gilmore, but take some pills, or cut your wrists. Keep the state out of it.

Gilmore, however, had his preferences. He would escape if he could. That was the best of the choices. But if he couldn't, he would accept execution, so he said. And if the courts gave him an unwanted reprieve, then and only then would he commit suicide. But in his mind, and he declared it often, suicide was the least attractive alternative.

For one thing, it was demeaning. It was not the same, went Gilmore's unstated argument, to do it yourself or have others do it. That was equal to the difference between announcing "I am wrong" or telling you "They say I am wrong." That was a clear difference. On reflection, there might be another.

For to die alone, by one's own hand, could take courage, but not so much as he would need to meet the hour of death in front of others. That would be an extreme test. Think of the terrors an actor must go through on first night if a play depends on his performance. Add the courage it will take to be prepared to step forward at the final curtain and stop four bullets with one's heart. That is an impossibly romantic role. Of course, Gilmore felt his life would begin with his death. "I lived a stupid life," he could have been saying. "Let me at least die well. That is the only way to redeem my pride."

It was in the whole tangle of these thoughts that I began to stammer on that television morning talking to Phil Donahue. "Yes," I said, "maybe we need a little capital punishment," and knew it was hopeless to explain. Capital punishment was embarrassing for the state, I could have said, and a meaningless punishment for ninety-nine out of a hundred men on death row—they had been there too long. Yet I also thought that once in a while, as a special solution, if a man or woman wished to die at the center of the stage, full of vanity, pride, and even some sense of atonement, well, that should also be a human right—to choose the most dramatic death possible, rather than the most delayed. If one believed in a soul that endured beyond one's body, the manner of one's dying might be the most important act of life.

All the same, the real question was still unanswered. Could capital punishment ever be justified when the condemned did not wish to die? Society, Ed Koch was still there to say, had a "right to demonstrate its sense of moral outrage against particularly heinous crimes."

Well, that, on further reflection, also begged the question. Such a remark assumed that society was good, whereas society might actually be in danger of breaking up. It could be clearer to say that society had not a right but a *need* to express its outrage. Maybe the grim truth was that society—this screaming gaggle of us all—was simply not large enough, generous enough, compassionate enough, no, not Judeo-Christian enough to tolerate a world where no killers were destroyed for their deeds. In that case, the abolition of all executions might be equal to extinguishing some last vital instinct of revenge. We might all sicken thereby a little further.

There are crimes, after all, which make one sick with rage. I saw a letter the other day from a woman whose two brothers were killed in a store. They had gone in to buy a bottle of liquor for a family celebration and had the misfortune to be caught in a stickup. They were tied together in a back room and stabbed until they died. The killers were captured on leaving. Got off with small sentences. They had "the most expensive lawyer in town."

One thinks of all that means, of all the ways in which money buys a piece of protection in every layer of society. What frustration we feel at the way morals and money lose their sharp edges in relation to each other. Society is afloat in a sea of corruption, so say we all, but there is also the instinct to flush it out. So occasionally, as part of that impulse, we look for a scapegoat. We have a profound need to find a murderer we can execute. His deed may be less horrible than the crime of the man next to him on death row, but by the particular local circumstances of the law, he is the man we have chosen to execute. Living amid all the blank walls of technology, we require a death now and again, we need to stir that foul pot. Needless to ask why we must learn over and over again that execution by the state looses a stench deeper than murder on the street. As the Greeks taught us, a country without a theater that dares to be profound is a weak society. So, unconsciously, we hold to the idea of capital punishment against all civilized arguments. Yes, like Greeks in the amphitheater viewing tragedy, we need—once in a while we need—an aesthetic upheaval that will be deeper than anything offered by our daily television and our money-laundered morals. That packaged entertainment and those flabby morals are the tranquilizers of all our suppressed insanity. So we face a frightful equation. Maybe we are not punishing the murderer so much as we are serving medicine to ourselves. Maybe a little capital punishment is better for society than a lot of repressed insanity. For when no one is killed by the state, then perhaps there is nothing to restrain all that is ready to fly loose in ourselves. In that case, capital punishment is a deterrent, but not for killers. It deters the common man from the impulse each day to become a little crazier.

That may be the nerve of our collective itch to get officials to commit murder for us, to demonstrate, that is, "our sense of moral outrage at particularly heinous crimes." We need the official bloodbath to restore ourselves to the idea that society is not only reasonable, but godlike.

That is cynical reasoning. A call for a little capital punishment. It is tonic to the average man's morals and good theater for all. Put in such words, the thought is vastly offensive.

Yet my instinct still tells me there is reason to it. Capital punishment may be one of our last defenses against the oncoming wave of the computer universe. Execution is irrational and ugly, it is uncivilized, it is wasteful of time, money, and emotion, yet it has one saving grace—it is primitive. It is a tribal ceremony. I tell myself it is historically true, it is overpoweringly true, that wars increase in scope as we grow too civilized. It is yet to be demonstrated that nuclear warfare is not the final expression of civilization. But if that is so, then our tribal ceremonies are part of our salvation, for they slow the speed with which we overcivilize ourselves right into our doom. It is frightening that we do not find it as hard to live in a world that liquidates millions as we do to confront the enormity of death when only one person is dying. That is a primitive ability. To look death in the face. Primitives do not have to surround the last hour with a hospital and its terminal machines.

Primitives, by our measure, may live like savages, but, compared to us, they go to war like angels. That is because they know more about the meaning of a single death. They know that one fatality can enlarge everybody who lived around the dead man, those who loved him and those who felt hate. Primitives go into battle with hideous cries, yet, so soon as the first warrior falls, the war, by convention, is over. The gods have spoken, and the issue has been decided. One death has become as vast in its significance as the sky. Indeed, for the primitive, there is no need to kill another until this death has been contemplated down to the last lay of the moldering bones.

Maybe something of that sort is necessary for a country like ours. Living with the civilized urgency to explain everything, we also have a secret need to live with questions that cannot be answered because they go too deep. In these bland, uneasy years when it all seems to be slipping away, perhaps we look for enigmatic figures who will haunt our consciousness after they are gone. Nobody is more mysterious than the murderer we have helped to execute.

Discovering Jack H. Abbott

(1981)

SOMETIME IN THE MIDDLE of working on *The Executioner's Song,* a note came from Morton Janklow, the literary agent. He was sending on a letter that had been addressed to him for forwarding to me. He assumed it was because our names had appeared together in a story in *People* magazine. In any event, the communication was by a convict named Jack H. Abbott, and Janklow felt there was something unusual in the fellow's letter. After I read it, I knew why he thought so.

An author will receive as many as several hundred letters a year from strangers. Usually they want something: Will you read their work, or listen to a life story and write it? This letter, on the contrary, offered instruction. Abbott had seen a newspaper account that stated I was doing a book on Gary Gilmore and violence in America. He wanted to warn me, Abbott said, that very few people knew much about violence in prisons. No author he had ever read on the subject seemed to have a clue. It was his belief that men who had been in prison as much as five years still knew next to nothing on the subject. It probably took a decade behind bars for any real perception on the matter to permeate your psychology and your flesh. If I were interested, he felt he could clarify some aspects of Gilmore's life as a convict.

There are unhappy paradoxes to being successful as a writer. For one thing, you don't have much opportunity to read good books (it's too demoralizing when you're at sea on your own work) and you also come to dread letter writing. Perhaps ten times a year, a couple of days are lost catching up on mail, and there's little pleasure in it. You are spending time that could have been given to more dedicated writing, and there are so many letters to answer! Few writers encourage correspondents. My reply to a good, thoughtful, even generous communication from someone I do not know is often short and apologetic.

Abbott's letter, however, was intense, direct, unadorned, and detached—an unusual combination. So I took him up. When you got down to it, I did not know much about violence in prisons, and I told him so and offered to read carefully what he had to say.

A long letter came back. It was remarkable. I answered it, and another came. It was just as remarkable. I don't think two weeks went by before I was in the middle of a thoroughgoing correspondence. I felt all the awe one knows before a phenomenon. Abbott had his own voice. I had heard no other like it. At his best, when he knew exactly what he was writing about, he had an eye for the continuation of his thought that was like the line a racing car driver takes around a turn. He wrote like a devil, which is to say (since none of us might recognize the truth if an angel told us) that he had a way of making you exclaim to yourself as you read, "Yes, he's right. My God, yes, it's true." Needless to say, what was true was also bottomless to contemplate. Reading Abbott's letters did not encourage sweet dreams. Hell was now clear to behold. It was Maximum Security in a large penitentiary.

Now, I was not the most innocent of tourists on trips into these quarters. I had, as I say, been working on *The Executioner's Song*, which apart from collateral reading in prison literature and trips to interview convicts and wardens had also provided me with Gilmore's letters to Nicole in the six months between his incarceration and his death. Those letters had their own penetration into the depths and horrors of prison life. Gilmore had his literary talents, and they were far from nonexistent. Still, he could not supply me with what Abbott offered. Gilmore, seen as a writer, rather than as a murderer, was a romantic and a mystic—ultimately, he saw incarceration as a species of karma. No matter how he might hate it, he also viewed it as the given. Life had its lights and shadows. Prison was the foul smell of the dark places, and maybe he had earned his sojourn there. That was the grim equation. Gilmore believed he would now find no happiness this side of death.

Out of Abbott's letters, however, came an intellectual, a radical, a potential leader, a man obsessed with a vision of more elevated human relations in a better world that revolution could forge. His mind, at its happiest, wanted to speak from his philosophical height across to yours. He was not interested in the particular, as Gilmore was, but only in the relevance of the particular to the abstract. Prison, whatever its nightmares, was not a dream whose roots would lead you to eternity, but an infernal machine of destruction, a design for the Dispose-All anus of a prodigiously diseased society.

The two men could not be more different. Gilmore, while always on the lookout to escape, still saw death as a species of romantic solution—he and Nicole could be together on the other side; Abbott, in contrast, might be ready by his convict's code to face death in any passing encounter, but he loathed death. It was the ultimate injustice, the final obscenity that society could visit on him.

Nonetheless, and it is one of those ironies that bemuses Abbott, he is the first to point out: " . . . if you went into any prison that held Gilmore and me and asked for all of the prisoners with certain backgrounds, both in and out of prison, backgrounds that include observed and suspected behavior, you will get a set of files, a list of names, and my file and name will always be handed you along with Gilmore's . . ."

Yes. Superficially, the morphology is close. Both were juvenile delinquents, both were incarcerated for most of their adolescence in state-supported institutions—as Abbott explained in his

early letters, the kids you knew in the juvenile home were equal
to relatives when you met them again in the pen—and both men
knew very little of liberty. At thirty-six, Gilmore had spent eighteen of the last twenty-two years of his life in jail; and Abbott,
while younger, had, proportionately, spent more. First imprisoned at twelve, he was out once for nine months, then imprisoned again at the age of eighteen for cashing a check with
insufficient funds. He was given a maximum of five years. As he
tells us in this work—it is no ordinary description of murder—he
then killed a fellow convict and was given an indeterminate sentence up to nineteen years. He has been in jail ever since but for
a six-week period when he escaped from Maximum Security in
Utah State Prison and was on the lam in America and Canada.
He has the high convict honors of being the only man to escape
from Max in that penitentiary.

There are a few other similarities between Gilmore and Abbott. Foremost, they are both convicts. They are by their logic
the elite of a prison population, part of the convict establishment as seen by the convicts, not by the authority—that is to say,
they are hard-core. They see themselves as men who set the code
for this city-state, this prison, that is occupied by a warden and
his security officers. Beneath that overarching authority, convicts
build their own establishment. They deal between themselves as
contending forces, they hold trials, they instruct the young, they
pass on the code.

There is a paradox at the core of penology, and from it derives
the thousand ills and afflictions of the prison system. It is that
not only the worst of the young are sent to prison, but the best—
that is, the proudest, the bravest, the most daring, the most en-
terprising, and the most undefeated of the poor. There starts the
horror. The fundamental premise of incarceration which Abbott
demonstrates to us, over and over, is that prison is equipped to
grind down criminals who are cowards into social submission,
but can only break the spirit of brave men who are criminals, or
anneal them until they are harder than the steel that encloses
them. If you can conceive of a society (it is very difficult these
days) that is more concerned with the creative potential of vio-

lent young men than with the threat they pose to the suburbs, then a few solutions for future prisons may be there. Somewhere between the French Foreign Legion and some prodigious extension of Outward Bound may lie the answer, at least for all those juvenile delinquents who are drawn to crime as a positive experience—because it is more exciting, more meaningful, more mysterious, more transcendental, more religious than any other experience they have known. For them, there is a conceivable dialogue. The authority can say: "Are you tough? Then show us you have the balls to climb that rock wall." Or travel down the rapids in a kayak, hang-glide—dare your death in any way that doesn't drag other people into death. Whereas for all those petty criminals who are not fundamentally attached to such existential tests of courage and violence, for whom crime is the wrong business, prison is not a problem. They can move with small friction from minimum security to prisons-without-walls to halfway houses. For them, a two-year sentence can even be a high school education. But the social practice of mixing these two kinds of criminals together is a disaster, an explosion. The timid become punks and snitches, the brave turn cruel. For when bold and timid people are obliged to live together, courage turns to brutality and timidity to treachery. A marriage between a brave man and a fearful woman may be exceeded in matrimonial misery only by a union of a brave woman and a fearful man. Prison systems perpetuate such relations.

Abbott doesn't let us forget why. I cannot think, offhand, of any American writer who has detailed for us in equal ongoing analysis how prison is designed to gut and corrupt the timid, and break or brutalize the brave. No system of punishment that asks a brave human being to surrender his or her bravery can ever work for the common good. It violates the universal stuff of the soul out of which great civilizations are built.

We do not live, however, in a world that tries to solve its prison problems. Even to assume we do is utopian. The underlying horror may be that we all inhabit the swollen tissues of a body politic that is drenched in bad conscience, so bad indeed that the laugh of the hyena reverberates from every TV set and is in danger of becoming our true national anthem. We are all so guilty at the way we have allowed the world around us to become more ugly and tasteless every year that we surrender to terror and steep ourselves in it. The mugger becomes the size of Golgotha and the middle class retires into walled cities with armed guards. Here, the prisons have wall-to-wall carpeting, and the guards address the inmates as "Sir," and bow. But they are prisons. The measure of the progressive imprisonment of all society is to be found at the base—in the state of the penitentiaries themselves. The bad conscience of society comes to focus in the burning lens of the penitentiary. That is why we do not speak of improving the prisons—which is to say, taking them through some mighty transmogrifications—but only of fortifying law and order. But that is no more feasible than the dream of remission in the cancer patient. To read this book is to live in the land of true and harsh perception—we won't get law and order without a revolution in the prison system.

Let me take it, however, from another tack. At one point in these letters Abbott speaks of how he obtained his education by reading books brought to him by his sister from a friendly bookstore outside. For five and a half years in Maximum Security he read, with an intensity he has carried over into his style, such authors as Niels Bohr and Hertz and Hegel, Russell and Whitehead, Carnap and Quine. Crucial to it all was Marx. We have the phenomenon of a juvenile delinquent brought up in reform schools who stabs another prisoner to death, takes drugs when he can, reads books in Maximum Security for five years until he can hardly stand, and then, like Marx, tries to perceive the world with his mind and come back with a comprehensive vision of society. The boldness of the juvenile delinquent grows into the audacity of the self-made intellectual. Only by the tender retort of the heart can we imagine what it must be like to live alone with so great a hunger and acquire the meat and bones of culture without the soup. Abbott looks to understand the world, he would dominate the world with his mind, yet in all his adult life he has spent six weeks in the world. He knows prison like the ferryman knows the crossing to Hades. But the world Abbott knows

only through books. He is the noble equivalent of Jerzy Kosinski's debased observer, Chauncey Gardiner, who learns about the
world through a TV set. Yet what a prodigious meal Abbott has
taken in. He has torn the meat of culture with his fingers, he has
crushed the bones with his own teeth. So he has a mind like no
other I have encountered. It speaks from the nineteenth century
as clearly as from the twentieth. There are moments when the
voice that enters your mind is the clear descendant of Marx and
Lenin untouched by any intervention of history. Indeed, Abbott,
who is half Irish and half Chinese, even bears a small but definite
resemblance to Lenin, and the tone of Vladimir Ilyich Ulyanov
rises out of some of these pages.

That offers a certainty. No one who reads this work will agree
with every one of Abbott's ideas. It is impossible. On the one
hand, he is the livid survivor of the ultrarevolutionary credo of
the Declaration of Independence, *"life, liberty, and the pursuit of
happiness."* Freedom and justice are oxygen to Abbott. He even
writes: "It has been my experience that injustice is perhaps the
only (if not merely the *greatest*) cause of insanity behind bars.
You'd be surprised to learn what a little *old-fashioned* oppression
can do to anyone." Hear! Hear! It is the devil's voice. We know it
is true as soon as we hear it. Of course, Abbott is also a Communist. What kind, I'm not clear. He seems to hold to Mao, and to
Stalin both, but vaguely. It is more clear that his real sympathies
are with the Third World, with Cuba, Africa, and Arab revolutionaries. How long he would survive in a Communist country I don't
know. It is obvious we would not agree on how long. We have written back and forth on this a little, but not a great deal. I no longer
have the taste for polemic that he enjoys. Moreover, I have not
spent my life in jail. I can afford the sophisticated despair of finding Russia altogether as abominable as America and more, but
then, I have had the experience of meeting delegations of Russian bureaucrats and they look like prison guards in prison suits.
I am free, so I can afford the perception. But if I had spent my
young life in jail, and discovered the officers of my own land were
my enemies, I would find it very hard not to believe that the officers of another land might be illumined by a higher philosophy.

I say this, and add that I am much more impressed by the literary measure of Abbott's writings on prison than by his overall analyses of foreign affairs and revolution. One is for me the meat and bones—the other is the soup he has not had. Yet I do not sneer. He has forged his revolutionary ideas out of the pain and damage done to his flesh and nerves by a life in prison. It is possible that he would be as much a revolutionary or more after ten years of freedom. Or an altogether different kind of man. I hope we have the opportunity to find out. As I am writing these words, it looks like Abbott will be released on parole this summer. It is certainly the time for him to get out. There is a point past which any prisoner can get nothing more from prison, not even the preservation of his will, and Abbott, I think, has reached these years. Whereas, if he gets out, we may yet have a new writer of the largest stature among us, for he has forged himself in a cauldron and still has half of the world to discover. There is never, when we speak of possible greatness in young writers, more than one chance in a hundred that we are right, but this one chance in Abbott is so vivid that it reaffirms the very idea of literature itself as a human expression that will survive all obstacles. I love Jack Abbott for surviving and for having learned to write as well as he does.

Marilyn Monroe's Sexiest Tapes and Discs

(1982)

UNACCOUNTABLY AND INCREDIBLY, Marilyn Monroe has emerged from the detritus of the insignificant, the burial ground of old movies. She is more vivid on the screen than others. She has more energy, more humor, more commitment to the part and to the playing—she *plays* the roles, she gives off the happiness that she is acting, and that is indispensable for any cheap entertainment.

She had intelligence—an artist's intelligence—and her taste by the end of her career was close to superb. She must have had a profound sense of what was whole in people and false, for her own characterizations were sound—she knew how to enter a scene with the full aura of the character she played, and so was able to suggest everything that had occurred on just the other side of the scene, the breeze she had smelled, the doorsill on which she stubbed her toe, the errant whimsy of a forbidden thought to be concealed, and five distractions appropriate to the character trailing like streamers. Even early she must have seen life as some sort of divine soup of situations where every aroma spoke of the primacy of mood.

She emerges even as we look at her movies today.

On Tape and Disc

Gentlemen Prefer Blondes (1953)

With Jane Russell, MM, Charles Coburn, Elliott Reid, Tommy Noonan. Directed by Howard Hawks. *(Magnetic Video cassette, color, 91 min., $59.95)*

Never again in her career will she look so sexually perfect as in *Gentlemen Prefer Blondes.* She will look more subtle in future years, more adorable, certainly lovelier, more sensitive, more lumi-nous, more tender, more of a heroine, less of a slut—but never again will she seem so close to a detumescent body ready to roll right over the edge of the world and drop your body down a chute of pillows and honey.

She dances with all the grace she is ever going to need when doing *Gentlemen Prefer Blondes,* all the grace and all the pizzazz— she is a musical comedy star with panache! "Diamonds Are a Girl's Best Friend!" What a surprise! And she sings so well Darryl Zanuck (head of Twentieth Century–Fox) will first believe her voice was dubbed.

She is a wonder in *Gentlemen Prefer Blondes.* She comes into the movie looking like a winner and leaves as one. If she had her first acting lesson not six years before, and had never been near to working on a New York stage, it has no significance before her grasp of cinema. She inhabits the frame even when she is not on. Just as she had once preempted the art of the still photographer and painted herself into the lens, now she preempts the director. In this picture, and in *Some Like It Hot,* to a lesser degree in *The Seven Year Itch* or *Bus Stop* or *The Misfits,* it is as if she has been the secret director.

She must have been the first embodiment of Camp, for *Gentle-men Prefer Blondes* is a perfect picture in the way early Sean Connery–James Bond movies were perfect. In such classics of Camp, which would arrive ten years and more after *Gentlemen Prefer Blondes,* no actor was ever serious for an instant, nor any situation ever remotely believable—the art was to sustain nonex-istence, counterexistence, as if to suggest that life cannot be comprehended by a direct look—we are not only in life but to the absurd side of it, attached to something else as well— something mysterious and of the essence of detachment. So in *Gentlemen Prefer Blondes,* she is a sexual delight, but she is also the opposite of that, a particularly cool voice which seems to say, "Gentlemen: Ask yourself what really I am, for I pretend to be sexual and that may be more interesting than sex itself. Do you think I have come to you from another place?" She could even be a visitor who has studied the habits of humans—the unhappy suspicion crosses our head that if she were a saint or a demon we would never know.

In any case, it is the first picture which enables us to speak of her as a great comedian, which is to say she bears an exquisitely light relation to the dramatic thunders of triumph, woe, greed and calculation: she is also a first artist of the put-on—she dra- matizes one cardinal peculiarity of existence in this century— the lie, when well embodied, seems to offer more purchase upon existence than the truth.

There's No Business Like Show Business (1954)

With Ethel Merman, Donald O'Connor, MM, Dan Dailey, John- nie Ray, Mitzi Gaynor. Directed by Walter Lang. *(Magnetic Video cassette, color, 117 min., $59.95)*

The script is patently inferior to *Heller in Pink Tights* (a vehi- cle Marilyn declined), and instead of playing with Frank Sina- tra (in *Pink Tights*), she has Donald O'Connor for a leading man. When she wears high heels, O'Connor looks six inches shorter. Worse, Ethel Merman is in the movie. Marilyn can hardly sing in competition with Merman. Dan Dailey, an old pro from the days of *A Ticket to Tomahawk* (which Marilyn ap- peared in briefly), is used to dancing at his best and hamming at his utmost in atrocious scripts. There is also Johnnie Ray, at the top of his vogue. She feels like an amateur among veterans. She is out of practice and had not made a movie in eight months, indeed, is only making this one as part of an arrange- ment to get *The Seven Year Itch.*

The Seven Year Itch (1955)

With MM, Tom Ewell, Evelyn Keyes, Sonny Tufts. Directed by Billy Wilder. *(RCA SelectaVision disc, CED, color, 105 min., $19.95; Magnetic Video cassette, color, 105 min., $59.95)*

Marilyn is plump, close to fat, her flesh is bursting out of every strap, her thighs look heavy, her upper arms give a hint that she will yet be massively fat if she ever grows old, she has a belly which protrudes like no big movie star's belly in many a year, and yet she is the living bouncing embodiment of pulchritude. It is her swan song to being a sexual object. She proves once again that she is as good as the actors she works with, and she and Tom Ewell do a comic march through the movie. As "The Girl Upstairs," a TV model in New York for the summer from Colorado, she creates one last American innocent, a pristine artifact of the mid-Eisenhower years, an American girl who *believes* in the products she sells in TV commercials—she is as simple and healthy as the whole middle of the country, and there to be plucked.

Bus Stop (1956)

With MM, Don Murray, Arthur O'Connell, Betty Field, Eileen Heckert. Directed by Joshua Logan. *(Magnetic Video cassette, color, 96 min., $59.95)*

Discarding preliminary sketches for her costume, she chose ratty clothes and looked for ripped stockings out of wardrobe with crude stitches, she purchased a sad small-town southern glamour by these funky clothes (a perfect piece of objectification), and brought to life some physical trappings of the biography she was to play, Cherie!, and thereby began to create a comic role so sad, so raunchy, so dazzling in its obliviousness to its own poverty of talent, that some would consider it her greatest movie. For certain, it is the only picture she ever made where she was ready to present a character independent of herself, even down to accent—it is not Monroe's voice we hear but the blank tones of a dumb southern drawl, she communicates continents of basic ignorance in each gap of the vowels, and her eyes roll and dart to the corners, as restless yet as lifeless as agitated marbles each time she talks about the promiscuities of her past. She has the blank schizoid fever of poor southern white trash, she is blank before moral dilemmas, blank before provocation, blank before dread—she suggests all the death that has already been visited upon the character in the mechanical, hard-remembered way she clicks the switch for her red spotlight during a song and dance. So *Bus Stop* becomes a vehicle for Monroe, but the rest of the movie suffers, the crowd scenes might as well have been done by a unit director from MGM, and much of the atmosphere established by supporting actors has the hyped-up hokey sound of bit parts in a stock company too long on the road.

Some Like It Hot (1959)

With MM, Tony Curtis, Jack Lemmon, George Raft, Pat O'Brien, Joe E. Brown. Directed by Billy Wilder. *(VidAmerica cassette, B&W, 120 min., rental only)*

That figure of immaculate tenderness, utter bewilderment, and goofy dipsomaniacal sweetness which is Sugar Kane in *Some Like It Hot* is Marilyn Monroe's greatest creation, in her greatest movie. She takes an improbable farce and somehow offers some indefinable sense of promise to every absurd logic in the dumb scheme of things until the movie becomes that rarest of modern art objects, an *affirmation*—the viewer is more attracted to the idea of life by the end of two hours. For all of Wilder's skill, and the director may never have been better, for all of first-rate performances by Tony Curtis and Jack Lemmon, and an exhibition of late-mastery by Joe E. Brown, it would have been no more than a very funny movie, no more, and gone from the mind so soon as it was over, if not for Monroe. She brought so good and rare an evocation it seemed to fit into the very disposition of things, much as if God—having put a few just men on earth in order to hold the universe together—was now also binding the cosmos with a few dim-witted angels as well.

The Misfits (1961)

With Clark Gable, MM, Montgomery Clift, Eli Wallach, Thelma Ritter. Directed by John Huston. *(Magnetic Video cassette, B&W, 124 min., $59.95)*

A young divorcee, Roslyn Taber (Marilyn), begins to live in the desert outside Reno with a middle-aged cowboy, Gay Langland, played by Gable, while two other cowboys, Eli Wallach and Monty Clift, begin to find her attractive, flirt with her, and apparently wait for her relation to Langland to end. After a time, the men go out to hunt for mustangs to trap and sell. It is one of the few ways left to earn a living that is "better than wages." Roslyn accompanies them, but is horrified at the cruelty of the capture and the pointless misery of the purpose. If these mustangs were once sold as riding horses for children, now they are canned as dogmeat. So Monroe has a war with Gable which is resolved (1) by his capture of the last mustang as a gesture to himself, plus (2) setting the horse free as a gesture to her. The film ends in such gestures. They drive off together to face a world in which there will be fewer and fewer ways to make a living better than wages.

The point is that *The Misfits* is a movie, particularly in its first half, that moves on no more powerful hydraulic of plot than the suggestion of one nuance laid like a feather over another—so it is closer to the nature of most emotional relations than other pictures. But its virtue is also its vulnerability. We see Roslyn and Langland come together, sleep together, set up home together, we feel the other two cowboys perching themselves on the edge of this relation, but no emotional facts are given, no setting of category or foundation, for the plot is never bolted down. We do not know exactly how Roslyn comes to feel for each man, nor how much she feels. The picture is even less precise than biography. Unlike other movies, we have no blueprint to the emotional line of her heart. Instead she seems to shimmer on the screen with many possibilities of reality. When she holds Monty Clift's head on her lap after he has been wounded in the rodeo, we do not know whether she is maternal or stirring for him, or both—nor is she likely to know what she feels. In life, how would she?

So the movie is different in *tone* than others, and she is altogether different from other actresses, even different from her performances of the past. She is not sensual here but *sensuous*, and by a meaning of the word which can go to the root—she seems to possess no clear outline on screen. She is not so much a woman as a mood, a cloud of drifting senses in the form of Marilyn Monroe—no, never has she been more luminous.

For Taping from TV

Ladies of the Chorus (1948)

With Adele Jergens, MM, Rand Brooks, Nana Bryant. Directed by Phil Karlson. (*B&W, 61 min.*)

A bad B movie about a young burlesque star (chaste!) daughter of an older burlesque star (classy) in love with a scion. It came out in 1948, and is the first movie where we can really see her; she sings, dances, acts, even has a catfight with hair pullings, slaps, shrieks, awkward blows reminiscent of girls throwing baseballs—the picture is terrible, but she is not. She is interestingly wooden in the wrong places (like a faint hint of the wave of Camp to come), and she sings and dances with a sweet vitality, even does her best to make one agree it is not absolutely impossible she is in love with Rand Brooks, the scion (who must certainly be the plainest leading man any ambitious ingenue ever was assigned to love), but what is most interesting in the comfort of studying this actress who is to go so far is the odd air of confidence she emits, a narcissism about her own potentialities so great it becomes a perfumed species of sex appeal as if a magnificent girl has just walked into a crowded room and declared, "I'm far and away the most beautiful thing here." Of course, she is not. Not yet. Her front teeth protrude just a fraction (like Jane Russell's), her chin points a hint, and her nose is a millimeter too wide and so gives suggestion of a suckling pig's snout. Yet she is still close to gorgeous in her own way, with a sort of I-smell-good look, I-am-wonderful look. She is like a baby everyone loves—how wise are the tunneled views of one's own hindsight!

Love Happy (1950)

With Chico, Groucho and Harpo Marx, Ilona Massey, Raymond Burr, Vera-Ellen, MM. Directed by David Miller. (*Color, 85 min.*)

In *Love Happy,* with Groucho Marx, Marilyn has a classic moment—the famous undulating movement of her hips is now unveiled for the first time in a movie. It is an uproarious moment in the movie—the wild call of a strange girl's ass to Groucho Marx—he engorges his cigar in a leer.

"What seems to be the problem?" he inquires.

"Men keep following me all the time." She exits, Mae West in one swinging pocket, Jean Harlow in the other. It is uproarious, but she may have been desperate. Twice hired, twice fired, and she is approaching the age of twenty-three—Elizabeth Taylor, who is four years younger, is already famous. So she puts everything she knows of provocation, exaggeration, and the nascent art of Camp into the swing—"Take me from behind, I'm yours," say her undulating hips.

River of No Return (1954)

With Robert Mitchum, MM, Rory Calhoun, Tommy Rettig. Directed by Otto Preminger. *(Color, 91 min.)*

A "Z cowboy film" is Monroe's concise description of *River of No Return.* She is the only woman and, surrounded by strong male actors, is also drenched in scenes with a boy actor and with a director who is famous for grinding actors' bones in the maw of his legendary rage. It is the most demoralizing movie in which Marilyn ever played a lead, and must be the worst of Preminger's pictures.

The Prince and the Showgirl (1957)

With MM, Laurence Olivier, Sybil Thorndike, Richard Wattis. Directed by Laurence Olivier. *(Color, 117 min.)*

The irony of *The Prince and the Showgirl* is that it is better than anyone has a right to expect from the (nightmarish) history of its making, but that is because Monroe is superb—will wonders never cease?

She is also lovely. Milton H. Greene is indeed a genius with makeup. Never will Marilyn exhibit so marvelous a female palette, her colors living in the shades of the English garden. A hue cannot appear on her face without bearing the tone of a flower petal. Her lips are rose, her cheeks have every softened flush. Lavender shadows are lost in her hair. Once again she inhabits every frame of the movie.

Of course, Olivier in his turn cannot fail to be excellent. He is too great an actor not to offer some final delineation of a Balkan archduke. If there are a thousand virtuosities in his accent, it is because his virtuosities are always installed within other virtuosities—a consummate house of cards. It is just that he is out there playing by himself. So one can never get to believe he is attracted to Monroe. (Indeed, he is most believable when he snorts, "She has as much *comme il faut* as a rhinoceros!") Willy-nilly, he is therefore emphasizing the high level of contrivance in the plot.

Let's Make Love (1960)

With MM, Yves Montand, Tony Randall, Frankie Vaughan; cameos by Milton Berle, Bing Crosby, Gene Kelly. Directed by George Cukor. *(Color, 118 min.)*

She never made a movie where she is so ordinary. A sad truth is before us again. Art and sex are no more compatible than they care to be. She is wan in the movie and dull.

Also on Tape

Marilyn Monroe videocassettes which Norman Mailer chose not to review in depth include:

All About Eve (1950)

With Bette Davis, Anne Baxter, George Sanders, Celeste Holm, MM. Directed by Joseph Mankiewicz. *(Magnetic Video cassette, B&W, 138 min., $79.95)*

Clash by Night (1952)

With Barbara Stanwyck, Paul Douglas, Robert Ryan, MM. Directed by Fritz Lang. *(Video Communications cassette, B&W, 105 min., $49.95)*

How to Marry a Millionaire (1953)

With MM, Betty Grable, Lauren Bacall, William Powell, David Wayne, Rory Calhoun. Directed by Jean Negulesco. *(Magnetic Video cassette, color, 96 min., $59.95)*

Marilyn Monroe (1967)

Documentary with narration by Mike Wallace. *(Karl Video cassette, B&W, 30 min., $45)*

Fallen Stars: Elvis and Marilyn (1963 approx.)

Documentary with narration by John Huston. *(Discount Video-tapes / Sound Video Unlimited cassettes, B&W, 60 min., $39.95)*

Marilyn also did *Right Cross* and *Home Town Story* for Metro. For Twentieth there was *The Fireball, As Young As You Feel, Love Nest, Let's Make It Legal, We're Not Married, Don't Bother to Knock, Monkey Business, O. Henry's Full House* and *Niagara*. They are all in varying degree unimportant pictures, and need little more description than their titles. *Love Nest* is worth a footnote in any history of cinema, for Jack Paar has a part in it, *We're Not Married* is comic, and *Don't Bother to Knock,* although a slow and disappointing piece of cinema, is worth study for a student of Monroe since she gives a serious performance in the part of a deranged girl with nuances of alternating numbness and hysteria, although she fails to project menace. It is a role she does not go near again. She has a classic stuntman's ride in an automobile with Cary Grant in *Monkey Business,* a scene with Charles Laughton in *Full House,* and a starring role in *Niagara,* in which she offers the only interest.

After her orgy of attention in *Gentlemen Prefer Blondes* and her skill in stealing *How to Marry a Millionaire* from Betty Grable and Bacall, she managed to get past *There's No Business Like Show Business* and *River of No Return* to go on to be the center of every production after (except for *Let's Make Love,* which has no center), dominating directors and running away with each movie. They have all, in varying degree, become *her* movies. Few prizefighters could point to such a string of triumphs.

The films she made through the last years of her life are her best, the fulfillment of an art. Her art deepened. She got better. Her subtlety took on more resonance. By *The Misfits* she was not so much a woman as a presence, not an actor, but an essence— the language is hyperbole, yet her effects are not. She appears in these final efforts as a visual existence different from other actors and so leaves her legend where it belongs, which is on the screen.

All the Pirates and People

———

(1983)

My dad was Scots-English; my mother's Dutch-Irish, strange combination. All the pirates and people who were kicked out of everyplace else.

—CLINT EASTWOOD

BACK IN 1967, I was trying to cast *The Deer Park* for Off-Broadway and needed a tall, young, clean-cut American to play the hero. Only you could not find talented actors in New York with such looks—they were all on the West Coast. One day, drinking a gloomy beer, I happened to glance at an old black-and-white TV set which had been muttering in the corner all afternoon and noticed a man on a horse. "There's the guy," I cried—it was much like a scene out of films one used to see—"that's the man we want. There's our Sergius O'Shaughnessy."

The director's name was Leo Garen, and he looked at me in pity. "Yes," he said, "he'd be wonderful. But we can't afford him."

"Why?" I asked. "It's a soap opera. He's probably dying to get into a play."

"No," said Garen, "this is an old rerun of *Rawhide*. The actor you're looking at is the hottest thing around right now."

That was my introduction to Clint Eastwood. Now, looking back on his years of starring in films which return prodigious profits, it is obvious he satisfies some notion in hordes of people of how an American hero ought to look.

NORMAN MAILER: I've seen an awful lot of presidential candidates, and you're one of the few people who could go far that way.
CLINT EASTWOOD: (laughs)
MAILER: I'm not kidding. There's one guy in five hundred who's got a presidential face and usually nothing else.
EASTWOOD: If I've got the presidential face, I'm lacking in a lot of other areas.
MAILER: Well, all lack it.
EASTWOOD: I don't feel I could get up and say a lot of things that I know I couldn't perform on. Yet they have to do that to win. The ones that are honest about what they can or can't do don't have a chance.

Let us assume we are strangers and searching about for a topic of conversation at dinner.

We discover we are both interested in Clint Eastwood.

Yes, I admit, I happen to know him.

Immediately, your mood improves.

Well, I say, I don't know him very well, but he's an interesting man. He's hard, however, to understand.

Do you like him?

You have to. On first meeting, he's one of the nicest people you ever met. But I can't say I know him well. We talked a couple of times and had a meal together. I liked him. I think you'd have to be around for a year before you saw his ugly side, assuming he has one.

It would take that long?

Well, he's very laid back. If you don't bother him, he will never bother you. In that sense, he is like the characters he plays in his films.

Since my new partner is a good listener, I begin to expatiate. I describe Eastwood on our first meeting. I talk about his tall pres-

ence, which is exceptional—exactly as one would wish it to be in
a movie star. He certainly has the lean, self-contained body that
you see only in the best dancers, rock climbers, competition ski-
ers, and tightrope walkers. His face has the same disconcerting
purity. You could be looking at a murderer or a saint.

Here, my partner makes a face.

No, I say, it's true. Men who have been in prison for twenty
years sometimes have such a look, and you can see it on monks
and certain acrobats with fine and tragic faces.

Is he very good-looking?

I'm not used to thinking of men as that good-looking, but
he is.

And you liked him?

He's marvelously friendly. Just saying hello. He has no fear of
others. At least, he shows none. I tell you, it was splendid. I rarely
liked a man so much on first meeting.

Good Lord. What did you talk about?

Well, Eastwood said right off, "Do you know I tried to get into
The Naked and the Dead back when they were making a movie of
it years ago, but they didn't want me."

"That's fair," I told him, "we tried to get you for *The Executioner's Song*. I wanted you to play Gary Gilmore."

Had he read the book, my dinner partner wanted to know.

I don't think so. Clint only answered: "What would you say
Gilmore was like?"

"Oh," I said, "he was a funny man, Gilmore. Very spiritual on
the one hand with a real mean streak on the other."

Eastwood gave a happy grin. "Sounds as if he would have been
just right for me."

That conversation took place outside a shabby Spanish-style
stucco motel near the beach in Santa Cruz, California. Eastwood
was on location making his latest movie, *Sudden Impact,* and the
small crowd watching us stood outside the company barrier.
They had been hanging around for hours in the hope they would
get a look at him. In the background you could smell boardwalk
popcorn and hear the downrush of the roller coaster after a long
clanking up the first rise. Some kids with orange hair were stand-

ing next to a black girl outside the movie company rope, and a couple of old ginks with slits in their sneakers and patience in their eyes were waiting beside blank-faced kids, all waiting behind the rope, never getting bored. Once in a while, Eastwood walked in and out of the movie trailer trucks or mobile dressing rooms parked along the side street off the motel, and it was then they would have their glimpse of him. He might even offer a line as he went by. "Still with us?" he would ask. "Oh, yeah, Clint," they would reply. Merely by standing behind this rope, they felt glamorous.

One fellow, tall, not bad-looking, with a dark suntan to set off his dark goatee, was brought up to Eastwood by one of the company people. "Clint, this fellow has a gift for you."

It was a short leather cape of the sort Eastwood used to wear in Sergio Leone westerns near to twenty years ago when Clint played the cowboy who had no name, rarely spoke, and walked about with the stub of a pencil-thin cigar in his mouth. A killer stared back at you then—the stills taken from those spaghetti westerns certainly made him famous in Italy, then all Europe, then the world.

Now, Clint Eastwood said softly to the man bearing him the gift, "You keep this."

"I want you to have it, Clint."

"Better not. You might change your mind in time to come."

"I never wear it," protested the man with the goatee. "This cape is right for you."

Eastwood, however, was accepting no gifts he would cast away later. That could leave a bruise on the mood. "No," he said softly, "I really don't need it. I have a number of capes already."

You make him sound good, my partner remarked.

Since we were warmed up, I went on about commanders in forward companies during the Second World War and how you could tell at once if they were respected from the mood that came off the first gun trained on your approach. Forward companies in Luzon lived on outposts miles apart in the hills and sometimes had no visitors for a week at a time. To drop in on them was a little like boarding a ship. You never had to guess about morale. The mood told you immediately how the men felt. If the company commander was well liked, morale was as high as the greeting you get from a large, happy, impressive, slightly crazy family. Everybody feels manic in the wealth of their people.

The same, I suggested, could be said of movie sets. They are able to offer great morale, awful morale, or anything in between. Eastwood might be renowned for bringing in pictures ahead of schedule and under budget, but he was also most popular with his crew. That was apparent. They adored him.

Of course, not everyone might wish to be adored by a movie crew. They have a great sense of humor for jokes that go with a few beers, but little tolerance for a fancy mix. They are good enough trade unionists to suspect that art is phony and would never trust any male who could not lift his own weight in movie equipment.

His crew obviously loved him. Eastwood could put back a few brews himself. Beer was his drink of choice. Besides, for movie crews, he had another virtue—he knew how to use animals. In the movie he was making now, there would be a big, doddering old English bull, fat, short-legged, asthmatic, pooped-out, and smelly. This dog would be a total hit onscreen. The script called for the English bull to piss on cue. At each right moment, the beast would raise one mournful leg and make water on a fallen villain. The crew loved the idea. That was cutting the mustard.

But how do you train an animal to do such things on cue, asked my partner.

I had put Eastwood to the same question. He came back with a glint in his eye. The modesty of the solution appealed to him. "Oh," he said, "you attach a monofilament to the leg and give a tug." He had to grin before the powers of conditioned reflex.

To fill the pause that followed, my partner now said: You do seem sure of a lot of things about Eastwood.

Well, I know him, I guess.

You said you didn't.

I do, I confessed. Eastwood is an artist. So I know him well. I know him by his films.

I also like his films, said my partner, but surely you aren't going to say he's much of an artist?

I'll go further. I'll say that you can see the man in his work just as clearly as you see Hemingway in *A Farewell to Arms* or John Cheever in his short stories. Hell, yes, he's an artist. I even think he's important. Not just a fabulous success at the box office, but important.

You do admire him.

No, I said, I'm angry at him. He doesn't know how good he is. I don't think he tries hard enough for what's truly difficult.

Did you tell him that at lunch?

No. He was making a movie.

Our discussion was now at an impasse. Besides, it was time to talk to the partner on the other side. So the conversation on Eastwood was never finished. I had to think about it later, however. A talented author once remarked that he discovered the truth at the point of his pencil in the act of writing. It occurred to me that I usually came across the truth while talking. I would say things and by the tone of my voice they would seem true or not. When I said Clint Eastwood was an artist, I liked the ring. It was true. It might also be true that he was a timid artist.

That made a nice paradox. For, by any physical terms, he was a brave man. Once, after a plane crashed at sea, he saved his life by swimming three miles to shore. He did a number of his own stunts in movies and learned to rock climb for *The Eiger Sanction.* The film was embarrassing, a prodigiously multicolored plot equal to ice cream on turnips, but Eastwood's rock climbing was good. He rode a horse well. He did car racing. He even looked, on the basis of *Every Which Way But Loose* and *Any Which Way You Can,* as if he might make some kind of boxer. He had a quick left jab with good weight behind it. He could certainly draw a gun. If it came to great box office movie stars competing in a decathlon, Eastwood would hold his own.

He was also capable of fine acting. With a few exceptions, he invariably understood his role and did a good deal with the smallest moves. Critics had been attacking him for years over how little he did onscreen, but Eastwood may have known something they did not.

The plot of a film works, after all, for the star. The more emotion that a story will stir in an audience, the more will the audience read such feeling into the star's motionless face. Sometimes the facial action of the movie star might offer no more movement than a riverbank, yet there is nothing passive about such work. A riverbank must brace itself to support the rush around a bend.

> I always was a different kind of person, even when I started acting. I guess I finally got to a point where I had enough nerve to do nothing. . . . My first film with Sergio Leone had a script with tons of dialogue, tremendously expository, and I just cut it all down. Leone thought I was crazy. Italians are used to much more vocalizing, and I was playing this guy who didn't say much of anything. I cut it all down. Leone didn't speak any English so he didn't know what the hell I was doing, but he got so he liked it after a while.

There is a moment in *Play Misty for Me* when Eastwood's character, an easygoing disc jockey, realizes that he has gotten himself into an affair with a hopelessly psychotic woman. As the camera moves in, his stare is as still as the eyes of a trapped animal. Yet his expression is luminous with horror. He is one actor who can put his soul into his eyes.

The real question might have little to do, however, with how much of an actor he could be. What separated Eastwood from other box office stars was that his films (especially since he had begun to direct them) had come to speak more and more of his own vision of life in America. One was encountering a home-grown philosophy, a hardworking everyday subtle American philosophy in film.

Burt Reynolds also gives us a private vision of the taste of life in America, but it is not so much a philosophy as a premise. Eat high on the hog, Reynolds suggests. The best way to get through life is drunk.

Since it's possible that half the male population of America under forty also believes this, Reynolds is endlessly reliable. Of

course, like many a happy drinking man before him, he takes no
real chances, just falls and smacko collisions. The car gets to-
taled, but Burt is too loaded to be hurt. He leaps to his feet, pulls
the fender off his neck with a sorry look, and we laugh. The best
way to get through life is drunk.

Eastwood is saying more. If you discount his two worst films in
these last ten years, *Firefox* and *The Eiger Sanction,* if you bypass
Dirty Harry, Magnum Force, and *The Enforcer* as movies made to
manipulate audiences and satisfy producers, you are also left
with *High Plains Drifter, The Outlaw Josey Wales, Every Which Way
But Loose, Bronco Billy,* and *Honkytonk Man.*

A protagonist in each of these five films stands near to his creator. Eastwood has made five cinematic relatives. They are spread
over more than a hundred years, from the Civil War to the present, and the action is in different places west of the Mississippi,
from Missouri to California. They are Okies and outlaws, truck-
ers, rodeo entertainers, and country and western singers, but
they come out of the odd, wild, hard, dry, sad, sour redneck wisdom of small-town life in the Southwest. All of Eastwood's knowledge is in them, a sardonic, unsentimental set of values that is
equal to art for it would grapple with the roots of life itself.
"When things get bad," says the outlaw Josey Wales, "and it looks
like you're not going to make it, then you got to get mean, I
mean plain plumb dog mean, because if you lose your head
then, you neither live nor win. That's just the way it is."

One has to think of the Depression years of Eastwood's childhood when his father was looking for work and taking the family
up and down the San Joaquin and Sacramento Valleys, out there
with a respectable family in a mix of Okies also wandering up
and down California searching for work. Those Okies are in
Eastwood's films, as must be the gritty knowledge he gained over
the seven years he worked on *Rawhide.* How many bit players and
cowboy stunt men passing through *Rawhide*'s weekly episodes
were also a part of that migrating country culture that was yet
going to present itself to us by way of CBs and pickup trucks and
western music? "You've got to outlast yourself" was the only way
to talk of overcoming fatigue. The words happen to be East-

wood's, but the language was shared with his characters, brothers in the same family, ready to share a family humor: it is that a proper orangutan will not miss a good opportunity to defecate on the front seat of a police cruiser, as indeed it did in *Every Which Way But Loose*. Small-town humor, but in *Honkytonk Man*, his last film before the one he was shooting now, it became art.

MAILER: How did you feel about *Honkytonk Man* before it came out?
EASTWOOD: I thought it was good, as good as I could do it. I did it in five weeks, five weeks of shooting, and I felt good about it. I felt it might find a small audience somewhere that might enjoy it. I wasn't looking for a big film. I just figured sometimes you have to do some things that you want to do and be selfish about it.

Honkytonk Man starts in the Oklahoma dust bowl of the Thirties and follows a drunk, all-but-destroyed country singer named Red Stovall on his car trip east to Nashville. He has been given an invitation to audition at the Grand Ole Opry and it is the most important event of his life. Red Stovall has very little left: ravaged good looks, a guitar, and a small voice reduced to a whisper by his consumptive cough. He's a sour, cantankerous, mean-spirited country singer who smokes too much, drinks too much, and has brought little happiness to man or woman, a sorry hero but still a hero. He will die before he will deviate from his measure of things. So he drives over the bumpy stones of his used-up lungs to get to the audition.

On stage at the Grand Ole Opry, out front before the producers, there in the middle of singing his best, he has to cough. Worse. He is so stifled with phlegm that he must stagger off the stage. The picture is about to end in disaster. Still, he is given a reprieve. A man who makes records is also at the audition. He has liked Red's voice and comes forward with a proposal. Red, given the treachery of his throat, can hardly perform before an audience, but maybe he can do a record session. They can lay the track between the coughs.

So he is able to sing on the last day of his life and makes one record before he dies. His whispery voice, close to extinction, clings to the heart of the film.

> So I lost my woman and you lost your man
> Who knows who's right and who's wrong?
> But I've still got my guitar and I've got a plan,
> Throw your arms 'round this honkytonk man.

> Throw your arms 'round this honkytonk man
> And we'll get through this night the best way we can.

It is as if every economy Eastwood has picked up in acting and directing found its way into the film. Something of the steely compassion that is back of all the best country singing is in the movie, and the harsh, yearning belly of rural America is also there, used to making out with next to nothing but hard concerns and the spark of a dream that will never give up.

Honkytonk Man was the finest movie made about country plains life since *The Last Picture Show,* and it stood up to that comparison because of what Eastwood did with the role. A subtle man was brought to life with minimal strokes, a complex protagonist full of memories of old cunning deeds and weary sham. It was one of the saddest movies seen in a long time, yet, on reflection, terrific. One felt a tenderness for America while looking at it. The miracle seemed to happen now and again. Once in a great while, movie stars become artists, and that was always moving. It gave a little hope. We are not supposed to get better once we are very successful.

MAILER: Those must have been incredibly tough years for you when you were scuffling as an actor.
EASTWOOD: Oh, I hated it, absolutely hated it. I tell people if you really want to do it, then you must be willing to study it and stick with it through all opposition and having to deal with some of the most no-talent people in the world passing judgment on you. They're going to pick the worst aspects of you or of anybody else that they cast. If you can take all that and keep grinding until some part comes along that fits you and your feelings, then

sometimes the odds will come up for you. But you have to have that kind of perseverance.

MAILER: How did you handle the rudeness?

EASTWOOD: I hated it. I wanted to pull people out of their seats and say, "Don't talk to me that way."

MAILER: I just realized that in a lot of the Dirty Harry movies, you've got a deep well of anger to dip into.

EASTWOOD: (laughs) Oh, yeah, it's easy. People think I play the anger well. All you have to do is have a good memory.

It would be agreeable to end right here. Not every movie star pays his dues, takes his bad years, becomes an artist, does it his way, and leaves us with an ongoing inclination for the dry wisdom of his stuff.

Eastwood, however, has another side. If his best movies come out of a real need to comprehend his part of our American roots, there is another category of film he makes, and most skillfully, which is full of manipulation. He also knows how to press the secret buttons in his audiences.

Art is democratic. It is the hope that you may arrive at a truth with your audience. Something happens in the heart of the ticket buyer exactly because there wasn't a calculated attempt to twitch his feelings like reflexes. Of course, art is thereby made difficult, and so it rarely works as well as manipulation.

The reviews for *Honkytonk Man*—the most quietly daring film Eastwood ever made—were, for the most part, cruel. Reviews usually came in bad for Eastwood films, but it did not matter. His films could bring in large box office with the most terrible reviews. *Honkytonk Man,* however, did not. It was a disaster critically *and* financially.

Eastwood once said, "I was never a discovery of the press," and the remark is crucial. He had been discovered by the box office. He could forgo favorable reviews but not good box office.

Now, after the jolting failure of *Honkytonk Man,* there was pressure from all sides to do another film about Dirty Harry Callahan. Of the five movies bringing in Eastwood's greatest profits, three had been about Dirty Harry Callahan, an outlaw cop who did things on his own. Callahan broke villains in two with his Magnum. Audiences cheered.

Eastwood had tired of making profitable movies about Dirty Harry Callahan. After filming three in the years between 1971 and 1976, he had shot none since. But now he accepted. He would act in and direct *Sudden Impact*.

> I wasn't intending to do any more of these characters. I never particularly wanted to. I thought I'd done all I can with it, and I might have, I don't know. But everybody kept asking about it.

One cannot say how much will be retained in the finished film, but the script of *Sudden Impact* shows us three men fatally shot in the groin by a woman. It is in retaliation for being raped by them. Dirty Harry knocks off eight sleazos himself. There are also six flashbacks to the rape.

It is a Dirty Harry Film. But for the new emphasis on women's rights (which moves Callahan to allow the girl to go free at the end), there are no new elements. The script gives us forty killings, rapes, fights, and other condiments. It is as full of ingredients as the first *Dirty Harry*.

That film bears summary. It is not just the amount of violent action, on average something new every three minutes, but the choice of items. There is something for everyone in *Dirty Harry*.

Right off, a girl swimming in a bikini is shot in a rooftop pool. We see the blood on her back. Soon after, a naked black is gunned down. He had to shoot the fellow, Callahan explains, because the man was chasing a girl up an alley while brandishing a butcher knife and an erection.

We hear of a thirteen-year-old girl buried alive. As proof of her existence, a detective holds up a bloodstained molar that has arrived in the mail. It was sent to her parents. Later, we will see the child removed from a manhole, nude, covered with dirt, dead, but chastely photographed.

A priest is seen in the sights of a sniper's rifle: when the priest moves, the sniper shoots a ten-year-old black boy instead.

A man ready to jump from a high ledge is informed by Dirty Harry that he will leave a mess on the pavement if he jumps. This so horrifies the prospective suicide that he threatens to throw up. Dirty Harry requests him not to vomit on the firemen below. He replies by trying to pull Harry with him.

Now, with the aid of another detective's binoculars, we look across into an apartment window. A naked girl opens her door to welcome a couple. They begin to make love. The sniper has them in his sights but is interrupted and guns down a cop instead. Then he shoots out a thirty-foot neon sign reading JESUS SAVES in flame-red letters.

We find the killer. His name is Scorpio, and he gets Dirty Harry—almost. Callahan has lost his guns, is down, and is having his face kicked in, but comes up with a last weapon, a long-bladed knife taped to his ankle. He throws it into the killer's thigh—to the hilt. The killer screams, staggers off. Harry picks up his Magnum, begins to track the man, finds him later, fires, hits him in the shin. Scorpio's leg is now broken. Harry steps on it to make him confess.

In between these episodes are quiet vistas of Callahan walking the street or going down long halls. Full time is taken for such shots. Despite its violence, the beat of the film is laconic. The movie is almost as open in its space as a western. Maybe that is why the violence works. For the movie, when seen, is considerably less graphic than this description of it. The violence is not so much unendurable as frequent and successful—like a cruise with many ports of call. Dirty Harry looks as clean and well turned out as any young senator with a promising future. In scenes where we see him striding down the street, he could be walking from one campaign stop to another. Eastwood knows the buried buttons in his audience as well as any filmmaker around. Is it out of measure to call him the most important small-town artist in America? One of the buried secrets small-town life is about is knowing how to press other people's buttons—that is, the ones concealed from themselves. That's why it takes so long for things to happen in a small town. Unless you're a genius, years can go by before you find each button.

MAILER: Does the question of moral responsibility weigh on you?

EASTWOOD: How do you mean?

MAILER: You can have arguments whether Dirty Harry reforms more criminals than he stimulates.

EASTWOOD: I never feel any moral problems with these pictures. I felt they're fantasy.

MAILER: Come on. In *Sudden Impact,* three men are shot in the groin by a woman. It's possible that some man or woman out there who never thought of doing that before, may now.

EASTWOOD: I don't think my movies are that stimulating. People in the audience just sit there and say, "I admire the independence. I'd like to have the nerve to tell the boss off or have that control over my life." In the society we live in, everything is kind of controlled for us. We just grow up and everything's kind of done. A lot of people are drawn to an original like Dirty Harry. The general public interpreted it on that level, a man concerned with a victim he'd never met. Like everybody says, "Boy, if I was a victim of violent crime, I'd sure like to have someone like that on my side. I'd sure like to have someone expend that kind of effort on my behalf." And I think a lot of people believe that there isn't anybody who's willing to expend that kind of effort if they were in that situation.

MAILER: There may not be.

EASTWOOD: There may not be. Right. That may be the fantasy— that there might be someone interested in my problem if I was ever in that spot. That preys on people's minds these days with crime in America, in the world. Jesus, is there somebody there, is there anybody there?

MAILER: Do you think this is one reason why blacks like your movies so much?

EASTWOOD: Well, maybe the blacks feel that he's an outsider like they felt they've been.

I let it go. He was making a film, and I did not know that I had the right to argue with a fellow artist when he was at work. Professionalism, in the absence of other certainties, becomes your guide.

Besides, I was not sure how I felt. Violence in films might have no more impact on future deeds than violence in dreams. Who could separate the safety valve from the trigger spring?

I let it go. I liked Clint Eastwood. Kin to him, I trusted my instincts. What if several hundred bodies were strewn across the thirty films he had made? It did not matter. In his movie gunfights, those bodies flew around like bowling pins. The violence happened so quickly that an audience was more likely to feel the kinetic satisfactions of a good strike in a bowling alley than savor the blood. Besides, nobody of virtue was ever killed by Eastwood. Perhaps he was right. Perhaps it was fantasy. How else account for the confident sense of duty in his person, his character, and his deeds?

What an American was Clint Eastwood! Maybe there was no one more American than he. What an interesting artist. He portrayed psychopaths who acted with all the silence, certainty, and gravity of saints. Or would it be closer to say that he played saints who killed like psychopaths? Not all questions have quick answers. Sometimes, it is worth more to dwell with the enigma. In the interim, he is living proof of the maxim that the best way to get through life is cool.

Huckleberry Finn, Alive at One Hundred

(1984)

IS THERE A SWEETER TONIC for the doldrums than old reviews of great novels? In nineteenth-century Russia, *Anna Karenina* was received with the following: "Vronsky's passion for his horse runs parallel to his passion for Anna" . . . "Sentimental rubbish" . . . "Show me one page," says *The Odessa Courier,* "that contains an idea." *Moby-Dick* was incinerated: "Graphic descriptions of a dreariness such as we do not remember to have met with before in marine literature" . . . "Sheer moonstruck lunacy" . . . "Sad stuff. Mr. Melville's Quakers are wretched dolts and drivellers and his mad captain is a monstrous bore."

By this measure, *Huckleberry Finn* (published a hundred years ago this week in London and two months later in America) gets off lightly. The *Springfield Republican* judged it to be no worse than "a gross trifling with every fine feeling. . . . Mr. Clemens has no reliable sense of propriety," and the public library in Concord, Mass., was confident enough to ban it: "the veriest trash." The *Boston Transcript* reported that "other members of the Library Committee characterize the work as rough, coarse, and inelegant, the whole book being more suited to the slums than to intelligent, respectable people."

All the same, the novel was not too unpleasantly regarded. There were no large critical hurrahs but the reviews were, on the whole, friendly. A good tale, went the consensus. There was no sense that a great American novel had landed on the literary world of 1885. The critical climate could hardly anticipate T. S. Eliot and Ernest Hemingway's encomiums fifty years later. In the preface to an English edition, Eliot would speak of "a master piece. . . . Twain's genius is completely realized," and Ernest went further. In "Green Hills of Africa," after disposing of Emerson, Hawthorne, and Thoreau and paying off Henry James and Stephen Crane with a friendly nod, he proceeded to declare, "All modern American literature comes from one book by Mark Twain called 'Huckleberry Finn.'. . . It's the best book we've had. All American writing comes from that. There was nothing before. There has been nothing as good since."

Hemingway, with his nonpareil gift for nosing out the perfect *vin du pays* for an ineluctable afternoon, was nonetheless more like other novelists in one dire respect: he was never at a loss to advance himself with his literary judgments. Assessing the writing of others, he used the working author's rule of thumb: If I give this book a good mark, does it help appreciation of my work? Obviously, *Huckleberry Finn* has passed the test.

A suspicion immediately arises. Mark Twain is doing the kind of writing only Hemingway can do better. Evidently, we must take a look. May I say it helps to have read *Huckleberry Finn* so long ago that it feels brand-new on picking it up again. Perhaps I was eleven when I saw it last, maybe thirteen, but now I only remember that I came to it after *Tom Sawyer* and was disappointed. I couldn't really follow *The Adventures of Huckleberry Finn*. The character of Tom Sawyer whom I had liked so much in the first book was altered, and did not seem nice any more. Huckleberry Finn was altogether beyond me. Later, I recollect being surprised by the high regard nearly everyone who taught American Lit. lavished upon the text, but that didn't bring me back to it. Obviously, I was waiting for an assignment from *The New York Times*.

Let me offer assurances. It may have been worth the wait. I suppose I am the ten millionth reader to say that *Huckleberry Finn* is
an extraordinary work. Indeed, for all I know, it is a great novel.
Flawed, quirky, uneven, not above taking cheap shots and cashing far too many checks (it is rarely above milking its humor)—
all the same, what a book we have here! I had the most curious
sense of excitement. After a while, I understood my peculiar
frame of attention. The book was so up-to-date! I was not reading
a classic author so much as looking at a new work sent to me in
galleys by a publisher. It was as if it had arrived with one of those
rare letters which says, "We won't make this claim often but do
think we have an extraordinary first novel to send out." So it was
like reading *From Here to Eternity* in galleys, back in 1950, or *Lie
Down in Darkness, Catch-22*, or *The World According to Garp* (which
reads like a fabulous first novel). You kept being alternately delighted, surprised, annoyed, competitive, critical, and finally excited. A new writer had moved onto the block. He could be a
potential friend or enemy but he most certainly was talented.

That was how it felt to read *Huckleberry Finn* a second time. I
kept resisting the context until I finally surrendered. One always
does surrender sooner or later to a book with a strong magnetic
field. I felt as if I held the work of a young writer about thirty or
thirty-five, a prodigiously talented fellow from the Midwest, from
Missouri probably, who had had the audacity to write a historical
novel about the Mississippi as it might have been a century and
a half ago, and this young writer had managed to give us a circus
of fictional virtuosities. In nearly every chapter new and remarkable characters bounded out from the printed page as if it were
a tarmac on which they could perform their leaps. The author's
confidence seemed so complete that he could deal with every
kind of man or woman God ever gave to the middle of America.
Jailhouse drunks like Huck Finn's father take their bow, full of
the raunchy violence that even gets into the smell of clothing.
Gentlemen and river rats, young, attractive girls full of grit and
"sand," and strong old ladies with aphorisms clicking like knit-
ting needles, fools and confidence men—what a cornucopia of
rabble and gentry inhabit the author's riverbanks.

It would be superb stuff if only the writer did not keep giving away the fact that he was a modern young American working in 1984. His anachronisms were not so much in the historical facts—those seemed accurate enough—but the point of view was too contemporary. The scenes might succeed—say it again, this young writer was talented!—but he kept betraying his literary influences. The author of *The Adventures of Huckleberry Finn* had obviously been taught a lot by such major writers as Sinclair Lewis, John Dos Passos, and John Steinbeck; he had certainly lifted from Faulkner and the mad tone Faulkner could achieve when writing about maniacal men feuding in deep swamps; he had also absorbed much of what Vonnegut and Heller could teach about the resilience of irony. If he had a surer feel for the picaresque than Saul Bellow in *Augie March,* still he felt derivative of that work. In places one could swear he had memorized *The Catcher in the Rye,* and he probably dipped into *Deliverance* and *Why Are We in Vietnam?* He might even have studied the mannerisms of movie stars. You could feel traces of John Wayne, Victor McLaglen, and Burt Reynolds in his pages. The author had doubtless digested many a Hollywood comedy on small-town life. His instinct for life in hamlets on the Mississippi before the Civil War was as sharp as it was farcical, and couldn't be more commercial.

No matter. With talent as large as this, one could forgive the obvious eye for success. Many a large talent has to go through large borrowings in order to find his own style, and a lust for popular success while dangerous to serious writing is not necessarily fatal. Yes, one could accept the pilferings from other writers, given the scope of this work, the brilliance of the concept—to catch rural America by a trip on a raft down a great river! One could even marvel uneasily at the depth of the instinct for fiction in the author. With the boy Huckleberry Finn, this new novelist had managed to give us a character of no comfortable, measurable dimension. It is easy for characters in modern novels to seem more vivid than figures in the classics but, even so, Huckleberry Finn appeared to be more alive than Don Quixote and Julien Sorel, as naturally near to his own mind as we are to ours.

But how often does a hero who is so absolutely natural on the page also succeed in acquiring convincing moral stature as his adventures develop?

It is to be repeated. In the attractive grip of this talent, one is ready to forgive the author of *Huckleberry Finn* for every influence he has so promiscuously absorbed. He has made such fertile use of his borrowings. One could even cheer his appearance on our jaded literary scene if not for the single transgression that goes too far. These are passages that do more than borrow an author's style—they copy it! Influence is mental, but theft is physical. Who can declare to a certainty that a large part of the prose in *Huckleberry Finn* is not lifted directly from Hemingway? We know that we are not reading Ernest only because the author, obviously fearful that his tone is getting too near, is careful to sprinkle his text with "a-clutterings" and "warn'ts" and "anywheres" and "t'others." But we have read Hemingway—and so we see through it—we know we are reading pure Hemingway disguised:

> We cut young cottonwoods and willows, and hid the raft
> with them. Then we set out the lines. Next we slid into
> the river and had a swim . . . then we set down on the
> sandy bottom where the water was about knee-deep and
> watched the daylight come. Not a sound anywheres . . .
> the first thing to see, looking away over the water, was a
> kind of dull line—that was the woods on t'other side;
> you couldn't make nothing else out; then a pale place in
> the sky; then more paleness spreading around; then the
> river softened up away off, and warn't black anymore . . .
> by and by you could see a streak on the water which you
> know by the look of the streak that there's a snag there
> in a swift current which breaks on it and makes that
> streak look that way; and you see the mist curl up off of
> the water and the east reddens up and the river.

Up to now I have conveyed, I expect, the pleasure of reading this book today. It is the finest compliment I can offer. We use an unspoken standard of relative judgment on picking up a classic. Secretly, we expect less reward from it than from a good contemporary novel. The average intelligent modern reader would probably, under torture, admit that *Heartburn* was more fun to read, minute for minute, than *Madame Bovary*, and maybe one even learned more. That is not to say that the first will be superior to the second a hundred years from now but that a classic novel is like a fine horse carrying an exorbitant impost. Classics suffer by their distance from our day-to-day gossip. The mark of how good *Huckleberry Finn* has to be is that one can compare it to a number of our best modern American novels and it stands up page for page, awkward here, sensational there—absolutely the equal of one of those rare incredible first novels that come along once or twice in a decade. So I have spoken of it as kin to a first novel because it is so young and so fresh and so all-out silly in some of the chances it takes and even wins. A wiser older novelist would never play that far out when the work was already well along and so neatly in hand. But Twain does.

For the sake of literary propriety, let me not, however, lose sight of the actual context. *The Adventures of Huckleberry Finn* is a novel of the nineteenth century and its grand claims to literary magnitude are also to be remarked upon. So I will say that the first measure of a great novel may be that it presents—like a human of palpable charisma—an all-but-visible aura. Few works of literature can be so luminous without the presence of some majestic symbol. In *Huckleberry Finn* we are presented (given the possible exception of Anna Livia Plurabelle) with the best river ever to flow through a novel, our own Mississippi, and in the voyage down those waters of Huck Finn and a runaway slave on their raft, we are held in the thrall of the river. Larger than a character, the river is a manifest presence, a demiurge to support the man and the boy, a deity to betray them, feed them, all but drown them, fling them apart, float them back together. The river winds like a fugue through the marrow of the true narrative which is nothing less than the ongoing relation between Huck and the runaway slave, this Nigger Jim whose name embodies the very stuff of the slave system itself—his name is not Jim but Nigger

Jim. The growth of love and knowledge between the runaway white and the runaway black is a relation equal to the relation of the men to the river for it is also full of betrayal and nourishment, separation and return. So it manages to touch that last fine nerve of the heart where compassion and irony speak to one another and thereby give a good turn to our most protected emotions.

Reading *Huckleberry Finn* one comes to realize all over again that the near-burned-out, throttled, hate-filled dying affair between whites and blacks is still our great national love affair, and woe to us if it ends in detestation and mutual misery. Riding the current of this novel, we are back in that happy time when the love affair was new and all seemed possible. How rich is the recollection of that emotion! What else is greatness but the indestructible wealth it leaves in the mind's recollection after hope has soured and passions are spent? It is always the hope of democracy that our wealth will be there to spend again, and the ongoing treasure of *Huckleberry Finn* is that it frees us to think of democracy and its sublime, terrifying premise: let the passions and cupidities and dreams and kinks and ideals and greed and hopes and foul corruptions of all men and women have their day and the world will still be better off, for there is more good than bad in the sum of us and our workings. Mark Twain, whole embodiment of that democratic human, understood the premise in every turn of his pen, and how he tested it, how he twisted and tantalized and tested it until we are weak all over again with our love for the idea.

The Hazards and Sources of Writing

_____

(1985)

KURT VONNEGUT AND I are friendly with one another, but wary. There was a period in our lives when we used to go out together a great deal because our wives like each other. Kurt and I would sit there like bookends. We'd be terribly careful with one another; we both knew the huge cost of a literary feud, so we certainly didn't want to argue. On the other hand, neither of us would be caught dead saying to the other, "Gee, I liked your last book," and then be met with a silence because the party of the second part could not reciprocate. So we would talk about anything else—Las Vegas or the islands of the Hebrides. We only had one literary conversation during such evenings in New York. Kurt looked up and sighed. "Well, I finished my novel today," he said, "and it like to killed me." When Kurt is feeling heartfelt he speaks in an old Indiana accent I can hardly reproduce. His wife murmured, "Oh, Kurt, you always say that when you finish a book," and he replied, "Well, I do, and it is always true, and it gets more true, and this last one like to killed me more than any."

Whatever could he have meant? I happen to know. It is the bond Kurt and I can count on. We understand each other in that fashion, which certainly provides a theme for the evening: "The Hazards and Sources of Writing."

When we contemplate the extraordinary terrain one must traverse to put a novel together, it may help to divide this region of endeavor into three self-contained lands: the techniques, the hazards, and the sources. We could speak of all the techniques, comprised of plot, of point of view and pace and novelistic strategies—but like an old mechanic, I have a tendency to mumble over such technical matters. "Put the thingamajig before the whoosits," is how I would probably state a practical literary problem to myself. Therefore, I am going to move over to the second and third parts of this most arbitrary division of the subject, and speak of the psychology—or, it may be closer to say, the existential state—of the novel writer, once having passed his or her apprenticeship. The years given over to becoming an established writer are subject to all the hazards of the profession—those perils of writer's block and failing energy, alcoholism, drugs, and desertion. For many a writer deserts his or her writing to go into a collateral profession in advertising or academia, trade journals, publishing . . . the list is long. What is not routine is to become a young writer with a firmly established name. Luck as well as talent can take one across that first border. Some do surpass the trials of acquiring technique and actually making a living at this bizarre profession. It is then, however, that less-charted perils begin.

I would like to speak at length of the hazards of writing, the cruelties it extorts out of mind and flesh, and then, if we are not too depressed by all these bleak prospects revealed, we can slip over to the last of the three lands, which is comparable to a kingdom beneath the sea, for it resides in no less a place than the mysterious dimension of our unconscious, the source of our aesthetic flights—and no human, no matter how professional, can speak with authority of what goes on there. We will be able only to wander at the edges of such a magnificent region and will have to be satisfied with the quickest glimpses of its wonders. No one can explore the mysteries of novel writing to their deepest source.

Let me commence with the hazards. I know something of them, and I ought to. My first published story came out forty-seven years ago, and the first novel I wrote that saw print is going to be forty-two this spring. Obviously, I have been accustomed to thinking of myself as a writer for so long that others even see me that way. I consequently hear one lament, over and over, from strangers: "Oh, I too would have liked to be an author." One can almost hear them musing aloud about the freedom of the life. How felicitous to have no boss and face no morning rush to work, how exciting to know the intoxications of celebrity. If those are superficial motives, people also long to satisfy the voice within which keeps repeating: "What a pity that no one will know how unusual my life has been! There are all those secrets I cannot tell!" Years ago I wrote, "Experience, when it cannot be communicated to another, must wither within and be worse than lost." I often ponder the remark.

Once in a while your hand will write out a sentence that seems true, and yet you do not know where it came from. Ten or twenty words seem able to live in balance with your experience. It may be one's nicest reward as a writer. You feel you've come near the truth. When that happens you can look at the page years later and meditate again on the meaning. So I think I understand why people want to write. All the same, I am also a professional, and there is another part of me, I confess, that is less charitable when strangers voice literary aspirations to me. I say to myself, "They can write an interesting letter, so they assume they are ready to tell the stories of their lives. They do not understand how much work it will take to pick up even the rudiments of narrative." If the person who has spoken to me in this fashion is serious, however, I warn them gently. "Well," I say, "it probably takes as long to learn to write as to play the piano." One shouldn't encourage people to write for too little. It's a splendid life when you think of its emoluments, but it is death to the soul if you are not good at it.

Let me keep my promise, then, and explore a little into the gloomier regions of my vocation. To skip at one bound over all those fascinating years when one is an apprentice writer and learning every day (at least on good days), there is in contrast an abominable pressure on the life of a mature novelist. For as soon as you finish each hard-earned book, the reviews come in—and the reviews can be murderous. Contrast an author's reception to an actor's. With the notable exception of John Simon, theater critics do not often try to kill performers. I believe there is an unspoken agreement that thespians deserve to be protected against the perils of first nights. After all, the actor is daring a rejection that can prove as fearful as a major wound. For human beings so sensitive as actors, a hole in the ego can be worse than a hole in the heart. Such moderation does not carry over, however, into literary criticism. *Meretricious, dishonest, labored, loathsome, pedestrian, hopeless, disgusting, disappointing, raunchy, ill-wrought, boring*—these are not uncommon words for a typical bad review. I remember, and it is thirty-eight years ago, that my second novel, *Barbary Shore*, was characterized by the massive authority of the reviewer at *Time* magazine as "paceless, tasteless, graceless." I am still looking forward to the day when I meet him. You would be hard-put to find another professional field where criticism is equally savage. Accountants, lawyers, doctors, engineers, perhaps even physicists, do not often speak publicly of one another in this manner.

Yet the unhappiest thing to say is that our critical practice may even be fair—harsh, but fair. After all, one prepares a book in the safety of the study. Nothing short of your self-esteem, your bills, your editor, or your ego is forcing you to show the stuff. You put your book out, if you can afford to take the time, only when it is ready. If economic necessity forces you to write somewhat faster than is good for you, well, everyone has their sad story. As a practical matter, not that much has to be written into the teeth of a gale, and few notes need be taken on the side of a cliff. An author usually does the stint at his desk, feeling not too hungry and suffering no pains greater than the view of the empty pad of paper. Of course, that white sheet can look as blank as a television screen when the station is off the air, but that is not a danger, merely an empty presence. The writer, unlike more active creative artists, labors in no immediate peril. Why, then, should open season not begin so soon as the work comes out? If talented authors were to have it better than other professionals and artists in all ways, there would be a tendency for talented authors to multiply, so the critics keep our numbers down.

In fact, not too many good writers do remain productive through the decades. There are too many other hazards as well. We are poked and jerked by the media to come in and out of fashion; each drop from popularity can feel like a termination to one's career. Such insecurity is no help to morale, since even in their best periods, all writers know one recurring terror. *Does it stop tomorrow? Does it all stop tomorrow?* Writing is spooky. There is no routine of an office to keep you going, only the white page each morning, and you do not know where your words are coming from, those divine words. So your professionalism at best is fragile. You cannot always tell yourself that fashions pass and history will smile at you again. In the literary world it is not easy to acquire the stoicism to endure, especially if you have begun as an oversensitive adolescent. It is not even automatic to pray for luck if it has been pessimism itself which gave force to your early themes. Maybe it is no more than blind will, but some authors stay at it. Over and over they keep writing a new book and do it in the knowledge that upon publication they will probably be savaged and unable to fight back. An occasional critic can be singled out for counterattack, or one can always write a letter to the editor of the book section, but such efforts at self-defense are like rifle fire against fighter planes. All-powerful is the writer when he sits at his desk, but on the public stage he may feel as if his rights are puny. His courage, if he has any, must learn to live with comments on his work. The spiritual skin may go slack or harden to leather, but the effort to live down bad reviews and write again has to be analogous to the unspoken, unremarked courage of people who dwell beneath the iron hand of a long illness and somehow resolve enough of their inmost contradictions to be able to get better. I suppose this is equal to saying you cannot become a professional writer and keep active for three or four decades unless you learn to live with the most immediate professional condition of your existence, which is that superficial book reviewing is irresponsible, and serious literary criticism can be close to merciless. The conviction that this condition is, on balance, fair has to grow roots deep enough to bear comparison to the life-view of a peasant who farms a mountain slope and takes it for granted that he was meant to toil through the years with one foot standing higher than the other.

Every good author who has managed to forge a long career must be able, therefore, to build a character that will not be unhinged by a bad reception. That takes a rugged disposition. Few writers are rugged when young. In general, the girls seldom look like potential beauty contest winners, and the boys show small promise of becoming future All-Americans. They are most likely to be found on the sidelines, commencing to cook up that warped, passionate, sardonic view of life which will bring them later to the attention of the American public. But only later. Young writers usually start as loners. They are obliged to live with the recognition that the world had better be wrong or they are wrong. On no less depends one's evaluation of one's right to survive. Thanks to greed, plastics, mass media, and various abominations of technology—lo, the paranoid aim of a cock-eyed young writer has as much opportunity to center on the ultimate target as the beauty queen's wide-eyed lack of paranoia. So occasionally young writers end up winning a place for a little while. Their vision has projected them forward—but rarely for long. Sooner or later, the wretched, lonely act of writing will force them back. Composition arouses too much commotion in the psyche to allow any writer to rest happily.

It is not easy to explain such disturbance to people who do not work at literature. Someone who has never tried fiction will hardly be quick to understand that in the study a writer often does feel godlike. There one sits, ensconced in judgment on other people. Yet contemplate the person in the chair: he or she could be hung over and full of the small shames of what was done yesterday, or what was done ten years ago. Old fiascos wait like ghosts in the huge house of the empty middle-aged self. Consciously or unconsciously, writers must fashion a new peace with the past every day they attempt to write. They must rise above despising themselves.

If they cannot, they will probably lose the sanction to feel like a god long enough to render judgment on others.

Yet the writer at work must not tolerate too much good news either. At the desk it is best if one does not come to like oneself too much. Wonderfully agreeable memories may arrive on certain mornings, but if they have nothing to do with the work they must be banished or they will leave the writer too cheerful, too energetic, too forgiving, too horny. It is in the calm depression of a good judge that one's scribblings move best over the page. Indeed, just as a decent judge will feel that society is injured if he or she gives an unfair verdict, so does an author have to ask constantly if he or she is being fair to the characters in a book. For if the author does violate the life of a character—that is, in the ongoing panic of trying to keep a book amusing, proceeds to distort the created people into more comic, more corrupt, or more evil forms than the writer secretly believes they deserve— well, then the writer is injuring the reader. It may be subtle injury, but it is still a moral crime. Few writers are innocent of such a practice; on the other hand, not so many artists can be found who are not guilty of softening their portraits. Some authors don't want to destroy the sympathy that readers may feel for an appealing heroine by the admission she shrieks at her children; sales might fly out the window. It takes as much literary integrity to be tough, therefore, as it does to be compassionate. The trail is narrow. It is difficult to keep up one's literary standards through the long, slogging reaches in the middle of a book. The early pleasures of conception no longer sustain the writer, who plods along with the lead feet of habit, the dry breath of discipline, and the knowledge that on the other side of the hill the critics—who also have their talent to express—are waiting. Sooner or later you come to the conclusion that if you are going to survive, you had better, where it concerns your own work, become the best critic of them all. An author who would find the resources to keep writing from one generation to the next does well to climb above the ego high enough to see every flaw in his or her own work. Otherwise, he or she will never be able to decide what are its merits.

Let yourself live, however, with an awareness of your book's lacks and shortcuts, its gloss where courage might have produced a real gleam, and you can bear the bad reviews. You can even tell when the critic is not exposing your psyche so much as turning his own dirty pockets out. It proves amazing how many evil reviews one can digest if there is a confidence that one has done one's best on a book, written to the limit of one's honesty, even scraped off a little of one's dishonesty. Get to that point of purity and your royalties may be injured by a small welcome, but not your working morale. There is even hope that if the book is better than its reception, one's favorite readers will eventually come to care for it more. The prescription, therefore, is simple: one must not put out a job with any serious taint of the meretricious. At least the prescription ought to be simple—but then, how few of us ever do work of which we are not in fact a bit ashamed? It comes down to a matter of degree. There is that remark of Engels to Marx, "Quantity changes quality." A single potato is there for us to eat, but ten thousand potatoes are a commodity and have to be put in bins or boxes. A profit must be made from them or a loss will certainly be taken. By analogy, a little corruption in a book is as forgivable as the author's style, but a sizable literary delinquency is a diseased organ, or so it will feel if the critics begin to bang on it and happen to be right for once. That will be the hour when one's creditors do not go away. I wonder if we have not touched the fear that is back of the writing in many a good novelist's heart, the hazard beneath all others.

This much said, we might quit with an agreeable moral reinforcement: one must do one's best to be honest. Unfortunately, there is more to be taken into account. Writing is like love. One never comes to understand it altogether. The act is a mystery, and the more you labor at it, the more you become aware that it is not answers which are being offered after a life of such activity so much as a greater appreciation of the scope of our literary mysteries. The ultimate pleasure in spending one's days as a writer is the resonance you can bring afterward to your personal experience. The mystery of the profession—where do those words come from, and how account for their alchemy on the

page?—can not only arouse terror at the thought of powers disappearing but may also inspire the happiness that one is in contact with the source of literature itself. Now, of course, we cannot
find direct answers to such prodigious questions. It is enough to
amuse ourselves by one or another approach to the problem. In
my college years, students used to have one certainty. It was that
environment gave the whole answer; one was the product of
one's milieu, one's parents, one's food, one's conversations,
one's dearest and/or most odious human relations. One was the
sum of one's own history as it was cradled in the larger history of
one's time. One was a product. If one wrote novels, they were
merely a product of the product. With this working philosophy I
did one book—it happened to be *The Naked and the Dead*—which
was wholly comfortable. I would not have known what an author
was suggesting by speaking of any of his or her works as uncomfortable. *The Naked and the Dead* seemed a sure result of all I had
learned up to the age of twenty-five, all I had experienced and all
I had read—the recognizable end of a long, active assembly line.
I felt able to account for each part of it.

Such an undisturbing view of the making of one's own literature was, however, soon lost. You must forgive me, but I am now
obliged—and inescapably, I fear—to speak of my own works. It is
because I am an authority about the particular conditions under
which they were written. That is the only matter on which I may
be an authority, and if I were to discuss the novels of other authors in the same manner, I would merely be speculating about
how they went at it. My own work I do know. I can say, then, that
the next book on which I embarked after *The Naked and the Dead*
was such a mystery to me that to this day I cannot tell you where
it came from. I used to feel as if this second novel, *Barbary Shore*,
were being written by someone else. Whereas *The Naked and the
Dead* had been put together with the agreeable effort of a young
carpenter able to put up a decent house because he is full of the
techniques and wisdom of those who built houses before him,
the text of *Barbary Shore* often felt as if it were being dictated to
me by a phantom in the middle of a forest. Each morning I
would sit down to work with no notion of how to continue. My

characters were strangers. Each day, after a few hours of blind work (because I never seemed to get more than a sentence or two ahead of myself), I would find that I had pushed my plot and people three manuscript pages further forward into their eventual denouement. Yet I never knew what I was doing nor where it came from. It is fortunate that I had heard of Freud and the unconscious, or I would have had to try to postulate such a condition myself. An unconscious mind was the only explanation for what was going on. I was certainly left aware, however, of two presences cooperating in a literary work—and the second, foreign to me, had the capacity to take over the act of authorship from the first.

Since then, I have not written a novel which did not belong to one category or the other. Some, of course, shared both. They came out of the deepest parts of my unconscious but were also the results of long, conscious preparation. I see *The Deer Park* and *Ancient Evenings* as fair subscriptions to these two categories, whereas my novel *The Executioner's Song* was so close to the facts of a real event that many would argue that it was not a novel at all. At the other extreme I find *Why Are We in Vietnam?* That work emerged in a voice not even remotely like my own. When I attempt to read it aloud to audiences, I am in need of an actor with a good Texas accent to step up from the audience and do the job instead. Yet I wrote that book in three happy and bemused months. Some novels take years, and some novels shift the weights and balances of your character forever by the act of writing them, but this work took only three months and passed through me with the strangest tones, wild and comic to an extreme. I used to go to my desk each morning, and the voice of my main character, a highly improbable sixteen-year-old genius—I did not even know if he was white or black, since he claimed to be one or the other at different times— would commence to speak. I had no idea where he came from nor where we were going. Such books make you feel like a spirit medium. I needed only to show up for work at the proper time and—I cannot call him he—*it* would begin to speak. One thinks of such books as gifts, compared with others; one hardly has to work at all.

Sometimes when I am feeling tolerant to the idea of karma,

demiurges, spirits of the age, and the intervention of angels, saints, and demons, I also wonder if being a writer over a long career does not leave you open to more than one source for your work. In a long career one may come forth with many values that are products of one's skill and education, of one's dedication, but I also wonder if once in a while the gods do not look about and have their own novels to propose and peer down among us and say, "Here is a good one for Bellow," or "That would have been a saucy dish for Cheever; too bad he's gone," or, in my own case, "Look at poor old Mailer worrying about his job again. Let's throw him something wicked."

Who knows? If we are for the most part sturdy literary engineers full of sound literary practice, cannot we also be agents for forces beyond our comprehension? Perhaps our books do on occasion come to us from sources we do not divine. I applaud the idea of that. Given our large and unrequited hungers, it is nice to believe that we can also be handed, in passing, a few gifts we do not quite deserve. How agreeable to feel akin to the force that put paintings on the walls of caves, set stonecutters to exactitudes that would permit Gothic arches, and gave the calculus to Newton's age. No, it is not so ill to sense that we are also heir to emanations from some unaccountable and fabulous source. Nothing lifts our horizons like a piece of unexpected luck or the generosity of the gods.

1990s

Review of *American Psycho*

(1991)

"THE COMMUNISTS," says someone at a literary party, "at least had the decency to pack it in after seventy years. Capitalism is going to last seven hundred, and before it's done, there will be nothing left."

If there is reality to *American Psycho,* by Bret Easton Ellis—if, that is, the book offers any insight into a spiritual plague—then capitalism is not likely to approach its septicentennial, for this novel reverses the values of *The Bonfire of the Vanities.* Where *Bonfire* owed some part of its success to the reassurance it offered the rich—"You may be silly," Wolfe was saying in effect, "but, brother, the people down at the bottom are unspeakably worse"—Ellis's novel inverts the equation. I cannot recall a piece of fiction by an American writer that depicts so odious a ruling class—worse, a young ruling class of Wall Street princelings ready, presumably, by the next century to manage the mighty if surrealistic levers of our economy. Nowhere in American literature can one point to an inhumanity of the moneyed upon the afflicted equal to the following description. I think it is best to present it uncut from the original manuscript:

> "Listen, what's your name?" I ask.
> "Al," he says.

"*Speak* up," I tell him. "Come on."

"Al," he says, louder.

"Get a goddamn job, *Al,*" I say, earnestly. "You've got a negative attitude. That's what's stopping you. You've got to get your act together. *I'll* help you."

"You're so kind mister. You're kind. You're a kind man," he blubbers. "I can tell."

"Ssshhh," I whisper. "It's okay." I start petting the dog.

"Please," he says, grabbing my wrist, but lightly, with kindness. "I don't know what to do. I'm so cold."

I ask him, "Do you know how bad you smell?" I whisper this soothingly, stroking his face. "The *stench*. My god . . ."

"I can't . . ." he chokes, then swallows, shaking. "I can't find a shelter."

"You *reek,*" I tell him again. "You *reek* of . . . *shit* . . ." I'm still petting the dog, its eyes wide and wet and grateful. "Do you know that? Goddamnit Al, look at me and stop crying like some kind of *faggot,*" I shout. My rage builds then subsides and I close my eyes, bringing my hand up to the bridge of my nose which I squeeze tightly, then sigh, "Al . . . I'm sorry. It's just that . . . I don't know, I don't have anything in common with you."

The bum's not listening. He's crying so hard he's incapable of a coherent answer. I put the bill slowly back into the other pocket of my Luciano Soprani jacket and with the other hand stop petting the dog and reach into the other pocket. The bum stops sobbing abruptly and sits up, looking for the fiver or, I presume, his bottle of Thunderbird. I reach out and touch his face gently, once more with compassion and whisper, "Do you know what a fucking loser you are?" He starts nodding helplessly and I pull out a long thin knife with a serrated edge and being very careful not to kill the bum push maybe half an inch of the blade into his right eye, flicking the handle up, instantly popping the retina and blinding him.

The bum is too surprised to say anything. He only opens his mouth in shock and moves a grubby, mittened hand slowly up to his face. I yank his pants down and in the passing headlights of a taxi can make out his flabby black thighs, rashed because of constant urinating in his pantsuit, the stench of shit rises quickly into my face and breathing through my mouth, on my haunches, I start stabbing him below the stomach, lightly, in the dense matted patch of pubic hair. This sobers him up somewhat and instinctively he tries to cover himself with his hands and the dog starts barking, yipping really, furiously, but it doesn't attack, and I keep stabbing at the bum now in between his fingers, stabbing the back of his hands. His eye, burst open, hangs out of its socket and runs down his face and he keeps blinking which causes what's left of it inside the wound to pour out, like red, veiny egg yolk. I grab his head with the one hand and push it back and then with my thumb and forefinger hold the other eye open and bring the knife up and push the tip of it into the socket, first breaking the protective film so the socket fills with blood, then slitting the eyeball open sideways and he finally starts screaming once I slit his nose in two, spraying me, the dog with blood, Gizmo blinking trying to get the blood out of his eyes. I quickly wipe the blade clean across his face, breaking open the muscle above his cheek. Still kneeling I throw a quarter in his face, which is slick and shiny with blood, both sockets hollowed out, what's left of his eyes literally oozing over his lips, creating thick, webby strands when stretched across his screaming open mouth. I whisper calmly, "There's a quarter. Go buy some *gum* you crazy fucking *nigger.*" Then I turn my attention to the barking dog and when I get up, stomp on its front paws while it's crouched down ready to jump at me, its fangs bared, and immediately crunch the bones in both its legs and it falls on its side squealing in pain, its front paws sticking up in the air at an obscene, satisfying angle. I can't help but start laughing and I linger at the scene, amused by this tableau. When I spot an approaching taxi, I slowly walk away.

Afterwards, two blocks west, I feel heady, ravenous, pumped-up, as if I've just worked out heavily, endorphins flooding my nervous system, my ears buzzing, my body tuning in, embracing that first line of cocaine, inhaling the first puff of a fine cigar, sipping that first glass of Cristal.

Obviously, we have a radioactive pile on our hands. Canceled by Simon & Schuster two months before publication at an immediate cost to the publisher of a $300,000 advance, picked up almost at once by Vintage Books, and commented upon all over the media map in anticipation of Christmas, although the book will now not come out much before Easter, we are waiting for a work with not one, not two, but twenty or thirty scenes of unmitigated torture. Yet the writer may have enough talent to be taken seriously. How one wishes he were without talent! One does not want to be caught defending *American Psycho*. The advance word is a tidal wave of bad cess.

The Sunday *New York Times Book Review* took the unprecedented step of printing a review, months in advance, on December 16. In the form of an editorial titled "Snuff This Book! Will Bret Easton Ellis Get Away with Murder?" it is by Roger Rosenblatt, a "columnist for *Life* magazine and an essayist for 'The MacNeil/Lehrer Newshour,'" who writes in a style to remind one of the critical bastinadoes with which *Time* magazine used to flog the ingenuous asses of talented young writers forty years ago.

American Psycho is the journal Dorian Gray would have written had he been a high school sophomore. But that is unfair to sophomores. So pointless, so themeless, so everythingless is this novel, except in stupefying details about expensive clothing, food and bath products, that were it not the most loathsome offering of the season, it certainly would be the funniest. . . . Patrick Bateman . . . is a Harvard graduate, twenty-six years old, is single, lives on Manhattan's Upper West Side, nurtures his appearance obsessively, frequents health clubs by day and restaurants by night and, in his spare time, plucks out the eyes of street beggars, slits the throats of children and does things to the bodies of women not unlike things that Mr. Ellis does to prose. . . .

But his true inner satisfaction comes when he has a woman in his clutches and can entertain her with a nail gun or a power drill or Mace, or can cut off her head or chop off her arms or bite off breasts or dispatch a starving rat up her vagina.

The context of these high jinks is young, wealthy, hair-slicked-back, narcissistic, decadent New York, of which, one only assumes, Mr. Ellis disapproves. It's a bit hard to tell what Mr. Ellis intends exactly, because he languishes so comfortably in the swamp he purports to condemn.

The indictment becomes more personal in *Spy,* December 1990, by a young—I assume he is young—man who calls himself Todd Stiles:

[Ellis] couldn't actually write a book that would earn attention on its merits, so he chose a course that will inevitably cause controversy and get him lots of press and allow him to pontificate, kind of like the novelist and critic Leo Tolstoi, on the question What is Art? *I am purposely exaggerating the way yuppie men treat women. That's the point,* he will say. *I meant to convey the madness of the consumerist eighties.* Not much could be more sickening than the misogynistic barbarism of this novel, but almost as repellent will be Ellis's callow cynicism as he justifies it.

In fact, Ellis has given a few indications that he is ready to justify it. For the "Arts & Leisure" section of the Sunday *Times,* December 2, 1990, he wrote a piece called "The Twentysomethings,
Adrift in a Pop Landscape."

> We're basically unshockable.... This generation has
> been wooed with visions of violence, both fictive and
> real, since childhood.
>
> If violence in films, literature and in some heavy-
> metal and rap music is so extreme ... it may reflect the
> need to be terrified in a time when the sharpness of
> horror-film tricks seems blunted by repetition on the
> nightly news.

It is obvious. Ellis wants to break through steel walls. He will
set out to shock the unshockable. And *Spy* writer Todd Stiles is
right—we are face-to-face once more with the old curmudgeon
"novelist and critic Leo Tolstoi" (who not so long ago used to be
known as Tolstoy). We have to ask the question once more: What
is art? The clue presented by Bret Easton Ellis is his odd remark
on "the need to be terrified."

Let me take us through my reading of the book, even though
the manuscript I read was close to two hundred thousand words;
the Vintage edition is bound to be shorter, for the novel is needlessly long—in fact, the first fifty pages are close to unendurable.
There is no violence yet, certainly not if the signature of violence
is blood, but the brain receives a myriad of dull returns. No one
who enters the book has features, only clothing. We will learn in
a while that we are in the mind of our serial killer, Patrick Bateman, but from the second page on, we are assaulted by such
sentences as this: "Price is wearing a six-button wool-and-silk suit
by Ermenegildo Zegna, a cotton shirt with French cuffs by Ike
Behar, a Ralph Lauren silk tie, and leather wing-tips by Fratelli
Rossetti." On page 5, "Courtney opens the door and she's wearing a Krizia cream silk blouse, a Krizia rust tweed skirt and silk
satin D'Orsay pumps from Manolo Blahnik."

By page 12, Price is "lying on a late 18th century French Aubusson carpet drinking espresso from a cerelane coffee cup on the floor of Evelyn's room. I'm lying on Evelyn's bed holding a tapestry pillow from Jenny B. Goode nursing a cranberry and Absolut."

Bateman's apartment has "a long, white down-filled sofa and a 30-inch digital TV set from Toshiba; it's a high-contrast highly defined model . . . a high-tech tube combination from NEC with a picture-in-picture digital effects system (plus freeze-frame); the audio includes built-in MTS and a five watt-per-channel on-board amp." We progress through Super Hi-Band Beta units, three-week eight-event timers, four hurricane halogen lamps, a "glass-top coffee table with oak legs by Turchin," "crystal ashtrays from Fortunoff," a Wurlitzer jukebox, a black ebony Baldwin concert grand, a desk and magazine rack by Gio Ponti, and on to the bathroom, which presents twenty-two name products in its inventory. One has to keep reminding oneself that on reading Beckett for the first time it was hard not to bellow with fury at the monotony of the language. We are being asphyxiated with state-of-the-art commodities.

Ditto the victuals. Every trendy restaurant that has succeeded in warping the parameters of the human palate is visited by the Wall Street yuppies of this book. For tens of thousands of words, we make our way through "cold corn chowder lemon bisque with peanuts and dill . . . swordfish meatloaf with kiwi mustard."

Themes will alternate in small variations. We pass from meetings at the office (where business is never transacted) to free-weight workouts in the gym, to Nell's, to taxi rides, to more descriptions of clothing, furnishings, accessories, cosmetics, to conference calls to expedite restaurant reservations, to acquaintances who keep mistaking each other's names, to video rentals and TV shows. We are almost a third of the way through an unending primer on the artifacts of life in New York, a species of dream where one is inhaling not quite enough air and the narrative never stirs because there is no narrative. New York life in these pages is circular, one's errands footsteps in the caged route of the prison bullpen. Bateman is living in a hell where no hell is external to ourselves and so all of existence is hell. The advertise-

ments have emerged like sewer creatures from the greed-holes
of the urban cosmos. One reads on addicted to a vice that offers
no pleasure whatsoever. One would like to throw the book away.
It is boring and it is intolerable—these are the worst and dullest
characters a talented author has put before us in a long time, but
we cannot get around to quitting. The work is obsessive—the
question cannot be answered, at least not yet: Is *American Psycho*
with or without art? One has to keep reading to find out. The
novel is not written so well that the art becomes palpable, declares itself against all odds, but then, it is not written so badly
that one can reject it with clear conscience. For the first third of
its narrativeless narrative it gives off a mood not dissimilar to living through an unrelenting August in New York when the sky is
never clear and rain never comes.

Then the murders begin. They are not dramatic. They are
episodic. Bateman kills man, woman, child, or dog, and disposes
of the body by any variety of casual means. He has penetrated to
the core of indifference in New York. Humor commences; movie
audiences will laugh with all the hysteria in their plumbing as
Bateman puts a body in a sleeping bag, drags it past his door-
man, heaves it into a cab, stops at a tenement apartment he
keeps as his private boneyard, hefts it up four flights of stairs,
and drops the cadaver in a bathtub full of lime. Smaller body
parts are allowed to molder in the other apartment with the concert grand and the ashtrays from Fortunoff. To visitors, he explains away the close air by suggesting that he cannot find just
where the rat has died. He gets blood on his clothing and brings
this soiled package to a Chinese laundry. A few days later, he will
curse them out for failing to clean his suit immaculately. The
proprietors know the immutable spots are blood, but who is to
debate the point? If you argue with a stranger in New York, he
may kill you.

So, Bateman's murders are episodic: Nothing follows from
them. His life goes on. He works out in the gym with dedication,
he orders shad roe and pickled rabbit's kidney with cilantro
mousse, he consumes bottles of Cristal with friends, and in discos he scores cocaine. Over one summer, he has an idyll in the

Hamptons with Evelyn, the girl he may marry, and succeeds in restraining himself from murdering her; he masturbates over porny videos, he tells a friend in the middle of an acrimonious meal that if friend does not button his lip, he will be obliged to splatter friend's blood all over the blond bitch at the next table, and, of course, the speech is heard but not taken in. Not over all that restaurant gabble, not in all that designer din. When tension builds, Bateman kills in the same state of loneliness with which he masturbates; for relief, he hires two escort girls and tortures them to death before going off to the office next morning to instruct his secretary on who he will be available to on the telephone, and who not.

The murders begin to take their place with the carambola sorbet, the Quilted Giraffe, the Casio QD-150 Quick-Dialer, the Manolo Blahnik shoes, the baby soft-shell crabs with grape jelly. Not differentiated in their prose from all the other descriptions, an odd aesthetic terror is on the loose. The destruction of the beggar is small beer by now. A boy who strays a short distance from his mother at the Central Park Zoo is killed without a backward look. A starving rat is indeed introduced into the vagina of a half-slaughtered woman. Is Bateman the monster or Bret Easton Ellis? At best, what is to be said of such an imagination? The book is disturbing in a way to remind us that attempts to create art can be as intolerable as foul manners. One finishes with an uneasy impulse not to answer the question but to bury it. Of course, the question can come back to haunt us. A novel has been written that is bound to rest in unhallowed ground if it is executed without serious trial.

So the question returns, what is art? What can be so important about art that we may have to put up with a book like this? And the answer leads us to the notion that without serious art the universe is doomed.

These are large sentiments, but then, we live in a world which, by spiritual measure, if we could measure it, might be worse than any of the worlds preceding it. Atrocities, injustice, and the rape of nature have always been with us, but they used to be accompanied by whole architectures of faith that gave some vision to our sense of horror at what we are. Most of us could believe in Catholicism, or Marxism, or Baptism, or science, or the American family, or Allah, or Utopia, or trade-unionism, or the synagogue, or the goodness of the American president. By now, we all know that some indefinable piece of the whole is not amenable to analysis, reason, legislative manipulation, committees, expertise, precedent, hard-earned rule of thumb, or even effective political corruption. We sense all too clearly that the old methods no longer suffice, if they ever did. The colloquies of the managers (which can be heard on any given TV night and twice on Sunday morning) are now a restricted ideology, a jargon that does not come close to covering our experience, particularly our spiritual experience—our suspicion that the lashings have broken loose in the hold.

In such a world, art becomes the remaining link to the unknown. We are far beyond those eras when the English could enjoy the spoils of child labor during the week and read Jane Austen on the weekend. Art is no longer the great love who is wise, witty, strengthening, tender, wholesomely passionate, secure, life-giving—no, Jane Austen is no longer among us to offer a good deal more than she will disrupt, nor can Tolstoy still provide us (at least in the early and middle work) with some illusion that life is well proportioned and one cannot cheat it, no, we are far beyond that moral universe—art has now become our need to be terrified. We live in the fear that we are destroying the universe, even as we mine deeper into its secrets. So art may be needed now to provide us with just those fearful insights that the uneasy complacencies of our leaders do their best to avoid. It is art that has to take the leap into all the truths that our media society is insulated against. Since the stakes are higher, art may be more important to us now than ever before.

Splendid, you may say, but where is *American Psycho* in all this? Is the claim being advanced that it is art?

I am going to try an answer on these lines: Art serves us best precisely at that point where it can shift our sense of what is possible, when we now know more than we knew before, when we feel we have—by some manner of leap—encountered the truth.

That, by the logic of art, is always worth the pain. If, then, our
lives are dominated by our fears, the fear of violence dominates
our lives. Yet we know next to nothing about violence, no matter
how much of it we look at and live with. Violence in movies tells
us nothing. We know it is special effects.

All the more valuable then might be a novel about a serial
killer, provided we could learn something we did not know before. Fiction can serve as our reconnaissance into all those jun-
gles and up those precipices of human behavior that psychiatry,
history, theology, and sociology are too intellectually encum-
bered to try. Fiction is indeed supposed to bring it back alive—
all that forbidden and/or unavailable experience. Fiction can
conceive of a woman's or a man's last thoughts where medicine
would offer a terminal sedative. So Ellis's novel cannot be dis-
qualified solely by a bare description of its contents, no matter
how hideous are the extracts. The good is the enemy of the
great, and good taste is certainly the most entrenched foe of literature. Ellis has an implicit literary right, obtained by the
achievements of every important and adventurous novelist before him, to write on any subject, but the more he risks, the more
he must bring back or he will leach out the only capital we have,
which is our literary freedom.

We have to take, then, the measure of this book of horrors. It
has a thesis: *American Psycho* is saying that the eighties were spiritually disgusting and the author's presentation is the crystalliza-
tion of such horror. When an entire new class thrives on the
ability to make money out of the manipulation of money, and
becomes altogether obsessed with the surface of things—that is,
with luxury commodities, food, and appearance—then, in effect, says Ellis, we have entered a period of the absolute manipulation of humans by humans: the objective correlative of total
manipulation is coldcock murder. Murder is now a lumber mill
where humans can be treated with the same lack of respect as
trees. (And scream commensurately—Bateman's main tools of
dispatch are knives, chain saws, nail guns.)

Such a massive thesis does not sit well on underdeveloped
legs—nothing less than a great novel can support a great, if mon-

strous, thesis. A good novel with too major a theme can only be crushed by the weight of what it is carrying. The test of *American Psycho* is whether we can ever believe the tale. Of course, it is a black comedy—that all-purpose cop-out!—but even black comedies demand an internal logic. If we can accept the idea that the political air turned flatulent after eight years with the hornpipe wheezes of the Pied Piper, we must also entertain the thesis that the unbridled manipulations of the money decade subverted the young sufficiently to produce wholly aimless lives for a generation of Wall Street yuppies. But was it crowned by the ultimate expression of all these meaningless lives—one total monster, a Patrick Bateman? Can he emerge entirely out of no more than vapidity, cupidity, and social meaninglessness? It does not matter whether a man like him does, in fact, exist; for all we know there might be a crew of Patrick Batemans at large in New York right now.

The demand is not that Bateman be factual but that he be acceptable as fiction. Do we read these pages believing that the same man who makes his rounds of restaurants and pretends to work in an office, this feverish snob with a presence so ordinary that most of his casual acquaintances keep mistaking him at parties and discos for other yuppies who look somewhat like him, can also be the most demented killer ever to appear in the pages of a serious American novel? The mundane activity and the supersensational are required to meet.

Bret Easton Ellis enters into acute difficulties with this bicameral demand. He is a writer whose sense of style is built on the literary conviction (self-serving for many a limited talent) that there must not be one false note. In consequence, there are often not enough notes. Even with writers as splendidly precise as Donald Barthelme, as resonant with recollected sorrow as Raymond Carver, or as fine-edged as Ann Beattie, there are often not enough notes. A book can survive as a classic even when it offers much too little—*The Great Gatsby* is the prime example forever—but then Fitzgerald was writing about the slowest murders of them all, social exclusion, whereas Ellis believes he is close enough to Dostoyevsky's ground to quote him in the epigraph. Since we are going to have a monstrous book with a monstrous thesis, the author must rise to the occasion by having a murderer with enough inner life for us to comprehend him. We pay a terrible price for reading about intimate violence—our fears are stirred, and buried savageries we do not wish to meet again in ourselves stir uneasily in the tombs to which we have consigned them. We cannot go out on such a trip unless we believe we will end up knowing more about extreme acts of violence, know a little more, that is, of the real inner life of the murderer.

Bateman, however, remains a cipher. His mother and brother appear briefly in the book and are, like all the other characters, faceless—we are less close to Bateman's roots than to his meals. Exeter and Harvard are named as parts of his past but in the manner of Manolo Blahnik and Ermenegildo Zegna—names in a serial sequence. Bateman is driven, we gather, but we never learn from what. It is not enough to ascribe it to the vast social rip-off of the eighties. The abstract ought to meet the particular. In these pages, however, the murders begin to read like a pornographic description of sex. Bateman is empty of inner reaction and no hang-ups occur. It may be less simple to kill humans and dispose of them than is presented here, even as real sex has more turns than the soulless high-energy pump-outs of the pornographic. Bateman, as presented, is soulless, and because we cannot begin to feel some instant of pity for him, so the writing about his acts of violence is obliged to become more hideous externally and more affectless within until we cease believing that Ellis is taking any brave leap into truths that are not his own—which happens to be one of the transcendent demands of great fiction. No, he is merely working out some ugly little corners of himself.

Of course, no one could write if art were entirely selfless. Some of the worst in us has also to be smuggled out or we would use up our substance before any book was done. All the same, a line is always in place between art and therapy. Half of the outrage against this book is going to come from our suspicion that Ellis is not creating Bateman so much as he is cleaning out pest nests in himself. No reader ever forgives a writer who uses him for therapy.

If the extracts of *American Psycho* are horrendous, therefore, when taken out of context, that is Ellis's fault. They are, for the most part, simply not written well enough. If one is embarked on a novel that hopes to shake American society to the core, one has to have something new to say about the outer limits of the deranged—one cannot simply keep piling on more and more acts of machicolated butchery.

The suspicion creeps in that much of what the author knows about violence does not come from his imagination (which in a great writer can need no more than the suspicion of real experience to give us the whole beast) but out of what he has picked up from *Son* and *Grandson of Texas Chainsaw Massacre* and the rest of the filmic Jukes and Kallikaks. We are being given horror-shop plastic. We won't know anything about extreme acts of violence (which we do seek to know if for no less good reason than to explain the nature of humankind in the wake of the Holocaust) until some author makes such acts intimately believable, that is, believable not as acts of description (for that is easy enough) but as intimate personal states so intimate that we enter them. That is why we are likely never to know: Where is the author ready to bear the onus of suggesting that he or she truly understands the inner logic of violence?

To create a character intimately, particularly in the first person, is to convince the reader that the author is the character. In extreme violence, it becomes more comfortable to approach from outside, as Bret Easton Ellis either chose to do, or could do no better. The failure of this book, which promises to rise occasionally to the level of the very good (when it desperately needs to be great), is that by the end we know no more about Bateman's need to dismember others than we know about the inner workings in the mind of a wooden-faced actor who swings a broadax in an exploitation film. It's grunts all the way down. So, the first novel to come along in years that takes on deep and Dostoyevskian themes is written by only a half-competent and narcissistic young pen.

Nonetheless, he is showing older authors where the hands have come to on the clock. So one may have to answer the question: What would you do if you happened to find yourself the unhappy publisher who discovered this book on his list two months before publication?

I am not sure of the answer. The move that appeals most in retrospect is to have delayed publication long enough to send the manuscript to ten or twelve of the most respected novelists in America *for an emergency reading*. Presumably, a number would respond. If a majority were clearly on the side of publication, I would feel the sanction to go ahead. To my knowledge, that possibility was never contemplated. A pity. Literature is a guild, and in a crisis, it would be good if the artisan as well as the merchants could be there to ponder the decision.

This is, of course, fanciful. No corporate publisher would ever call on an author, not even his favorite author, on such a matter, and perhaps it is just as well. A lot of serious literary talent could have passed through a crisis of conscience. How to vote on such a book? The costs of saying "Yes, you must publish" are fearful. The reaction of certain women's groups to *American Psycho* has been full of unmitigated outrage.

Indeed, an extract from one of the most hideous passages in the novel was read aloud by Tammy Bruce, president of the Los Angeles chapter of the National Organization for Women, on a telephone hotline. The work is described as a "how-to novel on the torture and dismemberment of women . . . bringing torture of women and the mutilation deaths of women into an art form. We are here to say that we will not be silent victims anymore."

While it is certainly true that the fears women have of male violence are not going to find any alleviation in this work, nonetheless I dare to suspect that the book will have a countereffect to these dread-filled expectations. The female victims in *American Psycho* are tortured so hideously that men with the liveliest hostility toward women will, if still sane, draw back in horror. "Is that the logical extension of my impulse to inflict cruelty?" such men will have to ask themselves, even as after World War II millions of habitual anti-Semites drew back in similar horror from the mirror of unrestrained anti-Semitism that the Nazis had offered the world.

No, the greater horror, the real intellectual damage this novel may cause is that it will reinforce Hannah Arendt's thesis on the banality of evil. It is the banality of Patrick Bateman that creates his hold over the reader and gives this ugly work its force. For if Hannah Arendt is correct and evil is banal, then that is vastly worse than the opposed possibility that evil is satanic. The extension of Arendt's thesis is that we are absurd, and God and the Devil do not wage war with each other over the human outcome. I would rather believe that the Holocaust was the worst defeat God ever suffered at the hands of the Devil. That thought offers more life than to assume that many of us are nothing but dangerous, distorted, and no damn good.

So I cannot forgive Bret Easton Ellis. If I, in effect, defend the author by treating him at this length, it is because he has forced us to look at intolerable material, and so few novels try for that much anymore. On this basis, if I had been one of the authors consulted by a publisher, I would have had to say, yes, publish the book, it not only is repellent but will repel more crimes than it will excite. This is not necessarily the function of literature, but it is an obvious factor here.

What a deranging work! It is too much of a void, humanly speaking, to be termed evil, but it does raise the ante so high that one can no longer measure the size of the bet. Blind gambling is a hollow activity and this novel spins into the center of that empty space.

How the Wimp Won the War

———

(1991)

ON AUGUST 2, 1990, it could be said that George Bush's media prospects were dire. The budget, prisons, drugs, inner cities, AIDS, crack, crime, and the homeless were exhibiting an obdurate, malicious, even perverse inclination to resist all solution.

There was also the $500 billion S&L scandal. While one could not yet speak of it as a cancer upon the presidency—no, not so bad as Watergate—still, it was a damn chancre at the least, and the president's son, whether innocent, guilty, or somewhat smudged, was going to be treated by the media for the next six months as a blot on the Bush escutcheon. The media would not be media if they did not have the instincts of a lynch mob. George Bush knew that well enough. He had spent eight years in the advanced course in media manipulation under Ronald Reagan, and you could hardly not learn a lot from Ronald Reagan, who worked on the notion that most Americans would rather be told they were healthy than be healthy.

Since this condition can inspire a good deal of free-floating anxiety, Reagan also recognized that the media had acquired the power of a shadow government, ready to cater to all the dread in American life. If a widow encountered an ax murderer in her bedroom, the lady's blood went onto the television screens that night, and the blood was sometimes as red as the ketchup in the commercial that followed. Ronald Reagan, the survivor of more than fifty B movies, understood that TV was the spirit of interruption—we were in the age of postmodernism, where anything could be connected to anything and sometimes gave you an interesting, that is, a new sensation. Ronald Reagan was ready to apply postmodernism to history and its retinue of facts. Henry Ford, who struggled with the concept when it was new, had said "History is bunk," and was ridiculed; Reagan took the notion out of the swamps. History was not bunk but chosen statements.

If you were president, you could tell stories that were not true, yet they, too, could become facts inasmuch as denial of the statement didn't carry one-quarter the heft of the initial declaration. It came down to knowing how to feed the media. The media were a valve installed in the governing heart of the nation, and they decided which stories would receive prominence. Reagan recognized that one had to become the valve within the valve. Otherwise, certain catastrophes could produce headlines equal to spurting arteries. They could pump away the plasma of your reputation. When 241 Marines were killed in Beirut by one bomb carried in one truck by one Arab terrorist on October 23, 1983, Reagan gave the order two days later to invade Grenada. A catastrophe must immediately be replaced by another act so bold that it, too, may end in catastrophe—that takes moxie!

Grenada worked, however. Nineteen hundred Marines conquered something like half their number of Cuban construction workers, and the media were banned from reporting events firsthand for the three days of the campaign. Then America celebrated the victory. A phenomenon ensued. The American public reacted as if the victory in Grenada had removed the shame of Vietnam.

Only a political genius can turn a debacle into a media success, and George Bush had studied Ronald Reagan with all the intensity of an unwanted child for eight hard years, taken his snubs, suffered the nitty-twit positions Reagan left him in, and the wimp slanders prevalent in the press. George Bush was keen, lean, competitive, and wanted the presidency as much as any vice president before him. Without it, he had nothing to anticipate but an enduring reputation as the ex-vice-presidential wimp. Male pride is insufficiently appreciated. It can approach earthquake force. George Bush was not to be stopped by the likes of Dole or Dukakis; George Bush knew that you win elections by kissing the great American electorate on the mouth—"I want a kinder, gentler nation"—and by kicking the opposition in the nuts.

Grenada may have demonstrated that the need for pride in one's patriotism was the largest unsatisfied love in American life, but the most feared nightmare in American life (now that the Evil Empire was benign) had to be the black criminal avenger whom good liberals were blind enough to let out of jail long enough to rape a white, doubtless Christian, female person. The case of Willie Horton was a real shitkicker's stomp, and the creative author, Lee Atwater, who happened to be an aficionado of black music, would subsequently develop a tumor in his head and would die last month. Who can say how much he felt inwardly condemned for conceiving and carrying out such a caper on a people whose music he loved.

George Bush cut his thin thread of congressional liaison to the Democratic Party with Willie Horton (and that would cost him later, since Democrats do control Congress), but then, he did not know at the time that Michael Dukakis would prove lead-footed as a candidate. Bush saw the immediate world head-on. Win the presidency. Do not debate the efficacy of overkill. Swear allegiance to the first precept of Ronald Reagan: *Be as shallow as spit on a rock and you will prevail.* Bush prevailed and entered the postmodern American presidency of crack, crime, AIDS—we have the list.

On August 2, 1990, however, the Iraqis invaded Kuwait, and Saddam Hussein entered American life.

Before it was all over, there would be people to suggest—King Hussein of Jordan, for one—that Saddam Hussein was provoked into crossing the border by Mubarak of Egypt, King Fahd of Saudi Arabia, the State Department, and presumably the CIA.

This is, of course, paranoid, which by writer's rule of thumb means not within the parameters of my piece. We will assume for the purposes of this reconnoiter through recent history that it was no more than George Bush's good luck for Saddam Hussein to misread a few signs en route to gobbling the Kuwaitis. That sort of error would not have been difficult to make. Saddam was endangered at home by problems as deep as the need of other people to see him dead, and he was surrounded by sycophants who would never indicate that an unhappy matter could be the leader's fault, a condition which is tonic for a leader's vanity, but does feed elephantiasis of the ego.

In addition, Saddam was a poet. "The mother of all battles" is a metaphor primeval enough to reach into the nightmares of every infantryman arrayed against him. No poet ever believes he or she is incapable of world-shaking moves. When you know the power of the word, you depend on it.

To strengthen this mix, the president of Iraq was a degenerate gambler. He had played all his life with table stakes larger than he could afford. That was his strength. Few men gain a sense of personal power greater than does a degenerate gambler who has not been destroyed by his vice. One tends to believe that God, or Providence, or some mysterious demiurge like Lady Luck, is enraptured with your presence on earth.

Hitler held to such beliefs; there may be no other explanation for him. So, by an extrapolation of his imagination, George Bush was able to speak of Saddam Hussein as Hitler, and that was certainly a page taken from the gnomic maxims of Ronald Reagan—a Muslim Hitler who comes to the stage as your foe can do a lot to save the American presidency.

Now, Saddam could conceivably have become as monstrous as Hitler. For that, however, he would have had to acquire Saudi Arabia, Jordan, and the Emirates, then Iran and Syria (two formidably indigestible items) plus Israel—a major war—and Egypt, and North Africa. There may not be the rudiments of enough administrative ability in all of Islam to take care of such an empire, temperamentally supercharged, technologically Third World, oil-rich, and revolution-rife; yes, if you can conquer all of

that in a decade, when Saudi Arabia alone is one-quarter the size
of the United States, then you are the equal of Adolf Hitler and
would doubtless exhibit the same cavernous disregard for the
deaths of whole millions of people; yes, putting Saddam Hussein
into the equation with Hitler was also a metaphor, but then,
George Bush was even competitive about that. Saddam Hussein
was Hitler, QED, and there would be no Munichs for George.

On a stripped budget, Hussein could have been stopped,
probably, from moving into Saudi Arabia by sending over a division of Marines with naval and air support. The troops could
have been kept—as they were, in fact, for months—hundreds of
miles south of the Kuwait border. It would have been effective
militarily if one wanted to avoid war; it would have drawn, precisely, a line in the sand.

George Bush, however, needed war. It would take no less than
that to dig into the macho meat of B-movie sentiments. As Ronald Reagan had delineated, this was the real emotional broth of
a majority of voting Americans—they had, after all, put in their
time growing up on the narrative reflexes of B movies, plus all
the A movies that happened to be no more elevated in sentimental vision than the B movies. George Bush could avoid war by
keeping a token force in Saudi Arabia—and who but the Kuwaitis would grieve for Kuwait?—but the prognosis suggested
poor media potential; the action could downgrade itself into
one headline blight after another. A task force underwriting
such a limited peace in the Middle East would hardly be large
enough to accomplish dramatic results. Incidents were bound to
occur. Carousing soldiers would sooner or later be killed by
Saudi policemen (which, in the absence of other news, would
loom as large as a tank battle). Governing America in company
with the media is like spending a honeymoon with your mother-
in-law's ear to the door. George Bush's aim was hardly going to
focus, therefore, on something as minimal as avoiding a war; his
goal was to save his presidency. For that, nothing less than a
major campaign would do.

Many a political leader has the ability to bear comparison to
Napoleon for a season. Maggie Thatcher had the Falklands in

1982, and it gave her eight and a half more years of political life. The president, abetted by the skills of his secretary of state, had a few such weeks in August 1990: showing precisely the sort of competence Michael Dukakis had advertised as his own first virtue, Bush and Baker succeeded between them in establishing UN sanctions against Iraq. Twenty-eight countries joined the coalition. A mighty and magnetic movement toward war got under way in America against an outraged liberal defense: "No blood for oil."

The liberals had the commonsense logic, the good ethics, the good morals, the antiwar pieties, the slogans, the demonstrations, and the inner conviction that they were on the side of the angels, but they were entering a trap larger and deeper than any of the moats ablaze with burning oil that Saddam Hussein had promised American troops. Intellectually speaking, liberal ideology had become about as stimulating as motel furniture. You could get through a night with it provided you didn't have to hang around in the morning. Liberalism was opposed to war, poverty, hunger, AIDS, drugs, corruption in high places, crowded prisons, budget cuts, sexism, racism, and opposition to gay liberation, but it had not had an idea in twenty-five years for solving any of those problems.

George Bush, however, had heard the music of the Pied Piper. He knew that Ronald Reagan had launched America on a fiduciary way of life once practiced by Marie Antoinette and various members of the French, British, and Russian aristocracy. One spent lavishly for one's pleasures, sold one's cherry orchards (a transaction we are, at present, arranging with the Japanese), and looked for entertainments that would offer new zest for life not only to the people who were attending the ball but to the populace watching outside. Reagan established the principle: you cannot be a good president unless you keep the populace entertained. Reagan understood what hard workers like Lyndon Johnson, Richard Nixon, and Jimmy Carter did not; he saw that the president of the United States was the leading soap-opera figure in the great American drama, and one had better possess star value. The president did not have to have executive ability nearly as much as an interesting personality. A touch of the selfish or the unscrupulous—just a touch!—might be necessary to keep a hero interesting.

Ronnie, of course, was perfect—the nicest movie actor ever to serve up his young manhood to losing the girl to the handsome guy who might not deserve her quite as much. His presidency was delivered from that hint of insipidity, however, by the presence of Nancy. She suggested more than a few touches of the cruel, the narrow, and the exclusive. So, they were interesting. You followed them. You kept waiting over eight years, like the rest of the American public, to see one small crack in the surface of their marriage. You never succeeded, but then, the rock-bottom aesthetic of the long-running soap opera is to keep the same anticipation alive.

George Bush, as the central figure in the new series, had a totally different problem. His wife was strong, decent, gracious, and an obvious helpmate, but George had to prove he was worthy of her. Overcoming the wimp burden could then prove a narrative asset. Given such parameters, he was not about to look for a draw with Saddam Hussein. Only wimps were eager to endure the headaches and the dull obsessional arguments that follow in the wake of a contest which ends without decision.

George Bush, in it for the win, knew that sanctions, now that he had them, were not likely to work. How was one to keep Saddam Hussein encysted within the embargo for the two long years, or three, that starving him out was going to take? There were already trouble spots in the UN firmament—Syria, then the Soviet Union, Morocco, Germany, and Japan. And what of such uncommitted or barely committed nations as Iran, Afghanistan, Cuba, and China? Constant vigilance would be required to accomplish, yes, what? Hussein would flood the world press with pictures of starving Iraqi children. Any Red Cross food that entered the country would feed his Republican Guard. Hussein could live with famine in large parts of Iraq—he would be busy making certain that his internal enemies suffered the famine. Meanwhile, he could play upon the passions of the Palestinians, and provoke the Israelis. For that matter, when the time was propitious, what would ever keep him from starting a war with Israel? Every Muslim leader in the coalition would then have to hold down his own people. From George Bush's point of view, maintaining sanctions would be about as sensible as going into a brothel to announce, "I'll be in town for the next year. I want you girls to promise that during this period you won't pick up a venereal disease." No, the sanctions had to be seen as an instrument, a staging area from which to prepare the shooting war.

Bush, undeniably adroit at such a game, managed to maneuver the Security Council of the UN into agreement: If Saddam did not agree to pull out of Kuwait by January 15, 1991, then the allied armies, ultimately 750,000 strong, were authorized by the UN to engage in combat with Iraq. A vote of approval still had to be taken in Congress, however, and was on January 12, 1991.

During the TV hours of watching that debate in the House and Senate, our writer-at-large was to discover surprising sentiments in himself. He was on the side of war.

He could not believe it, but he felt a lifting of his spirit. A few days later, the sentiment was confirmed by a whole sense of excitement that the war had actually begun. For a man who disliked news shows, he now listened to generals with as much as half an open ear. He knew that if he felt himself viscerally allied with this combat, then nearly all of America would be gung ho over it.

It had gone beyond morality. Some cures can be found only in the art of the binge. Was this the phenomenon at work now? Did the country need a war?

Well, it had also needed Ronald Reagan, and Grenada, and Panama, and our writer had been opposed to all three. Where, now, was the difference? Perhaps it was that the country kept getting worse and worse. All the American revolutions seemed to have degenerated into enclaves of jargoneers who were not even capable of debate if their opponent did not employ their jargon. No, it was worse than that. When one forced oneself to contemplate the phalanxes of the left, one by one, it could be seen that no effective left remained in the country. The trade unions were bureaucratic when they were not corrupt; the sexual left was confounded, fragmented, bewildered, and AIDS was a catastrophe; little power groups fought over the remains of gay liberation. The thought began to intrude itself into the mind of many an American that, no matter how tragic individual cases might be, not everyone who came down with AIDS was necessarily entitled to a medal. Women's liberation, contributing to no cause but its own, had grown tiresome. Their agenda was sexist: women were good, and men were no damn good.

Then there were the blacks. The Black Power movement of the sixties, intended to give blacks a more powerful sense of identity, had, in the absence of real social improvement, succeeded merely in moving whites and blacks even farther away from each other. Encapsulated among themselves (in direct relation to how poor they were), the blacks were now divided between a bare majority who worked and a socially unassimilable minority who did not. Legions of black youth were marooned in hopelessness, rage at how the rich grew obscenely rich during the eighties, and self-pity. If there was a fair possibility that black people were more sensual than white people, then the corollary was that they suffered poverty more. Sensual people who are poor can drown in self-pity as they dream of how much real pleasure they could enjoy if they had money. It is a point of view that will draw you to the luminous inner life of drugs. Afterward, the luminosity used up, the habit keeps one chasing the high through crime, for crime is not only quick money but the heady rewards of risk, at least when risk is successful. Prison, the unsuccessful consequence, comes to be seen as a species of higher education. It is a way of life for young blacks that does not gear into the working black community, and it has nothing whatever to do with the working white community. The Democratic Party had a hole in its flank from the spearhead of this problem, and the Republican Party had a hole in its head. Republican thoughts on the subject had run out long ago.

Mailer had decided that America—no matter how much of it might still be generous, unexpected, and full of surprises—was nonetheless sliding into the first real stages of fascism. The Left, classically speaking, might be the most resolute defense against fascism, but what was the Left now able to contest? No part of it seemed able to cooperate effectively with any other part, nor was it signally ready to work with the Democratic Party for any set of claims but its own. The Democratic Party was bereft of vision and real indignation, and, given the essential austerity of the Christian ethic, the Republican Party was never wholly comfortable with the idea that Americans like themselves ought to be that rich. They grew more and more choleric about the blacks. Their unspoken solution became the righteous prescription: if those drug bastards won't work, throw them in jail.

Of course, the jails were another disaster system. The best of them were overcrowded, and there were no budgets for new prisons. If avalanches of new prisoners came along, the only place for them would be camps, guarded by the military.

This was merely a scenario, no more than one more doomsday scenario as long as the economy held. Money could still soothe some crucial margin of every American's exacerbated feelings. Let the river of money go dry, however, and what would hold the country together? There might be revolts in the ghetto, curfews in the inner cities, and martial law.

It was hard to believe that Bush or any other Republican or Democrat could offer a solution to the real problem, which was that standards of craftsmanship were deteriorating among the American workforce. Our consumer products were not as good as they used to be. The Germans and the Japanese made better cars and better toasters. Their best engineers were working in consumer industries, while ours were being hired by the military-industrial complex. Given the shoddy show, one could blame corporate packaging, advertising, and TV; one could blame hedonism and its hangovers; one could blame drugs, blacks, labor unions; one could blame the Pied Piper. It did not matter whom you blamed. It was multiple choice, and all of the answers might be correct. The fact was that America was mired in grievances, miseries, miscalculations, slave history, and obsessions; the economy was reflecting it.

In fact, Mailer was surprised by himself. Something deep in him—which is to say, no longer censorable—was now saying: "The country needs a purge, a fling, some sacrifice of blood, some waste of the blood of others, some colossal event, a triumph. We need an extravaganza to take us out of ourselves. We are Romans, finally, and there is no moral force left among our citizens to countermand that fact. So this war will be a crucial vacation from the morose state of American affairs. If it succeeds, the country may even be able to face a few real problems again."

It was, at least, a perspective. A nation's ego might be not unlike the human ego: when its view of itself was able to lift, there was more human energy available; yes, energy liberated itself best under the aegis of a happy ego. By that logic, America needed to win a war.

On the night in early March when George Bush delivered his victory speech to Congress, he was welcomed with an ovation that rivaled any outpouring of approval Ronald Reagan had received in the same Capitol building—which is no small remark. He had not only won the war, but accomplished it with an astonishingly small loss of American life—a double victory for Bush. When it came to the sacrifice of one's own countrymen, the president was also a liberal. He had merely altered the slogan to "Virtually no blood for oil," and there was no more talk of tens of thousands of body bags having been ordered by the Pentagon.

The same could not be said, of course, for the opponent. There were no reliable figures for killed in action among the Iraqis; they may have lost twenty-five thousand, or was it twice that figure? In forty-two days, 88,500 tons of bombs and missiles were dropped or released by U.S. forces, a figure that does not include the combat sorties of the rest of the coalition nor U.S. and allied artillery. The overall tonnage then, one would estimate, came to well over 100,000 tons, more than enough to pulverize the will to fight of the Iraqi soldiers. Saddam Hussein's mother of all battles had been reduced to the child of submission. Those of his planes which had managed to fly flew, in large part, to Iran; his tanks were buried deep in sand, yet not deep enough. Heat-seeking missiles blew them up (since metal, it was quickly discovered, held the heat of the desert sun longer at night than the desert that covered it). A considerable portion of his Republican Guards, however, had never been committed to battle and so remained more or less intact for the family of battles that was going to take place in Iraq after the war. George Bush had taken the decision to accept a cease-fire before all of Iraq was left helpless. After all, what would there be in Baghdad then to oppose Iran? Iran in control of an Iraq without Saddam Hussein weighed in the balance as a heavier prospect for America than Saddam still in power with but one lung left.

So, of course, there were ironies. A war without ironies searing enough to brand one's moral flesh is not a real war. The triumph in the Gulf may in time be characterized by military historians as the massively prepared campaign that turned out to be no more than a technical run-through for war. One mighty coalition executing a brilliant military plan encountered no more than a desert horizon of prisoners who had been waiting for weeks to surrender. A technological Leviathan had overcome a magician of metaphors.

Other ironies followed. We had liberated Kuwait, but it was ecologically mutilated. The restoration during daylight hours of blue sky for black sky was going to cost a fortune—would it prove to be as large as the disbursements on the war itself? Sea life in the Gulf might or might not recover from that oil spill seven or eight times greater than the *Exxon Valdez* disaster. The metaphors of the dark poet had proved dark indeed. Vastly less massive than Hitler on the historic scale, Saddam had been ready nonetheless to revenge himself on the God who had not supported him; Saddam waged fire and destruction against nature. He would pull down the walls of the oil temple. In disaster, Saddam would be awesome. No one inhabiting Kuwait over the next few years would be able to cease thinking of his active vengeance, present in every acrid breath. The wrath of hell was in one's lungs.

It had taken seven months of sleeping through nightmares for

young American soldiers to find a balance between their morale
and their fears. The stiffening of their resolve to be ready to die
had turned out in the end to be no more than a gargantuan
poker bluff. They may have felt not unequal to those American
athletes training for the Olympic Games in 1980, who could not
go to Moscow because the Russians had invaded Afghanistan.
The Gulf soldiers were now going to live with obsession: What
would I have been like in combat if it had turned out to be as bad
as the minefields, the burning ditches, the barbed wire, and the
fields of fire that I contemplated in my dreams?

That was an obsession to live with for the rest of one's life.
After all, many of these American soldiers had been obliged to
put the will to fight together out of no more than a tautology of
truisms: we've got to get the job done so we can all go home. If
they found any higher moral sanction, it doubtless came from
admiring the will to work under excruciating conditions that
characterizes line play in the National Football League.

Of course, the soldiers seen on television had been carefully
chosen for blandness of affect. This was one campaign the military was not going to lose to the press. So the most interesting
war in two decades for Americans was obliged to wag along on
TV with talking heads and zoom-aways of fighter planes taking
off into the wild-rose yonder of the desert at evening. The Pentagon was the producer of this entertainment, and its ranks were
composed of solemn people. They were no part of that consumer economy, now as subtly sleazy as all the half-rented suburban malls; no, the military had not acquired most of the best
engineering minds for the last two decades, and then brooded
like serious men upon their own faults and shortcomings in Vietnam (first of which was that they had been too obliging to the
press), to make the same mistakes again; no, the consumer economy might not show the happiest comparison with the Germans
and the Japanese, but the military was prepared to prove that it
was now, by far, the finest fighting force on earth.

Military men live within life-missions of pride. Since their activities take place inside the enclaves of national security, part of
their ethic is to suffer in silence. Silently, the Pentagon had un-

dergone the ravages of congressional investigation into why it spent $600 on a toilet seat for one airplane and $1,600 on a wrench for another; the military had had to live with the general public cognition that the B-2 Stealth bomber was a monumentally expensive disappointment. All the while, the generals were obliged to keep silent with the knowledge that if all else in America might be getting worse, they were getting better.

How could George Bush not turn them loose? They were what we had to show for the Reagan years. From 1980 to 1988, the Pied Piper had spent $2.1 trillion on the military—which is four times the amount of the S&L scandal. Maybe we couldn't make cars and toasters anymore, but we had forced the Russians to spend, over these same eight years, $2.3 trillion, $200 billion more than ourselves, and the Soviets couldn't afford it at all. They couldn't even make decent soap.

The military, wounded by the shame of Vietnam and fortified by the budget, had become a superior fighting force as a corollary to the main Reagan strategy, which had been to wreck the Russians economically. In that, we succeeded, but at the cost of handing over economic hegemony in the world to Germany and Japan while we enlarged the list of our unsolvable crises in the cities.

Now that the Soviet Union had folded as a foe, all we had to show was the state-of-the-art strengths of our forces. So George Bush used them the first chance he had. The technological display was full of stardust. The F-117A Stealth fighter with its laser-guided bombs hit 95 percent of its targets. In numbers, it was only 2.5 percent of the U.S. aircraft, but it managed to account for 31 percent of the successful hits on its first day. Endless nuggets of such sparkling statistics were now floating about in the vitreous fluid of the media. Yes, the air war, discounting delays from bad weather and ignoring all lack of opposition, had been a massive success; the deep, if natural, fear of the Bush administration and the Pentagon that the ground troops might not be well motivated enough to fight the Iraqis did not have to be tested. George Bush had gone up to the great dentist in the sky, but none of his teeth had been pulled. We had probably dumped

some amount like 200 million pounds of explosive on Iraq and
Kuwait, and that came down to 10 pounds virtually per person
for all of 21 million people. Of course, the bombs and rockets
had not been directed against people, but all the same, the Pentagon was not releasing the figures. Those tonnages could yet
take on the long shadows of overkill. The country preferred instead to enjoy the victory.

In an appearance before state legislators at the White House
in March, George Bush went so far as to suggest that the ghosts
of Vietnam had been exorcised, and the shame of the past had
been overcome. The misery of losing a war to a Third World
power could be forgotten. Our great win in the Gulf could replace our obsession with Southeast Asia.

George Bush, however, might encounter some subtle troubles
with his thesis in time to come. If the nation was going to enjoy
the fruits of victory, which is to say a strengthening of the national ego that, one hoped, would be able to produce a new vigor
for tackling our problems, then maybe the war in Vietnam ought
not to be exorcised so quickly. The president was, after all, getting into the same slough of muddy reasoning as the liberals.
They had decided in advance that the Gulf War was a repetition
of Vietnam, and that had been a perfect example of American
thinking at its most simplistic. Now the Bush administration was
going to run with the same errors around the other end of the
ideological line. When you got down to it, the only similarity
between the two wars was that America had been in both of
them. One, after all, had been combat waged in the jungle, and
the canopy offered concealment to ground troops from planes
and much-restricted access to tanks. Soldiers encountered one
another face-to-face in deep shadows. In the Gulf, war had been
fought in the open vistas of the desert against a mad poet who
was hated by all too many of his own troops. In Vietnam, we were
allied against a people ready to die for a leader who not only
looked like a saint but embodied the travails of a long-delayed
liberation. He offered the idea that their deaths would not be in
vain, and that a more humane world would follow for their children. The Democrats had kept the war in Southeast Asia going

eight years beyond its time, and then Nixon kept it going for another six, and by the time we left Saigon, there was no future left for anyone over there. Two million Vietnamese had been killed, and the cadres of power-for-its-own-sake filled the gap. More than a million new deaths would follow in Cambodia, and oppression was everywhere.

Of course, we had a bad conscience concerning Vietnam. It was part of the national honor to remind ourselves that we, a great and democratic nation, had been capable of monstrous deeds. It revealed to us that America might never come to maturity, nor develop a culture rich enough and sufficiently resonant to counterbalance our technology. No, we might end as computer hacks and body louts—the last superlouts in the history of the world—but if we had a national conscience, and it would yet prevail, then we were obliged to live with Vietnam and keep measuring the cost. Bury the ghosts of that war too soon and the last irony of the desert sands would be released. That great news machine, which eats our history as fast as it is created, might even move so fast that our power to enjoy the success of the war in the Gulf could also be covered over prematurely and we could lose whatever good it was going to do our long-bruised view of ourselves. While it was a war that might yet make a difference for good or for ill in the tangled nests of the Middle East, it might also turn out to be no more than its own weight, a military exercise on a colossal level, panoramas of technical virtuosity in a moral thicket, and if that was all it was, then the news machine would damn sure eat it. The memory of Vietnam, however, is not going to disappear. Vietnam is embedded in our moral history.

Of course, before the Gulf War can even show a tendency to disappear, our commander in chief is going to bring it back. George Bush has promised to remind us of its existence and what we owe the people who fought in it. He will have a special celebration for our returning veterans as soon as this coming Fourth of July.

On that occasion, he will remind us of his war. He will. He will.

By Heaven Inspired

(1992)

ONCE AN AGREEABLE TEXAS TOWN, Houston had expanded so prodigiously since the Second World War that one could now think of
it as a gargantuan humanoid in a special effects movie (after the
humanoid has been dismembered by a magnum ray-gun wielded
by Arnold Schwarzenegger). Modern Houston sprawls over the
nappy carpet of Texas soil in shreds, bones, nerves, and holes, a
charred skeleton with an eye retained here, and there a pros-
thetic hand still smoking.

The megacity is, of course, not burned out; rather it is not yet
built. Except in parts. The parts are often called edge-cities, clusters of modern office buildings thirty or forty stories high with
nothing much around them. Five miles away, like an amputated
elbow of the humanoid, one can find another cluster of tall corporate structures in mirrored glass. Between one edge-city and
another, there are, occasionally, funky streets of old cottages or
middle-aged ranch houses to remind one of the more modest
homeowner passions that once belonged to the West; often these
streets come to an end by polluted creeks, or peter out on a
country road that will cross a rail track to run eventually next to
one or another elevated highway that races on into another

edge-city. Thirty-six by thirty-eight miles in dimension, fourth-largest urban center in the United States (never crowded except on superhighways), its pride is its absence of form. You can virtually find a nose on the hip bone, an ear on the navel, and all the eyes you would ever want in the blue-gray and gray-green mirrored walls of all those edge-city thirty-story glass phalluses with their corporate hubris pointing up into the muggy Texas sky. So it was a city fit for Republicans in August, since, like the GOP mind, it had never had any other sense of the whole than how to win elections.

This convention year, however, the Republicans could hardly take in what had happened to them. Under Reagan and Bush, they had, by their lights, produced gouts of great and phenomenal history, had ended the threat of nuclear war; now all too many Americans did not seem to care about such achievement, and lately they had been trashed by the Democrats. In consequence, they were as mad as a hive of bees just kicked over. Mary Matalin, the party press chief, had described the Democratic campaign as "lower than a snake's belly," an opening gun. "Those characters belong in the outhouse, not the White House" was but another of the shots fired at the first session of the convention as speaker after speaker with relatively minor credentials came fulminating to the podium.

It was an odd morning. The floor of a convention offers intensities of mood comparable to the stirring of a beast, but in these first hours, the animal looked too comatose to stir. It was an opportunity, therefore, to study the two-thousand-plus delegates and two-thousand-plus alternates at 10 A.M., hung over and/or depressed, their faces formed in the main (given much anal and oral rectitude) around the power to bite. Leading an honest hardworking responsible life, at work from nine to five over the middle decades of one's life, can pinch the mouth into bitterness at the laziness and license of others. If one had been a convict up for parole, one would not be happy encountering these faces across the table. Imagination had long surrendered its ghost to principles, determined and predetermined principles.

On the other hand, who had ever said that parole board offi-

cers were ideally equipped to run the country? Republicans sitting in their orderly rows of folding chairs, the aisles considerably
wider than the cramped turns on the floor of Madison Square
Garden, the Astrodome ceiling much higher, the vast floor lavishly carpeted, were a sullen, slow-to-settle audience. They did
not listen to the minor speakers—one rarely did unless he was
from one's home state—but they applauded moderately on cue,
and tried to contemplate the problems of the change that might
be in the air. The only speaker to wake them up all morning was
Alan Keyes, a dynamic black man running for the Senate in
Maryland. The Democrats, he asserted, had brought the poor to
a pass where they were "trapped in welfare slavery. It does what
the old slavery never could. It kills the spirit." So Keyes received
a standing ovation, but it was a lonely event in a congealed opening morning void of other excitement.

By the time of the evening session, however, the mood had
altered completely. Two events had intervened. George Bush
had come to town that afternoon, and earlier there had been a
jam-packed meeting at a "God and Country" rally at the Sheraton Astrodome across the street from the convention arena. Inside, in the Sam Houston Ballroom of the Sheraton, a
medium-sized hotel chamber with no significant decorations
other than a very large American flag, a small stage, and a podium, a crowd of delegates, evangelists, and fundamentalist congregations estimated as high as two thousand people were
standing with a remarkable display of patience as various speakers came up to promise the appearance of other speakers, and
singers performed, notably Pat Boone wearing a cream-colored
suit. The air was celebratory—the executive director of the Christian Coalition told the crowd in the happiest tones: "Within the
past hour, the Republican Party passed a pro-life, pro-family platform! We are here to celebrate a victory. The feminists threw everything they had at us, and they lost!"

The assembled were healthy-looking people in the main, with
a tendency, given the augmentations of marriage, to put on
weight, and a great many young fathers and mothers were holding infants in their arms, the parents cleanly dressed with domi-

ciled haircuts, fresh-washed faces perspiring now, not a
bad-looking group except for the intellectual torpor that weighed
on the enthusiasm of the room. The assembled bore resemblance to those faces one sees among daytime TV audiences, the
minds graceless, the eyes blank, the process of thought as slack-
jawed as chewing gum before the complexity of things. If they
were pro-life, and they were, it was because, whatever valid and
sincere reasons were present, they were also being furnished
with an intellectual rock; God—as the Republican platform they
had participated in shaping now told them—was present in every
pregnancy. "We believe the unborn child has a fundamental individual right to life which cannot be infringed. We therefore
reaffirm our support for a human life amendment to the Constitution, and we endorse legislation to make clear that the Fourteenth Amendment's protections apply to unborn children."
Pregnancy was an aspect of God's will and every embryo was
therefore a divine soul. A mighty certainty resided in this one
notion, enough to make abortion illegal again; indeed, they
called for a constitutional amendment to codify it as a crime of
murder. The consequences, if carried to legal conclusion, could
conceivably jail 1.5 million women a year (as well as hundreds of
thousands of doctors, nurses, and midwives), since such was the
number of abortions a year, but then the prohibitive logic of
these numbers could never prevail against their other knowledge.

"I think," said Sylvia Hellman, a member of the Christian Coalition from Dallas, to David Von Drehle of *The Washington Post,*
"that the media are actually good people who want to do good,
but they go at it from the human perspective, not God's."

She was a lady who could still present a hint of lavender from
that lost era before deodorant, dungarees, air-conditioning, and
parking-lot asphalt malls had come to America, and she added,
"In the Bible, which conservative Christians take literally, there
are rules to live by. Sometimes the rules demand that we do
things that don't make sense to us, but we find out later they are
best."

It would have taken a brutal turn of intellect to suggest to her faith that there were men and women who thought the Devil might have as much purchase on the sexual act as God, and, if so, then many a young girl with an unwanted pregnancy might feel that she possessed a devil in her heart, or was it the Devil she was bearing in her womb? By such livid light, the murder of an ogre within one might seem less unholy than encouraging such a presence to appear and deaden others in small measure daily by words and ugly deeds. The calculus of gestation is as much a moral labyrinth as the food chains of nature, but that is not a thought to propose to those who have found their piece of the eternal parchment. As Richard Bond, the Republican National Committee chairman (once George Bush's job), said to Maria Shriver, "We are America. These other people are not America."

Since nearly all two thousand people in the Sam Houston Ballroom were obliged to stand, not only visibility was limited at the rear, but audibility as well. One could hardly hear the Reverend Pat Robertson, presidential candidate in the Republican primaries of 1988, as he introduced Dan Quayle, but some words were more distinct than others, and the vice president, despite the towering religiosity of the hundreds of heads between, was heard to say, "It is a pleasure to be with people who are the real America." No need to describe the cheers. "I don't care what the media say. I don't care what the critics say. I will never back down." He would repeat that sentiment several times in days to come, and was always clean-shaven as he said it. Dan Quayle might have his slips of tongue and occasional misalignment of facts or letters, but one could not conceive of him ever missing a single hair when he shaved.

"Well," Pat Robertson had remarked earlier, "this is a resurrection here today," and it is true that nearly all of God's minions had been on their feet and unable to move for close to two hours: that had proved more impressive than the rhetoric. Robertson was, by now, quietly celebrated among the liberal media for the appearance of a fund-raising letter in which he had declared that the feminist movement "encourages women to leave their husbands, kill their children, practice witchcraft, destroy capitalism, and become lesbians." He had a cherubic face, and he beamed forth a good, warm, nonsexual Christian vitality with every smile and gesture. Perhaps he did not realize that his abusive language was calculated to drive feminists a little further into the precise roles he had cataloged.

George Bush arrived in Houston a little later and hastened to the American Spirit Pavilion, now the name for the born-again Astroarena, a ministadium and shopping center on one of the flanks of the Astrodome. There, before a crowd of fifteen thousand media, delegates, Astroarena mall shoppers, and assorted guests, he laid into his problems with a squire's wrath. This was no longer the George Bush who vomited at a Japanese state dinner, or suffered a paucity of thyroid from Graves' disease, or was loved by Americans less than they loved his wife—not at all the George Bush who failed to knock out old Sad-damn, or had to patty-cake with the religious right and be bollixed by abortion and AIDS and have to listen to the interminable inner-party debates whether to deep-six Dan Quayle, certainly not the George Bush who was asked to solve the economy when none of his economists had a clue how to begin without getting into Democratic Party measures (such as more federal spending). Put it that he had one problem larger than all the others: the cold war was over. Could one begin to measure how much George Bush owed the cold war?

These were endemic concerns as worrisome (in the pit of nocturnal reflection) as the chronic concerns of any responsible householder in his late sixties. But George Bush was not the man to sink into the natural pessimism of his condition. He did stand up for one idea, after all, and it was named George Bush. Neither the spirit of wisdom nor of insight, he was the soul of Waspitude, one man of the gentry born to fight. He could hear the clash of armor when crusaders met Saracens; he had his own taproot into the universe of guts, a soldier's bowels, a knight of embattlement. Of all the misperceptions of the liberal media (and they were legion!), none was so unfounded as the still-prevailing notion that he was a wimp.

Problems passed, worries ceased. Combat was the medicine beneath all other prescriptions. If George Bush stood for one

political idea other than himself, it was that America loved a
fighter, and if you could maneuver the other elements, by whatever means (which did not preclude kicking your opposite number in the nuts), why, brother, the electorate would vote for the
warrior every time.

So George Bush came to the podium of the American Spirit
Pavilion, and in that auditorium, with fifteen thousand supporters there to listen and whoop, he started with the reinstallation
of Dan Quayle.

It was part of his strategy. Perhaps it was the most honorable
part. If every poll had shown that Quayle was a liability fast approaching the drag of a sea anchor, if most of George's advisers
had all but begged him to take on a new dynamite vice president like Jack Kemp or Jim Baker or Cheney or Powell or
Schwarzkopf, or even Bill Bennett if you had to keep your conservatives happy, Bush consulted his own psychology. All things
being more or less equal, Americans not only loved a battler,
but they adored a warrior faithful to his own troops. If he was
to overcome the foe, how much more happiness he would find
in victory, and how much more virtue (an indispensable companion was virtue) if he kept Quayle with him. The essence of
noblesse oblige (which God knows you could not lose sight of
no matter what other options had to be picked up) was to do it
the hard way.

So he filled the sound of the word "Quayle" with whalebone.

Four years ago, Dan Quayle and I teamed up and I told
him then, speaking from some personal experience,
that the job of vice president was a real character builder,
and I was not exaggerating. But look, this guy stood
there and in the face of those unfair critics he never
wavered. And he simply told the truth and let the chips
fall where they may. And he said we need families to
stick together and fathers to stick around, and he is
right.

So when the establishment in Washington hears
about this, they get all uptight about it, about him; they

gripe about it—but folks in the real world understand, and they nod their head, and he has been a super vice president and he will be for another four years.

This was George right off the cuff, and his minutes at the po-dium turned into an event. The convention came to life. Our president was no longer wan, defensive, and intrinsically con-fined by abortion, health care, AIDS, drugs, and Saddamn still alive, not to speak of the economy (that subtly nauseated off-beat stomach of the nation); no, this was the George who could win any battle against any Democratic foe any time because he knew the American people and what they cared about and what they laughed about. It was autointoxication for sure, but then mountains are climbed by just these will-to-win guys.

I couldn't help but notice an interview my opponent gave to the *USA Today* last week. It was absolutely incred-ible. . . . He talked about how he's already planning his transition, figuring out who should be deputy assistant undersecretary in every Washington agency . . . and I half expected, when I went over to the Oval Office, to find him over there measuring the drapes. Well, let me say as the first shot out of the barrel, I have a message for him. Put those drapes on hold; it is going to be cur-tain time for that ticket. And I mean it.

Yes, curtains. The other guy played the saxophone, and every-one knows what that instrument is attempting to convey. It's just a blither-blather of illicit sex and farts.

For nine months the other side has had a one-way con-versation with the American people and now it's our turn—and they have called our great country a mockery and sounded the saxophone of change, and that sound sure sounds familiar. They say they want to shake up Washington, but they oppose limiting the terms of con-gressmen and that's a change, just changing the subject.

By evening, back in the Astrodome, the same delegates who had sat in despond all morning were ready for fun and more oratorical brimstone. The word was out. The president believed he could win. So the Astrodome was quick with laughter at each assault on Bill Clinton. "You know something," said Kay Bailey Hutchison, state treasurer of Texas, a tall handsome lady with a humorous scorn in her voice reminiscent of Ann Richards, governor of Texas, as she spoke of Bill Clinton, "I think he did inhale." The delegates took vastly to that idea.

Then came Senator Alan K. Simpson from Wyoming, mean as rawhide, lantern-jawed as Popeye. His manner suggested the serious pleasure to be found in tapping into the jugular; the delegates confirmed his premise. Simpson would remind America that Clinton's only reason for not fleeing America while the war in Vietnam happened to be on was that he did not wish to lose his "political viability." Contumely rested in those two words. "How many other times," jeered Simpson, "did you sell your political soul to maintain your political viability? . . . How are you going to pay the bill, Bill?"

Then came the first large event on Monday night in the Astrodome—Pat Buchanan's speech. Trounced repeatedly in the Republican primaries by Bush, having to contend with the full weight of the Republican establishment in state after state, and succeeding nowhere after the early good showing in New Hampshire, Buchanan had managed nonetheless to amass three million votes. Half of them must have been as hard-core in their conservatism as Buchanan himself. Since he had also brought a heart attack on himself following such expenditures of energy, Buchanan could speak with the gravitas gained from reconnoitering early mortality.

Unlike the majority of speakers who strode up to the pale and massive podium of the Astrodome only to be overwhelmed by the caverns and hollows of volume in that huge and amplified space, he did not get into the trap of bellowing out his lines. Most speakers had a tendency to exercise hortatory rights—to yell louder as one lost more and more of one's audience. So they sounded cranky as their applause lines failed to elicit large response. All bad orations, whether by actors or politicians, have this in common: the speaker becomes exactly equal to his text—there is no human space between, no subtext to give resonance to the difference between the person and what he is saying.

Buchanan possessed a good deal of subtext. He was pleasant-faced and, in the beginning, mild-voiced, and no audience can fail to hang on every word of a killer speaker when he is pleasant-faced. So they took in each phrase and cheered with happiness at nearly every applause line. Patrick Buchanan was off to a fine start.

> Like many of you last month, I watched that giant masquerade ball at Madison Square Garden where twenty thousand radicals and liberals came dressed up as moderates and centrists—in the greatest single exhibition of cross-dressing in American political history.

The convention was happy enough by now to reveal a curious side of itself. Conservatives might form the vitally motivated core, but these delegates were a far cry from the conservatives of 1964, who had been a group so openly hostile toward the media that after the first day, many a reporter did not venture out again onto the hate-filled floor of the Cow Palace in San Francisco.

Now, however, it was more like a TV game. The delegates booed references to the media with grins, not scowls. They were part of a TV audience, after all; you grin, you do not scowl. Besides, they were curious—these were real media people of the sort you can see asking questions on TV. To be around them, therefore, was to be anointed into the other church, the new fold, television.

Indeed, not until Buchanan began to talk about Hillary Clinton did an ugly underside to his speech begin to emerge:

> Elect me, and you get two for the price of one, Mr. Clinton says of his lawyer-spouse. And what does Hillary believe? Well, Hillary believes that twelve-year-olds should

have a right to sue their parents, and she has compared marriage as an institution to slavery—and life on an Indian reservation. Well, speak for yourself, Hillary.

We can allow her to do that. In 1979 she wrote the article to which Buchanan was referring. Here is the passage:

Decisions about motherhood and abortion, schooling, cosmetic surgery, treatment of venereal disease, or employment, and others [which] will significantly affect the child's future should not be made unilaterally by parents. Children should have a right to be permitted to decide their own future if they are competent. . . . In all but the most extreme cases, such questions should be resolved by the families, not the courts. . . . I prefer that intervention . . . should he limited to decisions that could have long-term and possibly irreparable effects if they were not resolved.

Buchanan, having paused for the cheers he received, went on with the attack.

George Bush was seventeen when they bombed Pearl Harbor. He left his high school class, walked down to the recruiting office, and signed up to become the youngest fighter pilot in the Pacific War. And Mr. Clinton? When Bill Clinton's turn came in Vietnam, he sat up in a dormitory in Oxford, England, and figured out how to dodge the draft. Which of these two men has won the moral authority to call on Americans to put their lives at risk? I suggest, respectfully, it is the patriot and war hero, Navy Lt. JG George Herbert Walker Bush.

By his own scale of measure, Buchanan also lacked moral authority. He, too, had not served in the Armed Forces. Nonetheless, Buchanan had inner sanction. He laid down a gauntlet:

My friends, this election is about much more than who
gets what. It is about what we believe, what we stand for
as Americans. There is a religious war going on for the
soul of America. It is a cultural war, as critical to the
kind of nation we will one day be—as was the cold war
itself.

If he had kept to that, one could have applauded him from
across the cultural divide, for he had performed the obligatory
task of the serious politician—he had defined the nature of the
conflict. The fact that his voice had begun to wear down into a
hoarse whisper made him only more effective in his peroration.
Each of his words now seemed to insist on a private physical toll;
so suffering, he spoke to a sentiment that no other politician of
either party would have dared to come close to uttering in public:

Friends, in these wonderful twenty-five weeks [of cam-
paigning] the saddest days were the days of the bloody
riot in L.A., worst in our history. But even out of that
awful tragedy can come a message of hope.

Hours after the violence ended I visited the Army
compound in south L.A. where an officer of the 18th
Cavalry that had come to rescue the city introduced me
to two of his troopers. They could not have been twenty
years old. He told them to recount their story.

They had come into Los Angeles late on the second
day; and they walked up a dark street where a mob had
looted and burned every building but one, a convalescent home for the aged. The mob was heading in to
ransack and loot the apartments of the terrified old
men and women. When the troopers arrived, M-16s at
the ready, the mob threatened and cursed, but the mob
retreated. It had met the one thing that could stop it:
force, rooted in justice, backed by courage.

Greater love than this no man hath than that he lay
down his life for his friend. Here were nineteen-year-old

boys ready to lay down their lives to stop a mob from molesting old people they did not even know. And as they took back the streets of Los Angeles block by block, so we must take back our cities, and take back our culture, and take back our country.

God bless you, and God bless America.

The public relations successes of Grenada and Panama must have emboldened Buchanan to believe that when it came down to it, Americans would concern themselves no more over the demolition of Harlem than with the disruption of any other Third World or Caribbean country. So, he was drawing his own line in the sand. If it took martial law, barbed wire, camps of detention, and Pentagon management of the media, then, by God, fellow Republicans, is that not a comfortable price to pay for walking carefree again on the street? The temptation would go deep for many an American. Would one care to see the results of a confidential poll on just this point? Inner-city unrest, however, would hardly be solved by his solution. For a religious man, Buchanan did not seem to comprehend that freedom which is obtained for a majority by amputating the rights of a minority leaves a slough of bad conscience, and so offers no more balance to heaven than to the streets.

Besides, his facts were off. The black and angry mob in South Central Los Angeles had not been about to attack the old black folks' home: no, as the Associated Press reported it, the National Guard had been slow to arrive. Following Buchanan on Monday night would come Ronald Reagan. With a few cuts, his text could have been delivered by many a senior Democratic statesman (if, indeed, there are any left besides Jimmy Carter). It was as if Reagan was looking to attain the eminence that is above politics.

In my life's journey over these past eight decades, I have seen the human race through a period of unparalleled tumult and triumph. I have seen the birth of Communism and the death of Communism. I have witnessed the bloody futility of two world wars, Korea, Vietnam,

and the Persian Gulf. I have seen television grow from a
parlor novelty to become the most powerful vehicle of
communication in history. As a boy I saw streets filled
with model-Ts; as a man I have met men who walked on
the moon . . .

Yet tonight is not a time to look backward. For while
I take inspiration from the past, like most Americans I
live for the future. So this evening, for just a few minutes, I hope you will let me talk about a country that is
forever young. This powerful sense of energy has made
America synonymous for opportunity the world over.
And after generations of struggle, America is the moral
force that defeated Communism and all those who
would put the human soul itself into bondage.

So it went. He gave credit to the Republicans for ending the
cold war: he chided the Democrats. "Our liberal friends," he
called them. What got liberals most upset were "two simple
words: Evil Empire." Though Reagan's popularity was great in
this hall, it was smaller outside. He had spoken of the "Evil Empire" too often, and now we were left with the bill. Part of the
profound confusion that hung over the political atmosphere of
America this election year is that we had gotten ourselves in so
much debt under Ronald Reagan. If he had come into office
promising to cut taxes, balance the budget, and beef up the military so that it could defeat the Evil Empire, the dire fact was that
our debt had expanded from $1 trillion in the time of Jimmy
Carter to $4 trillion now ($4 trillion, we can remind ourselves, is
4 million separate sums of $1 million each); yes, the truth was he
had spent it not to fight, but to bankrupt the Russians. We did
not wage a holy war so much as a battle of U.S. versus Soviet
military disbursements, and it had been needless. Once, under
Stalin, the USSR had been a charnel house for human rights,
but the monstrosities of the '50s had ebbed by the '70s into a
dull and daily oppression, a moribund economy, a corrupt bu-
reaucracy, a cynical leadership, and no capacity whatever, no
matter how large the vastly inefficient Soviet armies, to succeed

at world conquest. By 1980, when Ronald Reagan came to presidential office, the Evil Empire had been reduced to an immense Third World collection of backward nations incapable of defeating even one other Third World country like Afghanistan. So we had spent our trillions in the holy crusade of a Pentagon buildup against an enemy whose psychic and economic wherewithal was already collapsed within, and had pursued Communism into little countries, and wrecked their jerry-built tropical economies even as we were wearing out what was left of the Soviets', but it all cost us twenty times more than it had to. Our grandchildren would pay the bill.

The American public, however, had been as attracted to Reagan's scenarios as he was. So our vision of an Evil Empire did not vanish altogether until the fall of Communism itself. Then the fraud was out. Evil Empires, like dragons, slaughter millions in their last throes, but Eastern Europe and the Soviet Union went over to capitalism peacefully. Blood did not run in the streets. Caught in the middle of a long sleep, the American mind began to ask itself: Were we taken? Had there been, for a long time, something phony about the cold war? It might be that Ronald Reagan was the last person in America to realize that he had not won such a conflict, but had merely extended it.

With the conclusion of Reagan's speech, the first convention evening came to a close, and Bush's strategy could begin to be seen. In all of this long day with its double session, Clinton had been attacked scores of times, the nation had been celebrated, the Bush administration had been glorified, pro-life had been affirmed, and legal abortion denied. That conservative movement which had sought to get the government off the backs of the American people had now put its foot into the womb of the American woman. Yet, with all the rhetoric, not a new word, nor a new idea, had been brought forth on the economy. The overall strategy was clear. In court, if you have a weak case and can argue neither the facts nor the law, dedicate yourself to arousing the emotions of the jury.

If Clinton was going to base his campaign on improving the weak state of the economy, which certainly handed him the facts, then Bush would look to dig deep into the mother lode of American politics—patriotism. Since the Republicans had been mining such ore since the Second World War, the question was whether the vein had been played out. All the same, Bush could only try. What with his hardest campaign workers coming from the religious right, he could hardly debate in the center; his would have to be the war between the Patriots and the Bureaucratic Managers, between the warriors and the hedonists (read: faggots, feminists, lawyers, media).

In preparation, therefore, the president dropped in Tuesday morning at the Hamilton Middle School to observe a class of students who were giving a karate demonstration. In honor of the occasion, Chuck Norris, founder of "Kick Drugs Out of America" and the martial arts virtuoso of numberless blood-drenched films, a quiet, gentle fellow, Chuck Norris—he could afford to be!— presented a white karate jacket and an honorary black belt to the president who in turn called Chuck a "point of light." One down, 999 to go!

That Tuesday night at the convention, Newt Gingrich, the House minority whip who had exposed the House Bank scandal (and had then been embarrassed by the number, twenty-two, of his own overdrawn checks), was up at the podium declaring that the Democrats were trying to sell America "a multicultural nihilistic hedonism that is inherently destructive of a healthy society." He had his backing. On cue, delegates were holding up placards that read "If Hillary can't trust him, how can we?" and a marijuana leaf showed up on a poster with the caption, "Bill Clinton's smoking gun."

Nonetheless, the strategy worked but minimally on the second night. Jack Kemp spoke with reasonable effectiveness and Phil Gramm put his audience to sleep with the keynote speech. The theme for the third day, Wednesday, was Family Values, and it was introduced in the Republican Gala at noon. Four thousand wealthy Republicans, paying $1,000 each, came to lunch at the George Brown Convention Center in Downtown Houston (largest edge-city of them all), and in the huge main room, as large as a football field, and therefore commodious enough for four

hundred tables, the gentry of Texas and a few country clubs beyond had congregated in support of the president and First
Lady, who, after notables had been seated at the dais, entered
the festivities in a mock railroad train called the American Eagle
Express, a black and gold behemoth of a toy locomotive about
the size of a large stagecoach. On the rear platform of the obser-
vation car it pulled were standing the Bushes and Quayles, and
in their wake walked the Secret Service, as alert on this occasion
as attack dogs. All considered, it was a hairy maneuver: the facsimile of a train choo-chooed and whistled gaily as it trundled
through the aisles along the luncheon floor, but it left the president and his wife wholly exposed as they smiled and nodded and
occasionally reached out to shake hands with friends on either
side.

Standing near the locomotive as it crawled by, one had a fair
look at Barbara Bush, who was immensely animated and appeared capable of taking in a formidable amount of information
at once. Her eyes scanned every face within ten feet of her, and
she did not miss a dear acquaintance or those who were at this
hour somewhat less than friends, the smallest movements of her
eyes and lips indicating a welcome across the gap, or a small reminder that things between were not altogether in order. To be-
stow warmth or display rectification in one's greetings suggests
command of that spectrum of recognition that usually belongs
to royals. On reflection, that was no surprise. Barbara Bush did
not look like a First Lady so much as like a woman who could be
Queen of England, and that did little for George standing beside
her, since his absolute trimness of figure, reminiscent of George
VI, could also bring to mind King George's older brother, the
former Prince of Wales, Edward, the old dear haunted poof who
married Wallis Simpson, although George Bush, God knows, was
no way a poof, but possessed the genuine steel (no matter how
he might be cursed with that mild face and mild voice, and—said
the Democrats—his mild brain!). Nonetheless, it was a moment
to recall—Barbara Bush, as the Queen of America, or, better yet,
our queen mother.

Entered the chow in chuck wagons, pushed along by teenagers in cowhand and cowgirl outfits, the boys leaning on the heavy wagons with all their strength, while the girls, obviously not liberated, were taking it easy. And the gathering of four thousand, whose least costly denominator when it came to dress was the Neiman-Marcus boutique, was delighted by such campy re-creation of chuck-wagon roots, but of course, as was true so often of Republican promises, the wagons were but symbols for the food to come; the real grub came out later, carried by other files of cowhands and cowgirls toting stacks of round plastic plates and plastic covers with fried chicken and fritters within.

After a series of short remarks offering thanksgiving to those who had brought off this $4 million fund-raiser, Dan Quayle got up to speak. It was interesting to see him in such a venue. Feeling himself among friends, he was relaxed and not unhumorous, much in contrast to his situation on Monday night at the Astrodome when he had sat in a guest box listening to Buchanan and Reagan while photographers never ceased clicking away. Under those circumstances, it had been possible to notice that a part of his unique appearance, always so off-putting in spite of his good looks, could be due to the fact that his head was strikingly small. He also looked waxlike, but indeed, under the circumstances, who would not? To be obliged to sit for ten or fifteen minutes, then another twenty minutes, and permit not one vague or errant expression to cross one's face on penalty of having it immortalized in the papers the next day, meant that he could neither smile nor groan sympathetically at what Buchanan or Reagan said, but had to content himself with a tasteful clapping of his hands for fear that any grin or grimace allowed to slip out would reveal some leering depth within. If he had not been the epitome of a rich man's son, or, in his case, grandson, a simulacrum for president of the wealthiest house on fraternity row, one could even have felt something like sympathy for him.

Bush came to the podium as a very large American flag was unrolled behind him, and he gave a short zippy set of remarks full of one-liners: "I think the train beats the bus," and "You're gonna love Barbara's speech tonight," or "I am proud and honored to have Dan Quayle on my side." He spoke of Clinton's drapes and George Bush's curtains for that minority who had not heard it before. He told the crowd that one out of two delegates at the Democratic convention was "on a government payroll." He also flattered his people:

> This is our last big convention, the last time—you might say—around the track. It is great to come back home to Texas, come home to where it really began for us in the political sense. The friends we made here and throughout our lives are the friends who are in this room—some from Texas, some elsewhere, every one of whom we owe a vote of gratitude to—friends who have stood by us when times are great and when times are tough. Now, we are about to embark on the fight of our life . . . and one thing that is the most comfort is that through good times and bad, I have had you at my side.

There was a photographers' platform erected fifteen feet above the floor and a hundred feet from the podium, and it was jammed with echelons of TV cameras, perhaps so many as forty or fifty; crowded in was a second host of still cameras. Out of this intensely compressed workforce, a voice shouted, "Bullshit!"

Later, the heckler was reported as saying, "What are you going to do about AIDS?" but that was later. The first muffled sound was "Bullshit," and everyone at the lunch froze for an instant as if everyone belonged again to one American family and was passing through the hour when Jack and Bobby Kennedy and Martin Luther King had been killed, and Ronald Reagan and Gerald Ford wounded and shot at. Like all families who put together a fragile composure after the death of someone who inhabited the center of the home and circle, it was as if the air went pale.

"Bullshit," came another voice, "what are you going to do about AIDS?" and by then, security was up on the platform manhandling the malefactors, who proved to be two wan young men with the telltale pallor of the disease, their hair cut in a punk-rock clump, and sores on their faces; now they were hustled down the stairs from the photographers' platform and out the exit.

Bush picked up his discourse, but he was shaken—how could he not be? The moment one will be assassinated must become one of the hundred entrenched expectations in every public leader's life—unlike other crises, there is not much to prepare for; the angle of attack is never known. In the aftermath, Bush started to make a sour joke—with all else, he felt sour—"This is a crazy year when they can get credentials for this," he muttered, but other voices started up on the photographers' platform ("What are you going to do about AIDS?"), and now several of the new hecklers—second wave of the plan—waved condoms at the boutique crowd there for lunch, and security whammed and slammed the second group of hecklers down from the platform and out of the room, while Bush came up fast with a few figures on what his administration was spending on AIDS—one cannot be a major politician without having a statistics tape in one's head—and then he added, the room now feeling at last restored, "In my line of work lately, this seems normal. If anyone else has anything they would like to say while we are all standing . . ."

He went on. He told his audience that he was working on his acceptance speech. "To be honest, I can tell you that I have a few butterflies . . . but you can count on this, I look forward to this fight. I can feel it building in my blood."

It was the presence of AIDS that would build in the Astrodome that night, however, and not far from everyone's blood. Mary Fisher, a slim, blond, and undeniably lovely young lady with a delicacy of feature and a poignancy of manner, proceeded to give the Republican address on AIDS not long after prime time commenced. If a casting director had searched for a fine actress unlikely ever to have contact with the virus, he would have selected Mary Fisher if she had been an actress, but she was not. She was in a rare category, a Republican princess; her father, Max Fisher, eighty-four years old and reputedly worth hundreds of millions of dollars, had been a major fund-raiser for the party since the early days of Richard Nixon. Mary Fisher could speak of Georgette and Robert Mosbacher and Gerald and Betty Ford as her friends; indeed, the women were weeping and the men were wiping their eyes as she spoke. Before she was done, the Astrodome floor would be awash. She was not only lovely, but innocent, after all; she had caught the disease from her ex-husband before they separated. Now presumably, she would die and have to say farewell to her sons Max and Zachary, four and two.

The Democratic convention had heard from a man and a woman, Elizabeth Glaser, who was HIV-positive, and Bob Hattoy, with AIDS, and their speeches had similarly affected the Democrats' convention. There had been accusations that not enough had been done by the Bush administration to fight against AIDS, and Bill Clinton had declared that such a fight would be one of the central issues in his campaign.

Mary Fisher was the Republican answer, then, to Democrats, and she was effective beyond measure. Outside their gates, across the bordering street beyond the Astrodome, in a weed-filled vacant lot now named the Astrodomain and renamed Queer Village by the protesters themselves, there had been a riot on Monday night. A half dozen arrests and a number of beatings had been handed out "professionally" by the police after a few of the one thousand protesters had put up effigies of George Bush, set them afire, and then had begun smashing wooden police barricades to feast the fire. The police had charged in on horse and foot and a helicopter shook the sky overhead as chants of doggerel came up from the protesters. "A hundred fifty thousand dead," they began, "Off with George Bush's head!" and "Burn, baby, burn!" They cried to the effigy, "We're queer and we're here." One protester announced, "This shows how far we mean to take our anger," but then the anger was as bottomless as the rage that victims feel against hurricanes and earthquakes. "We're all innocent. Do you want to see me die?" had shouted one AIDS activist to Senator Alfonse D'Amato in a Houston church when D'Amato made the mistake of remarking on the tragedy of AIDS when it took the lives of innocent children. "What about us?" someone shouted back. "We're also innocent and we're going to die."

Well, they were innocent or they were guilty. It was the intolerable and unspoken question at the heart of AIDS. Many a Republican was harboring ugly thoughts. AIDS, went the whisper,
stood for Anal Injection—Dirty Sex! Out in Oregon a movement
was commencing against the gay nation. The Oregon Citizens'
Alliance had sent out mass mailings that said, "Homosexual men
on average ingest the fecal material of twenty-three different
men per year," which, if a particularly roto-rooter way of stating
that the average homosexual had twenty-three lovers a year, also
posed the riddle of how the Oregon Citizens' Alliance ever obtained their statistic. But the anxiety of homosexuals, borne in
private for who knows how many centuries, was now inflamed by
the enigma of nature. Was excrement a side-product of nature,
offensive to some, as the Democrats would doubtless have argued, or was Satan in everyone's shit? Which, in turn, was a way
of saying that the Devil was present more often in homosexual
than in heterosexual encounters—exactly the question that
blazed on the divide. We are dying, said the victims of AIDS, and
you have no mercy. Are you cold to our pain because we are the
Devil's spawn?—beware, then, for we will haunt you. That was
the question. Was the gay nation guilty or innocent, victims or
devils, damned by Jehovah or to be comforted by Christ? Were
such acts shameful or natural? The wheel of obsessive and unan-
swerable questions went round and round, and gay rage came
up from the bottomless funnels of the vortex. Was their illness
for cause in a world of immutable principles? Or was it the absurdity of a badly designed natural system that had not provided for
safe sex short of the damnable deadhead odor of a condom?

What had happened to American politics? Like Mr. Magoo, it
teetered on the lip of ultimate peril—which is to say ultimate
questions—and all the while a blood rage had been building in
the nation. "If I am young and dying of AIDS," went the credo
that was forming, "then I might as well go down in flames." Yes,
the riots were building, and the forces of the right, equally inflamed by the more and more vivid presence of the gay nation,
were out to extirpate—so went the secret agenda—all human
flesh that carried such a virus. Scenarios were germinating on

the other side of that hill of time which is ten years away. Scenarios, we know, are rarely put into production by the cosmic forces who make the real films of our lives, but let us contemplate the Republicans in this pass—an enormous congregation of the conservative-minded, who can be enumerated as the greedy, the spiteful, the mean-spirited, in party congress with the sincere, the godly, the principled, and the tidy, all philosophically unsuited to contemplate the nightmare of a disease that is not amenable to medical science and may or may not have the deepest moral roots; yes, the Republicans were paralyzed before the obscene enigma of AIDS and so when Mary Fisher spoke like an angel that night, the floor was in tears, and conceivably the nation as well, for instead of the Evil Empire, so nicely manipulable by American might—we always held the aces—now we lived on the edge of uncontrollables we did not know how to stir against—drugs, crime, abortion, race, disease. How much, nearly half of the nation at least, must have longed for Buchananite solutions: how bewildered was each angry soul of the right that there was no retaking of the disease of AIDS block by city block.

Into this stew of choked passions and muffled fears (where a city was now defined as a place you would not enter until you knew where you would be able to park your car and ascend by elevator to your event), into this ongoing panic came Mary Fisher with a message so old that the coruscated souls of the Republicans, nine-tenths barnacled by now in greed and wealth, cant and bad conscience, fury and fear, began to weep in longing for the old memory of Christ kissing the feet of the poor. How contradictory are our conventions! At this one, the most moving message of the four days came from a Republican princess who had the Republicans bawling their hearts out at sentiments usually characterized by the L-word:

> Less than three months ago, at Platform Hearings in
> Salt Lake City, I asked the Republican Party to lift the
> shroud of silence which has been draped over the issue
> of my HIV/AIDS. I have come tonight to bring our si-
> lence to an end.

I bear a message of challenge, not self-congratulation. I want your attention, not your applause. I would never have asked to be HIV-positive. But I believe that in all things there is a purpose, and I stand before you and before the nation gladly.

Tonight I represent an AIDS community whose members have been reluctantly drafted from every segment of American society. Though I am white and a mother, I am one with a black infant struggling with tubes in a Philadelphia hospital. Though I am female, and contracted this disease in marriage, and enjoy the warm support of my family, I am one with the lonely gay man sheltering a flickering candle from the cold wind of his family's rejection. . . . We may take refuge in our stereotypes but we cannot hide there long. Because HIV asks only one thing of those it attacks: Are you human? And this is the right question. Are you human? Because people with HIV have not entered some alien state of being. They are human.

I want my children to know that their mother was not a victim. She was a messenger. I do not want them to think, as I once did, that courage is the absence of fear; I want them to know that courage is the strength to act wisely when most we are afraid. . . .

To my children I make this pledge; I will not give in, Zachary, because I draw my courage from you. Your silly giggle gives me hope. And I will not rest, Max, until I have done all I can do to make your world safe, I will seek a place where intimacy is not a prelude to suffering.

I will not hurry to leave you, my children, but when I go, I pray that you will not suffer shame on my account. To all within the sound of my voice, I appeal: Learn with me the lessons of history and of grace, so my children will not be afraid to say the word AIDS when I am gone. Then their children, and yours, may not need to whisper it at all. God bless the children, God bless us all—and good night.

Marilyn Quayle came next. Had the coordinators been wholly unready for the impact of Mary Fisher's speech and so had not foreseen what a powerful effect it would produce upon the mean-spirited not to be mean-spirited for a little while? Or did the convention organizers possess the wisdom to know that Marilyn Quayle was ready to appear at the podium after anyone— Gorbachev, Saint Peter, Madonna—she would not be cowed by those who came before. She had, after all, the insularity of a duchess, an insensitivity to her surroundings so monumental that it was almost attractive—one of a kind!

So she gave her little speech with absolute composure; the only sign that not everyone in herself was right there at home and listening came from her logo—that is, her horsy smile—that peculiarly self-intoxicated stretch of lips and protrusion of teeth that came and went to a rhythm that had next to nothing to do with what she said. Her words might be pious, or reflective, or she might even attempt to be funny, "If only Murphy Brown could meet Major Dad—what a story," but then the smile would come, on the beat, off the beat; it was like the reflex learned in childhood to hold off tears when one is being scolded.

Her language, however, was always correct. When it came to being politically correct—as a Bush Republican, that is—who could approach her? Her speech was seamless, and her espousal of Republican womanhood could not be improved, nor injured: it was there, flat as Indiana. "Watching and helping my children as they grow into good and loving teenagers is a source of daily joy for me."

On the other hand, she was not a duchess for too little. She had a nasal voice that could drill into clay, and given her disconnected smile, she could have been the president of a garden society, birdlike for all her horsiness, elevated above dross, and spacey as a space station. Let us say farewell while listening to her encomiums to the royal couple:

> Because leadership has everything to do with character
> and unwavering commitment to principle, Dan and I
> have been deeply honored to serve these four years with

President and Mrs. Bush. America loves Barbara Bush
because she exemplified our ideal of a strong and generous woman, dedicated to her husband, her children,
and her nation. She is a model for all generations, a
woman I am proud to call a friend and our nation is
proud to call First Lady.

To say that the appearance of Barbara Bush at the podium was
the second if not the first most important event of the convention is to miss the point. Barbara Bush was also the major gamble
of the Bush strategy. The economy, no matter what quantities of
pork barrel were going to be brought up from the hold to feed
electoral mouths in September and October, was going to remain a problem antipathetic to solution. One might as well roll
the dice then with Barbara Bush, and pump up the advantage
the Republicans held in family values. It was certainly a gamble.
If America reacted with the cry—jobs, not happy hearths—then
the election could be lost. On the other hand, Barbara Bush was
the only exceptional card they had to play, and one could find a
logic to the bet—patriotism, the flag, and the family were, after
all, the values taught in elementary schools (even if they were
public schools), whereas politics only commenced (if it did) with
high school civics. So family values were gut-bets. Unless the
economy got so bad that people had to vote with their minds,
patriotism, the flag, and the family had a real chance to hit.
George could take care of the patriotism, but Barbara could de-
molish every Clinton position when it came to family values, and
you wouldn't even see the smoke. The beauty of it all was that she
was also an ameliorative and corrective force. If the good ship
GOP was lilted ten degrees further over to the right than it cared
to be, with every attendant impediment to responsive steering,
Barbara could ballast it back a little to the left. The pro-lifers had
kept cutting too hellish a swath in Houston that week, blockad-
ing abortion clinics so violently that forty-one of their religiosos
got arrested on Monday, and then were so bad in court that they
called the judge, who was a mother and a Catholic named
O'Neill, nothing less than "anti-Christ"—Jesus, it was enough to

make you swear. Ultrareligious Americans were not paying heed to the effect on the electoral result. After Judge O'Neill ordered Operation Rescue to keep a hundred feet away from Planned Parenthood clinics, one preacher even started praying for the judge to repent or she would "be stricken from the face of the earth." Somebody else left a stink bomb at Planned Parenthood. Besides, you couldn't have a crazy-looking father, holding his kid, scared frozen, by one hand, while he swings a seven-month fetus (still reeking of formaldehyde) with the other. Republican women were going to leave the party in droves. George understood female psychology. You don't allow something as ugly as a fetus to be waved in public—women do not like to advertise the disagreeableness of some personal and private functions. Dammit, the party needed amelioration concerning pro-life.

Barbara could provide it. Barbara would provoke the religious right hardly at all, because, after all, even they knew they needed her. Pat Robertson made a point of saying, "I can't believe the American people are so blind that they would want to replace Barbara Bush." Family values was the epoxy, then, to keep the party together, and Barbara could handle any press conference or podium assignment. Trust her every time. In with reporters from *The Boston Globe* and *The Washington Post* just a week ago, why, she blocked every thrust, and these were top-flight journalists, true hard-ons, honed!

BOSTON GLOBE: On abortion, I have to ask you something. Why is it so many of your friends think you are pro-choice?
BARBARA BUSH: I have no idea. I have no idea.
BOSTON GLOBE: Because you never expressed it to them? Never talked about it?
BARBARA BUSH: I've always felt that if I ran for president, George Bush would back me 100 percent. That's the best I can do. [So] we can't return to that. I've given my answer.

WASHINGTON POST: Well, I'm returning to it and I want you to tell me how the Republican Party which . . .
BARBARA BUSH: I don't know the answer.

WASHINGTON POST: . . . which wants less government in our lives . . .

BARBARA BUSH: I don't know the answer to your question and so, in all honesty, don't ask it. Pro or con. I just don't want to get into it. I've had it with abortion.

She could front any confrontation. The day before she had said, "It's a personal choice. . . . The personal things should be left out of . . . platforms and conventions." She had said that during a televised interview in a simple setting. The only picture in the room was on the end table next to her, and it was a framed photograph (signed, presumably) of Pope John Paul II. She could offer every indication to Republican women that she was their advocate for choice in the land, while reassuring the religious right by dint of her close respect for John Paul II—no champion of abortion was he!

Speak of presumption, let us leave these musings of George Bush to hack away at the matter on our own. Concerning abortion, Barbara Bush is leaving just the kind of mixed message that only a monarch can dare to send out. Mixed messages are the prerogative of kings and queens; they are supposed to represent the entirety of the populace.

That was just what she did in her speech on family values. It was no rhetorical gem. On the page, it read like one of those decaffeinated pieces of prose that used to blanket the old *Reader's Digest,* affirmative, highly simplified, and emotionally available to anyone whose IQ had managed to stay below 100. But the GOP, we can assume, was profoundly aware, along with Barbara Bush, that most of the electorate was right there, right under that magic number.

Virtually at her commencement, she paid lip service to other orators: "There is something not quite right here . . . speeches by President Ronald Reagan, President Gerald Ford, Secretary Jack Kemp, Senator Phil Gramm, and . . . Barbara Bush?!" It was evident already that despite her protestations, she was an exceptionally good speaker, and this because of one exceptional and virtuous ability—she could address tens of thousands of people as if they were not more than two or three individuals sitting across from her on a couch. This faculty is available to few, and it suggests she had managed some exceptional transcendence— a woman once sensitive about her stocky build and much-lined face, her dumpy presence once so remarked in relation to Nancy Reagan, had undergone, now that she in turn had become First Lady, so many rites of passage, that she was now possessed of a consummate ease in public. So she gave her audience in the Astrodome a satisfaction they had found nowhere else—a wholly comfortable, social, witty, and reigning queen in their midst; yes, Barbara Bush was politics in the deepest sense, even as is monarchy. Her confidence suggested that one thing at least was right in the world—herself! We vote for what looks right.

So the royal presence that the Reagans had imperfectly commenced, the Bushes had now developed. The presidency had become a monarchy. In place of landed estates or thousand-year-old families, we had endowed symbols—endowed by the psychic etching upon our values of our quick history and, intrinsic to us, our American entertainment. Our symbols and our heraldry were in our American West, our Cavalry, the Marines, the Air Corps, the spirit-of-the-fourth-quarter, Notre Dame, and the kind of family values that had come down to us from Queen Victoria and been brought over by boatloads of immigrants, a sense of propriety brought up to the mark now by Queen Mother Barbara, and our own not wholly overpowering King George, a fantasy of rich national theater. However, since Mr. and Mrs. Bush partook of it as only WASP gentry and WASP vigor can settle into a set of roles they are able to spend their lives living out, but will never name, a subliminal nourishment was there for that part of America which could hardly survive without the certainty of a single powerful and uplifting idea, the unvoiced sense that Barbara Bush was, for all effects, our queen and so could underwrite the religion beneath all other American religions—America itself. Well, thought the Republicans, we'll win by an avalanche if we can only keep the focus on Hillary versus Barbara, Hillary with her feminist intelligence and her hairband.

For the speech itself little registers in the text unless we bring the emoluments of her presence to it. Speaking of her husband, she moved him safely out of harm's way with queenly dispatch:

> I always feel wonderful when I get to talk about the strongest, most decent, most caring, wisest, and yes . . . handsomest man I have ever known . . . George Bush. Now I am here to thank hundreds of communities across the country for one of the great privileges George and I have had in the last four years . . . the chance to meet so many American families and to be in your homes. We have learned from you. And we look forward to meeting many more of you with four more years! We've met thousands of wonderful families, we include extended families . . . we mean the neighbors, even the community itself.

and gave the enumeration:

> Heroic simple mothers and fathers, and grandparents . . . now raising their grandchildren . . . we've visited literacy classes where courageous parents were learning to read . . . we've held crack babies and babies with AIDS . . . George and I have seen communities gather around parents with a gravely ill child . . . times in our lives when we, too, couldn't have made it without our neighbors . . . shared moments with [Persian Gulf families] . . . those yellow-ribboned towns not only wrapped trees and posts, they also wrapped their arms around their young families . . . as in our family, as in American families everywhere, the parents we've met are determined to teach their children integrity, strength, responsibility, courage, sharing, love of God, and pride in being an American. However you define family, that's what we mean by family values.

The Republicans in the Astrodome were delirious. They could believe in victory for the first time. Clinton's lead was vanishing even as the First Lady spoke. For there was depth to this gambit. It would appeal not only to all who were happy and fierce about their family, but one could probably add in a host of those loners bereft of family, plus the unhappy families that wished to be happy so much that their hearts tugged at the thought that it might still be possible. Family values was bound to exert a force on 75 percent of the vote—all the people who were in favor of Barbara.

> You may be exhausted from working a job . . . or two jobs and taking care of your children, or you may have put your career on hold. Either way, you may wonder, as I did every now and then, am I really doing the right thing? . . . Yes, you are . . . from the bottom of my heart I'm here to tell you that you are doing the right thing and God bless you for it.

Who would ever have believed there was any other side to her tonight? When the scandal about George had hit the fan just a week before the convention, and the media had been teeming with tales, not quite nailed down, of George and Jennifer Fitzgerald, Barbara Bush had called the reports "deceitful," "harmful," "mean," "ugly." That was to the media at large. To one interviewer, for whom she may have had a fond spot, she had laughed and said, "It's funny. Nobody ever asks if I've fooled around."

Who knew? With all the Republican candidates for '96, could she be wholly out of her mind if occasionally she had an errant thought or two about who might be added to the list? History, we know, has its own mordant sense of humor. Tonight, with seventeen children and grandchildren surrounding Barbara and George, the story about Woody Allen, Mia Farrow, and Soon-Yi was circulating happily among the Republicans. William Kristol, an able servant in the development of the Republican mind—he was Dan Quayle's chief of staff—was heard to remark at a press briefing, "I'm tempted to say Woody Allen is a good Democrat and leave it at that." Newt Gingrich looked to rake in the pot. "Woody Allen having nonincest with a nondaughter to whom he

was a nonfather because they were a nonfamily fits the Democratic platform perfectly."

William J. Bennett, the former secretary of education and the
drug czar for the Bush administration, was chosen to nominate
Dan Quayle, a well-thought-out selection since Bennett was reminiscent of Pat O'Brien in the movies of the thirties and forties
where he would play a tough priest. Bennett gave a quiet, principled, conservative speech and concluded with a dignified series of encomiums for Dan Quayle. He has succeeded, said
Bennett,

> in sparking needed debate about our most important
> social issue: the values by which we live and which we
> convey to our children. He has stood for family values.
> He has stood up against his critics. He has been princi-
> pled and courageous and in response he has been be-
> littled, but he has not been silenced. Through it all, this
> good and decent man has demonstrated grace and re-
> solve and resilience. He has earned our respect. And we
> should stand by our man.

On the following night, Thursday, last session of the convention, it was up to Dan Quayle to fit such specifications. No routine task. One would have needed the light forged by inner
contests with one's rage and anguish, and Quayle, from the day
he had been chosen by Bush in 1988, had been unable to take in
one breath that was not predeterminedly partisan. Embattled,
ridiculed, in liege to a wife who seemed twice as strong as he was
and eight times more opinionated, he had had a full term of
skirmishing with the media, and now, four years later, his petulance still leaked through. After a bow to the greatness of George
Bush, he said:

> I know my critics wish I were not standing here tonight.
> They don't like our values. They look down on our be-
> liefs. They're afraid of our ideas. And they know the
> American people stand on our side. That is why, when

someone confronts them, they will stop at nothing to
destroy him. To them I say: You have failed. I stand before you, and before the American people—unbowed,
unbroken, and ready to keep fighting for our beliefs.

To this he added extempore: "I'll never surrender, never quit,
never retreat," which was reminiscent of Churchill's speech after
Dunkirk, but then Churchill, quite as easily as Quayle, could
have been seriously influenced in adolescence by Thomas Hen-
ley's "Invictus": "Out of the night that covers me / black as the
pit from pole to pole / I thank whatever gods may be / for my
unconquerable soul."

Quayle might speak with defiance, but he still seemed not so
much unfinished as uncommenced. "It is not just a difference
between conservative and liberal," said Quayle, speaking with
the sanctimoniousness that no politician in America seemed to
have in greater supply, "it is a difference between fighting for
what is right and refusing to see what is wrong." That is probably
why he inspired such hostility in the media. A young, rich, good-
looking man does well not to be pious—piety, we sense, is not
convincing unless it is based on tragedy and dread. Even as he
threw down the gauntlet, he lacked dimension, a mediocre actor
reciting a line more powerful than the true register of his experience.

Besides, he lacked taste. He mashed tuna salad and blueberry
muffins into the same picnic baggie:

We have taught our children to respect single parents
and their challenges—challenges that faced my grand-
mother many years ago and my own sister today. And we
have taught our children about the tragedy of diseases
like breast cancer—which took the life of Marilyn's
mother. Marilyn and I have hosted an annual event
called the Race for the Cure of Breast Cancer. Two
months ago, twenty thousand runners, men and women,
young and old, joined us in the nation's capital to race
for the cure.

Let us give him credit, however, for the interesting point he did make. He was all for reforming the legal system. If he did not say how he would bring this about without government interference, he did, at least, point to one of the first of our economic ills:

> America has 5 percent of the world's population and 70 percent of the world's lawyers. I have nothing against lawyers—at least most of them. I'm a lawyer; I'm married to one. When we worked our way through night law school, Marilyn and I looked forward with pride to becoming part of the finest legal system in the world. But today our country has a problem: our legal system is costing consumers $300 billion a year. The litigation explosion has damaged our competitiveness; it has wiped out jobs; it has forced doctors to quit practicing in places where they are needed most. Every American knows the legal system is broken—and now is the time to fix it.

Yes, indeed, and would he lead the war against the nonproductive costs put into our economic system by all the law firms that did corporate work?

Packed around the floor under the podium, cheering every phrase, placards pumping, voices chanting, and with a high tropism for the nearest television lens, the Republican Youth Delegate Program, also known as the Youth Group, had been powering it up so masterfully for Dan Quayle that if one had not seen them do as much for Pat Buchanan, Ronald Reagan, Jack Kemp, Phil Gramm, and Lynn Martin, the impression could have developed that Quayle's address to the convention had gotten him off to a good start for '96. The essence of successful prostitution, however, even when it is merely spiritual, is an exaggerated if temporary enthusiasm for the client, and the Youth Group had certainly done as much for each of the other speakers. Two hundred strong, picked for Republican balance in gender and ethnicity—a judicious spotting of black, Hispanic, and Asian faces—they were Republican high school and college students who would be future politicians, and so were up each day by five in the morning and did not pack their convention gear until after midnight, a special corps bused from rally to rally and event after event, there to give life to the TV crews outside and inside the Astrodome.

They certainly did their best for Quayle, and if one did not discern the drop in intensity as one moved farther away from the podium, there would have been no way to explain the little economic fact that over in the Astroarena, down in the shopping center, Buchanan buttons were selling briskly, Kemp buttons modestly, and Quayle buttons were not moving at all. How severe are the findings of the competitive free market! By its stern laws and principles, the unsuccessful are equal to the undeserving. Quayle's buttons would be cast out on Friday.

Enter George Bush. Once again, as in 1988, he would have to give the speech of his life. Or so it was generally agreed. The feeling among Republicans was that family values had taken a full bite out of the Democrats' lead in the polls, and if George could deliver on this occasion, parity might be near.

Bush had fretted over the need to prove himself one more time. It was as if he could not overcome his resentment that he, the conqueror of the Persian Gulf, was still obliged to seek victory through oratorical splendor. Whatever his desires, he had ended as the focus of narrative interest for this four-day convention. Would he or would he not startle and encourage the nation with new ideas and new policies? Or would he fail to?

Thursday morning at an ecumenical prayer breakfast, he had said, "Tonight, I give my acceptance speech—and if it catches fire, it may give a whole new meaning to the burning Bush." A humorous remark, but a vain hope. He was too angry within: the delegates were treated instead to the smoldering Bush. If Clinton had failed to deliver a great speech and took fifty-four minutes to prove it, the same sentence could now be employed for George Bush except that he ate up fifty-eight minutes.

On reflection, there was a difference in the nature of their journeyman gifts at the podium. Clinton had elucidated a number of points and programs, even if he had felt obliged to do it

three times over; the president, having no new themes, provided
a hundred applause lines. In the beginning, response came
quickly and frenetically, his audience steamed up to hysteria not
only by the Youth Group, packed in whole compressions of young
humanity under his nose at the podium, but from the delegates
on the floor, superheated in the first minutes of this hour of climax, ergo George Bush had difficulties handling the din. His first
estimated ten minutes must have consumed twenty. Nor was he
simple and modestly appealing as he had been in '88 with Peggy
Noonan's speech. Tonight, the text read like a committee production, and by the end, a quiet pall was on the Astrodome, not
unreminiscent of Bill Clinton's last ten minutes at the Garden.

So it is pointless to do more than give a most restricted sam-
pling of what he offered. He had, after all, said it before, and
would say it again. His contribution to the problem of the economy was to tell again his tale of woe. Blame must fall on the head
of Congress. The speech, like his ideas, was scattered in bits and
pieces, a Broadway comedy which cashed laugh after laugh and
left its audience muttering, "What an empty show!" The longer
it went, the more one became aware that the center of narrative
interest, the philosophical content, was the one protagonist that
never appeared.

Here, then, is Bush's climactic speech presented in selected
snippets that will prove less injurious to him than the complete
text:

> This convention is the first at which an American presi-
> dent can say—the cold war is over, and freedom finished
> first. . . . I saw the chance to rid our children's dreams of
> the nuclear nightmare and I did . . . when Saddam Hus-
> sein invaded Kuwait. . . . What about the leader of the
> Arkansas National Guard—the man who hopes to be
> commander in chief? Well, while I bit the bullet, he bit
> his nails. . . . Sounds to me like his policy can be summed
> up by a road sign he's probably seen on his bus tour,
> SLIPPERY WHEN WET . . . Who do you trust in this elec-
> tion? The candidate who raised taxes one time or the

other candidate who raised taxes and fees 128 times, and enjoyed it every time?

Listening carefully in one of the VIP boxes above the floor was Jim Baker. Studying his expression, one could only decide that he was not the fellow to play poker with—by his expression you could not tell whether Baker was enthralled, appalled, or bored. As Bush went on, Baker proceeded to study the text of the speech with the concentration others might give to a musical score. Was he noting which lines produced more genuine response or less than he had anticipated?

> Now, I know Americans are tired of the blame game, tired of people in Washington acting like they are candidates for the next episode of *American Gladiators*. I don't like it either. Neither should you. But the truth is the truth. Our policies haven't failed; they haven't even been tried.

It was a long exercise in the use of the larynx to come from a man whose voice was sixty-eight years old, and he was beginning to whine—indeed, the timbre of complaint was beginning to remind one of Quayle.

He was near the end, however. It was time to produce a new sound:

> I believe that America will always have a special place in God's heart, as long as He has a special place in ours. And maybe that's why I've always believed that patriotism is not just another point of view. . . . Tonight I appeal to that unyielding spirit. . . . Tonight I say to you—join me in our new crusade—to reap the rewards of our golden victory—to win the peace—so that we may make America safer and stronger. . . .

The president could not help it that he felt contempt for the American people. They had been out there and down there for so long. There they were, that long way off, far from the number-less committee rooms where he had lived and mingled and made his purchase on history for two decades now.

The last hundred thousand of a quarter-million balloons floated down with the conclusion of his speech, and golden con-fetti gave an effulgence as it fell, a heavenly light to outline the podium as the singer offered "God Bless America."

Yes, God bless us—we need it. If fascism comes from the rot-ting away of a nation's virtue until words like "trust" mean "cor-rupt," then yes, we are going to need it.

The Best Move Lies Close to the Worst

(1993)

ONE MORNING AT THE Gramercy Gym on East Fourteenth Street in New York, a friend of one of our regulars came along to join us for the Saturday morning workout. He had never put on gloves before, but he was quietly confident. Having finished the New York City Marathon in close to three hours, he was even ready to get in the ring on his first day, and that was notable since it usually took a couple of months to build up to such a moment. Of course, the marathoner was in superb shape.

He sparred for three minutes with his friend and by the end of that round was too used up to go another. The answer was to be found in the special nature of boxing. If our visitor had been playing baskets one-on-one for the first time, or running after a tennis ball, he might have felt talentless, even foolish, but he would not have been wholly winded in three minutes.

Boxing, however, is not like other tests in sport between one athlete and another, it arouses two of the deepest anxieties we contain. There is not only the fear of getting hurt, which is profound in more men than will admit to it, but there is the opposite panic, equally unadmitted, of hurting others. Part of this second fear rests, of course, on the well-comprehended equation that the harder you hit your opponent, the more he is going to feel free to bang back on you, but it goes a long way beyond that. To be born into that middle class, which is two-thirds of America by now, is to be brought up not to strike others. Probably it is worth noting that General S.L.A. Marshall's classic study of infantrymen in battle for World War II, *Men Against Fire*, came to the conclusion that the large majority of soldiers in combat for the first time could not bring themselves to fire their rifles.

No surprise then if it is difficult to deliver a good punch. It not only requires about as much coordination as to throw a football in a spiral for thirty yards, but, in addition, the punch must find some inner sanction. You have to feel justified. The marathoner wore out because two wholly opposed anxiety systems had been working at full thrust in him. It is one thing to be frightened— some part of yourself can sometimes pull you through. When your cowardice and aggression are both in a flurry, however, quick exhaustion is the consequence.

Be it said that for professionals such opposed fears still exist—it is just that the ante has gone up. Now, you can kill a man in the ring or be killed yourself.

Muhammad Ali once paid a press-inspired visit to Floyd Patterson's training camp in the Catskills a few weeks before their championship match in Las Vegas, and on arrival proceeded to savage Floyd. "You're nothing but a rabbit," Ali told Patterson in front of the reporters, and then decamped in high operatic disgust. Patterson managed to throttle his visible perturbation down to a wry grin. "Well," he said, "I won't have to worry about motivation with that guy, will I?"

One can take one's pass at Ali's premise. For a man like Patterson, an overload of sanction could prove disastrous. He would feel too murderous. On the night that the bout took place in Vegas, Floyd was so tense that his lower back went out on him in the second round. He managed to keep on his feet, fighting from one contorted position after another until the contest was stopped in the twelfth round, but he never had a chance. Ali was a genius.

In the ring, genius is transcendent moxie—the audacity to

know that what usually does not work, or is too dangerous to attempt, can, in a special case, prove the winning move. Maybe that is why attempts are made from time to time to compare boxing with chess—the best move can lie very close to the worst move. At Ali's level, you had to be ready to die, then, for your best ideas.

For our pugilistic fold, however, out there on Saturday morning in the gray, grimy, now-closed Gramercy Gym, where even the ropes and the canvas were gray, and the windows, summer or winter, were a greasy patina of dishrag gray, it was enough that we were ready to show up, each at our own private frequency— some regularly once a week, some once a month, and all variations between—were, yes, ready to wake up on Saturday morning with the knowledge that no legitimate excuse was there on this occasion to get us out of it. We were not hung over, had had enough sleep, yes, we would have to show up. Nonetheless, it was also true that once there, one did not have to box; one could merely work out, hit the speed bag, the heavy bag, do sit-ups, jump rope, shadowbox, or even less—there were no rules, and no obvious rewards, and virtually no shame for doing too little, other than a faint and subtle queasiness concerning macho matters.

Or, one could get into the ring. Sometimes there were weeks in a row when you went one or, better, two three-minute rounds on every Saturday. It varied. No one judged anyone else. Given our separate lives, we were nonetheless not that unalike when it came to our guts and our skill. Most of us did not have a great deal of the latter. We were there to make delicate adjustments on our ongoing workaday ego. Sparring honestly for several weeks in a row, just that once-a-week submersion into three minutes or six minutes of high-speed (for us) boxing did wonders for the self-esteem one could bring back to one's social life.

Of course, most of us went our separate ways outside. We had among us a cabdriver, a bearded editor of a porny magazine, a high school English teacher who suffered a broken jaw one Saturday morning, and an actor who worked nights as a dealer in a gambling joint and purchased headgear with a vertical bridge to protect his handsome nose—which we all found ludicrous until he went on to become a star in a TV crime series.

We also had a couple of young writers and one Golden Gloves aspirant who lost his first and only bout, and we had an established older writer, myself. For the record, I didn't hang up my fourteen-ounce gloves until I was fifty-eight, but by then my knees were gone, I had beaten them half to death jogging on sidewalks, and if you cannot do a little running for the requisite three times a week, you certainly don't have the wind to box on Saturday. It does not matter then how much you know about boxing's systems of anxiety: the fact is that when you have no wind, you cannot be any kind of pugilist unless you are as sly as Archie Moore or as wise as George Foreman. For an average man to go into the ring without wind is equal to going in without blood. So I gave it up, I eased out of it, and have never felt as virtuous since.

We had others who came on Saturday morning, transients. A criminal lawyer was there for a few weeks and a Greek fencer who could never come up with a way to convert fencing to boxing, although he did muster a kind of long left jab. The friends of friends showed up for short periods, and there was one year when we had an instructor, a fast Puerto Rican bantamweight professional, who was too small and too good to impart anything to us that was not in slow motion. He had been brought in by José Torres, our resident dean, who used to enjoy sparring with all of us despite the fact that he had been light heavyweight champion of the world. Torres won his title from Willie Pastrano in 1965 by a TKO in the ninth round at Madison Square Garden and, after several successful defenses, lost it to Dick Tiger in 1966 in fifteen rounds in the same place in a very close fight.

Why Torres enjoyed getting in the ring with us, I never quite understood. It bore comparison to the bemused pleasure Colin Powell might take in teaching close-order drill to recruits. On the other hand, we all enjoyed being able to say we had been in with a former light heavyweight champion. He was impossible to hit and that was an interesting experience—you felt as if you were sharing the ring with a puma. Be it understood, part of his honor was not to hurt anyone. When you made a mistake, he would tap you. If you repeated the error, he would tap you harder. Defensive reflexes developed in the student. One's offense, however, had to fend for itself. Over ten years of boxing with José Torres I was able to catch him with a good right hand twice, and the first occasion was an event. He ran around the ring with his arms high in triumph crying out, "He hit me with a right—he hit me with a right!" unconscionably proud that day of his pupil.

It was thanks to José that we had the use of the gym. The management had provided him with the keys. When he did not show up on an occasional Saturday, a poet who lived in a fourth-floor loft above the third-story gym would let us in by opening his begrimed window long enough to drop a key down to us in a rolled-up sock, and when we climbed the stairs, the premises still reeked of the serious sweat of the professional and Golden Gloves aspirants who had trained there from Monday to Friday.

Such was our club. But for one or two clear exceptions, we were all more or less equal, and we went at it like club members. There were few wars, and most of us went out to eat and drink together afterward. We worked on what we considered most lacking, a better left hook, a sharper jab, a hook off the jab, a heavier or faster right hand. Some of us even ventured into combinations, but never too far. Mediocre condition was the scythe that cut into the rate of one's improvement. It is hard to describe how tired you can get in a three-minute round when you are forced to labor at your utmost. Two-minute rounds, the duration employed in the Golden Gloves for subnovices, would have been a considerably more satisfactory interval for us, but at the Gramercy, our bell was set on a three-minute professional interval, with only that quick sixty seconds of rest before it rang again. So we worked through three-minute rounds, and paid the price: the last thirty seconds of a three-minute round can get to feel as long as the first two and a half minutes. Going a couple of such rounds in a row (which total of six minutes is equal to a three-round subnovice bout), you often got tired enough to find it considerably easier to take the other's arm-weary punch to your head rather than to raise your own bone-dead arms in defense.

Ryan O'Neal came to join us, however, and our Saturdays were altered. Ryan was making a movie in New York that season, and José Torres was his friend; José had worked as a boxing adviser on *The Main Event,* a comedy O'Neal had made with Barbra Streisand. Now, each Saturday morning, after five days of shooting on his film, O'Neal would come into the Gramercy.

He was good enough to have been a ring professional. When they boxed, Torres could not play with him, and once Ryan even managed to catch José with a shot to the mouth that drew a little blood. That was equal to sacrilege. Torres nodded curtly and stepped out of the ring. It was a sizable rebuke. The retaliation he had chosen not to express was as palpable as the air in summer before a storm and O'Neal looked sheepish, like a man who is too far from home to be caught without a raincoat.

After that, he and José did not box too frequently, and when they did, all the parameters were kept in place. O'Neal began to work out instead with whoever was there. By our measure, he was in impressive condition. He would take us on serially, each of us going for a round or two depending on our ability to continue, and by the end of his workout he had boxed his way through eight to ten rounds against such easy opposition. Then he would go off to play racquetball with Farrah Fawcett.

Getting in the ring with Ryan O'Neal became not only the focus of each Saturday, but the point to what some of us had been half-looking to do for years, that is, get extended a little in the ring. Ryan could be mean as cat piss. Even when he was carrying a man, he would punish him, and when he had dislikes, he liked to take them out on the opponent. In spite of every love affair in his private life, public fodder for more than a decade to the gossip columns, Ryan had his dry spot—the puritanism of the Irish. He took a secret dislike to the bearded editor of the porny magazine who happened to be not much of a boxer. The editor was awkward in the ring, so it was not hard to play tricks on him. He had surprising stamina, however. Until Ryan came along, the pornographer had, in fact, the most notable stamina of any of us. Maybe Ryan equated that ability to sexual prowess and disapproved of its presence in so unworthy a vessel, maybe he just disliked hirsute New York lumpen intelligentsia, but, in any case, he all but disemboweled the man, throwing cruel left hooks to the stomach until the editor collapsed, still conscious, in the middle of the second round, wholly unable to go on. What made it worse was that the pornographer's lady love, a good-looking girl who worked in a massage parlor, was witnessing it all at ringside. Something in their love—and it was, after all, *their* love—was lost that day.

I happened to be next in the ring with Ryan, which proved to be my good luck. After every discharge of mean feelings, Ryan would turn angelic. A little ashamed, I expect, of what he had just done to the pornographer, he was not now boxing like a movie star—he certainly did not protect his face. Since the man he had hurt happened to be a sweet guy, extraordinarily optimistic about life (which is probably how he had gotten into pornography in the first place), I liked the editor. When I saw him take this beating, I recognized that I saw him as a friend. If this seems something of a digression, let me say that it helps to carry the auctorial voice around the embarrassment of declaring that I boxed better on that day than I ever did before, or since. I was in a rare mean mood myself, mean enough not to be afraid of Ryan, and—it is very hard to do any kind of good boxing against a superior without some premise to carry you—I was feeling like an avenger. And here was Ryan boxing with his face. It was hard not to hit him straight rights, and he reacted with all the happiness of seeing a beloved senior relative get up from a sickbed. In our first clinch, he whispered, "You punch sharper than anyone here."

"Go fuck yourself," I told him.

We fell into a mutually pleasing pattern. He would give me his face for a target, I would bop it, and he would counterpunch. He hit harder than anyone else in the club, but that was the day when my two systems of anxiety were in quiet balance, and I never enjoyed boxing as much.

Following that Saturday, Ryan and I took up predictable weekly behavior. I would invariably be the first to box with him (mainly, I think, so I could enjoy watching the others now that I was done) and he would continue to spar with his hands low, daring me to catch him. I would, often enough, and he would counterpunch. How much he took off his blows I do not know—at whatever level he gunned down his motors for me, his punches still took your head half around, or left a space in your gut, and I, in turn, reduced my punches very little for him. Whatever the equilibrium, we had found it, and it was as close as it ever came for me to gain some knowledge of how a professional might feel in a real bout for money with a hard-hearted crowd out there and the spirit of electricity in the ring lights. Damn, it was exciting. I even came to understand what it was to feel love for the man you were fighting because he had forced you to go a little beyond yourself, and I never took as many good punches or threw as many as in those one or two rounds each Saturday with Ryan O'Neal.

Life, in the form of Luce publications, caught up with this romance. Ryan, having produced my Saturday illumination, would then box with another three or four of us and kept to his habit— I always thought it was penance for having become a movie star—of showing that good-looking open face, so relatively easy to score upon.

There came a day when I popped him in the left eye a few times running and the boxers who came after me did approximately as much in the same place, and when he was done, he had a mouse. That little animal got into the papers. One of the gossip columns recounted how Norman Mailer had given Ryan O'Neal a shiner.

People magazine called up. They were ready to do a story. The dangers were obvious. We would all be famous for too little. So I turned the reporter from *People* over to José Torres. José would know how to protect Ryan.

He did. For my money, he protected him too well. "Ryan could have easily beaten Norman up," said Torres for publication— which was exactly true. I understood that it was true with all the hard objective core of my pride in being a writer who would always look into the eye of the truth, that severe gray lady, gray as the Gramercy Gym, but, José, José, I whispered within, how about a little transcendence?

Torres was much too agile, however, to sacrifice one friend altogether in order to protect another. So, for *People* magazine, he added: "Norman could whip Sly Stallone in one round."

"Yes," I said later to José, "and what happens when I run into Stallone?"

José shrugged. More immediate problems were usually waiting for him around any corner.

I do not recall if it was one year or two or three before I encountered Sylvester Stallone, but it did happen one night in a particularly dark disco with a raked floor.

"I understand," said Stallone, "that you're the guy who can beat me in one round."

He had never looked in finer shape.

"Yeah," I said, applying all the thickener I could muster to my voice, "I remember when José said that, I said to him, 'Yeah, swell, but what happens if I don't knock Stallone out in one round?' and José said, 'Oh, then he will *keel* you.'"

Stallone gave his sad, sleepy-eyed smile. "Mr. Mailer, I can assure you, I don't go around killing people."

It was gracious. One could only respond in kind. "Mr. Stallone," I said, "I don't go around getting in the ring with people who can do one-arm push-ups."

"Ah," he said sadly, "I can't do them anymore. I hurt my arm."

We grinned at each other, we shook hands. I think we were in silent league (for the modest good it could do) against the long reductive reach of the media.

Afterward, I would smile at the cost of such knowledge. It had taken me ten years of boxing to come up with a glimmer of pugilist's wit—what if I don't knock him out in the first round?— yes, one boxed for the better footing it could offer in the social world, and one could even believe, yes, absolutely, that boxing was one of the sixty things a man should learn if he is to get along in this accelerating world, so farewell, Gramercy Gym, gray lady of my late middle age, I will always be loyal to you.

Clinton and Dole: The War of the Oxymorons

(1996)

Oxymoron—n. [Greek *oxymoron,* fr. neut of *oxymoros,*
oxy- sharp, keen + *moros* dull, foolish]; a figure of speech
in which opposite or contradictory ideas are combined
(e.g., thunderous silence, sweet sorrow, purple yellow)

THEY WERE THE SAME AGE—which might be about all they had in
common. Still, Norman did remember their one meeting. It had
only lasted a couple of minutes, but sometime in the early nine-
ties, as one of the perks after a Folger Library gala, he was ush-
ered with a couple of authors into Dole's Senate office, a
predictable domain. It could boast of a gracious chamber, large
windows, a commodious balcony. On the instant of their meeting, he had, however, been surprised. Expecting an encounter
with a stern and somewhat wooden figure—the senator certainly
looked no less on television—he was taken aback. When they
said hello, Dole's eyes danced with private humor, as if he were
ready to say: "You don't know the first thing about me, Mailer."
It worked.

Novelists live for the moment when their imaginations come
alive, since such a moment can feel as good as a match being

struck in the dark. Afterward, he never discounted Dole. There had been too much light in the eye.

So he was not startled when surprises popped up in the last week before the San Diego convention. Indeed, he blessed the gods for having made him a writer of fiction. It might be that only a novelist could hope to understand this particular Republican candidate.

His confidence was that he was ready to make a few guesses concerning that inscrutable inner life Dole would hardly bring to an interview. Did one desire to comprehend the senator's motives? That seemed an effort worthy in itself. Be brave enough to divine him. What else, after all, was the domain of the novelist? So, he would write about Dole as if he understood him well.

All right, then. A plunge. One night in the mind of Bob Dole as he approaches San Diego in July 1996 to accept the nomination for president of the Republican Party.

They kept saying, "Character. Bring up the issue of character." Win on character? Didn't think you could. Didn't like politicians who looked to impress with character. Grated on him. Besides, certain things—damned if he would discuss them. Nitty-gritty of nursing. Being nursed. Pretty degrading.

Wounds of war come down to being helpless. Couldn't take care of himself for close to three years. Why talk about that? Shipped home in a body cast, lost one kidney, lost more than seventy pounds, lost control of this and that, whatever. Didn't look into a mirror those years. Hell of a cadaver looked back. Thirty-nine months to put hospitals behind him. His right arm would never move well. Never again. Had to keep a black pen clutched in his right fist so you wouldn't try to shake hands. Everybody knew that. Except they didn't. Always trying to shake hands.

Somebody told him of a writer named Ernest Hemingway who said, "Don't talk about it." He wouldn't. Keep what virtue you can retain. Don't put it on the air. Certainly nothing good. A man lies wounded. In real pain. Gets to know the air. All the air around him. Knows that forever. Air is as alive as you and me. So, keep what you have learned. Don't put it on the air. Keep that secret chamber. If no one knows your next move, your surprises can pick up some smack. But what surprises? Problems do not guarantee a solution. Still, the idea of Clinton beating him. That would be awful. Sweet Billy Clinton didn't have enough ethics to worry that he was betraying his ethics. Trouble was, Billy had one positive quality: his heart was in the right place. And it was big. Big as a field of cowflop. Hang around him, you take off your shoes, you put on boots. Billy could cry for others as quickly as another man zips up his pants. Of course, Billy's butt was owned by fat cats. Probably why his other part got inflamed so often. Heart and the other part were all that was left to him. Corporate suits owned Clinton's nuts. Dole was sure he could do better. Had lived with the big boys for a long time, and they didn't own his testicles. Just held a mortgage on them.

Unkind thoughts about Billy weren't going to get him anywhere, however. Not with people these days. They want you softhearted. Back to first principles. It's basic. Use an oxymoron. Put opposites together. Art of politics. Use every oxymoron you can get away with. Marry incompatibles. Get twice as many votes. Speak of family and freedom as if they are one. The virtues of the family are many, particularly at Christmastime. What isn't said: family happiness is obtained by losing a considerable amount of your freedom. Of course, there never was a dictator who failed to talk up the virtues of the family. But then fascists were emperors— emperors of the oxymoron.

Trying to copy Clinton might be an infectious disease, but he had caught Billy's bug. The kind of light you get from fever, he had it now. Wanted to win. Could do it if he played a good game. Had to keep telling himself: think it through.

After all, Republicans had one real achievement: They had made it impossible for that old Democratic Party to survive. Survive, that is, as their old Democratic Party. Reagan had run the debt up. Then Bush. Now it had gotten to where every Democrat who got in had to work to reduce debt. Had to dismantle their Great Society. Couldn't afford it anymore. Law of reversal. Now, a strong Republican could get away with running up a new deficit. Could claim it was the Democrats' fault. After all, wasn't it always Democrats who went to war? Then it took Republicans to make peace. Couldn't be otherwise. No Democrat can end a war. How could he? Republicans would beat him to death for lack of patriotism. For cowardice. By contrast, no Republican president could go to war without half of America getting full of distrust. Democrats, anyway. Look at Bush's trouble getting into war with Iraq. So, there's an edge. Only a Republican can run up a new deficit. Could be his surprise. Get elected on tax cuts. Extra money is as valuable to the American people as elixir of libido. Great stuff, elixir of libido.

Of course, they would say he was helping to bring about breakdowns in family values. Extra money could certainly lead to more infidelity. Well, you get elected and that gives you a bully pulpit. Try to undo the damage done getting elected. First things first.

Daring idea. But feasible. Larger your oxymoron, more chance it has. Cut taxes. Insist you can balance your budget. Brings the two halves of the Republican Party together. Certainly has to stimulate curiosity. People will ask, Does Dole succeed or fail on this promise? People want to know what happens next.

Of course, you don't want to get into details. Can't speak of cuts in Social Security or Medicare. Equal to being dead in the water. Only other real solution: end corporate welfare. Something to consider. It would take Dole to do it. Just like Nixon was the one to make peace with China. But you can't mention corporate welfare. Just say: I have the will. I have the will to do it. Trust me. When the debates come, look Clinton in the eye. The fat boy might melt. Nothing lost for trying. Will try it.

Well, tried it, announced it. Didn't work. No credibility. Not even for Dole. War wounds worth less these days. Credibility has to be reinforced. Buttressed. Consider it. Jack Kemp for running mate. Will guarantee credibility on your tax cut. Kemp's been talking about it for years. So, Dole-Kemp could wake this convention up. Tantamount to Mae West strolling down center aisle stark naked.

Dole-Kemp will do it. The trick is to keep telling yourself: an election campaign is not cut in stone. Not like legislation. For the Senate, you have to respect legislation. How can a nation survive all the bad bills that get passed if there aren't a few good ones? Keel of government. Underline that. As a legislator, you have to be responsible. Some of the time.

As a presidential candidate, it's opposite. Be ready to get away with what you can. Look at Reagan. Easier to catch a fly with your thumb and forefinger than to corner Reagan on a weak point. Emulate Ronnie. Don't look back. Most voters are not living in Kansas. So stop treating them as if they are smart enough to read character. Failing memory is the fastest-growing disease of the twentieth century. People do not wish to have to recall what was said five days ago.

All the same, don't go off half-cocked. Calculate media cost. They'll bring up those jokes. What were they? How long ago was that? He had said, "If Jack Kemp were smart, he would corner the market on hair spray instead of undergoing all that personal expense." Something like that. Kemp had an answer. Not a bad one. Talked about poor Bob Dole. Said how sad it was that this fire burned down Dole's house. However, Dole's library was saved. Both of his books were intact. That was nice, because Dole hadn't yet finished his coloring book.

Well, he couldn't laugh all the way home, not over that one. Kemp had upped the ante. Ergo, do unto others as they do unto you. Our good news, Dole had said, is that Jack Kemp and some of his supply-siders were in a bus crash. The bad news is that three of the seats were empty.

You could say he had gone too far. Had to watch that streak. Dark, Dole, dark. The media would swarm over those jokes. Still, it would keep everybody paying attention to Dole-Kemp. Do those two guys get along? Do they not? Will produce narrative interest. And Kemp will be loyal. For the next couple of months, anyway. Had to. Would want to be elected vice president. And no need to worry about a change of life in office. It's all in an old Italian saying. Heard it in Italy: revenge is a dish that people of taste eat cold. He could live with the joke about the coloring book.

Would Kemp accept his offer? Would Neil Armstrong refuse to take a first step for mankind? Dole knew political figures when they were making policy on the inside. Knew them when they were pushed outside. He had installed some fellows in good places. Had maneuvered a few gentlemen out. Been inside and outside himself. At one point, Nixon had turned chilly. That hurt. Practically speaking, you could call it one big crisis of identity. Left you feeling small.

Now Kemp had been out for a while. Called it living in his "wilderness years." But he was going to call Kemp back to the fray. That would do it. How could Kemp not love him? All the same, he couldn't approve of Kemp altogether. Talked too much. Very little Kemp wouldn't put on the air. Nonetheless! Dole-Kemp. A Mac Whopper of an oxymoron.

He was hearing it all over the place. An enthusiastic crowd was waiting for them. Good for warming the bones. In front of the courthouse in Russell, he introduced Kemp to a large group—all home folks. Called him an "American original." Of course, you could say that Dole was an American original. For that matter, so was Sweet Billy Clinton. Whatever. And Jack Kemp, when he got up to talk to the folks in Russell, mentioned that at lunch he had asked Bob Dole how long he wanted him to speak, and Dole had answered, "Kemp, you can speak as long as you want, but we're only going to be here for five more minutes. . . ."

We must prepare for a shock. We are going to move over to Jesse Jackson giving a speech on August 27 at the Democratic convention. Jesse Jackson may be our greatest orator, but his voice is sometimes muffled by all his withheld sounds—rage of frustration, clamped-down sobs of exasperation, the dark vibration of this year's patience compressed upon last year's patience. Sometimes you can hardly hear him. Truth, there are many whites who would not wish to hear him, a majority doubtless. Still, he said it on Tuesday night, August 27, 1996, in Chicago, like no one else happened to be saying it these days. Let us put up his words as a benchmark by which we can measure both conventions by

their resolute inability to look into the eye of the issues, the few
real issues:

> One-tenth of all American children will go to bed in
> poverty tonight. Half of all America's African American
> children grow up amidst broken sidewalks, broken
> hearts, broken cities, and broken dreams. The number
> one growth industry in urban America: jail. Half of all
> public housing built to last ten years. Jails. The top
> 1 percent wealthiest Americans own as much as the bot-
> tom 95 percent. . . . We must seek a new moral center.

The ghostly tone of the Democratic Convention in Chicago can
more easily be found, however, in the following speech:

> We Democrats believe that the family, fueled by values,
> must be restored to the central place in American life
> if we are to keep the dream alive. Yet families cannot
> thrive and pass on these beliefs if parents cannot bring
> home a decent, living wage for a hard day's work. . . .
> In this richest nation on earth, we still have not solved
> the problems of poverty . . . which tear away at the
> roots of strong families. . . . We have to make sure that
> reduced government spending does not single out just
> the poor and the middle class. Corporate welfare and
> welfare for the wealthy must be the first in line for elim-
> ination. . . . It is the entitlement state that must be re-
> formed and not just the welfare state. And we must do
> it in a way that does not paint all of government as the
> enemy.
> We are a big enough party—and big enough peo-
> ple—to disagree on individual issues and still work to-
> gether for our common goal: restoring the American
> Dream. I am a Democrat because I believe in that
> dream, and I believe we are the ones to keep it alive.

A liberty has been taken. Two words were changed. "Republicans" and "Republican" were altered to "Democrats" and "Democrat." The speaker was not in Chicago but in San Diego on Monday, August 12, and he was Colin Powell.

Given his remarks on corporate welfare, he is, in fact, to the left of the Democratic Party. Powell was, of course, to the left of the Republican Party as well—there was no other luminary in the GOP who spoke out against corporate welfare at the convention. A year earlier, that had not been so. John Kasich, head of the House Budget Committee, had been looking to wipe out the deficit by the year 2002. He also had to find no less than $200 billion to pay for the tax breaks promised in the Contract with America. For a time, he thought corporate welfare might even be the place to do it. Kasich said in an interview, "I think it is an absolute outrage that some of this crap is still in this budget, and it just infuriates me every day when I think about it."

It is not the sentiments of men that make history but their actions. Kasich came down from the mountain of $200 billion to $25 billion. Didn't get anywhere with that, either. By the time he stood at the podium in San Diego, he did not mention corporate welfare. Rather, he spoke of "reattaching our souls to one another," and "sending a clear message to God that He is being invited back into American life."

God, who is reputed to mark the fall of every sparrow, might not need an invitation.

Of course, the numbers involving corporate welfare are, to put matters in the politest form, full of discomfort. Stephen Moore of the right-wing Cato Institute has said, if we were able to get rid of all the corporate welfare spending programs, "we could cut our budget deficit in half."

We can also take a quote from a signally good article on corporate welfare in *The Boston Globe* on July 9, 1996: " 'Clinton initially wanted to make a strong statement on corporate welfare, but backed away,' an administration source said. He eschewed the words 'corporate welfare' in public, the source said, adding: 'He uses the phrase in private and cabinet meetings, but the phrase is too combative for him.' "

Shall we call it corpfare from now on? Corpfare the rich child; welfare the hungry child. We need not be surprised that the Democratic Convention was close to an overlay of the Republican convention.

The American political body had evolved into a highly controlled and powerfully manipulated democracy overseen by a new species of aristocracy formed at the junction of four royal families—the ten-thousand-dollar suits of the megacorporations, the titans of the media, the high ogres of Congress, and the upper lords of the White House. The inner disputes of a court with four such elements are not easy to follow, but their accords are clear.

Both parties were linked on balancing the budget, increasing the sentences on drug dealers, upgrading the best armed forces in the world and downsizing government (as if the two had no relation to each other!). Both parties would change welfare as we know it. No one asked whether anyone writing the specifications for those changes had any intimate knowledge about what life might be like on welfare.

There were, it is true, a few points of dispute: The Democrats, for example, were tougher on cigarette smoking among adolescents than were the Republicans, and the Democrats were certainly pro-choice. Family values would prevail in both parties except for those special cases where family values might interfere with megasize profits. There, in the realm of film, music, and health management organizations, family values could take a walk.

Given these similarities, we do not have to catalog the Democratic Convention activities either. Details are interesting when a dramatic turn in one event produces an unforeseen shift in another. None of that occurred. No riots, demonstrations, or protests offered enough impact to be closely followed by the media. Both conventions had been prepared so thoroughly for TV that an irony intervened. Except for the last night, the major networks refused to show more than an hour of convention time. The largest question for the media became: Who will win a larger share of the TV public during the prime-time hours on the first night of each convention?

The Republicans brought the deaf, the wounded, the victim of rape to testify to the honor and compassion of Bob Dole; on their initial network hour, the Democrats did not discuss politics at all. What a stroke! The genius of Dick Morris was once more confirmed. Focus groups had given him an ideal speaker for the first night, a nonpolitical person with immense TV impact, none other than Superman, Christopher Reeve, who had broken his neck taking his horse over a jump. In his *20/20* appearance with Barbara Walters last year, he had generated an enormous response. The Democrats, having no one available for their first night with status comparable to Colin Powell, chose Reeve, and he gave one of the best speeches of both conventions. Because everyone knew that he could not move his limbs, the stern small shifts of his lips as he intoned his hard-earned sentiments of compassion occasioned real oratorical intensity. He stirred large emotional depths in the audience, and much of that was in relation to how handsome he was, and how immobile. He was not unlike a mythic idol, human, but made of stone. As he spoke of the need for research, one could see that it was the plainest women who were weeping most. His voice, transmitted through a larynx mike, was stirring precisely because it was small and necessarily measured:

> We don't need to raise taxes; we just need to raise our expectations.
> We found nothing is impossible. That should be our motto. It's not a Democratic motto nor a Republican motto. It's an American motto. It's something we will have to do together. America is stronger when all of us take care of all of us.

At the end of Reeve's ovation, Clinton came in on the big TV screen. He was speaking from Columbus, Ohio, and looked as large as a big-time football coach at a Friday night rally. His mojo was working. Thanks to Christopher Reeve, the returns for the Democrats' first night had done almost as well as the Republicans' first night had with Powell and Nancy Reagan.

It is a true change of scene to go from Christopher Reeve to Barbara Boxer, for the senator from California was tiny and peppy,
and she wore very high heels. She talked a great deal about children. She was so devoted to their welfare that one wondered why
she seemed 1 percent phony. Later, one learned that she and
Dianne Feinstein, the other senator from California, voted on
the side of corpfare. It was, however, no evil deed. The bill to
take a whack at corporate welfare had been voted down 74 to 25.
So, Boxer and Feinstein were just two of 74 senators defending
the nest where the big birds hatched their eggs.

On Monday afternoon in the Sheraton Ballroom, Barbara
Boxer, at the podium, turned to Hillary Clinton on the dais and
said, "We're going to take back the Hill because of you." She saluted her. She added, "To my favorite First Lady of all time."
Barbara Boxer was the only one wearing red on the speaker's
platform, a primary red that gave a bounce to her black hair and
red lipstick. If you're tiny, flaunt it. It was also likely that she di-
eted with major passion. She was older than the new generation
but nonetheless had the look of the New Woman. She was the
instrument of her own will. She would make herself into what
she chose to be. It was possible that she did not understand that
one virtue we cannot acquire by an act of will is to improve our
minds in such a manner that we can improve the minds of others. Acts of will, on the contrary, tend to produce abilities that
oppress others. Piety, for example.

But we have strayed, we have moralized! (We are moralizing
among the moralizers.) And we have hardly declared where we
are, nor why. Hillary was having a session at Chicago's grandest
new hotel, where she was staying and where Bill would join her.
More than fifteen hundred people were present, 85 percent of
whom were well-dressed women. When she came forward to
speak, Senator Carol Moseley-Braun even waved her right arm in
the air like a prizefighter. But then their subject was the empow-
erment of women.

Hillary's speech soon followed. It was so easy for her. She had only to touch a button and the women would cheer and rise to their feet. "Doesn't it feel good to have a president who stood up against the National Rifle Association?" she asked. Cheers. Sound bites, one after the other. But then there were a great many TV people there. A sizable stand had been erected for them. Now, no matter how the TV would cut her remarks, there would always be a selling point. "I have listened to our women senators, and I say to myself, 'Go, girl, go!'"

To the huge roar that came up on this last, she added, "We are applauding women who ran for office to help affect the lives of men, women and children." If she had asked them to march all the way to the convention center, they might have sprouted a bouquet of blisters in their high heels, but they would have followed her. If she had asked them to bare their breasts, they would have shucked their blouses and their bras. They might be corporate ladies, but they were loyal troops. Command me—I am yours!

How the Republicans were enraged by Saint Hillary's army, so militant, so sure of themselves. Republicans had often been left with dry, hard-edged specimens of women or obese cuties with beehive hairdos, but then the GOP had been giving it all to the men for a century—giving it to their tycoons, to their military heroes, their white athletes, their independent-minded riflemen who believed in freedom (while relinquishing more of it every day to the spiritual depredations of the corporation). What depredations? Why, to list a few—plastic, high-rises, fluorescent lighting, and sealed windows in expensive hotels.

That was Monday afternoon. On Tuesday night when Hillary spoke at the convention, she was wearing a knit dress somewhere in hue between baby blue and royal blue. A perfect color for television, it reached out for your eye but did not burn it. Her hair was coiffed for the kind of dinner party only doyennes give in New York. Immaculate yet subtle was her hair, and well colored. In two decades, Hillary had moved half the distance from bottle-lens Rodham—the angry formidable dark-haired no-nonsense Yale Law School grind and soon young wife of young Governor Clinton—all the way over to a modest copy of Sharon

Stone. Hillary had become a blond actress. She was not yet a very good one, but she was certainly better than the average ingenue.

At the convention on Tuesday night, the delegates were expecting a powerful speech to burn out the power of the impression Liddy Dole had left at the Republican Convention. But Hillary was not competitive, not, at least, on this night. She had a quiet, caring, interested-in-your-doings family chat prepared, and she was not going to stray. She did her best to fulfill the role. But she was not all that compassionate. Ice blondes can hide a variety of faults—they cannot convince you of their loving care, however, when they are not feeling it.

> I want to talk about what matters most in our lives and in our nation—children and families. I wish we could be sitting around a kitchen table, just us, talking about our hopes and fears, and our children's futures. For Bill and me, family has been the center of our lives. . . .
>
> Of course, parents, first and foremost, are responsible for their children. . . . Just think about what many parents are responsible for on any given day: packing lunches, dropping the kids off at school, going to work, checking to make sure the kids get home from school safely, shopping for groceries, making dinner, doing the laundry, helping with homework, paying the bills, and I didn't even mention taking the dog to the vet.

One could see why so many Americans disliked her. She was decompressing the presidency. She was pretending to be near to the people, but the nature of her position made that impossible. We laugh at the English royals when they pay their visits to factory workers, but at least they remain royal. Hillary was pretending that she was one of us, and it was hardly true. One wanted political leaders who were full of passion for the people but were also noble and a touch aloof: FDR and Eleanor set the standard. That was easier to trust than someone who pretended to know which laundry detergent to use, or, even worse, was not pretending. She did know. What a waste of the upper faculties.

During the half hour she spoke, there were more than seventy references to children, to mother and father, to family. It no longer had anything to do with politics. There she was, absolutely in place, ice-blond, a saint to her gender even as she proceeded to talk about PTA solutions to profound problems. None of the real questions came into her purview, nothing about the sleazy quality of so many American products advertised to the hilt, nothing trenchant about the waste of the ghettos, the paucity of good wages among working people, the fever of global capitalism to send the profits to the top rather than sharing some of the wealth with those who worked to make the stuff.

To her credit, Hillary had succeeded in weathering the 400 blows aimed at her over the last four years. A weaker woman would have been in a sanitarium by now. She became stronger. We all know: if it does not kill you, it will make you stronger. Yet she had not become a nicer woman. Her ice-blond presence now offered the unhappy suggestion that acts of transcendence do not always lead us to the light. Saint Hillary and her Knights Templar were a force to emblazon one another, but they might not be exactly what the country needed. They were too eager to show that they could be the equal of any man in the corporation or the government. Probably they could. And so what? Women are as ugly as men when personal power is their life cause, their only real life cause.

If black people are often seen by some fearful whites as the wildest people in America, it is not as easily recognized that they can also be the most disciplined men and women. If that helps to explain why a million black people can march on Washington without one act of violence, it can also account for the genial affect with which they came to Chicago and stayed there through the week, never breaking their own good mood, even if aspects of the Clinton overdrive—all that moderate Republicanism— had to be heartbreaking to the majority of them. Many of the welfare women and children, who would soon be having cruel and heartless dealings with the local authorities in their states, might be friends of the delegates, or their neighbors, or even poor members of their own families. The word was out, however, among the brothers and sisters—we are here to celebrate how good our relations are with white Democrats.

And they were. One had to go back to the Fifties to recall a time when liberal whites and blacks had been so ready to have a good time together. Whatever Clinton's faults, political omissions, and betrayals, there was this to his credit—relations between blacks and whites, in the Democratic Party at least, were on the mend. Blacks knew the figures. At the Dole convention, about 3 percent of the delegates were black. In Chicago, the figure was about 19 percent. Now, however, blacks also knew that they were the Democrats' best chance for recapturing the House and the Senate. It could be done if they came out to vote in force.

So Clinton had gambled that blacks would accept his signing of the welfare bill. Many Democrats were unhappy that he signed, but they were certainly not mutinous. Where was there to go? They hoped, and some believed, that Clinton would fix the worst parts of the new welfare machine (not even yet designed) if he were reelected with a Democratic Congress. No voice, but for Jesse Jackson, rose in real wrath to declare: If welfare is to be cleansed at the bottom, why not have it fumigated at the top? Corpfare!

Silence prevailed. Since the fire was out of the Democratic Party, geniality took its place. Many of the black delegates liked Clinton. He was warm, he was good-hearted, he had tears in his eyes before the pain of others—he had been there to commiserate with black congregations after their churches were burned. If he was a sinner, he was also a churchgoer. (As you should be after you have sinned.) Of course, he was also sufficiently active as a sinner to salivate at the sight of a hotel room in a strange town, or, for that matter, in his own town. He was okay. He was alive, he was American, he had his good side, he had his bad side.

So the mood was genial. It was not a time to brood on the low state of the party. The Democratic Party, after all, had been in an unhealthy condition for years. In 1968 it had been torn in half by Vietnam. The slash of the wound still ran across the face of the party. And of late, its soul had been bruised. Inanition bruises the soul.

The years from 1992 to 1994 were a terrible time for the Democrats. A wholly quixotic effort to get gays into the military was followed by a yearlong sludge-filled effort to arrive at a medical health plan. It failed altogether. Did one have to go back to the Civil War to find battles where so much had been committed and so little gained?

After two years in the White House, it was clear that Clinton's past was a puddle and he was sitting in it. In consequence, the Democratic Party had been without a general. There was no one to lead them back to ground where they could fight the Republican Party. Instead, they all but joined it. The Democrats remained weak before the righteousness of the Republicans, whose blitzkrieg in 1994 had been underwritten by a fundamental public anger: there were too many indulgent poor people being supported on the taxes of the hardworking. Of course, the hardworking were often not too bright, especially the white men who had been brought up to succeed and believed, therefore, that to be hardworking was virtuous. It was, but it was not as virtuous as they thought. The top was taking more from the middle than the bottom was taking. The failure to recognize this (or the resolute cowardice not to recognize it) was also a failure of virtue.

On Thursday night, President William Jefferson Clinton came to the podium to present his acceptance speech. Rarely had he looked better or spoken with more vigor. His energy never waned. He had the charisma on that Thursday night to give a great speech and indeed he would have—if he had had a speech. But he didn't. He had a list of items, political items, most of them modest. He had, in effect, the kind of speech that a man running for mayor in a small city might give to the locals.

The wonder of it all, however, was that it took something like half the speech, a full thirty minutes, for the emptiness of the offering to become apparent. Clinton had risen in his person so completely above his text that he stood before the TV cameras of the world—tall, ruddy, handsome, vigorous, confident, even proud. His manner provided the assertion: he was going to do wonderful things for the country. But his text was offering less than any president had promised in a long time.

There is no need to quote at length from what he said. It is all pretty much the same, a demonstration of the inner life of political sin. Clinton's punishment for his sins was that he had become intellectually dull:

> We must require that our students pass tough tests to keep moving up in school. A diploma has to mean something when they get out (*applause*). We should reward teachers who are doing a good job, remove those who don't measure up. But in every case, never forget that none of us would be here tonight if it weren't for our teachers. I know I wouldn't. We ought to lift them up, not tear them down (*cheers*). With all respect, we do not need to build a bridge to the past, we need to build a bridge to the future, and this is what I commit to you to do (*cheers, applause*).
>
> So tonight, let us resolve to build that bridge to the twenty-first century, to meet our challenges and protect our values. Let us build a bridge to help our parents raise their children, to help young people and adults get the education and training they need, to make our streets safer, to help Americans succeed at home and at work, to break the cycle of poverty and dependence, to protect our environment for generations to come, and to maintain our world leadership for peace and freedom. Let us resolve to build that bridge (*applause, cheers*).

He mentioned that bridge more than fifteen times in the hour. It was his metaphor.

How good he looked! It did not matter what he said. He never lost his vigor. Still! Excitement began to ooze out of the occasion. The delegates had heard too many other speakers go on this week about children and the family. One felt at last as if one were trapped in one of the old (by now classic) MGM films, one of those well-made dung heaps of sentimentality. We were receiving the worldview of the long-gone Hollywood studio lot with its L. B. Mayer star and starlet system.

In an interview Clinton had done for *USA Today*, he had listed the books that had been "sources of real inspiration." He had shaped his values by those books. They were *The Meditations of Marcus Aurelius* and *The Imitation of Christ* by Thomas à Kempis. Christians should, Clinton said, "tend to their own soul's health before all else." There was *Moral Man & Immoral Society* by Reinhold Niebuhr, and that had influenced Clinton about "how you can deal with the question of personal integrity in public life." There was "Politics as a Vocation" by Max Weber. "If you have power over other people," suggested Clinton, "we risk our soul in the exercise of that power. It's a great call for humility."

Finally, there was his weekly reading of the Bible. He quoted Saint Paul: "It is the very thing I would not do that I do; the very thing that I would do that I do not" (Romans 7:15).

He was so bright. He was worthy of becoming a great character in a novel. It wasn't what he had done but what he had failed to do. Gogol would have enshrined him. He was perfect for *Dead Souls*. He had failed to go to the root of any problem. He had a mind that wonked and wonked, and none of the vehicles of thought that his reading brought to him had been able to make a real stir in his political world, not Marcus Aurelius, Thomas à Kempis, Reinhold Niebuhr, Max Weber, Saint Paul, Jesus, or Jehovah. If only just once he would say, "Look, I'm no good and I can prove it, but for a bad guy working in a very bad town, maybe I am entitled to say, 'I have accomplished one thing. I never gave up. I take a good punch. You can't keep me down.'"

Would he be ready to listen to a reply from someone else who was no good and could prove it? The words would go like this: "If you screw around a lot, it may do a great many things for you (increase your experience, expand your ego, and/or reduce your chances of getting cancer). It will certainly make you more knowing in the art of seducing the electorate, but in most cases, you cannot pretend that it is particularly good for the kids."

If Clinton beat Dole—and he certainly would, provided creatures from the president's past did not rise up out of the black lagoon—the credit could go to the last forty years of television. For a majority of TV-watching Americans, it was likely that Clinton was by now the most fascinating character to come along since J.R. That large share of America's viewers would not wish the Clintons to go off the air. For this is a TV entertainment with the potential to rise above all the video heights of the past, and even the Simpson case could pale before the future adventures of Bill and Hillary.

At the Point of My Pen

———

(1998)

I MAY NOT TELL YOU WHY I write—it could be too complicated for my mind—but I can tell you about my dear friend, my oldest friend, Jean Malaquais, and why he writes.

I remember how it was with him forty years ago when he was in his mid-forties and was working on a novel, *The Joker.* He would spend fourteen hours a day at his desk. Since he was punctilious about literary virtue to the point of vice, he would, what with deletions, corrections, and revisions, manage to advance his narrative two or three hundred words. One page a day for fourteen hours of horrendous labor. Since his powers of concentration were intense, it was, indeed, a labor for which no other adjective applied. Fourteen hours. Horrendous. I, a more self-indulgent writer, used to complain that a thousand words in three or four hours was hardly a fair bargain for me.

I asked him once, "Why do you insist on remaining a writer? With your intelligence, with your culture, you could be successful at so many things. Writing may not be a normal activity for you."

He happened to agree. "You are absolutely right," he said. "I am not a natural writer. There are even times when I detest this torture. I achieve so little of my aims."

His aims, needless to say, were immense. They were exactly at the center of the problem. "All right," I said, "why not do something else?"

"Never," he said.

"Never? Tell me why."

"The only time I know the truth is when it reveals itself at the point of my pen."

I have been thinking of Jean Malaquais's answer for forty years. I could go on at length about how I write to convey my anger at all that I think is wrong in this world, or I could speak of the mystery of the novelist's aesthetic—ah, to be able to create a world that exists on the terms one has given it!—or I could even, unlike Jean Malaquais, be able to say, "When it's a matter of making a living, you can't beat the hours." But finally, I subscribe to his reply. For me, it has the advantage of being incontestably true. The only time, right or wrong, that I feel a quintessential religious emotion—that the power of the truth is in me—comes on occasion when I write, no, even better: the only time I know the truth is at the point of my pen.

2000s

Social Life, Literary Desires, Literary Corruption

(2003)

ONE OF THE CRUELEST remarks in the language is: Those who can, do; those who can't, teach. The parallel must be: Those who meet experience, learn to live; those who don't, write.

The second remark has as much truth as the first—which is to say, some truth. Of course, many a young man has put himself in danger in order to pick up material for his writing, but as a matter to make one wistful, not one major American athlete, CEO, politician, engineer, trade union official, surgeon, airline pilot, chess master, call girl, sea captain, teacher, bureaucrat, Mafioso, pimp, recidivist, physicist, rabbi, movie star, clergyman, or priest or nun has also emerged as a major novelist since the Second World War.

What with ghostwriters, collaborators, and editors hand-cranking the tongues of the famous long enough to get their memoirs into tape recorders, it could be said that some dim reflection can be found in literature of the long aisles and huge machines of that social mill which is the world of endeavor—yes, just about as much as comes back to us from a photograph insufficiently exposed in the picture taking, a ghost image substituted for the original lights and deep shadows of the object. So, for every good novel about a trade union that has been written from the inside, we have ten thousand better novels to read about authors and the social activities of their friends. Writers tend to live with writers just as automotive engineers congregate in the same country clubs of the same suburbs around Detroit.

But even as we pay for the social insularity of Detroit engineers by having to look at the repetitive hump of their design until finally what is most amazing about the automobile is how little it has been improved in the last fifty years, so literature suffers from its own endemic hollow: we are overfamiliar with the sensitivity of the sensitive and relatively ignorant of the cunning of the strong and the stupid, one—it may be fatal—step removed from good and intimate perception of the inside procedures of the corporate, financial, governmental, Mafia, and working-class establishments. Investigative journalism has taken us into the guts of the machine, only not really, not enough. We still do not have much idea of the soul of any inside operator; we do not, for instance, yet have a clue to what makes a quarterback ready for a good day or a bad one. In addition, the best investigative reporting of new journalism tends to rest on too narrow an ideological base—the rational, ironic, fact-oriented world of the media liberal. So we have a situation, call it a cultural malady, of the most basic sort: a failure of sufficient information (that is, good *literary* information) to put into those centers of our mind we use for assessment. No matter how much we read, we tend to know too little of how the world works. The men who do the real work offer us no real writing, and the writers who explore the minds of such men approach from an intellectual stance that distorts their vision. You would not necessarily want a saint to try to write about a computer engineer, but you certainly would not search for the reverse. All too many saints, monsters, maniacs, mystics, and rock performers are being written about these days, however, by practitioners of journalism whose inner vision is usually graphed by routine parameters. Our continuing inability to comprehend the world is likely to continue.

———————

Being a novelist, I want to know every world. I would never close myself off to a subject unless it's truly repulsive to me. While one can never take one's imperviousness to corruption for granted, it is still important to have some idea of how the world works. What ruins most writers of talent is that they don't get enough experience, so their novels tend to develop a certain paranoid perfection. That is almost never as good as the rough edge of reality. (Franz Kafka immaculately excepted!)

For example, how much of the history that's made around us is conspiracy, how much is simple fuckups? You have to know the world to get some idea of that.

It's not advisable for a novelist, once he is successful!, to live in an upper-class social milieu for too long. Since it is a world of rigid rules, you cannot be yourself. There's a marvelous built-in reflex in such society. It goes: if you are completely one of us, then you are not very interesting. (Unless you have prodigious amounts of money or impeccable family.) If you have any en-trée, it's because that world is always fascinated with mavericks, at least until the point where they become bored with you. Then you are out. On the other hand, while in, even as a maverick, there are certain rules you have to obey, and the first is to be amusing. (Capote and Jerzy Kosinski come to mind.) If you start accepting those rules past the point where you enjoy going along as part of the game, then you are injuring yourself. Capote played consigliere to New York society until he could bear it no longer and then he commenced his self-destruction with *Answered Prayers*. Kosinski, who may have been the most amusing guest of them all in New York, committed suicide during an on-going illness.

I remember saying in 1958, "I am imprisoned with a perception that will settle for nothing less than making a revolution in the consciousness of our time." And I certainly failed, didn't I? At the time, I thought I had books in me that no one else did, and so soon as I was able to write them, society would be altered. Kind of grandiose.

Now, the things I've stood for have been roundly defeated. Literature, after all, has been ground down in the second half of the twentieth century. It's a gloomy remark, but consider that literature was one of the forces that helped to shape the latter part of the nineteenth century—naturalism, for example. One can fear that in another hundred years the serious novel will bear the same relation to serious people that the five-act verse play does today. The profound novel will be a curiosity, a long cry away from what great writing once offered. Where indeed would England be now without Shakespeare? Or Ireland without James Joyce or Yeats? If you ask who has had that kind of influence today in America, I'd say Madonna. Some years ago, the average young girl was completely influenced by her. She affected the way girls dressed, acted, behaved. So far, she's had more to do with women's liberation than Women's Liberation. I mean, for every girl who was affected by feminist ideology, there must have been five who tried to live and dress the way they thought Madonna did. They had their own private revolution without ever hearing about *Ms.* magazine.

Sometimes you write a novel because it comes out of elements in yourself that—no better word—are deep. The subject appeals to some root in your psyche, and you set out on a vertiginous venture. But there are other times when you may get into an altogether different situation. You just damn well have to write a book for no better reason than that your economic problems are pressing.

Tough Guys Don't Dance comes under that rubric. After I finished *Ancient Evenings,* I was exhausted. I also felt spoiled. So I did no writing for ten months. Unfortunately, my then publisher Little, Brown and I were parting company. (They weren't mad about authors who took eleven years on a massive tome like *Ancient Evenings.*) However, there was one more book owed to them. And my feeling was, Well, they won't want the book right away even if they have been paying me good money every month to write it and I haven't been doing the job. Reality had not tapped on any of my windows for all those months. If it sounds silly that a grown man could be that naïve, well, we are all, you know, somewhat less than our sophistication.

So, on month ten, they said to me in effect, "Are you going to give us a novel or will you repay us the money?" Now, I had to recognize that if I ended up owing them a year of sizable monthly stipends, I would never catch up with the IRS.

The only thing was to come up with a book in sixty days! I couldn't possibly give them nonfiction. The research would take too long—no, I had to do a novel that would be quick and comfortable. First thing, therefore, was to make a decision on whether to do it in first person or third. First person is always more hospitable in the beginning. You can give a sense of the immediate almost at once. It would be first person, then.

But where would it take place? New York is too complicated to write about quickly. Besides, given the constrictions of time, I had to know the place well. All right, it would have to be a book about Provincetown. At that time, in the early eighties, I had been going there off and on for forty years. For practical purposes, it was all the small town I would ever have.

What should it be about? Well, I could take my cue from *An American Dream*, make it a story of murder and suspense. But who would the narrator be? An easy decision: Let him be a writer. In first person, a writer is the single most cooperative character to deal with. Let him be between thirty-five and forty, frustrated, never published, bitter, quite bright, but not as bright as myself. After all, I had to be able to write this book in a hurry. Then, having subscribed to these quick guidelines, I thought if I had one pious bone in my body, just one, I would now get down and pray. Because I was still in trouble. Sixty days to produce a novel!

I set out. It's one of the few times I've felt blessed as a writer. I knew there was a limit to how good the book could be, but the style came through, and that is always half of a novel. You can write a very bad book, but if the style is first-rate, then you've got something that will live—not forever, but for a decent time. The shining example might be G. K. Chesterton's *The Man Who Was Thursday*. It has an undeniably silly plot unless you invest a great deal into it. A worshipful right-wing critic can do a blitheringly wonderful thesis on the symbolic leaps and acrobatics of *The Man Who Was Thursday*, but actually, it's about as silly as a Jules Verne novel. Yet the writing itself is fabulous. The style is extraordinary. The aperçus are marvelous. *The Man Who Was Thursday* proves the point: style is half of a novel.

And for some good reason, unknown to me, the style came through in *Tough Guys Don't Dance*. The writing was probably, for the most part, as good as I can muster. The plot, however, was just as close to silly. That was the price to pay for the speed of composition. The irony is that the book did not end up at Little, Brown. I was able to pay off my debt because Random House wanted me, and I have been with them ever since.

I expect we are now ready to talk about the writer's daily work.

Review of *The Corrections*

———

(2003)

I HAVEN'T LOOKED AT Jonathan Franzen's work yet, but by some reports, *The Corrections* is the first important novel that's come along in quite a while. Obviously, it has to be read if one wants any sense at all of what's going on in American letters. And I noticed when looking at the blurbs on the back that something like twenty writers and reviewers all gave their salute, and most of them were of Franzen's generation. Updike wasn't there; not Bellow, not Roth; I wasn't there—the oldest was Don DeLillo, who gave the smallest praise. The others were new, respected names like David Foster Wallace, Michael Cunningham, and a host of others, all contemporary. Apparently, *The Corrections* is the book of a generation that wants to wipe the slate clean and offer a new literary movement.

I think the younger writers are sick of Roth, Bellow, Updike, and myself the way we were sick of Hemingway and Faulkner. When I was a young writer we never talked about anyone but them, and that feeling grew into resentment. Since they had no interest in us, we began to think, Yeah, they're great—now get off the stage! We want the lights on us!

———

Since writing the above, I've read *The Corrections*. It is very good as a novel, very good indeed, and yet most unpleasant now that it sits in memory, as if one has been wearing the same clothes for too many days. Franzen writes superbly well sentence for sentence, and yet one is not happy with the achievement. It is too full of language, even as the nouveaux riches are too full of money. He is exceptionally intelligent, but like a polymath, he lives much of the time in Wonkville Hollow, for Franzen is an intellectual dredging machine. Everything of novelistic use to him that came up on the Internet seems to have bypassed the higher reaches of his imagination—it is as if he offers us more human experience than he has literally mastered, and this is obvious when we come upon his set pieces on gourmet restaurants or giant cruise ships or modern Lithuania in disarray. Such sections read like first-rate magazine pieces, but no better—they stick to the surface. When he deals with what he does know directly and intimately, which is the family at the core of his book—an old father, a late-middle-aged mother, two grown sons, and a daughter—he is an exceptionally gifted observer. What waste, however! Nothing much is at stake for us with his people. They have almost no changing relation to each other (considering that they have something like six hundred pages to work up a few new mutual stances). Three, maybe four of the five can legitimately be characterized as one-note characters—only the daughter, who becomes a passionate lesbian, has much to tell us. It is not only that—dare I use the old book reviewer's clichés?—they offer us very little rooting interest and are, for the most part, *dank*. Worse!—nothing but petty, repetitious conflicts arise from them. They wriggle forever in the higher reaches of human mediocrity and incarcerated habit. The greatest joy to lift from the spine of the book is the author's vanity at how talented he is. He may well have the highest IQ of any American novelist writing today, but unhappily, he rewards us with more work than exhilaration, since rare is any page in *The Corrections* that could not be five to ten lines shorter.

All this said, exceptional potential still remains. I think it is the sense of his potential that excites so many. Now, the success of

The Corrections will change his life and charge it. Franzen will begin to have experiences at a more intense level; the people he encounters will have more sense of mission, will be more exciting in their good and in their evil, more open at their best, more crafty in their use of closure. So if he is up to it, he will grow with his new experiences (which, as we ought to have some idea by now, is no routine matter), but if he succeeds, yes, he has the potential to become a major writer on a very high level indeed. At present, his negative characteristics predominate. Bellow and Company can still rest on their old laurels, I think I am almost ready to say, "Alas!"

Gaining an Empire, Losing Democracy?

(2003)

THERE IS A SUBTEXT to what the Bushites are doing as they prepare for war in Iraq. My hypothesis is that President George W. Bush and many conservatives have come to the conclusion that the only way they can save America and get if off its present downslope is to become a regime with a greater military presence and drive toward empire. My fear is that Americans might lose their democracy in the process.

By downslope I'm referring not only to the corporate scandals, the church scandals, and the FBI scandals. The country has gone kind of crazy in the eyes of conservatives. Also, kids can't read anymore. Especially for conservatives, the culture has become too sexual.

Iraq is the excuse for moving in an imperial direction. War with Iraq, as they originally conceived it, would be a quick, dramatic step that would enable them to control the Near East as a powerful base—not least because of the oil there, as well as the water supplies from the Tigris and Euphrates Rivers—to build a world empire.

The Bushites also expect to bring democracy to the region and believe that in itself will help to diminish terrorism. But I expect the opposite will happen: terrorists are not impressed by democracy. They loathe it. They are fundamentalists of the most basic kind. The more successful democracy is in the Near East—not likely in my view—the more terrorism it will generate.

The only outstanding obstacle to the drive toward empire in the Bushites' minds is China. Indeed, one of the great fears in the Bush administration about America's downslope is that the "stem studies" such as science, technology, and engineering are all faring poorly in U.S. universities. The number of American doctorates is going down and down. But the number of Asians obtaining doctorates in those same stem studies are increasing at a great rate.

Looking twenty years ahead, the administration perceives that there will come a time when China will have technology superior to America's. When that time comes, America might well say to China that "we can work together," we will be as the Romans to you Greeks. You will be our extraordinary, well-cultivated slaves. But don't try to dominate us. That would be your disaster. This is the scenario that some of the brightest neoconservatives are thinking about. (I use Rome as a metaphor, because metaphors are usually much closer to the truth than facts.)

What has happened, of course, is that the Bushites have run into much more opposition than they thought they would from other countries and among the home population. It may well end up that we won't have a war, but a new strategy to contain Iraq and wear Saddam down. If that occurs, Bush is in terrible trouble.

My guess though, is that, like it or not, want it or not, America is going to go to war because that is the only solution Bush and his people can see.

The dire prospect that opens, therefore, is that America is going to become a mega–banana republic where the army will have more and more importance in Americans' lives. It will be an ever greater and greater overlay on the American system. And before it is all over, democracy, noble and delicate as it is, may give way. My long experience with human nature—I'm eighty years old now—suggests that it is possible that fascism, not democracy, is the natural state.

Indeed, democracy is the special condition—a condition we

will be called upon to defend in the coming years. That will be
enormously difficult because the combination of the corporation, the military, and the complete investiture of the flag with
mass spectator sports has set up a prefascistic atmosphere in
America already.

The White Man Unburdened

————

(2003)

EXEUNT: LIGHTNING AND THUNDER, shock and awe. Dust, ash, fog, fire, smoke, sand, blood, and a good deal of waste now move to the wings. The stage, however, remains occupied. The question posed at curtain-rise has not been answered. Why did we go to war? If no real weapons of mass destruction are found, the question will keen in pitch.

Or, if some weapons are uncovered in Iraq, it is likely that even more have been moved to new hiding places beyond the Iraqi border. Should horrific events take place, we can count on a predictable response: "Good, honest, innocent Americans died today because of evil al-Qaeda terrorists." Yes, we will hear the president's voice before he even utters such words. (For those of us who are not happy with George W. Bush, we may as well recognize that living with him in the Oval Office is like being married to a mate who always says exactly what you know in advance he or she is going to say, which helps to account for why more than half of America now appears to love him.)

The key question remains—why did we go to war? It is not yet answered. The host of responses has already produced a cognitive stew. But the most painful single ingredient at the moment

is, of course, the discovery of the graves. We have relieved the
world of a monster who killed untold numbers, meganumbers,
of victims. Nowhere is any emphasis put upon the fact that many
of the bodies were of the Shiites of southern Iraq who have been
decimated repeatedly in the last twelve years for daring to rebel
against Saddam in the immediate aftermath of the Gulf War. Of
course, we were the ones who encouraged them to revolt in the
first place, and then failed to help them. Why? There may have
been an ongoing argument in the first Bush administration
which was finally won by those who believed that a Shiite victory
over Saddam could result in a host of Iraqi imams who might
make common cause with the Iranian ayatollahs, Shiites joining
with Shiites! Today, from the point of view of the remaining Iraqi
Shiites, it would be hard for us to prove to them that they were
not the victims of a double cross. So they may look upon the
graves that we congratulate ourselves for having liberated as se-
pulchral voices calling out from their tombs—asking us to take a
share of the blame. Which, of course, we will not.

Yes, our guilt for a great part of those bodies remains a large
subtext and Saddam was creating mass graves all through the
1970s and 1980s. He killed Communists en masse in the 1970s,
which didn't bother us a bit. Then he slaughtered tens of thousands of Iraqis during the war with Iran—a time when we supported him. A horde of those newly discovered graves go back to
that period. Of course, real killers never look back.

The administration, however, was concerned only with how
best to expedite the war. They hastened to look for many a justifiable reason. The Iraqis were a nuclear threat; they were teeming
with weapons of mass destruction; they were working closely with
al-Qaeda; they had even been the dirty geniuses behind 9/11.
The reasons offered to the American public proved skimpy, unverifiable, and void of the realpolitik of our need to get a choke
hold on the Middle East for many a reason more than Israel-
Palestine. We had to sell the war on false pretenses.

The intensity of the falsification could best be seen as a reflection of the enormous damage 9/11 has brought to America's morale, particularly the core—the corporation. All the organization

people high and low, managers, division heads, secretaries, salesmen, accountants, market specialists, all that congeries of corporate office American, plus all who had relatives, friends, or
classmates who worked in the Twin Towers—the shock traveled
into the fundament of the American psyche. And the American
working class identified with the warriors who were lost fighting
that blaze, the firemen and the police, all instantly ennobled.

It was a political bonanza for Bush provided he could deliver
an appropriate sense of revenge to the millions—or is it the tens
of millions?—who identified directly with those incinerated in
the Twin Towers. When Osama bin Laden failed to be captured
by the posses we sent to Afghanistan, Bush was thrust back to
ongoing domestic problems that did not give any immediate
suggestion that they could prove solution-friendly. The economy
was sinking, the market was down, and some classic bastions of
American faith (corporate integrity, the FBI, and the Catholic
Church—to cite but three) had each suffered a separate and
grievous loss of face. Increasing joblessness was undermining national morale. Since our administration was conceivably not
ready to tackle any one of the serious problems looming before
them that did not involve enriching the top, it was natural for
the administration to feel an impulse to move into larger ven-
tures, thrusts into the empyrean—war! We could say we went to
war because we very much needed a successful war as a species of
psychic rejuvenation. Any major excuse would do—nuclear
threat, terrorist nests, weapons of mass destruction—we could
always make the final claim that we were liberating the Iraqis.
Who could argue with that? One could not. One could only ask:
What will the cost be to our democracy?

Be it said that the administration knew something a good
many of us did not—it knew that we had a very good, perhaps
even an extraordinarily good, if essentially untested, group of
armed forces, a skilled, disciplined, well-motivated military,
career-focused and run by a field-rank and general staff who
were intelligent, articulate, and considerably less corrupt than
any other power cohort in America.

In such a pass, how could the White House fail to use them?

They would prove quintessential morale builders to a core element of American life—those tens of millions of Americans who had been spiritually wounded by 9/11. They could also serve an even larger group, which had once been near to 50 percent of the population and remained key to the president's political footing. This group had taken a real beating. As a matter of collective ego, the good average white American male had had very little to nourish his morale since the job market had gone bad, nothing, in fact, unless he happened to be a member of the armed forces. There, it was certainly different. The armed forces had become the paradigmatic equal of a great young athlete looking to test his true size. Could it be that there was a bozo out in the boondocks who was made to order, and his name was Iraq? Iraq had a tough rep, but not much was left to him inside. A dream opponent. A desert war is designed for an air force whose state of the art is comparable in perfection to a top-flight fashion model on a runway. Yes, we would liberate the Iraqis.

So we went ahead against all obstacles—of which the UN was the first. Wantonly, shamelessly, proudly, exuberantly, at least one-half of our prodigiously divided America could hardly wait for the new war. We understood that our television was going to be terrific. And it was. Sanitized but terrific—which is, after all, exactly what network and good cable television are supposed to be.

And there were other factors for using our military skills, minor but significant: these reasons return us to the ongoing malaise of the white American male. He had been taking a daily drubbing over the last thirty years. For better or worse, the women's movement has had its breakthrough successes and the old, easy white male ego has withered in the glare. Even the consolation of rooting for his team on TV had been skewed. For many, there was now measurably less reward in watching sports than there used to be, a clear and declarable loss. The great *white* stars of yesteryear were for the most part gone, gone in football, in basketball, in boxing, and half gone in baseball. Black genius now prevailed in all these sports (and the Hispanics were coming up fast; even the Asians were beginning to make their mark). We white men were now left with half of tennis (at least its male half), and might also point to ice hockey, skiing, soccer, golf (with the notable exception of the Tiger), as well as lacrosse, track, swimming, and the World Wrestling Federation—remnants of a once great and glorious white athletic centrality.

Of course, there were sports fans who loved the stars on their favorite teams without regard to race. Sometimes, they even liked black athletes the most. Such white men tended to be liberals. They were no use to Bush. He needed to take care of his more immediate constituency. If he had a covert strength, it was his knowledge of the unspoken things that bothered American white men the most—just those matters they were not always ready to admit to themselves. The first was that people hipped on sports can get overaddicted to victory. Sports, the corporate ethic (advertising), and the American flag had become a go-for-the-win triumvirate that had developed many psychic connections with the military.

After all, war was, with all else, the most dramatic and serious extrapolation of sports. The concept of victory could be seen by some as the noblest species of profit in union with patriotism. So Bush knew that a big victory in an easy war would work for the good white American male. If blacks and Hispanics were representative of their share of the population in the enlisted ranks, still they were not a majority, and the faces of the officer corps (as seen on the tube) suggested that the percentage of white men increased as one rose in rank to field and general officers. Moreover, we had knockout tank echelons, Super-Marines, and—one magical ace in the hole—the best air force that ever existed. If we could not find our machismo anywhere else, we could certainly count on the interface between combat and technology. Let me then advance the offensive suggestion that this may have been one of the covert but real reasons we went looking for war. We knew we were likely to be good at it.

In the course, however, of all the quick events of the last few months, our military passed through a transmogrification. Indeed, it was one hellion of a morph. We went, willy-nilly, from a potentially great athlete to serving as an emergency intern required to operate at high speed on an awfully sick patient full of frustration, outrage, and violence. Now in the last month, even as the patient is getting stitched up somewhat, a new and troubling question arises: Have any fresh medicines been developed to deal with what seem to be teeming infections? Do we really know how to treat livid suppurations? Or would it be better to just keep trusting our great American luck, our faith in our divinely protected can-do luck? We are, by custom, gung ho. If these suppurations prove to be unmanageable, or just too time-consuming, may we not leave them behind? We could move on to the next venue. Syria, we might declare in our best John Wayne voice: You can run, but you can't hide. Saudi Arabia, you overrated tank of blubber, do you need us more than ever? And Iran, watch it, we have eyes for you. You could be a real meal. Because when we fight, we feel good, we are ready to go, and then go some more. We have had a taste. Why, there's a basketful of billions to be made in the Middle East just so long as we can stay ahead of the trillions of debts that are coming after us back home.

Be it said: the motives that lead to a nation's major historical acts can probably rise no higher than the spiritual understanding of its leadership. While George W. may not know as much as he believes he knows about the dispositions of God's blessing, he is driving us at high speed all the same—this man at the wheel whose most legitimate boast might be that he knew how to parlay the part ownership of a major league baseball team into a gubernatorial win in Texas. And—shall we ever forget?—was catapulted, by legal finesse and finagling, into a now tainted but still almighty hymn: "Hail to the Chief"!

No, we will rise no higher than the spiritual understanding of our leadership. And now that the ardor of victory has begun to cool, some will see how it is flawed. For we are victim once again of all those advertising sciences that depend on mendacity and manipulation. We have been gulled about the real reasons for this war, tweaked and poked by some of the best button pushers around to believe that we won a noble and necessary contest when, in fact, the opponent was a hollowed-out palooka whose monstrosities were ebbing into old age.

Perhaps he was not that old. Perhaps Saddam made a decision to go underground with as much wealth as he had spirited away, and would fund al-Qaeda or some extension of it in a collaboration of sorts with Osama bin Laden—a new underground team, the Incompatible Terrorist Twins. That is a hypothesis as mad as the world we are beginning to live in.

Democracy, more than any other political system, depends on a modicum of honesty. Ultimately, it is much at the mercy of a leader who has never been embarrassed by himself. What is to be said of a man who spent two years in the air force of the National Guard (as a way of not having to go to Vietnam) and proceeded—like many another spoiled and wealthy father's son—not to bother to show up for duty in his second year of service? Most of us have episodes in our youth that can cause us shame on reflection. It is a mark of maturation that we do not try to profit from our early lacks and vices but do our best to learn from them. Bush proceeded, however, to turn his declaration of the Iraqi campaign's end into a mighty fashion show. He chose—this overnight clone of Honest Abe—to arrive on the deck of the aircraft carrier *Abraham Lincoln* on an S-3B Viking jet that came in with a dramatic tailhook landing. The carrier was easily within helicopter range of San Diego but G.W. would not have been able to show himself in flight regalia, and so would not have been able to demonstrate how well he wore the uniform he had not honored. Jack Kennedy, a war hero, was always in civvies while he was commander in chief. So was General Eisenhower. George W. Bush, who might, if he had been entirely on his own, have made a world-class male model (since he never takes an awkward photograph), proceeded to tote the flight helmet and sport the flight suit. There he was for the photo op looking like one more great guy among the great guys. Let us hope that our democracy will survive these nonstop foulings of the nest.

Immodest Proposals

(2004)

IN DECEMBER 2000, George W. Bush became president by dint of a Supreme Court decision warped shamelessly in his direction. He may have lost the popular vote, but he won the game. In compensation for a limited intellectual spirit, he now placed his reliance on big-money advisers who were used to playing with high stakes.

Tax cuts for the rich characterized the first eight months of his administration. In that period he also took more vacations than any U.S. president before him. Chalk it up to the callow distress of encountering his massive ignorance of the new job. In the wake of 9/11, however, came an unmitigated run of White House mendacity calculated to carry us into war. If our Democratic candidate could ever be fortunate enough to run exclusively against George W.'s misdeeds, there is small chance he would fail to win. In the last century no Republican president, not George W.'s father, nor Reagan, Nixon, Hoover, Coolidge—we can go all the way back to Taft, Teddy Roosevelt, and McKinley—had put together such an enrich-the-rich set of political actions. Nonetheless, we Democrats face a near to insurmountable irony. George W. is a popular, even a populist, president. All too many of the public love him, love him still. We have to overtake a war president with an immense campaign chest who manages to keep ahead of the skunk trail of an abominable record.

We have, for example, suffered the highest number of private bankruptcies in any twelve-month period of our history, in company with the highest number of home foreclosures in the past thirty years. Even as two million Americans were losing their jobs, unemployment benefits were not extended. We have the largest budget deficit in U.S. history, a projected half a billion dollars coming up. Half of the nation is outraged over the lies that embedded us in Iraq.

For those whose pride in America runs deep, this sense of alienation from our country is full of woe, sharp as a divorce. The United States now feels like two nations, and Iraq is there to remind us daily of our surrealistic hubris. Boorish arrogance carried the day. Confident we could bring American-style democracy to the Middle East, we proceeded to ignore an entrenched establishment of mullahs who see American democracy as the literal embodiment of Satan.

It is possible that George W. has never grown up, and the same may be true for half of us in America. This, indeed, is the greatest obstacle to the Democrats winning the election in 2004. We have to recognize the possibility of two entirely different kinds of presidential campaigns. At the time of this writing, George W. Bush's popularity has begun to decline. If that continues, the Democrats can win by running against the economy.

If, however, unemployment diminishes and the stock market shows signs of new life, if our situation in Iraq looks less like a quagmire and the road map to peace between Israel and the Palestinians has not fallen apart, then Bush's personal popularity can rise again. At that time it will behoove the Democrats to try to win every serious voter. No longer can we address ourselves to our own side only, no, we will be obliged to look for open-minded Republicans as well. There are a number of serious conservatives who have been appalled by a leader who speaks like an android and plays Russian roulette with our economy and foreign affairs. In a close election the Democrats have to pick up a significant number of conservative and independent voters, and that is possible provided—and this proviso is the crux of the matter—we are able to demonstrate that the spiritual values in our politics go deeper than the Republicans'.

Given the size of the endless and complex debates between and within the two parties concerning the multitudinous problems of labor, farming and foreign trade, this memo will restrict itself to the following subjects: Bush's Virtual Reality, the Corporate Economy, advertising and education—the last two closely affect each other—then the trinity of oil, plastics, and the ecosystem, followed by such social issues as prison, abortion and gay liberation, welfare and the safety net, after which we can take a look at foreign policy, homeland security, and terrorism.

These topics, given their complexity, can hardly be satisfied by a memo, but one or two suggestions may prove of future interest provided we win the election in 2004.

A New American Belief System: Virtual Reality

So why did Bush and company go to war? The probable answer is that an escape was needed from our problems at home. Joblessness gave no sign of going away, and corporate greed had been caught mooning its corrupt buttocks onto every front page. The CIA had become much too recognizable as an immense intelligence apparatus whose case officers did not speak Arabic, and the stock market was offering signs that it might gurgle down to the bottom of the bowl. An easy war looked then to be George W. Bush's best solution. What he needed and what he got was a media jamboree that provided our sweet dose of patriotic ecstasy. Bush would give us *The Twin Towers, Part Two—America's Revenge*. We had all seen Part One—the audacity of the terrorists, the monumental viciousness of the attempt, and its exceptional filmic success—who will ever forget the collapse of those monoliths? The TV viewer had been overpowered by the kind of horror that belongs to dreams. One was witnessing what seemed a video game on a cosmic scale. Worse! The exploitation film

had finally come alive! Two gleaming corporate castles disinte-
grated before our eyes. Two airplanes did it. David had struck
Goliath, and David was on the wrong side. The event had gone
right into the nervous system of America, but Bush now had his
mighty mission, and he knew the game that would handle it—
Virtual Reality.

Virtual Reality is built on whatever parameters have been laid
into it. The predesigned situations plus the responses permitted
within the limits of the game—steering a car on a video screen,
for example—measure your success or failure. Virtual Reality is
then a closed system, a facsimile of life. You have fewer choices,
and the choices have been laid out for you in advance.

In life we encounter not only parameters but chaos. Closed
systems forbid unexpected patterns, confusion, and all that
seems meaningless. They declare what the nature of reality can
be. In that sense Communism was Virtual Reality and religious
fundamentalism is still another spiritual settlement within a totally structured system. Obviously, if you live in such a matrix, it
helps if you believe the parameters were established by a higher
authority.

Ergo, Bush's decision to invade Iraq came from the Lord. Virtual Reality decided which conclusions we would obtain before
we went in. We had all the scenarios in hand. We were prepared
for everything but chaos.

Given our human distaste for chaos, Virtual Reality is the
choice of every ethical system that looks for no difficult questions, especially if they lead to even livelier and more difficult
questions. The emphasis is always to go back to the answer you
had before you started.

So Bush laid out the parameters. There was a hideous country
out there led by an evil madman. This monster possessed huge
weapons of mass destruction. But we Americans, a brave and
militant band of angels, were ready to battle our way up to the
heavens. That was our duty. Safeguard our land and all other
deserving lands from such evil.

Stocked with new heroes and new dragons, Bush was quick to
sense that his presentation would be lapped up by half the

nation—all those good Americans who were longing for the pleasure of being able to cheer for America again. He turned churchgoing into high drama. September 11 had transmogrified him from a yahoo out of Yale to an awesome angel. We were in a war against evil. A spiritual adventure, full of slam-bang.

Truth, it may have been Bush's political genius to recognize that the U.S. public would rather live with Virtual Reality than reality. For the latter, out there on the sweaty hoof, bristled with questions, and there were no quick answers. Whereas Virtual Reality gave you American Good versus Satanic Evil—boss entertainment!—evil was now easy to recognize. Everything from Islamic terrorists to hincty Frenchmen. Freedom Fries! Be it said that TV advertising, with its investiture into the nerves and sinews of our American senses, had long been delivering Virtual Reality into our lives—all those decades of sensuous promises in the commercials.

The Welfare of the Rich

A Swedish multimillionaire, talking to his American guest, could not keep from complaining how steep were his taxes. Yet, by the end of the evening, warmed, perhaps, by his own good liquor, he reversed course and said, "Do you know, there is one good thing about all these taxes. I am able, at least, to go to bed and know that nobody in Sweden is tossing all night on an empty stomach. I can say that much for our safety net, I do sleep better."

Perhaps the time has come for Americans to stop worrying about the welfare of the rich. For the last two decades, the assumption has grown more powerful each year that unless the very well-to-do are encouraged to become wealthier, our economy will falter. Well, we have allowed them to get wealthier and wealthier and then even wealthier, and the economy is faltering. Apparently, the economic lust of the 1990s has unbalanced the springs. Might it not be unnatural, even a little peculiar, to concern ourselves so much about the needs of the rich? The rich, as Scott Fitzgerald tried to suggest to Ernest Hemingway, are not like you and me. They are not. They know how to make money. They do not need incentives. Making money is not only their gift but their vital need. That is their vision of a spiritual reward. Not only is their measure of self attached directly to the volume of their gains, but the majority of them know how to stay rich. They are highly qualified to take care of themselves in any society, be it socialist, fascist, banana republic, or chaotic. Whether they live in a corporate economy relatively free of government or with a larger government presence, they will prosper. They can withstand an American safety net. And they may even sleep better.

In the half century since World War II, Americans have seen the Corporation become more and more powerful, usually with the aid of the government. Under Clinton—to name one Democratic sin—there were unconscionable periods of Corporate Welfare. They took place even as we were stripping welfare from the poor. It was outrageous. By the end of the 1990s, it was out of control. An all-out competition began among top executives to see who could become the Champion of the Golden Parachute. The 1990s became a study in edema-of-the-ego among once-responsible CEOs. We have yet to measure the size of that damage to our economy.

Capitalism works best when there is true competitive pride in the quality of one's product. But marketing has now stepped in. The impulse to put your acumen, your daring, your prudence, and your energy into making something better than it was before has given way to a lower desire. It has become more rewarding to market successfully a sleazy piece of goods. More skill is required at manipulating the public.

A basic choice has to be made. Are we Democrats ready to attack the Corporate Economy we all helped to create? It is open to attack for its marketing practices and its egregious profit taking. There is, by now, no real alternative to taxing the rich and ending the tax cuts. If we do not call on new imposts, we will not be able to create a health system for all, plus a safety net. So we have to reinvigorate the argument that a well-funded active government is not creeping socialism. Rather, the return of government as a major partner in our economic existence could bring some quietus to the greed, overmarketing, and slovenliness of the Corporate Economy. Through emphasizing taxation of the vices and indulgences of corporate business, we will also be able to claim that we are improving its capacity to make a profit. Indeed, this claim might have the added advantage of being true. Something in most of us, including the profiteers, is violated when the gap between rich and poor yawns before us. There is no way to justify the right of any executive to make five hundred times more than his lowest-paid worker. That kind of inequity belonged to the Pharaohs. It could be debated whether a decent ratio is ten to one, or fifty to one, but a disproportion of five hundred to one pokes rudely into a spiritual core most of us still possess. It is time to say again: Let's tax the rich. Let's tax their incomes, their dividends, their offshore investments, their perks, their concealed expenses, their padded accounts, their promotional squanderings, their limousines, their boats, their airplanes, their entertainments, their death tax, yes, even their advertising.

Maybe it is time to recognize that there is a sculptor's art to taxation. The body of national production can be worked into better shape by judicious choices once the government becomes again a serious partner in the economy. Once again, let us not be paralyzed by the fear of being called socialist. We are not. Historically, we Democrats have been for small business, the family farm, the honest labor union, whereas capitalism, if allowed to become too free of the restraints of government, becomes Corporate Capitalism, plus agribusiness, plus corrupt unions, plus— not least—a manic stock market. Capitalism is unhealthy when most of the money is made from other money.

To restore the promise of American democracy, we would do well to search for the viability of small business, the return of the family farm, and the cleaner labor union. During the presidential campaign, we can do no more than hint at such claims. But is it too much to hope that we Democrats will come up with a candidate who will have the personal integrity to convince both liberals and some conservatives that, while they will not find support for each and every one of their favorite political desires, they will still have the satisfaction of working toward a less lunatic America? If even one-tenth of the Republican vote were to move over to the Democrats, victory could be assured. The question opens: What could such a candidate offer to both sides that might excite them enough to pass over their parochial demands?

The devil has to be in the details. Tax write-offs, tax rebates, tax moratoria have been used repeatedly to enrich corporations, but our real need is to restrict tax relief to those enterprises that benefit the whole economy rather than a privileged corner of it. In a time of worrisome joblessness, why not reduce taxes for all businesses in direct proportion to the number of new jobs they create? Indeed, the obverse can also be effective. Any business that chooses to pare its working force to take in immediate profit could give up a proportion of the new and extra income in added taxes. If it will be argued that such an emphasis on sophisticated taxation will be steering the federal government's nose into every business, the answer is that American capitalism brought this upon itself. As a system, it works considerably better than Communism, but it has its own built-in vices. The free market is not an economic miracle. If Communism failed ultimately because the degree of selflessness demanded of human beings was not enough to counteract the self-enriching urges of the human ego, so capitalism in its turn has demonstrated that greed is no magic elixir, but, to the contrary, greed is greed, and can drive its acolytes into economic hysteria. There is a human balance between self-interest and selflessness. It is not only possible, but likely, that a powerful desire is developing in America to become more honest about ourselves and less overheated in our patriotism. For what is excessive patriotism but unadmitted dread that all too much is wrong?

Education Reform: Kill the Noise, Cut the Glare

While it is sometimes remarked that the poor performance of children in public schools is linked to watching TV for several hours a day, another factor, more invidious, is not mentioned:

the constant insertion of commercials into TV programs. There used to be a time in childhood when one could develop one's power of concentration (which may be the most vital element in the ability to learn) by following a sustained narrative, by reading, for example. Now a commercial interrupts nearly all TV presentations every seven to twelve minutes. The majority of our children have lost any expectation that concentration will not be broken into.

Our plank on education will, of course, parade forth the predictable nostrums—new schools, smaller classes, higher salaries for teachers. We can attack George W. Bush's program, No Child Left Behind, which shows no signs of working. Whatever programs we offer are bound to do less harm than No Child Left Behind, but the basic problem—TV commercials—will remain. It would probably do more good if a portion of the proposed funds for public school education could replace fluorescent lighting in just about every classroom with old-fashioned light-bulbs. The unadmitted truth is that every human alive loses personal appeal under the flat illumination of a fluorescent tube. Children can hardly feel as ready to learn when everyone around them, including their teacher, is a hint ghastly in skin tone.

We are, of course, not ready to tell the electorate that TV advertising has become an albatross upon the American spirit with its instruments of persuasion—noise, disjunction, mendacity and manipulation. Is it possible, given the federal government's soon ravenous need for new kinds of funds, to consider a special tax on advertising? Since the radical right will at once be screaming that this is an attack on free speech, we could term it removal of a business deduction, a penalty for those advertising expenses that go beyond standard industry practice. However phrased, there is no reason for a healthy economy to need to encourage hyped-up marketing for shoddy products. One example we do not dare suggest, not as yet, is to take a good look at the heavy competition in marketeering among the fast-food chains. Very much alike are all of them, and they serve the same social purpose—inexpensive meals quickly available. If they could be encouraged to cease advertising against one another, our children might be spared untold hours of inroads on their attention (plus the accompanying inclination to grab a snack and get a little more obese). Besides, the money saved by the chains, given restrained merchandising, could go into the real risk of competition. Let it depend on the improved quality of their wares!

To War on All Garbage That Does Not Rot

If we are to appeal to conservatives and environmentalists alike, we could suggest that we are in need of an enlarged Food and Drug Administration to explore the long-term effects of nonbiodegradables on public health. Plastic, after all, derives from what was once the waste products of oil. It might even be fair to say that plastic is the excrement of oil, but that would be an abuse of language. Organic excrement can nourish the earth, whereas plastics do not decompose for thousands of years if at all and never revitalize one acre of soil. Meanwhile, our children are raised from infancy with toys composed of synthetic materials in constant contact with their fingertips and their lips. What does that do to them? Such research is, of course, a long way down the road, but our plank could address the ecological problems that plastic refuse presents to the environment. Why not suggest higher rates of taxation on throwaway items that inundate our town and city dumps, there never to decompose?

Of course, the depredations that oil brings to the environment may be the leading problem our civilization faces in the century ahead and therefore is larger than our present readiness to recognize problems that do not have ready solutions. If all too many Americans don't like any question that takes longer than ten seconds to answer, it can be replied that we now have the president we deserve.

Let's Pay for Our Vices—but Don't Put All of Them in Cells

Prisons! The problem owes half its weight to drug laws of the early 1970s that criminalized marijuana possession. The fear then was that America would become a nation of young druggies. We didn't. We became instead a land of air, soil, and river pollution. (The anal emissions of warehoused pigs took over our prairie.) Meanwhile, our prisons were overstuffed with young convicts. Since America is hardly ready to legalize drugs (and empty those prisons by half), there are some unhappy figures to deal with.

In 2003 our inmate population set a record—2,166,260. We have the ratio of incarceration you would expect from Third World tyrannies. Our penitentiaries are loaded with drug offenders serving long sentences for minor infractions.

Can we dare propose that the nation, given the financial relief it would afford, begin to release a good number of minor offenders? A pilot program to explore the question is feasible, even for a convention plank. Some inmates might be released for drug treatment. Marijuana smokers, and petty dealers, could, for example, be given parole on the premise that they would pay a fine if caught continuing their habit or their trade; if they did not have the funds to meet the penalty, they would be required to perform community service for modest pay until the debt is satisfied. To counter the objection that government moneys were being disbursed to excuse a vice, it could be pointed out that we invariably pay for such easy vices as cigarettes and whiskey. Do they or do they not kill more people than marijuana?

Abortion: What Are a Woman's Rights?

Roe v. Wade probably repels more good conservatives than any other item in the liberal canon. Yet a serious and intimate recognition of the question could serve a new Democratic administration. Indeed, it is imperative. The present state of the argument strips all humanity from the equation. Those for the Right to Life see every pregnancy as God's will, God's intention: ergo, the abortionist and his patient are both evil. Defenders of *Roe v. Wade* view abortion as a woman's right yet sully their position by postulating that abortion is not killing a future human being if it takes place within the first three months, or in the first six months, or whenever. It is a stand to weaken one's intellectual self-respect.

Is it possible to agree that abortion is indeed one more form of murder and yet is still a woman's right? If God's will is flouted, it is the woman, not the society, who will pay the price. That would be a huge and indigestible political move if it were ever stated just so. Yet as a species, we humans commit murder all the time, not only in war but by way of the meat and fish and fowl we send daily to our machines of extermination. Every piece of flesh at our tables was slain.

Such an argument is obviously not suited for travel in public. Lambs and cattle are not to be compared to humans, and war protects our endangered land, etc. Since the Right to Life will continue to insist that pregnancy is the direct expression of God's will, let us approach that as the true field of battle for this debate. Sex, given its appeal, its mystery, its extravagances, its explorations, its commitments, its adventures—be they sordid or illuminating—sex by its unique entrance into our most private thoughts, compulsions, pleasures, and, yes, terrors, is for most humans an arena where we are aware of a presence that seems divine, but we are also sensitive often to another presence. Some fornications feel diabolically inspired. The question is begged in its entirety when we say "God's will." A pregnancy can seem a blessing to one woman and a nightmare to another. Most women are haunted by the fear of losing a child in their womb, but there will always be a minority who find themselves drawn to abortion. They are haunted by an opposite terror, the fear that they have conceived a monster.

If that becomes a woman's deepest sentiment within a pregnancy, who has the authority to declare she is in error? She is, after all, convinced that her oncoming creation is evil. This may be the extreme case, but what of the woman who knows that her vanity is still so consumed with the need to maintain her youth and freedom that she senses how badly she would rear her child? A woman can have an honest recognition that she is too selfish or too timid or in too desperate a situation to bring an infant into the world. That much self-honesty can become the first step in becoming more human or, at least, more adult. For rare is the woman who has an abortion without suffering her private horror.

The counterattack to the Right to Life is that no man has the authority to forbid abortion until we come to the end of all wars. Otherwise, since God is always on our side in war, it must be God's desire that we look to exterminate strangers en masse. Such slayings are highly organized, of course, but they are first cousin to terrorism. We are killing people we know nothing about. We are also destroying full-grown humans into whom God may have put much interest and much intent.

Gay Marriage: Family Values?

Civil marriage for homosexuals is one more problem to divide liberals and conservatives. The prejudice runs deep. Most heterosexual men and women feel they have paid a life price to duty and responsibility by the act of getting married. So their resentment is profound. Why should gays enjoy the pleasures of the sybaritic yet have the civil and economic protections of marriage as well? The answer—and it will take more than one presidential election before these matters can be discussed openly—is that mutual comprehension and tolerance between heterosexuals and gay people may begin to come into being only after gay couples have taken on the yoke of marriage and, by adoption, children. Indeed, the saving irony to convince a few conservatives is that the desire among certain homosexuals to seek out the constraints of marriage does speak of an innate pull toward domestic cohabitation.

Besides, there is a more forceful argument. It is that in a democracy, everyone feels the need to find out who they are, what they are, and in which ways they can live and identify themselves. Is this not the theme underlining the Pursuit of Happiness? It is worth adding that every child adopted by a gay couple no longer has to spend his or her years in an orphanage. If that child might face special difficulties because the parents are gay, the question to ask is whether the problems encountered will prove more dire than growing up in an institution.

The Bush Credo: War Is More Godly Than Welfare

It is still an outrage. Compared with other industrial powers, we do not have a comprehensive safety net. Indeed, much of the brouhaha over affirmative action is but the visible tip of the iceberg. Relatively restrained, the opponents of affirmative action give barely a hint of the deeper aversion many of them feel toward blacks and, to a lesser degree, Hispanics.

The real target has always been social welfare. There were men and women on the right who were enraged that whole sections of the population seemed content to raise large one-parent families and live off the government. Since their anger was often fueled by their own hard lives, they found it obscene that others did not have to work as conscientiously.

Let us eschew the bona fide reply that not all idle hands were happy to live with welfare. Once again, it is worth taking up the right-wing argument on its merits. They would be the first to say that work is a blessing. Let us assume it is. By such logic, the real suffering for those on welfare is, precisely, that they are deprived of that blessing. For the average human, white or black, man or woman, it is probably more difficult to live on the dole than to work. Boredom and shame do the work instead on the soul.

Can we stare into the center of the real moral issue? A nation indifferent to social welfare, a land so fevered with the free market that it would forgo all safety nets, a country without concern for its poorest members, deserving or undeserving, has become a society with distorted values. Whether one is full of belief in a higher authority or feels no belief, the basic notion, all flaws granted, is that democracy is still a system which assumes all human beings are of value. The concept is noble. But if the emphasis is on our own rights at all costs and we have become so swollen in our egomania that we are indifferent to the homeless sleeping on the street, even furious at the fact of their existence, what kind of freedom are we then offering to the tyrannized of other countries? Bogged down in the grease-soaked sands of Iraq, we have transported ourselves to a future of large taxation to small purpose. We will have to pay off Bush's extravagances. Why? Was it, at worst, that if all else failed, we could keep our budget deficit so big that we would never be able to provide a safety net? One of the answers to why we are at war in Iraq may be there. The harshness in the voice of the talk radio motor-mouths gives a clue.

Foreign Policy: Get Us Off the Dance Floor

We are at a major turn in our history. It is possible that the Republican and Democratic Parties are at the edge of an upheaval of ideologies, a schism in each of our two major political configurations that will bend every one of our notions to Left or to Right. Will old-line GOP financial conservatives be in serious conflict with their own radical right? Will there be existential Democrats in rebellion against the rigidities of political correctness?

Ever since FDR, the Democratic Party has been internationalist. So were most Republicans. The power of their corporate center enabled them to withstand intense isolationist sentiments in their own ranks.

Following the end of the Cold War, the triumph of the corporate economy encouraged a vanity until recently that the corporation is a morally estimable body. One manifestation of this sense of superiority is physical presence. The world is now teeming with aesthetically neutered monuments—precisely, those high-rise hotels and offices that surround every major airport and capital in the world, those monotonous, glassy behemoths coming forth as the virtuous architecture of the new corporate religion, an El Dorado of technology.

One fundamental error has begun to rock the globe. It was assumed by us that the most powerful of these corporate entities, that is to say, America, knew what was best for the rest of the world. The United States was ready to solve the problems of every nation, all of them, all the way from old Europe to the flea- and fly-bitten turpitudes of the Third World.

It could be remarked that the men who set sail with Columbus in 1492 had more idea of where they were going. The best to be said for the gung-ho capitalistas of the Bush administration is that they taught us all over again how extreme vanity is all you need to sail right off the edge of the world.

You cannot bring democracy to tyranny by conquest. Democ- racy can be neither injected nor imposed. It comes into exis- tence through a long rite of passage. It has achieved its liberty by the actions of its own martyrs, rebels, and enduring believers. It is not a system, it is an ennoblement. Democracy must come from within. Brought into oppressed nations by way of external force, it collides with all the habits those tormented populations were obliged to develop, those humiliating compromises that came from submitting to an ugly and superior force. Now all of that has been jammed into an abruptly ground-up gruel of chopped psychic reflexes, even as a strange people arrived from outside in mighty machines with guns attached, new people whose motives one could not trust. How could one? The prevail- ing law within a tyranny is to trust nobody. There have been too many shameful adaptations within oneself, as well as decades of long-swallowed rage. The recollection of humiliations early and late has been incorporated into the psychic core. Existence has been imprisoned too long in the virtual reality imposed by the tyrant.

We did not have an administration who could comprehend that. We came in with our guns, our smiles, and our assumption that democracy was there to hand over to these Iraqis. Our gift! Our form of virtual reality, superior to yours!

The truth is, we don't belong in any foreign country. We are not wise enough, honest enough with ourselves, nor a good enough nation to tell the rest of the world how to live—indeed, such a nation has never existed. But even if we were just so fabu- lous, so unique, other humans would still not be ready to savage their national pride for the dubious joy of receiving our crusade against evil. We would do well to become a little more aware of Christian militancy that marches into war against any evil but its own.

Homeland Security: Will We Ever Learn to Live with Arithmetic?

The time has come to solve our own problems, our ongoing American problems. We have a direct need to focus on ourselves over the coming span of years and thereby become less displaced from reality. For we are the most mighty of all the nations, and we are secure. Despite all, we are relatively secure. We can absorb new terrorist attacks if they come. We do not need military invasions into foreign lands to protect us. From 1968 through 2000, the world suffered an average of 425 terrorist incidents a year, resulting in an average of 321 deaths annually. In 2001, however, came 9/11. Three thousand lives were lost. A huge number. Yet in that same period, 1968 to 2001, Americans suffered more than forty thousand deaths each year from auto accidents. So even in 2001, there were thirteen times as many deaths resulting from auto accidents as from terrorist attacks. If it be asked why such focus is now being put on automobile mortalities, it is because such tragedies are not without analogy to losing one's life to a terrorist. You leave your home, you kiss your wife goodbye, and you are dead ten minutes or ten hours later. For those left to grieve, there seems not enough reason to such death. Not enough logic! More than any other event in our lives, our own demise excites just such a need for logic in those who remain. Lung cancer, we know, kills 155,000 people a year. That is nearly four times more than automobiles, but we can comprehend that. We are ready to decide that cigarettes or working with asbestos has something to do with it. But death without any grip on an explanation bothers people more. It does no good to tell ourselves that 2.4 million people die each year in America. We are fixed on the three thousand lost humans of 9/11. They seem more important. In truth, they have been so important to America that we have come to what may be another point of no return. Will we continue to protect our freedoms, or will we conclude that all effort must go to saving ourselves from every conceivable form of terrorist attack? The second course pursued to conclusion will lead to nothing less than a unique variety of fascism. Brownshirts or Blackshirts will not be needed. Our only certainty is that whatever it will be called, fascism will not be the word. Should Bush remain in office, we can count on virtual reality to suggest the face of the new regime. But then, that is the essence of fascism—you must give the populace a version of cause and effect that has very little to do with how things are.

The question, then, is whether we will be brave enough to dispense with foreign adventures. We know, or we should know, that any nation looking to attack us has to face the might of our armed forces. Any nuclear attack from North Korea or Iran would be an absolute disaster for either. Our power to retaliate is awesome. When it comes to terrorist attacks, however, we are also at the mercy of our deteriorating relations with the rest of the developed world. Military forays are not the answer—you do not wipe out terrorists with airplanes and tanks. Rather, we will be obliged to use—that dreaded term!—collective efforts to build an international police force ready to guard against major attacks comparable to 9/11. Even the best of such collaborative organizations will not prevent small terrorist acts, any more than a local police force can root out all local crime. But to be able to counter a terrorist effort on the scale of the Twin Towers, a global police system with a worldwide network of informants can be developed. It is one thing for terrorists to succeed in suicide bombings; it is another for them to find the necessary cadres, skills, and materials to bring off an immense coup against the sophisticated forces of proscription that can be put in place. Al-Qaeda took several years to prepare 9/11! Since we will, however, never be able to prevent all minor attacks, it is illogical to be ready to sacrifice our remaining liberties in order to search for a total security that will never come to pass. Terrorism, in parallel with cancer, is in total rebellion against established human endeavor. If democracy ever did begin to work in Iraq, the incidence of terrorist acts would, doubtless, increase. Suicide bombers are stimulated by the presence of the enemy, whether that presence is foreign soldiers or a political system that is anathema to their beliefs. Should Islam ever take over America, our own Christian fundamentalists would be the first to become terrorists.

American freedom now depends on what we learned in elementary school. We must live with arithmetic! Over the last three years, 850 Israelis have been killed in suicide bombings, ambushes, sniper attacks, and gun battles. That, by rough calculation, is one Israeli in 20,000 for each of those three years. If we in America were to suffer at the same rate, we would, given our population, which is roughly fifty times as great as Israel's, suffer approximately 14,000 deaths a year. That comes to one-third of our American loss of life from automobile accidents. Short of a major disaster, we are not likely to face 14,000 such deaths a year. We do not have the daily problems that Israelis have with Palestinians and Palestinians with Israelis. We have more freedom to explore into what we can become as a nation.

Fighting the Mind That Is Inside the Brain

Karl Rove, the man whom many consider the mind inside George W. Bush's brain, is on record with his hopes for a twenty-year reign of the GOP. If that is not to take place, the need of the Democrats—it is worth repeating—is to be able to appeal to the best and most thoughtful of the conservatives. The time has come for us to understand that not everyone to the right is on the hunt for more money, more power, more conquest, and more worship of the flag. Not every conservative is for suburbs scourged by blank-faced malls, nor is every conservative ready to cheer every corporation that puts its name on a new stadium for professional athletes. Not every conservative believes that our God-given mission is to needle the serum of democracy into nations with no vein for democracy. No, there are conservatives who believe that the United States has been boiling up an unholy brew under the lid of the corporate pot, conservatives who believe that educating our children is degenerating into a near to autistic mess, conservatives who do not think that all the answers to crime can be solved by building more prisons. No, there are even conservatives who would argue, just like Democrats, that no matter how much we spend on our schools, they don't seem to be working. There are conservatives who have sensitive feelings on these matters—as sensitive as the Democrats', by God. Yet neither side knows how to speak to the other.

Still, this variety of conservative—decent not bigoted, open to discussion rather than given over, body and soul, to talk radio—is also aghast at the uneasy but real possibility that George W. Bush might be the worst and most unqualified president America has ever had. Yes, such conservatives, whatever their number, are in the same state of inanition and ideological impotence as all those Democrats who cannot believe where the country is going. Let us as Democrats consider the possibility that such conservatives can also be part of a future in which Democrats draw their political sustenance from the best ideas of Left and Right. At present, that is not easy to believe, but there are new political conceptions in the air, ideas that have not been hardened into the iron load of ideology that sits upon the elephant's head and the donkey's saddle. This country was founded, after all, on the amazing notion (for the time) that there was more good than evil in the mass of human beings, and so those human beings, once given not only the liberty to vote but the power to learn to think, might demonstrate that more good than evil could emerge from such freedom. It was an incredible gamble. All society until then had assumed that the masses were incapable of exercising a wise voice and so must be controlled from the top down.

That wager has remained alive through the two centuries and twenty-odd years of our national existence, and often it has seemed that the result was affirmative. Now doubt is with us again. In 2004 we will face what could become the most important election in our history. Since our candidate will never have funds to equal the bursting coffers of an opposition inflamed by power, bad conscience and all the virtual reality of religious fundamentalism itself, the election will be a most furious contest between their money, self-righteousness, and mental rictus scalding down on us, versus our hope that moral revulsion still exists in more than half of our voting public, enough to let us succeed, despite all our own impurity, in overthrowing the corporate colossus on the other bank. May our wit be clean, our indignation genuine, and our ideas new enough and fine enough to pierce the caterwaul of political advertising that will look to flood our campaign down the river and over the falls.

The Election and America's Future

(2004)

A VICTORY FOR BUSH may yet be seen as one of our nation's unforgettable ironies. No need to speak again of the mendacities, manipulations, and spiritual mediocrity of the post–9/11 years; the time has come to recover from the shock that so abysmal a record (and so complete a refusal to look at the record) looks nonetheless likely to prevail. Who, then, are we? In just what kind of condition are the American people?

A quick look at our movie stars gives a hint. The liberal left has been attached to actors like Warren Beatty and Jack Nicholson. They spoke to our cynicism and to our baffled idealism. But the American center moved their loyalties from the decency of Gary Cooper to the grit and self-approval of John Wayne. Now, we have the apotheosis of Arnold Schwarzenegger. He captured convention honors at the Garden in the course of informing America, via the physicality of his presence, that should the nation ever come to such a dire pass as to need a dictator, why, bless us all, he, Arnold, can offer the best chin to come along since Benito Mussolini. Chin is now prepared to replace spin.

In 1983, during the formative years of spin, 241 Marines were blown up by one terrorist blast in Beirut. Two days later, on October 25, Reagan landed 1,200 marines in Grenada, which is 3,000 miles away from Beirut. By the time that the invasion force grew to 7,000 Marines, the campaign was over. The United States lost 19 dead, while 49 soldiers in the Grenadian army perished on the other side, as well as 29 Cuban construction workers. Communism in the Caribbean was now kaput (except for the little matter of Castro and Cuba). After this instant victory over a ragtag foe, Reagan was stimulated enough to accept his supporters' claim that America had now put an end to our shame in Vietnam. Reagan understood what Americans wanted, and that was spin. It was more important to be told you were healthy than to be healthy.

Bush-and-Rove enlarged this insight by an order of magnitude. They acted on the premise that America was prodigiously insecure. As an empire, we are nouveaux riches. We look to overcome the uneasiness implicit in this condition by amassing megamoney. The sorriest thing to be said about the United States, as we sidle up to fascism (which can become our fate if we plunge into a major depression, or suffer a set of dirty-bomb catastrophes), is that we expect disasters. We await them. We have become a guilty nation. Somewhere in the moil of the national conscience is the knowledge that we are caught in the little contradiction of loving Jesus on Sunday, while lusting the rest of the week for megamoney. How can we not be in need of someone to tell us that we are good and pure and he will seek to make us secure? For Bush-and-Rove, 9/11 was the jackpot.

The presidency is a role, and George, left on his own, might have become a successful movie actor. Kerry's task by now is to scourge Bush's ham machismo. But how? Kerry's only real opportunity will come as he steps into a most constricting venue— the debates. Kerry has to dominate Bush without a backward look at his own dovish councils—"Don't be seen as cruel, John, or you will lose the women!" To the contrary—Kerry must win the men. He has to take Bush apart in public. By the end of the debates, he has to succeed in laying waste to Bush's shit-eating grin and present himself as the legitimate alternative—a hero whose reputation was slandered by a slacker. That will not be routine. Bush is the better actor. He has been impersonating men more manly than himself for many years. Kerry has to convince some new part of the audience that his opponent is a closet weakling who seizes on inflexibility as a way to show America that he is strong. Bush's appeal is, after all, to the stupid. They, too, are inflexible—they also know that maintaining one's stupidity can become a kind of strength, provided you never change your mind.

There is a subtext which Kerry can use. Bush, after all, is not accustomed to working alone in hostile environments. He has been cosseted for years. It is cruel but true that he has the vulnerability of an ex-alcoholic.

People in Alcoholics Anonymous speak of themselves as dry drunks. As they see it, they may no longer drink, yet a sense of imbalance at having to do without liquor does not go away. Rather the impulse is sequestered behind the faith that God is supporting one's efforts to remain sober.

Giving up booze may have been the most heroic act of George W.'s life, but America could now be paying the price. George W.'s piety has become a pomade to cover all the tamped-down dry-drunk craziness that still stirs in his livid inner air.

These gloomy words were written before the first debate on September 30. They were followed by an even gloomier final flourish:

> Through this era of belly-grinding ironies, the most unpalatable may be that we have to hitch our hopes to a series of televised face-offs whose previous history has seldom offered more than a few sound bites for the contestants and apnea for the viewer. God bless America! We may not deserve it, but we could use the Lord's help. Bush's first confidence, after all, is that the Devil will never desert him in his hour of need. His only error is that he thinks it is the Son who is speaking to him.

The debate, however, offered surprising ground for optimism. Kerry was at his best, concise, forceful, almost joyous in the virtuosity of his ability. He was able to speak his piece despite the Procrustean bonds of the debate. And Bush was at his worst. He looked spoiled. He was out of his element. He was tired from campaigning. There are times when a man has campaigned so much that he is running on hollow. Even Bush's face had become a liability. He looked cranky and puckered up. For years, he had been able to speak free of debate, always able to utter his homey patriotic gospel without interruption. Now in the ninety minutes of formalized back-and-forth, with the camera sometimes catching his petulant reactions while Kerry spoke, he looked unhappy enough to take a drink.

Most of this was seen on a big state-of-the-art television set, and the verdict seemed clear. Kerry had won by a large margin. Bush's only credit was that he had gone the distance without making any irremediable errors. Kerry's poll numbers seemed bound to increase.

Only one caveat remained. The first twenty minutes of the debate had been seen on the kind of modest-sized set that most of America would be using. On that set, one saw a somewhat different debate. Karl Rove had scored again. However it had been managed, the placement of the cameras favored Bush. His head took up more square inches on the screen than Kerry's. In television, that is half the battle. Kerry looked long and lean as he spoke out of what seemed to be a medium shot, whereas Bush had many a close-up.

This advantage partly disappeared on the large set. There, each man's expression was clear, and their relative strengths and weaknesses were obvious. On a small set, however, some of the cinematographic advantage went the other way.

We will have to wait for the polls. Will they be as skewed as the camera angles? We seem to be living these days in a kaleidoscope of ironies. Is the worst yet to come? If it is a close election, the electronic voting machines are ready to augment every foul memory of Florida in 2000. Perhaps it is no longer Jesus or Allah who oversees our fate but the turn of the Greek gods to take another run around the track. When it comes to destiny, they were the first, after all, to conceive of the Ironies.

Comment on the Passing of George Plimpton

———

(2004)

THE MEMORIAL SERVICE for George Plimpton at the Cathedral of St. John the Divine proved memorable. There were something like ten speakers and most of us—I do include myself—were good. It was all George's fault. He was one man it was easy to talk about, and we had known him for decades. If the best speech of all was given by his son Taylor, that was as it should have been—a father would want and expect just that while listening from the other side. If there is anything to such a notion, I am sure George had his ear well cocked.

When it came my turn—I confess to being surprised by what I said. It was as if my voice was leading my thoughts. Obviously, since I had not put it on paper, there is no written record, but I believe I can recall most of what I said. It centered on the notion that George had represented a part of New York which many in the audience knew well. There were few people, after all, who were acquainted with that many large and small figures in the city. Moreover, given the several generations at *Paris Review* alone, George was on good terms with the old, the young, and every variety in between. So this became the core of what I discovered myself saying. I declared that there may have been no one in the city who was loved so much by so many people. I spoke then of the shock when Sarah Plimpton called on the morning following the night of George's end to tell us the news. My wife and I felt close to Sarah, perhaps closer than we felt to George. Ergo, I was stunned by the pain I felt. By God, I realized, I loved George, I really did.

So many such reactions are only felt after the fact. That opened a perception for me. I began to think of how we love each other in New York. Over the years, there are so many people with whom we have social relations, hundreds, certainly, over the decades, and for some we do feel a kind of love, a limited love that I would call New York love. Yes, exactly. It is there as a full sentiment of love yet it is wholly circumscribed. Which is to say that when we encounter this kind of old friend or acquaintance, the moment can feel as good, pure, and sweet as love, we are so pleased to be with them. Yet it is a love without a present history. Nothing further is given to it, nothing exceptional comes out of it, we are just happy to see that person again and know that they are there. I repeat: it is New York love. In this city, we all know so many people that it is impossible to have deep relations with more than a few. So we love in capsule a good fifty or a hundred of our friends, and that even becomes one more nourishment one can offer and receive from love.

George must have inspired that kind of feeling in countless people. How we all felt good on running into George, so many of us, and the best is that he was worthy of it, for he never took anything from anyone I know without giving back more with his charm, his exceptionally good and subtle manners, his anecdotes, his brio, his verve, and his rare talent—there was so much in life he was able to enjoy. More than anyone I knew. So, yes, three cheers. Maybe in the old rich sense of the word, he was a gentleman, the best gentleman most of us ever got to know.

On Sartre's God Problem

(2005)

This year marks the centenary of the birth of Jean-Paul Sartre, the great philosopher of existentialism and a definitive model of the intellectual engagé. The Paris-based daily *Libération* asked a group of writers to comment on the philosopher's legacy. Norman Mailer was among the contributors. His remarks are reprinted below.

—ADAM SHATZ

I WOULD SAY THAT SARTRE, despite his incontestable strengths of mind, talent, and character, is still the man who derailed existentialism, sent it right off the track. In part, this may have been because he gave too wide a berth to Heidegger's thought. Heidegger spent his working life laboring mightily in the crack of philosophy's buttocks, right there in the cleft between Being and Becoming. I would go so far as to suggest Heidegger was searching for a viable connection between the human and the divine that would not inflame too irreparably the reigning post-Hitler German mandarins who were in no rush to forgive his past and would hardly encourage his tropism toward the nonrational.

Sartre, however, was comfortable as an atheist even if he had no fundament on which to plant his philosophical feet. To hell with that, he didn't need it. He was ready to survive in midair. We are French, he was ready to say. We have minds, we can live with the absurd and ask for no reward. That is because we are noble enough to live with emptiness, and strong enough to choose a course which we are even ready to die for. And we will do this in whole defiance of the fact that, indeed, we have no footing. We do not look to a Hereafter.

It was an attitude; it was a proud stance; it was equal to living with one's mind in formless space, but it deprived existentialism of more interesting explorations. For atheism is a cropless undertaking when it comes to philosophy. (We need only think of Logical Positivism!) Atheism can contend with ethics (as Sartre did on occasion most brilliantly), but when it comes to metaphysics, atheism ends in a locked cell. It is, after all, near to impossible for a philosopher to explore how we are here without entertaining some notion of what the prior force might have been. Cosmic speculation is asphyxiated if existence came into being ex nihilo. In Sartre's case—worse. Existence came into being without a clue to suggest whether we are here for good purpose, or there is no reason whatsoever for us.

All the same, Sartre's philosophical talents were damnably virtuoso. He was able to function with precision in the upper echelons of every logical structure he set up. If only he had not been an existentialist! For an existentialist who does not believe in some kind of Other is equal to an engineer who designs an automobile that requires no driver and accepts no passengers. If existentialism is to flourish (that is, develop through a series of new philosophers building on earlier premises), it needs a God who is no more confident of the end than we are; a God who is an artist, not a lawgiver; a God who suffers the uncertainties of existence; a God who lives without any of the prearranged guarantees that sit like an incubus upon formal theology with its flatulent, self-serving assumption of a Being who is All-Good and All-Powerful. What a gargantuan oxymoron—All-Good and All-Powerful. It is certain to maroon any and all formal theologians who would like to explain an earthquake. Before the wrath of a tsunami, they can only break wind. The notion of an existential

God, a Creator who may have been doing His or Her artistic best but could still have been remiss in designing the tectonic plates, is not within their scope.

Sartre was alien to the possibility that existentialism might thrive if it would just assume that indeed we do have a God who, no matter His or Her cosmic dimensions (whether larger or smaller than we assume), embodies nonetheless some of our faults, our ambitions, our talents, and our gloom. For the end is not written. If it is, there is no place for existentialism. Base our beliefs, however, on the fact of our existence, and it takes no great step for us to assume that we are not only individuals but may well be a vital part of a larger phenomenon that searches for some finer vision of life that could conceivably emerge from our present human condition. There is no reason, one can argue, why this assumption is not nearer to the real being of our lives than anything the oxymoronic theologians would offer us. It is certainly more reasonable than Sartre's ongoing assumption—despite his passionate desire for a better society—that we are here willy-nilly and must manage to do the best we can with endemic nothingness installed upon eternal floorlessness. Sartre was indeed a writer of major dimension, but he was also a philosophical executioner. He guillotined existentialism just when we needed most to hear its howl, its barbaric yawp that there is something in common between God and all of us. We, like God, are imperfect artists doing the best we can. We may succeed or fail—God as well as us. That is the implicit if undeveloped air of existentialism. We would do well to live again with the Greeks, live again with the expectation that the end remains open but human tragedy may well be our end.

Great hope has no real footing unless one is willing to face into the doom that may also be on the way. Those are the poles of our existence—as they have been from the first instant of the Big Bang. Something immense may now be stirring, but to meet it we will do better to expect that life will not provide the answers we need so much as it will offer the privilege of improving our questions. It is not moral absolutism but theological relativism we would do well to explore if our real need is for a God with whom we can engage our lives.

Myth Versus Hypothesis[*]

———

(2006)

SINCE HIS REELECTION, George W. Bush has been more impressive in his personal appearances, more sure of himself, more—it is an unhappy word in this context but obligatory—he seems more authentic, more like a president.

I would warrant that before this last election he has always been the opposite of what he appeared to be, which is to say that he has worked with some skill to pass himself off as a facsimile of macho virtue. That is not unlike a screen star who has been alcoholic but is now, thanks to AA, a dry drunk who is able to look tough and ready on the screen. He never wavers when in peril. He is inflexible.

I would assert that inflexibility is not actually at the root of the president's character. Inflexibility serves, instead, to cover any arrant impulses that still smoke within. Of course, to keep all that stuff to oneself is not a happy condition for a commander in chief.

If we contrast George W. to his parents, it is probably fair to

* The following was a speech given to the Nieman Fellows on December 6, 2004, by Norman Mailer.

say that his father was manly enough to be president but seemed unable to escape his modesty. Indeed, for all one knew, it was genuine. While at Andover, he must have sensed that he was not quite bright enough for the job. Barbara Bush had, doubtless, more than enough character to be First Lady, yet so long as she was obscured by the obliterative shadow cast by Nancy Reagan, she was seen as not elegant enough. In turn, their oldest son, George, in contrast to his father, was neither an athlete nor a fighter pilot. While at Andover he was a cheerleader. That, in itself, might have been enough to drain some good part of his self-respect. It is not easy to be surrounded by football players when you are just as tall and large as most of them, but are not as athletic. The son, out of necessity perhaps, developed his own kind of ego. He turned out to be as vain as sin, and as hollow as unsuccessful sin.

If this sense of Bush's character is well based, then one must accept the increment of strength that victory offers to such a man. He now feels as entitled to national respect as the dry-drunk screen star after a box office smash. One can see the magnitude of George W.'s personal happiness now. The smirk is gilt-edged these days.

In contrast, the woe one encounters among Democrats is without parallel. Just as no president, not even Richard Nixon, was so detested, so was the belief implicit, just the week before the election, that no matter how deadlocked the polls, it was inconceivable that Bush could triumph. This conviction was most intense among the young. Now, the prevailing mood among many young Democrats is not unlike the disbelief that attends the sudden death of a mate or a close friend. One keeps expecting the deceased to be sitting at the table again. Or, the doorbell will ring and there he will be. But, no, he is not there. Bush is the victor, not Kerry. It is analogous to the way people who have been kidnapped by the intensity of a dream have to keep reminding themselves on awakening, "I am not in Katmandu. I am in my own bedroom. There will be no deliverance from George W. Bush. I will have to see his face for the next four years."

Of course, if Kerry had won Ohio and so had become president despite a deficit of several million votes, the situation down the road could have proved disastrous for Democrats. Kerry, given his 50-50 stand on the war, would have had to pay for all of Bush's mistakes in Iraq. He would then have inherited what may yet be Bush's final title: Lord Quagmire.

The truth is that neither candidate proved ready to say why we are really there. Indeed, why? Why, indeed, are we in Iraq? It is likely that a majority of Americans are looking for that answer, no matter whom they voted for.

Undeniably, I am one of them. I have probably spent a fair part of the last two years brooding over this question. Like most large topics which present no quick answers, the question becomes obsessive.

Let me make one more attempt. I would ask, however, that you allow me to do it through the means by which I think. I do not come to my conclusions with the mental skills of a politician, a columnist, a journalist, an academician in foreign relations or political science—no, I brood along as a novelist. We novelists, if we are any good, have our own means.

What may establish some mutuality with this audience, however, is that we do have one firm basis in common. Good novelists and good journalists are engaged, after all, in a parallel search. We are always trying to find a better approach to the established truth. For that truth is usually skewed by the needs of powerful interests.

Journalists engage in this worthy if tricky venture by digging into the hard earth for those slimy creatures we call facts, facts that are rarely clear enough to be classified as false or true.

Novelists work in a different manner. We begin with fictions. That is to say, we make suppositions about the nature of reality. Put another way, we live with hypotheses which, when well chosen, can enrich our minds and—it is always a hope—some readers' minds as well. Hypotheses are, after all, one of the incisive ways by which we try to estimate what a reality might be. Each new bit of evidence we acquire serves to weaken the hypothesis or to strengthen it. With a good premise, we may even get closer to reality. A poor one, sooner or later, has to be discarded.

Take the unhappy but superexcited state that a man or woman can find themselves in when full of jealousy. Their minds are quickened, their senses become more alert. If a wife believes her husband is having an affair, then every time he comes home, she is more aware of his presence than she has been in previous weeks, months, or years. Is he guilty? Is the way in which he folds his napkin a sign of some unease? Is he being too accommodating? Her senses quicken at the possibility that another woman—let us call her Victoria—is the object of his attention. Soon, the wife is all but convinced that he is having an affair with Victoria. Definitely. No question. But then, on a given morning, she discovers that the lady happens to be in China. Worse. Victoria has actually been teaching in Beijing for the last six months. Ergo, the hypothesis has been confuted. If the wife is still convinced that the husband is unfaithful, another woman must be substituted.

The value of a hypothesis is that it can stimulate your mind and heighten your concentration. The danger is that it can distort your brain. Thoughts of revenge are one example. The first question may be: Am I too cowardly to exercise this revenge? One can wear oneself down to the bone with that little suspicion. Or, one's moral sense can be activated. Does one have the right to seek revenge? Hypotheses on love usually prove even more disruptive. The most basic is, of course: Am I really in love? Is this love? How much am I in love? What is love, after all? To a family man, the question can become: How much do I love my children? Am I ready to sacrifice myself for them? Real questions. Questions that have no quick answer. Good hypotheses depend on real questions, which is to say questions that do not always generate happy answers.

Patriotism offers its own set. For some, it is not enough to wave a flag. The people in fascist countries always wave flags. So, some Americans are still ready to ask whether it is false patriotism to support our country under any and all conditions. Others, a majority, no doubt, seem to feel that one's nation demands an unquestioning faith, and so you must always be ready to believe that the people of our nation are superior—by their blood alone—to the people of other nations. In that sense, patriotism is analogous to family snobbery. Indeed, one can ask whether patriotism is the poor man's equivalent of the upper-class sense of inbred superiority.

These questions can provoke us to ask: What is the nature of my country now? Do we have the right to be in Iraq? Why are we there?

Before we look at the familiar answers that have been given to us by the administration, the media, and the opposition, allow me an excursion. What intrigues me most about good hypotheses is that they bear a close relation to good fiction. The serious novel looks for situations and characters who can come alive enough to surprise the writer. If he or she starts with one supposition, the actions of the characters often lead the story some distance away from what was planned. In that sense, hypotheses are not only like fictions but can be compared to news stories— once the situation is presented, subsequent events can act like surprisingly lively characters ready to prove or disprove how one thought the original situation would develop. The value of a good hypothesis, like a good fiction, is that whether it all turns out more or less as expected, or is altogether contrary, the mind of the reader as well as the author is nonetheless enriched.

A good novel, therefore, like a good hypothesis, becomes an attack on the nature of reality. (If attack seems too violent a notion here, think of it as intense inquiry.) But the basic assumption is that reality is ever changing—the more intense the situation, the more unforeseeable will be the denouement. Reality, by this logic, is not yet classified. The honor, the value of a serious novel rests on the assumption that the explanations our culture has given us on profound matters are not profound. Working on a novel, one feels oneself getting closer to new questions, better ones, questions that are harder to answer. It's as if in writing novels, you don't assume there are absolutes or incontrovertible facts. Nor do you expect to come to a firm or final answer. Rather, the questions are pursued in the hope they will open into richer insights, which in turn will bring forth sharper questions.

Let me then repeat the point. Novelists approach reality, but they do not capture it. No good novel ever arrives at total certainty, not unless you are Charles Dickens and are writing *A Christmas Carol.* Just so, few hypotheses ever reach verification. Not every Victoria teaches in China.

This much laid out, I am almost ready to leave this substantial introduction to what I am yet going to say. Before I do, however, let me present a lagniappe, not necessary for my argument, but there for its flavor. So, I would claim that the most interesting bond between hypothesis and serious fiction is that they both have something to say about sex and the social forms it takes. For a long time, I've amused myself with the notion that the poem, the short story, and the novel can be compared to phases of sex. The short poem, certainly, is analogous to a one-night stand. It may come off as brilliant, or it can be a bummer. A love affair of reasonable duration is, all too often, like a short story. What characterizes most short stories is that they look to suggest something forthright by the end. In their crudest form, when young men write their early pieces, the last sentence almost always has its echo of "He felt old, and sad, and tired." By analogy, it may be fair to say that few affairs come to an end without being characterized—usually uncharitably—by the participants. Marriage, however, like a novel, is closer to a metamorphosis of attitudes. The end of one chapter may leave the husband and wife ready to break up; they cannot bear each other. In the morning, which commences the next chapter, they discover to their mutual surprise that they are back in the sack. Reality varies from chapter to chapter.

I expect I have used this little excursion to suggest that those of us who do not hold fundamental beliefs often approach our sense of reality by way of our working hypotheses, or by our various literary forms. It is certainly true that on the road to Iraq, we were offered more than a few narratives for why we were so obviously hell-bent for war.

In the beginning, some said that George W. Bush was trying to validate his father by occupying Baghdad—others argued that he wished to appear superior to George H. W. Two opposed hypotheses. Each made a neat one-page article for one or another magazine.

Another hypothesis which soon arose was that such a war would be evil. Shed no blood for oil. That became the cry. Quite likely, it was correct in part, at least, but it was as harsh in argument as the prose of any ill-written tract. Others offered a much more virtuous reason: conquering Iraq would democratize the Middle East. Problems between Israel and Palestine could be happily settled. In the event, this proved to be nearer to Grimm's fairy tales than a logical proposition.

In its turn, the administration presented us with weapons of mass destruction. That lived in the American mind like an intelligence thriller. Would we locate those nightmares before they blew us up? It became the largest single argument for going to war. Colin Powell put his political honor on the chopping block for that assertion. He is still holding his head in his hands.

There were other hypotheses—would we or would we not find Osama bin Laden? Which became a short story like "The Lady, or the Tiger?"—no ending. On the eve of war, there was a blood-cult novel in the night. It was Shock and Awe—had we driven a quick stake through the heart of Saddam Hussein? Good Americans could feel they were on the hunt for Dracula.

Vivid hypotheses. None held up. We did not learn then and we still do not begin to agree why we embarked on this most miserable of wars. Occam's Razor does suggest that the simplest explanation which is ready to answer a variety of separate questions on a puzzling matter has a great likelihood of being the most correct explanation. One answer can emerge then from the good bishop's formula: it is that we marched into a full-sized war because it was the simplest solution the president and his party could find for the immediate impasse in which America found itself. (Besides, a war would authenticate his Florida presidency.) Yes, how much we needed a solution to our developing problems.

The first problem, which could yet become the most worrisome, was that the nation's scientific future, and its technological skills, seemed to be in distress. American students at STEM studies—S-T-E-M: science, technology, engineering, and mathe-

matics—no longer appeared to be equal to those Asian and European students who were also studying advanced courses at our
universities. For pleasure-loving American students, STEM subjects may have seemed too difficult, too unattractive. Moreover,
the American corporation was now ready to outsource its own
future, even eager to do so. Given drastically lower factory wages
in Third World countries, there may have appeared no alternative to maintain large profits. All the same, if American factory
jobs were now in danger of disappearing, and our skills at technology were suffering in comparison to Europe and to Asia, then
relations between American labor and the corporation could go
on tilt. That was not the only storm cloud over the land.

Back in 2001, back before 9/11, the divide between pop culture and fundamentalism was gaping. In the view of the religious
right, America was becoming heedless, loutish, irreligious, and
blatantly immoral. Half of all American marriages were ending
in divorce. The Catholic Church was suffering a series of agonizing scandals. The FBI had been profoundly shaken by moles in
their woodwork who worked for the Soviets and a Mafia killer on
close terms with their own agents on the scene.

Posed with the specter of a superpower, our own superpower,
economically and spiritually out of kilter, the best solution
seemed to be war. That would offer an avenue for recapturing
America—not, mind you, by unifying the country, not at all. By
now, that was close to impossible. Given, however, that the country was deeply divided, the need might be to separate it further
in such a way that one's own half could become much more powerful. For that, Americans had to be encouraged to live with all
the certainties of myth while bypassing the sharp edge of inquiry
demanded by hypothesis.

The difference is crucial. A hypothesis opens the mind to
thought, to comparison, to doubt, to the elusiveness of truth. If
this country was founded in great part on the notion that enough
people possessed enough goodwill, and enough desire for
growth and discovery to prosper, and this most certainly included
spiritual and intellectual discovery, then, or so went the premise,
democracy could thrive more than monarchy or theocracy.

Of course, all these political forms depend on their myths.
Myths are tonic to a nation's heart. Once abused, however, they
are poisonous. For myths are frozen hypotheses. Serious questions are answered by declaration and will not be reopened. The
need is for a morality tale at a child's level. Good will overcome
a dark enemy. For the Bush administration, 9/11 came as a deliverance. The new myth even bore some relation to reality. There
was no question that Islamic terrorists were opposed to all we
stood for, good or bad. They did call us the Great Satan. But
even this was not enough. The danger presented by this enemy
had to be expanded. Our paranoia had to be intensified. We
were encouraged to worry about the security of every shopping
mall in America. To oppose the fears we generated in ourselves,
we had to call on our most dynamic American myths. We had
had, after all, a lifetime of watching action films.

The possibility of weeding terrorists out through international
police action never came into real question. We needed much
more than that. War is, obviously, a mightier rallying ground
than a series of local police actions. Yet half of America was opposed to our advance toward war with Iraq. Half of us were asking one way or another: "How much goodness has America
brought to the world? How much has it exploited the world?"

The president, however, had his own imperatives. Keep America fixed on myth. So he went all the way back to Cotton Mather.
We must war constantly against the invisible kingdom of Satan.
Stand at Armageddon and battle for the land. This was fortified
by a belief which many Republicans, some of the most intelligent and some of the most stupid, accepted in full. It was the
conviction that America was exceptional, and God had a special
interest in America. God wanted us to be a land superior to
other nations, a realm to lift His vision into greater glory. So the
myth of the frontier, which demanded a readiness to fight without limit, became part of our exceptionalism. "Do what it takes."
No matter how deeply one was embedded in near to inextrica-
ble situations, one would complete the job—"Bring 'em on."
The myth was crucial to the Bush administration. The last thing
it needed was to contend with anything like a real approach to
reality.

   This attempt to take over the popular American mind has certainly not been unsuccessful, but it does generate a new and major hypothesis which would argue that the people of the United States were systematically, even programmatically, deluded from the top down. Karl Rove was there to recognize that there were substantial powers to be obtained by catering to stupid stubborn people, and George W. Bush would be the man to harvest such resources. George W. understood stupid people well. They were not dumb, their minds were not physically crippled in any way. They had chosen to be stupid because that offered its own kind of power. To win a great many small contests of will, they needed only to ignore all evidence. Bright people would break down trying to argue with them. Bush knew how to use this tool. With a determination that only profound contempt for the popular mind can engender, we were sold the notion that this war would be honorable, necessary, self-protective, decent, fruitful for democracy, and dedicated to any and all forms of human goodness. I would suggest that there was close to zero sincerity at the top. The leaders of this country who forced the war through were neither idealistic nor innocent. They had known what they were doing. It was basic. Do what it takes. They had decided that if America was to be able to solve its problems, then the country had to become an empire. For American capitalism to survive, exceptionalism rather than cooperation with other advanced nations had become the necessity. From their point of view, there had been ten lost years of initiatives, ten years in the cold, but America now had an opportunity to cash in again on the great bonanza that had fallen its way in 1991 when the Soviet Union went bankrupt in the arms race. At that point, or so believed the exceptionalists, America could and should have taken over the world and thereby safeguarded our economic future for decades at least with a century of hegemony to follow. Instead, these exceptionalists had been all but consumed with frustration over what they saw as the labile pussyfooting of the Clinton administration. Never have liberals been detested more. But now, at last, 9/11 had provided an opportunity for America to resolve some problems. Now America could embark on the great adventure of empire.

These exceptionalists also happened to be hardheaded realists. They were ready to face the fact that most Americans might not have any real desire for global domination. America was pleasure-loving, which, for exceptionalist purposes, was almost as bad as peace-loving. So, the invasion had to be presented with an edifying narrative. That meant the alleged reason for the war had to live in utter independence of the facts. The motives offered to the American public need not have any close connection to likelihoods. Fantasy would serve. As, for example, bringing democracy to the Middle East. Protecting ourselves against weapons of mass destruction. These themes had to be driven home to the public with all the paraphernalia of facts, supposed confirmative facts. For that, who but Colin Powell could serve as the clot-buster? So Powell was sold a mess of missile tubes by the CIA. Of course, for this to work, the CIA also had to be compromised.

So we went forward in the belief that Iraq was an immediate threat, and were told that hordes of Iraqis would welcome us with flowers. Indeed, it was our duty as good Americans to bring democracy to a country long dominated by an evil man.

Democracy, however, is not an antibiotic to be injected into a polluted foreign body. It is not a magical serum. Rather, democracy is a grace. In its ideal state, it is noble. In practice, in countries that have lived through decades and centuries of strife and revolution and the slow elaboration of safeguards and traditions, democracy becomes a political condition which can often withstand the corruptions and excessive power seeking of enough humans to remain viable as a good society.

It is never routine, however, never automatic. Like each human being, democracy is always growing into more or less. Each generation must be alert to the dangers that threaten democracy as directly as each human who wishes to be good must learn how to survive in the labyrinths of envy, greed, and the confusions of moral judgment. Democracy, by the nature of its assumptions, has to grow in moral depth, or commence to deteriorate. So, the constant danger that besets it is the unadmitted downward pull of fascism. In all of us there is not only a love of

freedom, but a wretchedness of spirit that can look for its opposite—as identification with the notion of order and control from
above.

The real idiocy in assuming that democracy could be brought
to Iraq was to assume that its much-divided people had not been
paying spiritually for their compromises. The most evil aspect of
fascism is that all but a few are obliged to work within that system
or else their families and their own prospects suffer directly. So
the mass of good people in a fascist state are filled with shame,
ugly memories of their own small and occasionally large treach-
eries, their impotence, and their frustrated hopes of revenge.
Willy-nilly, their psyches are an explosive mess. They are decades
away from democracy. There is no quick fix. Democracy has to
be earned by a nation through its readiness for sacrifice. Ugly
lessons in survival breed few democrats.

It is all but impossible to believe that men as hard-nosed, in-
ventive, and transcendentally cynical as Karl Rove or Dick
Cheney, to offer the likeliest two candidates at hand, could have
believed that quick democracy was going to be feasible for Iraq.

We are back to oil. It is a crude assertion, but I expect Cheney,
for one, is in Iraq for just that reason. Without a full wrestler's
grip on control of the oil of the Middle East, America's economic
problems will continue to expand. That is why we will remain in
Iraq for years to come. For nothing will be gained if we depart
after the new semioppressive state is cobbled together. Even if we
pretend it is a democracy, we will have only a nominal victory. We
will have gone back to America with nothing but the problems
which led us to Iraq in the first place plus the onus that a couple
of hundred billion dollars were spent in the quagmire.

Let me make an attempt to enter Cheney's mind. I think, as
he sees it, it will be crucial to hang in at all costs. New sources of
income are going to be needed, new trillions, if for nothing else
than to pay for the future social programs that will have to take
care of the humongously large labor force that will remain en-
demically jobless because of globalism. That may yet prove to be
the final irony of compassionate conservatism. It will expand the
role of government even as it searches for empire.

Cheney's looming question will be then how to bring off some sizable capture of Iraq's oil profits. Of course, he is no weak man, he is used to doing what it takes, no matter how it smells, he is full of the hard lessons passed along by the collective wisdom of all those Republican bankers who for the last 125 years have been foreclosing on widows who cannot keep up with the mortgage on the farm. Cheney knows. You cannot stop a man who is never embarrassed by himself—Cheney will be full of barefaced virtue over why—for the well-being of all—we have to help the Middle East to sell its oil properly. We will deem it appropriate that the Europeans are not to expect a sizable share since, after all, they do not deserve it, not given their corrupt deals with Hussein under so-called UN supervision. Yes, Cheney will know how to sell the package for why we are still in Iraq, and Rove will be on his flank, guiding Bush on how to lay it out for the American people.

It seems to me that if the Democrats are going to be able to work up a new set of attitudes and values for their future candidates, it might not be a bad idea to do a little more creative thinking about the question for which they have had, up to now, naught but puny suggestions—which is, How do you pick up a little of the fundamentalists' vote?

If by 2008, the Democrats hope to come near to a meaningful fraction of such voters, they will have to find candidates and field workers who can spread the word down south—that is, find the equivalent of Democratic missionaries to work on all those good people who may be in awe of Jehovah's wrath but love Jesus, love Jesus so much more. Worked upon with enough zeal, some of the latter might come to recognize that these much-derided liberals live much more closely than the Republicans in the real spirit of Jesus. Whether they believe every word of Scripture or not, it is still these liberals rather than the Republicans who worry about the fate of the poor, the afflicted, the needy, and the disturbed. These liberals even care about the well-being of criminals in our prisons. They are more ready to save the forests, refresh the air of the cities, and clean up the rivers. It might be agonizing for a good fundamentalist to vote for a candidate who did not read the Scriptures every day, yet some of them might yet be ready to say, "I no longer know where to place my vote. I have joined the ranks of the undecided."

More power to such a man. More power to all who would be ready to live with the indecision implicit in democracy. It is democracy, after all, which first brought the power and virtue of good questions to the attention of the people rather than restricting the matter to the upper classes.

Long may good questions prevail.

Original Publication and Permission Credits

The essays in this book have been previously published in the following publications:

American Review: "Genius"; *Big Table:* "Quick Evaluations on the Talent in the Room"; *Dissent:* "From Surplus Value to the Mass Media," "Introducing Our Argument," "The White Negro," "What I Think of Artistic Freedom"; *Esquire:* "The Best Move Lies Close to the Worst," "An Evening with Jackie Kennedy," "The Mind of an Outlaw," "Our Man at Harvard," "Some Children of the Goddess," "Superman Comes to the Supermarket," "Suicides of Hemingway and Monroe"; *George:* "Clinton and Dole: The War of the Oxymorons"; *The Harvard Advocate:* "Comment on the Passing of George Plimpton"; *International Herald Tribune:* "Gaining an Empire, Losing Democracy?"; *Look:* "Looking for the Meat and Potatoes—Thoughts on Black Power"; *Michigan Quarterly Review:* "The Hazards and Sources of Writing"; *The Nation:* "On Sartre's God Problem"; *National Guardian:* "A Credo for the Living"; *The New Republic:* "By Heaven Inspired"; *New York:* "Before the Literary Bar"; *The New York Review of Books:* "Discovering Jack H. Abbott," "The Election and America's Future," "Punching Papa," "Tango, Last Tango," "The White Man Unburdened"; *The New York Times Book Review:* "Huckleberry Finn, Alive at One Hundred"; *The New York Times Magazine:* "Christ, Satan, and the Presidential Candidate: A Visit to Jimmy Carter in Plains"; *One:* "The Homosexual Villain"; *Parade:* "All the Pirates and People," "Until Dead: Thoughts on Capital Punishment"; *Partisan Review:* "Black Power"; *Playboy:* "The Crazy One," "Immodest Proposals"; *Vanity Fair:* "How the Wimp Won the War," "Review of *American Psycho*"; *Video Review:* "Marilyn Monroe's Sexiest Tapes and Discs"; *Village Voice:* "Nomination of Ernest Hemingway for President: Part I," "Nomination of Ernest Hemingway for President: Part II," "On Lies, Power, and Obscenity," "Raison d'Être"; *The Big Empty* (New York: Nation Books, 2006): "Myth Versus Hypothesis"; *Cannibals and Christians* (New York: Dial, 1966): "Our Argument as Last Presented"; *The Prisoner of Sex* (New York: Little, Brown, 1971): "Millett and D. H. Lawrence"; *The Spooky Art: Some Thoughts on Writing*, edited by J. Michael Lennon (New York: Random House, 2003): "Review of *The Corrections*," "Social Life, Literary Desires, Literary Corruption"; *Why I Write: Thoughts on the Craft of Fiction*, edited by Will Blythe (Boston: Back Bay, 1998): "At the Point of My Pen."

Grateful acknowledgment is made to the following for permission to reprint previously published material:

GEORGES BORCHARDT, INC.: Excerpt from *Sexual Politics* by Kate Millett, copyright © 1969, 1970, 1990, 2000 by Kate Millett. Reprinted by permission of Georges Borchardt, Inc., on behalf of the author.

GROVE/ATLANTIC, INC.: Excerpts from *The Wretched of the Earth* by Franz Fanon, copyright © 1963 by *Présence Africaine*. Used by permission of Grove/Atlantic, Inc. Any third party use of this material outside of this publication is prohibited.

HAL LEONARD CORPORATION: Excerpt from "Honky Tonk Man," words and music by Johnny Horton, Howard Hausey, and Tillman Franks, copyright © 1956 by Universal-Cedarwood Publishing. Copyright renewed. All rights reserved. Reprinted by permission of Hal Leonard Corporation.

HARPER'S BAZAAR U.S.: Excerpt from "Born 1930: The Unlost Generation" by Caroline Bird (*Harper's Bazaar*, February 1957). Reprinted courtesy of Harper's Bazaar U.S.

ALFRED A. KNOPF, AN IMPRINT OF THE KNOPF DOUBLEDAY PUBLISHING GROUP, A DIVISION OF RANDOM HOUSE LLC AND POLLINGER LIMITED: Excerpt from *The Plumed Serpent* by D. H. Lawrence, copyright © 1926 by Alfred A. Knopf, a division of Random House LLC and copyright renewed © 1954 by Frieda Lawrence Ravagli. Copyright © 1987 The Estate of Frieda Lawrence Ravagli. Digital rights are controlled by Pollinger Limited. Reprinted by permission of Alfred A. Knopf, an imprint of the Knopf Doubleday Publishing Group, a division of Random House LLC and Pollinger Limited.

ANDREWS KURTH LLP: Excerpt from a speech delivered by Barbara Bush at the 1992 Republican National Convention. Reprinted by permission.

THE NEW YORK TIMES: Excerpt from "Snuff This Book" by Roger Rosenblatt (*The New York Times*, December 16, 1990), copyright © 1990 by *The New York Times*. All rights reserved. Reprinted by permission and protected by the Copyright Laws of the United States. The printing, copying, redistribution, or retransmission of this Content without express written permission is prohibited.

OFFICE OF COLIN POWELL: Excerpt from a speech delivered by Colin Powell at the 1996 Republican National Convention. Reprinted by permission.

ANN ROVERE: Excerpt from "Letter from Los Angeles" by Richard Rovere. Reprinted by permission of Ann Rovere.

VINTAGE BOOKS, AN IMPRINT OF THE KNOPF DOUBLEDAY PUBLISHING GROUP, A DIVISION OF RANDOM HOUSE LLC: Excerpt from *American Psycho* by Bret Easton Ellis, copyright © 1991 by Bret Easton Ellis. Reprinted by permission of Vintage Books, an imprint of the Knopf Doubleday Publishing Group, a division of Random House LLC.

Acknowledgments

———

I would like to thank the Mailer family and David Ebershoff, Random House executive editor, for the generous opportunity to edit this volume. A nod of deep friendship and gratitude goes to J. Michael Lennon, authorized biographer of Norman Mailer (*Norman Mailer: A Double Life,* 2013), who was particularly gracious and cogent in providing strategic inclusion suggestions as well as acquisition strategies. Caitlin McKenna, Random House editorial assistant, was exceptionally helpful in assisting with the assembly and transmission of essays and other critical segments. My special thanks and warm appreciation to M. Allison Wise, managing editor of *The Mailer Review,* for her painstaking and meticulous assistance in locating challenging, elusive manuscripts and assisting in generating faithful copy text. And to my wife, Cary Sipiora, my inexpressible gratitude for her unrelenting support.

PHILLIP SIPIORA

Index

About the Author

———

Born in 1923 in Long Branch, New Jersey, and raised in Brooklyn, NORMAN MAILER was one of the most influential writers of the second half of the twentieth century and a leading public intellectual for nearly sixty years. He is the author of more than thirty books. *The Castle in the Forest,* his last novel, was his eleventh *New York Times* bestseller. His first novel, *The Naked and the Dead,* has never gone out of print. His 1968 nonfiction narrative, *The Armies of the Night,* won the Pulitzer Prize and the National Book Award. He won a second Pulitzer for *The Executioner's Song* and is the only person to have won Pulitzers in both fiction and nonfiction. Five of his books were nominated for National Book Awards, and he won a lifetime achievement award from the National Book Foundation in 2005. Mr. Mailer died in 2007 in New York City.

About the Editor

———

PHILLIP SIPIORA is a professor of English and film studies at the University of South Florida. He is the author or editor of four books and has lectured nationally and internationally on twentieth-century literature and film. He is a longtime scholar of Norman Mailer and the editor of *The Mailer Review*.

About the Type

This book was set in Baskerville, a typeface designed by John Baskerville (1706–75), an amateur printer and typefounder, and cut for him by John Handy in 1750. The type became popular again when the Lanston Monotype Corporation of London revived the classic roman face in 1923. The Mergenthaler Linotype Company in England and the United States cut a version of Baskerville in 1931, making it one of the most widely used typefaces today.